Hester Lynch

(MRS. THR

MRS. THRALE AND HER DAUGHTER HESTER
(QUEENEY), c. 1781

Painted by REYNOLDS *Oil on canvas 140.4 cm. × 148.6 cm.*
Gift of Lord Beaverbrook. Beaverbrook Art Gallery, Fredericton, N.B., Canada

Hester Lynch Piozzi

(MRS. THRALE)

BY

JAMES L. CLIFFORD

SECOND EDITION

With a new introduction

BY

MARGARET ANNE DOODY

COLUMBIA UNIVERSITY PRESS
NEW YORK
1987

Columbia University Press Morningside Edition 1987
Columbia University Press
New York

© *1987 Oxford University Press*
© *1987 New introduction—Margaret Anne Doody*

First Edition 1941
Second Edition 1952
Reprinted with Corrections and Additions 1968
Reissued in paperback with additions to 1968 reprint

Library of Congress Cataloging in Publication Data
Clifford, James Lowry, 1901–
Hester Lynch Piozzi (Mrs. Thrale).
Reprint. Originally published: 2nd ed. Oxford
[Oxfordshire]: Clarendon Press, 1968.
Bibliography: p.
Includes index.
1. Piozzi, Hester Lynch, 1741–1821—Biography.
2. Authors, English—18th century—Biography.
3. London (England)—Intellectual life—18th century.
I. Title
PR3619.P5C5   1986   828'.609 [B]   86–14749
ISBN 0–231–06389–X

Printed in Great Britain

PREFACE TO SECOND EDITION

IN the more than eleven years since the first edition of this biography much new evidence concerning Mrs. Piozzi has become available. *Thraliana* has been admirably edited by Professor Katharine C. Balderston. Well over two hundred new letters from Mrs. Thrale to the Burneys may now be consulted. And the dramatic discovery of the original manuscript of Boswell's *Life of Johnson* makes it possible to evaluate more accurately his treatment of his rival.

There is little in the new material, however, which fundamentally changes our understanding of Mrs. Piozzi's character. While it reinforces and elaborates, it does not alter the main outlines of the story. Consequently, instead of rewriting the entire volume, I have preferred to reproduce the first edition by lithography, making only such minor changes as are necessary to correct typographical errors and obvious errors of fact.

Although little new material has been added to the text, readers will find in the additions to the 'Select Bibliography' references to the more significant of the recent discussions of Mrs. Piozzi. In the notes I have not attempted to bring up to date the statements of ownership of manuscripts. A few major changes, nevertheless, may be indicated here. The whole of the famous R. B. Adam collection, and most of the Piozzian holdings of the late Mr. A. Edward Newton are now in the possession of Mr. and Mrs. Donald Hyde. Those of the late Sir Randle Mainwaring are owned by his son, Mr. Hugh Mainwaring. Unfortunately I do not know the whereabouts of the papers listed as the property of the late Mr. and Mrs. Herbert Evans of Brynbella.

Because of the method involved in reprinting the book, it has proved impossible to revise thoroughly the sections dealing with Boswell and Mrs. Piozzi. For some objections to my conclusions, readers are referred to the review-article by Professor F. A. Pottle and Dr. Charles H. Bennett in *Modern Philology* for May 1942. So far as possible, all errors of fact have been eliminated, but in order to reconcile our differences of interpretation it would have been necessary to rewrite large sections of the text. Although I willingly soften some of my remarks about Boswell's handling of the evidence, I still am not convinced that his later expansions of his original notes have the same validity as have the notes themselves or the expansions made a short time after the conversations took place. In the controversial passages in Chapters XII and XVII, therefore, readers should always bear in mind these unresolved differences of opinion.

Thanks are due again to Dr. L. F. Powell and to Professor Allen T. Hazen for help in correcting various minor errors.

J. L. C.

COLUMBIA UNIVERSITY
March, 1952

NOTE TO THE CORRECTED IMPRESSION

FOR this second impression of the second edition only a few textual changes have been made, and there has been no attempt to indicate all recent shifts of ownership of manuscripts. One correction, however, can now be made. The papers listed as the property of the late Mr. and Mrs. Herbert Evans of Brynbella are now in the National Library of Wales, Aberystwyth.

J. L. C.

November 1967

PREFACE TO FIRST EDITION

MY introduction to Mrs. Piozzi came through that Prince of Johnsonians, Mr. A. Edward Newton. He stimulated interest in the 'Light Blue Stocking', and later generously allowed me to make use of the riches of his great manuscript collection. Actual research was begun at the suggestion and under the direction of Professor Ernest Hunter Wright of Columbia University. For the past eight years he has given me continued encouragement and help, for which I express deep appreciation. I also owe much to Professors Harry Morgan Ayres, Hoxie N. Fairchild, Roger Sherman Loomis, Elliott V. K. Dobbie; and to the trustees of Columbia University for the grant of a Cutting Travelling Fellowship which enabled me to spend the year 1935-6 in England.

From the beginning, Professor Frederick A. Pottle of Yale University has been unsparing with aid and suggestions; and, although not always agreeing with my treatment of Boswell, he has, together with Dr. Charles H. Bennett, carefully read through the pages in proof. Others at Yale who have given valuable assistance include Professors Chauncey B. Tinker, Edmund T. Silk, and Allen T. Hazen. Mr. James M. Osborn read the first draft of this book, and has never slackened in his friendly encouragement. It is difficult to express my debt to Professor George Sherburn, now of Harvard University. As 'guide, philosopher, and friend', he has been untiring in criticism and advice, and has been the greatest single influence in shaping this work.

It is impossible to name all the other American scholars who at various times assisted my research, but I wish particularly to thank Professor Katharine C. Balderston for generously taking time from her editing of Thraliana to read my manuscript and offer many valuable suggestions; and Professors Elizabeth Manwaring, Edward L. McAdam, Richard L. Greene, Amos A. Ettinger, R H Heindel, Dr. Robert Metzdorf, Dr. Philip Gove, and Mr. G. S. Alleman.

In England I have received the kindest, most generous co-operation. Dr. R. W. Chapman has allowed me to consult his voluminous file of Johnson's letters, and has continuously supplied me with information. Professor D. Nichol Smith has without stint given me the advantage of his wide knowledge and sound critical judgement. Dr. L. F. Powell's inexhaustible Johnsonian lore and careful and enthusiastic reading of proof have been invaluable. I can only repay his friendly aid with a deep and lasting affection. To Dr. Henry Guppy of the John Rylands Library, Manchester, I wish to express my gratitude for every possible assistance in consulting that great collection of Piozziana; also to Dr. Moses Tyson and Dr. Frank Taylor of the same institution. Special thanks are also due to Mr. F. Bateson; to Mr. H. W. Bromhead, the Streatham antiquarian; to Mr. F. Harrison of Brighton; to Mr. P. Laithwaite of Lichfield; to Mr. A. L. Reade of Blundellsands; to Dr. Ernest Sadler of the Mansion, Ashbourne; to Mrs. Phyllis Rowell of Gough Square; to Mr. J. Alun Thomas of St. Asaph; and to Mr. and Mrs. Herbert Evans, the hospitable occupants of Brynbella.

Possessors of Piozziana everywhere have been most courteous in allowing me to consult their treasures. I wish particularly to express my thanks to Lord and Lady Lansdowne, Lord Harmsworth, Sir Randle Mainwaring, Mr. S. C. Roberts, Mr. Frederick Vernon, Major C. A. Carlos Perkins, the late Mr. D. F. Pennant, the late Mrs. A. M. Knollys, the late Miss Susan Mainwaring, Mr. and Mrs. C. F. Colman, Mr. and Mrs. Hubert Miller, the late Mr. O. Butler Fellowes, Mr. Lindsay Fleming, Mr. Oswald Bourne, Mr. Robert Roberts; in the United States to the late Mr. R. B. Adam, Col. Ralph Isham, Dr. A. S. W. Rosenbach, Mr. Albert B. Ashforth Jr., Mr. Abel Cary Thomas, the late Mr. Wilton Lloyd Smith, Mr. J. P. Morgan, Mr. Oliver Barrett. To the Henry E. Huntington Library I am indebted for permission to consult the Thraliana diary; and to the Viking Press for the right to quote from the Boswell Papers. Officials of the British Museum, the Bodleian Library, the National Library of Scotland, the National Library of Wales, the Victoria and Albert Museum, the Johnson House, Gough Square, Johnson's Birthplace at Lichfield, the Morgan Library in New York, the Columbia, Yale and Harvard University Libraries, and others, who must be nameless, have tirelessly shown me all the valuable materials in their possession.

My list of acknowledgements would not be complete without the long-suffering relatives and friends who have listened, commented, and encouraged. Only a few may be named: Mr. and Mrs. George O. Clifford, Mr. Robert D. Orr, Mrs.

Samuel Orr, Mrs. Samuel C. Mitchell, and Mr. and Mrs. Richard L. Hanson. My greatest debt of all I owe to my mother, who has not only supported me in every possible way throughout the long weary labours of composition, but has made these labours lighter by her judicious criticisms and constant faith in the final result. To her this volume is dedicated, in loving recognition that without her help it could never have been completed.

J. L. C.

LEHIGH UNIVERSITY

September, 1940

CONTENTS

LIST OF PLATES xii

ABBREVIATIONS xiii

INTRODUCTION, 1941 XV

NEW INTRODUCTION, 1986 . . . XX

PART I
HESTER LYNCH SALUSBURY

I. Daughter of Wales (before 1758) . . . 3

II. Heiress of Offley (1758–63) 25

PART II
HESTER LYNCH THRALE

III. Streatham and Southwark (1763–6) . . 49

IV. Beginning Diarist (1766–70) . . . 66

V. Depression (1770–3) 88

VI. Travels and Tragedy (Jan. 1774–Apr. 1776) . 111

VII. Widening Acquaintance (Apr. 1776–Feb. 1778) . 139

VIII. Troubles with Master (Mar. 1778–June 1779) . 160

IX. The Last of Master (June 1779–June 1781) . 177

X. Widow (June 1781–Sept. 1784) . . . 203

PART III
HESTER LYNCH PIOZZI

XI. *The Florence Miscellany* (Sept. 1784–Aug. 1785) . 235

XII. *Anecdotes of Dr. Johnson* (Sept. 1785–May 1786) . 255

XIII. Travel on the Continent (Mar. 1786–Mar. 1787) 277

XIV. England Again (Mar. 1787–Mar. 1788) . . 293

xv. Johnson's Letters (1788) 314
xvi. London Society and Travel (Mar. 1788–Dec. 1789) 331
xvii. Streatham Renewed (Jan. 1790–Apr. 1794) . 352
xviii. Brynbella (1794–1801) 375
xix. Gout (1801–9) 406
xx. Bath-Blue (1809–21) 426
EPILOGUE 457
APPENDIXES 461
SELECT BIBLIOGRAPHY 470
ADDITIONS TO SELECT BIBLIOGRAPHY . . . 474
INDEX 477

PLATES

Mrs. Thrale and her Daughter Hester . . . *frontispiece*
Mrs. Salusbury . . . . . . *facing p.* 44
Queeney—aged Twenty Months . . . . ,, 70
A Page from the Children's Book, June 18, 1773 . . ,, 104
Supposed Caricature of Henry Thrale . . . ,, 162
Gabriel Piozzi . . . . . . ,, 308
Hester Lynch Piozzi . . . . . ,, 406
John Salusbury Piozzi Salusbury . . . . ,, 434

ABBREVIATIONS

WHEN quoting from unprinted sources I have given the owner of the manuscript each time, except for long series (still intact) of letters to the same person, and for important journals. The ownership of these, instead, is given in Appendixes C, D, and E. In consequence, whenever the source and date of the quotation are given in the text, no footnote is deemed necessary. If the date is not mentioned in the text, it is included in a note. For example, practically all of Mrs. Thrale's letters to Johnson are in the John Rylands collection, and all of her letters to Queeney are in the possession of Lord Lansdowne; consequently, when these sources are used no reiteration of their ownership seems required. Similarly, references to the Children's Book, which is an unpaged but chronological journal, give the date of entry only.

In referring to the manuscript material in the John Rylands Library, Manchester, England, I have adopted a special notation. 'Ry. 540, 75', for instance, indicates that the letter may be found in John Rylands English MSS., volume 540, item 75.

When using printed sources, I have attempted to give the exact reference as succinctly as possible, and have used certain contractions for the standard authorities. The more important are listed below:

Adam Libr. The R. B. Adam Library Relating to Dr. Samuel Johnson and His Era (Buffalo, N.Y., 1929–30).

Blunt R. Blunt, Mrs. Montagu, 'Queen of the Blues' (London, 1923).

Life J. Boswell, The Life of Samuel Johnson, LL.D., ed. G. B. Hill, revised and enlarged by L. F. Powell (Oxford, 1934).

Private Papers. Private Papers of James Boswell from Malahide Castle, ed. Geoffrey Scott and Frederick Pottle (privately printed, 1928–34).

Broadley A. M. Broadley, Dr. Johnson and Mrs. Thrale (London, 1910).

Early Diary of F. Burney. The Early Diary of Frances Burney, ed. A. R. Ellis (London, 1907).

D'Arblay, Diary. Diary and Letters of Madame D'Arblay, ed. Austin Dobson (six volumes, London, 1904–5).

Letters Letters of Samuel Johnson, LL.D., ed. G. B. Hill (Oxford, 1892).

John. Misc. Johnsonian Miscellanies, ed. G. B. Hill (Oxford, 1897).

Hayward   *Autobiography Letters and Literary Remains of Mrs. Piozzi (Thrale),* ed. A. Hayward, 2nd edition (London, 1861). See pp. 471–2.

Thraliana, ed. Hughes. *Mrs. Piozzi's Thraliana,* ed. Charles Hughes (London, 1913).

Letters to Pennington. The Intimate Letters of Hester Piozzi and Penelope Pennington 1788–1821, ed. O. G. Knapp (London, 1914).

H. More, *Memoirs.* W. Roberts, *Memoirs of the Life and Correspondence of Mrs. Hannah More,* 2nd edition (London, 1834).

Seeley   L. B. Seeley, *Mrs. Thrale Afterwards Mrs. Piozzi* (London, 1891).

Whalley, *Corr. Journals and Correspondence of Thomas Sedgewick Whalley D.D.,* ed. H. Wickham (London, 1863).

INTRODUCTION, 1941

OF the many women who have made a place for themselves in English literary history perhaps none has been more often the subject of controversy than Hester Lynch Piozzi, the friend of Dr. Johnson, the rival of Boswell, the sprightly, irrepressible Mistress of Streatham. In her own time she was a well-known figure in London society, with steadfast friends and a host of bitter enemies. To-day, even in the perspective of over a century, she still arouses ardent admiration or intense dislike. The late Professor Sir Walter Raleigh once remarked to Mr. A. Edward Newton, after examining some of Mrs. Piozzi's papers, 'What a dear, delightful person she was! I have always wanted to meet her'; and Mr. Newton himself declared that of all the feminine writers of English literature he would most like to have known Mrs. Piozzi.[1] Yet, in contrast, the late Lord Lansdowne called her 'a woman essentially vain, vulgar, and false, intolerable as a parent and rightly kept at a distance by her offspring'.[2]

What was there about this eighteenth-century brewer's wife which even in the twentieth century can arouse such intense feeling? Why does it seem impossible to arrive at any general estimate of her character? These are some of the questions which I hope to answer in the present biography.

There is one obvious reason why Mrs. Piozzi is difficult to understand. Throughout her life she was a bundle of contradictions, a chameleon changing colour with her varying surroundings. Consequently, any over-emphasis on the years just preceding her second marriage makes her appear giddy, self-centred, and unstable; yet a similar concentration on her early life with Thrale or her last years with Piozzi shows an intelligent woman, self-sacrificing, and dependable. Random excerpts from her letters are apt, therefore, to be misleading, for it is not possible to make an accurate estimate of her character simply by examining a portion of her correspondence. She habitually showed a different side of her nature to each person to whom

[1] A. E. Newton, *The Amenities of Book-Collecting and Kindred Affections* (Boston, 1918), pp. 186, 221.
[2] The Marquis of Lansdowne, *Johnson and Queeney* (London, 1932), p. xxvii.

she wrote, choosing her mood to suit the character of her correspondent. In order to gain a complete picture of her facile mind, one must examine not only the social letters, but those devoted to business, family, and literature as well, and, above all, her diaries and journals. Unfortunately, too many critics in the past have formed their opinions after the reading of only a few series of letters, and the result has been a one-sided and distorted portrait, either too sentimentally pleasing or too harshly severe.

To consult all the existing evidence about Mrs. Piozzi, however, is no easy matter, and perhaps it has been the sheer magnitude of the task which has discouraged most of her biographers. Thousands of her letters, as well as scores of her diaries and commonplace books, are preserved in libraries and family archives throughout Great Britain and the United States. Of these only a few have been accurately published, and the remainder have been so widely dispersed by a series of sales that they have not been easily available for study. In 1909 the prospect of ever securing all the facts seemed so doubtful that Mr. A. M. Broadley remarked that the scattering of Mrs. Piozzi's manuscripts would in all probability 'prove an insurmountable barrier to the completion of Johnson's biography, as well as to the compilation of an exhaustive work dealing with the life and correspondence of one of the cleverest and most entertaining of the many feminine letter-writers who flourished between 1760 and 1820'.[1]

A difficulty, however, is sometimes a challenge, and I must confess that it has been the thrill of the search, almost as much as an abounding interest in the lady, which has lured me on. So for years I have followed the trail of her manuscripts across the United States and over part of Europe, to most of the places in which she lived—to Streatham, Southwark, Brighton, Bath, Wales, and Italy—returning sometimes disappointed and empty handed, but more often rewarded with new and interesting information. Although some treasures have perhaps eluded me, treasures which may become fascinating quarry for Johnsonians of future years, the results of the long quest have in many ways more than justified the effort expended. I cannot but remember particularly my good fortune in Mrs. Piozzi's own beloved Vale of Clwyd in North Wales, where an almost unbelievable series of coincidences culminated in the opportunity to study numerous documents the existence of which was

[1] A. M. Broadley, *Doctor Johnson and Mrs. Thrale* (London, 1910), p. 88.

then unsuspected. Elsewhere, too, the collectors of Johnsoniana have been more than generous, so that, as a general estimate, I have been able to read at least 2,500 letters written by Mrs. Piozzi and over 2,000 addressed to her, most of which have never been published.[1] It has been my good fortune, also, to consult numerous manuscript diaries and journals, the one of chief importance being the so-called 'Children's Book', kept by Mrs. Thrale from 1766 to 1778 during her early friendship with Johnson, in which she recorded the domestic joys and griefs of the Thrale household. Through the courtesy of the owner, I am now privileged for the first time to make full use of this record, which reveals certain qualities of the Mistress of Streatham heretofore largely disregarded by all her biographers. The other little-known sources include an unpublished five-volume literary autobiography compiled by Mrs. Piozzi expressly for her adopted heir, John Salusbury; her later 'New Common-Place Book'; seventeen smaller diaries with brief notations of daily events; and a large collection of miscellaneous business papers and occasional jottings.

Still the most important authority for her life is the six-volume diary and commonplace book, Thraliana, which Miss Katharine C. Balderston is now editing for the Huntington Library. I have been courteously allowed to consult this great repository and to quote directly from the original manuscript rather than from the unreliable printed versions of Hayward and Hughes. But since the work in its entirety will soon be available, I have felt it advisable to copy as little as possible from it, and instead to use the accounts recorded in her other journals, which often repeat in the main the same evidence. Throughout, however, references have been given to the entry dates in Thraliana.

Apart from the difficulty of discovering all the extant Piozziana, another problem confronts the biographer of Mrs. Piozzi. How much credence can be placed in the evidence thus found? How valid are her accounts when compared with those of other writers of the day? No doubt most critics will answer without hesitation that she cannot be implicitly believed unless supported by other evidence—to which in part I must agree. But what has not been emphasized enough is the fact that neither can most of her contemporaries—at least in their published recollections. Nearly all of our accepted authorities on the Johnson era are also suspected. For instance, Fanny Burney's

[1] For a general list of these letters and journals see Appendixes.

Diary often represents, not what the young girl wrote at the time, but what the ageing Mme D'Arblay thought proper to be printed.[1] So too, Boswell's day-by-day accounts in the *Life* do not always coincide precisely with his own original notes; and Anna Seward's printed letters are very different from those actually sent through the post.[2] These are only typical examples, but they serve to show how careful we must be in quoting from these generally accepted sources. Unless we can examine the original manuscript itself, we can seldom be sure whether the printed page represents the original impression of the writer or merely a later revision of that opinion for publication.

It is particularly important, when examining remarks about Mrs. Piozzi, to know whether a given statement was made before or after 1784, the year of her second marriage, since the animosities aroused by her union with the Italian musician colour nearly all opinions after that date. For this reason I have felt it imperative to use contemporary evidence, and to disregard, so far as possible, recollections printed long afterwards. In quoting from Boswell I have attempted to use his original notes, whenever they have been preserved, rather than the printed *Life*. Furthermore, I have tried to avoid the use of the later reminiscences of other writers, unless they correspond with unquestionable evidence.

Mrs. Piozzi herself provides an excellent example of variable reliability, for though the accounts of her early life written as an older woman are not always accurate, her day-by-day entries in diaries and journals are for the most part authoritative. Hence in assembling the story of her life, I have tried to use actual letters and contemporary jottings wherever possible. Unfortunately, for the years of her childhood and youth it is still necessary to trust to later memories, but these I have tested with all available objective evidence. Where there are differences, I have assumed the contemporary reference to be correct; where the discrepancy is negligible or where there is no conflict, I have accepted the familiar version as genuine.

It may be necessary to add a word concerning my treatment of the text of unprinted sources. Feeling that by normalization

---

[1] A. E. Newton, *Reflections on the Character of Madame Thrale Piozzi*, privately printed, Daylesford, Pa., pp. 3–7.

[2] Anna Seward's letters were printed in 1811 from 'copies' which she had preserved. A comparison, however, with the actual letters sent to Mrs. Piozzi (now in the John Rylands collection) shows that the printed versions have been completely rewritten. And not only did Miss Seward alter the phraseology but, with some incomprehensible subtlety, the dates as well. See also pp. 306–7, 317, 344.

much of the flavour as well as the accuracy of eighteenth-century accounts is lost, I have followed the original spelling, punctuation, and capitalization. But since Mrs. Piozzi's picturesque calligraphy cannot be completely reproduced except by facsimile—it was her custom to indicate excitement or anger by varying the size, colour, and shape of the words—the exact written form has not always been followed. I have decided to make no attempt to indicate eccentric positions of letters, and to be wholly consistent, I have not even recorded 'superior letters'. Thus, contractions such as w^d, M^r, and ye have been printed as wd., Mr., and ye. Only in special cases, where ambiguity might otherwise result, has this general principle been violated.

In regard to the general plan employed, I have found it impractical to adhere throughout to a strict chronological order. For such a 'tripsy' lady, as she once called herself, the repetition of her many moves about England makes dull reading. On the other hand, I have felt that a semi-chronological treatment presents a better picture of her life than any simple telescoping of past, present, and future. It might possibly have been simpler to combine all the evidence about Mrs. Thrale's relations with her children into one painful chapter, but such a concentration would have distorted the essential truth. The seemingly endless series of births, illnesses, and deaths gradually affected her character, so that only by viewing the succession of troubles, interspersed as they were with pleasant social diversions, can we see the picture of later events in its true perspective.

If it is objected that the intimate details of the family life of an eighteenth-century brewer are not sufficiently interesting to warrant such minute care, I can answer only that Dr. Johnson himself would have welcomed such a chronicle. When he was in the Hebrides with Boswell, and was told that at Tobermory he would see the man who had written the history of the Macleans, Johnson replied: 'I'd rather hear the history of the Thrales.'[1] This is the history of the Thrales.

J. L. C.

---

[1] Boswell, *Tour to the Hebrides*, ed. F. A. Pottle and C. H. Bennett (New York, 1936), p. 302.

INTRODUCTION TO THE 1986 IMPRESSION

BY MARGARET ANNE DOODY

'I HAVE somewhere heard or read, that the Preface before a book, like the portico before a house, should be contrived, so as to catch, but not detain the attention of those who desire admission to the family within. . . .'[1] So Hester Lynch Piozzi begins the 'Preface' to her *Anecdotes of the Late Samuel Johnson, LL.D.* and I cannot do better than remind myself and my reader that this Introduction is merely a portico before a house constructed by James L. Clifford, wherein those who desire admission may meet Hester Lynch Piozzi, once Mrs. Thrale. The revised second edition (1968) of the biography furnishes the present text, but Clifford's biography was first published in 1941. It is gratifying to realize that as early as 1941 one of the most notable and thorough scholars of the eighteenth century should give such detailed attention to a woman of the period. No one familiar with the other work of James L. Clifford can be surprised at the care taken in the research; all others who write on Mrs. Piozzi after him must take account of what he did, and rely on his discoveries. Above all, he paid the woman the compliment of thinking her worthy to be written about. Here we see, not Mrs. Thrale the amusing companion of Dr. Johnson, but Hester Lynch, a woman with a full life before and after her association with Johnson, a personage in her own right.

It is my object briefly to introduce that personage again, emphasizing some points that Clifford does not stress while referring to authors who have written on Hester Lynch Piozzi since Clifford's book last appeared. Above all, since Clifford did not regard the duties of the biographer as including those of the literary critic, I have thought it right to discuss with some particularity the qualities of her written works—and especially the published works. In an era such as ours in which women's writing is of considerable interest, her claims as an author have a new and potentially sympathetic audience. I

[1] 'Preface' to *Anecdotes of the Late Samuel Johnson, LL.D.* (London: T. Cadell, 1786), p. v.

should add that my quotations do not overlap with those used by Clifford, and that we diverge slightly in some opinions. I do share in his liking and admiration for Hester Lynch Piozzi and wish, as Clifford wished, to help to bring this always-controversial figure back to the light.

It is a salient fact about Hester Lynch, née Salusbury, that she was a Welshwoman. As Clifford points out, she prided herself on being a descendant of Katherine of Beraine, 'Mam Cymru', the mother of the Welsh people. It has not, I think, ever been noticed how consistently Samuel Johnson surrounded himself with friends from the Celtic regions of Britain. Among these, Boswell (Scotland), Goldsmith, and Burke (both of Ireland) immediately come to mind. Among Johnson's women friends too we find Charlotte Lennox, née Ramsay (Scotland), and Anna Williams (South Wales). Hester Lynch saw herself as a true Welshwoman: 'I find a great Resemblance between the two Nations [Scotland and Wales] in a hundred little Peculiarities, & the Erse sounded so like my own native Tongue that I wished for Erudition to prove the original Affinity between them',[1] she wrote to Sophia Weston (later Mrs. Pennington) in 1789. If she considered Welsh 'her own native Tongue', she was a transplanted Celt, and like so many of the Welsh felt the pull of homesickness that makes the traveller return—as she tried to do in establishing herself and Gabriel Piozzi at Brynbella. Like Johnson's other transplanted Celtic friends, when she chose she could regard English society with the sharp satiric eye of the foreigner.

If she was a transplanted Welshwoman, she was also a transplanted gentlewoman. Despite the precariousness of her assumed inheritance, and the parental lack of money, young Hester Lynch Salusbury was trained to think of herself as a lady and an heiress; and she was bred in country pursuits and domestic affairs, including the care of poultry and the work of the dairy. Such pursuits did not mean her other talents went unvalued. She says proudly that she was her parents' 'Joynt Play Thing', taught 'till I was half a Prodigy'.[2] She learned

---

[1] HLP to Sophia Weston (later Mrs. Pennington) 1 Sept. 1789, MS letter in Firestone Library, Princeton, in grangerized edition of Knapp, *The Intimate Letters of Hester Piozzi and Penelope Pennington 1788–1822*, MS AM 14613.

[2] 'Biographical Anecdotes', HLP's holograph MS of 36 pages, was originally intended as prefatory material for a new edition of the *Letters*; the title written on the front cover is 'Letters from Dr Sam: Johnson | publish'd by | Hester Lynch Piozzi 1788 | with Trifling | Biographical Anecdotes | of the Editor | Committed to the Care, & consign'd to the Honour | of | Sir James Fellowes | by his Obliged Friend | H. L.

Spanish and Italian from her mother and aunt, and was allowed to take lessons in Latin and rhetoric from Arthur Collier. Domestic and intellectual pursuits no more conflicted for her than they did for that other country gentlewoman, Clarissa Harlowe, heroine of a novel Hester admired. But Hester's marriage in 1763 meant a decided change.

Clifford has explained the circumstances surrounding Hester Lynch's marriage to Henry Thrale, and indicated her unhappiness in reluctantly yielding to the wishes of her uncle and her mother. Clifford says 'she never made any pretence that her decision originated from any other feeling than prudence', and he adds that 'it would have been difficult to find a bride and groom who were more temperamentally unsuited to each other'.[1] Perhaps even Clifford does not sufficiently emphasize the misery in this union. Hester's 'prudence' can be misinterpreted, as if the girl herself, careless of temperaments, willingly chose a prudent match. Walter Jackson Bate, ignoring Clifford's hints, has recently taken that line: 'The marriage, in short, was not a love match; nor, like so many other eighteenth-century marriages, was it expected to be.' And if Thrale were unfaithful, then, according to Bate, 'Mrs. Thrale, like other wives of the time, accepted this, and, at least externally, did not seem too hurt.'[2]

It seems right to stress that Hester Lynch Thrale did not take her marriage in this matter-of-fact way. She was appalled by what had happened to her. She was a Clarissa who lost the family battle, tamely and correctly choosing filial obedience; such virtue was not rewarded. At some level she felt she had betrayed herself. The 'Biographical Anecdotes' which she wrote in 1815 give a full idea of the nightmarish unreality of the wedding, and the cold stagnation and dread that characterized for her the early part of the marriage. At the age of seventy-five Hester is still rebelling against the marriage inflicted on her when she was twenty-two. She remembers everything with bitter clarity. The match seemed hurried on, against her will, by her uncle and her mother; Henry Thrale himself displayed no interest in his intended bride:

Piozzi Bath | Dec^r: 1815'. Reprinted in Hayward, *Autobiography, Letters and Literary Remains*, this is the material referred to by Clifford as 'Adam ms', then in the Hyde Collection and now in Firestone Library, Princeton (MS 3891.8.313); pp. 5–6.

[1] Clifford, see below, pp. 44, 49.

[2] Walter Jackson Bate, *Samuel Johnson* (New York and London: Harcourt Brace Jovanovich, 1977), p. 413.

My Uncle went himself with me to Church; gave me away—dined with us at Streatham Park—returned to Hertfordshire, wedded the Widow—& then, scarce ever saw, or wrote to either of us; leaving me to conciliate as I could—a Husband who was indeed much kinder than I counted on, to a *plain Girl* who had not one Attraction in his Eyes & on whom he never had thrown five Minutes of his Time away,—in any Interview unwitness'd by Company— even till after our Wedding Day was done!!

In this biographical manuscript addressed to Sir James Fellowes Hester does not go into details about Thrale's mistresses, but she does emphasize that her husband was surrounded by hard and high-living companions, including Sir Simon Lutterell 'afterwards known to all the Town by the emphatic Title *King of Hell*'. The men made merry in their own way and ignored the bride; she had to cultivate the oddest if most accessible member of the party, the Roman Catholic Dr. Fitzpatrick, 'a very sickly old Physician'.[1] She had no place and no influence, and was given no affection and no occupation. Thrale kept 'a famous Pack of Foxhounds at a Hunting Box near Croydon:—but it was Masculine for Ladies to ride &c'. Allowed no part in his pleasures, she could not at that point take an interest in her husband's business; Thrale's clerks 'scarce dar'd approach *him*—much less come near *Me*; whose Place he said was either the Drawing Room or the Bed Chamber'.[2] The heavy years of childbearing gave her some importance, but when Johnson first knew the couple Mrs. Thrale was living a life she found greatly restricted. Johnson himself noticed something of this, especially in a disagreeable remark made before Hester and her mother: 'Doctor Johnson now Introduced among us; told me once—before *her* Face who deeply did resent it; that I lived like My Husband's kept Mistress,—shut from the World, its Pleasures, or its Cares.'[3]

Years later, after Johnson's death, a satiric piece entitled *Bozzy and Piozzi; or, The British Biographers, A Town Eclogue* was to take Mrs. Piozzi to task, not only for writing the *Anecdotes of Johnson*, but for writing at all. Johnson's ghost is made to exhort her to 'Give up her *anecdotical* inditing, / And study *housewifry* instead of *writing*'.[4] Not content with this travesty of the views of the real Johnson, who had a high opinion of women's capacities, 'Peter Pindar' repeats the charge at the end:

[1] 'Biographical Anecdotes', MS p. 22.
[2] Ibid., p. 24.
[3] Ibid., p. 25.
[4] 'Peter Pindar' [John Wolcot], *Bozzy and Piozzi; or, The British Biographers, A Town Eclogue* (London: G. Kearsley and W. Foster, 1786), p. 26.

A happy knowledge in a *pye* or *pudding*,
Will more delight your friends, than all your *Studying*.
One cut from *ven'son*, to the heart can speak
Stronger than *ten quotations* from the *Greek*.[1]

These clichés are irritating enough in themselves, but there is
an extra irony in their inapplicability to Hester's situation
during her life as Mrs. Thrale. She knew all the arts of
housewifery and they proved useless to her. 'We kept the finest
Table possible at Streatham Park; but *his* Wife was not to *stink
of the Kitchen* so I never knew what was for Dinner till I saw
it.'[2] The lack of control in her own household must have been
very demoralizing, and the whole situation at first very dis-
orienting. The former Miss Salusbury of Offley Park had had
to make a violent adjustment to life in the urban house by the
brewery in Dead-Man's Place, Southwark. She learned from
Doctor Fitzpatrick 'what had determined my Husband's
Choice to *Me* till then a standing Wonder',[3] and that was her
willingness to live in Southwark. Mr. Thrale had asked several
other women to marry him, but they had all refused to live in
the Borough; perhaps Hester in the country had known too
little to object. Even Streatham Park was, after all, not a true
estate but an extensive version of a rich burgher's suburban
villa. The new Mrs. Thrale tried to keep some poultry there,
but the brewer was not interested in the arts and crafts of a
country gentlewoman, any more than he was concerned with
or pleased at her scholarship and writing.

The cultural shock of accommodating herself to a different
class and a different way of life must have been severe. Both
consciously and unconsciously the woman metamorphosed into
brewer's wife maintained the identity of a gentlewoman, with
aristocratic contempt for simpering middle-class manners and
twopenny gentility. She looked down on Thrale and his family,
and they must have known it. She herself was left in solitude;
the absence of women friends (save for her mother) during
most of Mrs. Thrale's married life is striking, as she valued
female friendship highly. Eventually Thrale brought home
Johnson and others members of the Club, but this was at a time
when the mistress of the house was undergoing frequent
pregnancies, enduring the loss of children, and nursing a sick

[1] Ibid., p. 52.
[2] 'Biographical Anecdotes', p. 24.
[3] Ibid.

mother. To be required to perform as hostess is not quite the same thing as acquiring friends—although Henry Thrale was correct in divining her talents as a hostess. Her education and the confidence of her original class enabled her to do what Thrale's own sisters could not have done.

Bearing children was the work for which Henry Thrale had chiefly required a wife. Mrs. Thrale bore twelve children, of whom six died at birth or in early infancy. The son and heir Harry died in 1776 at the age of ten. The birth of the next child after Harry's death was not greeted with joy. Hester wrote to Samuel Johnson on the birth of Cecilia (the last child born of the Thrale union who lived to grow up):

> I am alive after a very rough Labour, and a very vexatious Disappointment; however we must be patient if not contented . . . it is—to me at least— far better than no Child at all: & the little Gipsy is so eminently large, strong & handsome that she promises to make us all possible amends for her Sex. She is the finest Child I ever had . . . so much for our Cicely. M[r]. Thrale says I must take the more Care of myself for having done my Business so ill. . . .[1]

There is poignancy in the interjected 'to me at least'; to Hester, if not to her husband, a live girl is better than a stillbirth. Beneath the light tone we can sense her resentment that producing a girl child should be considered a failure; we can hear, too, a subtle appeal to Johnson for a sympathy she was not to obtain from her husband.

The friendship between Hester Lynch Thrale and Samuel Johnson is the most noted fact about her life. At the time, and even long after Johnson's death, the friendship was the topic of amused speculation, even of obscene jests. Few can seriously have believed that there was sexual intercourse between the two, but some contemporaries apparently genuinely expected that after Thrale's death the widow would marry the elderly and ill Johnson. What is certain is that the friendship went very deep indeed with both parties, far deeper than many sexual 'affairs'. And if the friendship was one of the most important experiences of both their lives, it was more important for Samuel Johnson than for Hester Thrale.

In her *Anecdotes of Johnson* the writer, now Mrs. Piozzi, reminds us that the friendship with Johnson was not of her seeking. At this point she is writing defensively, wishing to

[1] HLT to Dr. Johnson, 12 Feb. [1777], MS in Firestone Library Princeton, MS AM 14675.

explain the break in that friendship for which she has been blamed. But in the tone and metaphor of the writing we can feel that she associated the relationship with Johnson with the 'yoke' and 'confinement' of her first marriage:

> Veneration for his virtue, reverence for his talents, delight in his conversation, and habitual endurance of a yoke my husband first put upon me, and of which he contentedly bore his share for sixteen or seventeen years, made me go on so long with Mr. Johnson; but the perpetual confinement I will own to have been terrifying in the first years of our friendship, and irksome in the last. . . .[1]

Samuel Johnson found the relationship with Mrs. Thrale emotionally fulfilling, while to the much younger Hester Thrale the relationship with Johnson, mentally stimulating as it was, always meant added emotional responsibility, especially 'when he found himself particularly oppressed with diseases incident to the most vivid and fervent imaginations'.[2] John Wain has written shrewdly and sympathetically of the inequity of their relationship in its best days:

> All men, in the end, make impossible demands on women, and Johnson's demands on Hester Thrale were no exception. He told her of his own anxiety and misery, but he did not like having to hold still while she told him of hers. He clutched at her hand while walking through the valleys of his own private Inferno; she had to walk through hers alone. . . . Johnson listened for hours at a time to Boswell's confessions and emotional outpourings. But when he was with Mrs. Thrale it was his turn to do the talking.[3].

As Wain points out, Johnson, who at least in theory believed a husband's whoring was no sin against the wife, could never have wished to condole with Hester Thrale over her husband's chronic infidelity. We now know from Hester's Journal that Henry Thrale's infidelity led to recurrent bouts with venereal disease, posing not only vexation but some rather grim threats to his wife. A good wife, of course, as all the conduct books preached, never complains of her husband to anyone. But Johnson had an immediate emotional investment in choosing to believe that the Thrales were happy together. He seems to have adopted the couple—both younger than himself—as substitute parents.

[1] HLP, *Anecdotes*, p. 293.
[2] Ibid., p. 294.
[3] John Wain, *Samuel Johnson* (London: Macmillan, 1974; New York: The Viking Press, 1975), p. 269.

Samuel Johnson's demands on Mrs. Thrale seem in part demands for a mother-love he had not known from his own severe and rather elderly mother. Martine Watson Brownley, in her recent study of the ways in which Mrs. Thrale fostered Johnson's creative powers, 'mothered his mind', sees in Johnson's life with the Thrales an emotional arrangement that economically satisfied his desires for both dependence and freedom. Hester Thrale was to supply not only unconditional maternal love but also a semi-maternal discipline, order, the control that helped Johnson to work. But such discipline was acceptable from her because Mrs. Thrale herself must visibly submit to her husband.

What had developed was a situation ideal for Johnson. On the one hand, he craved feminine company, affection, and 'petticoat government'—Thrale [i.e. Hester] noted that '*I* should not have the same Power myself over Johnson's *Spirits* . . . if I were not a Woman.' At the same time, Johnson feared female power in certain ways: 'Nature has given women so much power that the law has very wisely given them little'. . . . Johnson could submit willingly to Thrale's discipline without being threatened, because he knew that it was ultimately illusory.[1]

A situation ideal for Johnson was not necessarily so for Hester Thrale. And both parties carried considerable emotional baggage in connection with ideas of either 'mother' or 'child'. The maternal/filial elements invoked in their relationship provided, Brownley feels, the ultimate cause of the violent dissolution of that relationship.

A desire for maternal presence does not cancel out an erotic element in the love Johnson felt for Hester Thrale. That he felt in some deep sense betrayed is evident in his lashing out at her over Piozzi, and an anguished sense of rejection is evident in his protesting too much: 'I drive her quite from my mind!'[2]

Johnson uttered these words to Fanny Burney, another friend who broke with Hester Lynch over the marriage to the Italian musician. The only close female friend among the Johnson group that frequented Streatham, Frances Burney had won Mrs. Thrale's respect and affection. Hester made the

---

[1] Martine Watson Brownley, '"Under the Dominion of *Some* Woman": The Friendship of Samuel Johnson and Hester Thrale', in *Mothering the Mind*, ed. Ruth Perry and Martine Watson Brownley (New York and London: Holmes & Meier, 1984), p. 73.

[2] See Clifford below, p. 239; see Frances Burney, *The Diary and Letters of Madame D'Arblay*, ed. Charlotte Barrett, 7 vols. (London: Henry Colburn, 1854), ii. 274.

mistake of confiding her feelings about Piozzi to Fanny, not realizing that the unmarried novelist of thirty was, for reasons to do with her own childhood, more likely to share the panic of Hester's children than to comprehend the passion of the woman. Dr. Charles Burney, his former obsequiousness turned to treachery, egged Fanny on to break from the woman. Dr. Burney had reason to be sensitive on the subject of music-masters and rich widows. Fanny became treacherous too. Yet the novelist Burney in her *Cecilia* (1782) had depicted the loveless and frustrating marriage between the stiff Compton Delvile and the intelligent, wilful, unhappy Mrs. Delvile, showing that Burney had learned something from observing the Thrales. And to that fictional marriage she allowed dissolution.

The real mystery about Hester lies not in her relation to Henry Thrale or to Samuel Johnson but in that to her children. Why were the daughters so cold—even harsh—to such a warm-hearted woman who was so proud of them? Queeney, on whom her mother so doted, is a particular puzzle. She seems so haughty, so ungenerous to a mother who lovingly recorded all her *bons mots* from infancy. Patricia Meyer Spacks can see nothing but gloom and anger in *Thraliana*, and takes very seriously Hester's own occasional speculations as to whether she herself is unlovable.[1] Spacks thinks, evidently, that Hester Lynch *was* unlovable, but the evidence of the many people attracted to her goes against that. People are still attracted by the wit, liveliness, inventiveness, and spontaneity of the personality behind *Thraliana*. The daughters might feel outshone by a mother too sparkling. The peculiar coldness that seems to emanate from Queeney, however, could be understood only if we could know the daughters' feelings about Henry Thrale; they must have loved him more than his wife ever did. Yet Queeney, in postponing her own marriage until the advanced age of forty-four (older than her mother had been when she married Piozzi) showed that she had taken note of her mother's life. Queeney married in time to have one child, no more, successfully avoiding her mother's experience of youth spent as one long period of dangerous and exhausting breeding.

At one juncture the trials of childbearing plunged Hester Lynch Thrale into serious depression. In 1779 her husband's poor health meant that she herself, though heavily pregnant,

---

[1] Patricia Meyer Spacks, *The Female Imagination* (New York: Alfred A. Knopf, Inc., 1975), pp. 253–66.

was called upon to cope with the brewery's problems. This must have stimulated unpleasant memories of the near-ruin of 1772, when Hester (then pregnant also) had had to work to save the brewery, her husband so shocked and depressed that he was unable to do anything. Hester then had relied on her mother, who contributed her savings, and on Johnson, who admired both women:

our Philosophical Friend embracing her—exlaimed that he was equally charmed by her Conduct, & edified by her Piety. Fear not the menaces of Suicide said he; the Man who has two such Females to console him, never yet killed himself—& will not *now*.[1]

This is a pretty clear indication that Henry Thrale did feel suicidal in 1772. Now in 1779 there was a milder repetition of the panic, and the exertion may have been the cause of Hester's miscarriage in August. For some while she was haunted by the fear, or belief, that she was about to die. If Henry Thrale felt suicidal in 1772, perhaps Hester played with suicide in the dark recesses of the mind in the late summer of 1779. She found expression for her feelings in a private satire, 'Three Dialogues on the Death of Hester Lynch Thrale, Written in August 1779'. As she explains in her 'Preface',

One of Dean Swift's happiest Compositions is certainly the little poem on his own Death. My Death would be a slight Event indeed compared with his—it would I think just bear three Dialogues among the people I chiefly lived with, & some of them are insignificant enough too.[2]

Her low opinion of her husband's relatives and some of his associates comes out in that last clause. The first 'Dialogue' deals with the more famous friends, including Burke, Mrs. Montagu, and Johnson. Dr. Johnson turns loudly against William Weller Pepys for reviving sorrow by alluding to the deceased Mrs. Thrale, but Johnson seems the only one of the company affected by her loss; rebuked, Pepys flies to Mrs. Montagu for sympathy:

MRS MONTAGU. Ay! flew out—did not he we heard him quite across the Room; why he burst in your hand like an overcharged Musket, & you seem

---

[1] 'Biographical Anecdotes', p. 27.
[2] HLT 'Preface' to 'Three Dialogues on the Death of Hester Lynch Thrale', in *Three Dialogues by Hester Lynch Thrale*, ed. M. Zamick, reprinted from *The Bulletin of the John Rylands Library* (Jan. 1932), (Manchester: Manchester University Press, 1932), p. 23.

a little shattered by the Recoil too I protest,—but he has had a Loss you'll allow—Mrs. Thrale, among her other Qualifications, had prodigious strong Nerves—and that's an admirable Quality for a friend of Dr. Johnson's.

PEPYS. Oh Madam I have been stunned by him at Streatham many a Time, and Mrs. Thrale not content with his loud Voice would make me exert my own Lungs very often till I have been quite Ill after it—how She could bear such bawling, & not be totally divested of all Delicacy was a constant Source of Wonder to me—I used to tell her that She put me in Mind . . .

MRS. MONTAGU. Bless me! yes, She had remarkable good Nerves, & yet carried off so suddenly—pounced by Death like a Partridge upon the *Wing*—caught in one of her *Flights* Mr. Pepys.

PEPYS. Charming! Charming! Bravo! Bravo!

[*And now he runs about telling everybody what Mrs. Montagu said last—while Johnson, enquiring what the happy Sallie was & hearing it repeated—leaves the Room, and the Conversation is changed to a worthier Subject.*][1]

This 'First Dialogue' may have been influenced by Fanny Burney's recently completed play, *The Witlings*, whose progress Mrs. Thrale had followed closely. Charles Burney forbade his daughter to think of having her play produced, partly from fear that Mrs. Montagu would take offence at a portrait of herself in 'Lady Smatter'. Mrs. Thrale, who thought herself in part a model for 'Lady Smatter' and generously didn't mind, is able in her private dramatic squib to ridicule Mrs. Montagu even more closely.

She also ridicules herself, stepping outside herself so that the qualities she delineated in more straightforward autobiographical moments emerge comically interpreted (or misinterpreted) as 'strong Nerves' (there is too an implicit statement that Johnson could and did get on her nerves). Hester Lynch found relief from her mood of despair in crisp but mordant comedy which allows her obliquely to present death as at least an escape from her present company. Self-pity is transformed by wry indirection. Hester was almost entitled to her later boast: 'I never was good at *pouting* when a Miss; and after fifteen years are gone one should know the value of Life better than to *pout* any part of it away.'[2] If she believed that self-pity was tiresome, that was partly because she basically distrusted the capacity of others to sympathize. Our essential human

---

[1] 'First Dialogue', p. 27.
[2] HLP to Sophia Weston 10 July 1789, MS in Firestone Library, Princeton; see Oswald G. Knapp, ed., *The Intimate Letters of Hester Piozzi and Penelope Pennington 1788–1822* (London: John Lane, The Bodley Head; New York: John Lane Co.; Toronto: Bell & Cockburn, 1914), pp. 20–1.

nature does not dispose us to sympathy; as she wrote in her commonplace book 'Minced Meat for Pyes', 'I do not think there is any such thing as *natural Pathos*: Tho' Man is a Teardropping Animal; in a Savage State none fall I believe but for *himself. . . .*'[1]

Hester Lynch possessed much of the tough-mindedness of the eighteenth century. A constant play of irony about herself and others is one of her most 'Augustan' qualities. She had a warm heart and at times an impulsive head, but it seems wrong to term her 'romantic' or 'sentimental' as even Clifford sometimes tends to do. Such terms are ways of getting rid of the feminine forms of her Augustanism. What makes Hester Lynch disconcerting is not sentiment but the aggressive comic turn of mind, the insight that sees connections in a flash of disenchantment.

Clifford, commenting on these three 'Dialogues', regrets that Hester 'never tried her hand at a full-length play'.[2] But she did try plays. Her masque, *The Two Fountains a Fairy Tale*, its story a radical revision of a fairy tale by Johnson (1766), was shown to Sheridan and Kemble in 1789. Earlier, she had begun a comedy, *The Humorist*, taken from a French play. And at some point in the 1780s she completed a two-act comedy, *The Adventurer*. It would have been natural for Hester to think of making some money and a name by writing for the stage in a period when women dramatists were often successful. But these abortive plays, all unpublished at present, exhibit no sense of dramatic structure, and are most likely to interest us as reflections of their author.

In *The Two Fountains*, the two breast-like magic fountains, associated with wishing and with life itself ('Source of Pleasure! Source of Pain! / Life with all its Wishes vain!'), are in the keeping of Lilinet the Fairy and her court. The young mortal Floretta is allowed to drink of the wishing fountain. She desires

> A Lover to my Taste . . .
> Unlike these Lords by which I live surrounded
> Rude and unletter'd as their vassal Hinds
> . . . 'Mid such Companions what Society
> Can your Floretta find?

---

[1] In HLP, 'Minced Meat for Pyes' as excerpted in *Piozzi Marginalia Comprising Some Extracts from Manuscripts of Hester Lynch Piozzi and Annotations from her Books*, ed. Percival Merritt (Cambridge, Mass.: Harvard University Press, 1925), p. 86.

[2] Clifford, below, p. 180.

We can hear Hester retracing her youthful intense desire for another kind of marriage from the marriage to Henry Thrale. But in the play, the world of feminine mutual help and sympathy, of fairies, wishes, and fountains is countered by the baleful figure of the tyrant Oberon, who has the power to send any elf to one of Derwent's dripping caves 'Till to a Petrifaction candy'd'. Oberon's masculine power is another expression of the petrifying masculine principles of rigidity, law, and stagnation which are termed 'Reality' at the end and which, without any particular dramatic logic, Floretta sadly decides she must obey: 'Social Duty best can bind / To its proper path the Mind'.[1] Female sexual desire and mental initiative—and dreams—are illicit and unwholesome, like superstition.

The Adventurer reflects the feelings and inner debates of 1781–2, and perhaps was first designed then. In this comedy the handsome widow with three thousand a year, Lady Rental, is in love with the poor 'adventurer' Ferdinand, even when she discovers that he has had 'low' occupations (as a riding master, an apothecary, and an usher at a school). She soliloquizes:

> Oh that he were a Gentleman by Blood, as he is by Sentiment! What low Profession could then taint his Honour? Yet how are the Professions he has exercised such *low* ones? I am ashamed to be making thus Excuses to myself for loving a Man bred a Scholar and a Soldier . . . here he comes, my Heart confesses his approach.

The eventual discovery that Ferdinand is the illegitimate son of Lord Harry Forrester surprisingly suffices to make him an English 'Gentleman by Blood'; the widow is able to unite with her 'honourable Adventurer' with the approval of her friends— in fiction as not in life. The play expresses resentment against the constrictions of custom. Lady Rental meditates on the lack of true independence in the world:

> Independence! how often have I heard that Word! & how little do I yet understand it? My Father, a wealthy & luxurious Merchant . . . cursed the Weather, ensured his Ships, & prayed for Independance: my Husband a Country Baronet teized me six Years about his Mother in law's Joynture wishing it would once drop that he might secure Independance. Perhaps in some humours I too have been Puppet enough to follow the same Phantom; here I stand however, rich in Purse, passable in Person, unconnected and uncontrolled; am I therefore possessed of Independance?—Not a Whit: the World will exercise Authority. . . .[2]

---

[1] John Rylands Library, Thrale-Piozzi manuscripts; *The Two Fountains* (a rough working version) is MS 649; quotations are from Act I, p. 5ʳ; p. 6ᵛ; Act II, p. 16ᵛ; p. 23ʳ.

[2] John Rylands Library, *The Adventurer*, MS 652; quotations are from Act II sc. 2, p. 12ʳ; Act I, sc 2, pp. 5ᵛ–6ʳ.

The shrewd impatient tones remind us of the author's self. Lady Rental is a self-portrait of Hester in mid-life, as Floretta in *The Two Fountains* is a presentation of herself in girlhood. Hester's plays show that she had ways of escaping the censor, but only momentarily. The author cannot let her imagination run riot, and anxiously satisfies the proprieties. The writing of a play seems to Hester Lynch a means of portraying her own situation, expressing velleities; she has not the feeling for characters and action in themselves that make the dramatist. One feels that any made-up stories interested her only in rare moods, and did not really attract her authorial self. She never showed much interest in purely fictional creation. The plays show that she associates fiction-making with wishing, and with constricted forms of self-expression; she is better off when she can allow herself the free play of an interest in history and current affairs.

If not a writer of fiction, she had always seen herself as an author. In her teens she sought a published (if secret) identity:

When I was about 13 14 and 15 Years old . . . I took a fancy to write in the S^t: James's Chronicle—unknown to my Parents and my Tutor too; it was my Sport to see them reading, studying, blaming or praising their own little Whimsical Girl's Performances—but such was their Admiration of one *little Verse Thing*, that I could not forbear owning it. . . .[1]

The 'little Verse Things' were the easiest pieces with which to win not only the approval she craved but the publication she always wanted. Throughout her life Hester wrote verses. Yet, despite the moderate success of 'The Three Warnings', which Johnson included in the compilation for Anna Williams, there are few symptoms of the true poet in Hester Lynch's verse-writing. She was, however, decidedly always an author, if often a frustrated one. Her real interest was in non-fictional prose; she cared for combinations of observations and ideas. For many years much of her writing was occasional, random, and private. But keeping *Thraliana* was not really all she wanted to do. When she got the chance, she turned her eyes to a wider scene.

What kind of writer did Hester Lynch truly want to be? Looking at her works we can see that there is much about her of the humane journalist, the kind that has long articles published in serious magazines today. Ultimately she aspired to be a historian and a philologist. The kind of writing that she

---

[1] 'Biographical Anecdotes', p. 29.

most cared for is, unfortunately for her, the kind that requires formal training in preparation, that needs libraries, the challenge of classroom debate, and the fostering criticism of acute readers. Novelists and dramatists of both sexes in any century can do without higher education; perhaps they are the stronger without it. Fanny Burney did not need it. But the historian needs the training of the schools, not only for the acquisition of languages (always the first point of education in the eighteenth century) but for instruction in sifting evidence and constructing argument. Hester Lynch had acquired a number of languages, but she began her true writing career as Hester Lynch Piozzi, in full middle age, without having been sufficiently taught the arts of argumentative construction, and without having been challenged as to leapt-to conclusions. Yet she was endowed with a witty and powerful mind, and with considerable knowledge, as well as experience of life. She was not wrong in believing that she could use that mind in writing. If Clifford's biography has a fault, it is in its not quite allowing the seriousness of Hester Lynch Piozzi's career as a writer. For all the impediments in her pursuit of her career, she accomplished a little more, perhaps, than Clifford is willing to allow.

It was after her new life with Gabriel Piozzi had begun that Hester Lynch felt able to venture into full-length publication. Gabriel Piozzi should be given some credit for 'mothering' her mind. It was of course neither of her two husbands but Johnson who was the subject of her first book. The first issue of *Anecdotes of Johnson* sold out on the first day of publication, but that was because of a mania for Johnson, and curiosity about his ladyfriend.

Always a rich mine for Johnson biographers, though formerly decried in favour of Boswell's *Life*, the *Anecdotes* may at present be returning to visibility and esteem. William McCarthy has made some serious claims for Hester Lynch Piozzi's biographical work:

> Five years before Boswell's *Life* and independently of his published *Tour*, she is here practicing the very method of seemingly unfiltered, candid-shot detail that Boswell is usually credited with inventing. If this claim seems exaggerated, we need only recall that the initial scandalous success of the *Anecdotes* was of precisely the same kind, and arose from the same causes, as those of the *Tour* and the *Life*. ... In writing of Johnson's boyhood on the model of Rousseau's she brings into view the psychological, pre-Freudian Johnson who is, we now know, really there to see (he is present, for instance, in many *Rambler* essays) but who has hardly any place in Boswell's innocent

vision. She is also doing something for which she has never been given credit: an avant-garde experiment in English biography. The credit for biographical innovation has traditionally gone all to Boswell.[1]

These claims are justified. Piozzi's *Anecdotes* is an innovative work. Reviewers did feel similar shocks on perusing first Piozzi, then Boswell. The shock appears to have been somewhat greater in the case of the *Anecdotes* because the author was a woman, and a woman betraying a sort of father, a sort of lover. The book's appearance led to hostile attacks, and a revival of all the abuse heaped on Hester at the time of her second marriage—hostile and even obscene abuse in which her rival James Boswell took a leading part, as Mary Hyde has chronicled in *The Impossible Friendship*.

Undaunted, Hester Lynch Piozzi published *Letters to and from the Late Samuel Johnson* (1788), a book which showed beyond doubt what an important friend and intellectual companion she had been to Johnson. Boswell took his revenge by producing his *Life of Johnson* (1791) in which Mrs. Thrale hardly figures save as a silly person on the fringes of Johnson's world, who exists to be contradicted.

The *Anecdotes* has a kind of mordant honesty in its treatment of both Johnson and the author, and in her discussion of the nature of her performance and her necessarily limited knowledge of her subject: 'Mine is a mere *candle-light* picture of his latter days, where every thing falls in dark shadow except the face, the index of the mind; but even that is seen unfavourably, and with a paleness beyond what nature gave it.'[2] There is a rugged beauty about her Johnson, and considerable tenderness as well as toughness in her *chiaroscuro*. *Anecdotes of Johnson* is a strong and not a sweet book. The marriage to Piozzi and the baptism by the fires of publicity that accompanied it were both of value to Hester. She had not only acquired a lover, companion, and supporter, she had also shaken off the trammels of English gentility. The loss of both feminine anonymity and bourgeois respectability served to harden her into an

---

[1] William McCarthy, *Hester Lynch Piozzi: Portrait of a Literary Woman* (Chapel Hill, N.C., and London: University of North Carolina Press, 1985), pp. 117–18. This excellent new study came out just before this went to press; coincidences of opinion are to be attributed to the truth of both our views. McCarthy had earlier recorded his opinion that HLP's book on Johnson is 'considerably more pungent and probing' than Boswell's *Life* ('Hester Piozzi' entry in *A Dictionary of British and American Women Writers 1660–1800*, ed. Janet Todd (London: Methuen and Co., 1984), p. 255).

[2] HLP, *Anecdotes*, p. 244.

author. In the published work of her mature years she is never
tempted into the treacliness of the softly ladylike.

Hester Lynch Piozzi continued to publish under her new
name, and to write new books which did not derive their
literary identity from her association with Johnson. Her next
book is a tribute to her second marriage, and a subtle panegyric
upon experience and liberty. In *Observations and Reflections Made
in the Course of a Journey through France, Italy and Germany* (1789),
she did not adopt the device (customary among travel-writers
and particularly useful to women) of presenting the book as a
collection of letters. Instead, she explains defiantly in her
'Preface' that she had no friends in England at the time with
whom to exchange pleasantries:

> I have not thrown my Thoughts into the form of private letters; because a
> work of which truth is the best recommendation, should not above all others
> begin with a lie. My old acquaintance rather chose to amuse themselves with
> conjectures, than to flatter me with tender inquiries during my absence: our
> correspondence then would not have been any amusement to the Public . . .'[1]

Separating herself, in the freedom of bitterness, from the
modest epistolary device, she adopts and creates an authoritative voice. She allows herself to intertwine observation, historical fact, speculation, jokes, feelings, and judgements. She can
move from description of Venice, its buildings 'illuminated as
I saw them last night by the moon at full, rising out of the sea'[2]
to description of the Venetian Senators in their red robes to a
historical and moral generalization: 'It is observable that all
long robes denote peaceful occupations, and that the short coat
is an emblem of a military profession, once the disgrace of
humanity, now unfortunately become its false and cruel
pride.'[3]

Ellen Moers has suggested that Hester Lynch Piozzi was an
important influence on Mrs. Radcliffe and thus on the new
Gothic fiction in her 'unconventional, distinctly female travel
book'.[4] It *is* a distinctly female travel book. Hester Lynch
Piozzi maintains an interest in the arts of peace and particularly in the productions of women, as also in women's various
experiences of life. She observes that a nun of her acquaintance
is not particularly interested in visitors, and comments 'one is

---

[1] 'Preface', *Observations and Reflections Made in the Course of a Journey through France, Italy
and Germany*, 2 vols. (London: A Strahan and T. Cadell, 1789), vol. i, pp. vi–vii.
[2] Ibid., p. 151.
[3] Ibid., p. 159.
[4] Ellen Moers, *Literary Women* (New York: Anchor Press/Doubleday, 1977), p. 194.

always more important in one's own eyes than in those of others; but no one is of importance to a Nun, who is and ought to be employed in other speculations.'[1] More remarkable than individual observations on the women seen abroad is the pattern of references to women in the very texture of the writing. Hester Lynch Piozzi not only introduces quotations from women writers like Lady Mary Wortley Montagu, but also employs numerous illustrations and metaphors taken from the feminine world. For instance, she says that while Venice's black gondolas 'give an air of melancholy at first sight' they are utterly un-sorrowful, and then illustrates contrast in adding 'It is like painting the lively Mrs. Cholmondeley in the character of Milton's Pensive Nun. . . .'[2]

Throughout, there is an air of personal exploration, and the flow of a lively consciousness coming across external facts that are vivid if disconcerting, facts sometimes failing to live up to book-nurtured expectations. Hester Lynch Piozzi's description of crossing the Alps (which deserves to be anthologized and was doubtless an influence on Radcliffe) records an Augustan relief in the face of expected disillusion. The experience can honestly be said to be grand; it gives the mind 'a sensation of fulness never experienced before, a satisfaction that there is something great to be seen on earth—some object capable of contenting even fancy'.[3] This of course makes claims for a capacious mind and a fancy not easily contented.

In her travels in Italy Hester Lynch Piozzi is conscious that she is coming not as the tourist but as the relation, finding in a sense a new home, and needing to understand it: '*I* ought to learn that which before us lies in daily life, if proper use were made of my demi-naturalization.'[4] There is, she makes us understand, a personal urgency in her recognition of this old land which she is seeing under new and unusual auspices. The bridal experience itself is of course a feminine one, sharply distinct from the experience and expectation of the male traveller glancing at classic ground and modern pleasures. Her book celebrates a marriage, attachment, 'demi-naturalization'.

Living in Gabriel Piozzi's country with new relatives and carrying on her life in another language was no hardship to the new Signora Piozzi. She knew a number of languages—and

---

[1] *Observations and Reflections.*, i. 3.
[2] Ibid., pp. 159–60.
[3] Ibid., p. 36.
[4] Ibid., p. 67.

had she not grown up hearing two tongues, English and Welsh, before acquiring others in her youth? She was fascinated by languages, and she had some 'learning' which in the eighteenth century meant knowledge of Latin and Greek. These were the languages which represented male power, and a learned lady could inspire hostility and unease. As recently as 1914 Oswald Knapp is comically reluctant to believe that Mrs. Piozzi really knew Greek, but has to admit that all the evidence indicates that she did, though not instructed in it in her youth.[1] Fanny Burney felt that learning Latin would look too conspicuously erudite and unladylike, and dropped the lessons Johnson was giving her and Queeney; Hester Lynch had no such qualms, and towards the end of her life began to acquire Hebrew. Her Celtic background as well as her education stimulated her interest in word derivations and relationships; unlike the average Englishwoman, a Welshwoman cannot take her own language for granted. The journals and letters have constant quick observations on words and their meanings:

> Did not Virgil mean by his Epithet *Puniceis* to *Rosetis* in the fifth Eclogue the rose of Tyrian Dye! the *Punic* or Damask Rose. I perswaded Johnson to believe it one Day at Streatham as we read the Eclogue together—in the Year 1769.—[2]

> This evening a chair will carry me to M^{rs}. Holroyds to meet Two other Females whom Richardson taught the Town to call old Tabbies, attended says he by young *Grimalkins*; now that's wrong: because they are young Tabbies, & when grown Grey—are *Gris Malkins*, I suppose.[3]

Hester Lynch enjoyed collecting puns in different languages and noticing other people's use (and pronunciation) of words, as well as speculating about derivations. These interests combine in an ambitious work, *British Synonymy; or, An Attempt at Regulating the Choice of Words in Familiar Conversation* (1794). The problems of her husband and other Italians with the tricky pseudo-synonyms of English justified an endeavour which soon became more than a simple handbook. In her 'Preface' the author again remembers her own national origin: 'I shall have

---

[1] 'But in her Commonplace Book ... written only for her own amusement, occur several Greek phrases, and an epigram of some length, with a translation, apparently her own. And it is noteworthy that the Greek is written with the breathings and accents, in the clear firm hand of one well used to the script, very unlike the tentative efforts of a beginner' (Oswald G. Knapp, *The Intimate Letters of Hester Piozzi and Penelope Pennington*, p. 10).

[2] *Thraliana: The Diary of Mrs. Hester Lynch Thrale (later Mrs. Piozzi), 1776–1809*, ed. Katharine C. Balderston, 2 vols. (Oxford: Clarendon Press, 1951) i. 31.

[3] HLP letter to Sir James Fellowes, Bath, 1815; MS in Firestone Library, Princeton, MS AM 17952.

an honour to boast, and like my countryman Glendower in
Shakespeare's Henry the Fourth, *have given our tongue an helpful
ornament.*[1]

British Synonymy is desirous of honour, extensive, and idiosyn-
cratic. The sufferings of Louis XVI have made too deep an
impression on the author's mind, and King Louis' head turns
up where one least expects it. The treatise, however, has the
merits as well as the defects of being opinionated. Reading it
gives one an often enjoyable sense of contact with a lively mind
to whom words are perpetually fascinating. Her excursions are
often efforts to connect literature, social life, and facts of
speech, as in the entry under 'Sentiment':

a person who, as Addison's Sempronius says of Cato, is grown ... *ambitiously
sententious*, has been of late derided by the appellation of a man of SENTI-
MENT—in allusion, as I suppose, to Mr. Sheridan's play. Favourite dramas
have, among the English, a temporary influence over the language that
would amaze us. The Duke of Buckingham's Rehearsal drove out of
fashionable company the silly phrase of *Egad and all that*; and I have been told
that Dryden's Sir Martin cleared the elegant tables of their favourite
intercalation *in fine, Sir*. New ones meanwhile spring up every day, like these,
dully to take their turn and be forgotten, to the no small incumbrance of
conversation. ... for living, as Collins said, under the dominion of a word,
whether SENTIMENT, or *rage*, or *bore*. ... or whatever absurdity determines
choice, must surely be a despicable mode of proving our good breeding. ...
Indeed the pedantry of a drawing-room is no less offensive than that of a
college, or an army coffee-house, or a merchant's compting-house;—all are
tedious and disgraceful, and should be swept away.[2]

Yet for all her contempt for clichés, she has some feeling for
sound colloquial slang; she regrets, for instance, that the
schoolboy phrase 'a blunt' for a dull person cannot be used: 'a
blunt, is so good, that I sigh for its removal into social life, where
blunts are exceedingly frequent and we have no word for
them.'[3] In her pursuit of words she gives interesting glimpses of
the customs and habits of the age, as, for example, under the
entry 'Fat':

A corpulent man or woman is said to be FAT, when we have no mind to
soften matters—and tell them that their embonpoint is agreeable. ... But for
the comfort of those who delight to see mind triumph over body, we have the
famous miller of Billericay in Essex, who by dint of resolute temperance, or
rather a strictly abstemious diet, did actually reduce himself from the
enormous weight of twenty-nine stone to twelve only. ... And 'tis said that a

---

[1] 'Preface' to *British Synonymy; or, An Attempt at Regulating the Choice of Words in
Familiar Conversation*, 2 vols. (London: G. G. and J. Robinson, 1794), vol. i, p. vi.
[2] Ibid., ii. 243–4.
[3] Ibid., i. 177.

gentleman of fortune . . . is at this moment determining to follow so excellent an example.—Let not however any thing which he does, or I say, tend to approve or even palliate a folly often committed by young ladies, who, to prevent their being called FAT, ruin their health and beauty too, which best consists in PLUMPNESS—and which when once lost can never be restored.[1]

The author's moral imagination is frequently apparent, most strikingly perhaps in the careful delineation of the difference between 'luxury', 'sensuality', 'voluptuousness', and 'debauch'. Her essay describing a man perfectly luxurious and totally free of sensuality is an ingenious creation of a moral horror—the portrait of someone as remote from all virtue as free from sensual vice.[2] The author's political beliefs, everywhere apparent, are not simply conservative, and are in keeping with general moral and humane concerns:

TO MANUMIT . . . implies the power of doing an act with our own hands, and must shortly become useless; for who can MANUMIT when servitude shall be no more? When the human soul however is SET FREE from all corporeal temptations, by the dissolution of that body which contains it, how will theirs rejoice that have from pure motives, from honest and generous principles, contributed towards EMANCIPATING the Blacks, and DELIVERING them FROM SLAVERY![3]

British Synonymy is a book that offers many pleasures; it is a good book to dip into. It can be recommended to those wishing to find out how eighteenth-century people might have thought about a variety of matters. The section on 'Fancy' and 'Imagination', for instance, is crisp, useful, and surprising; not dwelling too long on Milton's *Paradise Lost* as a work of imagination and Pope's *Rape of the Lock* as 'a work of exquisite FANCY', the author moves to a discussion of the difference between the terms as used in medicine:

We are taught by medical students to believe, that such is the near connection between soul and body—each one feels injuries offered to the other with an acute and immediate sensibility. . . . they point out to our enquiries . . . patients labouring under a chlorotick habit, or confirmed anorexia—who find themselves subjected by those disorders to the force of IMAGINATION in such a manner as to create in them new and unaccountable FANCIES for food, rejected by persons in perfect health, as odious and offensive. . . .[4]

The little excursion into medical belief about mind–body relation and medical use of terms throws some real light on the

---

[1] Ibid., pp. 231–2.
[2] Ibid., pp. 404–15.
[3] Ibid., p. 193.
[4] Ibid., pp. 221–3.

eighteenth century's response to 'imagination'. Above all, *British Synonymy* gives us the pleasure of contact with a mind that has thought about the experience of her age as that experience is moulded by and reflected in current language.

Hester Lynch Piozzi's last major work is *Retrospection: or, A Review of the Most Striking and Important Events, Characters, Situations, and Their Consequences, Which the Last Eighteen Hundred Years have Presented to the View of Mankind* (1801). One can see in Piozzi's works a kind of progression, almost a programme, if unconsciously developed at first. From an account of persons and anecdotes she turned in her *Observations and Reflections* to places and events. *British Synonymy* examined language and meanings. Now in her history of the world (more particularly of the West) she could ambitiously combine all these interests, and connect persons, places, events, anecdotes, and languages. In her 'Preface' Hester Lynch Piozzi defends her introduction of light material, and the book's general focus:

Half a moment will suffice to prove, that whilst the deep current of grave history rolls her full tide majestick, to that ocean where Time and all its wrecks at length are lost: our flashy *Retrospect*, a mere *jet d'eau*, may serve to soothe the heats of an autumnal day with its light-dripping fall, and form a rainbow round. Did no such book catch the occurrences, and hold them up, however maimed and broken, before the eyes of our contemporaries, we really should very soon forget all that our ancestors had done or suffered. . . .

The same kind and encouraging Publick . . . shall take [it] as it is; and if they feel themselves pleased with the colours presented in the varying changeful mass, will try to hinder some critick's heavy hand from breaking it; remembering that an opal loses all its power of playing before the eye, soon as a crack is made in its thin surface.[1]

The waterfall, the rainbow, and the opal are very expressive eighteenth-century images, speaking the virtues of variety and movement and life as against stasis and death. The reference to 'grave history' is mocking, for all history speaks our progress, individual and collective, to the grave, and we are all alike swept on that dark stream towards the end of time—but the would-be majestic tones of historians are false and hackneyed. *Retrospection* is, as it were, a memoir, as if the world (or rather, the Western part of it) since the time of Christ were an individual person, capable of looking back on a long but none-too-happy life. This approach is an aspect of the basic strategy.

[1] HLP, 'Preface' to *Retrospection: or, A Review of the Most Striking and Important Events, Characters, Situations, and their Consequences, Which the Last Eighteen Hundred Years Have Presented to The View of Mankind*, 2 vols. (London: John Stockdale, 1801), vol. i, pp. viii–xi.

Retrospection has a main thesis and several decided and original themes. Its major thesis would find no favour today outside fundamentalist circles, though it is related also to what we have heard from Spengler. Hester Lynch Piozzi believed that recent events, especially in France, proved the truth of biblical prophecy, and that the last days were approaching. (Among other things, she believed the Jews were soon to be recalled to the Holy Land.) Her history is a quietly apocalyptic book. She also believed very sincerely that the nature of history is ultimately to point out the inadequacy of a life without Christ, illustrating the pitiful failure of the hopes of the flesh and the pride of men. Her tone is not one of disillusion but of lack of illusion. Just as a man or woman over sixty (so the tone suggests) ought to be able to look back on life and times without self-deception, so we ought to acknowledge the truth about the interesting but untidy past. History shows no grand human progress towards perfection; human nature is ever asserting its uglier aspects. Neither is there any great good time to which we can look back—Imperial Rome or Merrie England. As William McCarthy says, 'In *Retrospection* she attempted nothing less than to answer to Gibbon's Whig, and "Infidel," *History*; the book failed in part because it was perceived to have overstepped the generic limits allowed to women writers—"a series of dreams by an old lady" one reviewer scornfully called it.'[1] Fortunately, perhaps, Hester Lynch Piozzi had anticipated the severity of the critics, as she showed in her burlesque criticism supposedly by the *Critical Review*:

tho' the lively Lady herself was not stagger'd as it appears when she took a Birds Eye View of such immense Extent—we confess *our* limited Capacities can with difficulty understand the Work. ... For tho' we have been lately accustomed to the Style of *Female* Dramatists, *Female* Wits, Female Politicians & Female Astronomers,—It has not been quite in our Practise to travel wth. y^e *fair* Creatures thro' the *Dark Ages* . . . or follow in their Train to present Times, unravelling by fancied Clews spun by themselves the inexplicable Labyrinth of Events. . . . But . . . M^{rs}. Piozzi upon the Strength of a Three Years Tour thro' Italy, & Three more pass'd in Meditation upon its distant Beauties, strongly contrasted by her present Prospects in the County of *Flint*, North Wales—bursts on us in the character of *Serene Instructress* wth. regard to

---

[1] McCarthy, *Portrait of a Literary Woman*, p. 239. McCarthy, the first critic to treat *Retrospection* seriously and at length, sees in it an anticipation of Marxist history-writing and praises the 'remarkably unsentimental and sophisticated' analysis of the English Revolution of 1688 (p. 246). See also his entry in Todd dictionary.

Religion & Politics—both which She prudently squares to Court Notions & Episcopal Ideas.[1]

Her parodic critique shows that Hester Lynch at the age of sixty had the same keen perception of how others might see her that she had exhibited in the earlier 'Three Dialogues'; the parody also shows that the book was a very conscious and deliberate engagement with affairs, and knowingly risk-taking.

Hester Lynch Piozzi's history is indeed alike antagonistic to progressivist Whig History, to radical reformist optimism, and to the elegiac grandeur of a Gibbon. But it certainly is not the result of a mean prudence that squares itself 'to Court Notions'. The anecdotes repeatedly prove the recurrent exhibition of human absurdity, injustice, and cruelty. Human history is indeed very real; our ancestors did do and suffer, and not to make formulae for historians. At the same time, history is a divine comedy with a slightly inadequate cast.

The author is interested in changes in social life and manners, including those that affect women; she notes, for instance, the establishment of the first boarding-school for girls in England. She takes account of card games, table manners, new tastes in gardening. Naturally, there are developments of which she approves (within measure). But she does not believe in an improvement in human nature:

After the year 1600, our *retrospective* eye will not see gross and prominent offence so often. The superfic[i]es of life began to obtain a smoothness little known before. Language, morals, religion, manners, all were soon covered with a coat of varnish, that has employed men ever since to *rub it in* and *hide*, not *take away*, defects from the sub-stratum.[2]

She treats her own period of the mid-eighteenth century with considerable caution and suspicion:

Yet were the thirty years we are reviewing [i.e. 1750–80], oddly polluted by unnatural falsehood and people not contented to *tell* lies, *lived* in them. George Psalmanazar, who had eaten raw flesh and worshipped the sun ... was scarce cold in earth before new fictions, new fables perplexed us. An obscure girl, by a meanly constructed tale, set London in a fever of discordant opinions; and the mayor, who wished to punish what he deemed perjury, scarcely escaped with life from her adherents ... and some years after that, the Douglas cause drawn to disgraceful length; showed that high birth was no security against suspicion of a black imposture. Strange literary fraudulence was found in Lauder, charged on Macpherson, and proved

[1] HLP in 'Minced Meat for Pyes', quoted in Merritt, *Piozzi Marginalia*, pp. 77–9.
[2] HLP, *Retrospection*, ii, 119.

clear on Chatterton. Junius, clad in complete darkness, darted malignant, and yet undetected flashes of wit and anger through the gloom. . . .[1]

The implication seems to be that if the eighteenth century excelled in dishonesty it perhaps lied to itself, most of all in its belief in its progressive success. This is a refreshing view of a period which prided itself on its sincerity and its *honnêtes hommes*.

There are a number of personal touches, some striking: 'Forgiveness is a virtue too good for Pagans, somehow—I feel as if I grudged it them.'[2] There are some quite witty shafts: 'Sir Richard Steele gave weekly instructions to climb the hill Difficulty by some short cut, or easy path to Fame.'[3] Hester Lynch Piozzi allows herself to be irreverent and unconventional.

One of the more unconventional themes is a constant if unobtrusive defence of women. This shows itself in the advocacy of women's achievements, such as the protest in favour of 'the Princess Anna Commena' and her 'female eloquence' against Gibbon's strictures.[4] Piozzi also quietly insists on bringing women into the account, as in the discussion of Anne of Brittany. In her account of her own century she introduces the murderous Mary Blandy and the inoculation-bringing Lady Mary Wortley Montagu. She reminds us of the ever-present beauty of Frances Stuart: 'Remembrance of her symmetrick form is even yet preserved among us, by the figure of Britannia on a half-penny.'[5]

Retrospection is really a feminist history. Like *Observations and Reflections* it has a texture of references and images taken from feminine experience. In its major strategies, as in its parts, it is a female challenge to the interpretation of history that serves the ends of power. She writes in deliberately feminine language, for instance, about the Europeans' discovery of the Americas: 'soon as a new world opened itself to their inordinate desires, they fell upon it like untaught children on a toy-shop—tasting, and breaking, and knocking all in pieces.'[6] The whole is not only a retrospection but a retaliation, as Hester Lynch Piozzi serves up history with a difference.

The sense of the unchanging perversity of human behaviour

[1] Ibid., pp. 436–7.
[2] Ibid., i, 31.
[3] Ibid., ii, 317.
[4] Ibid., i, 273.
[5] Ibid., ii, 305.
[6] Ibid., p. 59.

and experience went very deep with Hester Lynch. One of the best annotations to *Retrospection* is found in a letter to Sir James Fellowes in 1816. Sad that her home of fifty years is to be sold by auction, Hester yet observes that the auctioneer is handsome, and this, in one of her characteristic turns of association, reminds her of a story told to Cicero:

> There is an old story of Balbus when Quaestor at Seville, throwing an Auctioneer to the Lyons in his Menagerie, because a Female Friend who was selling up her Possessions, complain'd to him that the Auctioneer was so ugly & deformed, he frighted all Buyers away. Our People will lose no Bidders by that fault: but is it not odd that the World with all its *Fluctuations*, should have undergone so little *Change?*
>
> Always Vexations, Disappointments, and inadequate Anger, for what can hardly be helped: tho' the Mode of expressing that Anger is alter'd by the different Situations of Society—[1]

It is the modes of experiencing our 'inadequate Anger' that mark history, though the eruptions of anger, largely impotent and useless, change little in the fluctuations wrought by unchanging life. That letter expresses Hester's grimmer outlook, but it typifies her views and style, in the focus upon anecdote and the turns of comic tones to underlying sadness.

It is a pity that all this good material should be lost. The new edition of *The Correspondence of Hester Lynch Thrale Piozzi (1784–1821)* now being prepared by Edward A. and Lillian D. Bloom will bring to everyone's attention Hester's powers as a letter-writer, displaying the strength as well as the vivacity of her observations. But it is time to rescue the Piozzi works written for publication. Perhaps we can hope in the not-too-distant future to possess an anthology of excerpts from her chief works, a *Hester Lynch Piozzi Reader*. Such an anthology should include at least one of the chapters on the eighteenth century in *Retrospection*, and extensive passages from *Observations and Reflections*, and from *British Synonymy*, as well as excerpts from verses and dramas and of course from journals, commonplace-books, and letters. There is a deal of interesting writing to be found in the works of—what shall we call her? She has been clogged by marital titles; we first hear of her as 'Mrs. Thrale' but it is not much improvement to call her 'Mrs. Piozzi'—and that persona did not come into being until 1784. History teaches us that the name of 'Mrs.' is a sad impediment to full literary fame, and that a Charlotte Brontë will always be

---

[1] HLP to Sir James Fellowes, 18 Apr. 1816, MS in Firestone Library, Princeton, MS AM 14675.

more valued than a *Mrs.* Gaskell. Hester Lynch Thrale as Mrs. Thrale figures as the subject of others, but as Hester Lynch Piozzi she wrote and published for herself—the self she signed with a flourish 'H:L:P:'. It is not the serviceable 'Mrs. Thrale' or the flighty 'Mrs. Piozzi' whose marriage caused such a scandal but the essential, thoughtful, tough-minded Hester that we can meet and understand in the writings. And that is the Hester we encounter and see developing through the changing modes of experience in the biography by James L. Clifford that you are about to read. The portico, I hope, serves both for use and ornament, but it is the house that matters.

M.A.D.

EDITOR'S NOTE

Although in the present printing no alterations have been made in the text or footnotes, there are a number of other changes. The original frontispiece, now known to be not a portrait of Mrs. Thrale, has been replaced by an authenticated portrait. Captions for the illustrations have been corrected where ownership has changed. Appendices B and C have been brought up to date, an important note inserted in Appendix D, and the *Additions to Select Bibliography* enlarged by Professor Doody to include those works which have appeared since the 1968 reprint was published.

Virginia I. Clifford
1986

HESTER LYNCH SALUSBURY

I

A DAUGHTER OF WALES

'WHY, sir,' says Quaint in Vanbrugh's *Aesop*, 'I'm a Herald by nature; my mother was a Welchwoman'; and when he is pressed further for information about his country, he describes Wales as a place where 'every man is born a gentleman, and a genealogist'.[1]

It is well to remember this national trait when considering the subject of these pages, for it has been said of Mrs. Thrale that the only topic upon which she could be dull was her family history.[2] Though always ready to laugh at her own pretensions, she consumed many hours attempting to trace her ancestry into the dim past. And even if many of her genealogical claims cannot be substantiated to-day, the elaborate family tree which she devised is not wholly a figment of her imagination, for she came of a celebrated Welsh family, of which she might well be proud.[3]

---

[1] Vanbrugh, *Aesop*, Act III, Scene 1.

[2] Broadley, p. 4. Introductory essay by T. Seccombe.

[3] In later life Mrs. Piozzi copied out her family tree a number of times, notably in Mainwaring Piozziana (an account written for her adopted heir in 1810–13), in Thraliana, in Cecilia Mostyn's copy of Yorke's *The Royal Tribes of Wales* (sold at the Anderson Galleries, New York, May 4, 1933), and for the Countess of Orkney, Dec. 31, 1801 (now in the Nat. Lib. of Wales, Aberystwyth). Another copy, written for Lord Keith in a different hand, is now in my possession, the gift of the late Mrs. Knollys. Since Mrs. Piozzi was continually gaining information, these accounts do not agree in all details. Welsh genealogy is a very complicated matter, and it is impossible for anyone not an expert to write with any certainty about it. Consequently I have relied throughout on what would appear to be the most authoritative account of Mrs. Piozzi's ancestry, the article by Sir John Ballinger, 'Katheryn of Berain', *Y Cymmrodor*, xl (1929), 1–42. Complete genealogical charts are included with this article. Much ink has been spilt over Mrs. Piozzi's claim to royal blood, but present scholarship admits her descent from Henry Tudor, though not by a legitimate line (but see Broadley, pp. 280–3, and the *Athenaeum*, Feb. 2, 1861, p. 164; Feb. 23, 1861, p. 264). In other parts of the elaborate family tree which she constructed there are errors, but usually these mistakes do not materially weaken her major lines of descent. These errors, too, can usually be traced to generally accepted Welsh authorities of the day, such as Thomas Pennant, her distant cousin. In Mrs. Piozzi's possession (now in the John Rylands Library) were over 330 deeds, grants, conveyances, rentals, wills, bonds, and other documents having to do with her family. The earliest in this collection is a grant by Thomas Salusbury the younger on June 30, 1490, to Thomas, son of Richard Billinge. From this mass of evidence some day a trained genealogist may construct a complete and accurate family tree of the Salusbury family. A number of

The Salusburys had been prominent for centuries, though the claim that the supposed founder of the house, Adam de Salzburg, had come to England in the eleventh century with the Conqueror is undoubtedly pure conjecture. It is certain, however, that members of the family had been active in the Crusades and in the Wars of the Roses, that a Salusbury was one of the first Governors of Denbigh under Henry II, and that another gallantly held the Castle for Charles I during the Civil War.

The most illustrious of her ancestors was the celebrated Katherine of Beraine, called 'Mam Cymru'—Mother of Wales —because of the number of her descendants. Granddaughter of an illegitimate son of Henry VII; said to have been recognized as a cousin by Queen Elizabeth, whose gifts are still preserved as family treasures; married in turn to members of four of the most powerful families in North Wales—Salusbury, Clough, Wynn, Thelwall; willing to leave behind the children of her first husband when emigrating to the Continent with her second, but using them later as pawns to further her own ambitions; ruling them and her grandsons with a rod of iron; she was a man's woman, more gifted with sharpness of wit and charm of manner than with the more homely household virtues. Many legends have gathered about her, the most amusing of which is the romantic story told by Pennant of her speed in accepting a second and a third husband after the death of her first.[1] There were other tales, too, of her generosity and goodness, her many lovers, even her false and murderous disposition. It is impossible to separate the true from the false, but possibly, like her distant granddaughter, she was a mixture of forceful decision and wilful femininity not easy to characterize by any simple generalization.

The future Mrs. Piozzi was descended from Katherine both through her father, John Salusbury, and her mother, Hester Maria Cotton. Frequent intermarriages between cousins had mixed both the family tree and the property, and strangely

the later papers have notes on the back in the hand of Dr. Johnson, showing that Mrs. Thrale evidently discussed the question with him. Johnson, like the others, may have been bored, but he patiently examined all her old family records.

[1] T. Pennant, *A Tour in Wales*, ii (1784), 26. According to this story, Katherine refused Wynn, who escorted her from the church after the funeral of her first husband, Sir John Salusbury, because she had already accepted the proposal of Sir Richard Clough, who had brought her to the ceremony. But, so the tale runs, she promised Wynn that should she ever be left a widow again, he would be her third—and so he was. The story is shown to be merely a variation of an old folk legend, and chronologically impossible in the case of Katherine, by Professor Carleton Brown in *Poems by Sir John Salusbury and Robert Chester* (E.E.T.S., Extra Ser. cxiii, 1914), p. xiv. See also Ballinger, op. cit., pp. 6–8.

enough, it was her mother who traced her lineage back to Sir John Salusbury, Katherine's first husband, while her father traced his back to Sir Richard Clough, the second. Thus it was that about the beginning of the eighteenth century the Salusbury estate of Lleweney, so called from the old Bavarian Lion which adorned the coat of arms, came into the family of Salusbury-Cotton, while the Clough estate of Bach-y-Graig, with the spectacular six-story house of Dutch bricks, which the superstitious Flintshire natives thought built by a demon, was held by their distant relatives the Salusburys. The master and mistress of Lleweney were Sir Robert Cotton, a man of wealth and distinction in the country, and his wife, Lady Betty Tollemache. Living with them was his unmarried sister, Hester Maria, a talented, attractive woman, with a considerable fortune in her own right, who had consistently refused all suitors because her heart had long been given to her improvident cousin and neighbour, John Salusbury of Bach-y-Graig.[1]

This John was a wayward but appealing character. Born in 1707,[2] he lost his father four years later, and with two younger brothers was brought up by an indulgent mother. Many of the faults of the man are directly traceable to this lack of restraint when a child. He was given the best of educations, first at Whitchurch School, later at Trinity Hall, Cambridge, which he entered at seventeen. He became a Fellow Commoner of his college in 1728, and received the M.A. degree the same year.[3]

[1] The following account of the parents of Hester Lynch Salusbury is based largely on statements written much later by their daughter. These accounts appear in Thraliana, in the Mainwaring Piozziana (see p. 429, n. 4), and in an autobiographical sketch written at the express desire of her executor, Sir James Fellowes, in Dec. 1815. This last (now in the collection of Mr. R. B. Adam) was printed by Hayward in 1861, and has been used as the chief authority for her early life ever since. In such a late version, however, the chronology is apt to be vague. The most complete account, and the earliest, is to be found in Thraliana, April 1778. Wherever possible these reminiscences have been checked from actual contemporary documents available among her family papers in the John Rylands Library and elsewhere, and the later accounts have only been used when they do not seem obviously inconsistent with the available facts.

[2] In a copy of *The Ladies Calling* (now at Brynbella), once owned by Lucy Salusbury, the following entries appear in the front: '1707 John Salusbury was born The first day of September at three o'clock in the morning on Monday'; '1708 Thomas Salusbury—12th December'; '1709/10 Harry Salusbury—19th March'; '1711 William Salusbury—22nd day of 1ober and dyed the 9th day of January 1711-2.' In the back of this same book is listed the birth of her only grandchild, Hester Lynch Salusbury.

[3] I am indebted to Mr. C. W. Crawley, Fellow of Trinity Hall, for information concerning John Salusbury's college records. In the admissions book of Trinity Hall, Cambridge, for 1724 appears the entry 'ad. Pen. 3 July. ad. Sch. 5 Jan. 1724/25; ad. F. C. 28 April 1728. taken off 20 Decr. 1732'. He was thus admitted Pensioner on July 3, 1724, Scholar Jan. 5, 1725, Fellow Commoner Apr. 28, 1728,

Later he seems to have cut something of a figure in Welsh society, as Captain of the local Militia and Deputy Lieutenant for the County of Denbigh.[1] He also mixed in the world of fashionable London. He appears to have led a mildly adventurous life, though not one so lurid as his daughter would have us believe, for the startling tales of his early affairs set down in her diary many years later read more like a Fielding romance than real history.[2] Certainly a careful study of his own family papers hardly supports the rakish portrait she has painted. Quick-tempered, imprudent, and wild he undoubtedly was, but his own letters and diaries do not show a dissipated adventurer.

John's second brother, Thomas, had also been educated at Trinity Hall, Cambridge, became a Fellow of his college in 1732, and then resided in London at Doctors' Commons.[3] Harry, the third brother, rendered something of an imbecile as the result of an accident, was content to remain rooted to the Welsh soil. The expensive education of the two elder boys, together with their extravagant life in London, had been financed by loans and mortgages on the family property, for the Salusburys were not wealthy like their cousins the Cottons.

Some of the money they had managed to borrow from Sir Robert Cotton,[4] who had always been friendly, and who, as Lord Lieutenant of the County of Denbigh, had given John the commission in the Militia. The story goes that he took John abroad with him, paying all the expenses, merely from delight in his company;[5] but how long they travelled on the Continent,

and taken off the books Dec. 20, 1732. As Mr. Crawley points out, the dates in the register do not prove actual residence, but merely indicate change of status. The degrees taken were not recorded in any college registry, these appearing only in the University records. Mr. Crawley sums up the facts which can be derived from the records. 'The entries show at least that Salusbury was both intelligent and well-to-do; his admission as a Scholar suggests the first, his admission as a Fellow Commoner, the second (since it meant higher fees).' Lucy Salusbury, John's mother, had been well educated herself. The pupil of the famous astronomer, Halley, she saw to it that her sons had the best instruction. (See letter from Mrs. Piozzi to Sir James Fellowes, July 7, 1819.) John and Thomas were together at Cambridge part of the time, when they 'slept together as they delighted to tell, & their Cat Tyger on the Bed'. (Mainwaring Piozziana, I. viii.)

[1] Ry. Charter, 1231, 1232. Both appointments were made on Feb. 10, 1734/5, by Sir Robert Salusbury Cotton, Bt., Lord Lieutenant of the County of Denbigh.

[2] Thraliana, Apr. 1778.

[3] Thomas Salusbury was admitted as a Pensioner at Trinity Hall, Cambridge, in 1726, Scholar in 1728, received the degree of LL.B. in 1734, LL.D. in 1740, and was a Fellow of the college from 1732 to 1751.

[4] Ry. Charter 1004 is a bond from John Salusbury to Sir Robert Cotton for £600, dated Feb. 28, 1736/7. On the back Dr. Johnson later wrote: 'the time of payment does not appear.'   [5] Thraliana, Apr. 1778.

or when each returned, cannot be determined. Nor is it certain how much we may believe concerning the French Marquise at Lyons who is supposed to have squandered her fortune on the handsome, romantic English traveller. This seems more like a bit of colourful gossip than the stuff of authentic biography. It is certain, however, that by the end of 1738 John Salusbury was back in England, thirty-one years old, and if possible poorer than before. The Bach-y-Graig estate would bear no further mortgaging, and his personal credit had long since been extended past the breaking-point.

One obvious recourse for a handsome, penniless gentleman of fashion was marriage to an heiress. John had probably always known Sir Robert's sister, Hester Maria; she was almost his own age, and he may have been in love with her for many years. She, for her part, had certainly not lacked other opportunities, but though no longer young she was still waiting for her dashing cousin. If only he would accept her hand and devotion, she was quite willing to dissipate her fortune in settling his debts. For obvious reasons her brothers opposed the match, for while the improvident John Salusbury might be a pleasant companion, he was not a desirable brother-in-law. But since Hester Maria was of age and determined to have her way, there was little they could do, except to wash their hands of the whole affair.

Early in 1739, then, Hester Maria sent Thomas Salusbury to Wales to make a list of his brother's obligations,[1] and when the task had been satisfactorily concluded, on February 13, 1738/9, a marriage settlement was signed in London.[2] Shortly afterwards, John Salusbury and Hester Maria Cotton were married. His mother, Lucy Salusbury, wrote on February 19 from Bach-y-Graig to her new daughter-in-law to 'wish all Joy

---

[1] Ry. 530, 22. Thomas Salusbury to 'Mrs. Hester Cotton at Mrs. Lewis's House near Montague House, Bloomsbery, London'. It was written from Bach-y-Graig, and is postmarked Feb. 12 (probably 1738/9). Practically the whole of the letter is taken up with an account of paying his brother's bills with money sent by Miss Cotton.

[2] The settlement (Ry. Charter, 1008) indicates that Hester Maria Cotton's liquid capital amounted to £2,500, of which £1,200 was immediately to be used in settling encumbrances on the estate of John Salusbury. The later statements that her fortune was £7,000 or £10,000 (Thraliana, Apr. 1778, and Hayward, ii. 9) were probably exaggerations on the part of her daughter, or may refer to additional real estate or the value of annuities. Hester Maria did enjoy an annuity of £125 a year for the life of her mother, Mrs. King. Her trustees insisted that John Salusbury should place certain of his properties, free from encumbrances, in trust for his wife as her marriage portion. Some of the capital was thus used to pay off mortgages on certain farms, listed as her jointure.

& Happyness to attend you for Ever', and added her thanks
for taking poor Jack, 'without which hee Could not have
lived'.[1]

By the time the more pressing of the Salusbury debts had been
settled, Hester Maria's liquid capital was dissipated. Despairing
of help from Sir Robert and the Cottons, and lacking any ready
money of their own, the couple were obliged to give up any
thought of a house in London, and sought instead an economical
retreat in the country. To the newly married pair love in a
cottage may possibly have had an idyllic sound. Accordingly,
they rented a house from Sir Thomas Hanmer, about three
miles north-west of Pwllheli in the most distant part of Caernarvonshire, and close to an inheritance from which John still
received a small income.[2] Clothing, furniture, and all the
necessities were sent to them from Bach-y-Graig by John's
mother, and in the spring of 1739 the bride and groom made
the long journey to their new home.

The next few years were spent quietly at Bodvel Hall, as the
farm-house was called, and there, after one or two disappointments, their first and only child was born, between four and
five o'clock in the afternoon of January 16, 1740/1.[3] (This is
old style reckoning. Mrs. Thrale in later years always celebrated her birthday on January 27.) On February 10 she was
christened Hester Lynch Salusbury in the neighbouring church
of Llanner—the first name Hester after her mother, the second
an obvious but vain attempt to secure aid from her maternal
grandmother, whose maiden name was Lynch.[4]

For a man used to the pleasures of London society, life in
western Caernarvonshire was insupportably dull. Even if John
Salusbury was something of a scholar and a lover of nature (the
celebrated naturalist and traveller, Thomas Pennant, always
maintained that his interest in natural history had been first
aroused by his distant cousin John Salusbury),[5] his tempera-

[1] Ry. 530, 60.   [2] Mainwaring Piozziana, i. ix; Thraliana, Apr. 1778.
[3] The birth is recorded in her grandmother's book (see p. 5, n. 2). On the
same page, Mrs. Piozzi wrote in her later bold hand, 'St in 1803 still lives, to
thank God for the Virtues of her dear Parents, and Grandmother . . . Brynbella 9:
May 1803.' The date of birth is given as recorded, in what is called old style dating.
Differences between the old and new style calendar always seem to have bothered
Mrs. Piozzi, and she often misstated her own age, even in Thraliana.
[4] The actual entry in the old parish record of baptisms and burials reads,
'Hester Lynch the Daughter of John Salusbury of Bachegraig Esqr. and Hester his
wife was Baptized ye 10th February [1740/1]'.
[5] T. Pennant, *Literary Life* (1793), p. 1. The actual volume of ornithology
presented to Pennant when about twelve years old by John Salusbury still exists.
See L. F. Powell, *The Library*, 4th Ser. xix (1938), 131–2.

ment was unsuited to continued rustic retirement. The years of chafing sharpened a temper already irascible, and he quarrelled frequently with his self-sacrificing wife, who willingly slaved and economized for his sake. 'She made her own Candles, Salted her own Meat, iron'd her own Linen & her Husband's & mine', wrote her daughter long afterwards, '& if he wd. have been but good humor'd protested that she shd. have been happy'.[1] He found little to occupy his time except drinking with his neighbour Dick Lloyd and playing with his infant daughter. Both parents delighted in watching the gradual development of their only child. '*I* was their Joynt Play Thing,' Hester Lynch later wrote, '& although Education was a Word then unknown, as applied to Females; They had taught me to read, & speak, & think, & translate from the French, till I was half a Prodigy.'[2] In those dreary early years at Bodvel the mind of the future Blue-Stocking was moulded.

Meanwhile, since John's mother continued to live extravagantly at Bach-y-Graig, and Thomas associated with men of fashion in London, all attempts to save money proved fruitless. Inevitably there was the necessity for further borrowing to meet their continued expenditure. Actually, the only part of the Salusbury property not already completely mortgaged consisted of certain farms which had been cleared of debt at the time of John's marriage and set aside as his wife's jointure. Now, by dint of bullying and persuasion, she was finally prevailed upon to allow her portion to be attached, the major share of the receipts going to Thomas for London expenses.[3] The Salusbury sons had been brought up 'never to possess an *undivided* Guinea',[4] and Hester Maria was now a Salusbury.

In February 1745 Lucy Salusbury died,[5] and John was nominal head of Bach-y-Graig, but this made little difference to the impoverished family. Consequently, Hester Maria with her little daughter remained at Bodvel, still struggling to make ends meet and to calm the perpetually ruffled temper of her husband. It was obvious that there could be no hope of improvement in the Salusbury finances; their only prospect of getting away from their drab surroundings lay in a reconcilia-

---

[1] Thraliana, Apr. 1778.
[2] Adam MS. (Hayward, ii. 10). That the child must have been considered something of a prodigy is shown by a copy of Ogilby's translation of Homer presented to the four-year-old girl by George Shakerley in 1745 (now at the Johnson house in Gough Square, London).
[3] See letters to John Perkins in the autumn of 1773, and Thraliana, Apr. 1778.
[4] Mainwaring Piozziana, i. viii.
[5] Lucy Salusbury was buried in Tremeirchion church, Feb. 14, 1745.

tion with her family. Possibly Sir Robert Cotton, now a
childless widower, had regretted the quarrel with his favourite
sister and was now longing to see his little niece. Perhaps after
all these years his anger might be appeased; at least there was
no harm in investigating. Advances were made through
common friends, and finally Sir Robert sent a friendly note
to the despairing exiles. Then, some time about 1747, little
Hester Lynch, under careful supervision, dispatched a letter to
the distant uncle she had never seen. The ruse was successful
enough to secure a cordial invitation from Sir Robert to visit
old Lleweney Hall, an invitation which was accepted with
alacrity.

Just when the Salusburys permanently left Bodvel is uncertain. They were probably still there in May 1747,[1] although
by the middle of the summer they had certainly sold most of
their household effects and journeyed back to Flintshire.[2] Here
for the first time Hester Lynch saw the domain of her Salusbury
ancestors. Remembering the event long afterwards, she wrote
how 'we came to the *Old Hall* hung round with Armour, which
struck my infant eyes with wonder & delight'.[3] And in the later
account, with naïve pleasure at her own precocity, she added
that when she was established in the house,

My Uncle soon began to dote on Fiddle as he called me in Fondness, & I certainly did not obtain his Love by Flattery—as I remember well this odd Tête a Tete Conversation—Come now Dear
said he, that we are quite alone, tell me what you expected to see
here at Llewenney. I expected replied I, to see an old Baronet.
Well! in *that* your Expectation is not much disappointed—but why
did you think of such stuff? Why just because Papa & Mamma
were always saying to me & to one another at Bodvel, what the
Old Baronet would think of this & that.—They did it to fright me
I see now; but I thought to myself that Kings & Princes were but
men; and God made *them* you know Sir; & *they* made Old Baronets.
—Incomparable Fiddle! exclaimed my Uncle;—You will see a Mr
& Mrs Clough at Dinner today—Do you know how to spell Clough?
No, was the Reply; I never heard the Name: but if it had been spelt
like *Buff* you would not have asked me the Question. They write it
perhaps as we write *Enough*—C, l, o, u, g, h.

Although the baronet was delighted with his new-found niece,

[1] In the Rylands collection is an excise receipt dated Pwllheli, May 23, 1747,
Received of John Salusbury—of Bodvel—£2 for one two-wheel Carriage—'of
which he has this Day given notice'. It may even be possible that this carriage was
intended to transport his goods back to Flintshire.
[2] Thraliana, Apr. 1778.   [3] Adam MS. (Hayward, ii. 11).

he could not live peaceably with his irritating brother-in-law. Again and again John, no doubt feeling humiliated by his dependent position in the household, let his temper override his judgement and quarrelled violently with his host. The suggestion that he should secure some foreign post, leaving his wife and daughter to share the old baronet's fortune, was more than he could bear. 'No, no, Sir Robert, was the haughty Answer: If I go for a Soldier, Your Sister shall carry the Knapsack:—& the little Wench may have what I can work for.'[1] As it was obvious that the two men could not remain longer under the same roof, the Salusburys planned to go to London with the help of Sir Robert, after a possible short stay at Bach-y-Graig.

A letter survives, written by Sir Robert Cotton to his sister, directed from his other estate of Combermere on November 9, 1747.[2] He begins by alluding to his recent arrival there, and to his pleasure at hearing that Mrs. Salusbury had 'got safe home', and then referring to their projected journey to London, adds that he had written to have his London house made ready for them. 'Any House of mine is at your Service', he insists, and though confined to his room with a fit of gout, hopes they will stop at Combermere on their way. The letter is a friendly, affectionate message, giving the number of 'Fidle's Benefit Ticket', relating news of her parrot, and ending with the line: 'I expect a Letter soon from Hetty, a line from her or You will give great satisfaction to Dear Sis, Your most affectionate Brother & faithful Servant R. S. Cotton.' There is not a word of John Salusbury in the entire letter. Sir Robert had forgiven his sister and practically adopted his little niece, but he would never pardon the man who had ruined their lives. His chief interest was the little girl who might be his heir, and in a postscript, scribbled at the bottom of the sheet, appears a clue to the child's early tastes. 'I have some French Books here for Hetty, but she will be over-stockd with Presents of yt. sort from others.' Not yet seven, Hester Lynch was already an avid reader, and French books had become more suitable presents than dolls.

The Salusburys reached London in December 1747, at first lodging in King Street, Soho, and later in the Cotton house in

[1] Ibid. 12.
[2] Ry. 530, 6. The date is '9ber ye 9th 1747', which I have interpreted as standing for November. Nevertheless, on the back is written in Johnson's hand, 'Octr. 9, 1747 Sir R. C. to Mrs. S.' For information about Combermere, see N. H. Hignett, in *Cheshire Life* (May 1936), pp. 9-29.

Albemarle Street.[1] Naturally the city was full of excitement for
the eager child, whose experiences so far had been of fields and
animals rather than buildings and people. No wonder those
first months made an impression she never forgot. And John
Salusbury's fashionable friends were apparently amused and
delighted with the ingenuous child.

I became [she wrote] a Favourite with the Duke & Duchess of
Leeds, where I recollect often meeting the famous Actor Mr. Quin,
who taught me to speak Satan's Speech to the Sun in Paradise lost;
and when they took me to see him act Cato—I remember making
him a formal Courtsy, much to the Dutchess's Amusement—perhaps to that of the Player; I was just *six* years old—and we sate in
the Stage Box: where I kept on studying the Part with all my
little Power—not at all distracted by the Lights or Company, which
they fancied would take my Attention. The Fire Works for the
Peace of Aix la Chapelle were the next sights my Fancy was Im-
press'd with, We sate on a Terrace belonging to the Hills of Tern
—now Lord Berwick's Family;—& David Garrick was there &
made me sit in his Lap feeding me with Cates &c—because having
asked some one who sate near, why they called those Things that
flew up *Gerbes* in the Bill of Fare? *I* answer'd, because they are like
Wheat Sheaves you see, & Gerbe is a Wheat Sheaf in French.[2]

While Hester Lynch and her mother stayed on in Sir Robert's
London house, John Salusbury returned to Flintshire in an
attempt to bring some order out of his tangled affairs. But, as
usual, he seemed only to make matters worse. As far back as
1731 he had become involved in an attempt to sink a mine for
lead and copper on his property, when he and his brother
Thomas fell into the hands of swindlers who claimed to have
found a rich lead deposit at Hebden.[3] Always searching for
some simple way to regain his lost fortune, he proved an easy
dupe for the mining promoters with their prospects of sudden
riches; instead of gaining he lost a considerable amount of
money in the enterprise.

Since John Salusbury's own affairs had now become desperate, the only hope of the family lay in Sir Robert Cotton. The
rich, childless baronet, having broken with his only brother,
who also had married without his consent, now openly declared

---

[1] Thraliana, Apr. 1778. Yet on Jan. 27, 1795, she referred to having spent her
birthday at Lleweney with her uncle, Sir Robert Cotton, in 1748.

[2] Adam MS. (Hayward, ii. 13).

[3] See Ry. Charter 1190, 1191, and letters from Bridge, Ry. 531, 532. The
original agreement to sink a lead and copper mine on the Hebden property was
signed Oct. 14, 1731, but the enterprise in succeeding years proved a constant
drain on the Salusburys' resources rather than a money-maker.

he would generously provide for his little niece in his will. But the promises proved vain. The will was never made, and when in August 1748 Sir Robert died suddenly, his brother, Sir Lynch Salusbury Cotton, inherited the entire estate.[1] The child never forgot her mother's anguish and her father's violent temper upon receipt of the news. They were plunged again into complete despondency.

Something drastic had to be done, for the Salusburys were faced with the possible loss of their entire property. Yet John, the lovable companion, was incapable either of thrift or business enterprise, and his brother Thomas was too indolent to try to bring order out of the chaos. As early as April 1748, Edward Bridge, John's agent in Flintshire, had discussed with them the advisability of selling much of the furniture and personal effects at Bach-y-Graig to pacify some of his creditors, but as long as Sir Robert lived nothing had been done. Now there seemed no other way out of their difficulties. To be sure, Sir Lynch Cotton was friendly and allowed them to remain at the Cotton home, Albemarle Street, until little Hester Lynch came down with a light attack of smallpox, or perhaps chicken-pox, when the Salusburys were forced to leave these comfortable quarters and move to lodgings in Great Queen Street, Lincoln's Inn Fields. After that they lived in a few rooms, oppressed with debt, harassed by creditors' threats, and fearful of complete ruin. Finally, in one last attempt to effect a settlement, Thomas Salusbury spent the month of January 1749 in Wales interviewing creditors who demanded immediate payment.[2]

At this moment one of John's former intimate companions proposed a way for him to better his condition. The Earl of Halifax, sometimes styled the 'Father of the Colonies', had long been interested in fostering the growth of English settlements in North America and, on becoming head of the Board of Trade in the autumn of 1748, immediately planned an expedition to Nova Scotia. What was more logical than that the impoverished John Salusbury should seek his fortune in the New World,

---

[1] In 1810 Mrs. Piozzi wrote in the Mainwaring Piozziana (i. x), 'Miss Bridge you know, says the Will was made, & burned by my Uncle Lynch; I hope it was not so.' Sir Robert Cotton died Aug. 27, 1748. In Thraliana (Apr. 1778) Mrs. Thrale indicates that his death occurred in May, and in her Biographical Anecdotes for Sir James Fellowes she gives the impression that the death quickly followed their arrival in London. Later recollections must of necessity be vague. It is possible that Sir Robert suffered a stroke in May which prevented him from joining the Salusburys in London as planned, but did not die for several months.
[2] Letters from Bridge to various members of the Salusbury family (Ry. 531, 532). See also Thraliana, Apr. 1778.

occupying a post of importance directly under Cornwallis, the Governor! When Bridge, the Flintshire agent, heard the news, he was greatly alarmed, fearing the effect upon the uneasy creditors. John's departure from England might even lead to a crisis. Before he could voice his objection, however, the decision had already been made, and preparations for the great adventure kept the Salusburys busy during April and early May 1749. Sir Lynch Cotton lent John £200 for expenses, and a host of friends were profuse in advice and encouragement.[1]

A wide-eyed little girl of eight watched all the bustling with excitement—the familiar belongings of her father, packed in large boxes for the hold of the mysterious ship. The father, on the contrary, about to sail away from those he loved to an unknown land, grew less eager as the day approached. John Salusbury was not the stuff of which pioneers are made. He had languished at Bodvel with his family to cheer him; how could he endure the hardships of the colony without them? Only the desperate financial condition at home made him willing to endure the separation. After tearful farewells, he set out from London some time in May 1749, and on the 29th just before sailing from Plymouth, he wrote a pathetic letter to his wife.

To Live an individual,—Not thought of by any body—is of all Others the most Forelorne State: and, Except Thy Dear self, life, I am the very Man. I think, perhaps, I could have Cas'd Aside my own Honour, ambition, call it what you will For the Happyness, the Joy of being always with thee: But then, not to be able to Live up to Thy Rank. . . .

God Bless thee, My Dear Life, take Care of thy self and the poor little Girl—If it was for My sake onely—My onely Hope—My onely Comfort—that we may be Once more Happy—Truely never to part again: And I trust in the Almighty it shall Be So Amen. Hold up thy Heart Dear Love. Please God we shall meet Again: what greatly assists to support mine Is—that I am out of the reach of their Snears or Insults—and Fairly Practice Every Honest Endeavour to gain an Independancy. The twenty Nin'th of May, no Happy Day to me—nor any other, absent from my Dear Love![2]

After John Salusbury sailed away for distant Nova Scotia, Hester Lynch and her mother spent their time for the most part

---

[1] In a letter from Mrs. Salusbury to Sir Thomas of Jan. 3, 1765 (Ry. 530, 30), she refers to Sir Lynch Cotton as having lent £200; yet in Thraliana, Apr. 1778, Mrs. Thrale maintained that £100 was secured from Sir Lynch and £100 from Dr. Bernard Wilson. See also letters from Dr. Crane and Lord Halifax (Ry. 530).

[2] Ry. 530, 37. According to Thraliana (May 3, 1790) John Salusbury left London, Wednesday, May 3.

with various relatives. The summer could usually be passed at Lleweney, where Sir Lynch Cotton always made them welcome, or with the child's grandmother, the former Lady Cotton, who lived at East Hyde, not far from Luton in Bedfordshire.[1] At East Hyde Hester Lynch learned to love horses, and to ride.

When my Mother hoped I was gaining Health by the Fresh Air, I was kicking my Heels on a Corn Binn, & learning to drive of the old Coachman, who like every body else small & Great, delighted in taking me for a *Pupil*. Grandmamma kept four great ramping War-horses; *Chevaux entiers* for her Carriage, with immense long Manes & Tails which we buckled & Combed—& when after long Practice I shewed her & my Mother how two of them (poor Colonel & Peacock) would lick my hand for a lump of Sugar or fine white Bread, much were they amazed! much more when my skill in guiding them round the Courtyard on the Break, could no longer be doubted or denied—tho' strictly prohibited for the future.[2]

During the winters mother and daughter usually boarded with a Mrs. Hayne, a Methodist milliner in Charles Street, St. James's Square.[3] Having no regular income except her annuity of £125 a year, Mrs. Salusbury was forced to live as economically as possible.

The girl's education was almost entirely in the hands of her mother. French, writing, and arithmetic were her principal studies, interrupted for long periods when illness or social affairs intervened. At times in the winter she was a temporary pupil at a large school in Queen Square.[4] Mainly, however, her intellect was allowed to develop as it would, unfettered by the discipline of regular schooling, a fact which may account for the erratic mind of the later Mrs. Thrale.

As Bridge, the steward, had feared, John Salusbury's depar-

[1] Lady Cotton was daughter of Sir Thomas Lynch, and had been possessed of a large fortune in Jamaica. At fifteen years of age she had been married to Thomas Salusbury-Cotton, and by him had a large number of children, one of whom was Hester Maria Cotton, the wife of John Salusbury. When left a widow at thirty-seven years old, she deeply offended her children by marrying a second time, a certain Captain King. After the death of King she was reconciled to her children, and thus provided another refuge for the wife and daughter of the distant colonist. Many years later, when her own daughters strongly disapproved of her second marriage, Hester Lynch must have remembered the similar experience of her grandmother. (Hayward, ii. 14, 15.)
[2] Adam MS. (Hayward, ii. 15, 16).
[3] Thraliana, Apr. 1778. Addressed there by Bridge in Mar. 1750 (Ry. 531, 9). During the winter of 1751 it seems probable that because of Mrs. Salusbury's health she and her daughter spent some months in Hampstead. Here the ten-year-old girl read all through Livy in French, as well as Rapin and Plutarch. See Mrs. Piozzi to Queeney, May 22, 1796 (Lansdowne MS.), and Thraliana.
[4] Hayward, ii. 14.

ture roused his creditors, who demanded a foreclosure on the farms of Ty-mawr and Ty-coch.[1] Early in 1750, in answer to Bridge's long pleading letters, and by dint of some mysterious economy, Mrs. Salusbury raised a small emergency fund, hoping to avert the loss of the property, but Thomas Salusbury, who had been left a power of attorney to transact all affairs in his brother's absence, seemed indifferent, perhaps thinking the effort useless, certainly trusting to other plans to save the tottering family fortune.

Close to East Hyde, at Offley Park, in Hertfordshire, lived Sir Henry Penrice, Judge of the Admiralty Courts, with his only daughter Anna Maria, who had taken a fancy to the tall, good-looking Doctor in the Commons. Thomas, gallantly overlooking the fact that Miss Penrice stammered and was subject to epilepsy—he dwelt instead on her accomplishments of mind and beauty of spirit, not forgetting that she was heiress to a very large fortune—was quick to respond to her advances.[2] Bridge might well write to Mrs. Salusbury: 'I am afraid the Doctor has bent his thoughts more upon Miss Penrice than taking care of his poor Brother's affairs.'[3] Even the actual foreclosure in May, when the farms were completely lost, made no impression on the ardent Thomas Salusbury, for although negligent in business matters, he was no laggard in pursuit of Miss Penrice. For once in his life he was feverishly energetic, and this one burst of unwonted exertion was rewarded by ease and luxury for the rest of his life. After assiduous wooing and persistent negotiations, Sir Henry's consent was finally gained and the marriage arranged. In 1751 Sir Henry retired from the Bench; his son-in-law succeeded to his position as Judge of the Admiralty and to the accompanying Knighthood.[4] As Sir Thomas Salusbury, he cut more of a figure socially, though financially he was still dependent on his wife's expectations.

At first the news from John Salusbury in Nova Scotia was encouraging. The colony seemed to prosper, and John in his capacity of one of His Majesty's Council, and Register and Receiver of His Majesty's Rents, was active and important.

[1] In June 1749 Bridge sold most of the furniture at Bach-y-Graig to raise money with which to pacify the creditors, but to no avail (Ry. 531, 6, &c.).
[2] Thraliana, Apr. 1778.
[3] Ry. 531, 9; Mar. 1, 1750. On May 23 Bridge wrote that the properties had been lost because of the mismanagement of Thomas. Later letters tell of the desperate shifts used to save Bach-y-Graig itself.
[4] Cussans, History of Hertfordshire (1874–8), ii. 104. Sir Henry Penrice had been a widower for twenty-five years, and his only daughter, Anna Maria, was thirty-three years old at the time of her marriage to Thomas Salusbury.

Pleased and delighted, Lord Halifax wrote affectionate and heartening letters. But soon the tide turned, for life in the barren, newly founded settlement was hard. Chafing under confinement as the long winter months dragged slowly by, the men continually quarrelled, fought duels, or engaged in undercover intrigue for the political posts. John Salusbury's journal and his letters were filled with the unhappy complaints of a homesick exile.[1] In July 1750 he wrote to his wife:

My Heart akes when I write to thee—when and where will this Letter find thee—God Knows. Please God we shall once more meet, never to part again. . . . I constantly Attend our Court but had rather be with thee in a Cottage than at the Head of All our American Affairs without thee. . . .

John was beginning to see that acquiring a fortune in the new colony would be difficult. Many officials did make their way, but it was usually by dishonest means and through unsavoury political manœuvring, to which he would not stoop. He acknowledged himself a miserable, penniless exile, a complete failure, but he nevertheless took pride in remaining a gentleman. On September 20 he wrote: 'I have now declined their money employment—knowing I will be Honest *think* it too much trouble: on that footing not worth while to have Governments Money in keeping.' In letters and diaries his only thought now was how soon he might return to those he loved, his constant grievance that the Governor would not release him; for he would not leave without permission. Finally, in August 1751 his pleas proved successful, and he sailed joyfully for England.

At home John found conditions little changed, and his own position as difficult as ever. His brother's marriage to the Penrice heiress, while it had improved the prospects of the entire family, had so far provided no ready money. As his agent, Bridge, expressed it, the credit of the Salusbury family had 'sunk down to the Lowest Ebb'. Thus he was thrust once again into interminable meetings with his creditors and desperate shifts to keep what was left of his patrimony.[2] Lord

[1] John Salusbury's Nova Scotian journals (Ry. 615) exist in eight small notebooks. A large number of passages in them are underscored with red ink, for what purpose it is not quite clear. On the outside are various notes in the hand of Dr. Johnson. The inference from these markings is that at a later date Mrs. Thrale may have contemplated some publication from her father's diaries, and with the aid of Johnson selected the passages to be printed. All John Salusbury's letters to his wife may be found in Ry. 530.

[2] The tenants in Tremeirchion were actually served with ejectments (Ry. 531,

Halifax, too, was greatly disappointed in the news that John had brought of the fate of the colony. Halifax urged him to return to Nova Scotia with new instructions for the management of the settlements, and as England proved so unfriendly John allowed himself to be persuaded. In June 1752 he again set sail from Plymouth for the New World.

With the second departure of John, the two 'Hettys', mother and daughter, returned to their old practice of making protracted visits to various relatives. It was by all odds the most pleasant and economical life for persons in their restricted circumstances. Another hospitable refuge was now provided at Offley, the home of the Penrices and Sir Thomas Salusbury, and on May 31, 1752, Lady Salusbury wrote to her sister-in-law, 'you will always be welcome here, when, and as often, and for how long, or little time you please, and I beg of you to make no ceremony, for it makes no difference to me'.[1] Her letter ended with an amusing little vignette of English country life. There was a large number of guests in the house, including Lady Cotton, and,

to entertain all this good Company we had a Cock-fighting, which diversion I never saw before; it rained a little, and I doubt my poor Father catch'd a cold looking at them, for he is lamer today than yesterday, but My lady desir'd me to observe it was not her fault that he sat in the rain.

Point is given to the story when it is known that Sir Henry Penrice died this same year, possibly from the cold caught watching the cock-fighting. At his death his only daughter inherited the entire estate, valued, according to the *Gentleman's Magazine*, at £150,000.[2] Sir Thomas, at least, would have no more financial worries.

But the news from Halifax was still disappointing. John wrote to his wife on October 16, 1752:

You know I am but a bad manager, besides that I have been Cheated, downright Cheated of forty pounds; it is true I saw it, but could not Help my self, it vexed me indeed—but the story is too long to tell thee now. So that for the time to come—I shall draw on Tom for what I shall expend Here, but will take Care that my salary shall always be sufficient to answer it. Never will have any thing more to do with the Paltry Rascalls Here. . . .

14), and a copy of the writ, which was saved by Mrs. Thrale, has written on it in Dr. Johnson's hand, 'debt and difficulty' (Ry. Charter 1203). The property was only saved by a loan of £2,000 by Miss Elizabeth Mostyn.
  [1] Broadley, p. 104.
  [2] *Gent. Mag.* xxii (1752), 385. Sir Henry Penrice died Aug. 10, 1752, aged 75.

It was the old story of the incompetent gentleman, with no training in business or experience in trade, trying to compete with others better fitted to wrest a livelihood from the bleak shores of North America. In spite of every effort honestly made, he finally returned to England in the summer of 1753, not 'worth a Groat', more deeply in debt than ever, and utterly dejected.

This time, however, John found affairs in England less desperate. Sir Thomas was willing, after some show of reluctance, to use his wife's inheritance to help support his elder brother and to settle some of his most pressing debts. The letters from Bridge thus gradually became less frantic, and for the next few years there was a lull in the financial troubles which had so harassed the Salusburys in the previous decade.

Since the estate of Bach-y-Graig, barring any direct male heirs of John Salusbury, was entailed on Thomas and his sons, the latter was not actuated by wholly unselfish motives when he paid off the mortgage. Apparently John would never have a son to perpetuate the name, so that it was of vital importance to Sir Thomas to save the estate from foreclosure. When the liability was finally paid off, probably in the summer of 1755, John signed various papers admitting indebtedness to his brother for the whole amount.[1] At the time it was probably merely a matter of form, and with Sir Thomas as direct heir there was no prospect or intention that the money should ever be repaid. Many years later, however, this transaction was to prove disastrous to John's daughter.[2]

The years following John Salusbury's final return from Nova Scotia were uneventful for his family. For a time the Salusburys were in lodgings in Jermyn Street, St. James's; then in a pleasant house in Dean Street, near St. Anne's, Soho.[3]

---

[1] In a legal document, dated Aug. 19, 1755, Miss Mostyn and John Salusbury turned over Bach-y-Graig to Sir Thomas Salusbury. Later additions dated Nov. 8, 1779, show that the document was brought forward in Chancery in the suit between Dame Sarah Salusbury and the Thrales (Ry. Charter 1013). On Apr. 6, 1756, Bridge wrote describing a complete survey which had been made of the Bach-y-Graig property (now at Brynbella). According to Bridge the actual Bach-y-Graig estate was only 190 acres, but altogether John Salusbury had been possessed of 568 acres of meadows and pastures, and 70 acres of woodlands.

[2] See pp. 211, 214, Chapter X.

[3] Indicated by letters from Bridge, &c., and Thraliana, Apr. 1778. Occasionally they visited various watering-places. During the summer of 1758 the family spent some time at Weymouth, where Hester Lynch met the famous Dr. Warburton. In a letter (now in the collection of Mr. Frederick Vernon) of Aug. 29, 1758, Herbert Lawrence wrote to Miss Salusbury:

I don't know whether I should congratulate you or Doctor Warburton on

Released from financial worries, established once more in a house, with several servants, they were able to face the world with more assurance. Although it was galling to John to be so dependent upon his younger brother, for the time there were no serious quarrels. Long months were spent visiting at Offley, where Hester Lynch was the spoiled darling of the entire family. Sir Thomas's marriage had brought him no children, and with his wife's increasing ill health, it became more and more certain that he would have none. For this reason his brother's child began to assume added importance as a possible heir.

Lady Salusbury, in spite of many physical weaknesses, was a cultivated woman, with a special interest in Romance languages, and her delight in reading Italian and Spanish literature was soon communicated to her niece. Already reading French fluently, the latter turned to the other Latin tongues with avidity. 'Study', she wrote in after years, 'was my delight, and such a patroness would have made stones students.'[1] By the middle of 1757 Hester Lynch had begun to keep all her personal accounts in Italian, and even wrote letters to her aunt in the same language. Laboured first drafts of these letters, written when she was about fifteen, give some insight into the girl's reading at the time. (In one she refers to Rapin's *L'Istoria d'Inghilterra* and Tasso's *La Gerusalemme liberata*.)[2] For exercises in translation Lady Salusbury set her the task of turning various papers of the *Spectator* into Italian.

But it was Spanish which particularly attracted the romantic girl, the graceful fluency of the language appealing to her imaginative taste. At the suggestion of her aunt and her mother, who had herself some little knowledge of Spanish, Hester Lynch tried her hand at various translations. The Lisbon earthquake of 1755, which had turned the eyes of many Englishmen to the Peninsula, had particularly interested Lady Salusbury in that part of the world. Consequently, at the suggestion of her mother, Hester Lynch translated a Spanish sermon preached by a certain Isaac Netto on February 6, 1756,

your acquaintance with each other—pray was not that the Doctor's motive for going to Weymouth? I think it cou'd never be to add salt to his Satire, for the Sea Water is reckon'd good against the Itch of every Kind, and the Itch of writing is a Disease the Doctor does not wish to be cur'd of.

[1] Hayward, ii. 17. I have in my possession a battered little copy of four French dialogues, printed in Paris in 1684, and having written in the front, 'Hester Lynch Salusbury her Book 24th May 1756. Price 2d.'

[2] Ry. 616. In the pocket of her daily diary for 1757. See also Ry. 629, 15.

and dedicated it to her aunt.[1] Lady Salusbury, vastly pleased, wrote affectionately to her niece:

I am extremely oblig'd to you for the pains you have taken in Translating the Spanish Sermon, it has given me infinite pleasure I assure you; & as your Uncle will be in Town next Week, I desire you will tell him what Books in any Language you shou'd like, or Ornaments for your Person, or any thing else that wou'd be most agreable to you, & he will take care you shall have them, but I beleive you had better choose them yourself, & bring him in the Bill, tho' indeed I think the Sermon is above Reward, so I beg you will not be sparing in your Demands, I shall take great care of it as the first thing that was ever Dedicated to me, except as Reader.[2]

In spite of the fact that the fifteen-year-old girl was something of a prodigy, considering the normal education of the time, she was also endowed with normal feminine desires. It is amusing to know that it was not books, but rather a 'set of pearl and garnet ornaments', which was the 'shining recompense' chosen.[3]

Hester Lynch was particularly fond of the novel, *Don Quixote*, and for practice tried her hand at a new English rendering of some of the most amusing sections.[4] Similarly, with the encouragement of her father, she completely translated into English the life of Cervantes by Don Gregorio Mayans y Siscar.[5] She even spent tedious hours in making a queer, crabbed English version of a learned Spanish dissertation on the God Endovellicus.[6] Its thirty-nine closely scribbled pages of jumbled quotations and arguments concerning various attempts to decipher the ancient religion of Spain make it an odd farrago indeed. Even the commendation of the Reverend Edward

---

[1] Hayward, ii. 17, 18. The actual printed copy of the sermon which Hester Lynch used in making the translation is in the Rylands collection (Ry. 697, 35). See also Ry. 629, 9.

[2] Ry. 616. The letter is dated Offley Place, July 22, 1756.

[3] Hayward, ii. 18. The ornaments were later given to her daughter, Queeney.

[4] Translated in Dec. 1756 or Jan. 1757 (Thraliana, Sept. 1776). The manuscript of the entire 45th chapter of *Don Quixote*, with miscellaneous leaves of other parts, still exists (Ry. 625). I am indebted to Mr. Richard Locke Hanson for aid in determining the accuracy of the translation.

[5] Two manuscripts of this translation are to be found in the Rylands collection (Ry. 626, 627). The first is in the hand of H.L.S.; the other in a more regular copy-book style. On the outside of the latter Mrs. Piozzi wrote: 'This was translated by H. L. Salusbury from the Spanish in the year 1756 I believe or rather 1755—it was copied over by Thos. Cotton her first Cousin a Boy at School.' The date of composition, ascribed many years later, like a number of her late reminiscences cannot be accepted without reservation. As in the case of a number of her poems, a somewhat later date than the one she claims is more probable. Wishing to accentuate her own precocity, she possibly was not too accurate in dating her earliest compositions. [6] Ry. 628.

Clarke,[1] who should have known better, would hardly make a modern reader continue to the end. And Mrs. Piozzi herself, coming on the little note-book many years later, was struck by the queer mixture of fact and fancy, and wrote on the outside 'This was a strange thing for a Child to do. It was written in the year 1755 or 1756—at latest, by H. L. Salusbury.' For the most part the extant manuscripts of these translations show that her knowledge of the Spanish tongue was extensive, if not very accurate; and while evidently not intended to be rigidly literal, the versions do not always reproduce exactly the original meaning. They are remarkable performances for a young girl, but cannot be considered anything more than that.

More usual for a young girl was the keeping of a diary. The earliest which has survived among her papers was written in 1757.[2] It is merely a bare outline of everyday occurrences, kept in an ordinary commercial note-book called 'The Daily Journal: or The Gentleman's Complete Annual Accompt Book'. Nevertheless, the brief entries give some insight into her pleasant life in London; of the visits, the parties, the games, the dancing lessons with her master Mr. Leviez, the oratorios, the gifts from her kind uncle and aunt. A few quotations may suffice: January 11, 'Won at the Goose -1/ Mr. Richardson came, play'd with us at Shuttle Cock and at ye Goose'; January 12, 'Nobody came, nor nothing done but playing'; January 26, 'Went to Duke Street in ye Morning, in the Evening Lady, Miss & Mrs. Wynns, Mr. Clifford supp'd here'; February 3, 'Went with Lady Wynn to ye Play of the Suspicious Husb.'; February 10, 'My Father din'd at Sir Lynch's & quarrelld with my Lady Cotton'; February 22, 'Din'd at Ld. Halifax's Company ye Sir Roger, Lady Betty Archer, Dr. Crane Sir Thomas Salusbury'; March 21, 'Staid at Home nothing remarkable happend this day spent no money at all for a wonder'; March 23, 'Pd. for going to ye Opera 5/'; March 29, 'Dressed, went to Miss Scarletts Ball, danc'd Minuet wth. Mr. Lane & 2 with Captn. Batton'; March 30, 'went out a walking expected Mr. Leviez who disappointed me according to Custom'.

These few extracts are enough to show not only her daily

---

[1] Dr. Collier, some time between 1760 and 1763, wrote to Hester Lynch: 'Clarkius pro tua translatione Libri de Deo Endovelico tibi multum Laudis indicavit.'

[2] Ry. 616. In 1752 John Salusbury had written from Nova Scotia to his wife (Ry. 530, 45), 'God Almighty Bless thee my Dear Love and Poor little Girl—bid Her—continue Her Journal', but whether the 'Journal' referred to was a diary or a long series of notes to be sent her father is not clear.

life but also something of the character of the diarist herself. Even in this early laconic record is foreshadowed the future indefatigable diarist. Some phrases are so characteristic that they could have been written sixty years later. 'Spent no money at all for a wonder', 'Staid at Home all Day, Coughed terribly', might as well have been written by the ageing Blue-Stocking in her comfortable house at Bath in the year 1817 as by the adolescent Hester Lynch in Dean Street in 1757. The terse, pointed description and the half-humorous introspection are identical; even the subject-matter is unchanged—society, health, books. Only the setting is different.

Of her personal appearance we have few descriptions. Bridge wrote in 1758, when she was seventeen, 'I am sorry to hear Miss Salusbury is so short, but hope she has not done growing'. All her life she remained under normal height. Her features were too pronounced for feminine beauty, the nose long and sharp, the mouth wide and firm. Her hands were large and muscular, and to these 'Salusbury fists', as she called them, she later ascribed the strength and masculine quality of her handwriting. But if she had no great claim to beauty, the vivacity of her manner and the expressiveness of her features gave her an air of charm and attractiveness.

Unfortunately no portraits of the youthful Hester Lynch have survived, if indeed any were ever made. She may, nevertheless, have posed as a model for Hogarth, who was one of John Salusbury's London friends.[1] In 1759 Hogarth was at work on his painting, *The Lady's Last Stake*, which he had begun as a commission from Lord Charlemont.[2] Over fifty years later Hester Lynch, then an old lady, wrote several accounts of the painting of this picture, in all of which she claimed to have been the model for the single female figure. In one she maintained that the artist first sketched her head one day at her uncle's; in another that it was on a visit to Hogarth's studio in Leicester Fields that he got her to sit to him.[3] The version recorded in her New Common Place Book in 1815 is:

It was painted for *me* when I was quite a Girl, but he said I *should* be like it—and as he thought he discover'd in me an ardor for Play—this was meant as my Preservative—for Says he You *are* 15, but you *will* be five and Twenty. He lost his Life however,

---

[1] Hayward, ii. 309; Broadley, p. 262.
[2] A. Dobson, *William Hogarth* (1907), pp. 124–5, 157.
[3] See Hayward, i. 44; ii. 28, 309; a letter to Queeney, Mar. 28, 1812 (Lansdowne MS.); E. Mangin, *Piozziana*, p. 11; and *Gent. Mag.* xcii (Dec. 1822), 486–7.

& I my Picture. It was exhibited in 1814—& I stood & cried over it.[1]

The discrepancies in the accounts, and the known fact that the painting was undertaken not for her but for Lord Charlemont, have largely discredited her assertions. Yet more recent investigations indicate that there probably is some truth behind her story. Hogarth made two distinct versions of the painting, and spent some time engraving a plate which he did not live to complete.[2] It is possible, then, that one of the three may have been promised to Hester Lynch, and that she read too much into the promise. Additional proof may be found in the fact that the features of the lady in the original oil-painting closely resemble those of the later portraits of Mrs. Thrale.

Hester Lynch always remembered the artist affectionately.

Many were indeed the lectures I used to have in my very early days from dear Mr. Hogarth, whose regard for my father induced him perhaps to take notice of his little girl, and give her some odd particular directions about dress, dancing, and many other matters interesting now only because they were his.[3]

He also told the Salusburys much about an acquaintance of his, the famous Samuel Johnson, and aroused the girl's desire to see this astounding man. Hogarth's admiration for the author of the *Rambler* was unlimited. His conversation, he said, 'was to the talk of other men, like Titian's painting compared to Hudson's'. Hester Lynch was impressed with the eulogy and vaguely hoped some day to meet such a remarkable person. But before her dream was realized she came under the influence of another scholar who, even more than Johnson, was to mould her mind and character.

[1] p. 111. Now in the possession of Mr. A. Edward Newton.
[2] There are two versions of the painting which seem to be authentic, one now belonging to Mr. J. P. Morgan, and the other to the Duke of Richmond and Gordon. See the *Connoisseur* (Jan., 1936), pp. 41–2. It is not exactly clear for whom the second version was painted. While attempting to engrave a plate from the painting, Hogarth kept one original in his possession for some time. Finally, when he could not bring the woman's head to suit his taste he gave up the idea. It may possibly have been at this time that he sketched Hester Lynch's head while at her uncle's, as related by Mangin. The writer of the article in the *Connoisseur*, after referring to Mrs. Piozzi's claims, adds: 'The conflicting stories have tended to discredit both, although it is still possible that the discrepancies could be reconciled with the aid of further evidence'; and G. C. Williamson, in *English Conversation Pictures* (1931), p. 8, insists, 'it is quite a possible thing that both of Mrs. Piozzi's stories may be accurate'.
[3] *John. Misc.* i. 240–1.

II

THE HEIRESS OF OFFLEY

1758-1763

WITH her eager curiosity and thirst for information, Hester Lynch had largely educated herself under the guidance of two women, her mother and her aunt. At seventeen, so Lady Salusbury thought, it was time for more thorough instruction.[1] Probably at her insistence, Dr. Arthur Collier was persuaded to give the young girl regular lessons in Latin.

Dr. Collier was a man of some mental ability—no doubt inherited from his father, the philosopher—but of erratic character.[2] In 1758 he was fifty-one years old, a sentimental bachelor, maintaining comfortable quarters in chambers of Doctors' Commons, near those of Sir Thomas Salusbury. He had been reasonably successful in his chosen profession of the law, but enjoyed spending his leisure hours in discussing the classics with attractive young ladies. Among these was Sarah Fielding, to whom he taught Greek, much to the annoyance of her brother Henry, who disapproved of the higher education of women.[3] On his

[1] It is not certain when Collier began his instruction. Seeley, in *Mrs. Thrale*, p. 9, from evidence given in Hayward, ii. 43, states that it was in 1757, but I have been unable to find conclusive contemporary evidence to establish this date. Few early letters between the two have survived, and those which have are undated. 1758 or 1759 would seem to me more probable.

[2] For information about the elder Arthur Collier, who simultaneously with Berkeley arrived at the same conclusions about the nature of matter, see R. Benson, *Life of A. Collier* (1837). For a description of the young Collier see C. Coote, *Sketches of the Lives of English Civilians* (1804). Coote described the doctor as 'ingenious, but unsteady and eccentric'. Dr. Collier was born October 13, 1707, and died May 23, 1777. In 1758, therefore, he would have been fifty-one years old and Hester Lynch seventeen, so that her later recollection of his being sixty-four when she was sixteen cannot have been literally true (Hayward, ii. 18). Possibly he may jokingly have once referred to himself as almost four times her age, which a half century later would have crystallized into definite figures. In the first volume of Thraliana Mrs. Thrale gives a detailed description of her former tutor.

[3] See Ry. 533, 16. Collier's sisters were very friendly with the Fielding family: Jane, the author of *The Art of Ingeniously Tormenting*, saw Henry Fielding off on his last fatal voyage to Lisbon; and Margaret accompanied him all the way (W. L. Cross, *History of Henry Fielding* (New Haven, 1918), iii. 24). The novelist had other more cogent reasons for detesting Dr. Collier, since in various business dealings, according to his biographers, Fielding felt he had been grossly cheated by the doctor. See Cross, ii. 42-4; also *N. & Q.*, 12th Ser. ii (Aug. 5, 1916), 104-6.

visits to Offley Collier had probably been attracted to the gifted Hester Lynch and gladly accepted her as a pupil.

At first the tutor found her more enthusiastic than thorough, and as a result she made slow progress. Collier wrote in despair:

My Dear Child You are enough to make a Parson Swear, and I wont write a word of Latin more to you till you learn your Accidence at lest, and know what ought to be nominative and what accusative case before and after verbs. What can be the matter? there must be something strangely wrong in your Head that so plain and simple a doctrine will not make its way into your understanding: In the very first sentence of your yesterdays Letter there are but seven words and six faults.[1]

He was not an indulgent instructor and insisted from the beginning on diligent study of the rules of grammar. He spent hours in transcribing elaborate tables and charts of declensions for her use,[2] and made her write letters to him in Latin, to which he replied in the same language. He was determined she should be a sound classical scholar.

Unfortunately, her letters to Collier have not survived, but over a hundred of his replies were kept by the sentimental girl.[3] And these carefully composed Latin epistles are not dry reading, since they are more concerned with family matters than with details of syntax. It may have been that Collier soon found his student more interesting than the assigned lessons. Certainly, like Swift with Vanessa, the elderly man became fascinated by the rapid unfolding of his pupil's mind, while she for her part found her wise and polished tutor so much more attractive than the unlettered and awkward youths of her own age that he rapidly assumed first place in her heart. Such a connexion had its dangers (as Swift had discovered), but in the early years of their attachment the accord between student and teacher was complete. She worked assiduously at her lessons, and he affectionately took an interest in all her other activities. He became her confidant, her adviser, her idol.

Collier grew increasingly proud of his fair disciple and introduced her to many of his scholarly friends, even insisting that they read her compositions. One of his friends was James Harris, the author of well-known philosophical and gram-

[1] Ry. 534, 103. Undated, but without doubt early in the correspondence. All quotations in this chapter from Collier's letters are taken from Ry. 534.
[2] Ry. 630. One exercise is on Greek grammar.
[3] See n. 1. The majority of the letters were undoubtedly sent back and forth between their two homes in London.

matical treatises. Mrs. Thrale later told the story that when
Harris took his seat in the House of Commons, Charles
Townshend said to his next neighbour, 'Who is this Man? I
never saw him before.' The friend replied, 'Why, Harris the
author, that wrote one book about Grammar and one about
Virtue.' 'What does he come here for?' replied Townshend, 'he
will find neither Grammar nor Virtue *here*.'[1] Harris in 1760
sent the young student a copy of his *Hermes, or a Philosophical
Inquiry Concerning Universal Grammar*, interleaved with blank
pages so that she might write down her remarks and questions
as she read.[2] Other prominent people, too, were interested in
her: Sarah Fielding sent verses full of high compliment;[3] the
famous Dr. Oliver of Bath, when shown one of her poems, was
moved to dash off eight four-line stanzas of unstinted praise;[4]
the Rev. Edward Clarke sent her Spanish books;[5] Dr. Mather
explained astronomical observations;[6] and Dr. Bernard Wilson
criticized one of her French translations.[7] From such associations Hester Lynch acquired a taste for literature, for criticism,
and for metaphysics. Collier possessed an original mind and
in his gentle way loved speculative argument. Listening to the
long philosophic wrangling of her tutor and his cronies prepared the impressionable girl for the later discussions at
Streatham.

These excursions into Latin grammar and philosophical
speculation had not lessened her interest in modern languages,
however, and in London she continued her study of French
under the supervision of Dr. Parker, later chaplain to George III.
Possibly at his suggestion she attempted a translation of Louis
Racine's 'Épitre I sur l'homme', as well as of some letters to

---

[1] Hayward, ii. 29, 31. Also Ry. 629, 6. This version of the anecdote, written
down by Mrs. Thrale about 1770, differs slightly from the one given in the *D.N.B.*
[2] These four volumes, interleaved with notes, were sold by Broster in the sale
of Mrs. Piozzi's library in Manchester, Sept. 17, 1823, and following days. Opposite the dedication Mrs. Piozzi had written: 'Dr. S. Johnson said that in this dedication, consisting of but 30 lines, there were 6 Grammatical faults—and these fellows
(says he) will teach Philology.' Compare *John. Misc.* i. 187. From Thraliana, it
would appear that she did not meet Harris until much later; yet from Hayward,
ii. 29, one might infer that she had listened to the conversations of Harris and
Collier.
[3] Mainwaring Piozziana, i. 25.
[4] Ry. 656, 2a. Dr. Oliver was the inventor of the Bath-Oliver biscuit.
[5] Ry. 534, 77.
[6] Ry. 536, 14. On the outside is written: 'Dr. Mather's complts. to Miss Salusbury & has sent her the Observations as made at the different places He mentioned.' Dr. Mather was possibly the Rector of Whitechapel who died in 1768.
[7] Ry. 624. See p. 28, n. 1. Dr. Wilson at his death in 1772 left Mrs. Thrale
a fairly large bequest.

and from the French poet.[1] A rough draft of this work was shown to Dr. Parker, who replied in January 1760 (?):

The Performance upon careful Perusal greatly exceeds my Expectation; though my Expectation was very high, and always will be, of every thing wch comes from dear Miss Salusbury; the best and fairest Pupil that I could ever boast of. I must desire therefore, and insist upon it, that you go through the other Book in the same Manner. I am sure you do more than Justice to the Author. For I never saw any French Poetry that was so nervous, or that pleased me so much as your Translation.[2]

In her rendering of 'Épitre I sur l'homme' Hester Lynch used the heroic couplet, a metre in which she had already acquired some facility. It is not certain when she first began scribbling poetry of her own, but probably it was at an early age, for not many talented young people in those days could resist imitating Prior and Pope with neatly turned epigrams and hackneyed moral observations. If her later accounts may be believed, she sent some of these compositions anonymously to the newspapers, and enjoyed watching the actions of her elders when they saw the lines in print.[3]

Although her early poems have little intrinsic merit, they do indicate in an interesting way the nature of her studies and reveal something of the literary preferences of the mid-eighteenth century. Hester Lynch was aware of the revolutionary forces at work in the world, and in 1758 wrote 'Moral Stanzas from Rousseau', in which she repeated the simple tragedy of natural man.[4] For the most part, however, she was content to follow the models offered by the Queen Anne writers, at least in the matter of diction and verse form. Like so many others she demonstrated how easy it is to imitate Pope, and how impossible it is to do it well. Her attempts were made even more difficult by her temperament; for being instinctively romantic, she could not resist diluting the standard themes with infusions of the popular melancholy of the day. This is clearly shown in a

[1] Ry. 624. This consists of a series of loose sheets on which is a later note stating that the translation was made by H.L.S. at a very early period, perhaps when thirteen years old. It seems more reasonable to date the work shortly before 1760.

[2] Ry. 536, 23. Dated only 'Jany. 15', but references to the military campaign of Count Dann and the King of Prussia offer some clue to the year. The translation was probably made from L. Racine, *Poésies Nouvelles*, Tome second, Paris, 1747.

[3] Hayward, ii. 28. The *St. James's Chronicle* had not been started when Hester Lynch was fifteen, so that her account cannot be literally true.

[4] Ry. 646, 11. Her early poems may be found in a variety of places. Some appear in Thraliana, in the volumes of Mainwaring Piozziana, in two special collections of manuscript poetry now owned by Dr. Rosenbach, and in two volumes in the Rylands collection (Ry. 646, 647).

long didactic verse-epistle, concerned with the fate of an old
horse named Forrester, which she addressed to her uncle, Sir
Thomas Salusbury. The poem begins with the lines:

> The setting Sun declar'd the Close of Day,
> And Philomela tun'd her parting Lay;
> The Dew began to drop, the Owl t'affright,
> And Evening Objects grew upon the Sight;
> The Winds were still, and Nature seem'd inclin'd,
> To sooth the Sadness of a pensive Mind;[1]

Sir Thomas apparently encouraged his niece in experiments
of this kind, since she sent a number of other long poems of a
similar nature to him during the happy years at Offley. Some
passages indicate real ability. For instance, midway in her long
descriptive poem 'On the Fall of the great Ash Tree in Offley
Park' appear the lines:

> But when the Plains no more rich Gleanings yield,
> And the light shade flies transient o'er the field.
> When the Heat quivers on the fallow Grounds,
> And the stanch Pointer beats the Flinty Rounds;
> Who scorns with Head high held, the sultry Heat,
> And treads the Stubble with unfeeling Feet:
> How happy then beneath thy shade to shun
> The vigour of the fierce Meridian Sun!
> Far off to see the dazzling Splendours play
> While every Flow'r reflects a double Ray
> And the bright Stubble glitt'ring in our Eyes
> Forms a gay Contrast to the Azure skies,
> While the refreshing Turnips vivid Green
> Revives the sight and variegates the Scene.[2]

A doting uncle and an admiring family thought these effusions
admirable, and applauded her every effort. Thinking back
many years later to this time, she wrote:

> I was now completely a spoyl'd Child, and wrote Odes for the
> Peace & Verses upon every, & upon no Occasion. Imitations of
> English Poets too, which I fancied tolerable; but which on looking
> over my Copies of late, appeared to me Insupportable.[3]

She was not far wrong in her final estimate of the poetic
value of her 'Irregular Ode in Praise of the English Poets',[4] but
the piece does give an indication of the critical opinion of the
time.

> Nor has her Fame, nor Genius felt decay,
> From hobbling Chaucer, down to tuneful Gray.

[1] Ry. 646, 13.   [2] Ry. 647, 2. The poem is here dated Feb. 10, 1760.
[3] Mainwaring Piozziana, i. 19.   [4] Ry. 646, 23–31. Written in 1759.

She began her ode with a Spenserian stanza of the usual eighteenth-century type. Then in order came imperfect imitations of Shakespeare, Milton, and Dryden. With Pope, however, she was on surer ground.

> To scourge the wicked, and the wise to mend,
> Raise falling Virtue, and her Cause defend;
> See Pope appear, who could alone explore
> Worlds then unknown, and paths untrod before;
> Mark the nice spot where Vice and Virtue join'd
> And fix the ruling Passion of the Mind;
> Then stoop to celebrate Belinda's Name,
> And consecrate his own—eternally to Fame.

The ode ended with a message for those who disdainfully maintained that the present had no writers to compare with the glorious past.

> Nor has the Muse forgot to sing,
> Nor has She yet forsook her fav'rite Isle;
> Some Modern Bards there are can strike the String,
> And draw from Phoebus an approving smile:
>   Why then ingrate
>   Complain of Fate
>   As wanting in poetic Fire?
> While easy Marriott tunes the vocal Lyre,
> While Gray, that great Original we own,
> And gentle Mason sits sublime, on Nature's peaceful Throne.

The inclusion of Marriott with Mason and Gray, as one of the contemporary rivals of Shakespeare and Milton, requires some explanation. Like Collier, James Marriott was one of Sir Thomas's legal friends and an intimate member of the Salusbury circle. In his younger days he had no small pretensions as a poet, publishing several volumes of verse;[1] later he achieved distinction as Vice-Chancellor of Cambridge University, was knighted by George III, and became Judge of the Admiralty Court in 1778. At the time when Hester Lynch wrote of him, he was about thirty, and from all accounts gay and volatile in temperament.

With the roving eye of youth, Marriott had found the clever Hester Lynch something more than an appreciative critic with whom to discuss poetry. But his attempt at a sentimental flirtation was violently cut short by her irate father. John

---

[1] Marriott had published volumes of poems in 1755 and 1760. Some of his verses also appear in Dodsley's collection in vols. iv and vi. He later wrote three papers in *The World*, Nos. 117, 121, 199.

Salusbury refused to believe that his daughter was grown up, and flew into a rage at the sight of a love-letter which Marriott had directed to the girl. Immediately he dispatched a fiery reply.

Sir

My Daughter shewed me an extraordinary letter from you; she resents the ill treatment as conscious that she never gave any pretence to take such liberties with Her. I think it hard that insolence and Impudence should be suffered to interrupt the tranquil state of Youth and innocence.

I therefore insist on no altercations—no more trash on the subject: But should you continue to insult my poor child, I do assume the Father, I shall take the Insult to myself;—be then most certainly Assured that I will be avenged on you—much to the detriment of your Person and—So Help me God.

John Salusbury[1]

This ended Marriott's wooing, but her father could not keep away other unwelcome lovers, try as he would, for Hester Lynch was nineteen and attractive.

The suitors, it must be admitted, were not all lured by Hester Lynch's fascinating manner or her ability to translate French and Spanish, for she was now the acknowledged heir of Sir Thomas and future mistress of Offley Park. Except for these prospects, however, she was practically penniless. Her father was almost entirely dependent on his brother even for everyday expenses,[2] and her mother's inheritance had long been spent. Even the annuity from her grandmother had ceased at her death in December 1758. What was more of a disappointment, the former Lady Cotton had left the Salusburys no money in her will, considering Hester Lynch well provided for as heiress of her rich uncle.[3] At the time, the girl's future seemed assured, and when, a few months afterwards, Lady Salusbury died and

---

[1] Now in the collection of Mr. R. B. Adam. It is printed in Broadley, p. 105. The letter is addressed to Marriott, Doctors' Commons, London, but the postmark is blurred, only 'Ia 11' being discernible. From another letter of Marriott's to Hester Lynch, of June 30, 1763, sending back the earlier letter, 'recd. near three years ago', the year would seem to have been 1760.

[2] Hester Lynch's account book (Ry. 616), kept in Italian, for 1761 shows that the family's total income for this year was about £600, a large part of the receipts being listed as from Sir Thomas. The family's condition was slightly improved by the gradual receipt of Mrs. Salusbury's share in the estate of her half-brother, Cotton King, which, when finally settled several years later, brought several thousand pounds to each of his heirs. (Ry. 530, 599, &c.)

[3] Ry. Charter 1235 is a copy of the will of Dame Philadelphia Cotton, dated Nov. 3, 1756, with a codicil added May 6, 1758. Mrs. Salusbury received plate &c., but no substantial bequest, the estate going to other children and grandchildren. See also the letter from Bridge of Jan. 6, 1759 (Ry. 532, 74).

left all her fortune to Sir Thomas, it appeared even more secure.¹ Her uncle treated her as his adopted daughter, was proud of her accomplishments, and exhibited her to his guests, just as he did his favourite horses. As she later recollected, 'Every Suitor was made to understand my extraordinary Value. Those who could read, were shewn my Verses, those who could not, were Judges of my Prowess in the Field.'²

Hester Lynch's thoughts were far from matters of love and marriage, for her kindly tutor, Dr. Collier, held all her affection. 'A friendship more tender', she wrote, 'or more unpolluted by interest or by vanity, never existed; love had no place at all in the connection, nor had he any rival but my *mother*. *Their* influence was of the same kind, and hers the strongest.'³ So she ridiculed the suitors attracted by her prospects, and mimicked others to make the older man laugh. One was a rich young merchant in the Dutch trade named Clifford, who was introduced by her uncle's business agent, Mathias.⁴ Another, who never forgave her scorn, was a distant cousin, Thelwall Salusbury, the curate of the parish adjoining Offley Park.⁵

Though in her fancied security she could laugh at the self-interested devotion of her admirers, her own future was not so certain as it appeared. Despite the seemingly peaceful atmosphere at Offley there smouldered embers of resentment ever ready to burst into flame. It was galling to John Salusbury to be dependent on his younger brother for everything, and his temper provoked a continual round of quarrels. The inevitable explosion finally occurred late in 1761.

The year had begun pleasantly enough. In March Lord Halifax was nominated Lord Lieutenant of Ireland, and during the summer he proceeded in a leisurely manner to Dublin to take up his duties. He was accompanied part of the way by the two Salusburys, who delighted in this opportunity to show their friend the beauties of Wales. After the tour John remained in Flintshire, while Sir Thomas speedily returned to Offley, where Hester Lynch and her mother kept him company for the remainder of the summer, little realizing that this was to be their last happy vacation in Hertfordshire.

¹ It had been rumoured as early as 1758 that Sir Thomas was going to settle £30,000 on his niece when she married (letter from Bridge, Ry. 532, 73).
² Adam MS. (Hayward, ii. 18).   ³ Hayward, ii. 18–19.
⁴ Mainwaring Piozziana, i. 26. Also referred to in a letter to Queeney, May 26, 1806 (Lansdowne MS.). I need hardly add that unfortunately I can claim no relationship to this early suitor for Miss Salusbury.
⁵ See letter to Queeney, July 23, 1805. It was Thelwall Salusbury who later induced Sir Thomas Salusbury to disinherit his niece.

Two new acquaintances, who must have seemed amiable enough on their first visits to Offley that summer, were destined to be the causes of their woe. The first was the Honourable Mrs. King, a widow from Wellbury, who had settled near by, and who immediately exerted all her blandishments in an effort to attract the rich, sporting widower, Sir Thomas.[1] Since the girl's only chance of an advantageous position in the world was to inherit Offley and the Penrice possessions, there was intense jealousy from the start between the charming widow and the Salusbury ladies, which turned to active hatred when Sir Thomas appeared to be susceptible.

The second new acquaintance whose introduction altered the situation at Offley was a handsome young London gallant named Henry Thrale, whom Sir Thomas had met on one of his expeditions to the city and had eulogized to the ladies upon his return:

what an excellent, what an incomparable young Man he had seen— who was in short a Model of Perfection: ending his Panegyric by saying that he was a *real Sportsman*. Seeing me disposed to laugh, he looked very grave, said he expected us to like him—& that seriously. The next Day Mr. Thrale follow'd his Eulogist; and applied himself so diligently to gain my Mother's Attention—ay & her Heart too: that there was little doubt of her approving the Pretensions of so very shewy a Suitor—if Suitor he was to *me*; who certainly had not a common share in the Compliments he paid to my Mother's Wit, Beauty, & Elegance.[2]

Henry Thrale, during his first visit, made a good impression on everyone, with the possible exception of Hester Lynch. His father, he informed them, had been born of poor parents in the neighbourhood of Offley, and he won the admiration of the natives by presenting five shillings to a poor boy, because he felt sure his father had been just such a lad. By hunting with Sir Thomas, paying court to Mrs. Salusbury, and flattering the local gentry, he soon had Offley at his feet.

Boswell has given a good account of the ancestry of Thrale and of his father's rapid rise to wealth and prominence, though his family may not have been so poor or so mean as either Mrs. Piozzi or Boswell has insisted.[3] Both the Laird of Auchinleck

---

[1] Sarah Burroughs, daughter of Samuel Burroughs, a Master in Chancery, and widow of the Hon. William King of Wellbury, Lord Kingston's brother. For a full account of her romance with Sir Thomas, see Cussans, *History of Hertfordshire*, ii. 98, 99, 104.

[2] Adam MS. (Hayward, ii. 19–20). The chronology of this period is derived from Thraliana, Apr. 1778.

[3] Boswell, *Life*, i. 490–4. A payment of £66 to Margaret Thrale, Apr. 10, 1707,

and the descendant of Katherine of Berain looked down on the middle-class ancestry of the Thrales. Thrale's grandmother's brother, Edmund Halsey, son of a miller at St. Albans, had run away to London to make his fortune towards the close of the seventeenth century, married the daughter of the owner of the Old Anchor Brewery in Southwark, and proved so successful that he was able to marry his daughter to Sir Richard Temple, later the first Lord Cobham. The latter, best remembered as the friend of Pope and the creator of the gardens at Stowe, inherited Halsey's brewhouse at his death and after some delay sold the property to his wife's cousin, Ralph Thrale, for £30,000. Mrs. Piozzi later claimed that he had paid the money out of his savings as an employee of the brewery; Boswell, that he gave security on the property and discharged the debt in eleven years out of the profits.[1] In any case, Ralph Thrale made an ample fortune from the business, entered Parliament in 1741, and became a substantial, respected man of affairs. There is a story current in Streatham to-day that the Duke of Bedford allowed him to enclose over a hundred acres of ground on Tooting Common, in exchange for a constant supply of ale and porter to be delivered for a period of ten years to Woburn Abbey, the Duke's seat in Bedfordshire. No doubt it was by some such means that Ralph Thrale did secure the property at Streatham, where he built a fine, solid country house. His only son, Henry, and his three daughters were given every advantage which money could buy.

The exact date of the son's birth is not known, but it was probably in 1728 or 1729, since he matriculated at University College, Oxford, in June 1744, giving his age as fifteen.[2] The

for money lent upon credit on the land tax (now owned by Myers & Co., 102 New Bond St.) would not indicate absolute poverty. Monuments in St. Albans Church show the family to have been of some consequence there. But see J. H. Busby, 'The Hertfordshire Descent of Henry Thrale', *N & Q*, 13 Nov. 1948, pp. 495–8.

[1] *Life*, i. 490–1, 555. Boswell quotes Johnson as saying that Ralph Thrale worked at the brewery for twenty years at a salary of six shillings a week. In an old account book still held by the Barclay Perkins Co. entries in the year 1693 show that Thrale's salary was already one pound a week. Later he must have received even more, though it is doubtful whether he could have saved enough to purchase the brewery from earnings. Possibly in this instance both Boswell and Mrs. Thrale are partially right.

[2] On Thrale's epitaph, composed by Dr. Johnson, the year of birth is given as 1724. See H. W. Bromhead, *The Heritage of St. Leonard's Parish Church, Streatham* (1932), p. 24. Johnson must have received his information from the family, but a search for baptismal records has, as yet, not been successful in verifying this date. On June 4, 1744, Thrale was entered at University College, Oxford, giving his age as fifteen, and on June 6 his name appears in the University records, again as fifteen years old. From this evidence it would appear more likely that he was born

statement has also been made, unsupported by any credible evidence, that before going to the University he was at Eton for a time.[1] While at Oxford, he was provided with a generous allowance and encouraged to associate with members of the nobility. The business connexion with Lord Cobham brought him into early acquaintance with the Cobham cousins, the 'Young Patriots', and as a result of these friendships Henry Thrale was familiar with the occupants of Stowe, Hagley, and other great country houses. As was not uncommon, young Thrale left Oxford without a degree, and then made an extended tour of Europe with William Henry Lyttelton, later Lord West-cote. Ralph Thrale, it is said, paid the expenses of both travellers, no doubt feeling that the social prominence of young Lyttelton would provide valuable connexions not only on the tour but throughout his future life.[2] After his return to England Henry Thrale led the life of a gay man about town, more interested in the amusements of London than in his father's business in Southwark.

In Henry Thrale were combined two opposite tastes: a scholarly appreciation of good literature and a delight in sensual pleasures. His inseparable companion was the Irish play-wright and wit, Arthur Murphy. Since Murphy knew inti-mately all the places of amusement in London, and Thrale had all the money that was needed, the two men in their leisure hours led a life of gay excess. They played madcap jokes on the famous Gunning sisters, spent nights in the fashionable sporting resorts, and frequented the green-rooms and gambling-houses of the day.[3] Drunkenness was never one of Thrale's weaknesses, for in May 1760 Murphy wrote to Garrick, 'You stand engaged to Mr. Thrale for Wednesday se'ennight. You need not apprehend drinking; it is a very easy house.'[4] When his father died in 1758, leaving him sole owner of the brewery, Henry threw himself whole-heartedly into business affairs, to the great surprise of many of his old associates. He began, too, to think of a political career, and in 1754 and 1760 made strenu-ous, though unavailing, efforts to obtain for himself a seat in

---

about 1729. In Thraliana, June 1805, Mrs. Piozzi indicates that Thrale may not have known his own age.

[1] The records of Eton for this period are very meagre. I am indebted to Mr. R. A. Austen-Leigh for the information that Henry Thrale's name does not appear in the only extant lists for this period, those of 1742 and 1745.

[2] Hayward, i. 10. See also my letter in *T.L.S.*, Dec. 30, 1939, p. 755.

[3] In numerous entries in her journals Mrs. Thrale shows that she had heard many stories of their questionable affairs. See Hayward, ii. 81, and New Common Place Book, p. 74.   [4] *Garrick Correspondence*, i. 116.

Parliament.[1] In 1761, when he first came to Offley, Henry Thrale was a handsome well-educated business man, with the typical merits and vices of his class. To Hester Lynch he must have been a new type, surrounded as she had been by Welsh gentlemen, legal scholars, and clerics.

When John Salusbury returned from Wales, late in the summer of 1761, he was not left long in ignorance of the new forces at work at Offley, for the disappointed curate, Thelwall Salusbury, slyly let him know of Sir Thomas's flirtation with the widow King, and of his design to marry his niece to the wealthy brewer from Southwark. High words immediately followed, and John swore he would not have his daughter 'exchanged for a Barrel of Porter'.[2] Further disputes, rendered more acrimonious by the ever present menace of the widow, strained relations to the breaking-point, and late in 1761 the John Salusburys left Offley in high dudgeon.

As a farewell to this beloved country home Hester Lynch wrote a long descriptive poem in heroic couplets, called 'Offley Park'. She concluded it with an effusive compliment to her uncle and significant allusions to his dead wife, the kindly Anna Maria. Apparently Hester Lynch was well aware of the perils which threatened her.

The winter of 1762 was not a pleasant one in Masefield Street, St. Anne's, where John Salusbury was now living with his family. The situation was rendered more uneasy, as Hester Lynch later related, by the 'Visits from Mr. Thrale—to my Mother—render'd more terrifying to *me* every Day from Papa's Violence of Temper'.[3] Yet the break was not complete, for during the summer the two brothers so far forgot their differences as to make an extended trip to Wales together.[4]

In the midst of this family tension Hester Lynch continued her lessons with Dr. Collier and her writing of poetry. She composed verses on the king's nuptials in 1761, an elegy on Collier's dog Pompey, who had been her only rival in the doctor's affections, and a fable translated from the French of Mme Barnard.[5] These and other poems she copied over and over into her later Journals, sure that they were unusual, and

[1] For the earlier attempt at Abingdon, see *Jackson's Oxford Journal*, May 5, 12, 1753; and *John. Misc.* i. 292–3. For 1760 see B.M. MS. 32916—238–44.
[2] Adam MS. (Hayward, ii. 20).   [3] Ibid. 21.
[4] Referred to in Collier's Latin letter to his pupil of Saturday, Aug. 7 [1762] (Ry. 534, 17).
[5] Mainwaring Piozziana, i. 10–15, 27–9, &c. Johnson is quoted as saying that her song on the king's nuptials 'was not worse than that of my Contemporary Bards'. The Epistle from Pompey is dated Sept. 3, 1761, in Ry. 647, 3.

hoping that some day they might bring her fame. She was interested, too, in the literary movements of the day. At the appearance of Macpherson's Ossianic poems, she was 'half frantic', like so many of her contemporaries, with admiration. Here was a style which fused classic diction with vague romantic yearning just to suit her taste, and she was not slow in trying her hand at the new form.[1]

Her contributions to the newspapers also included political squibs, rather daring in their tone. Certainly her letter called 'Albion Manor', which appeared anonymously in the St. James's Chronicle for July 24, 1762, did give some grounds for the affectionate epithet of 'vilissima Whiggula'[2] contained in one of Collier's Latin Letters. Signed only 'Thomas ——', it purports to be the bluff, honest account of 'Albion Manor', as told by an old steward. The political satire is obvious, and the description of the new master of the manor and his 'dirty Scotch Boy Steward' is a palpable hit at young George III and the detested Bute. Amusingly written, the characterization is more sure than one would have expected from a young lady of twenty-one.

The delight at seeing her production in print and the praise of her immediate friends stirred Hester Lynch to further literary efforts. During the summer of 1762 her tireless pen was unusually active, the chief production being an elaborate 'Ode on the Blessings of Peace', which she says was later in the autumn 'in the Hands of the famous Doctor Arne our great Musical Composer of those Days—in order to be set & sung at Ranelagh for one of the grand Fêtes exhibited there in honour of the Peace'.[3] But her ode was never to be sung at Ranelagh, for a domestic crisis in the Salusbury family forced its withdrawal.

Affairs in Masefield Street were rapidly reaching a critical stage. Thrale kept up his attentions to the mother, while ignoring the father and daughter, and John Salusbury's temper was on the verge of explosion. He had taken an intense dislike to Thrale from the start, and from later entries in his daughter's diaries it is easy to understand his attitude. Although the young man was no worse, indeed, much better, than the usual wealthy London rake of the day, Thrale was not the sort

---

[1] Ry. 647, 11. On the back of this imitation is a note telling what it is in the hand of that arch-foe of Macpherson, Dr. Johnson. Also see New Common Place Book, p. 46.

[2] A letter from Herbert Lawrence of Aug. 7, 1762 (Ry. 535, 5), leaves no doubt as to the authorship of the contribution. Lawrence assured her he was unacquainted with the identity of the writers of several answers which had appeared, but insisted his friend Wilkes had no hand in the matter. Collier referred to the squib in his letter of Aug. 7 (Ry. 534, 17).   [3] Mainwaring Piozziana, i. 46.

of husband that John wished for his only daughter. So the sight of his wife openly approving and his daughter a trifle dazzled by this rich suitor drove the excitable Welshman almost off his head. And the knowledge that Sir Thomas was still flirting with the widow King did not add to his peace of mind. Meanwhile Hester Lynch, the centre of the turmoil, was in despair, and found her only relief in confiding in her devoted tutor. Collier's Latin letters constantly refer to the nervous irritation of her father, and when Thrale's name appears, it is always as an ominous menace to the happiness of the family group.

Late in the year came a crushing blow, the tragic climax to the domestic woes of the past few years. Long afterwards Hester Lynch herself remembered that

A Note came sent in a sly Manner from Dr. Collier to tell me— (it was written in Latin) that Sir Thomas would certainly marry Mrs. King the Sunday following—and beg'd I would not say a Syllable till the next Day, when *he* would come, & break the dreadful Tydings to my Father.

My Countenance however shew'd—or his Acuteness discerned, something he did not like: an Accusation follow'd, that I received clandestine Letters from Mr. Thrale, a Circumstance I had certainly every just Reason to deny, & felt extremely hurt, of Course at seeing myself disbelieved. After a fruitless & painful Contest for many Hours of this cruel Evening—my Spirits sunk, I fainted—& my Father—gaining possession of the fatal Billet—had to ask *my* Pardon—poor unhappy Soul! & in this fond Misery spent we the Hours till 4 o'clock in the Morning. At 9 we rose—He to go across the Park in search of my Maternal Uncle Sir Lynch Salusbury Cotton, from whom, & from Dr. Crane Prebendary of Westmr. he meant to seek Counsel & Comfort;—Me, to the Employment of calling our Medical Friend Herbert Lawrence to Dinner by a Billet of earnest Request—*All of us* were *Ill*,—but by the Time he came, my Father died—& was brought us home a Corpse—before the Dining hour. This was December 1762—Fifty Three Years ago exactly—Yet are not my Feelings blunted!![1]

Such was the tragic end of John Salusbury. Wayward and choleric he may have been at times, and economically incompetent, but he was always adored by his family and a little circle of intimate friends.[2] Even his brother, shaken for once

---

[1] Adam MS. (Hayward, ii. 21). Further details will also be found in a letter to Queeney, Feb. 28, 1811. John Salusbury died Dec. 18. See *Gent. Mag.* (1762), p. 601.

[2] Letters from Lord Halifax, Dr. Crane, and others show their grief (Ry. 530). Bridge wrote to Sir Thomas on Dec. 21 a letter of condolence in which he called John a 'real sincere good man' (Ry. 532, 100).

from his own selfish indifference, was genuinely affected, and proved comforting and helpful. He showed his goodwill by again clearing his brother's debts and offering to take care of his sister-in-law and niece, who were now in a most precarious financial condition. According to the previous legal arrangements Bach-y-Graig now became the property of Sir Thomas, though it would return to Hester Lynch should he leave no heir. Charged against the estate was a small yearly allowance of £200 for Mrs. Salusbury and a wedding portion of £2,000 for the daughter. This was the sum total of their inheritance.[1] But Sir Thomas, under the impulse of grief, was lavish in promises, and wrote on Christmas Day, a week after the calamity, that since he had 'always Intendd the Girl to Have ten Thousand pounds', he would make up the estate to that total and include a jointure for Mrs. Salusbury.[2]

Mrs. Salusbury soon found, however, that the knight's promises were not always followed by action. And when he continued to procrastinate, various friends of the family were moved secretly to attempt a little coercion. Dr. Crane on February 3, 1763, wrote to Hester Lynch, in a letter which he vainly requested her to burn:

I did not trouble you in my last, having not seen Lord Halifax, with telling you that I had desired his Lordship to take the first opportunity to talk to Sir Thomas in the same manner I should do.

Lord Halifax has been with me to day, & told me that he gave Sir Thomas his Opinion last thursday on the point & in the manner I desired him, & that Sir Thomas promised him to act accordingly, of which I hope you have found the Effects.[3]

As time wore on, Sir Thomas continued to delay, and Mrs. Salusbury desperately turned her hopes to the proposals of Henry Thrale. She had gradually come to believe that in him lay their only salvation. On the other hand, Hester Lynch herself had not yet been won over, probably because of the opposition of her father and Dr. Collier, who still had confidence in the promises of Sir Thomas and wished no rash action taken until these financial details were settled.[4] With mother and tutor taking opposite sides, Hester Lynch was in a difficult position.

Whether for this reason or not, there were signs that the bond

---

[1] See Ry. 534, 53, a letter from Collier explaining the exact provisions of the will. Mrs. Piozzi's pride doubtless made her increase the amount of her heritage in later accounts (Hayward, ii. 22).   [2] Ry. 530, 26.

[3] Ry. 536, 6. Dr. Crane had been tutor in the household of Lord Halifax.

[4] Hayward, ii. 18.

between pupil and teacher was becoming strained. A hint appears in the early letters of 1763, and on April 5, after a lapse of some time, Collier wrote (this time in English at her request) to defend himself against her reproaches for coldness.[1] 'After so free and unconstrain'd a Correspondance as ours has so long time been, and the passing of above two Hundred Letters between us within this last twelvemonth', he began, the sudden break in their correspondence had come as a distinct shock, especially since she held him responsible. Collier defended his action, and in turn accused her of changeable moods and incomprehensible behaviour. With impassioned fervour he asked for some explanation:

But where thought I, is gone that tongue that talked but t'other day so sweetly! Where are all those friendly cordial Hopes, and wishes vanished! . . . For Gods Sake, my Dearest Angel, dont put me again upon Metaphysical disquisitions, and general abstracted reasonings about the mutabilities of the female Heart.

He had thought her the one shining example of her age who had 'escaped the general contagious failings of her sex'; now that faith was rudely shaken. (How ironical that exactly twenty years later another disillusioned tutor was to wonder if he had made the same mistake!) Collier would have been the first to deny being in love with his pupil, but his next letters have the querulous tone of an injured lover. There is the same complaint and suspicion, the same longing for return of affection. Irritably on April 17 he suggested ending her Latin lessons.

As to these same Verba Substantiva I think I would not have you plague your self any more about the matter, for they won't make one a bit younger Richer, or Handsomer, and the only women that I ever knew made much of the matter all lived to be old maids.

This time the rift in the tender friendship was speedily mended, and when, late in April, Hester Lynch with her mother visited her maiden aunts, Sophia and Sidney Arabella, in Bath, Collier kept her informed of the gossip in London. Referring to the excitement over Wilkes and the *North Briton*, he amusingly commented in his letter of May 4 that he was glad to hear that even 'against the grain' she was 'likely to become a good Honest Tory at last'. He continued the old affectionate by-play, and a few days later ended a note with the wish that her 'sweet

[1] This and the following letters from Dr. Collier, all originally written in English, may be found in Ry. 534, 35–72. The majority are undated, but from internal evidence can be accurately placed.

Impetuosity' would let him know when to expect her return. All the while he was trying his best to further his pupil's interests with Sir Thomas. Though we must piece together the record of the endless negotiations solely from his letters, the situation seems clear, and we can easily imagine the wily Mrs. King pulling the wires which frustrated the doctor at every move.

The chief business of Collier's letter of May 4 had been to give his opinion that 'all matters are over between the widow & the Knight', and to pass on the joyful news that Sir Thomas was actually ready to pay all their outstanding bills. But he was too optimistic. The ladies were again in London by May 14, beginning anew the attempt to placate Sir Thomas, who must have suspected his friend of conspiring against him. Collier wrote hurriedly:

> But as the Knight went abroad, and I could not trace his goings, I was afraid of meeting Him at your House, which I know would but Increase his Jealousie of our Caballing as He would call it against Him so do not expect to see me till I am sure He is fixed somewhere else or is gone out of Town. . . .
>
> I find this man will not give me any opportunity of saying more to Him, and keeps out of the way of both your mother and Sir Lynch.

Collier was determined to persuade Sir Thomas to settle a fortune on his niece before he married a second time, knowing too well how intolerable would be the girl's situation dependent on the good graces of an aunt whose enmity was apparent. Hester Lynch herself was not unaware of this danger, and it kept her in a state of seething excitement. Perhaps some of John Salusbury's irascibility had been inherited by his daughter, for Collier laughingly admitted that he had seen 'Lions and Tygers', but his 'sweetest Angel in a passion' was even more frightening. If only she would have patience, he insisted, all would be well.

The doctor tried in every possible way to force Sir Thomas to act; but when he urged Hester Lynch to write a submissive letter to her uncle to smooth the way, her Welsh pride revolted and she refused to follow his suggestion. In every message he related some long conversation with the knight either about her claims on the Bach-y-Graig estate or the necessity for immediate action to settle her fortune. Of one talk he wrote:

> Thursday morn. last as we were coming Home in the coach together from the Tavern, I asked Him if He had seen his sister, He replied He had—That He intended to make your Three, as

He said Ten, whenever you married, and allow your mother Three
or four. Now dont stop here but read on—Make up when she is
married said I—How for God sake would you have Her maintain
the rank and condition of a woman of that fortune in the meantime?
No. no. If you do any thing, Pray put them both off your Hands
immediately, take the Estate to yourself and be a free man, and then
you will have some comfort of each other: and if you will tell me
what you intend to do, I will save you all farther trouble about the
matter. But I think you should make Madam a compleat Four—
well then says He I Intend to do so—But I cant pay the Ten in this
month yet—well said I, if it be not this Three months that need
make no alteration, only settle matters at present—well well said
He, I will. . . .

The slow negotiations disgusted the impetuous girl. Feeling
sure her uncle's promises were not to be relied upon, she fell
to dreaming of supporting herself as a writer. Collier, who knew
too well the difficulties of such a life, was not at all impressed.

Dont let your aspiring ambitious spirit be allways thinking of a
Garret, I think a good nine Hundred pounds a year without deduction and a good House &c. &c. &c. may serve you and your
mother pretty well till something better falls.

Sir Thomas, however, still resisted all appeals, and openly
avoided his intimate friend.

This man is an Eel; for would you think it, tho: we live next door
to each other I have never been able to catch a moments opportunity of saying a word upon the subject, till last night as we were
going from your House together in the Coach, when I asked Him
if He had settled any thing as yet about you and your mother:
He said No.

Refusing to be discouraged, Collier had the bonds made up
according to their former conversation, but could not get Sir
Thomas to sign, even when confronting him with the actual
documents embodying what he had promised. Instead, Sir
Thomas insisted that he would give his niece ten thousand
pounds when she married with her mother's consent, and until
then allow her two hundred a year; but that was all he ever
intended or would agree to do. After a long account of the
ensuing quarrel, Collier ended with the complaint: 'He is the
perversest mule I ever had to deal with.' The next day Collier
wrote again in despair:

I want to see you sadly: and sadly I may say indeed: The Man I
find means not one word He Says, and I am now convinced this
same Sr. Honesty's a very dirty, Base, ungenerous, low-designing

man, and so from this time forth I shall forever Hold Him. I cannot
write all that I have to say, But He kept me awake the greatest part
of last night, for I find that after all his filthy protestations of affection, His Puffy promises and Declarations, He will allow—He'll
give if—He'll do most wondrous things—But nothing certain—and
so we Broke off our Discourse. surely such men are not of God
almighty's making—and so I have done with Him.

Yet he still continued scheming, hoping for a change of heart.

Then came the denouement. Collier wrote in haste that he
had had a long conversation with Sir Thomas, who had told
him everything about his relations with the widow. All the
doctor's suspicions were relieved, and he ended by admitting
that the knight had proved that he had not been 'acting so
foolish and unaccountable a part as I before Imagined'. But
Mrs. Salusbury and her daughter had lost faith in the vacillating Sir Thomas, and were disgusted at the gullibility of the
doctor. On the back of this letter appears the comment in the
hand of Hester Lynch: 'last Letter but *one* my Mor. very angry
with the D.'

More and more Mrs. Salusbury was becoming convinced
that Collier's opposition to Thrale and his attempts to secure
a final settlement from Sir Thomas resulted from a selfish
desire to keep his pupil's affection. At her time of life the
mother had few romantic illusions, and felt that if her daughter
married a wealthy, handsome young man, it would be a happy
solution of their problem. She determined to remove the only
obstruction which stood in her way. Collier's next letter was
his last. On it is written in Hester Lynch's hand: 'The last I
ever rec'd from Dr. Collier as my Mother would not permit
me to answer it or see the Dr. anymore.' Caught in the mesh
of suspicion and jealousy, the once devoted friends were forced
to part. The man who had moulded her character in its most
impressionable years disappeared for ever from her life.

With Dr. Collier out of the way, Mrs. Salusbury was finally
able to convince her daughter that their best interest lay in
accepting the proposal of Henry Thrale. It is not very clear
just why Thrale was so eager to marry Miss Salusbury; he
obviously was not in love with her, and had made no effort to
gain her affection. In fact, throughout he had seemed studiously
to avoid her. Possibly it was the ten thousand pounds which he
knew her uncle had promised as a dowry. Or perhaps it was
his admiration for her mother, Mrs. Salusbury. Certain it is
that when he was about to propose, he addressed himself to

mother and daughter together. On June 28, 1763, Thrale wrote:

Mr. Thrale presents His most respectfull compliments to Mrs. & Miss Salusbury & wishes to God He could have communicated His Sentiments to them last night, which is absolutely impossible for Him to do to any other Person breathing; He therefore most ardently begs to see Them at any Hour this afternoon, & He will at all Events immediately enter upon this very interesting Subject, & when once begun, there is no Danger of His wandering upon any other: in short, see them, He must, for He assures them, with the greatest Truth & Sincerity, that They have murder'd Peace & Happiness at Home.[1]

At last his collective love-making met with success, for Hester Lynch reluctantly made up her mind to acquiesce in her mother's desires. Marriage to some one being the condition of her uncle's generous offer, it seemed obvious that Thrale was the most likely candidate. But she never made any pretence that her decision originated from any other feeling than that of prudence.

Once his niece had shown her docility by agreeing to marry the man of his choice, Sir Thomas finally transformed some of his promises into deeds. To this end Thrale proved a better advocate than Doctor Collier. Thus, in a draft of a letter probably written to Richard Lloyd in the latter part of July 1763 or early August, Hester Lynch wrote:

Sr. Thos. has given me a Bond for £10,000 on my Marriage with my Mother's Consent alone not his. till when he obliges himself by the same Bond to pay me £200 per ann. for my present support; & on this Bond which was obtain'd from him with evry difficulty to all my Friends who were so kind to interest themselves most warmly in my favr., particularly Sr. Lynch Cotton, Ld. Halifax & other Gentlemen of whom you have never heard—I am perfectly content to rely especially as my Uncle is on the point of being married himself to a fine young widow whose nearer Claim to his property & Affections must necessarily destroy mine: however while Heaven is pleased to spare me my Mother's Life, I shall think myself full as happy under her gentle Guidance as in the possession of that Coronet you so kindly wished me, thinking me I believe much more ambitious than I am.[2]

That Hester Lynch was not enraptured over her approaching

---

[1] In the collection of Mr. R. B. Adam. On the back is written in the hand of Mrs. Thrale, 'Mr. Thrale's first Proposal of Marriage to H. L. Salusbury.' A sorrowful love-letter from her old suitor Marriott on June 30, 1763, would seem to indicate that he suspected the good fortune of his rival (Broadley, p. 106).

[2] Ry. 533, 2.

MRS. SALUSBURY

Painted by ZOFFANY *(Portrait of John Salusbury on the wall)*
Now in the possession of the Earl of Shelburne

nuptials is plainly shown in trial drafts of letters written to one of her aunts at Bath, announcing her engagement.[1] The longer one begins: 'With what Spirits I us'd to sit down to write to my Dear Aunt Sidney, & how slowly my Pen moves this Even.' Hardly the excited rapture of a girl in love! Nor is what follows more ecstatic: 'That the Man my Mother most approves should have luckily fix'd on me for choice seems partly that peculiar Interposition of Providence. . . . Our mutual Preference of each other to all the rest of the World, that Preference not founded on Passion but on Reason, gives us some Right to expect some Happiness.' The shorter draft similarly tells of her mother's partiality for Thrale, and ends with the poignant admission: 'His real & grateful Regard for Her is no small proof of His Understanding—nor ought lightly to be esteem'd by me. I somehow can add no more.'

It was duty and not desire, regard for her mother's happiness and not her own inclinations, Hester Lynch maintained, which led to her decision to marry Thrale. Romance and sentiment were to be renounced, rational submission to take their place. And this rationalization of love and duty was the theme of her last poetical effort as a maiden, 'Imagination's Search after Happiness', which appeared in the *St. James's Chronicle* for September 10, 1763.[2] She tried hard to convince herself, but it was a half-hearted effort.

Throughout September Thrale and Sir Thomas were busy arranging the details of her settlement: the brewer, as a good business man, obtaining the most advantageous terms possible, and the knight, once the decision had been made, protecting his niece's interests as best he could. The settlement was finally drawn up and signed on October 9 and 10.[3] It expressly stipulated that upon the marriage of Henry Thrale and Hester Lynch Salusbury, in consideration of her fortune of ten thousand pounds, he was to grant to two trustees the estate of Crowmarsh in Oxfordshire for ninety-nine years, the income from which was to be divided, £200 to his wife and the remainder to himself. Should he die, however, she was to receive as her jointure £400 per year from this property and £13,400 from his other estate. The agreement also provided security for the

---

[1] Ry. 533, 1. Very effusive letters from Sir Lynch Cotton show that her judicious choice was welcomed by her relatives (Ry. 530, 15–18).

[2] This fable from the French was published anonymously, and, she maintained, was later included in many of the magazines of the month.

[3] The present résumé is derived from an abstract of this settlement (Ry. Charter, 1236).

trust and arranged separate inheritances to possible children of the union. Often misunderstood by later attorneys, it was obviously considered at the time a just and well-designed marriage settlement by all concerned.

After these important business details were settled, on October 11, 1763, in St. Anne's Church, Soho, Hester Lynch Salusbury became the wife of Henry Thrale.[1] Sir Thomas Salusbury gave away the bride, and after the ceremony the whole wedding party journeyed to the bridegroom's home at Streatham for dinner. It was only on her wedding day that Hester Lynch saw for the first time the house where the most eventful years of her life were to be spent.

[1] P. Merritt, *Piozzi Marginalia* (1925), p. 9.

HESTER LYNCH THRALE

III

STREATHAM AND SOUTHWARK

1763–1766

THE estate to which Henry Thrale brought his bride was known as Streatham Place or Streatham Park. Some six miles from London on what is now the Tooting Bec Road, it faced directly on to Tooting Upper Common. A sweeping drive of a hundred yards led from the lodge gates to a compact three-story brick house, surrounded by a park of about a hundred acres. At the back of the home were farm buildings, domestic offices, green-houses, stables, and an ice-house. Behind these and to the west was the kitchen garden with forcing-frames for grapes, melons, peaches, and nectarines. Streatham Place was a comfortable country house, though far removed from the luxurious mansion it later became; for it then had no spacious parlour or library, no extensive lawn, pond, or summer-house. These were added as the family and income increased.[1]

Up to this time the young couple had scarcely exchanged more than a few words alone—one reason perhaps why they welcomed the companionship of Mrs. Salusbury and a cousin, Hester Cotton, who remained with them for a while.[2] Indeed it would have been difficult to find a bride and groom who were temperamentally more unsuited to each other. Henry Thrale was essentially a business man, matter-of-fact and unemotional, with the cynicism of his rakish companions in London. Hester Lynch, on the contrary, had been a precocious child, petted and admired by an adoring family who had led her to believe that she was an unusual person with remarkable gifts as a poet.

[1] See Thraliana, Oct. 12, 1790, Sept. 17, 1791. References to the long succession of improvements may be found in her correspondence with Johnson. For Susan Burney's description of Streatham in later years see Early Diary of F. Burney, ii. 255. See also H. W. Bromhead, The Heritage of St. Leonard's, Streatham, pp. 39–45. A detailed description of the estate is there given, derived from a large-scale plan of the grounds 1825, attached to a release, dated Apr. 28, in Fee of Freehold and Covenant to surrender copyhold on its sale by the Thrale daughters. A traced copy, made by Mrs. Bromhead, is included, together with many other items of interest about the estate.

[2] Hayward, ii. 22.

Sentimental, intensely introspective, artistic, she was the anti-thesis of her husband.

Although she had never made any pretence of being in love with Thrale before their marriage, she had a woman's confidence that she could capture his affections once the two were thrown together in the intimacy of married life. The romantic girl dreamed of turning her stolid husband into a devoted lover. She later wrote of these early days:

I was now a married Woman: young enough to be proud of being such,—& silly enough to expect that my husband's heart was to be won by the same empty Tricks that had pleased my Father & my Uncle. so I wrote Verses in *his* Praise instead of *theirs*—& while we remained at Streatham between Octr. 11th—our Wedding Day, & the Time we went to Southwark for the Winter: (while he was at Harrow on a Visit—& I sate at home to *spin*) *This* was my Amusement.

> While Harrow's happier Groves detain
> Your lingering Steps from Streatham's Plain;
> To think or write of ought were vain
>   But Harrow on the Hill:
>
> In vain as home last Night we flew,
> The varied Landschape lay in View;
> No Object could my Eyes pursue
>   But Harrow on the Hill:
>
> As much in Vain my Wheel I seize,
> My Temper—not my Flax I teize;
> No subject now My Thoughts can please
>   But Harrow on the Hill:
>
> And while my Heart in earnest burns,
> Your Stay the murmuring Spindle mourns,
> Impatient till my Love returns
>   From Harrow on the Hill.[1]

Thrale, however, was incapable of responding to such poetic effusions, and his wife found her advances coldly ignored or disdained. She added:

These sentimental Jeux D'Esprit I had been so long accustom'd to, that It seemed odd when I observed them repress'd as Impertinent, or rejected as superfluous: but it was Natural to try, & try again: so Instead of Dressing showily, or behaving usefully—I sate at home & wrote Verses.—my *next* Effort Doctor Johnson praised

---

[1] Mainwaring Piozziana, i. 50, 51. Owing to a tendency to colour and sentimentalize everything she wrote, in these later recollections she may have placed too great emphasis on the incompatibility with Thrale, but undoubtedly there must have been some basis for her accounts.

as a very pretty one: though he did not see it till Years after it had been presented—neglected, & forgotten.

The '*next* Effort', an Ode to a Robin Redbreast, written at Streatham Park in December 1763, again reflected her wistful yearning for married happiness. The poem was an irregular Pindaric of the type so common at the time, and the central section ended with the stilted lines:

> Of nuptial Bliss record the Sweets,
> And sing of Streatham's calm Retreats;
> Her long-drawn Walk, her Piny Grove,
> Where Happiness delights to rove,
> Where Love and Peace and Pleasure join
> A Wreath round Hymen's Brows to twine:
> Where You like me have most Delight to prove,
> The Joys of Rural Life and Sweet Connubial Love.[1]

Even if Thrale was apparently unmoved by this metrical wooing, it is not hard to understand why his wife still spent so much time with poetry. She had very little else to do. Neither Thrale nor his mother-in-law was willing for her to enter the social life of London, and her favourite outdoor sport had to be given up because Thrale thought riding too masculine.[2] Nor was she allowed to interfere with the domestic arrangements of the house, for Thrale claimed the kitchen as his own province, and his wife later admitted that she never knew what was being prepared for dinner until she saw it on the table. The brewer considered that a woman's place was in the drawing-room or the bedchamber. The bride was thus driven to study and writing in order to occupy herself during the long autumn months of 1763.

Another reason was that she was left very much alone, for Thrale drove almost every day to the brewery. With the coming of cold weather, however, he grew tired of the long drives, neither comfortable nor safe on the deserted, wintry roads. Earlier in the year, on one of his trips, he had been robbed of thirteen guineas, his watch, and silver shoe-buckles.[3]

[1] Mainwaring Piozziana, i. 53. On the back of a copy of this poem (Ry. 647, 4) is a note in Johnson's hand, 'On the Red breast at Streatham Dec. –63', indicating that he had examined the poem at some later date.

[2] Hayward, ii. 24. Thrale was much interested in hunting, and kept a pack of fox-hounds at a hunting box near Croydon. Possibly his objections to his wife's riding may be explained by the fact that his earlier mistress, Polly Hart, had been a very skilful rider. (See *Westminster Magazine*, i (1773), 178.)

[3] *St. James's Chronicle*, May 3–5, 1763. On Aug. 12, 1763, Samuel Beaton was executed at Kennington Common for robbing Henry Thrale (*Gent. Mag.* xxxiii. 411).

So, in January 1764, he moved to his home at Southwark, next to the brewery in Dead-Man's Place.[1]

This house, also never seen by Mrs. Thrale before her marriage, was not in a fashionable residential district. It was south of the Thames, close to the site of the old Globe theatre where many of Shakespeare's plays were first produced. In Elizabethan times the region had been one where theatres and brothels carried on their somewhat interrelated amusements, but during the seventeenth and eighteenth centuries it had changed into a centre of business and manufacture. The elder Thrale had thought it best to occupy a house near to the brewery, to keep a closer watch on its affairs, and his son approved this plan. The men were unaffected by the dreary surroundings, but it is not surprising that the young wife found them dull. The story now reached her that Thrale's choice of a bride had been influenced by her willingness to live in Southwark. According to one account, he had considered several other heiresses, each of whom had been reluctant to reside so far from Hanover Square.[2] Hester Lynch could not have afforded such independence, even if she had been given a choice. Although she disliked the Borough, she never openly rebelled, and good-humouredly made the best of her bargain.

Mrs. Thrale later recalled that first winter:

> Our Society at the Borough House was exceedingly circumscribed. Few People would come to so strange a Place—few indeed *could* come; but as we kept Two Equipages I had it always in my Power to go out. My mother however thought the closer I kept home the better.[3]

The move to town had separated mother and daughter for the first time, for Mrs. Salusbury now returned to her house in Dean Street, Soho. There her daughter drove every day to keep in touch with her old friends. One morning, on her regular visit, she found her mother in tears because of the death of her sister, Sophia Cotton, at Bath. At the request of another aunt, Mrs. Thrale wrote a short inscription for a memorial tablet at Weston, which was some slight return for a legacy of £500.[4]

The only company who found their way to Southwark were Thrale's family and bachelor friends. Except for Arthur

---

[1] *Thraliana,* April 1778. For information about Southwark and the Anchor Brewery see Charlotte Boger, *Southwark and its Story* (1881); E. W. Brayley, *The History of Surrey* (Dorking, Ede), App., pp. 10–18; *The Wine and Spirit Trade Record,* Oct. 16, 1935, pp. 1246–56.   [2] Hayward, ii. 24; *Thraliana,* Apr. 1778.
[3] *Mainwaring Piozziana,* i. 55.
[4] Ibid., p. 54. For a copy see Ry. 530, 8.

Murphy, the witty Irishman, they did not meet with Mrs. Thrale's approval. Neither the facetious George Bodens nor the notorious Simon Luttrell proved congenial or attractive. (It was said of the latter that he once challenged his own son, Wilkes's opponent in the famous Middlesex election, who refused to fight him, 'not because he was his father, but because he was not a gentleman'.) Dr. Fitzpatrick, a sickly physician, was also an intimate friend of the household.[1] Here, too, came her husband's three handsome sisters, Lady Lade, Mrs. Nesbitt, and Mrs. Plumbe, who had married wealthy London business men, and had little interest in poetry or scholarship. With their new sister-in-law they maintained a casual intercourse, but because of such divergent tastes were never intimate or affectionate.

In the meantime relations with her uncle, Sir Thomas, had again become strained. After giving his niece to the man of his choice, Sir Thomas proceeded with his own love affair and less than a month later married the widow King.[2] The long-dreaded alliance was now a reality. Since neither Mrs. Thrale nor her mother could ever forget the black hours which fear of the marriage had brought to John Salusbury, they petulantly refused to call on the new wife. Bitterly resenting the affront, Sir Thomas took the only available means of retaliation by refusing to pay Mrs. Salusbury the annuity which he had promised at the time of her daughter's marriage. He even kept back the small payments from the Welsh property provided in his brother's will. Although Sir Lynch Cotton and Bridge both interceded in an effort to make peace, they were unsuccessful.[3] The ladies were stubbornly determined not to make the first move, and Sir Thomas, who felt himself the injured party, saw no reason to humble himself.

The winter of 1764 passed uneventfully,[4] but by spring, with

---

[1] Hayward, ii. 23. Many anecdotes of Bodens appear in Thraliana.

[2] Sir Thomas wrote to Thrale from Offley on Nov. 4, 1763, to acquaint him with the marriage (Ry. 530, 29), and added that everyone who had thought proper to ask him had known of his intentions long ago.

[3] A scribbled first draft of a letter from Mrs. Thrale in Southwark to Edward Bridge, dated May 19, 1764, is in the Rylands collection (Ry. 533, 3). Mrs. Thrale's justification for her behaviour is that her uncle had never called on her mother since his marriage, and had avoided them when in London, though she herself had seen him occasionally with other people. Mrs. Salusbury, even if she received no financial aid from Sir Thomas, was not wholly dependent on her son-in-law, since recent legacies from other members of her family provided enough to keep up her house in Dean Street. During the summers, however, she always lived with the Thrales at Streatham.

[4] Very little contemporary evidence has survived for the year 1764. On Apr. 15

the knowledge that she was to have a child, Mrs. Thrale assumed in the household a position of more importance. A wife's primary duty, according to Thrale, was to produce an heir to carry on the business after him, and now that she was expectant his hopes were high. The following summer was spent quietly at Streatham Park; then because of her condition they moved back to Southwark early in September. Here, the Thrales' first child, a girl, was born on September 17, 1764.[1] On the 24th, in St. Saviour's Parish Church, Southwark, she was christened Hester Maria in honour of her grandmother.

The birth of a daughter must have been disappointing to Thrale. What his wife's feelings were we cannot tell; she was too busy during the autumn looking after her first-born either to think of recording her impressions or to consider the future.

The young mother's complete preoccupation with the affairs of the nursery did not last long. Among her husband's old friends, Mrs. Thrale had been immediately attracted by the amusing Arthur Murphy, who, although Thrale's companion in many a reckless adventure, had a serious side to his nature. He was a popular dramatist, a fair classical scholar, and a sound and versatile writer; he was also the intimate friend and companion of many of the best-known men of the day, including Samuel Johnson. Johnson, for his part, had a special fondness for the mercurial playwright, whom he affectionately called his 'dear Mur'. It is not surprising to find Murphy wishing to bring his two friends together—to introduce the popular brewer and his wife to the Great Cham of literature. Some years later, in Thraliana, Mrs. Thrale told the story of this introduction.

It was on the second Thursday of the month of January 1765. that I first saw Mr. Johnson in a Room: Murphy whose Intimacy with Mr. Thrale had been of many Years standing, was one day dining with us at our house in Southwark; and was zealous that we should be acquainted with Johnson, of whose moral and Literary Character he spoke in the most exalted Terms; and so whetted our desire of seeing him soon, that we were only disputing *how* he

her old friend Dr. Bernard Wilson sent Mrs. Thrale his translation of *Monsieur de Thou's History of his Own Time* (first translated by Wilson in 1729), adding his regard 'for a Lady of her distinguishing Accomplishments and uncommon Literature few being qualified to make so good an use of so excellent an Historian . . .' (Ry. 891, 6). A few other letters addressed to Mrs. Thrale this year are extant, and indicate that among other interests she acted as patroness for James Merrick who was publishing a paraphrase of the Psalms (Ry. 536, 15, &c.). Three letters from Eliz. Surman, discussing literature and poetry, also indicate that Mrs. Thrale was aiding the writer's brother to find a position. Miss Surman added that she kept Mrs. Thrale's replies as treasures in her strong box. (Ry. 536, 40–2.)

[1] Children's Book. (See p. 70, n. 2.)

should be invited, *when* he should be invited, and what should be the pretence. at last it was resolved that one Woodhouse a Shoemaker who had written some Verses, and been asked to some Tables, should likewise be asked to ours, and made a Temptation to Mr. Johnson to meet him: accordingly he came, and Mr. Murphy at four o'clock brought Mr. Johnson to dinner.[1]

Another description of the dinner was also written long afterwards by the shoemaker poet, Woodhouse.

I was informed, at the time, that Dr. Johnson's curiosity was excited, by what was said of me in the literary world, as a kind of wild beast from the country, and expressed a wish to Mr. Murphy, who was his intimate friend, to see me. In consequence of which, Mr. Murphy being acquainted with Mrs. Thrale, intimated to her that both might be invited to dine there at the same time; for till then, Dr. Johnson had never seen Mrs. Thrale, who, no doubt he also much desired to see.[2]

We may well imagine the shock with which Mrs. Thrale first saw the huge, lumbering form of the Doctor. Murphy, to be sure, had warned her, giving 'general cautions not to be surprised at his figure, dress or behaviour',[3] but even with this preparation her first reaction must have been one of astonishment. Johnson's eccentricities are familiar to everyone, the twitching frame, the nervous hypochondria, and the voracious appetite. And because of these, many women at first sight were prejudiced against Johnson. So, for example, the wife of 'Hermes' Harris was shocked by his 'dreadful voice and manner' and awkward carriage. He was, she maintained to her son,

---

[1] *Thraliana*, Sept. 18, 1777. The original notation came, no doubt, from one of her early journals. Mrs. Piozzi in the *Anecdotes* (*John. Misc.* i. 232) places her first meeting with Johnson in 1764, but Thraliana is undoubtedly a more accurate source. To anyone brought up under the old system of dating, where the winter months were considered to be still a part of the previous year, it would have been a very easy mistake to think of January 1765 as 1764. Similarly Thomas Pennant wrote 1764 on the title-page of his manuscript volume entitled *Tour on the Continent*, although he did not set out from London until Feb. 19, 1765 (*T.L.S.*, Aug. 20, 1938, p. 543). Mrs. Thrale is probably wrong, however, in ascribing the day of the first meeting to Thursday, Jan. 10. In Johnson's diary for 1765 (recently discovered by Col. Isham) the first mention of the Thrales (spelled Trails) occurs on Wed. Jan. 9. The next reference comes on Tuesday, Jan. 29, and the one following on Mar. 18. Johnson's record, on the other hand, is very incomplete, and after Jan. 10 lists no engagements throughout the winter for Thursdays; consequently it is no conclusive evidence against Mrs. Thrale's later assertion that he came to Southwark regularly every Thursday. In his diary Johnson may, in the case of the Thrales, have listed only the special visits in addition to his regular weekly invitation. See also *Life*, i. 520–1. Dr. E. L. McAdam has provided some of the above details.

[2] *Adam Libr.* iii. 263. The letter was written by Woodhouse to Wm. Mudford, July 28, 1809. See also *Blackwood's Mag.* xxvi (1829), 748–55.

[3] *John. Misc.* i. 233.

'more beastly in his dress and person than anything I ever beheld. He feeds nastily and ferociously, and eats quantities most unthankfully.'[1] Mrs. Thrale was more discerning. If at first she was annoyed at Johnson's lack of polish, she soon forgot such faults in admiration for his conversation and wonder at his kind heart. Besides, the quiet domestic life of the past year and a half was beginning to bore her, and she welcomed someone to fill the place of Collier and his friends with discourse of literature and philosophy.

We know little of that first dinner at Thrale's house in the Borough,[2] but undoubtedly Johnson was delighted with the meal, and with his host and hostess. What more could any man wish? The Thrales were equally pleased with their guest, and she wrote: 'We liked each other so well that the next Thursday was appointed for the same Company to meet—exclusive of the Shoemaker.'[3] Throughout the rest of the winter of 1765, Johnson dined at the Thrales' every Thursday.

Mrs. Thrale was properly flattered at playing hostess to so celebrated a figure as Johnson, for she had some of the instincts of the lion-huntress; but no doubt she would not have been so zealous in her ministrations had she not been personally attracted to the man himself.[4] And Johnson would not have journeyed weekly to Southwark merely for a dinner if he had not also been interested in his host and hostess. Henry Thrale was more than a brewer. His friend Murphy wrote of him: 'His education at Oxford gave him the habits of a gentleman; his amiable temper recommended his conversation, and the goodness of his heart made him a sincere friend.'[5] Though never a ready talker, he delighted to hear others carry on an argument at his table. Mme D'Arblay, much later, maintained

---

[1] *Letters of the First Earl of Malmesbury* (1870), i. 302. Mrs. Harris wrote from Twickenham, Apr. 20, 1775. Johnson's inattention to everything else about him while eating is described by Joseph Cradock (*John. Misc.* ii. 61). See also *Life*, i. 468.

[2] In a letter to Wm. Mudford, Aug. 29, 1810, Mrs. Piozzi herself retold the story of her first meeting with Johnson. She added, Johnson's 'Injunction to him [Woodhouse] about the Spectators struck me very forcibly. Give Nights & Days Sir said he, to the study of Addison'. (Original letter in the Adam collection; printed in *Blackwood's Mag.* xxi (1829), 754–5.) See also *John. Misc.* i. 233. Johnson evidently gave the shoemaker poet advice similar to that later incorporated into the life of Addison. Another topic possibly discussed that evening was the poetry of Milton. Woodhouse, as an old man, related to Mudford a somewhat questionable story of Johnson's bitterness when referring to Milton. See Wm. Mudford, *Critical Enquiry into the Writings of Dr. Samuel Johnson* (1803), p. 37.

[3] See p. 55, n. 1; also *John. Misc.* i. 233.

[4] Mrs. Thrale always insisted that she never made a lion of Johnson. See Hayward, i. 49.   [5] *John. Misc.* i. 423–4.

that Thrale found 'a singular amusement in hearing, instigating, and provoking a war of words, alternating triumph and overthrow, between clever and ambitious colloquial combatants'.[1] Mrs. Thrale herself gives evidence that as a young man her husband was gay and voluble, far from the stolid, unresponsive being of later years. It must always be remembered that it was many years afterwards that Johnson is reported to have replied, when asked about Thrale's conversational ability, 'Why, Sir, his conversation does not show the minute hand; but he strikes the hour very correctly.'[2] As for Mrs. Thrale, she was vivacious and attractive, and not afraid to dispute at length with her famous visitor. While she poured tea from a seemingly inexhaustible tea-pot,[3] she delighted to chat about the latest pamphlet, the merits of some poet, or the most recent bon mot going the rounds in London. Her lively and unaffected talk provided, as did Boswell's, a perfect foil for Johnson's remarks.

According to Mrs. Thrale's later recollections, Johnson was at this time considering a translation of Boethius. Mentioning the project to his hostess, he laughingly suggested that she do the 'Odes', setting her the task of producing one for each Thursday, the day on which he regularly came to dinner.[4] In the easy familiarity of the Thrale home the work was begun in due course, and a number of the *Metres* were rendered into English verse. Every week she would pass over to him her translations written out on small cards, many of which still exist. For sport she and Johnson translated the sixth *Metre* of the third book together, each doing alternate stanzas. In all Johnson alone completed three *Metres*, Mrs. Thrale produced about six, and they collaborated on at least five others.[5]

---

[1] D'Arblay, *Memoirs of Doctor Burney* (1832), ii. 104–5.

[2] There are several versions of this story. *John. Misc.* ii. 169, 374. For Thrale's early gay character see Hayward, i. 10.

[3] It is interesting to note that one of Mrs. Thrale's tea-pots, later sold in the Streatham sale, had a capacity of more than three quarts. It was of old oriental porcelain, painted and gilded. (J. Marryat, *Collections towards a History of Pottery and Porcelain* (1850), p. 289.) On the other hand, the tea-pot now in the possession of the Johnson House in Gough Square, London, is very small indeed.

[4] *Letters to and from Johnson* (1788), Preface, p. vi. See also Hayward, ii. 86. Mrs. Thrale's own dating of 1765, though very early, has been accepted because this winter Johnson is supposed to have dined regularly with the Thrales every Thursday. In later years he had become more of a regular inmate of the house.

[5] Originally Mrs. Piozzi had intended to print all of these *Metres* in her edition of Johnson's letters (1788). At the last minute, however, after the sheets had all been printed, it was decided to cancel all of Mrs. Piozzi's own efforts, and publish only those in which Johnson's hand could be traced. Samuel Lysons's copy of the edition, now in the possession of Lord Harmsworth, contains the cancelled pages.

Perhaps Johnson did not take the matter very seriously; but the episode serves to show how much he must have been attracted to his new acquaintance, as it also indicates a certain regard for her scholarly attainments. The project, however, was soon given up. As Mrs. Thrale later recorded, 'we went however but a little Way in the Business, because some poor Author had engaged in the Work—& he fear'd our Publication would be his Hindrance'.[1] She treasured up the scraps which had been written and published Johnson's contributions in her edition of his letters in 1788.

Except for sprightly conversations with her new friend, and the care of her baby, the winter of 1765 followed the usual pattern of monotonous domesticity. With the coming of spring the Thrales moved out to Streatham. By this time Mrs. Thrale was again with child, and was having more trouble than before.[2] It was probably because of her ill health that the family went to Brighton late in the summer.

Johnson had been urged by the Thrales to join them in Sussex, but wrote on August 13 apologizing for not being able to accept their invitation. Busy as he was on the proofs of his edition of Shakespeare, he could not leave London, though the prospect of a holiday with such agreeable companions was a strong temptation. He promised, nevertheless, to come as soon as he could dismiss the work from his hands; and then added:

I am afraid to make promises even to myself; but I hope that the week after the next will be the end of my present business. When business is done, what remains but pleasure? and where should pleasure be sought, but under Mrs. Thrale's influence?[3]

Unfortunately before Johnson could join the Thrales at Brighton they had hurriedly returned to the house in Southwark. Two considerations probably brought about this sudden change of

Metres 1, 3, and 4 of book 1, and 1, 3, and 7 of book 2, entirely the work of Mrs. Thrale, were omitted. (Original MS. versions of these verses may be found in Ry. 538, and in the possession of Mr. L. Fleming, Bognor Regis.) Positive proof of the collaboration of Mrs. Thrale and Johnson on at least one Metre is provided in the facsimile of the original draft of Metre 3, book 3, in Broadley, p. 114. Johnson's lines in Metre 12, book 3, were probably dictated to Mrs. Thrale, as is shown by her original copy (Ry. 538).

[1] Mainwaring Piozziana, i. 68; also Letters to and from Johnson, Preface, p. vi. For a discussion of this episode see the edition of Johnson's poems by D. Nichol Smith and E. L. McAdam.

[2] Children's Book. For description of this journal see p. 70, Chapter IV.

[3] Unless otherwise noted, Johnson's letters may be found in Hill's edition, 1892. Further evidence of the connexion of Johnson and the Thrales this summer is the fact that Mrs. Thrale had in her possession early page-proofs, with many corrections in the author's hand, of Johnson's Preface to his edition of Shakespeare (Ry. 653).

plans: Mrs. Thrale's approaching confinement, and her husband's political ambitions. Henry Thrale had long wished to represent Southwark in Parliament. As we have seen, as early as 1754 he had offered himself for a possible vacancy;[1] now the death on September 16, 1765, of Alexander Hume, one of the members for the Borough, at last provided the opportunity for which he had been waiting. Thrale rushed to Southwark and, after a meeting with some of the electors on September 23, announced his candidature.[2]

On the 27th, in the midst of all the bustle and excitement of the approaching election, Mrs. Thrale gave birth to another daughter, who was baptized Frances at St. Saviour's Church on October 3. Four days later the child died suddenly,[3] but in the activity arising from her husband's entrance into politics Mrs. Thrale had little time for mourning. She early learned that busy matrons could not afford the luxury of grief.

Mrs. Thrale's account of this period, recorded later in the *Anecdotes*, is rather vague. She indicates that Johnson, who had not been told of their precipitate return to London, made the trip to Brighton only to find his host and hostess gone. Disappointed and enraged, he wrote them a letter expressing his anger at such inhospitable treatment. However, when Murphy, acting as conciliator, explained the reason, Johnson was soon mollified, and, as Mrs. Thrale wrote, 'from that time his visits grew more frequent'.[4] In the stress of political campaigning, moreover, Thrale found his new friend's powers of literary persuasion a valuable asset.

During October and November the Borough was assiduously canvassed, and finally Thrale's opponent, Durant, decided to withdraw from the contest. Despite this, Thrale printed an address in the newspapers on November 21, soliciting the voters' favour on election day. There is in existence a copy of this appeal to the worthy electors of Southwark with proof corrections in Johnson's hand. The newspaper version, how-

---

[1] See p. 36, n. 1.

[2] See *Public Advertiser* and other papers of Sept. 23, 24, 1765. Thrale's first advertisement was repeated in the issues of Sept. 25, 26, 27, 28, 30. Another address, thanking his supporters for their encouragement during the canvass, was printed by Thrale Oct. 1, and was repeated in the papers throughout October and early November.

[3] *Children's Book*. According to Mrs. Thrale, the child died 'of the watery Gripes' which was undoubtedly ordinary infantile diarrhoea. I am indebted, throughout the following chapters, to Dr. Ernest Sadler, of the Mansion, Ashbourne, for aid in interpreting the illnesses of the Thrale children.

[4] *John. Misc.* i. 233.

ever, does not embody these changes. It may be assumed, therefore, that even if Johnson did not compose the original draft, he at least revised the wording at a later time, possibly for a broadside to be distributed by hand throughout the borough.[1]

On December 20 the papers announced that Thrale would be chosen without opposition, and on the 23rd he was officially returned a member of Parliament.[2] Although Johnson may not have supervised the early announcements of his friend's candidature, he was solely responsible for his last address. Thrale's final acknowledgement to his constituents on December 24 was expressed in the sonorous phrases of the *Dictionary*.

Gentlemen

Having received the unusual honour of an unanimous Election, it may justly be expected that I express my Gratitude to my worthy Constituents. I therefore return you thanks for the favour of your Suffrages, of which I hope never to give you reason to repent. For I shall think it the highest happiness to preserve by a constant and uniform attention that concord of which this numerous and opulent Borough has given on this occasion so laudable an Example[3]

The fact that Johnson was willing to give his time to these election affairs shows how quickly he had identified himself with the concerns of the Thrale household. No doubt he must have been greatly pleased at his friend's entry into Parliament, confirming as it did his own high estimate of the man. Even if Thrale's political career was to prove far from spectacular, it at least gave him an enhanced standing in the community.

Political and maternal duties could not keep Mrs. Thrale from her old occupation of scribbling verses; nor was she ever backward about showing them to other people. That Johnson read many of her youthful attempts during the early months of their friendship is proved by the fact that a number of the original drafts have notes on the back in his handwriting.[4]

---

[1] *Public Advertiser*, Nov. 21, 1765. The address is dated Nov. 20, and was repeated in the issues of Nov. 22, 23, 25. The copy with Johnson's proof-corrections is now in the possession of Mrs. Herbert Evans, Brynbella.

[2] *Public Advertiser*, Dec. 20, 1765, &c. In this issue appeared another address from Thrale, possibly drafted by Johnson.

[3] The original draft of this address in the handwriting of Johnson is now in the possession of Mrs. Herbert Evans, Brynbella. The manuscript shows several words and phrases corrected, and the address was printed as written, except for capitalization and punctuation and the addition of 'my sincere' between 'you' and 'thanks' in the second sentence, in the *Public Advertiser*, Dec. 24, 1765 (repeated Dec. 25, 26). (See also miscellaneous collection of newspaper clippings referring to this election in the Adam collection.)

[4] Chiefly in the John Rylands collection.

Possibly Mrs. Thrale's verses reminded him of those of another lady, the blind Welsh poetess, Anna Williams, who shared his dwelling in Fleet Street. In spite of the fact that Johnson had written proposals for printing a subscription volume of Miss Williams's poems as far back as 1750, the years had slipped by without anything being done. Finally, in the winter of 1766 something spurred him into action. New plans were made for publication, additional subscriptions secured, and a printer engaged.[1]

At the last minute it was found that the number of poems was hardly sufficient to fill the volume which Johnson had engaged to print. He turned at once to Mrs. Thrale.

Have you any Verses by You—said he to me—which have never been seen? I show'd him a Tale that I had written the Week before & he liked it so well it was seized on Instantly, & called *The Three Warnings*.[2]

Johnson was pleased with this contribution, but still more was needed.

He said Come Mistress, now *I'll* write a Tale and your Character shall be in it; so he composed The Fountains in the same Book, a Performance little known, and in few hands—I guess not *whose* except my own;—and bid me translate Boileau's Epistle to his Gardener which I did: and the Work turn'd out a Thin flat Quarto, which it appears sold miserably: I never saw it on any Table but my own. Tis *now* however become a Curiosity.

Miss Williams's *Miscellanies*, which appeared in April 1766, certainly caused no stir at the time, and is to-day a rarity.

Mrs. Thrale's contribution, the 'Three Warnings', when later reprinted in other collections of verse, achieved some popularity.[3] It is her best-known poem, and several generations

---

[1] *Life*, ii. 26; Courtney and Nichol Smith, *Bibliography of Samuel Johnson* (1925), pp. 111–12.　　　　　　　[2] Mainwaring Piozziana, i. 57, 61.

[3] The poem was included in Pearch's collection of *Poems by Several Hands* (1770), iii. 258–62 (also in later editions), at which time the authorship was definitely ascribed to Mrs. Thrale. The poem was circulated in a chap-book, *Abbas and Mirza an Eastern Story to which is added the Three Warnings*, price Threepence (Chelmsford, printed and sold by I. Marsden, no date). 'The Three Warnings' was published separately by George Gower at Kidderminster in 1792. It was reprinted frequently in popular anthologies: The *British Poetical Weekly* (Huddersfield, 1799), ii. 5; *British Female Poets*, ed. Bethune (1848); *English Poetesses*, ed. E. S. Robertson (1883), &c. According to Mrs. Piozzi the poem was translated into German, and into Italian by the Marquis de Pindemonte (Lansdowne MS. letter of Solstice, 1805, and *Queeney Letters*, p. 202). It became a popular poem for public recitation. In a letter from Mrs. Thrale to Johnson, from Bath, Apr. 20, 1780, she referred to a reading of the Tale by a public lecturer (Ry. 540, 93). On Mar. 19, 1795, L. Chappelow wrote to Mrs. Piozzi that Holman was to read the poem in a series at

of readers have been familiar from their schoolroom days with
old Dobson, the hero.[1] The plot, a variation of a well-known
folk-tale motif, was not original,[2] being, as she admitted, the
favourite anecdote of old Sir Charles Wager, retold in easy
octosyllabics.

Death had promised Farmer Dobson three warnings before
his final visit, and when the time arrived, Dobson demanded
his warnings. Death in turn asked the farmer a few pertinent
questions.

'I little thought you'd still be able
To stump about your farm and stable;
Your years have run to a great length,
I wish you joy, tho', of your strength.'
'Hold,' says the farmer, 'not so fast,
I have been lame these four years past.'
'And no great wonder,' Death replies.
'However, you still keep your eyes;
And, sure, to see one's loves and friends,
For legs and arms would make amends.'
'Perhaps,' says Dobson, 'so it might,
But latterly I've lost my sight.'
'This is a shocking story, faith,
Yet there's some comfort still,' says Death.
'Each strives your sadness to amuse,
I warrant you have all the news.'
'There's none,' cries he: 'and if there were,
I'm grown so deaf, I could not hear.'
'Nay, then,' the spectre stern rejoin'd,
'These are unjustifiable yearnings;
If you are lame, and deaf, and blind,
You've had your three sufficient warnings.
So come along, no more we'll part,'
He said, and touched him with his dart.
And now old Dobson, turning pale,
Yields to his fate—so ends my tale.[3]

Mrs. Thrale's only other contribution to Miss Williams's
Miscellanies was her translation of the 'Epistle of Boileau to his
Gardener', which was effectively written in the heroic couplet.
Soon after the publication of these poems attempts were made

Free Mason's Hall which was much advertised (Ry. 562, 24). See also *European
Mag.* x (1786), 5.
   [1] See reference by Miss Miriam A. Ellis, *Fortnightly Review* (Aug. 1903), p. 269.
   [2] See *N. & Q.*, 3rd Ser. ii (Dec. 14, 1867), 482.
   [3] Seeley, *Mrs. Thrale*, pp. 49–50. The poem is also printed in Hayward, ii.
165–9.

to trace in them the hand of Johnson.[1] Yet there is no reason to question the lady's independent authorship, for while some of the lines may be Johnson's, or corrected by him before publication, Mrs. Thrale had previously shown herself quite capable of writing the poems unassisted.

Besides the help Johnson gave in collecting subscriptions and in adding to the meagre supply of verses written by Miss Williams, he contributed the Preface, several short poems, and the fairy tale called 'The Fountains'. As has been mentioned already, Johnson told Mrs. Thrale that in this story he would describe her character. She always believed he had done so, as is shown by remarks in her letters and books; indeed, her copy of the *Miscellanies* has numerous annotations in the margins comparing Floretta with herself.[2] One should be careful, however, not to see in his characterization more than Johnson actually intended.

In the story, Floretta was given the right to drink either from the spring of joy or from the spring of sorrow, and thus to attain her most ardent desires. She tried, in rapid succession, beauty, a faithful lover, the right to have her own way, wealth, and even wit; but when envy and jealousy rendered all of these unendurable, she successively drank each one away, except wit, with a draught from the fountain of sorrow. Finally, when even long life proved futile, Floretta resigned herself calmly to the course of nature. Probably all Johnson wished was to make his hostess realize that most worldly ambitions were hollow, and he took this means of advising her to be content with the talents God had given her.

Throughout the winter of 1766 Johnson was probably a constant visitor in Southwark, though we have no accurate

---

[1] *John. Misc.* ii. 353, note; quoted from Prior, *Life of Malone*, p. 413. S. Lysons is in this case given as authority for the statement; yet in his own scrap-book of clippings, when pasting in the story printed in the *Morning Post* for Mar. 21, 1788, Lysons wrote next to the clipping, 'Not true S.L.' (See p. 124, n. 1, Chapter VI.)

[2] Now in the collection at Johnson's Birthplace, Lichfield. In Nov. 1815 Sir James Fellowes jotted down from Mrs. Piozzi's conversation various recollections concerning 'The Fountains'. According to this account,

'Dr. Johnson wrote the beautiful Tale of the "*Fountains*" in a short time in the library at Streatham whilst Mrs. Thrale was sitting by him, telling her that he would describe her as "Floretta" and that it would serve to fill up the book about to be published for the benefit of Mrs. Anna Williams the blind lady entitled "*Miscellanies in Prose & Verse*" 1766. The lines scored in the Tale of the Fountains were by H.L.P.—'

(Adam collection). It is greatly to be doubted whether Mrs. Thrale actually supplied any parts of Johnson's Tale, though she may possibly have suggested some points of the characterization. The writing probably occurred in Southwark rather than Streatham, but this too is not certain. See also Hayward, ii. 444–5.

record of his movements.¹ He was living at the time in his house in Johnson's Court with the strange medley of companions caricatured by Macaulay. Life in this household, with the objects of his charity constantly quarrelling among themselves, could hardly have been cheering to the ailing moralist, who was subject to black fits of melancholy. The drab atmosphere of his home provided no antidote for his sombre moods. While occasional dinners with congenial friends, or meetings of the Club, with Burke, Reynolds, and Goldsmith, might rouse his spirits for a few hours, the greater part of his time was spent in brooding dejection. Some time in the first half of 1766 Johnson suffered a severe breakdown; he became so morbidly depressed that he would not stir out of his house for many weeks together, and as Mrs. Thrale later expressed it, 'he often lamented to us the horrible condition of his mind, which he said was nearly distracted'. It was so distressing that,

when we waited on him one morning, and heard him, in the most pathetic terms, beg the prayers of Dr. Delap, who had left him as we came in, I felt excessively affected with grief, and well remember my husband involuntarily lifted up one hand to shut his mouth, from provocation at hearing a man so wildly proclaim what he could at last persuade no one to believe; and what, if true, would have been so very unfit to reveal.

Mr. Thrale went away soon after, leaving me with him, and bidding me prevail on him to quit his close habitation in the court and come with us to Streatham, where I undertook the care of his health, and had the honour and happiness of contributing to its restoration.²

Exactly when Johnson accepted the Thrales' invitation for a prolonged stay at Streatham is uncertain, but we know definitely from his own journal that he was there from the latter part of June to the 1st of October 1766.³ This was a turning-point in his life. Friendship quickly ripened into intimacy, and for the next sixteen years Johnson spent the greater part of his

---

¹ From Boswell's records of Feb. 1766 (*Life*, ii. 5–16), it appears that he saw Johnson during week-ends, a fact which lends further support to Mrs. Thrale's assertion that Johnson came to them regularly every Thursday, and possibly on other days in the middle of the week.

² *John. Misc.*, i. 234.

³ The problem of Johnson's illness and first domestication at the Thrales is considered by Dr. L. F. Powell in Appendix F, *Life*, i. 520–2. Without further evidence it seems difficult to harmonize Mrs. Piozzi's account with the fairly cheerful tone exhibited by Johnson in his letters to Langton in March and May 1766; yet these letters may have been written in lucid intervals. See also *Life*, ii. 25. Johnson's mental instability this spring is clearly shown in the entry in his diary for Mar. 29, 1766 (printed by R. B. Adam in *Pages from Johnson's Diary*, Buffalo, 1926).

time with the Thrales either at Streatham or in Southwark. He grew to think and speak of both these houses as 'home', and constantly referred to his host and hostess as his 'Master' and 'Mistress'. To all intents and purposes Johnson became a member of the Thrale family.

IV

BEGINNING DIARIST

1766–1770

THE domestication of Samuel Johnson at Streatham brought a welcome change for Mrs. Thrale, who had been forced since her marriage to lead a comparatively secluded life and expected to be content with household and maternal duties while her husband continued to enjoy the diversions of London alone. Johnson once frankly told Mrs. Thrale, in her mother's hearing, that she lived like a kept mistress, 'shut from the world, its pleasures, or its cares'.[1] Now for the first time she had some one in the home who was willing to spend hours in literary conversation or to lend a sympathetic ear to tales of household perplexities. Thrale, as we have seen, had no patience either with her complaints or with her enthusiasms. Because of Johnson's presence, too, other interesting visitors began slowly to find their way across the river to Southwark or to Streatham. Thrale's bachelor cronies who, with the exception of Arthur Murphy, could hardly have felt at ease with the author of *Rasselas*, were seen less frequently. Instead, a more distinguished company took their place. Baretti, Sir Joshua Reynolds, Goldsmith, and the Burkes made the acquaintance of the Southwark brewer and came to his house to dine.[2] Thus Mrs. Thrale had Johnson to thank not only for kindly counsel in the house, but also for bringing his famous friends to her drawing-room. Her mind need stagnate no longer in petty cares or dull gossip.

On the other hand, she soon found that there were objectionable features in the arrangement. Although Johnson might feel that it was a mistake for a talented woman to give all her days to affairs of the family, he never advocated complete

[1] Hayward, ii. 25. Johnson used to tell her that while she was feeding her chickens she was starving her own understanding (Ry. 585, 14).

[2] In only one instance is there any contemporary evidence proving just when each was introduced. In Sir Joshua Reynolds's note-books (now at the Royal Academy, London) the name of Thrale first appears among the lists of business and social engagements on Sept. 2, 1766.

emancipation, and made it a settled rule always to support
the husband in any serious argument. And even his literary
conversation was not unalloyed pleasure, for his love of talk,
combined with perpetual insomnia, made him prolong the discussions far past the usual bed time, and Mrs. Thrale was often
compelled to be his long-suffering companion.[1] Furthermore,
the open dislike shown by her own mother for the great man
resulted in constant friction. Mrs. Salusbury was interested
in current topics and derived particular enjoyment from reading and discussing news from the Continent. To Johnson such
preoccupation with doubtful news of the day was a waste of
time, and he continually teased her about her credulity. This
much is certain, but we may be inclined to question the story
which Mrs. Thrale tells of his writing misleading accounts of
imaginary battles in central Europe and inserting them in Mrs.
Salusbury's favourite newspaper.[2] The situation was not improved when Mrs. Salusbury's dog Belle committed the unpardonable sin of devouring Johnson's buttered toast while he
was holding forth to her daughter. It was only after a long
succession of family sorrows that Johnson and Mrs. Salusbury
got over this early prejudice and became devoted friends.

Living with the Thrales resulted in a change in Johnson too.
Never before had he enjoyed day after day the luxury and comforts of a well-to-do household. He was assured of the best of
food, spacious grounds for exercise, efficient service for all his
needs, and a congenial group of companions deferring to his
wishes. The early years of privation had left their mark on
both his disposition and his huge frame, sharpening his tongue
as well as his appetite. Now in the happy, tranquil life at

---

[1] *John. Misc.* i. 231. See also p. 149.

[2] Ibid., p. 235. Sir Brooke Boothby corroborates the story, hardly credible
though it may seem. He told Robert Anderson (who recorded it in his *Life of
Samuel Johnson* (3rd ed., Edinburgh, 1815), p. 322) that Johnson one day at Lucy
Porter's related,

that a lady of his acquaintance implicitly believed every thing she read in the
papers; and that, by way of curing her credulity, he fabricated a story of a
battle between the Russians and Turks, then at war; . . . The lady, however,
believed the story, and never forgave the deception; the consequence of which
was, that I lost an agreeable companion, and she was deprived of an innocent
amusement.

According to the story, Johnson even claimed that the Russian Ambassador sent
in great haste to know where the printer had received his intelligence. Baretti
also gives evidence of the early jealousy between Johnson and Mrs. Salusbury.
In a note to the 1788 edition of Johnson's *Letters* (British Museum) he wrote:
'Johnson could not much bear Mrs. Salusbury, nor Mrs. Salusbury him, when
they first knew each other But her cancer moved his compassion, and made them
friends.'

Streatham Johnson relaxed and gradually became a different person. His health improved both physically and mentally; even his outward appearance was altered.

Thrale was responsible for this last and most obvious metamorphosis. He was the Master of Streatham, and since his word was law in the household, even Johnson dared not disobey. It was Thrale who saw to it that Johnson's clothes were clean and in order, that he put silver buckles on his shoes, that he changed his shirt more often than formerly. On occasions a servant stood outside the dining-room with a fresh wig, so that the result of Johnson's habit of reading too close to the candle might not be apparent to the guests.[1] Moreover, only the Master could curb Johnson's dogmatic assertions. Mrs. Thrale tells us that at least once her husband cut short one of his pronouncements with a curt—'There, there, now we have had enough for one lecture, Dr. Johnson; we will not be upon education any more till after dinner, if you please.'[2] That Johnson would accept such a reproof is evidence of the respect he had for his host and his willingness to conform to the rules of the Streatham family.

The months of idleness throughout the summer of 1766, during which he was provided with all the fresh fruit and vegetables he could consume (his idea of perfect luxury), partially restored his health and good spirits.[3] The change so delighted the Master and Mistress of the mansion that they began to consider their guest as a permanent addition to the family. Having sampled the pleasure of his wise companionship and seen him rejuvenated by good living, they were averse to going back to the old casual intercourse. Consequently, even during the winter, when they were in town next to the brewery, they expected Johnson to spend at least part of the week with them. As Mrs. Thrale wrote, Dr. Johnson 'soon became something like a regular Inmate of the House at Southwark, where Mr. Thrale fitted him up an Apartment over the Counting House Two Pair of Stairs high—& called it the *Round Tower*'.[4] Here Johnson was comfortably installed, and naturally began to think and speak of the borough, as well as Streatham, as 'home'. The following summer he wrote to Mrs. Thrale from Lichfield:

Though I have been away so much longer than I purposed or expected, I have found nothing that withdraws my affections from

[1] Hayward, i. 16.   [2] *John. Misc.* i. 339.
[3] *Life*, ii. 25; *John. Misc.* i. 234.   [4] Mainwaring Piozziana, i. 56.

the friends whom I left behind, or which makes me less desirous of reposing at that place which your kindness and Mr. Thrale's allows me to call my *home*.[1]

As might have been expected, Johnson was soon interested in all the affairs of the household, with the library, of course, one of his chief concerns. Even so early as this year we find him purchasing a stray volume of 'Saurin on the Bible' which Mrs. Thrale marked, 'An odd volume bought at a sale for 2 s. 9 d. by Dr. Johnson, for Streatham Park Library, 1766'.[2] Later he assisted his host in making wholesale additions to his stock of reference works, being given *carte blanche* to expend comparatively large sums of money to make the collection at Streatham as comprehensive as possible. On one occasion he wrote to Mrs. Thrale:

I have now got more books for Mr. Thrale than can be carried in the coach, and, I think, he may better send a cart than we can get one, because he may send with it baskets or sacks for the smaller volumes. We have of all sizes more than four hundred.[3]

Johnson was not interested solely in the food, the conversation, and the books at his new abode; he was soon involved in the concerns of the nursery as well. In 1766 little Hester Maria was too small to attract much attention, but the next year Mrs. Thrale ended a fable written about her little daughter with the lines:

> There—should her Prattle once beguile,
> Judicious Johnson of A Smile,
> You'd soon confess your Cares repaid,
> And wonder at the Progress made.[4]

Johnson's love for young people was an element in his character which Boswell almost completely ignored, and it is in his relations with the Thrale children that we see the old man in his kindliest role. He aided in their education, watched their

---

[1] July 20, 1767.

[2] The volume was sold with Cecilia Mostyn's effects in Brighton in 1857 (*Brighton Herald*, Oct. 17, 1857). In a letter to Queeney, May 12, 1807, Mrs. Piozzi wrote that 'Saurin's *Sermons* were bought for me long ago by a well-meaning Friend, who I set to purchase me the *Dissertations*'.

[3] *Adam Libr.* i. 152; May 21 (no year). Though impossible to date with certainty, this note undoubtedly belongs in the early 1770's, possibly after the building of the new library in 1773. According to Mme D'Arblay (*Memoirs of Doctor Burney*, ii. 79), Thrale once gave Johnson £100 with which to purchase volumes for the library.

[4] Mainwaring Piozziana, i. 93. There is some confusion as to the dating of this poem. In various places it is dated 1767 and 1776, but the earlier seems more probable.

growth with affectionate concern, and grieved over their ill health. He almost looked upon them as his own. First place in his heart was always held by the eldest—'Miss Hetty' as he first referred to her, then 'Queen Hester', which was shortened to 'Queeney'. Although her mother had other pet names which she used continually, such as 'Hetty' and 'Niggy', it is as 'Queeney' that the child moves serenely across the pages of Johnson's letters and her mother's diaries.

Mrs. Thrale was inordinately proud of the little Queeney. She engaged the celebrated Zoffany to paint the child when only twenty months old seated on a pillow by the side of the dog Belle.[1] Possibly at Johnson's suggestion, she decided to keep a special journal devoted to accounts of the child's education and physical growth. This was called the 'Children's Book or rather Family Book', and the first entry was made on Queeney's second birthday:

This is to serve as a Memorandum of her Corporeal & Mental Powers at the Age of two Years, to wch she is arriv'd this 17: Sept: 1766. She can walk & run alone up & down all smooth Places tho' pretty steep, & tho' the Backstring is still kept on it is no longer of Use. She is perfectly healthy, of a lax Constitution, & is strong enough to carry a Hound puppy two Months old quite across the Lawn at Streatham. also to carry a Bowl such as are used on bowling Greens up the Mount to the Tubs. She is neither remarkably big nor tall, being just 34 Inches high, but eminently pretty. She can speak most Words & speak them plain enough too, but is no great Talker: she repeats the Pater Noster, the three Christian Virtues & the Signs of the Zodiac in Watts's Verses; she likewise knows them on the Globe perfectly well. She can tell all her Letters great & small & spell little Words as D, o, g, Dog, C, a, t, Cat &c. She knows her nine Figures & the simplest Combinations of 'em as 3, 4, 34, 6, 8, 68, but none beyond a hundred. She knows all the heathen Deities by their Attributes & counts 20 without missing one.[2]

The nature of the new record is readily apparent in this first entry. It was to contain the indisputable proofs of the remarkable gifts of her children; but as the years progressed, more and more autobiographical material crept in, and the journal gradually came to serve also as a release for her own emotions.

---

[1] A print made from this portrait is now in the possession of Mrs. Herbert Evans, Brynbella, by whose kind permission it is reproduced here.

[2] 'The Children's Book, or rather Family Book', unpublished MS. of 186 pages, 8vo, begun Sept. 17, 1766, and continued to the end of 1778. It is now in the possession of Sir Randle Mainwaring, Hafod-y-coed, St. Asaph, North Wales, who has kindly given permission for the printing of the following extracts.

QUEENEY—AGED TWENTY MONTHS

From a print after a portrait by ZOFFANY

Whereabouts unknown

It was impossible for Mrs. Thrale to be objective about anything, least of all her own family affairs. As a result, during the
next decade the Children's Book became almost a diary, and
we consult it to-day as the one indispensable narrative of this
period. For the first few years, however, the entries are few,
devoted solely to accounts of births, illnesses, and the accomplishments of her rapidly increasing family.

The next baby, born in Southwark on February 15, 1767,
was a son who was named Henry Salusbury. Thrale's hopes
for an heir were at last realized, and the happy mother ended
the entry in the new journal with the jubilant phrase, 'he appears
likely to live thank God'.[1] During the remainder of the winter,
with two infants to care for, Mrs. Thrale was kept busy and
contented, her chief and absorbing preoccupation still being
the mental development of her first-born. On March 17, 1767,
she wrote another long description of Queeney's attainments in
the Children's Book. Although only two and a half years old,
Queeney was, according to the account, a marvel of precocity,
with a varied knowledge of geography, grammar, mathematics,
and religion. 'Certainly uncommon performances', indeed, for
a child so young! Soon an extra little blue book was filled with
further mental acquisitions of the prodigy,[2] who, the proud
mother felt, would certainly some day shine in the intellectual
world.

The affairs of the nursery largely monopolized the time of
Mrs. Thrale for the next year. As Johnson was away in the
Midlands for almost six months, the literary discussions at
Streatham flagged. It was not until late in October 1767 that
he was back 'home', seeking comfort and cheer after the death
of his mother's old companion, Catherine Chambers. By this
time Mrs. Thrale, whose winters were spent in a chronic state
of pregnancy, was miserable and dispirited herself. Johnson's
presence in the house thus proved a blessing both to the young
wife and to the great man, since literary chat would always
drive away their morbid thoughts.

Before the child appeared, however, the Thrales were thrust
into serious political embroilments by the approaching dissolution of Parliament. Early in 1768 Thrale was anxiously canvassing the borough, for although reasonably sure of his seat he
wished to take no chances. Johnson was again called upon to

---

[1] The child was christened Mar. 3 at St. Saviour's Church, Southwark, his
sponsors Mr. Nesbitt, Mr. Plumbe, and Mrs. Salusbury.

[2] Children's Book, Sept. 17, 1767, Brighton.

draft announcements for the newspapers, and even when he went for a short visit to Oxford he was actively in touch with the situation. On February 29 he wrote to Mrs. Thrale: 'Though I do not perceive that there is any need of help, I shall yet write another advertisement, lest you might suspect that my complaisance had more of idleness than sincerity.'[1] Not only did he send the required address, but he also, at the insistence of his Mistress, wrote a letter to be shown to a Mr. Pennick, whose vote was in doubt.

On March 8, at a general meeting in the borough, Thrale was renominated, and he spent the next few days campaigning strenuously. Because of the disturbance aroused by the proceedings against Wilkes, the election of 1768 was unusually violent. The city was in a tumult, with mobs everywhere, outbreaks in the streets, carriages stopped by the rioters and the occupants made to shout for Wilkes and Liberty. The borough, too, was seething with continuous excitement, and since Thrale with quiet determination opposed the patriots, the contest was taxing to his family. Although not particularly worried over the result, Johnson wrote again from Oxford on the 14th: 'If I can be of any use, I will come directly to London.'[2] By this time, however, Thrale felt fairly certain of success. Mrs. Thrale, on the other hand, was not so sanguine: worried and fretful, within a few weeks of the birth of her fourth child, she morbidly imagined the worst, and was confident that all was lost. Finally, on the 23rd, the polling was completed, and Thrale was elected at the head of the list.[3]

Worn out with the suspense and excitement, Mrs. Thrale soon after moved to Streatham, where on April 1 she gave birth to another girl, duly christened Anna Maria in honour of her great aunt, the first Lady Salusbury. The name was doubtless a gesture of peace towards Sir Thomas, though it probably only served to make his second wife more implacable.

The election of 1768 did not end the unrest in London, and

---

[1] *Adam Libr.* i. 91. With his letter to Mrs. Thrale of Feb. 29 Johnson included an election address which was printed in the London papers of Mar. 3, 1768, signed by Thrale. In the *Gazetteer* the address was repeated in the issues of Mar. 4, 5, 7, 8. See also *Letters*, No. 196, &c.

[2] *Letters*, No. 197. Further election addresses signed by Thrale had appeared in the newspapers, but there is no direct evidence that they were drafted by Johnson. One address appeared in the *Gazetteer* of Mar. 9, 10, 11, 12, and another in the same paper Mar. 15, 16, 17, 18, 19, 21.

[3] Polling began on the 21st and was concluded on the 23rd. Thrale expressed his thanks for support in the *Gazetteer* for Mar. 23, and on the 24th added his appreciation for the election.

the problems of the day provided a constant topic of conversation in the home of the Member for Southwark. Mrs. Thrale's feelings about Wilkes and the Friends of Liberty were mixed. Her husband, a loyal henchman of Lord North, was shocked by the riotous methods of the Middlesex electors, but, in contrast, some of her old intimates, notably Herbert Lawrence, were hand-in-glove with the party of Wilkes. During the following summer Lawrence kept her supplied with clippings from the papers of poems and articles which he had written to further the popular cause, and finally she herself became so much interested that she dashed off an epigram for the *Public Advertiser* of July 20, 1768, pointing out an analogy between Wilkes and the ancient Egyptian Ichneumon.[1] The next year she published in the same paper an amusing nursery rhyme which she had scribbled in a spare moment.[2] 'A was an Alderman, factious and proud' began the doggerel; then on through the alphabet Mrs. Thrale amusingly pointed out political morals for the edification of the public. Later she asserted that George Steevens claimed this witty sally as his own, and that it was this pretension which first bred suspicion of his truthfulness in the mind of Johnson. The poem is not important enough to make or break the literary reputation of either claimant, but the resulting jealousy is probably one reason why Steevens never became a member of the Streatham circle.[3]

In maintaining her husband's parliamentary position, Mrs. Thrale continually entertained powerful constituents and party allies at her dinner table, and finding it difficult to identify them all, often kept lists of their names on the back of her menu card.[4] She had also, on occasions, to find positions for relatives of loyal adherents[5] and to help make arrangements for food to be sent to party rallies.[6] For his part, Johnson was glad either to solicit support or to use his pen in the service of his host. Some time later, when the excitement caused by the expulsion of Wilkes and the arbitrary election of Colonel Luttrell had plunged London into a state of uproar, Johnson wrote his favourite political dissertation, *The False Alarm*, to excuse the government's high-handed attempt to disfranchise the

---

[1] See also Ry. 535, 8; 646, 133.
[2] *Public Advertiser*, Aug. 4, 1769; see also Mainwaring Piozziana, i. 71.
[3] Hayward, i. 56.
[4] Original note now in the possession of Mr. L. Fleming, Bognor Regis.
[5] See pp. 119–20, Chapter VI.
[6] Mentioned in a letter to Johnson, undated, but obviously Sept. 20, 1777 (Ry. 540, 73).

voters of Middlesex. According to Mrs. Thrale, the pamphlet
'was written at our house between eight o'clock on Wednesday
night and twelve o'clock on Thursday night; we read it to Mr.
Thrale when he came very late home from the House of
Commons'.[1] In spite of the fact that Johnson's enemies always
maintained that he wrote this and other political pamphlets
in return for his government pension, it seems almost certain
that some of them, at least, were merely intended to aid Thrale
and his friends in critical times. It may even be doubted that two
or three would ever have been completed had it not been for
the urgings of the Southwark household.[2] Johnson's contribution was to express in forceful style the conservative sentiments
which he had always cherished and which he heard constantly
at the Thrale dinner table. He did this so well, moreover, that
some of his admirers felt that such ability should be put to wider
use, and sought to obtain for him a place in Parliament.
Hawkins is authority for the statement that Thrale himself once
tried actively to further the scheme, but that nothing came of it,
largely because Lord North feared Johnson's stout independence
might be embarrassing.[3]

The tie between Johnson and Mrs. Thrale was gradually
growing stronger. To her he brought with delight each new
literary curiosity which came his way; to her he confided his
pain and suffering; to her he turned for tender nursing whenever he was ill. In the spring of 1768, while she was confined
at Streatham after the birth of Anna Maria and he was ill at
Oxford, he wrote: 'I have been really very bad, and am glad
that I was not at Streatham, where I should have been troublesome to you, and you could have given no help to me.'[4] Absence
always made him think fondly of his adopted family, and he
insisted a month later: 'I count the friendship of your house
among the felicities of life.'[5] The next year under similar
circumstances he wrote:

That I should forget you, there is no danger; for I have time
enough to think both by night and by day; and he that has leisure
for anything that is not present, always turns his mind to that which
he likes best.[6]

It was to his dear Mistress that his mind turned on any and

---

[1] *John. Misc.* i. 173; *Life*, ii. 111; *Johnson Bibliography*, pp. 114–15.
[2] See also p. 117. On Apr. 1, 1775, Baretti told Dr. T. Campbell that not one of
Johnson's political pamphlets would have seen the light 'had it not been for
Mrs. Thrale & Baretti who stirred him up by laying wagers &c.' (See p. 122, n. 3.)
[3] *Life*, ii. 137.   [4] Apr. 19, 1768.
[5] May 23, 1768.   [6] May 18, 1769.

every occasion. Nor was she oblivious of the advantages of this association with one of the greatest men of her time. By this year she had embarked on her career as a recorder of Johnsonian anecdotes, and thus had begun almost as early as Boswell to preserve memorabilia of their hero.

For example, in September 1768 the Thrales took Johnson with them on a short tour through Kent. They spent his birthday, the 18th, in Townmalling, but were back in Streatham a few days later. Among Mrs. Thrale's miscellaneous papers is a reference to this trip.

We had taken Mr. Johnson a little Tour into Kent for the benefit of his health, & soon after our return he went to Town for a day or two during which time I went into his Apartment to see that all was left as it should be and found in an open drawer not even shut together these remarkable Lines of which I could not forbear taking a Copy, this Night 23: Septr. 1768.
'Sept: 18: 1768 at night Town Malling in Kent. I have now begun the sixtieth year of my life. how the last year has passed I am unwilling to terrify myself with thinking. this day has been passed in great perturbation, I was distracted at Church in an uncommon degree, and my distress has had very little intermission . . .'[1]

Mrs. Thrale's curiosity could not withstand the invitation of an open drawer. (It would be ungenerous not to believe that the drawer was at least partially open!) Some years later Boswell's wife refused to take advantage of a similar opportunity, much to the annoyance of her husband.[2]

During the long quiet days in the country Johnson confided to Mrs. Thrale much about himself. Finding her a ready and sympathetic listener, he even confessed his morbid secret fears of insanity. The sole repository of the secret, she did not betray the trust; in Thraliana, she never wrote all the details. In this instance Mrs. Thrale showed her loyalty by locking in her memory for ever that 'Secret far dearer to him than his Life'.[3]

[1] Ry. 543, 25. The complete quotation from Johnson's Prayers and Meditations may be found in *John. Misc.* i. 47–8. At Townmalling they visited Mr. Francis Brooke who later stood sponsor for Susanna Thrale. See also *Letters*, No. 538.
[2] Boswell, *Tour to the Hebrides*, ed. Pottle and Bennett (1936), p. 34.
[3] *Thraliana*, May 1779. She wrote:
It appears to me that no Man can live his Life quite thro', without being at *some* period of it under the Domination of *some* Woman—Wife Mistress or Friend . . . our stern Philosopher Johnson trusted me about the Years 1767 or 1768— I know not which just now—with a Secret far dearer to him than his Life . . .
This may be an allusion to his fear of insanity, or to possible masochistic tendencies. See the discussion by K. C. Balderston in *The Age of Johnson* (Yale University Press, 1949), pp. 3–14.

But she did record for posterity a few of his remarks made this year, such as the following:

always carry some little Book in my pocket and take it out at odd Times when nothing else was going forward, it has been by that means chiefly added he [that a]ll my knowledge has been gained ex[cept w]hat I have pick'd up by running [about] the World with my Eyes open to Obser[vation]; A man is seldom in a humour to [go to] his Book Case, set his Desk and [devot]e himself seriously to Study, but a [reten]tive Memory will answer all [. . .] & a fellow shall have strange Credit [shew]n him for Knowledge, if he can but [rem]ember striking Passages from various [Boo]ks, & keep the Authors separate in [his] Head.[1]

Characteristic advice from a man who saw no reason to read every book through to the end!

Mrs. Thrale's records for this period are fragmentary. It is possible that by this time she was keeping various journals, but the evidence is not conclusive. Nor do we have many allusions to the Thrales by other people of the day; few letters mentioning them have survived, and scarcely any references in diaries or journals. One glimpse, however, of the everyday life at Streatham may be found in a letter written by the German traveller, Peter Sturz, who was in London in August 1768, where he met a number of well-known people. Johnson, having invited George Colman to bring Sturz to see him, proceeded to forget all about it. But on August 18 the two found Johnson at Streatham, where they joined in a serious discussion about English speech. In writing his account of the day, Sturz described his trip to the landed estate of 'Herrn Thrailes, dessen Frau griechisch zum Zeitvertreib liest'.[2] Though to the stranger Mrs. Thrale appeared a female scholar of the deepest 'blue', she was probably merely puzzling out easy passages in Greek; she made no pretence to knowledge of the language. We know from various accounts, on the other hand, that she was proficient in Latin and, despite the later sneers of Boswell, had a wide, if cursory, acquaintance with the Latin classics.[3]

---

[1] Ry. 629, 7. See description, p. 85. The page is torn, and the conjectural supplements are by Dr. Moses Tyson (*J. Rylands Bulletin,* xvi (1932), 11). Compare with *John. Misc.* i. 181–2.

[2] Helferich Peter Sturz, *Kleine Schriften* (Leipzig, 1904), p. 97. Sturz gives an interesting account of Johnson's conversation, and its forceful style is obvious even in the German rendering. See also *T.L.S.*, Feb. 10, 1940, p. 80.

[3] Boswell quoted Johnson as saying that Mrs. Thrale's learning was 'that of a school-boy in one of the lower förms' (*Life,* i. 494). Yet Mangin (*Piozziana,* p. 12) insists that he considered her a good scholar; and in our own day Miss Marjorie Nicolson (*Huntington Library Bulletin,* x (1936), 132), when discussing Mrs. Piozzi's

While Sturz gives us an interesting sample of the conversation at Streatham, it was not until some time later that a more celebrated recorder jotted down notes of the discussions in the Thrale home. For various reasons, chiefly because during the past few years he had rarely been in London, James Boswell and Mrs. Thrale did not meet until 1768. Even then their acquaintance was apparently the result of chance, for Johnson does not seem to have been active in bringing his two admirers together. In the spring of this year, however, the young Scot, who had just published his Corsican travels and was bursting with importance, visited Johnson in Oxford and, late in May, eagerly welcomed him upon his return to London. Boswell probably looked forward to many conversations during the remainder of his stay in London, but Johnson was not content to linger in town when Streatham and the Thrales lured him away. Consequently, when Boswell came one day for a visit, he found his friend waiting for Mrs. Thrale to take him out to the country. There, 'before Mr. Johnson's court', the meeting took place. Boswell was not long in making the most of the occurrence, and, as he remembered, jumped into her coach, 'not I hope from impudence, but from that agreable kind of attraction which makes one forget ceremony'.[1] Nor was he slow in making clear their rivalry, even in this first encounter. 'I told you, Madam, that you and I were rivals for that great man. You would take him to the country, when I was anxious to keep him in town.'[2] It was prophetic that even in this introduction there should have been a hint of antagonism, one day to develop into bitter enmity. Moreover, this 'polite and obliging' interchange in the busy street led to no immediate friendship. Boswell made no move to follow his idol to the country, if indeed he was invited, and it was not until his next visit to London, almost a year and a half later, that he found his way out to Streatham.

Long afterwards he described this visit in the *Life*:

I had last year the pleasure of seeing Mrs. Thrale at Dr. Johnson's one morning, and had conversation enough with her to admire her talents, and to shew her that I was as Johnsonian as herself. Dr. Johnson had probably been kind enough to speak well of me, for this evening he delivered me a very polite card from Mr. Thrale and her, inviting me to Streatham.

marginalia, makes the statement that she was a woman of 'more than average education, of broad, if not deep, reading'.
[1] *Boswell's Letters*, ed. C. B. Tinker, ii. 313. Dated July 9, 1782.
[2] Ibid. i. 173. Dated Sept. 5, 1769. See also *Life*, ii. 77.

On the 6th of October I complied with this obliging invitation, and found, at an elegant villa, six miles from town, every circumstance that can make society pleasing. Johnson, though quite at home, was yet looked up to with an awe, tempered by affection, and seemed to be equally the care of his host and hostess. I rejoiced at seeing him so happy.[1]

The conversation which followed ranged from good-humoured pleasantry about Scotland, Garrick's talent for light poetry, the truth of historical facts, Whitefield's oratory, to the weakness of the Corsicans in their war with the Genoese. Boswell clearly shows that, despite the awe with which Johnson was regarded, Mrs. Thrale was not afraid to battle with him on literary matters. For instance, although not unaware of the merit of the poet Prior, Johnson on this occasion mercilessly attacked his love verses.

Mrs. Thrale stood to her gun with great courage, in defence of amorous ditties, which Johnson despised, till he at last silenced her by saying, 'My dear Lady, talk no more of this. Nonsense can be defended but by nonsense.'

If silenced for the moment, Mrs. Thrale remained unconvinced, and was quite ready to take up the argument again at a future time. She revered her guest's knowledge, but no man could make her hold her whirligig tongue when she disagreed with his opinions. And probably it was just this bravado which aroused Johnson's admiration, for he hated a timorous opponent; in fact her vigorous repartee seldom failed to rouse him from the slough of his own sombre thoughts.

In Boswell's accounts of talk at Streatham we see the social and literary Mrs. Thrale, but, as has already been pointed out, there was the maternal Mrs. Thrale as well, who can only be understood from a reading of her own journal, the Children's Book. Even a casual perusal cannot fail to convince anyone of the constant devotion of the young mother. Begun ostensibly as an expression of pride in her progeny, the entries during the next few years slowly changed into a heart-rending story of illness and frustration. Even in the early pages not all was unalloyed joy, for Mrs. Thrale wrote of Queeney on December 17, 1768:

Hester Maria Thrale is this Day four Years & a Quarter old; I have made her up a little red Book to which I must appeal for her Progress in Improvements: She Went thro' it this Day quite well. The Astronomical part is the hardest. She can now read tolerably,

[1] *Life*, ii. 77–8.

but not at sight, and has a manner of reading that is perfectly
agreable free from Tone or Accent. At 3 years & a half however
she wrote some Cards to her Friends with a Print taken from the
Picture which Zoffany drew of her at 20 Months old: but as I lay
in soon after, the writing was totally forgotten, & is now all to begin
again. She has this day repeated her Catechism quite thro', her
Latin Grammar to the end of the 5 Declensions, a Fable in Phaedrus,
an Epigram in Martial, the Revolutions Diameters & Distance
of the Planets: she is come vastly forward in Sense & Expression
& once more I appeal to her little red Book. with regard to
her Person it is accounted exquisitely pretty; her Hair is sandy,
her Eyes of a very dark blue, & their Lustre particularly fine; her
Complexion delicate and her Carriage uncommonly genteel. Her
Temper is not so good; reserved to all, insolent where she is free,
& sullen to those who teach or dress or do anything towards her.
Never in a Passion, but obstinate to that uncommon Degree that
no Punishment except severe smart can prevail on her to beg
Pardon if she has offended.

Having inherited the character and temperament of her father,
Queeney seems from earliest childhood to have inspired mingled
admiration and irritation in her mother. So in the confidential
pages of the Children's Book Mrs. Thrale alternated between
delight in the little girl's astonishing gifts and perplexity over
her lack of spontaneous affection.

So far as possible, Mrs. Thrale tried to superintend the education of her children herself; but frequent ill health and the
confusion resulting from yearly additions to the nursery often
made this difficult. Early in 1770 she remarked:

Hester Maria Thrale was four Years and nine Months old when
I lay in of Lucy; and then I first began to teach her Grammar
shewing her the Difference between a Substantive and an Adjective
as I lay in Bed; she has made since then a Progress so considerable,
that she this Day 1: Feb: 1770 persed the first Couplet of Pope's
Iliad, beginning of her own accord at the Vocative Case . . .

Again, on her daughter's sixth birthday, September 17, 1770,
Mrs. Thrale wrote:

She is tall enough for her Age, elegantly shaped, and reckoned
extremely pretty. Her Temper continues the same too; reserved
and shy with a considerable Share of Obstinacy, & I think a Heart
void of all Affection for any Person in the World—but Aversion
enough to many:—her Discretion is beyond her Years, and she has
a solidity of Judgement makes me amazed. her Powers of Conversation and copiousness of Language are surprising even to me
who know her so well, & She yesterday cited me the Story of

Cleopatra's dissolving the Pearl as an Instance of Prodigality. She read and persed to Dr. Goldsmith yesterday & he wonder'd at her Skill—She has a little Compendium of Greek & Roman History in her Head; & Johnson says her Cadence, Variety & choice of Tones in reading Verse are surpassed by nobody not even Garrick himself: it was Pope's Ode to Musick that She read to Johnson Goldsmith heard her read the Messiah.

On January 30, 1771, the proud mother recounted that Queeney had been examined by Mr. Bright, of the Abingdon Grammar School, who had been astonished at her skill in parsing some lines from Dryden's *Virgil*. In addition to this precocious scholarship, Queeney was well trained in household pursuits. She could, her mother noted, 'do the common Stitch upon Catgut & has actually worked Doctor Johnson a Purse of it'. But it was the child's innate good sense and steadiness of character which were most unusual in one so young. The tiny Queeney

could be trusted with a little Brother or Sister as safely as any Person of twenty Years old, & had such a Share of Discretion, that three Days ago being somewhat hot & uneasy with a troublesome Cold, & I had recommended Turnips, Apples or Other light vegetables to her rather than more feverish Food. We happend to have some Company at Dinner who officiously help'd her to Plum Puddan She took it therefore & looked pleas'd keeping it before her till she observ'd her Friend engaged in Talk, & then beckoning a servt. she sent it quietly away—for said she to me afterwards, I knew it was not fit for me to eat, but one could [not] disoblige Mr. such a one by a *peremptory* Refusal—*those* were her *words*.

On and on runs the enthusiastic account, though always qualified by complaints of the unresponsive nature of her daughter. Once, after a description of her son Harry, Mrs. Thrale added that he was 'so amiable besides that even Queeney loves him, who is of no loving Disposition'.[1] While the eldest naturally was given most space in the Children's Book, the annals of the others are almost as detailed. Harry, who was openly affectionate, was the life and joy of the household. He was strong and manly, with the 'honestest & sweetest Temper in the World'.[2] Of tiny Anna Maria, her mother related on January 1, 1770, that

She could kiss her hand at 9 Months old, & understand all one said to her: could walk to perfection, & even with an Air at a Year old, & seems to intend being Queen of us all if she lives which I do not expect she is so very lean—I think she is consumptive.

[1] Feb. 15, 1771.   [2] Dec. 1, 1769.

Anna Maria was the acknowledged favourite of her grandmother, Mrs. Salusbury, who accordingly during the winter took the child to live with her in Dean Street, possibly to give her special care.

The next addition to the Thrale nursery was entered thus in the Children's Book:

Lucy Elizabeth Thrale was born 22: June 1769. large strong and handsome likely to live: her sponsors were Mrs. Salusbury, Mrs. Cotton of Bath & Dr. Saml: Johnson who insisted on her being Elizabeth.

Johnson, in memory of his beloved wife, had been anxious to have one of the Thrale children named Elizabeth, and at the birth of the last child, over a year before, he had written to Mrs. Thrale, 'I design to love little Miss Nanny very well; but you must let us have a Bessy some other time.'[1] This time Johnson was to have his way, and Lucy Elizabeth entered the world under his sponsorship. He evidently took a proprietary interest in his god-daughter, for he wrote on July 6, 'I hope my little Miss is well. Surely I shall be very fond of her. In a year and half she will run and talk. But how much ill may happen in a year and half!'

Johnson was right; in the Thrale nursery much ill could happen in a year and a half, as time would show.

As usual, during the latter part of the summer of 1769 the Thrales went to Brighton, and this year for the first time they persuaded Johnson to join them there for a long visit. Both Mr. and Mrs. Thrale were fond of the Sussex coast, he of the hunting on the Downs, and she of the sea bathing. Planning to come often to the watering-place, Thrale had purchased in October 1767 a low, 'stone-coloured' house with bay windows in West Street, Brighton, which was to be their autumn home for many years.[2] Johnson, on the contrary, did not share his

---

[1] Apr. 19, 1768.

[2] I am indebted to Mr. Frederick Harrison of Brighton for copying the following entry from the Court rolls.

15th October, 1767. A general Court Baron. Thomas Friend, Lord of the Manor (Brighthelmston) Charles Gilbert, Steward. Henry Thrale admitted on Surrender of Josiah Dornford. Heriot 6d. Henry Thrale appeared by Charles Scrase. Josiah Dornford held that 'cottage' and garden with appurtenances in the east side of West Street, formerly Wheelers and Halfpennys also Howells.

Mrs. Piozzi, on Mar. 30, 1791, surrendered the house to her youngest daughter Cecilia Margaret. It was finally pulled down in 1871. In the Brighthelmstone Directory for 1800, 64 West Street is listed as a lodging house, 'Esther Thrale:— Two parlors; 3 bedrooms; 6 servant's bedrooms.' For a description of the house see an article by Mr. Harrison in the *Southern Weekly News* (Brighton), Nov. 14, 1931.

friends' enthusiasm; he was too confirmed a city man to delight
in any country resort.[1] But however much he may have longed
inwardly for the peaceful talk of Streatham or the congenial
company at the Mitre, outwardly he threw himself into the gay
life about him. On one occasion he drew startled exclamations
of approval from a professional 'dipper' for the stoutness of his
swimming,[2] and he rode many a long mile over the Downs with
Thrale's hunting acquaintances. Perhaps no praise ever proved
quite so acceptable as that of William Gerard Hamilton, who
called out one day upon the Downs, 'Why Johnson rides as well,
for aught I see, as the most illiterate fellow in England.'[3]

After the visit to Sussex, during the autumn of 1769, the
Thrales were at Streatham, and throughout the winter of 1770,
as usual, in Southwark. With the passing years Mrs. Thrale
was beginning to see that the life of an eighteenth-century
mother was complex; for while year by year new infants were
brought into the world, many were far from robust and lived
only a short span. Thus little Anna Maria, Mrs. Salusbury's
favourite, began before she was two years old to exhibit terrifying symptoms, 'fits of languor and screaming succeeding each
other by turns', the spells sometimes throwing her into delirium.
The doctors, diagnosing the disease as dropsy of the brain, gave
the distracted mother no hope, and on March 20 the child
died.[4] Her grandmother was so distressed at the loss that she
fled to Bath for a change of scene and did not return until May.

It is well known that whenever Johnson was in a particularly
serious or despondent mood, he relieved his feelings by writing
a prayer. Depressed by the tragic death of her child, Mrs. Thrale
followed his example, and selecting a small red note-book[5] to
serve as her repository, made the first entry:

It is not till we have been heartily afflicted that we seem to feel
the *Pleasure* of praying, it is done as a mere *Duty* by the prosperous . . .

The next seven pages are filled with personal supplications to
the Almighty, in the form of an original litany. A few of the
responses show what she considered to be her own worst faults.

> From Pride Insolence and an overweening Carriage,
> from Vanity & a Delight in vain Amusements
> Good Lord Deliver me!

---

[1] Mrs. Piozzi wrote to Miss Willoughby, Aug. 25, 1820: 'Doctor Johnson said
that after the full flow of London conversation, every place was a blank' (Hayward, ii. 456).

[2] *John. Misc.* i. 224. See also Hayward, ii. 444.   [3] Ibid., p. 288.

[4] Children's Book. Death was probably due to meningitis.

[5] In my possession. 42 pages, 7 in. × 5 in., only seven pages written upon.

> From the peculiar Vices of those with whom I associate,
> & from those of the Time & Place I live in,
> Good Lord deliver me.

Other fervent pleas in her prayers were that God might preserve her surviving children, her husband, her friends, and bring prosperity to her family. That she was deeply moved is evident; but after this first burst of inspiration the impulse flagged, and the remaining pages of the journal are blank.

In spite of the long illness and death of little Anna Maria, Mrs. Thrale herself had been in better health throughout the winter of 1770 than at any time since her marriage. Though in her usual condition, she wrote:

> I passed this last winter chearfully too, to what I ever did a winter since I was married: for I have been at an Oratorio, the first Theatre I have set foot in, since my eldest Daughter was born; & this Time she went with me: I never have dined out, nor ever paid a visit where I did not carry her, unless I left her in bed; or to the Care of servants (except asleep).[1]

Even a devoted mother was glad of some diversion.

When Mrs. Salusbury returned to London in May, she could not bear to go back to Dean Street where her little grandchild had died, and instead took a place at Croydon until the Thrales could move to Streatham. Mrs. Thrale drove over to see her mother every day; and on May 22, returning from her visit, she sat chatting until late in the evening with her husband and Johnson. Suddenly she was taken ill, and early next morning gave birth to a small, feeble child, born two months before its time. The strain of the past few months had taken a heavy toll. At first the little girl, whom they called Susanna Arabella, was not expected to live, being so 'miserably lean and feeble indeed, quite a mournful Object'; but to the great surprise of all in the household, she began to gain strength. The following August her mother was able to record in the Children's Book:

> She lives however & Doctor Johnson comforts me by saying She will be like other people; of which however if She *does live*, I make very great doubt . . . but is so very poor a Creature I can scarce bear to look on her.

As soon as possible after the premature birth of Susan, the Thrales moved out to Streatham, where they remained for the remainder of the summer, except possibly for a short trip to

[1] Children's Book, Mar. 21, 1770.

Brighton.[1] The nursery now had four occupants: Hester Maria,
or Queency as she was usually called; Henry, the only son;
Lucy Elizabeth, Johnson's godchild; and Susanna Arabella.
Frances and Anna Maria had died. Six children in seven years
had been an excessive strain, but apparently the mother thought
it nothing out of the ordinary. She had found time also to
write some poetry and to cultivate the respect and comradeship
of possibly the best-known literary figure of the time. All in all,
she probably considered herself a fortunate and happy woman
and counted her marriage a success. From an alliance arranged
for financial reasons such as hers, no woman could expect much
more. For the time, even her vague yearnings for romance were,
if not satisfied, probably stilled.

By 1770 the change in the character of guests entertained in
the Thrale home was almost complete. The old rakish companions of Thrale's bachelor days had disappeared, and now
an increasing number of gifted and famous members of London's literary and artistic set could be counted among their
friends. Johnson, to be sure, was the bait which drew across
the river to Southwark and out to Streatham the best-known
painter of his time, Sir Joshua Reynolds; the greatest actor,
David Garrick; the most versatile writer, Oliver Goldsmith;
and the most powerful force of the political opposition, Edmund
Burke. For long periods of time these and others of Johnson's
circle could find him only at the house of the Thrales and, if
they wished to keep up their intimacy, were literally forced to
accept the invitations of the ambitious member of Parliament
and his wife. As a typical example, the previous autumn,
when Boswell was preparing to leave London to return home
to be married, he wrote to Johnson at Streatham, asking him
to come in to the city for a farewell meeting. Loath to leave
the comfort of the country, Johnson replied: 'I find it will less
incommode you to spend your night here, than me to come to
town. I wish to see you, and am ordered by the lady of this
house to invite you hither.'[2] Hence Boswell had to drive all the
way out to Streatham to say good-bye.

The absence of Johnson from his former haunts was somewhat resented by his old friends, as Goldsmith clearly shows in

---

[1] On July 28, 1770, Johnson wrote from Ashbourne,
I have taken a place in the coach and shall be, I hope, in London on Friday,
and at Streatham on Saturday. The journey to Brighthelmston makes no part
of my felicity, but as I love those with whom I go, and those I shall love equally
in any other place.
(Sotheby Sale, June 2, 1908.)   [2] *Life*, ii. 110.

his poem, "The Haunch of Venison'. Johnson and Burke, the poet complains, are continually absent, 'the one with his speeches, and t'other with Thrale'.[1] But this did not mean that Goldsmith and the others were unwilling to accept Thrale's invitations; either at Streatham or Southwark they were sure of an excellent dinner, efficient service, and stimulating conversation. Every thing possible was done to make up for the distance travelled, for the Thrales were united in one desire— to number among their intimates the most interesting people of the day. They did not toady to the merely rich or noble; their one requirement was that their guests be witty and well informed. In time, to be sure, they began to count among their acquaintances members of the court circle and of the exclusive Blue-Stocking salons; but at first those who filled their dining-room were men who had risen to positions of eminence through their intellectual powers.

It will be noted that this society was largely masculine. Not until much later did Mrs. Thrale draw about her gifted members of her own sex; for the time she remained the one feminine attraction in a circle of men. Having the instincts of a true diarist, she was tempted to write down comments and anecdotes of the brilliant talk heard at her table. Now that the novelty of domestic and maternal duties was beginning to wear off, she longed to try her hand at something different. By this year, she was keeping a number of journals devoted to various interests: the Children's Book, containing only incidental references to Johnson, Goldsmith, and the others, and at least two others filled with literary and political anecdotes. This is not mere surmise on our part, for in addition to the complete Children's Book, a few scattered pages from the other journals have survived.

In the John Rylands collection, among the mass of miscellaneous fragments in her handwriting, are several leaves evidently torn from old note books. One has written on it:

These Anecdotes are put down in a wild way just as I received or could catch 'em from Mr. Johnsons Conversation, but I mean one day or another to digest and place them in some order: as the poor Egyptian gather'd up the relicks of a broken Boat and burning them by himself upon the Beach said he was forming a Funeral Pile in honour of the great Pompey.—may it be long before that day comes.[2]

---

[1] *Goldsmith's Works*, ed. Gibbs (1884), ii. 49.
[2] Ry. 629, 1. Approximately 7 in. × 5 in. in size.

Two others, evidently from the same source, contain excerpts from Johnson's conversation and are obviously the first drafts of accounts later published in her *Anecdotes*. They do not, however, contain any dates or references which would allow us to say with certainty when this collection of Johnsonian remarks was begun.

With these pages, also, are other sheets from a slightly larger book, containing for the most part anecdotes of other famous people.[1] On one occurs the oft related tale of James Harris's election to Parliament; on another the tragic rumour of the suicide of Mr. Yorke after he had accepted the seals of Lord Chancellor from George III, in January 1770; on another a distressing story of Goldsmith's weaknesses. Fortunately, for this Mrs. Thrale gives a definite date, September 16, 1770, the day before Queeney's sixth birthday. Furthermore, since the page is numbered 96, we may be safe in assuming that it was cut from a compilation begun some time before. Referring probably to the ease with which Goldsmith could be disconcerted, Mrs. Thrale recorded:

... Delicacy on the other, but Johnson (for he was by) would not suffer it to go off so, and said the Dr. was only awed from fear of a reply, for continued he were Goldsmith to light upon a dumb man he would be wonderfully severe on him—this blow Murphy follow'd so closely, & struck the little Dr. so forcibly & so repeatedly that though I saw that day & have often seen Instances of his Malevolent disposition, made still more acrimonious from his unequall'd rage of shining in Conversation I could not avoid pitying him when I saw him so humbled under the lash of a man who though so far superior to him in Friendship Honour & every manly Virtue, in Person, Address, and every pleasing Quality, is not to be compar'd with him as a Writer, nor will be set in Competition with him by Posterity— Poor little Dr. how he does disgrace himself! and disgrace those Parts but for the possession of which even the Dog would be in haste to forsake his Company. 16: Sept: 1770.[2]

Thus Mrs. Thrale corroborates Boswell in his claim that Goldsmith's great failing was a desire to shine in conversation at any cost. She appreciated his genius, but could only be repelled by such displays of jealousy.

From these fragmentary pages it seems obvious that Mrs. Thrale now had at least three separate note-books: one to contain the sayings of Dr. Johnson, another for stories of other celebrities, and the last for intimate references to her own family.

---

[1] Ry. 629, 5, 6. Approximately 8 in. × 6 in. in size.   [2] Ibid. 6.

The busy woman was launched on her long career of diarist and commentator. From this time until the end of her life she was never without several repositories in which to jot down all she thought worthy of remembrance, either about others or about herself. She was determined to be remembered through her friendships with celebrated men; she little realized that with such commemoration would come enmities and notoriety for herself, rather than fame.

V

DEPRESSION

SEPTEMBER 1770–DECEMBER 1773

AS we have seen, the bond between Mrs. Thrale and Johnson was developing fast into a deep affection. She found him a constant inspiration, someone to revere as a parent and to pamper as a child, and he openly returned her warmth of feeling. She noted in her smaller book:

> [Spe]aking once of His friendly affection for me, [he s]aid kindly, I do certainly love you better [tha]n any human Being I ever saw —better I th[ink] than even poor dear Bathurst, and esteem you more, though that would be unjust too, for I have never seen you in distress, & till I have I cannot rank you with a Man who acted in such trying situations with such uniformity of Virtue.[1]

He was soon to see his Mistress in real distress, and the experience would not change his opinion. But for a time, during the year 1771, the Thrale household enjoyed a pleasant interlude of comparative peace.

From the Children's Book we might be tempted to conclude that Mrs. Thrale gave all her time to the rearing of her children; from Boswell that her days were spent in endless literary chat; yet as a matter of fact she had numerous other interests almost as engrossing. She had always to keep in mind her husband's political plans, and soon his business affairs as well. A further responsibility arose for Thrale's sisters and their children, who seem to have depended largely on the relatives at Streatham for advice. The nephews, Sir John Lade and Ralph Plumbe, unlike their cousin Queeney, were not noted for unusual intelligence, and often served as the butt of family jokes;[2] but their education was a problem which enlisted the kind offices of Johnson,[3] as well as of their uncle and aunt.

---

[1] Ry. 629, 7. The page has been torn, and the reconstructed readings are made by Dr. Moses Tyson. See p. 76, n. 1.

[2] See Ry. 539, 3.

[3] See J. D. Wright, *J. Rylands Bulletin*, xvi (1932), 72–4. A number of letters from the schoolmaster, Henry Bright, to Johnson and the Thrales about Ralph Plumbe are also in the Rylands collection. See also *Letters*, Nos. 226, 226. 2.

Mrs. Thrale also occasionally attended concerts and oratorios. Although with no particular ear for music, she probably liked to be seen in fashionable gatherings, and the bustle of going across the river served to enliven the monotony of Southwark life. Sometimes Johnson's dislike of being left alone made him accompany her, though he had even less taste for music. So he attended an oratorio performed at Covent Garden on March 8, 1771,[1] where his 'contemptuous Clatter' during the music kept her continually annoyed. She little suspected what he was doing until their return from the theatre, when he repeated a set of Latin verses composed during the oratorio. In characteristic fashion he set her the task of translating them by breakfast the next morning, a challenge to which she was easily equal. Her lines, though as Johnson asserted, they turn the meaning 'inside out' in the last stanza, are worth reprinting as an epitome of the great man's mood.

> When threescore years have chang'd thee quite,
> Still can theatric scenes delight?
> Ill suits this place with learned Wight
>   May Bates or Coulson cry!
>
> The Scholar's Pride can Brent disarm?
> His heart can soft Guadagni warm?
> Or scenes with sweet delusion charm
>   The climacteric Eye?
>
> The social Club, the lonely Tower,
> Far better suit thy midnight Hour,
> Let each according to his power
>   In worth or wisdom shine.
>
> And while Play pleases idle Boys,
> And wanton mirth fond youth employs
> To fix the mind and free from Toys
>   That useful task be thine.[2]

Such literary by-play was no novelty in the Thrale home. Johnson was always ready to improvise stanzas, whether on a lady's gown and hat, an acquaintance's bad poetry, or his own

[1] Ry. 543, 27. See also Mainwaring Piozziana, i. 78–9; *John. Misc.* i. 196–8; Thraliana, Dec. 1777. The oratorio given Mar. 8 was the *Messiah* with Guadagni and Mrs. Pinto (Brent) as the principal singers. In later recollections this became mixed in her mind with an English opera by Dr. Arne, possibly *Artaxerxes*, given on Apr. 6.
[2] Ry. 543, 27. A slightly different version was published in the *Anecdotes* (*John. Misc.* i. 197.), where also may be found Johnson's Latin verses. See also Mainwaring Piozziana, i. 79.

ill health.[1] Sometimes the verses were in Latin, sometimes in sonorous English, sometimes in the most obvious doggerel. A few years later, on his Mistress's birthday, when she came into his room complaining that now she was so old nobody sent her verses any more, he rose to the occasion and rattled off the well-known impromptu beginning:

> Oft in danger, yet alive,
> We are come to thirty-five;[2]

> .　　.　　.　　.　　.

Then, as she was copying the verses, Johnson laughingly remarked, 'you may see what it is to come for poetry to a Dictionary-maker; you may observe that the rhymes run in alphabetical order exactly'.

Besides their common love for poetry, Johnson shared with Mrs. Thrale an interest in the marvels of science and medicine. Each delighted in tales of scientific discovery and longed to try personally the remarkable experiments of the new philosophers. Indeed, nothing pleased Johnson more than to mix various coloured solutions, or to fuse metals in a fiery furnace. With the enthusiastic support of his hostess he planned to set up a laboratory at Streatham, and during the next summer in the Midlands he collected a number of specimens of ores suitable for smelting. Then he asked Mr. Thrale to set aside about a hundred loose building bricks with which to construct a special oven.[3] The best place to carry out the experiment, he suggested, would be 'the pump-side in the kitchen garden'. After his return to Streatham they did try fusing some refractory ore in the new-made furnace, and the huge experimenter must have been an

---

[1] See *John. Misc.* i. 190–8, 260, 281. Also *Queeney Letters*, xiii. In the edition of Johnson's poetry by Nichol Smith and McAdam the problems involved in Mrs. Piozzi's versions of Johnson's occasional verse are discussed. For this reason it has seemed wise not to repeat the evidence here.

[2] *John. Misc.* i. 259–60. See above. In Thraliana, Dec. 1777, and May 1778, Mrs. Thrale indicates that the verses were written in 1777, but in Mainwaring Piozziana, i. 79, she gives the date as 1776. Actually Mrs. Thrale was thirty-five years old in Jan. 1776, and from internal evidence of the poem itself, and considering the condition of the Thrale household, this year would seem the correct one. Nevertheless, it must be admitted that during these years Mrs. Thrale was somewhat vague about her own age, on occasions appearing to consider herself born in 1742 rather than 1741. We must remember that the change from the old method of reckoning to the new was upsetting to many people. Mrs. Thrale had been born in Jan. 1740, according to the old dating; and 1741, according to our modern standards. In later years remembering that she must add a year, because of the calendar change, it was easy to make a mistake and adjust in the wrong direction. Johnson would naturally accept her statement of age without suspicion.

[3] *Letters*, No. 264; *John. Misc.* i. 307. See also the amusing and fairly accurate account in C. E. Vulliamy's *Mrs. Thrale of Streatham*, pp. 81–6.

awesome sight, grimy from feeding the roaring fire, and mutter-
ing as he poured the molten metal from the ladle. But alas
for the dreams of the amateur alchemist! One day, just as the
flame was hottest, and admiring children and servants gathered
close to watch and wonder, Thrale returned unexpectedly from
London. Fearing a disastrous explosion, he put an end to
further operations, and from this time forth Johnson's scientific
inquiries were restricted to such non-explosive materials as
orange skins and nail parings.[1]

The Thrales had remained quietly at Streatham throughout
the summer of 1771, while Johnson visited Ashbourne and
Lichfield. In July Mrs. Thrale was miserable, day by day
expecting another child, her condition more distressing and
oppressive than usual. At such a time Johnson apparently
expected Queeney, who was nearly seven, to share some of the
burden of the correspondence. The little girl, however, was
not to be moved, and her mother wrote on July 22:

> Queeney has at last squeezed out a kind word, She says that she
> has no word kind enough to write, but will make you some sort of
> amends when I am laid up, by a Letter all her own. Harry is glad
> that Queeney is sulky he tells me, for now he knows Mr. Johnson
> will love him best when he comes home.[2]

Later the same day Mrs. Thrale gave birth to another daughter
who was named Sophia. To her mother's delight, the child
was large and healthy and appeared 'likely to live'. The news
was quickly transmitted to Ashbourne; whence Johnson dispatched a charming letter to his dear Queeney on July 29:

> Please to tell little Mama, that I am glad to hear that she is well,
> and that I am going to Lichfield, and shall come soon to London.
> Desire her to make haste and be quite well, for, you know, that you
> and I are to tye her to the tree, but we will not do it while she is
> weak. Tell dear Grandmama that I am very sorry for her pain.
> Tell Papa that I wish him joy of his new Girl, and tell Harry that
> you have got my heart, and will keep it.[3]

Apart from the accounts of their ill-fated scientific pursuits,
our knowledge is scant about the life of the Thrales during the
last months of 1771 and the winter of 1772.[4] Even when Boswell

---

[1] *Life*, ii. 330–1; iii. 398; iv. 204.
[2] Unless otherwise noted all quotations from Mrs. Thrale's letters to Johnson
are from Ry. 539–40.
[3] *Queeney Letters*, p. 5.
[4] During this autumn Johnson was much at Streatham (*Goldsmith's Letters*, ed.
Balderston, p. 104); and James Beattie was an occasional visitor (*Life*, ii. 148;
Broadley, p. 123).

came to London in the spring, he did not record much about them, for although in his letter to Johnson of March 3, announcing his proposed visit to England, he sent 'best compliments to Mr. Thrale's family',[1] he was still a bit shy of these new acquaintances. In an affectionate reply, however, after reiterating his own partiality, Johnson named Mrs. Thrale among those in London who loved the distant Boswell.[2] Yet if Johnson in this instance was trying to promote good feeling between his two friends, his efforts were not at once effective. Boswell arrived in London on Thursday, March 19, and finding that Johnson was in Southwark, made no move to follow him there.

It appears to have been Johnson's habit to spend the weekends in his house in Johnson's Court and the middle of the week with the Thrales in Southwark. Consequently, Boswell arranged to see him only on the days spent in his own home, though occasionally they met also at the house of Paoli, Oglethorpe, or some other common acquaintance in town. It was nearly a month after his arrival, on April 22, that he took a boat across the Thames to sample Johnson's mid-week conversation.[3] Soon after, he returned for another visit, and his reception on these occasions proved so warm that he came on May 11 to say good-bye, even though Johnson was absent. His memorandum for the day indicates that, after much talk about the great man, Mrs. Thrale cordially invited Boswell to bring his wife from Scotland with him the following year. On the surface it seemed the beginning of a fast friendship.

Boswell found the happy life at the Thrales' 'capital', but he was there just before the *débâcle*. In little more than a month the entire complexion of affairs was changed, all because of a reckless speculation of Thrale's. Up to 1772 Mrs. Thrale had had nothing to do with her husband's business concerns, since she had no interest in the brewery except as it furnished the income necessary for their household expenses; now, suddenly, circumstances forced her into taking an active part in the management. While in many respects a good business man, Thrale was never content with ordinary returns on his investment, being driven into immoderate expansion of his plant by an inordinate ambition to outdo every other competitor in

---

[1] *Boswell's Letters*, ed. Tinker, i. 187. The original letter, one of the few of Boswell's letters to Johnson which have survived, is now in the Adam collection. A comparison with the printed version (*Life*, ii. 145) reveals Boswell's method of treating his own letters when preparing them for publication.

[2] *Life*, ii. 145.   [3] *Private Papers*, ix. 16, 256, 266.

England. He easily fell a prey to the schemes of an inventor named Humphrey Jackson, who claimed to have discovered a new method of brewing which eliminated malt and hops. Without adequate preliminary trial Thrale risked his whole year's output by the introduction of this new process, and lost heavily when it failed. Jackson also had other disastrous schemes in which Thrale became involved. As Mrs. Thrale wrote,

He had perswaded him to build a Copper somewhere in East Smithfield—the very Metal of which cost 2000£—wherein this Jackson was to make Experiments & conjure some curious Stuff, which should preserve Ships' Bottoms from the Worm; gaining from Government Money to defray these mad Expenses. Twenty enormous Vats, holding 1000 Hogsheads each—costly contents!— Ten more holding a *Thousand Barrels* each were constructed to stew in this pernicious Mess, & afterwards erected on I forget how much Ground, bought for the ruinous Purpose.[1]

To make matters more desperate, the failure of a great banking house in June 1772 threw the city into a financial panic. Business after business in London collapsed, and, according to the *Gentleman's Magazine*, universal bankruptcy was expected.[2] Since Thrale's extravagant misadventures had used all his available capital and spoiled his year's supply of beer, he had nothing to sell, and ruin stared him in the face. The shock was so great that he was completely stunned and rendered incapable of any action. In this emergency his family and friends came to the rescue. Johnson, throughout July and August, was constantly at Streatham, aiding the others with advice and help.[3] Mrs. Thrale was expecting another child, but the necessity of raising money to run the brewery was so urgent that she was forced to disregard her own condition. Consequently she interviewed mutinous clerks and drove all the way to Brighton to beg six thousand pounds from Mr. Scrase, an old gouty solicitor who had been an intimate friend of Ralph Thrale.[4] What was more, all of Mrs. Salusbury's savings were immediately put to use; Lady Lade lent five thousand pounds, and a Mr. Rush an

---

[1] Adam MS. (Hayward, ii. 25–6). For information about the scientist, Jackson, see *Thraliana*, ed. Balderston.

[2] *Gent. Mag.* xlii (1772), 292–3; see also Johnson's letter of Oct. 19, and the *Public Advertiser*, June 15, 20, 21, 1772.

[3] Miss Williams wrote to Mrs. Percy on Aug. 5, 1772: 'Doctor Johnson is constantly at Stratham, but whenever he comes to town asks me, if I know how Mrs. Piercey does' (*Adam Libr*. iii. 261).

[4] *Thraliana*, Apr. 1778, and Hayward, ii. 27. It is possible that the hurried trip to Brighton occurred another year and in later recollections became mixed with the affairs of 1772. See p. 166. Definite proof that Scrase was one of those lending Thrale money this year is found in a contemporary note-book for 1773. (Ry. 616.)

additional six thousand. In this way the immediate disaster was averted, but hanging over them still, according to Mrs. Thrale, were debts of one hundred and thirty thousand pounds, besides the borrowed money.[1]

Mrs. Thrale had rushed in to save the threatened family credit, but at sad cost to herself. On September 15, exhausted by constant worry, she gave birth to another daughter, and shortly after added this poignant note in the Children's Book:

Septr. 1772. Penelope Thrale was born—liv'd but 10 hours, looked black & could not breathe freely—poor little Maid! one cannot grieve after her much, and I have just now other things to think of—this has been a sad Lying In: . . . every thing going wrong well! as old Townsend says God mend all!

The business crisis of this summer left a lasting mark on Thrale. Until this time he had profited from every specula-tion, and had kept pyramiding his gains until he felt he could not fail; then suddenly everything seemed swept away. And the fact that he owed his salvation largely to the women of his household did nothing to salve his injured pride. Moreover, since the price of grain continued to rise, conditions remained precarious. Endless worry about the dark present and dubious future made Thrale moody and taciturn, and he never recap-tured the spirit of his younger days. The silent Thrale described by Boswell and Fanny Burney was created in the catastrophe of 1772.

As another consequence of the crash, Johnson and Mrs. Thrale were increasingly active in the affairs of the brewery. Once initiated into the mysteries of trade during the emergency, they insisted on sharing in the permanent management. John-son's letters for the next few years contain many references to the problems of the business—the price of malt and the harvest of wheat.

This financial *débâcle* was but the beginning of a long series of family troubles, the chief of which was the illness of Mrs. Salusbury, who for over a year had been troubled with increas-ing pain in the breast. Many friends suggested remedies, hoping to find an effective cure, and so little was known of cancer at the time that Johnson actually wrote to Mrs. Thrale asking if some mineral water recommended by Bennet Langton was being used. He added, 'it may perhaps do good, at least it may be tried. I am sure I wish it success.'[2] But no mineral water

[1] Hayward, ii. 27.
[2] Original letter of June 25, 1771, now at Johnson's birthplace, Lichfield. This

could bring relief to Mrs. Salusbury, whose anguish relentlessly grew worse. In the autumn of 1772, feeling that she probably had only a short time to live, she began to divide a few cherished possessions. She wanted Johnson to have something as a remembrance, and before he set out for Lichfield and Ashbourne in October, chose for him a chair-tapestry, worked by Mrs. Thrale when she was a little girl.[1] The years of close association had cleared away foolish misconceptions and substituted a sincere admiration which grew stronger to the end.

On November 3, several weeks after Johnson had gone, the Thrales moved in to Southwark, leaving Mrs. Salusbury with various attendants at Streatham. Economy was the new watchword, and Mrs. Thrale wrote to Johnson the next day that she and her mother had now

parted with a resolution to contend who shall live the cheapest; my folks I believe think my head is turned I do so scold & bluster about, and but that Abdalmelech the Turk was before hand with me, the name of *Skin Flint* would have been made for me.

But despite his wife's efforts to save money, Thrale's disposition remained surly, and he refused to rouse himself even to placate a dissatisfied client. As Mrs. Thrale confided to Johnson,

Mr. Thrale will not stir now he is in Town, nor can all the influence I have over him make him speak a kind word to a Customer when he knows it would save him a house—You see this is a *private Letter*.[2]

With her mother sick at Streatham and her husband morose at Southwark, Mrs. Thrale dashed back and forth between the two homes, so anxious and unhappy that her temper became uncertain, and it is no wonder that she showed the strain by occasional irritable treatment of her children.[3] Besides, since Johnson was away, she missed her one sympathetic adviser, and was forced to console herself by writing him complaining letters. Everyone looked forward to the time when the separation would be over; yet Johnson lingered on in Ashbourne with Dr.

passage was omitted from the printed version (*Letters*, No. 253). Langton's letter, dated June 10, 1771, recommending the Malvern water, is in the Adam collection (*Adam Libr.* iii. 149).
[1] Ry. 539, 11. Johnson thanked Mrs. Salusbury for the present in his letter of Oct. 15, just before setting out for Ashbourne (No. 278. 3). See also p. 426.
[2] [Nov.], 7, [1772]. The letter is misdated 'Sat. 7 Oct.', but from internal evidence it must be November.
[3] *Queeney Letters*, xxv, 7. Mrs. Thrale's irritable remark to Queeney, recorded in the latter's letter to Johnson of Nov. 24, 1772, shows the state of the mother's nerves at the time.

Taylor. On November 14 he replied, 'If I am wanted at the Borough I will immediately come, if not, be pleased to give me leave to stay the month with him'.[1] Never concealing her impatience to have him home, Mrs. Thrale two weeks later reminded him that the round tower was kept constantly aired for his return.[2] Finally on December 2 she urged him to come as soon as he could, since both she and her Master had much to consult him about. The Thrales had grown to rely so heavily upon their famous guest that they felt they could do nothing without his advice. Her summons reached him in Lichfield and though Lucy Porter was 'wheedling for another week',[3] he obediently returned to London by way of Birmingham and Oxford. This time, however, Johnson's presence did not prove helpful, for he himself soon fell ill with gout, complicated by a bad cough.

Although the financial crisis and the death of her child had made the year 1772 a troubled one, the following year was to be even worse. Mrs. Salusbury was in continual pain, and Mrs. Thrale spent most of her time at Streatham trying to add to her comfort. It seems to have been Mrs. Thrale's practice this winter to come in town every Tuesday for a brief stay at the Borough house, and it was Johnson's custom to dine with her there. The last Tuesday in January, however, he was unable to come, and penned a despairing complaint of grumbling and coughing through sleepless nights in his solitary sick-room. By the middle of February he was better and able to move about again, and on the 19th asked her permission to accept an invitation from Sir Joshua Reynolds for the next Tuesday.[4]

Mrs. Thrale's days in London were often given over to the affairs of the brewery, where conditions were still precarious. And even though confined to his house in Johnson's Court, Johnson was apparently her ever-ready counsellor; for in January, after interviewing a long succession of clients, Mrs. Thrale noted in a small memorandum book devoted to business, 'I went to Mr. Johnson yesterday: he approved of all I had done

---

[1] Sotheby Sale, Jan. 22, 1907.   [2] Nov. 30, [1772].
[3] Sotheby Sale, Jan. 30, 1918.
[4] See *Letters*, Nos. 293, 294. Northcote, who did not perceive the true reason for Johnson's request, in his *Life of Sir Joshua Reynolds* (1818), i. 277, cited the instance as an example of the flattery Johnson chose to pay to Mrs. Thrale. It probably only meant asking her to change their customary Tuesday engagement. Northcote also recorded an interesting event which probably occurred about this time (i. 317). This was a dinner given by Thrale at the brewery to Reynolds, Johnson, Goldsmith, Garrick, Burke, Baretti, and others 'who dined on beef-steaks broiled on the coppers, seated in a newly made brewing vessel, sufficiently capacious to contain the company conveniently'.

& all my Master had done'.[1] In February she added a long conversation with Perkins about her husband's infatuation with the scheming Jackson, and ended, 'Mr. Johnson shall know ab. ye boyling the Hoops—no acct. ever checkt with Jackson . . .' In early March she was even forced into acting as intermediary in a dispute with a man named Alexander, who claimed fraud on the part of Mr. Thrale and threatened a lawsuit. In this case, after repeated meetings and conferences with Johnson, she arranged a compromise, but nothing served to raise her spirits, since there was always the oppressive feeling that some new trouble would crop up as soon as one was settled.

All the while Mrs. Salusbury remained dangerously ill, and when on March 11 Mrs. Thrale returned to Streatham after arguments with Alexander, she found her mother so much worse that she sent for Dr. Thomas, who kept a school near by, to give her the Holy Sacrament. Momentarily expecting the end, Johnson wrote kind letters of sympathy and condolence. Mrs. Salusbury rallied, however, and a few days later Mrs. Thrale was able to write of her mother's unexpected improvement. But there were other barbs to wound her heart in the cruel silence of her 'tyger hearted' husband.

You saw the Leave we took, & He has never sent me a Scrap since to ask or tell me anything, nor would I firmly believe if I remain'd *here*, or in *Siberia* six Russian Winters—but he will come tomorrow of Course. Your Letter is like yourself, so wise, so good, so kind: I have read it twenty Times I dare say, and resolved to take the Advice when the Event shall require it—[2]

In the Children's Book on the 21st she made the agonized entry, 'nobody can guess what a Winter this has been to me, & big with Child too again God help me!'

In addition to these trials Mrs. Thrale was now startled by an outbreak of newspaper scandal attacking her husband. She probably had few illusions about his faithfulness, but it was humiliating to have his affairs made the subject of public gossip. As we have seen, Thrale combined the cultivated instincts of a gentleman with the loose standards of the fashionable world. There is evidence that he was not immune to

---

[1] Ry. 616. In the memorandum book for 1773 Mrs. Thrale made numerous notes of clients of the brewery interviewed and the problems involved, which indicate that in January 1773 she was particularly active. In February she wrote that Perkins 'says while Jackson possesses Mr. T's heart nothing but ruin can be hoped'.

[2] To Johnson (Ry. 539, 19. Mar. 19, 1773). Also 17 and 18.

the diseases often attendant upon such indulgences.[1] His wife accepted all this as perfectly normal, as what any woman might expect from a handsome husband who professed no open adoration of his lawful wife. She even welcomed into the home circle the young and sickly Jeremiah Crutchley, whom (according to her story) Thrale considered to be his own son.[2] And Johnson, the strict moralist, did not seem to expect his host to observe the same rigid code he prescribed for himself, being willing to esteem the man though he was aware of the flashing Polly Hart who was the recipient of Thrale's diamonds.[3] To Johnson the soberness of his host's home life doubtless compensated in some measure for any lapses in London; nevertheless he must have been sadly annoyed to see Thrale's roving disposition openly discussed in the public print.

The *Westminster Magazine* for March 1773, in a section called the 'Court of Cupid', printed the so-called 'Memoirs of Miss H—t, alias Mrs. R—d—h, Mr. Th—le, and Sir Edward D—g'.[4] According to this account Miss H—t, the daughter of a dancing master, had fallen into the widespreading arms of a Borough brewer, 'more famed for his amours than celebrated for his beer', 'Th—le' (the story continued) had established the nymph in a rural bower, where for a time she was the leader of his gay cronies. However, she soon tired of one lover, and the remainder of the memoirs related the further adventures of this notorious courtesan of the early 1760's.

The same magazine in June dug up further sensational episodes in Thrale's personal history.[5] This time it recounted the adventures of a 'Mrs. D—n', daughter of a hostess who kept a celebrated porter house near St. Clement's Church. Again it was the amorous brewer who lured this girl from the tap-room. 'Mr. Th—le did not come in the machine of his occupation, a dray, but in a chariot', and it was not long before the susceptible maid capitulated. For a time she too was surrounded by every luxury; yet her reign was short, for (as the account continued)

---

[1] In the Children's Book, Sept. 7, 1776, writing of another illness of her husband, Mrs. Thrale added, 'Mr. Thrale's having been infected about seven years ago when he put himself under Daran's Care to whom he gave fifty Guineas for curing him of a Venereal Complaint in the Urethra . . .' (probably gonorrhea). See also p. 164, n. 3.

[2] Hayward, i. 144; also see p. 205, n. 4.

[3] Hayward, ii. 441 (a letter to Sir James Fellowes, June 18, 1819); Common Place Book, p. 191; E. Mangin, *Piozziana*, p. 178. Polly Hart is described in the *Meretriciad* (6th ed., 1765), p. 17.

[4] *Westminster Magazine or the Pantheon of Taste*, i. (1773), 178. Published Apr. 2.

[5] Ibid. (1773), 374.

'great pleasures too often pall and cloy; and Mr. Th—le, who was forever the dupe of a *Duenna* (who was always springing new game to divert his fancy and indulge his passions) had procured him a new favourite, the celebrated Mrs. R—.'

Thrale's past having proved so productive, the scandal-mongers hit upon the idea of traducing his present home life. On April 7, 1773, when Boswell called on Goldsmith, the latter showed him two paragraphs from a newspaper, 'how an eminent Brewer was very jealous of a certain Authour in Folio, and perceived a strong resemblance to him in his eldest son'.[1] Both Boswell and Goldsmith were shocked at the gross insinuation about Johnson and the Mistress of Streatham, particularly since they realized that among people who did not know the principals involved the story might gain some credence. Mrs. Thrale soon learned that friendship with a great man involved penalties as well as privileges.

This scandal in the papers and magazines made worse Thrale's already ruffled temper, and his subordinates were made to suffer from his frayed nerves. Writing to Johnson on April 10, Mrs. Thrale wondered if their Master's heart had lost all feeling: 'Perkins caught me alone yester morning and complained to me how coursely Mr. Thrale treated poor Lester, whose Life was made very unhappy by perpetual affronts.' The remainder of the letter was filled with details of the persecution of the clerk, and ended,

Oh My Dear Mr. Johnson! and is it really possible that a Mind like yours can by the mere Impulse of friendship be made to take interest in such trumpery stuff—for the sake of the importance it is of to—H: L: Thrale.

Johnson did care, and never failed to give comfort and encouragement.

In spite of all this turmoil, a romantic interlude served to divert Mrs. Thrale's mind, for a time, from her own troubles.[2] Her husband's niece, Fanny Plumbe, though only fifteen, had fallen in love with Jack Rice, son of the former High Sheriff of Surrey; but Alderman Plumbe, the girl's father, though he had no valid reason for objecting to young Rice, violently opposed

---

[1] *Private Papers*, vi. 92.
[2] Part of this episode has been told by Miriam A. Ellis in 'Some Unedited Letters of Mrs. Thrale', *Fortnightly Review* (Aug. 1903), 268–76. The original letters are now held by Myers & Co., London. Mrs. Thrale's unpublished letters to Johnson supply the remaining information necessary to piece together the story. (Ry. 539.)

their marriage. Mrs. Thrale wrote to Johnson on April 19, telling how they had become involved.

Mrs. Plumbe & her Daughter & young Mr. Rice the Girls Lover are now here, begging my Masters Influence over old Sammy or his Consent for the Clandestine Marriage—My Mother herself will be interested in the Affair I think as the Women cry to her most dismally, and if you will come over at 2 or 3 o'clock on Wednesday next to Southwark & lend your kind assistance we will try to prevail on this silly old Man to agree to their Union or be content with what may follow his absurd Refusal. Can we do anything without you?

Deaf to all persuasion, 'Old Sammy', the Alderman, remained obdurate and even threatened to lock up his daughter. Mrs. Thrale, who was torn between her romantic disposition and her conviction that she should uphold the right of parental authority, was much surprised when Johnson refused to admit such absolute power for a father and insisted that a child, on some occasions, should act for himself.[1] Nevertheless, she lent young Rice her copy of *Rasselas* to teach him patience—strange diet (we might think) for a distracted young lover! Since Rice's father was willing and able to support his son, Thrale finally acquiesced in his niece's elopement. Accordingly the young couple, chaperoned by Dr. Thomas the schoolmaster, left for Holland on May 23 or 24.

When Alderman Plumbe discovered his daughter's absence he was frantic, and assuming that his brother-in-law had driven the lovers to Scotland, poured his full anger on the Thrales. As Mrs. Thrale commented to Fanny shortly afterwards, the Alderman turned 'his Wrath upon our House, where we stood a regular Siege'. The next few days were spent in nervous suspense, Mrs. Plumbe certain that her daughter had gone to the bottom of the Channel, and her husband violent in denunciation. Mrs. Thrale wrote to Johnson, 'I am hurried out of my Life; it will be *Calamity Thrale* in good earnest by & by', and several days afterwards she added, 'I have not seen Mr. Thrale this Week, & if he knew all I suppose we should not see him for a fortnight'. Evidently he thought it good policy to stay out of reach of his infuriated brother-in-law, while his wife held the fort. She found only one bright spot on the horizon—'the Children are well and happy—no Lessons now'. Later on, when news came of the safe arrival of the party at Calais, the tension relaxed. Shortly afterwards the couple were married in Holland, and

[1] *Letters*, No. 308; Ry. 538, 4.

returned to England in July, by which time 'Old Sammy' had been pacified, though insisting on a second ceremony in England.[1]

As soon as she heard of the marriage, Mrs. Thrale composed a long letter of advice to young Rice, and while we have no record of his response to her counsel, she herself thought it valuable enough to include when publishing her correspondence with Johnson, many years later.[2] The tenets laid down reveal her own attitude towards marriage: the young husband must not expect the first warmth of passion to endure; he should rather turn to the polishing of his loved one's mind; distinction in wit, knowledge, and virtue should be more desired than furniture and equipage; he should not indulge every wild wish of his lady's heart, but she ought never to suspect that she grows less pleasing to him; his superiority must always be seen though never felt. Reason, the matron insisted, was much more important than passion.

While the excitement of the elopement kept Streatham in a turmoil, Johnson remained in London, his health worse than usual. Consumed with longing for the country and his 'governess' there, he wrote to Mrs. Thrale:

My nights are grown again very uneasy and troublesome. I know not that the country will mend them; but I hope your company will mend my days. Though I cannot now expect much attention, and would not wish for more than can be spared from the poor dear lady, yet I shall see you and hear you every now and then; and to see and hear you, is always to hear wit, and to see virtue.[3]

The illness ended in a fever which caused an acute inflammation in his good eye. On May 29 he pleaded again: 'my eye is yet so dark that I could not read your note . . . I wish you could fetch me on Wednesday. I long to be in my own room.'[4] Although possibly not overjoyed at having another invalid in the house, Mrs. Thrale, in pity and obedient as usual to his every wish, carried him out to Streatham. By this time the eye was in a serious condition; in fact Baretti insisted on June 5 that he had been told that unless Johnson took the greatest care there was grave danger of his losing his sight.[5]

---

[1] Fanny Rice was married at fifteen, in quick succession gave birth to thirteen children, and a few weeks after the last, in Oct., 1790, she died at the early age of thirty-two. See *Miscellanea Genealogica et Heraldica*, 3rd Ser., i. 101.
[2] *Letters to and from Johnson* (1788), i. 96–103. The original of the letter is Ry. 38, 7. See also p. 320, n. 1.   [3] May 17, 1773.
[4] Sotheby Sale, Jan. 30, 1918. Beattie noted on June 1 that Johnson had gone to Streatham (M. Forbes. *Beattie and His Friends* p. 79).
[5] *Adam Libr*. iii. 15.

On his return Johnson found the Thrale household much upset, for Mrs. Salusbury was daily growing weaker and nearing the end of her suffering. Necessarily he was left alone for long periods, a prey to his own despondent thoughts, and being unable to read, found his sole consolation in composing Latin verses. One set of these has survived, a long poem addressed to Dr. Lawrence, which Mrs. Thrale found time to transcribe in odd moments snatched from her nursing.[1] Further evidence of the melancholia under which he was labouring may also be found in a long undated message in French, probably written at this time for delivery inside the house. Obviously something of a mystery,[2] this letter shows Johnson more than usually wrought up when writing to his Mistress. He begins by referring to the 'solitude profonde' in which he must pass much of the time; he begs to be given written orders, what he may do and what is forbidden; he refers even to the possibility of his being locked up in actual confinement. Rules for diet are requested. With obvious agitation the sick man pleads:

Est ce trop de demander d'une ame telle qu'est la vôtre, que, maîtresse des autres, elle devienne maîtresse de soy-même, et qu'elle triomphe de cette inconstance, qui a fait si souvent, qu'elle a negligèe l'execution de ses propres lois, qu'elle a oublièe tant de promesses, et qu'elle m'a condamnè a tant de solicitations reiterèes que la resouvenance me fait horreur.

Among Mrs. Thrale's undated letters is one which seems to be the answer to this.

What Care can I promise my dear Mr: Johnson that I have not already taken? what Tenderness which he has not already experienced? . . . You were saying but on Sunday that of all the unhappy you was the happiest, in consequence of my Attention to your Complaint; and today I have been reproached by you for neglect.[3]

She urges him to stop brooding in secret.

I am sorry you are obliged to be so much alone; I foresaw some Ill Consequences of your being here while my Mother was dying thus; yet could not resist the temptation of having you near me, but if you find this irksome and dangerous Idea fasten upon your fancy,

[1] Mainwaring Piozziana, i. 81–4; see also *Letters to and from Johnson*, ii. 415–18. Mrs. Thrale translated the lines, or rather imitated them, adding, 'They are—as Pope's Father used to say of his Son's Poetry—They are good Rhymes.'
[2] J. D. Wright, *J. Rylands Bulletin*, xvi (1932), 33–4, 62–5. Johnson's French accents were not in accord with modern practice. See also *Thraliana*, i. 384.
[3] Ry. 539, 30. The letter has no date or address, and is written in a more formal hand than usual. There is a possibility that it is not the original note.

leave me to struggle with the loss of one Friend, and let me not put to hazard what I esteem beyond Kingdoms, and value beyond the possession of them.

Mrs. Thrale saw that Johnson needed to get away from Streatham, where the shadow of death hovered over her mother's sick-room. 'Dissipation', she wrote, 'is to you a glorious Medicine, and I believe Mr. Boswell will be at last your best Physician.' She was sure that carrying out his long-discussed trip to the Hebrides would do more for him than all the doctors in London, and the next few months were to prove the wisdom of her suggestion.

By June 12 it became apparent that Mrs. Salusbury was dying. Murphy and Baretti came out to express sympathy and offer their aid, but there was nothing further anyone could do.[1] The end came on June 18, and on the same day in the Children's Book Mrs. Thrale set down a moving account of the preceding week, with the tragic event of the morning as poignant climax.

She slept very easy in the night, but had as usual all the Windows open, the Morng. however shewed a still more visible Alterration in her Countenance & at 7 o'clock her Utterance was quite gone. She try'd to take her Coffee but there was no passage Harry had the Toast as he always had, & after Prayers the Children read the Lessons to her as usual—She heard & understood us all perfectly well: however I saw we must send for Mr. Thrale as Life ebbed apace, & dispatched a Messenger accordingly: I then called up Mr. Johnson who when he felt her Pulse wonder'd at its Vigor but when he observed the dimness of her Eyes and universal languor, he leaned on the bed, kissed her Cheek, & said in his emphatical Way—May God bless you Dear Madam for Jesus Christ's sake. at these Words She looked up and smiled wth. a sweet Intelligence that express'd Hope, Friendship & Farewell—all at once.[2]

Mrs. Thrale was prostrated by the loss of her mother. With her death the last link with childhood was gone. To whom could she now talk of Bodvel, of Offley, and the happy days at East Hyde; to whom confide the bright remarks of her own

---

[1] Mrs. Thrale wrote in the Children's Book that on June 13 Murphy, who had not seen Mrs. Salusbury for three weeks, found her much altered. He said:
'You have already kept your Mother too long, dear Madam,—you must now part very soon, and I confess I wish the Crisis over for your sake.' I liked Baretti's speech better—it was 'God bless you dear Madm. & give *you* patience & *her Patience*, and as long a Continuance as both may be able to bear.'

[2] As an example of Mrs. Thrale's accuracy in setting down contemporary events, compare this account from the Children's Book with Johnson's version written about the same time (*John. Misc.* i. 66). Mrs. Salusbury died intestate. In my possession is a letter of administration, taken out by Mrs. Thrale, dated Aug. 12, 1773, and with a note on the back in the hand of Johnson, telling what it is.

children, or the little annoyances of the household? For the first time she was completely adrift from all the old ties.

> Sir Thos Salusbury has long ago cast me off, & Mr. Thrale & Mr. Johnson are the mere Acquisitions of Chance; which chance, or change of Behaviour, or Intervention of new Objects or twenty Things besides Death can rob me of. One solid Good I had & that is gone—my Mother!

As his wife was in such a distressed state of mind, Thrale was probably glad of an excuse to leave the gloomy house. Accordingly he went up to Oxford to witness the installation of Lord North as Chancellor of the University, and while there stayed with Johnson's friend, Chambers, at New Inn Hall. On this occasion Lord North took advantage of his new position to pay off a number of political debts, and his pliant henchman Thrale was rewarded with the degree of Doctor of Civil Law.[1] Beattie and Sir Joshua Reynolds were also honoured by the University at this time for accomplishments more obvious to later generations than those of the Southwark brewer. But whatever the justification, the testimonial must have been gratifying to Mrs. Thrale, for after the newspaper scandal of the previous spring it was a salve to her pride to have her husband given an honorary degree in such distinguished company.

Shortly before the death of Mrs. Salusbury Thrale had begun extensive improvements to the house at Streatham: a new library wing was added, many rooms entirely remodelled, among others the one always occupied by Johnson.[2] Driven out of his comfortable abode, Johnson, therefore, spent most of July, 1773, in London, leaving Mrs. Thrale more often alone.[3]

---

[1] A full account of the Encaenia is given in *Jackson's Oxford Journal*, Sat., July 10, 1773. On Thurs. 'Henry Thrale Esq. Member of Parliament' is listed among those receiving honorary degrees. On Friday Reynolds and Beattie were given their degrees. See also Forbes, *Life of Beattie* (1806), i. 267. Possibly Thrale and Reynolds saw a good deal of each other on this occasion; at least during the late summer and autumn of 1773 Reynolds was a much more frequent guest at Streatham than formerly. (See p. 66, n. 2.)

[2] Mentioned in the Children's Book, June 18, 1773.

[3] Johnson was occasionally at Streatham. In a small note-book for 1773 (Ry. 616), Mrs. Thrale wrote on July 8:

> Perkins came hither to dine with Mr. Johnson & me: from him I gatherd 1st. that we are absolutely now in debt to our Hopmen 18,000 L, 2d that we buy dearer than other people by reason of our requiring such long Credit, 3dly that Mr. Thrale has not done trying Experiments . . .

The next day Mrs. Thrale went to the Compting House where Perkins showed her the account books. Some indication of the various people who had loaned Thrale money appears: Lady Lade, Count Viry, Scrase, Hankin, &c. Johnson, according to her record, was at Streatham also on the 18th.

She slept very easy in the night, but had as usual all the Windows open, the Morn. however shewed a still more visible Alter:ration in her Countenance & at 7 o'clock her Utterance was quite gone. She try'd to take her Coffee but there was no passage Harry had the Toast as he always had, & after Prayers the Children read the Lessons to her as usual — She heard & understood us all perfectly well: however I saw we must send for Mr. Thrale as Life ebbed apace, & dispatched a Messenger accordingly. I then called up Mr. John:son who when he felt her Pulse wonder'd at its Vigor but when he observed the dimness of her Eyes and universal lan:guor, he leaned on the bed, kissed her Cheek, & said in his emphatical Way — May God bless you Dear Madam for Jesus Christ's Sake. at these Words she looked up and smiled wth a sweet. Intelligence that express'd Hope, Friendship & Farewell — all at once!

A PAGE FROM THE CHILDREN'S BOOK

JUNE 18, 1773

Now in the Hyde Collection

Though heartbroken, her impulse was to seek relief in action, not in melancholy brooding, but her first effort at diversion scarcely proved successful. On July 26, with her husband and Queeney, she went up the Thames to Richmond for the day, only to find on her return that Harry was feverish and with a rash. Soon all five children were down with the measles, and she wrote to Johnson warning him not to come back to the house if he was not immune.[1]

Whether Johnson heeded the warning and remained away from Streatham we cannot tell, but at least it is certain that with his home in the country turned into a sick ward, he began to make active plans for the proposed journey to Scotland. Though he had promised this year to explore the Hebrides with Boswell, he was loath to start, and Boswell, a little dubious of the promise, wrote on July 29 to Thrale to '*launch* him from London'.[2] Fortunately Chambers was going north at this time; consequently in his company, on August 6, Johnson began the most memorable expedition of his life.

Boswell's inimitable record of this trip contains very little about the Thrales; there was no reason that it should have been otherwise. Yet occasional notes show what a hold the family at Streatham had on the great man's affections.[3] Johnson refused to let Boswell joke at his intimacy with Mrs. Thrale, nor would he have her health drunk in as coarse a beverage as whisky. Whenever letters reached him, hers were the ones he most eagerly devoured. At Skye he penned the well-known Latin Ode, addressed to the Mistress of Streatham, the last verses of which reflect Johnson's mood at the time, and are here printed in Lord Houghton's rendering.

> Through paths that halt from stone to stone,
> Amid the din of tongues unknown,
> One image haunts my soul alone,
>   Thine, gentle Thrale!
>
> Soothes she, I ask, her spouse's care?
> Does mother-love its charge prepare?
> Stores she her mind with knowledge rare,
>   Or lively tale?

[1] Dated only 'Tuesday 27:', but obviously July 1773, since Mrs. Thrale gives in the Children's Book a long account of the measles.
[2] Ry. 542, 1.
[3] Boswell, *Tour to the Hebrides*, ed. Pottle and Bennett (1936), pp. 105, 302, 348, &c. This edition is printed from the original manuscript of Boswell's journal, acquired by Col. Ralph Isham.

Forget me not! thy faith I claim,
Holding a faith that cannot die,
That fills with thy benignant name
These shores of Sky.[1]

Throughout September and October Johnson's long descriptive letters to 'Thralia dulcis' kept her informed of the progress
of his tour. That he gave so much time to these letters is further
evidence of his devotion. Even his vivacious companion could
not make him forget his 'home'.

In the meantime, while Johnson scrambled about the Highlands of Scotland, Mrs. Thrale was vainly trying to find some
diversion to forget the sorrows of the spring. About the middle
of August, as soon as the measles were conquered, she invited
Sir Joshua Reynolds, Goldsmith, Beattie, and others out to
dinner, and shortly afterwards with Thrale and Queeney she
went for a ten-days' visit to Lady Lade at Windsor.[2] But the
children remained dispirited and fretful, and to make matters
worse new troubles beset her—this time outside the family circle.

Perkins, the chief clerk at the brewery, had in August been
dispatched to Ireland on business, but on his way arranged to
stop in Wales to see the old Salusbury properties there. It will
be remembered that the estate of Bach-y-Graig would legally
descend to Mrs. Thrale should her uncle, Sir Thomas Salusbury,
leave no male heir. Like his first, the Knight's second marriage
had brought him no children, and with his increasing ill health
the question of ownership began to assume more importance.
Accordingly, Perkins had been given introductions to Bridge
and others in Flintshire, and had been instructed to see the
house of Bach-y-Graig which, Mrs. Thrale wrote, 'your little
Friend Harry so often tells you will be his'.[3]

The enmity between Mrs. Thrale and Lady Salusbury had
never lessened during the past ten years.[4] Each suspected the

---

[1] Hayward, i. 37. There are in all five stanzas to the poem. The original
Latin Ode may be found in Boswell's *Tour to the Hebrides* (*Life*, v. 158) and in Mrs.
Piozzi's *Anecdotes* (*John. Misc.* i. 259).

[2] See M. Forbes, *Beattie and His Friends*, p. 90, and the Children's Book, Nov. 24,
1773. When Mrs. Thrale was away, the children were left in charge of a maid,
Sally, and 'Old Nurse', whose name was Tibson.

[3] This letter, dated Aug. 29, 1773, is the first of a series of letters written by Mrs.
Thrale to John Perkins. The original letters are now in the possession of Major
C. A. Carlos Perkins, through whose kindness the following extracts have been
made possible. All succeeding references are to this correspondence.

[4] In Thraliana, Mrs. Thrale recorded that some time after 1770 she had driven
to Offley to see her uncle, who had received her in a friendly manner. Lady
Salusbury, however, had been so angry that it had only intensified her vindictive
feeling.

other of trickery; and in September Mrs. Thrale was confirmed in her suspicion when Sir Thomas's agent came to Flintshire and to Streatham, attempting to get possession of all legal documents pertaining to the Welsh property.[1] At almost the same time the news arrived of her uncle's serious illness, which convinced her that the crisis was imminent. As Mrs. Thrale wrote to Perkins in Ireland on September 22,

should his Sickness be critical, it would be ten Times unlucky; for I am now so near my Time that I durst not hazard a Journey to Offley at any rate, and these Ladies that Bridge told you of, would have him all to themselves.

The next letter to Perkins on the 28th, which reported her uncle better, serves to illustrate the variety of annoyances she encountered in trying to aid her husband with the business, for not only had she to secure new capital for the brewery and pacify the clerks, but even to recapture dissatisfied customers. Of one of these last she wrote, 'I called on him today however, and by dint of unwearied Solicitation, (for I kept him at the Coach side a full half hour) I got his order for six Butts more as the final Tryal.'

Suddenly, late in October, the news came which she had been dreading: Sir Thomas Salusbury was dead and had left Offley and his entire personal estate to his wife. Although the loss could not have been a surprise, it was a great shock, since as long as her uncle lived there had always been a possibility that, with reconciliation, she might again take the position which she had been brought up to consider her rightful due. Sir Thomas's will extinguished all such vain expectation; a long line of distant, impoverished cousins in Wales were designated as residuary legatees before her.[2]

In the settled gloom following this disappointment, on November 8 another son was born, who was christened Ralph

---

[1] See letter from Bridge, Oct. 18, 1772, enclosing a demand from Sir Thomas to hand over all deeds, &c., to his agent (Ry. 532, 106). Mrs. Thrale wrote to Perkins on Sept. 14, 1773,

Sir Thomas's Agent Mr. Mathias has been with me enquiring for Papers relating to the Estate; I protested I had none, and referred him wholly to Robson, whose sagacity will I doubt not soon discern what they can want with such matters.

In his letter of Aug. 25, 1773, Johnson wrote to Mrs. Thrale from Banff advising her not to wage open war upon her uncle. This passage, omitted in the printed version, may be found in the original letter now in the Morgan Library, New York City.

[2] News of Sir Thomas's death and adverse will was received in letters from Mathias and others, Oct. 30, 1773 (Ry. 530, 32-4). Baretti and Dr. Crane wrote of their astonishment at the will (Ry. 541, 1; 536, 8).

after his grandfather. He was large and healthy, but his mother found him 'heavy, stupid and drowsy', and suspected that her vexations of the past six months had left their mark on him. Lying in bed, convalescing, she again had leisure to worry about the Welsh estate. Accordingly, she instructed Perkins, who was on his way back from Ireland, to hurry again to Flintshire to represent her interests and claims. On November 18 she began a letter to him with the plaint: 'This letter though written on my Pillow will be long as it will enumerate my many Vexations.' That he was near Wales at this crucial moment was a fortunate circumstance, and she reminded him that she depended entirely on his skill and discretion.

My Uncle disbursed Mortgages to a large Amount which I understand Lady Salusbury intends to recharge, if she can come at the Writings necessary to prove their Payment. of these Writings I now know nothing, but wish I knew that they *were all burned* in old Bridge's *parlour Fire* or wish at least that *you* knew it and I would be content.

As many of the obligations had been originally assumed for Sir Thomas's personal use, there had never been any intention that the claims should be repaid;[1] but Mrs. Thrale knew that it would be impossible to prove this in a court of law.

Would it not grieve one now to have this vile Mortgage recharged by Fraud and Violence a second Time? as it certainly will if this Harpy of a Woman can lay her claws upon the *Writings*—Let it therefore be your kind Care to secure *them* somehow.

Where her worldly interests were concerned, Mrs. Thrale's conscience was somewhat elastic. Once convinced that she was in the right, she had little difficulty in persuading herself that any procedure was legitimate. In this particular instance, however, all her scheming was in vain, for ultimately Lady Salusbury fully established her claim.

To her great relief Thrale seemed not at all disturbed over the loss of Offley Park and the considerable property which went with it, and did not blame her for the misfortune. She even felt that he was pleased not to be indebted to his wife for such a large fortune, which would still further have wounded his pride. On the other hand, Mrs. Thrale could not be calm in the face of mischance, and admitted to Johnson that she was 'as angry & as sorry' as could be.[2]

[1] For an explanation of the origin of this mortgage see Chapter I, p. 19.
[2] Oct. 31, 1773.

It must not be supposed that even in the last two years of depression Mrs. Thrale had not found time to continue her practice of writing down comments on her children. There were always peaceful intervals between calamities, and the Children's Book still proved a repository for accounts of mingled pleasure and pain. Early in 1773 Mrs. Thrale had recorded that Queeney, though not yet nine years old, had so much common sense that her mother often consulted her in household matters. As an example of her perspicacity, she added:

we were reading a strange Story in the papers t'other day of a Murder at Bristol when Queeney objected to the strangeness of some Circumstances, which says she renders the Person's Guilt very disputable—Well done Queeney! exclamed Dr. Johnson, thou shalt be upon the grand Jury.[1]

On another occasion Mrs. Thrale recorded:

I hate Dr. Goldsmith says Harry one Day to his Sister, because he does not love Mr. Murphy—I hate him too says she he is so disagreeable; let us however, while we talk of hating so freely, have a Care of Dr. *Beat'ye*.[2]

When Queeney was nine years old, Mrs. Thrale felt that it was time her precocious daughter had the benefit of expert teaching in modern languages. Consequently, on October 17 she noted that on that day Queeney had begun to study Italian with the famous linguist, Joseph Baretti.[3] He was too independent and too prominent a man to become a regular tutor, but at Johnson's suggestion a plan was devised whereby the Italian could stay whenever he liked at the Thrale house, and teach Spanish and Italian to the eldest daughter. It was a very loose and unbusinesslike arrangement, open to many objections from the start. For a few years, nevertheless, it provided the indigent Baretti with a comfortable home and Queeney with the best Italian instructor in all England. According to his own account Baretti at times also read Spanish with the Master of the household and aided the Mistress in translating Italian songs, but it is doubtful whether his instruction of the older members of the family was ever very extensive. Baretti, a brilliant, if sometimes overbearing conversationalist, proved, however, a valuable addition to the Thrales' dinner table.

---

[1] Children's Book, Mar. 21, 1773.
[2] Ibid. The incident is recorded in July 1776, after the death of Harry, but must have occurred before Goldsmith's death.
[3] Ibid. See notations of Sept. 17 and Oct. 17, 1773. For further discussion of Baretti's relations with the Thrales see L. Collison-Morley, *Giuseppe Baretti* (1909), pp. 269, 344-9, &c.

Although Queeney's mature intelligence continued to be the chief source of wonder, Harry and Lucy were Mrs. Thrale's favourites. But little Lucy was also a source of constant anxiety, for ever since the child was six months old she had had a 'running from her Ears' which the doctors had not been able to check. Johnson had added to the mother's fears by telling of a friend of his who had died from a similar ailment.[1] Except for this recurrent ear infection her mother could find no fault in the lovely child, and the year before had written in the Children's Book:

Lucy is very saucy, but wonderfully amiable; I am indeed accused of a partial Fondness towards her, but she is so lovely one cannot resist her coaxing—Queeney never would be fondled, nor delight in any Caresses I could give her, she has a Heart wholly impenetrable to Affection as it should seem, & Lucy is softness & kindness itself.[2]

One child, at least, satisfied her longing for love, but the pleasure in this instance was short-lived.

In the autumn of 1773 Lucy became seriously ill. At first the doctors diagnosed the trouble as the after-effect of measles, but when the child failed to rally they became genuinely alarmed. From her symptoms we to-day recognize mastoiditis, but even the best physicians then knew no way to cope with this infection. A succession of doctors, Pinkston, Bromfield, Lawrence, and James, plied her with rough purges, blisters, leeches, and bleedings, until the poor child was wild with delirium. More blisters and leeches only seemed to prolong the agony, until death finally released her on November 22. Affectionate little Lucy was no more, and her loss was a tragic finale to a terrible year. On December 31 Mrs. Thrale listed her afflictions at length in the Children's Book, ending with the poignant cry, 'So Farewell to all I formerly loved—to my Mother, my House in Hertfordshire, my lovely Lucy—and to this accursed Year 1773'.[3]

[1] Children's Book, June 22, 1771. Mrs. Thrale wrote that the story 'shocked me dreadfully tho' I took no Notice but it lay on my spirits all that Day & Night —& this Morning I can scarce bear to think on't'.
[2] Dec. 9, 1772.
[3] After a long list of her recent troubles Mrs. Thrale added,
    As I have now no soothing Friend to tell my Grief to, it will perhaps sink the sooner into Insensibility; Dr. Johnson is very kind as can be, & I ought to be thankful that Mr. Thrale does not, as most Husbands would—aggravate by Insult and Anger the Sorrows of my Mind.

VI

TRAVELS AND TRAGEDY

JANUARY 1774–APRIL 1776

FOLLOWING the years of almost continuous disaster there came some peaceful intervals, but so long as Mrs. Thrale brought infants into the world in rapid succession, only to lose them one by one, and Thrale retained his speculative attitude towards business, life was sure to be full of heartaches. Furthermore, even when her children were well and happy, she had to nurse and comfort Johnson, who, whenever he was indisposed or irritable, turned to his dear Mistress for the sympathy which seldom failed him. So on February 7, 1774, he wrote to Boswell, 'I have, indeed, for some weeks past, been very ill of a cold and cough, and have been at Mrs. Thrale's, that I might be taken care of.'[1] It was a rare month that did not find some sickness at Streatham or Southwark.

Gradually, however, Mrs. Thrale discovered ways to emancipate herself somewhat from the dull round of nursery and household duties. For one thing, the education of her young ones did not take up so much time as formerly. The sickly and backward Susan was sent to Mrs. Cumyns' school in Kensington, and, when at Streatham, Harry was a day scholar of Dr. Thomas. Queeney, the mother left more and more to the teaching of Baretti. The instruction was not all scholarly, apparently, for the next year Mrs. Thrale noted in the Children's Book:

Queeney begun to learn to dance this Week of Mr. Abingdon, who studied under my old Master Mr. Leviez: I used to say I would teach this Science to my own Family but these frequent Pregnancies disable me.[2]

But if she was forced to secure professional training for her son and elder daughters, it did not mean that she failed to watch their progress with the usual pride. Constant questioning and examinations kept her fully aware of all they were learning or forgetting, and she added numerous refinements of her own.

[1] *Life*, ii. 272.   [2] Jan. 25, 1775. See also p. 22, Chapter I.

Having a sensitive ear, upon which eccentricities of speech made an immediate impression, Mrs. Thrale was determined that her own children should have no colloquial handicaps—that no cockneyisms should creep in. She was shocked when the well-known Pepys brothers pronounced idea 'idear',[1] for no such vulgarity was tolerated in her household. Many years afterward she remembered an amusing conversation arising from her crusade against uncouth speech.

I teised my children so to pronounce Window & Fellow instead of the Cockney method Winder & Feller—that one day the Boy said Look Sister there's a Ladder—Fye, fye, cries the Girl it is a Laddow.[2]

Johnson, constantly in the house, also took an active part in rearing the children. Queeney, the eldest, naturally occupied most of his attention, but Harry and Susy were also great favourites. It was probably at his suggestion that Queeney began her collection of natural specimens, since he saw to it that she had a special cabinet made to hold the treasures, and on every trip tried to secure some new object to add to them.[3]

The great moralist often undertook to explain to the young people the true principles of religion. On one occasion when he had been speaking of Heaven's joys as being wholly intellectual, 'some of them said—What Pleasure can *such* Joys give to "Grinning Jack" Sir?—a poor half-witted Cowman that we kept—Oh replied he "Jack may *Improve* perhaps"'.[4] Another day, Mrs. Thrale recorded,

when my son was going to school, and dear Dr. Johnson followed as far as the garden gate, praying for his salvation, in a voice which those who listened attentively could hear plain enough, he said to me suddenly, 'Make your boy tell you his dreams: the first corruption that entered into my heart was communicated in a dream.' What was it, Sir? said I. '*Do* not ask me,' replied he with much violence, and walked away in apparent agitation.[5]

His ever-ready advice embraced other things than religion. He insisted that reading was so important that even foolish books were better than none at all. 'Doctor Johnson said always,—Get your Children into Habits of loving a Book by every possible means; You do not know but it may one Day

---

[1] New Common Place Book, p. 147.
[2] A marginal note in a copy of Pegge's *Anecdotes of the English Language* (1803), p. 69 (now at Brynbella).
[3] *Queeney Letters*, xiv; see also Ry. 891, 32.
[4] New Common Place Book, p. 37.
[5] *John. Misc.* i. 159.

save them from Suicide.'[1] This counsel was hardly needed, for Mrs. Thrale was more apt to over-emphasize scholarly training than to neglect it. Many years afterwards, looking back over her early life, she wondered if she had not been wrong in trying to cram knowledge into the youthful minds of her daughters;[2] but at the time she had no doubts. She was determined that her children should be mentally and morally superior, and she devised many amusing schemes to accomplish this end. To stimulate learning, she kept little coloured note-books filled with the passages to be memorized. To offset any possible tendency to future excess, she always gave medicines in wine, 'that they might constantly annex disagreeable Ideas with that Liquor'.[3]

Sometimes Mrs. Thrale's punishment took a physical form. Baretti, in his later 'Strictures', undoubtedly exaggerates the harshness of her treatment, but there is no reason to question his assertion that to enforce obedience she often resorted to blows from her 'Salusbury fist'.[4] Holding that children should be governed strictly by their parents (in which belief she was supported, for the most part, by Johnson), she felt that for their own good her daughters must learn to obey without question, and that if they did not, immediate punishment was necessary. But she was not a cruel tyrant.

Other interests arose to divert her mind from the affairs of the nursery, for in the spring of 1774 the Thrales and Johnson were discussing the possibility of taking a long tour together. Money was flowing into the brewery; Mrs. Thrale was in good health; everything seemed propitious. At first the Continent was suggested, chiefly because Johnson and the Mistress of the household, neither of whom had ever been outside the British Isles, both greatly wished to see Italy and the antiquities of Rome. It is evident that Thrale may have seriously considered such a journey, since Boswell, in his letter of May 13, wrote as if it were a settled fact. But the expedition to Italy never took place. Instead, Thrale decided that his wife's inheritance of the old Salusbury property in Wales made it imperative that they postpone any European travel, and visit that part of the island first.

Before setting out for Wales, Johnson probably spent some time in examining Mrs. Thrale's family papers. At her sugges-

---

[1] New Common Place Book, p. 243. [2] Broadley, p. 50
[3] New Common Place Book, p. 42.
[4] See Chapter XV, pp. 322-4, for a discussion of Baretti's 'Strictures'.

tion he read through, not only the legal documents having to do
with Bach-y-Graig, but also the long series of letters from Bridge
and numerous members of the Salusbury family. Once started,
he even looked over a number of her letters from Collier and her
father's Nova Scotian diaries. Over two hundred of these papers
have endorsements in his handwriting.[1]

Throughout June 1774 preparations for the journey were in
progress. The younger girls were left with Mrs. Cumyns in
Kensington; Harry instructed to spend his days at Thomas's
school in Streatham; 'old Nurse' given charge of the baby; and
Baretti charged with the task of keeping a vigilant eye on them
all and writing regular accounts of their health. Still,[2] it was with
some misgivings that on Tuesday, July 5, Mrs. Thrale set out
with her husband, Queeney, and Johnson for distant Wales. Never
before had she planned to be gone so long from her nursery,
and she imagined all sorts of accidents which might happen.

Beginning a journey of several months, she decided to keep
a separate diary of the tour.[3] Extending from July 5 to September 30, 1774, it is the first of her travel journals, and though it
may not have the insight of her later continental observations,
it reveals a mind already sensitive to new surroundings and
unfamiliar customs. The record is a day-by-day account of the
places they visited and the men and women they met, with her
penetrating comments on both. She recounts how, in their
own coach, with four fast horses, they jolted along over the
country roads, first to Lichfield and Ashbourne to see Johnson's
old friends, then on to Sir Lynch Cotton's estates of Combermere and Lleweney. After lingering for some time in the Vale
of Clwyd, the travellers penetrated as far into Caernarvonshire
as Pwllheli and saw Mrs. Thrale's birthplace a few miles away.
Although much of her account of this trip is merely a descriptive
chronicle of events, a large part is also given over to her own

---

[1] For the most part in the John Rylands collection. These include old deeds,
legal papers, and letters from Bridge, Lloyd, and members of the Salusbury family.
Since one letter containing his handwriting on the back is dated Aug. 3, 1773, it
seems probable that Johnson's examination of all the papers came after this date.

[2] Of Baretti's affectionate, friendly letters, giving news of the children, those of
July 9, 21, Aug. 4, 12, 13, Sept. 26 have survived. Four have been printed by L.
Piccioni, Baretti Epistolario (1936), pp. 127-32.

[3] The full text of Mrs. Piozzi's Welsh Journal may be found in A. M. Broadley's
Dr. Johnson and Mrs. Thrale (1910). Included is a reprint of Dr. Johnson's diary
kept during the same tour, together with much biographical material relating to
the Thrales. A comparison with the original manuscript, now in the collection of
Mr. A. Edward Newton, shows that Broadley's editing is not entirely trustworthy.
See also L. F. Powell's edition of Johnson's Welsh Journal in Life, volume v. 427-60.

feelings. Among the scenes and playmates of her childhood, she found it impossible not to fill many pages with sentimental recollections. It was never easy for Mrs. Thrale to write anything without some personal vagary creeping into the entry, and these intimate flashes are often the most interesting portion of her journals. Thus on Tuesday, August 9, while visiting at Lleweney, she wrote:

I expected letters from home and had none I have not Mrs. Cotton's even sweetness of temper, so I am come into my own room to cry. She loves her children as well as I do, but she would not have cried from fretful impatience like me. Why does every body on some occasion or other perpetually do better than I can?

Five days later came another complaint:

Queeney has a weight over her eyes today again. I hear Harry has had a black eye, and Ralph cut his teeth with pain, but I have nobody to tell how it vexes me. Mr. Thrale will not be conversed with by *me* on any subject, as a friend, or comforter, or adviser. Every day more and more do I feel the loss of my Mother. My present Companions have too much philosophy for me. One cannot disburthen one's mind to people who are watchful to cavil, or acute to contradict before the sentence is finished.

Travelling with Dr. Johnson, Thrale, and Queeney was not unalloyed pleasure. Thrale loved prospects, but the near-sighted Johnson when confronted with a breath-taking panorama preferred to keep his eyes fastened on the pages of a book. Besides, neither of the two men had expected to find much of interest in Wales, and they were not disappointed. As a result, Mrs. Thrale, with the pride of a true Welshwoman, was chagrined and hurt at their obvious dislike of her country. Nor were the men hesitant at expressing their distaste, so that the amenities fell heavily upon Mrs. Thrale, and she was 'obliged to be civil for four'.[1]

To offset the times when Johnson was churlish and irritable, however, there were happy occasions when he was agreeable and kindly. Thus at Pwllheli she recorded:

We went to the little town of Pwllhely, where Mr. Johnson would buy something, he said, in memory of his little Mistresses' Market Town; he is on every occasion so very kind, feels friendship so acutely and expresses it so delicately that it is wonderfully flattering to me to have his company. He could find nothing to purchase but a Primmer.

---

[1] *D'Arblay Diary*, i. 130.

To reconcile such varying accounts it must be remembered that she wrote down just what came to her mind at the moment. If she had a pleasant day and her companions agreed with her, they were the most charming persons in the world, and life itself absolute perfection. If, on the other hand, one of Johnson's or Thrale's remarks irritated her, she openly showed her indignation in her diary.

Through September the party made its way by easy stages back to London, a number of incidents on the way provoking caustic entries in Mrs. Thrale's journal. Their reception by the Lytteltons at Hagley was not so cordial as they had expected, and a visit to the Burkes at Beaconsfield was rendered less enjoyable by the hard drinking of their host and his friends. At Beaconsfield came the unpleasant news that Parliament had been dissolved, which meant that Thrale was faced with an immediate canvass for re-election. This was upsetting for Mrs. Thrale, who had been looking forward to a quiet autumn at Streatham, where, as she expressed it, she could have kissed her children 'and cuffed them by turns', and where they could always have had a place to play. Instead she would have to be 'shut up in that odious dungeon, where nobody will come near me'.[1] But she did not allow personal whims to affect her loyalty, and shortly after their return on September 30, she threw herself energetically into the campaign.

The election of 1774 was another desperate battle with the supporters of Wilkes, and Southwark was the scene of continuous rioting. On Tuesday, October 4, Mrs. Thrale sent a hurried scrawl to Johnson:

We lead a wild Life, but it will be over tomorrow seven-night; the Election will be carried, but not so triumphantly as I hoped for: some are stupid, and some are sullen. no less than four Candidates besides my Master—the Patriots have the Mob of Course. Do not think of seeing us till the Storm is over, unless you call for half an hour & hear News &· tell some. I write surrounded by people making a noise & scarce know what I say but that I am very busy.[2]

Johnson did not remain aloof while the excitement was intense. He drafted at least one of Thrale's announcements,[3]

---

[1] Broadley, p. 219. Upon their arrival in London on Friday, Sept. 30, Johnson remained in town, while Mrs. Thrale hurried to Kensington and Streatham to see her children. That day in the Children's Book she noted her pleasure at finding all well and improved. After spending the week-end in the country, she drove in to Southwark, leaving Queeney and Baretti in charge at Streatham.

[2] For a description of the riots at the close of the poll see *The Gazetteer*, Oct. 12, 1774.

[3] The original draft of one address in Johnson's handwriting is in my possession

and when the issue seemed doubtful dashed off a pamphlet called *The Patriot* to combat the arguments of the mob. It 'was called for', he wrote to Boswell, 'by my political friends on Friday, was written on Saturday'.[1] He was also quite capable of entering good humouredly into the amusing by-play of a political campaign. It was in this year, as he accompanied Mrs. Thrale on one of her canvassing expeditions, that a rough fellow seized his venerable beaver hat in one hand, and clapped him on the back with the other, while crying out, 'Ah, Master Johnson, this is no time to be thinking about *hats*.' 'No, No, Sir,' replied the Doctor in a cheerful tone, 'hats are of no use now, as you say, except to throw up in the air and huzza with,' accompanying his words with a true election halloo.[2]

Although Mrs. Thrale always professed to be bored with the duties of electioneering, it may be suspected that when actually launched she enjoyed the infectious fever of the contest. It is certain that she did everything in her power to aid her husband's cause, soliciting every voter in the Borough, and using all her blandishments to influence the result. This year the voting was close; but on October 18 Thrale was officially returned, second on the poll, and with naïve pride Mrs. Thrale remarked in the Children's Book that her husband's best friends admitted he owed his success to his wife's efforts. 'The truth is', she added complacently, 'I have been indefatigable.'

When the strenuous competition was over, she was glad of a few days' rest at Streatham. As soon as she felt strong again, she rode over to Kensington to arrange for the return of Susan and Sophy, who all this time had been left at Mrs. Cumyns's.[3] On the way, in Hogmore Lane, her horse fell while at a smart gallop, and she was thrown and painfully injured, her side being forcibly struck by the pommel of the saddle and her lip cut almost through. She was immediately carried to Mrs. Cumyns's where she melodramatically took final leave of her

---

(printed in *Life*, ed. Powell, v. 460, note 2). Dated Oct. 1, it first appeared in the *Daily Advertiser* and other papers on Oct. 3, 1774 (repeated on the 4th). On the 6th another announcement appeared in the papers, requesting 'Votes, Interest, and Support on the Day of Election' (repeated on the 7th, 8th, 10th), and on Oct. 14, after the poll, Thrale printed public thanks for his election. All three addresses may have been written by Johnson, though we have definite proof only of the first.   [1] *Life*, ii. 288.

[2] *John. Misc.* i. 293; *Thraliana*, autumn 1777. Another incident that undoubtedly occurred at this election is related by Laetitia Matilda Hawkins in her *Memoirs* (1824), i. 65–6.

[3] The account of this accident was written in the Children's Book on Nov. 12, 1774, at which time she referred to it as occurring 'about a Week ago'; Johnson wrote on Oct. 20 describing the fall as 'two days ago' (*Adam Libr.* i. 187).

whimpering daughters, sure that the accident would be the end
of herself and the child she was bearing. Badly bruised, with
two black eyes and a swollen jaw, she was a pitiable sight; but by
good fortune not seriously hurt. On her return home the same
day, however, she frightened the rest of the family by suddenly
collapsing. Queeney kept out of the way, Harry cried continuously, and Thrale was unusually tender—perhaps, she commented, having realized her worth anew after the valuable
service during the campaign. Although she soon recovered
from the fall, Mrs. Thrale carried one visible reminder to her
grave, for when her lip healed a deep scar was left at the right
side of the mouth. As an old lady, when artists painted her
portrait, she always insisted on having this scar appear in the
picture.

While still in the country she decided to inoculate the year-
old Ralph against small-pox. None of the other children had
been much affected by a similar inoculation, but little Ralph
became extremely ill with a mass of running sores, and it was
even feared he was dying. On December 8 Mrs. Thrale wrote
in despair in the Children's Book:

Oh Lord Oh Lord! what shall I do? Johnson & Baretti try to
comfort me, they only plague me—Up every Night and all Night
long again!—well if this don't kill me & the Child I carry, sure we
are made of Iron.

By the 19th the worst was over, and Ralph began to recover,
but his mother found him sadly altered, so languid and listless
that he seemed to have no strength left. The next day, when
they moved in to Southwark, she recorded her fervent wish:
'God give us a quiet Winter!'

As soon as the immediate crisis of Ralph's illness had passed,
she became absorbed, as usual, in a variety of projects: literary,
philanthropic, and social. In December, as a special favour
granted only to the King and to herself, she read Johnson's
account of his Hebridean tour, at least a month before Boswell
and the general public.[1] She also had an early view of the new
political pamphlet, *Taxation No Tyranny*.[2] At the same time she
aided her famous guest in a number of charitable schemes.

Johnson's kind heart and active generosity have always been
recognized; a similar kindliness on the part of the Mistress of
Streatham has unfortunately often been overlooked. Mrs.
Thrale served as a member of the committee of management

---

[1] *Life*, ii. 509. See also lot 224, Sotheby Sale, Jan. 30, 1918.
[2] Ry. 539, 38.

of 'The Ladies' Charity School for Training Girls as Servants', the same school in which Johnson and the blind Anna Williams took such an interest. In a later letter to Mrs. Thrale Johnson actually wrote of it as 'your charity school'.[1] She was a warm supporter of the Lying-in Hospital and other public philanthropies, but more to her liking were private benefactions to deserving unfortunates. She seems continually to have besought her friends and acquaintances on behalf of some unfortunate boy or girl. Since Thrale was usually too busy to be bothered, his wife was forced to carry on her schemes, *sub rosa*, with the aid of those more amenable. In one instance, when trying to secure a non-freeman's presentation to a city charity school for the son of Harry's old nurse, she ended her plea to Johnson: 'Mr. Thrale knows I am always tormenting my Friends about this Time of Year—for they present only at Easter—so I dare not say a word to him about it.'[2] On another occasion the draft of one of her solicitations ends with the admission, 'Mr. Thrale will not even read my Letter and only wonders at my Assurance in supposing I can have the least Interest with Mr. Harley.'[3]

Sometimes, to be sure, her efforts were expended in attempts to secure positions for relatives of voters in the borough, and then her husband was more interested. One such project, several years before, had resulted in an amusing fiasco. At a time when the Queen was expecting another child, Mrs. Thrale had written to obtain the position of wet-nurse in the royal nursery for the wife of one of Thrale's constituents. In typical fashion, however, her desire to write a clever letter proved fatal to her plan, and she was forced to apologize through Doctor Bromfield.

I sometimes beg favours of you but seldom one like this: it is to see Dr. Hunter for me and to tell him how much I am mortified at his misunderstanding a passage in a letter I had lately occasion to write Lady Effingham recommending a Wet Nurse to the Queen . . . but the Doctor has unfortunately objected to a passage in my letter and I fear I have done my friend more mischief than I can easily repair: I have no means of getting at Dr. Hunter but thro' you or I would not be this troublesome, but do tell him that I think her a young Woman of Merit, that I have no suspicion of her Virtue being corrupted at Court nor no thought of the Court being a place of corruption: but that people return to their homes uneasily

---

[1] *Letters*, No. 883. For information about the Charity School, see Broadley, pp. 96, 121, and *The Speaker*, Mar. 22, 1890, pp. 311–12.

[2] Ry. 539, 34. Undated.

[3] Ry. 533, 4. Dated May 27, 1774. The note has to do with Carter's son. See next page. For Harley see *Letters*, i. 304.

from a Life of less employment and more delight must be obvious to
every Observer and that was really all I said . . .[1]

Mrs. Thrale's rattling wit was apt to involve her in difficulties,
whether she spoke or wrote. But she never could keep from
saying what she thought, no matter what the consequence.

Sometimes her struggles proved unavailing through no fault
of her own. As an example, about this time one of the chief
objects of Mrs. Thrale's beneficence was the family of an
indigent riding master in the Borough named Carter, the son
of a gentleman, but reduced to a pitiable state by a series of
misfortunes. In 1774 Mrs. Thrale wrote a number of letters
to influential acquaintances in an attempt to get Carter's son
admitted to Christ's Hospital, the famous Blue Coat School.[2]
The riding master himself was even a more difficult problem.
Living in an unfashionable part of the town, he had few pupils,
and with a large family to support he had fallen deeply into
debt. Johnson became concerned and finally evolved a plan
which at first sight seemed the perfect solution of the unfortunate man's difficulties. Some years before, Oxford University
had been presented with a bequest from the family of Lord
Clarendon to establish a riding school at the University; why
not secure the post of instructor in the proposed academy for
Carter? Late in February 1775 Johnson made a trip to Oxford
to investigate the matter and to use his influence in obtaining
the appointment. His reports being favourable, Mrs. Thrale
sent Carter, who scarcely dared stir out of his house 'except on
Sundays' and then haunted her 'with his doleful Looks', to
Oxford for an interview.[3] Because of unforeseen obstacles, however, both Carter and Johnson were forced to return with little
accomplished. In the end the funds available proved insuffi-
cient, and the University scheme had to be abandoned;[4] but
though their more ambitious efforts on behalf of the poor riding

[1] Hunter-Baillie Collection, Royal College of Surgeons, London. The letter is
dated Apr. 22, 1770. With it is the original letter of Mrs. Thrale to Lady Effingham
of Mar. 29, 1770, in which the remarks on the possible bad effect of court life on
Mrs. Newby are certainly over-stressed. (Mrs. Newby was a niece of Samuel
Croxall, the poet.)

[2] Drafts of some of her solicitations may be found in Ry. 533, while answers from
C. R. Bromfield, John Durand, and Wm. Herne are in my collection, as is also a
trial draft of a begging letter directed to an unnamed lord, in the handwriting of
Johnson.

[3] Every move is described in Mrs. Thrale's letters to Johnson (Ry. 539, 36–45)
and in his replies. See also Thraliana, late 1777.

[4] The Clarendon bequest was not used until the middle of the nineteenth century, and then to build a scientific laboratory. See *Life*, ii. 527–8; also *J. Rylands
Bulletin*, xx (1936), 270–1.

master were fruitless, the Thrales and Johnson continued to give temporary aid to the improvident family.

Philanthropy may have occupied some of Mrs. Thrale's time, but her chief interest outside the nursery was society and conversation. Still the company at Streatham and Southwark was preponderantly masculine, made up of business and political connexions of her husband and the famous friends of Johnson. These last, indeed, should have been enough to content any hostess. To receive letters of compliment from Edmund Burke,[1] visits from Sir Joshua Reynolds and the Scotch poet and philosopher James Beattie,[2] pamphlets and gossip from Dr. Michael Lort, the Cambridge Greek scholar,[3] was a triumph indeed for the wife of a Southwark brewer. One well-known guest, however, who had often been present would never again sit at her table. Mrs. Thrale had not been greatly impressed by Dr. Goldsmith, had indeed thought little of his talk, but his death had come as a shock. Boswell was right when he wrote to Thrale, 'Poor Goldsmith will be much missed at your literary parties'.[4]

Gradually Mrs. Thrale was meeting other people whose friendship she had long desired. It was with delight that she dispatched a note to Johnson on February 5, 1775.

I wonder when we shall have any Leisure from our Engagements to chat with each other. Today I hear you dine with Mr. Paradise, so I will take this Afternoon to go out a'visiting. tomorrow Mr. Thrale entertains two or three of the People concerned in Crossby's Affairs, so when I have sat the Dinner out, & said a few civil Things to my Company I shall go to drink Tea with Jack & Fanny Rice with whom I shall go to the Comic Mirror at Night to hear the Dialogue between Doctor *Anecdote* and Mrs. *Thalia*—If you will meet me at home when I return from that Nonsense we shall have

---

[1] Two letters from Burke to Mrs. Thrale during the spring of 1774 still exist. One is of May 5 (*Adam Libr.* iii. 42), the other of June 20 (lot 344, Sotheby Sale, Dec. 6, 1904). In the former, Burke referred to Mrs. Thrale's great partiality to Mrs. Burke and himself, and admitted that this had made him presume to bring two friends with them when they came that day to dine. In the second, he informed her that his friend Mr. King would like to be introduced.

[2] The Thrales had first met Beattie in 1771. The kindly, courteous poet and philosopher became a pronounced favourite with Mrs. Thrale, and she jokingly told Johnson that if ever she had another husband it would be Beattie (*Life*, ii. 148; also Broadley, p. 123). In 1773 he was again in London and on Aug. 13 Sir Joshua Reynolds and his sister brought him out to Streatham for dinner, when Goldsmith, Baretti, and Sir Thomas Mills were also present (M. Forbes, *Beattie and His Friends*, p. 90).

[3] Ry. 544, 1. Also see Thraliana, May 1777, and *Queeney Letters*, p. 255.

[4] *Boswell's Letters*, i. 203. Many anecdotes about Goldsmith were recorded in the first volume of Thraliana.

something to laugh about. on Wednesday we dine with Sir Joshua Reynolds according to an Invitation he sent hither on Saturday to ask us to meet Mrs. Montagu so I am like Miss Jenny in the Journey to London telling how tomorrow we see the new Pantomime & the next day dine with the Duchess of Distinction &c. I like however that you should always know where I go & what I do that you may either approve me or scold me which is the next best as the one shews your Partiality the other your Friendship.[1]

To become acquainted with the famous Mrs. Elizabeth Montagu opened up a new vista for Mrs. Thrale's ambitions, bringing within reach the world of the Blue-Stockings into which Thrale's wealth and her own vivacious conversation had not yet provided the necessary entrée. Besides, Johnson was every year becoming more valuable bait. Though he might still shock the sensibilities of fashionable Mrs. Harris, he was growing more presentable in dress and less ferocious in manner and would not be so difficult to fit into the society presided over by the 'Queen of the Blues'.

Two intimate records, those of Boswell and of an Irish clergy-man, Dr. Thomas Campbell, give us a picture of the Southwark life of the Thrales during the winter of 1775. Boswell, on this year's trip to England, had been given a 'general invitation' to dine in the Borough 'when not otherwise engaged',[2] and often took advantage of the privilege. Dr. Campbell, who it was reported had come to London for the express purpose of meeting Johnson, kept almost as complete an account of his experiences in the Thrale circle.[3] On March 14 he called at Southwark for the first time, where he found the lady of the house very learned, and joining 'to ye charms of her own sex ye manly understanding of ours'. After this he dined at intervals with the Thrales, once on the 25th, when 'there were 10 or dz gentlemen & but one lady besides Mrs. Thrale'. Campbell recorded much of interest about Johnson, Baretti, and others, but except for some com-ments on his hostess's doubtful taste in repeating the Doctor's *bons mots* before his face, he had little to say about Mrs. Thrale. On the 25th he did, however, describe in detail the dinner, which he found excellent:

first course soups at head & foot removed by fish & a saddle of

---

[1] I have been unable to find any references in the newspapers to the dialogue mentioned. Jenny appears in Cibber's version, *The Provoked Husband*.

[2] *Private Papers*, x. 158.

[3] A *Diary of a Visit to England in 1775, by an Irishman*, with notes by Samuel Raymond, M.A., Prothonotary of the Supreme Court of New South Wales, was published by Waugh and Cox, Sydney, New South Wales, in 1854, and re-edited from the original manuscript by me in 1947 (Cambridge University Press).

mutton—second course a fowl they called Galena—at head, & a capon—larger than some of our Irish turkeys at foot—Third course four different sorts of Ices viz. Pineapple, Grapes, raspberry, & a fourth—in each remove there were I think fourteen dishes—The two first courses were served in massy plate.

At least twice Campbell and Boswell met at the Thrales, and as a result we have two independent accounts of the same occasion. In one instance it is fortunate for the reputation of each diarist that there is corroboration for some rather dubious stories of Johnson's vulgar remarks which were related by Murphy.[1] When these remarks were quoted, Mrs. Thrale undoubtedly was not in the room; when she was in the party, the topics of conversation ranged from marriage with an inferior to Gray's poetry and Murphy's accuracy of narration.[2] As usual Boswell portrays Mrs. Thrale strenuously opposing Johnson in argument, for she refused to be awed either by his reputation or by the violence of his pronouncements. Johnson was in good form; he had just received his degree of Doctor of Laws from Oxford, and though he affected to depreciate its importance, he was at heart vastly pleased with the honour. Rarely using the title himself, he now acquiesced in the distinction from his friends.

During these years Boswell and the Thrales were ostensibly on the best of terms, but it is already possible to see the beginning of future rivalry. On April 8 Boswell notes:

Mr. Thrale told me, I am not sure what day, that there is a Book of *Johnsoniana* kept in their Family, in which all Mr. Johnson's sayings and all that they can collect about him is put down. He told me they had seen—[Hector], a Surgeon at Birmingham, who was a Schoolfellow of Mr. Johnson's, had some of his exercises, and could tell a great deal about him, and that he had promised to give them a great deal. I must try to get this *Thralian* Miscellany, to assist me in writing Mr. Johnson's Life, if Mrs. Thrale does not intend to do it herself. I suppose there will be many written.

> Be there a thousand lives,
> My great Curiosity has stomach for 'em all.[3]

Undoubtedly Thrale's reference was to the early journal in which his wife had been recording Johnsoniana since the late seventeen-sixties, but it is possible that there may have been

---

[1] Boswell and Campbell give substantially the same version of the conversation. See *Private Papers*, x. 172 ff., and Campbell's diary for Apr. 1, 1775.
[2] *Private Papers*, x. 158 ff.
[3] Ibid. x. 200.

another collection of which we have no trace. A writer in a
newspaper, indeed, later maintained that

the preservation of Johnson's Memorabilia being first begun at
Thrale's house, where an octavo, full of blank paper, was placed on
one of the shelves in a common room, for every person in the family
to note each remarkable saying of Doctor,—who, once attracted by
the splendid binding, to open the book, observed, not without
evident complacency, 'Upon my word I did not think I had so
much point about me.'[1]

How much credence to place in this vague newspaper story
it is impossible to estimate. Unlikely as it sounds, the experiment may possibly have been tried, although it is doubtful if
anyone else in the family ever aided the mistress of the household in writing down anecdotes of their famous guest. But the
knowledge that some volume existed was enough to rouse
Boswell's interest and to put him on his guard.

His jealousy of the Thrales showed itself in more ways than
one, and the next year, when he thought his idol badly treated,
he wrote in his journal:

After all, though his intimacy in Thrale's family has done him
much good, I could wish that he had been independent of it. He
would have had more dignity. For undoubtedly he is at times under
some restraint and submits to circumstances not quite agreable,
that he may not lose that intimacy.[2]

On her side, the lady was at times inclined to be a trifle
facetious about her Scotch rival. Several years later she commented to Johnson: 'I am glad Mr. Boswell is with you—
nothing that you say for this Week at least will be lost to Posterity.'[3] Yet on the surface all was serene. It was easy to like
the effervescent, amusing Boswell, of whom she once wrote that
he would 'make Ashbourne alive better than three Hautboys &
the Harpsichord; and in Sewards Phrase will *do more* for one'.[4]
He was the most good-humoured of guests, ever ready to please,
and full of spontaneous fun. Even if she did later grow to feel
that he was an insincere friend, she was always glad to welcome
him whenever he crossed the river to the Borough. On one
such visit (in 1776) Boswell described his greeting:

My reception here was truly flattering. At once I had chocolade

---

[1] Included in a scrap-book kept by Samuel Lysons (now in the collection of
Professor C. B. Tinker). A similar account appeared in the *Morning Chronicle*,
Jan. 7, 1785, in which it was stated that Murphy, Goldsmith, and Hawkesworth
had aided in filling the volume with anecdotes.
[2] *Private Papers*, xi. 212.
[3] Sept. 18, 1777.   [4] Sept. 16, 1777.

before me, and Dr. Johnson was in full glow of conversation. I was
elevated as if brought into another state of being. Mrs. Thrale and
I looked to each other while he talked (Baretti having soon left the
room), and our looks expressed our congenial admiration of him.
I said to her, 'This is *Hermippus redivivus*. I am quite restored by him,
by transfusion of Mind.' Mr. Thrale joined us, and cordially
wellcomed me.[1]

In the spring of 1775 Boswell even lent Mrs. Thrale his
manuscript journal, kept during the famous trip to the Hebrides. Perhaps he thought that if she once sampled his genius for
Johnsonian narration it might forestall a future contest; at least
it might lead to an opportunity for him to consult her Johnsonian records in return. But no such idea had entered her
mind, for Mrs. Thrale, after reading the long manuscript
which nearly blinded her, was strangely non-committal.[2]

From the verbatim notes of Boswell and Campbell we can
reconstruct the easy give and take of conversation in the Thrale
home—conversations so well known and so accessible that there
is no need to repeat them here. Throughout them all the witty,
talkative hostess plays a major role, with her vivacity, her
refusal to be silenced even by the weighty assertions of more
scholarly visitors, her keen interest in people and literature.
This is the Mrs. Thrale of tradition. On the other hand, in
these accounts we catch no glimpse whatsoever of the worried,
maternal Mrs. Thrale; for even when driven almost frantic by
family problems, she showed her dinner guests only the glittering front of the literary hostess. Yet in April 1775 Mrs. Thrale
was within a few weeks of the birth of her tenth child, and
besides was uneasy about her second son, Ralph. On April 14
the boy was shown to Pott, the eminent surgeon, who gave his
opinion that the trouble was in the brain, and that the child
was suffering from a serious complaint which had affected his
intellect.

Oh how this dreadful sentence did fill me with Horror! [Mrs.
Thrale wrote in the Children's Book] & how dismal are now the
thoughts of all future Connection with this unhappy Child! a
Thing to hide & be ashamed of whilst we Live: Johnson gives me
what Comfort he can, and laments he can give no more . . . Oh
Lord give me patience to bear this heaviest of all my Afflictions.

The prospect of a feeble-minded son was a frightful shock to
a woman who gloried in her own mental faculties.

---

[1] *Private Papers*, xi. 134–5.
[2] Although she wrote to Boswell on May 18, 1775, about his manuscript, she
made few comments to Johnson in her letter of May 20, 1775.

Late in April she moved her family out to Streatham, where on May 4 another daughter was born who was named Frances Ann. The child was small and delicate, though seemingly unaffected by her mother's recent troubles. Slow in recovering her strength, Mrs. Thrale was in a highly nervous state throughout May. To escape a complaining wife, her husband found it advisable to remain as much as possible in London, a procedure which did not improve her temper, and she protested to Johnson: 'I could pout myself for a Penny to see my Master never come near me but on those Days that he would come if I had never been born—Saturday, Sunday & Monday.'[1] She had other grievances, too, which she continued to confide to the same correspondent when he set out for Oxford and Lichfield. Thrale, she felt, was supporting the wrong candidate in an election; and there was difficulty about her mother's epitaph which Johnson had long before engaged to write but with his usual procrastination had not completed. Even when the epitaph did arrive she found it too long. Everything seemed to combine to aggravate her petulance; but, as usual, it was an easy step from desperation to perfect contentment. On June 16 she admitted to Johnson that her husband had been right about the election.

My Master is apt to be right and I apt to be perverse & self opinionated . . . Mr. Thrale is right in another Affair, he has found out that the Letter of the Epitaph may be made less, and then the stone will hold more; he will not have your Writing or my Mother's Praises curtailed he says. All this you may be sure obliges me & I am in the best humour now, as well as the best Health in the World.

Not even worry about Ralph, who at the doctor's suggestion had been sent with a nurse to Brighton to try sea bathing, could long depress her spirits. Throughout late June and early July her correspondence with Johnson was regular and full of interest. The Doctor wrote of his continued efforts on behalf of Carter, of Lichfield gossip, and of Dr. Taylor's bulls. She, in return, told of Carter's bad luck with his horses, of her children's health and activity, and of the exciting time at the Thames regatta. Keeping Queeney up until six o'clock in the morning after that entertainment was news indeed. She was anxious, however, to have him home.

I shall be wondrous glad [she wrote on June 29] to see you—though I write every thing so I shall have nothing to tell: but I shall

[1] May 20, 1775.

have you safe in your Bow Window to run to, when any thing comes in my head, and you say that's what you are kept for you know.

On July 4, with her husband, Queeney, and Harry, Mrs. Thrale drove to Brighton to see Ralph. Finding the child much worse, she called in Dr. Lucas Pepys for consultation, who tried blisters, baths, and stimulants of various kinds, but to no avail. In despair she wrote to Johnson:

This poor unfortunate Child will dye at last—The Matter which discharged from his Ear was it seems a temporary Relief, but that was all over when I came down & the Stupor was returned in a most alarming Manner: he has however violent fits of Rage—proceeding from Pain I guess—just as Lucy & Miss Anna had—Kipping says the Brain is oppressed of which I have no doubt: What shall I do? What can I do? has the flattery of my Friends made me too proud of my own Brains? & must these poor Children suffer for my crime? I can neither go on with this Subject nor quit it.[1]

Whenever Mrs. Thrale was particularly upset, she sought diversion outside her home. This time, since she could do nothing for Ralph except await the end, she dashed about Brighton with feverish abandon. 'I opened the Ball last Night', she added to Johnson,—'tonight I go to the Play: Oh that there was a Play or a Ball for every hour of the four & twenty!'

On the 8th Thrale insisted that she return with the others to Streatham, where she immediately confided her unhappiness to Johnson. There were even greater worries than leaving her little boy to die in Sussex:

it is the horrible Apprehension of losing the others by the same cruel Disease that haunts my affrighted Imagination & makes me look on them with an anxiety scarce to be endured. If Hetty tells me that her Head achs, I am more shocked than if I heard she had broken her Leg.

It seemed to her as if a curse had been laid upon her children and that none of them would survive this terrible brain ailment. Remembering that one of Johnson's relatives had had a little girl similarly afflicted, Mrs. Thrale urgently inquired if she was still alive.

Word soon came that Ralph was sinking, and she rushed back to Brighton on the 13th only to find the child dead. A post-mortem examination showed the child's brain 'almost dissolved in Water; & something amiss too in the original Conformation of the Head—so that Reason & Life both might, had we known all been despair'd of from the very first'.[2] This

---

[1] Date uncertain (Ry. 539, 46).　　　[2] Recorded in the Children's Book.

poor boy at least was 'better dead than alive'; but the loss of
a son was a cruel blow indeed.

Nevertheless she wrote to Johnson on the 18th of her resolve

to be thankful to God and chearful among my Friends again till
new Vexations arise. Baretti has been very good, and taken Care
of my little ones like a Nurse while I was away, & has not failed
writing to me &c. & I am sorry I was so peevish with him. I came
home Yesterday Mr. Thrale has been in Town ever since I was gone,
but would not come home to me last Night but went to Ranelagh
I hear, however I will not be peevish any more for it torments
nobody but myself.

Although she determined to throw off her distress, whenever
any of her children complained of a headache for years afterwards, the old haunting fear returned. Losing three children
from the same mysterious trouble in the head could never be
forgotten. Her one longing now was to see her confidant again,
to pour out her cares into his sympathetic ear. 'I think you
shall never run away so again,' she ended her letter of the 18th,
'I lost a child the last Time you were at a distance.' Everything seemed to go wrong when Johnson was absent.

While at Brighton on this melancholy errand, Mrs. Thrale,
following Johnson's advice, had had a long conversation with
Mr. Scrase, the old solicitor, who had come to the rescue of
the brewery three years before. With the death of one son,
and as she thought the possible extinction of the whole family,
it was important that some settlement should be made of her
Welsh property. The substance of this talk with Scrase she
wrote down immediately, 'not caring', as she admitted to
Johnson, 'to trust either my Memory or my Veracity—so you
& I may both be sure that what I read to you is true'. She
added that she had named Johnson and Cator her trustees, '&
that is the wisest thing I have done in it'.[1] This summary of
Mrs. Thrale's talk with Scrase, together with their later correspondence, explains in detail the legal arrangements which were
finally made in regard to Bach-y-Graig. With quixotic impetuosity Mrs. Thrale wished to settle her Welsh property
permanently on her eldest son, with 'remainder' to the sons of
her daughters, or other heirs of her husband. When Scrase
mildly suggested that should Thrale and her children die she
might presumably have children by a second husband, she was

---

[1] July 18, 1775. The actual summary of their talk, written down by Mrs. Thrale
at the time, still survives (Ry. 600, 23).

shocked at the idea. Such a contingency seemed perfectly absurd, and Mrs. Thrale was determined to ignore it. But the kindly old solicitor knew too well the uncertainty of human relationships. So on July 30 he wrote to Thrale himself, objecting to the proposed plan as very improper. 'It is expressly Mrs. Thrales Idea,' he insisted, 'her first Object, after providing for her Children, to give you all she has in the world in the fullest extent.' Scrase urged that no absolute entail be set up—that the settlement be so arranged that '*you & Mrs. T. during your Joint Lives* may at any time revoke or alter the Limitations proposed'.[1]

Throughout the discussion Mrs. Thrale had required that nothing definite should be decided until the return of Dr. Johnson, who lingered on in Ashbourne and Lichfield. Instead of returning as she so wished, he wrote long, affectionate letters full of advice and comfort. Sometimes he wondered what would become of this correspondence, and on August 2, when asking her, point blank, if she kept his letters, admitted that he thought he should like to read them in later years.

For though there is in them not much history of mind, or any thing else, they will, I hope, always be in some degree the records of a pure and blameless friendship, and in some hours of languour and sadness may revive the memory of more cheerful times.

Finally, by August 17, Johnson was back at Streatham, and with a few minor exceptions gave his approval to the agreement as suggested by Scrase and drawn up by Robson the attorney. Mrs. Thrale kept discretionary power over her estate, an arrangement for which she was one day to bless Scrase. On September 5, when the document was signed, Johnson found himself one of two trustees in technical control of the Salusbury estate of Bach-y-Graig.[2]

In several of his letters throughout the summer Johnson had asked whether the Thrales intended to go to Brighton as usual for the autumn season. Never particularly enjoying the Sussex resort, he undoubtedly hoped for some more interesting journey. Baretti, too, was eager to introduce his friends to the delight of continental travel, with himself as cicerone. Mrs. Thrale was well, for once not expecting a child; all the surviving children appeared healthy; and it seemed an auspicious time. Though Italy was too far, Paris might easily be enjoyed during

[1] Ry. 600, 26.
[2] A photostatic copy of this settlement is in the National Library of Wales at Aberystwyth.

the favourable months before winter set in. Accordingly, the same company which had toured Wales the summer before set off on September 15 for France, with the addition of Baretti, who, speaking French fluently, acted more or less as a courier for the party and kept accurate accounts of all the minor expenses.[1]

Again Mrs. Thrale kept a separate journal devoted to the tour.[2] She began: 'Notwithstanding the Disgust my last Journey gave me, I have lately been solicitous to undertake another. So true is Johnson's Observation that any thing is better than Vacuity.' In day-by-day entries she told as before the itinerary which they followed and the people and places visited. And while her vivid picture of the France of Louis XVI has more general interest for us than the former accounts of Welsh scenery, many of the best touches are still autobiographical.

At first the foreign language was something of a hindrance, for despite her reading knowledge of French she had the usual difficulty with the spoken word. Johnson refused to attempt the vernacular, but found many people willing to converse with him in Latin. So at Rouen he had a long talk with an interesting abbé, and Mrs. Thrale noted:

We supt this Night with Madame du Perron & her Circle of Wits, where Johnson once more met his Friend the Abbé & entered into a most ingenious Argument with him concerning the demolition of the Jesuits. Mr. Thrale was enchanted with the Conversation & I never knew his Judgment fail: I had myself no Power to attend to their Talk, I had so much trouble to make myself understood; which however I contrived to manage somehow.[3]

Soon, however, she was able to rattle away easily, if not grammatically, to the Frenchmen whom she met, and once amusingly added:

Our two agreeable Foreigners came [in] after the Italian Comedy, and we had a good Deal of Literary Chat, sometimes in English, sometimes in French, sometimes in Latin, sometimes in Italian; we all made Mistakes & those Mistakes made us laugh—[4]

At the beginning, while filling her diary with comments, she

---

[1] Baretti's detailed account of expenses is in my possession. Together with Mrs. Herbert Evans and Dr. L. F. Powell, I also have a number of the French bills for purchases made on this journey.

[2] *French Journals of Mrs. Thrale and Doctor Johnson*, ed. by M. Tyson and H. Guppy (Manchester, 1932). Since this excellent edition of the French journal is easily available, only a short account is included here.

[3] Ibid., pp. 84–5.   [4] Ibid., pp. 106–7.

was chary of attempting generalizations. Indeed, she wrote,
'I will relate only what I see—which can hardly fail of being
true'.[1] There was much to see: the churches, shops, theatres,
even the Queen of France attending a theatrical performance.
On Mrs. Thrale's first visit to the Continent it was natural that
she should be greatly impressed by the differences in manners
and social conventions. English travellers throughout the
eighteenth century (and perhaps in other centuries) were not
noted for their sympathetic desire to understand strange customs, and Mrs. Thrale had the usual insular distaste for many
things she saw. What seemed to her 'intolerable Grossness'
brought the remark:

The Youngest and prettiest Ladies of the Court will hawk and
spit straight before them without the least Attention to Delicacy, &
today at the Horse Race we were shewn a Woman of Condition
riding astride wth: her thick Legs [totally] uncovered except by
her Stockings [ye whiteness of] which attracted all Eyes to look on
them.[2]

Even trade was unfavourably criticized.

The Shops here at Paris are particularly mean & the Trades-
people surly & disagreeable; a Mercer will not shew you above
half a Dozen Silks & those he will not cut,—they run in Pieces for
Gowns & you are obliged to buy all or none.

Frank in deriding what she considered vulgar or inconvenient,
she was as open in commending what she thought elegant and
suitable, even occasionally trying to learn rather than merely
to pass hasty judgement. At an Italian play, the buffoonery of
which disgusted her, she was willing to agree with Baretti 'that
to criticise a Comedy without knowing the Characteristicks of
the Nation is impossible', and ended her account with the
admission 'I therefore returned home, not entertained—because
my Taste differs from theirs, but not disappointed, because I
have gained some Knowledge'.[3] As the years went by, she was
to develop more and more of this objective ability to accept
foreign customs differing from her own.

The days passed rapidly in the glow of Parisian life: visits
to the churches, to convents, and to the theatre; long conversations with new-found acquaintances; even a trip to Versailles
for a view of the royal family at dinner (vastly pleased she was
here to have the Queen ask questions about little Queeney).

---

[1] Ibid., p. 94.   [2] Ibid., pp. 100–1.   [3] Ibid., pp. 109–10.

Throughout the trip she and Johnson kept up an amusing badinage, teasing each other about personal preferences and dislikes. One evening late in October, when the others of the party had gone to the theatre, she noted, 'I was not well enough to venture so Mr Johnson sat at home by me, & we criticised & talked & were happy in one another—he in huffing me & I in being huff'd.'[1] She did not confine all her repartee to the immediate family. One *bon mot* even made its way back to London, and was printed in the newspapers.

The French, it seems, exult very much upon our inability to subdue the Colonists. A French gentleman, who sat near to Mrs. Th—le at an Opera in Paris, asked her when she thought the Americans would be conquered? 'Upon my word', said the lady, 'that is a question not easily to be answered: When America belonged to the French, the English found no difficulty in subduing it; but now that it is defended by our countrymen, the task of conquering it is not so easy.'[2]

In Paris Mrs. Thrale could gratify one of her favourite passions—that for pictures. Graphic art had always appealed to her more than either music or architecture, and she was transported by her first real view of great Italian paintings. Titian, Raphael, the Bolognese school, brought rhapsodies from the astonished novice. In her journal for October 6 she made the entry: 'This has been my happiest Day hitherto; I have spent it with English Men & among Italian Pictures.' For the next month she continually commented on what she saw in the galleries, and on the last day in Paris she spent three hours in the Palais Royal looking again at the Orleans collection.

The 1st of November the travellers left Paris, and having slowly made their way back to England by way of Chantilly, Cambray, Douay, Lille, and Dunquerque, they were safely settled once again at Streatham by the middle of the month.[3] This first short visit to France had widened Mrs. Thrale's perspective, had given her a taste for European travel and Italian pictures, and had strengthened her determination some day to visit other parts of the Continent.

Immediately upon her return to England she was precipitated again into anxiety and the care of a sick child, when the seven-months old Frances Ann became seriously ill in an

[1] *French Journals*, p. 143.
[2] *Morning Chronicle*, Nov. 27, 1775; *Weekly Miscellany* (Dec. 1775), p. 285, &c.
[3] On Nov. 18, shortly after their return, Thrale presented an address to the King from the Merchants of Southwark (*Morning Chronicle*, Nov. 20, 1775).

epidemic of influenza. The mother's first thought was that, like the others, the trouble was in the brain, but Dr. Lawrence insisted that this time there were different symptoms. Whatever the cause, the child grew steadily worse, and died on December 9, her death being presently followed by that of the nurse who had principally taken care of her.

Through these dark days Mrs. Thrale's one continual comfort was her nine-year-old son, Harry.[1] The year before she had written of him in the Children's Book:

A better or finer, a wiser or kinder Boy than Harry cannot be found: he goes to Jenning's free School here in Southwark, & is half adored by Master and Scholars, by Parents & Servants—by all the Clerks—by all his Friends and Acquaintance. he has Charity, Piety, Benevolence; he has a desire of Knowledge far above his Years, and is perpetually passing by Boys of ten Years old at the same School: he always does his Exercise at a Night in my Dressing room, and we always part after that is over pleased with each other —he is so rational, so attentive, so good; nobody can help being pleased with him.[2]

All the affection which she had lavished on her darling Lucy was now concentrated on the sturdy boy. The devoted mother was more amused than shocked to find that while she was in France he had been severely punished at Loughborough School for telling bawdy stories to the other boys. She admitted he was a bit 'too *forward* in *some* things', particularly in his reading.

The other Day Bob Cotton was saying how he had saved some Lady on Horseback from great Danger— Oh ho cries Harry I'll warrant you'll marry her at last as Tom Jones did Miss Sophy Western! Lord Child say'd I didst thou ever read Tom Jones?— Yes to be sure replies Harry One *must* read Tom Jones, & Joseph Andrews.[3]

Yet she was proud of his ability to construe Ovid, and recorded that he 'does his Tasks with a degree of Intelligence that Dr. Johnson says is not common even at 12 years old'. With a happy, open disposition, the boy was a universal favourite.

On February 15, 1776, Harry was allowed to ask his own company for a birthday party.

His selection was Murphy, Perkins & Tom Cotton, to whom I added a friendly Atty. here in the Borough, & Count Mannucci who we knew at paris came in by Chance. he landed Yesterday.

---

[1] Children's Book. Two letters from Harry, directed to his mother in Paris, dated Oct. 14 and 21, 1775, are in the collection of Sir Randle Mainwaring.
[2] Jan. 20, 1775.   [3] Nov. 25, 1775.

Old Perney & little Blake from Loughboro' House filled up our heterogeneous Mess of Company, & Johnson was here of Course; he *does* love little Harry!

There were even more exciting things to think about than her son's wit and good humour, for since the French excursion had proved so pleasant it was decided that the same group should go to Italy in 1776. Baretti again was to act as courier, and he immediately set to work to make all necessary arrangements. Writing to friends and relatives in Italy, Baretti explained about the preparations and added interesting comments about the various members of the party. Thrale, he insisted, was a thorough gentleman, never out of humour for a minute.

He only speaks a very little French, unlike his wife, who talks French and Italian fluently, without troubling about their quality, and likes to talk them, and is bright and lively. She is, however, shocked at the least offence against religion or morality, for she is very fond of her Bible.[1]

Suggesting to his brother that there be a supply of old books about, Baretti added that the lady understood Latin perfectly, that like her husband she was interested in agricultural affairs, was very fond of her chickens, understood the making of cheese and butter, and liked to talk familiarly with the country people. Of little Queeney he added that he loved her seven thousand times more than he had ever loved anyone else.

In another letter, written in March, Baretti explained that the travellers were to set out on April 8 in three four-wheeled chaises. The three Thrales, Johnson, and himself would occupy two of them, and in the other would be a maid and a groom, with another servant to follow on horseback. A German courier was to precede the party, and other temporary servants would be secured in the various cities in which they stayed. Baretti hinted that, although the brewer had a tendency to economy, he intended to be comfortable when travelling.[2]

Johnson was greatly excited at the prospect and wrote to Boswell to hasten his coming to London, as they were soon to depart. He wished to have his company on a farewell visit to friends in Oxford, Lichfield, and Ashbourne before setting out on the long journey from which a man of his age might never

---

[1] Translated in L. Collison Morley's *Giuseppe Baretti and His Friends* (1909), p. 289. The original version may be found in Giuseppe Baretti, *Epistolario*, ed. L. Piccioni, ii (Bari, 1936), 149. See also *Life*, iii. 470–1.
[2] Collison Morley, p. 286; Piccioni, ii. 160.

return. Boswell obligingly hurried south, and on March 19 they left for the Midlands.[1]

Suddenly, while plans for the Italian tour progressed apace, a dreadful catastrophe in the Thrale family threw everything into the utmost confusion. Mrs. Thrale's dramatic account in the Children's Book minutely describes every detail.[2] On Wednesday, March 20, all was well in the household. The next day, after Susan had been brought home from Mrs. Cumyns' for a week, Queeney complained of feeling ill.

Harry however had seen a play of his Friend Murphy's advertised, & teized me so to let him see it that I could not resist his Importunity, and treated one of our principal Clerks to go with him: he came home at 12 o'clock half mad with delight, and in such Spirits Health & Happiness that nothing ever exceeded: Queeney however drooped all Afternoon, complained of the Headack & Mr. Thrale was so cross at my giving Harry leave to go to the play, instead of shewing him to Sir Robert; that I passed an uneasy Time of it, and could not enjoy the praises given to Susan, I was so fretted about the two eldest. when Harry came home so happy however, all was forgotten, & he went to rest in perfect Tranquillity—Queeney however felt hot, & I was not at all pleased with her, but on Fryday Morning the boy rose quite chearful & did our little Business with great Alacrity. Count Mannucci came to Breakfast by Appointment, we were all to go shew him the Tower forsooth, so Queeney made light of her Illness & pressed me to take her too. There was one of the Ships bound for Boston now in the River with our Beer aboard—Harry ran to see the blaze in the Morning, & coming back to the compting house—I see says he to our 1st. Clerk—I see Your Porter is good Mr. Perkins; for it *burns* special well. Well by this Time we set out for the Tower, Papa & Mannucci, & the Children & I: Queeney was not half well, but Harry continued in high Spirits both among the Lyons & the Arms: repeating Passages from the English History, examining the Artillery & getting into every Mortar till he was as black as the Ground. . . . From this Place we drove to Moore's Carpet Manufactory, where the Boy was still active, attentive & lively: but as Queeney's looks betray'd the Sickness She would fain have concealed, we drove homewards; taking in our way Brooke's Menagerie, where I just stopped to speak about my Peafowl: Here Harry was happy again with a Lyon intended for a Show who was remarkably tame, & a monkey so beautiful & gentle, that I was as much pleased with him as the Children: here we met a Mr. Hervey who took notice of the Boy how *well* he look'd, Yes said I, if the dirt were scraped off him:

That night Harry went to bed as perfectly well as at any

[1] *Life*, ii. 423, 24, 38.
[2] The record fills twelve pages, and was written probably on Apr. 9, 1776.

time in his life, but Queeney was still feverish and drooping. On the 23d the boy had breakfast, as he loved to do, with the young clerks at the brewhouse, seemingly in the best of health:

After this he returned with two peny cakes he had bought for the little Girls, & distributed them between them in his pleasant Manner for Minuets that he made them dance.

All this while Mrs. Thrale was waiting on her eldest daughter and tutoring Sophy till the clock struck ten. Then Molly the maid came to tell her that Queeney was better, but 'Harry making a Figure of 5:10 so we always called his manner of twisting about when anything ailed him'. At first no one was especially alarmed, but later, when his mother saw the boy's 'Sickness increase, & his Countenance begin to alter', she sent out a servant,

with orders not to come back without *some* Physician—Jebb, Bromfield, Pinkstan or Lawrence of Essex Street, whichever he could find: in the mean time I plunged Harry into Water as hot as could easily be borne up to his middle, & had just taken him out of the Tub, & laid him in a warm bed, when Jebb came, & gave him 1st. hot Wine, them Usquebaugh, then Daffy's Elixer, so fast that it alarmed me; tho' I had no Notion of *Death* having seen him so perfectly well at 9 o'clock.

In spite of everything the Doctor could do with emetics and poultices, Harry continued to grow worse throughout the morning. Even then only the mother, who was 'all confusion distress & perplexity', thought his illness serious,

& Mr. Thrale bid me not cry so, for I should look like a Hag when I went to Court next Day—he often saw Harry in the Course of the morng. and apprehended no danger at all—no more did Baretti, who said he should be whipt for frighting his mother for nothing.

Then suddenly the symptoms became worse, and by the middle of the afternoon the boy was dead, undoubtedly from a ruptured appendix.

Summoned back by news of the calamity, Baretti found the household in disorder. He later described the terrible scene:

Mr. Thrale, both his hands in his waistcoat pockets, sat on an arm-chair in a corner of the room with his body so stiffly erect, and with such a ghastly smile in his face, as was quite horrid to behold. Count Manucci and a female servant, both as pale as ashes, and as if panting for breath, were evidently spent with keeping madam from going frantic (and well she might) every time she recovered from her fainting-fits, that followed each other in a very quick succession.[1]

For the rest of that day and the two following Mrs. Thrale remained in a state of complete collapse. Lady Lade kindly took the younger children to Kensington, but Queeney, who had been ailing before, was too ill to be moved.

When, on March 28, Harry was buried at Streatham, there was interred with him all the hope and pride of the Thrales. To the distracted mother nothing seemed left but to try to save the life of her eldest daughter, to salvage one treasure from the wreck of their prospects. Dr. Jebb recommended immediate change of scene, and after several sleepless nights, Mrs. Thrale in desperation decided to take her daughter to Bath. Accepting Baretti's offer to accompany them, she made ready to start on the 29th. Just as they were setting out, Johnson arrived.[2] He had heard the tragic news in Lichfield, and after a hasty trip to Ashbourne had hurried back to be of service to his friends. Shocked to find his Mistress about to leave on a journey, according to Baretti, he did not offer to take the Italian's place on the melancholy expedition; instead Johnson thought best to remain behind to comfort the father.

That hurried drive to Bath was a distressing one, even if Baretti was indefatigable in diverting Queeney's languor 'with all the Tricks he could think on'.[3] Nor was Bath much better at first, for Mrs. Thrale and Baretti, both nervous and on edge, were soon at each other's throats. Queeney had for years been troubled with worms, for which the only successful remedy seemed to be a mild type of 'tin pill'. Mrs. Thrale, like Dr. Johnson, delighted in doctoring herself and all connected with her, but Baretti had the strong man's fear and distaste for all medicines. He flew into a tantrum when he found the mother giving Queeney 'tin pills' against the advice of Dr. Jebb. A violent quarrel ensued, which neither ever forgot or forgave, although Mrs. Thrale the next morning presented her opponent

---

[1] G. Baretti, *Prefazioni e Polemiche*, ed. L. Piccioni (Bari, 1933), p. 336 (reprint of first Stricture in the *European Magazine* of May, 1788).

[2] Boswell indicates (*Life*, iii. 6) that Johnson was hurt at finding his Mistress on the point of departure, just as he arrived. If this is so, he did not show his pique in letters to Mrs. Thrale. The exact date of their setting out is not clear. In the Children's Book she indicates that it was the morning of the 30th; yet Boswell and Johnson returned to London on the 29th. Boswell's letter of condolence from Mr. Dilly's in the Poultry, dated Friday, Mar. 29, 1776, is certain proof of this fact. Possibly, since the wording of the passage in the Children's Book is not explicit, Mrs. Thrale may have referred to their arrival at Bath on the 30th rather than their departure from Southwark.

[3] Children's Book (see p. 135, n. 2).

with a leather memorandum book to show she was willing to overlook the incident. Baretti's strong words rankled deep, however, as she admitted in a later letter to Johnson.[1]

After a week at Bath, Queeney was so much improved that they hastily returned to London by Easter Sunday, April 7.[2] Baretti was in a frenzy to know how this tragedy would affect the plans for the Italian journey. Insisting that after so many arrangements had been made the Thrales would look ridiculous if no trip at all were taken, he pleaded that nothing be changed. But Thrale had lost all heart for the journey. On April 9, when Mrs. Thrale went out to Streatham, she left the two men still arguing, but later in the day she wrote to Johnson that her Master held to his purpose to give up the tour, and that Baretti 'teizes no more'. With all hope extinguished in the death of his only son, Thrale's mood was that of black despair. During his wife's absence at Bath he had even refused to have Johnson with him in the Borough house where he brooded alone. Finally on the 9th the dam of his emotions gave way. 'Mr. Thrale has seen your Letter', his wife added to Johnson, '& shed Tears over reading it—they are the first he has shed—I can say no more—' In the Children's Book she concluded her account: 'So ends my Pride, my hopes, my possession of present, & expectation of future Delight.' 'Childless with all her Children—wants an heir'—is it any wonder that the Mistress of Streatham felt herself pursued by a relentless and vindictive fate?

---

[1] Bath, May 3, 1776. *Letters to and from Johnson* (1788), pp. 316–19. See also Baretti, *Prefazioni e Polemiche*, op. cit., pp. 338–41.

[2] *Private Papers*, xi. 231. Boswell records seeing Mrs. Thrale and her daughters on this day.

VII

WIDENING ACQUAINTANCE

APRIL 1776–FEBRUARY 1778

STUNNED by the sudden death of their only son, the Thrales had no inclination to set out on a continental journey. But some change of scene was necessary to restore the health and spirits of the grief-stricken family. Accordingly Bath, which had proved so beneficial immediately after the catastrophe, was substituted for Italy, a change which naturally proved a great disappointment to Johnson. He philosophically approved the decision, however, in contrast to Baretti, who was very angry. Having gone to some expenditure of time and money to make the necessary arrangements for the tour, Baretti felt himself cheated and aggrieved. To make up this loss, Thrale presented him with a hundred guineas, which salved his purse, if not his pride.[1]

About the middle of April 1776, with Queeney and Johnson, the Thrales set out for Bath, where they found lodgings in the Corner House on the North Parade. Mrs. Thrale thus described their arrangements in the Children's Book.

> Mr. Thrale slept on the 1st. Floor next the Dining room, Johnson slept on the 2d. Floor, so did Queeney, so of course did I: and there were some dirty Irish people lodged in the Parlours. I think says Hetty our House is like the Tree in Sophy's Fable Book. The *Eagles* inhabit the Top, the *Fox* possesses the Middle, & the *pigs* wallow at the bottom.

In recent letters of condolence Johnson had advised his Mistress not to indulge in grief. 'Remember', said he, 'the great precept, *Be not solitary; be not idle*', and later, 'Keep yourself busy, and you will in time grow cheerful.'[2] She now religiously followed this advice, and instead of remaining closely secluded threw herself into the diversions of the place. She realized that the best way to forget was to push on to new interests.

She did not lack agreeable companions. Boswell, who had

---

[1] Hayward, i. 103–8. See also *French Journals*, pp. 252–5, and Collison Morley, pp. 292–301.   [2] *Letters*, Nos. 466, 470.

never been at Bath, decided this would be a good opportunity to see it in the company of his friends. He arrived on the 26th and secured a room at the Pelican Inn close to their lodgings. Mrs. Thrale also encountered her old childhood playmate and distant cousin, Miss Margaret Owen, from Penrhos near Shrewsbury, whose simple, unaffected good humour, combined with Boswell's exuberance, helped to drive away despondency.[1] In a congenial, entertaining group, free from household cares, Mrs. Thrale found the life at Bath much to her liking.

Queeney and Johnson, on the other hand, were not so favourably impressed. When someone asked the eleven-year-old girl what she thought of the Rooms and the company, she replied: 'I think the Room very like the *South Sea house*; & the Company—very like *the Clerks*.'[2] On another occasion, when Mrs. Thrale pointed out to her daughter the famous Mrs. Macaulay, the child replied, 'I have seen the two great Literary Ladies—Mrs. Montagu & Mrs. Macaulay; and I have seen—that one wears *Black Wool* in Her Ears, and that the other—wears *White*.' This was what Baretti called Queeney's 'laconism'. Nor did Johnson find much to interest him in the crowded, bustling place. There was too much idle chatter and not enough thinking to suit his taste, and he was not sorry to be called back to London to help his friend, Dr. Taylor, on a legal matter. Promising to return as soon as the business was settled, he left on May 3.

Mrs. Thrale could never cut herself off entirely from maternal worries, for shortly after Johnson's departure word came from Kensington that her two younger daughters had the chicken-pox. As she wrote to Johnson on the 8th, the illness, 'though a trifling Thing in any other Family, might for ought I knew prove fatal in my ill fated House'. Fortunately, however, word had come the next day that they were recovering, so that she could add, 'I believe one Night's crying will do—& that I have already had'. Letters from Baretti, who made frequent trips to Kensington to see the girls, also helped to calm her fears.[3]

Throughout May 1776 the Thrales continued at Bath, while Johnson put off his return, giving as a reason the insistence of Dr. Taylor. Finally, towards the end of the month, after visit-

---

[1] Miss Margaret Owen of Penrhos was almost the same age as Mrs. Thrale. She died unmarried at Shrewsbury on Oct. 25, 1816, aged 73. See B. G. Charles, 'Peggy Owen and Her Streatham Friends', *Cornhill Mag.* clx (1939), 334–51. Also *Gent. Mag.* (May, 1833), p. 418.

[2] This and the following anecdotes were recorded in the Children's Book.

[3] Baretti wrote on May 11, 12, and 17 (Ry, 541, 6, 7, 8).

ing Stonehenge, Southampton, and Portsmouth, the travellers returned to London. Upon leaving home in April, the Thrales had dismissed most of their servants, and they were now faced with the prospect of securing a new staff. But it was some time before Mrs. Thrale was able to get Streatham running smoothly, for immediately after her return she was stricken with cholera morbus.[1] On June 7, though still weak, she scribbled a note to Johnson, informing him of her improvement in health, but suggesting that since he was suffering from gout, he had better not come home until he was well.

What should we do together if both want nursing? for I have here no Superfluity of Conveniencies at present, nor have had Time or Ability to get any about me.

Actually it was not until late in June that Mrs. Thrale had her family all about her again at Streatham. Sadly she could not but remember that the year before there had been six children and that now there were only three. In twelve short months she had lost two sons and a daughter.

About the 1st of July, when Thrale went off for a short fishing holiday, his wife decided to send him news of the household in the form of a verse epistle in the easy rhythm of Christopher Anstey's *New Bath Guide*.

> While you are amused with your Rickmansworth Fishing
> And see the Red Trout look so crimson the Dish in
> What says my dear Master to our pleasant fancy
> Of trying to emulate great Mr. Anstie?
> That we by some means for your sport may provide
> You may read as you travel this new *Streatham Guide*;
> Here then we begin—our Adventures rehearse
> Which can't be more easy in Prose than in Verse;
> For where there is nothing to tell 'tis much better
> To make all the bustle one can with a Letter:
> So to Wickam on last Monday morning we drove
> To carry our Compliments, Service, and Love;
> Mrs. Nesbit was just driven out at the Door,
> But had left Master Arny, the Dogs & Miss More
> With a young tawny Brat of their new Commodore.
> They offered us Cherries, Tea, Coffee and Cake,
> But few of their Bounties would Queeney partake;
> And for my part I fretted that Poppet and Ramper,
> Had had for no purpose so silly a Scamper.
> I ask'd of their Butler, and heard he was nice,
> Possessing no Virtue, if charged with no Vice;

---

[1] Her illness is described in the Children's Book.

Not an Englishman stout, nor an Irishman bony,
But a man half a miss, a perfumed Macaroni:
They discard him with Pleasure—why we should receive
Is more than my Wit can find out—with your leave,
Unless the mere name of Nesbitt contains
Some strange hidden power of warming one's Brains;
And they themselves fancy that Albert's wise man
Will put their Affairs on a wonderful Plan:
Since this Fellow then seems only something to titter at
I vote for the Man you say liv'd with Vansittart;
And I wish he'd make haste at our Table to wait,
Get matters in order, and brush up the plate,
For on Saturday next Lady Cotton & they come,
Besides a whole Troop I invited from Wycombe,
And we shall look desperate foolish indeed,
If of Plate and of Servants we stand so in need.
Well! so much for Business, 'tis time to be telling
What mischief our matters Domestic have fell in;
Our Dogs by the Tulippomania possest,
Everlastingly fighting, will give us no Rest;
Our Pea-Chickens droop, and our Pheasants don't lay
And the Weather's uncertain for cutting the Hay;
But the Children are happy, unless perhaps Hetty
While conning her lesson for Mr. Baretti;
If Johnson and he would come home with some news
My Letter'd have much better chance to amuse;

.   .   .   .

I would willingly now close my Letter to you
But more serious Misfortunes will plead for their due
Our Friend Mrs. Parker's in real Distress
Send somebody over—you can do no less.
Her Sister was burnt in last Monday's sad Fire
If you send a Man over he'll further enquire;
But oh my dear Love! what a sad World is this!
The Sorrow so frequent, so scanty the Bliss;
That one cannot one's Cares for a moment beguile
Nor draw from one's Husband an innocent Smile,'
But the gloom of Concern over shadows our Day, ·
And shews us that Man was not made to be gay.[1]

From this it seems evident that Baretti, although irritated
with the Thrale family, still continued his instruction of

[1] Volume of manuscript poetry in the possession of Dr. A. S. W. Rosenbach.
Also Mainwaring Piozziana, i. 87–91. The date has been ascertained from internal
evidence, particularly the fire at Mr. Booth's house which occurred on Saturday
morning, June 29, 1776 (*Morning Chronicle*, July 1, 1776). Mrs. Thrale's note to
Johnson of July 2 refers to Baretti's expected return on that day (Ry. 540, 61). The
word 'Tulippomania' is made up from the name of the Thrale's bitch, Tulip.

Queeney. But he was nearing the limit of his endurance. From the beginning of the arrangement, three years before, he and Mrs. Thrale had been antagonistic. Even in the early days of their acquaintance her admiration for his literary ability, and the physical comfort which he secured in the Streatham household, had barely sufficed to keep the two from irreconcilable quarrels. Everyone sensed this mutual distrust. Johnson himself had remarked to Boswell, earlier in the year:

> Mrs. Thrale did not like Baretti, nor Baretti her. But he was the best teacher of Italian that she could have for her daughter, therefore she kept him in the house. Baretti was well entertained and well paid, therefore he staid in the house. He lived there as at an Inn. I suppose he meant, gave value for what he got, and did not mind whether the Landlady liked him or no.[1]

Baretti resented the lady's pretensions to wit and learning, and he was especially indignant at what he considered her cruel treatment of her children. In the matter of discipline the two could not agree Mrs. Thrale believing that physical punishment was often necessary to secure obedience, Baretti advocating complete indulgence. He represented the type of bachelor who adored all young girls and imagined that affection was all that was necessary to insure docility and effective co-operation. With a mother and tutor holding such divergent opinions, there is little wonder that there was friction. Mrs. Thrale was positive that Baretti was constantly inciting his pupils to rebel, and he insisted that her severe punishment ruined all his efforts to teach by kindness.[2] Of course the children welcomed their tutor's open advocacy, being quick to use him to gain more indulgences for themselves. Yet it is significant that while his underhand thwarting of Mrs. Thrale helped to widen the natural breach between mother and daughters, there is no unprejudiced evidence that his devotion was rewarded by any unselfish attachment on their part.[3]

Following the indefinite postponement of the Italian tour,

[1] *Private Papers*, xi. 202; Mar. 26, 1776.
[2] Hayward, i. 103-9.
[3] Susan Burney wrote Aug. 1, 1779, to Fanny of a trip to Streatham, when she and Queeney had some talk. Susan recorded. 'She was to meet Mr. Baretti that day, with Mr. and Mrs. Thrale at *Mr. Caters*, I think, and did not seem much delighted by the idea' (*Early Diary of F. Burney*, ii. 259). Shortly after the quarrel, in July 1776, Mrs. Thrale noted in the Children's Book that Queeney apparently had 'no great Kindness for any body. Baretti endeavoured by flattery, Caresses, & even by inciting her on all occasions to Oppose my will, & shake off my Authority, to obtain her Friendship:—but in vain! when he was gone she could not suppress her Joy'.

and with little likelihood of any permanent annuity from Thrale, Baretti's feelings for the whole family, with the exception of his beloved *Esteruccia*, turned to active dislike. The teaching became more desultory, and his absences from the house longer and more frequent. The final break came the first week in July 1776. Thrown into a frenzy by various arguments over servants and guests, the Italian quietly packed his effects to be sent after him to London, and on the morning of July 6 stalked off to the city without taking leave.[1] This was his way of asserting his independence. For her part, Mrs. Thrale was not sorry to see him go; the household would be quieter and her daughters more amenable without his interference. She little suspected, however, what a bitter form his hatred would take in the future.

The tragic mortality of her children left Mrs. Thrale exhausted and disillusioned. No longer could she throw herself with untiring enthusiasm into the education of her daughters. On July 23, 1776, Sophia, the youngest, was five years old, and her mother recorded in the Children's Book:

> She Has read three Epistles & three Gospels: I do not make her get much by heart: The Thing is—I have really listened to Babies Learning till I am half stupefied—& all my pains have answered so poorly—I have no heart to battle with Sophy: She would probably learn very well, if I had the spirit of teaching I once had . . .

The child, she felt, had good parts and a desire to please, but,

> I will not make her Life miserable as I suppose it will be short—not for want of Health indeed, for no Girl can have better, but Harry & Lucy are dead, & why should Sophy live? The instructions I labor'd to give *them*—what did they end in? the Grave—& every recollection brings only new Regret. Sophy shall read well, & learn her Prayers; & take her chance for more, when I can get it for her. At Present I can not begin battling with Babies—I have already spent my whole Youth at it & lost my Reward at last.

It probably seemed to Mrs. Thrale that the cause of all her trouble was some fatal taint in the Thrale blood; but from the standpoint of modern medicine, we may suspect that the weakness was less one of inheritance than of exhaustion from too rapid a series of childbirths.[2]

---

[1] Hayward, i. 105; Collison Morley, pp. 296–301.

[2] Dr. Ernest Sadler informs me that from his examinations of the evidence he feels that there is no certainty that the children's deaths were caused by any inherited taint. Thrale's occasional venereal disease does not seem to have been passed on to his wife or children. Dr. Sadler maintains that it was the frequent and rapid bearing of children (a common cause of delicacy in children) which rendered them susceptible to outside infections. He adds: 'Of the 12 children, 7 followed the

Of the three girls still living, Queeney, Susanna, and Sophia, the elder two had always been cold and unsympathetic. Mrs. Thrale once described them:

Susan's Temper is not good, she denies her Knowlege to avoid exhibiting; Mr. Johnson says she is therein the wiser—I do not suspect her Wisdom, I suspect her for having no natural Compliance in her Disposition . . . There is something strangely perverse in Queeney's Temper, full of Bitterness and Aversion to all who instruct her . . . Sophy is more like other people's children; of a soft gay Disposition—thanks one for a Cake & cries if she gets a Cuff; the others put one in Mind of what my Father said of a Wench that lived with us in old Times—'Tis all one to this Girl if she is kiss'd or kick't She can but hate one and she does that naturally.[1]

Queeney and Susan resembled their father in stolid common sense and unresponsiveness. Her own favourites, the high-spirited Anna Maria, the affectionate Lucy, and the manly Harry had been of a different temperament, more congenial to her own. She continued to be proud of Queeney and the others, but her heart was buried in the graves of Lucy and Harry. It is significant that in later years she often referred to the three elder as 'Mr. Thrale's daughters' or the 'Miss Thrales'. Almost she seemed to regard them as not of her own flesh and blood. The younger ones were kept away at school as much as possible, and gradually the mother gave less and less time to the affairs of the nursery. Since her children were doomed, there was no reason to waste her life in useless struggles; instead, she deliberately sought more diversion in the role of literary hostess and woman of fashion.

Mrs. Thrale's early journals had been, ostensibly, records of her family and famous friends. Now came the impulse to turn from writing about her children, her husband, her guests, to something more definitely autobiographical. So on September 15, 1776, she began a new journal with the entry;

It is many Years since Doctor Samuel Johnson advised me to get a little Book, and write in it all the little Anecdotes which might come to my Knowledge, all the Observations I might make or hear, all the Verses never likely to be published, and in fine ev'ry thing which struck me at the Time. Mr. Thrale has now treated me with a Repository,—and provided it with the pompous Title of Thraliana; I must endeavour to fill it with Nonsense new and old.

previous one within 14 or 15 months; several of them after 13 months, one of them after only a year, and one even as early as 11 months. Small and puny children would be likely to be born under such conditions. The strongest of all, the one who lived longest, was Hetty, the eldest, which is what one would expect.'

[1] Children's Book, Dec. 21, 1776.

It is true that anecdotes of other people and remembrances of past events were to play a considerable part in the new record, but for the first time she herself was to be the principal subject. The whole tone of Thraliana is personal; yet, strictly speaking, it is more a commonplace book than a diary. For one thing, in the early volumes there is no semblance of chronology, many of the entries being copied from earlier records without reference to dating. Even in the later volumes the chronology is often obscure, and frequent long gaps of time in which nothing apparently was set down render it often difficult (though by no means always impossible) to conjecture the day when the entry was made.

On one occasion, when Johnson suspected she was spending much of her time writing in Thraliana, he urged her to be careful of dates:

As you have now little to do, I suppose you are pretty diligent at the Thraliana, and a very curious collection posterity will find it. Do not remit the practice of writing down occurrences as they arise, of whatever kind, and be very punctual in annexing the dates. Chronology you know is the eye of history; and every man's life is of importance to himself. Do not omit painful casualties, or unpleasing passages, they make the variegation of existence; and there are many transactions, of which I will not promise with Æneas, *et hæc olim meminisse juvabit.* Yet that remembrance which is not pleasant may be useful. There is however an intemperate attention to slight circumstances which is to be avoided, lest a great part of life be spent in writing the history of the rest. Every day perhaps has something to be noted, but in a settled and uniform course few days can have much.[1]

Johnson's concern about disregard to dates also extended to her correspondence. He continually called her attention to this fault, though occasionally guilty himself of the same lapse, and at the close of one of his letters added a postscript, 'Now there is a date; look at it.'[2] Nevertheless, neither his suggestion of regular numbering of her letters, nor that of daily entries in her journal, was adopted until many years later.

The manuscript of Thraliana, as it exists to-day, is in six volumes quarto, and comprises well over 1,600 pages in Mrs. Thrale's clear, forceful hand.[3] It covers the period from 1776 to the last of March 1809, though it is not the only record for these years. Saintsbury calls Mrs. Thrale 'the most feminine'

---

[1] Sept. 6, 1777.   [2] Apr. 25, 1780; see also *Life,* i. 122–3.

[3] Thraliana is now in the Huntington Library, Pasadena, California, and was edited by K. C. Balderston (Clarendon Press, 1942; new edition, 1951).

of writers,[1] and her chief journal goes far to justify this assertion. It has been well called 'a delightful jumble of family troubles, gossip, scandal, political events, amusing tales, and serious reflections'.[2] Her sentimental nature is apparent throughout, and the rapturous exclamations and fulsome epithets, 'Dear Dr. Johnson', 'Poor dear Dr. Burney', 'Poor pretty Siddons', which so annoyed Macaulay, still seem affected. Excessive sentiment, however, was rampant in the theatre and in much of the popular literature of the time, and we must not blame Mrs. Thrale too severely for adopting this mode of expression of her day.

We may arraign her for a more serious defect which constantly appears in her diaries. She is apt to colour too highly her accounts of people and of occurrences. Her own family was not spared this distortion. For this reason her father, John Salusbury, has always had the reputation of being an unconscionable rake and adventurer, and only to-day are we able to get at the truth. Other individuals and incidents throughout Thraliana have also suffered some misrepresentation from her innate love of dramatic effect. Harsher words have been used for this tendency of Mrs. Thrale; yet the fact that she could not help giving a personal tinge to everything she wrote does not completely discredit the evidence. Remembering this idiosyncrasy, a judicious reader can usually sift and evaluate for himself; and after every sifting much remains that is convincing and that cannot be found elsewhere.

Thraliana does not consist entirely of anecdotes. As might be gathered from the first entry, it is a queer compilation, representing all the ideas and miscellaneous items which Mrs. Thrale wished to remember. Nor is it all in prose, for countless occasional verses of her own and her friends are included. Separated from the people and incidents which gave it birth, much of this society verse makes dull reading to-day, but it is characteristic and at times amusing. Interspersed with the poetry and contemporary anecdotes are many more personal entries. Some of these perhaps represent merely the fashionable gush of the day, but the larger part accurately express her own feelings. She was naturally of a romantic turn, and Thraliana offered a release for pent-up emotions. Neither her husband nor Johnson was of the type to approve of the vapours of sentiment, and after her mother's death she had none to whom she might unburden all her troubles and boast of her triumphs.

---

[1] *The Peace of the Augustans*, p. 232.   [2] *Thraliana*, ed. Hughes, p. 11.

As a result, her journal became the only complete outlet for her confidences.

Yet Thraliana was not kept solely for the diarist herself. Always she must have had in mind the usefulness of the information she was recording for future generations. Many passages she undoubtedly felt to be too intimate for the public eye, and intended to excise them before her death (a number of pages have been cut from the original manuscript, either by Mrs. Piozzi or by someone else), but from the beginning she probably had ultimate publication, in some form or other, in mind.[1] She meant to describe her circle of interesting friends, and at the same time explain herself, to some far-away, later reader.

Into the first volume of Thraliana Mrs. Thrale copied numerous anecdotes from her earlier journals, sometimes revising the phraseology as she copied. The few pages of these early records now known to have survived indicate this revision.[2] What became of the original versions? Did she continue to use them, as she did the Children's Book? Or were they destroyed, page by page, when their contents were transcribed into the larger journal? At present it is impossible to tell. The possibility that they still exist provides a tantalizing mystery.

The remainder of 1776 was spent partly at Brighton, which Johnson as usual found dull, and partly at Streatham.[3] Early in December Miss Owen came for a visit, and in order to give Queeney and her a sight of some plays and operas, the three

---

[1] In May 1789 she wrote in Thraliana: 'I wonder if my Executors will burn the Thraliana.' See also *French Journals*, p. 21, n. In Nov. 1818 she wrote in her New Common Place Book:

'Revisal of one's past Life!! Doctor Johnson who always profess'd an Aversion to Canting—did not surely cant himself when he advised me to keep a Register of Events, Conversations, &c, and said how pleasant it would be to me on Revisal! and I stupid Dunce! never had the Wit to reply, "Why Sir, you don't like reviewing your own Life; why should I at your Age like it better?" he always said looking back on past Days was dreadful to him:—& then counsel'd me to make a Thraliana. I have looked into mine since I brought it from Brynbella—read 12 Pages—and lost my Sleep for a Week. Nothing should keep me from burning the whole to Night, but respect for my Executor's Profit or Amusement——but I have tied it up tight, & will *review* my past Life no more: any other Suicide would be less painful, and I do not wish to shorten Existence at 79 Years old—but so many Opportunities for Good were surely never, no *never* flung away as by H. L. Piozzi. not that I consider my Life as an unhappy one—Oh God forbid! infinitely more happy than the Lives of infinite Numbers who deserved better and made better returns to the Giver of ev'ry Blessing;—but bitter to Remembrance & hateful to *review*.'

Mrs. Piozzi's final reaction, however, to re-reading episodes in her past was not adverse. See p. 445, n. 1.

[2] See pp. 76, 85–8. Even the Children's Book was culled for anecdotes of Johnson and Queeney.

[3] *Life*, iii. 93. For Mrs. Thrale's chief worry this autumn see p. 164, n. 3.

ladies took temporary lodgings for a week in Parliament Street.[1] It was on this expedition that Mrs. Thrale made arrangements with the well-known music teacher, Dr. Burney, to give lessons to Queeney. She may have known Burney for years, but now, as her daughter's instructor, he became an intimate of the Thrale household, and with his perennial good spirits he was soon a general favourite. Mrs. Thrale found him of advantage in many ways, particularly as a companion for Johnson in the early morning hours. In her usual condition, she was unable to stand the strain of the late vigils which her guest's insomnia and constant tea drinking rendered necessary. Years later she could still remember her misery in sitting up with Johnson until her legs began to swell as big as columns.[2] Now when Dr. Burney was in the house she could slip away to bed whenever so inclined.

Mrs. Thrale was expecting her eleventh child, and strangely this time was more oppressed by vague forebodings than ever before, having a premonition that she would finally bear another son, but not survive the ordeal. She tortured herself with wondering how brief would be the mourning and whom Thrale would choose for his second wife. 'Poor Mr. Johnson would have the greatest Loss of me', she commented,

and he would be the most sensible of his Loss: he would willingly write my Epitaph I am sure if my Husband would treat me with a Monument; which I do believe he would too, if any body would press him to it before the first Year was out—after *that* he would be married again, & his second Lady would perhaps make Objections.[3]

In such a morbid state of mind she was delighted to have Miss Owen agree to stay on through the winter. As Mrs. Thrale wrote to Johnson on January 12, 1777, 'it is a vast Comfort to have a Lady about me—and I have had none so long'. Johnson himself was of little help in cheering her despondency, for in London he was suffering from insomnia and 'difficulty in breathing'. Writing on the 15th that he had been bleeding himself for relief, he ended with the plea that she take him out to Streatham on Friday. 'I do not know but clearer air may do me good; but whether the air be clear or dark, let me come to you.' But his Mistress was in no condition to welcome another invalid in the house, and hurriedly replied:

Here is Dr. Burney come & says you are very ill: Oh sad! oh

---

[1] Children's Book, entry of Dec. 13, 1776.
[2] Mrs. Piozzi to Queeney, Oct. 31, 1809 (Lansdowne MS.).
[3] Children's Book, Jan. 7, 1777.

sad! indeed I am very sorry; and I unable to nurse you—for Goodness sake do as Dr. Lawrence would have you & be well before you come home—and pray don't be bleeding yourself & doing yourself harm—my Master is very angry already.[1]

In spite of her fears Mrs. Thrale on February 8 was safely delivered of another daughter, who, at the insistence of her friends Mrs. Strickland and Miss Owen, was named Cecilia Margaretta. Mrs. Thrale was scarcely recovered when Queeney fell ill. This time, discouraged by her own past failures, the mother took her child immediately into town to consult Dr. Jebb. She would not again take chances with her own remedies. Fortunately Queeney was soon well, and with her mother and Miss Owen ready to enjoy the gaiety of London Society.

In the preceding years Mrs. Thrale had gradually become acquainted with some of the so-called 'Blue-Stocking Circle'.[2] This group of talented people who preferred conversation to cards or fashionable assemblies had as its leader Mrs. Elizabeth Montagu, 'Queen of the Blues'. Her splendid conversaziones were considered the last word in literary brilliance, though they were perhaps not so amusing as those of her intimate friend Mrs. Vesey, whose impulsive character had earned for her, among her associates, the name of 'The Sylph'. Effervescent, absent-minded, and delightfully absurd, the latter's one preoccupation was in managing to keep her guests from forming a large, stiff circle. Mrs. Montagu and Mrs. Vesey were the chief Blue-Stocking hostesses; but among their friends were Elizabeth Carter, the scholarly translator of Epictetus, whose piety, headaches, and puddings were proverbial; the ingenious maker of paper flowers, Mrs. Delany; the polite Mrs. Boscawen; and the homely Mrs. Chapone, well known for her friendship with the novelist Richardson and for her letters of advice to young ladies. The chief masculine supporters included the Master in Chancery, William Weller Pepys, of the long nose and London accent, who was termed 'Prime Minister to Mrs. Montagu'; his brother Sir Lucas Pepys, the famous physician; and William Seward, hypochondriac dabbler in physics and literature. On the fringe were Horace Walpole, Soame Jenyns, and the other wits.

---

[1] Ry. 540, 86. Undated, but apparently answered by Johnson on Jan. 16, 1777.
[2] For a general discussion of the Blue-Stocking movement see Ethel R. Wheeler, *Famous Blue-Stockings* (1910); Julia Kavanagh, *English Women of Letters* (1863); G. and P. Wharton, *Queens of Society* (1860); Mrs. A. K. Elwood, *Memoirs of the Literary Ladies of England* (1843), &c. Byron violently attacked the Blue-Stockings in Canto V of *Don Juan*.

Mrs. Thrale, the wife of the Southwark brewer, was never unreservedly accepted into the inner circle of the Blue-Stockings. It seems probable that she never even met Mrs. Delany; nor did she ever become intimate with Mrs. Vesey, Mrs. Chapone, or Miss Carter. Yet if she was not of the *élite*, she became a powerful rival of the 'Queen', and by later generations was considered one of the leaders. She was a true 'Blue', if not technically a 'Blue-Stocking'.

With Mrs. Montagu she was closely associated for a number of years. From the beginning of their acquaintance Mrs. Montagu had conceived a high opinion of her, and shortly after Harry's death had written to Beattie: 'Her uncommon endowments and love of literature expose her to the illiberal jests of the ignorant and idle, but her life is rational, usefull, decent. Can those who ridicule her say as much of theirs.'[1] For her part, Mrs. Thrale was delighted to number among her friends such a distinguished person of her own sex. She had frankly admitted to Johnson in January, 'Mrs. Montagu's Visit—at any Time a Favour, will now be a Charity.'[2]

Throwing off the despondency of the winter, Mrs. Thrale was very gay during the spring of 1777 and delighted in showing Miss Owen all the sights of London. On March 19 Johnson asked:

Did you stay all night at Sir Joshua's? and keep Miss up again? Miss Owen had a sight—all the Burkes—the Harris's—Miss Reynolds—what has she to see more? and Mrs. Horneck, and Miss.

Johnson added: 'You are all young, and gay, and easy; but I have miserable nights, and know not how to make them better; but I shift pretty well a-days, and so have at you all at Dr. Burney's to-morrow.' So on March 20 Mrs. Thrale and Dr. Johnson were for the first time in the same room with Fanny Burney, the shy, retiring daughter of the fashionable music master. Although the elder woman scarcely noticed

---

[1] Apr. 12, 1776 (original letter in the Aberdeen Univ. Library). Mrs. Montagu added that she was that morning going to visit 'poor Mrs. Thrale, who has lost her only son'. Again, on Aug. 12, 1777, Mrs. Montagu described a dinner at Streatham to Mrs. Vesey:

We had a most elegant dinner at Mr Thrales, and the best of all feasts, sense, and witt, and good humour. Mrs Thrale is a Woman of very superior under-standing, and very respectable as a Wife, a Mother, a Friend, and a Mistress of a Family. Mr Thrale has a fruit garden and Kitchen Garden that may vye with the Hesperians gardens for fruit and flowers.

(Blunt, *Mrs. Montagu*, ii. 269.)

[2] Ry. 540, 94. Streatham, Sunday 12. Undoubtedly Jan. 1777, since it answers Johnson's of Jan. 11, 1777 (No. 505. 2).

the silent girl, the latter long remembered every detail of this memorable meeting and, as was her custom, wrote a long account of the party a few days later to her confidential adviser, 'Daddy' Crisp. 'Mrs. Thrale', she wrote, 'is a very pretty woman still; she is extremely lively and chatty; has no supercilious or pedantic airs, and is really gay and agreeable.'[1] Fanny's portrait of the great Dr. Johnson, on the other hand, was not so complimentary, for his unusual exterior and ponderous manner at first caused nothing but astonishment. With unerring skill she pictured him preoccupied with a book, utterly oblivious of the musical entertainment, and finally teased by the irrepressible Mrs. Thrale into making silly remarks. That day the same company had been asked to dine with Mrs. Montagu, and Fanny recorded an amusing argument between Johnson and Mrs. Thrale as to whose invitation had been most flattering.

'*Your* note', cried Dr. Johnson, 'can bear no comparison with *mine*; I am *at the head of the Philosophers*, she says.'

'And I', cried Mrs. Thrale, '*have all the Muses in my train*!'

Mrs. Thrale and Johnson might joke about their invitations from Mrs. Montagu, but they were vastly pleased to receive them just the same.[2]

The 'Queen of the Blues' was anxious to have the great literary dictator in her circle, and during these years assiduously attempted to gain his friendship. Once, writing to Mrs. Thrale about Johnson, his good spirits, and her delight in his conversation, Mrs. Montagu ended with the admission: 'he is very coy, & very cruel, and I am always courting him, & always get a denial. I cannot but say he is very polite, but I want him to be tender.'[3] With great ladies Johnson was always a trifle formal; he could be flattering and amusing, but never intimate. With Mrs. Thrale, on the other hand, he was different; her informality and lack of ostentatious refinement put him at his ease and drew out the tenderness which the others could not inspire. The talk of the two women contrasted as sharply as their background. Mrs. Thrale once made the comparison:

---

[1] *Early Diary of F. Burney*, ii. 152.

[2] Mrs. Montagu's letters to Mrs. Thrale were always couched in the most complimentary terms. In a letter of Jan. 15 (no year) she wrote: 'you have all the virtues that make solitude tranquill, & all the talents that make society pleasant & lively, so that you may chuse freely, but pray have a little compassion for us, who, perhaps, have only those qualities which pass in a Crowd' (Ry. 551, 5).

[3] Ry. 551, 3. Jan. 14 (no year).

'Mrs. Montagu's Bouquet is all out of the Hot-house—mine out of the Woods & Fields & many a Weed there is in it.'[1]

It seems likely that it was in March, 1777, that Mrs. Thrale first went to Court. At the time of Harry's death she had referred to the prospect of such a presentation the next day; but that, of course, had been given up. Her comment, when the event was finally over, is revealing:

the Ceremony was trifling, but I am glad it's over; one is now upon the footing one wishes to be—and in a manner free of the Drawing Room, I confess I am pleased at having been there.[2]

Johnson, in his reply, agreed that her presentation had certainly been 'delayed too long'.

Throughout the spring Mrs. Thrale's social ambitions continued to soar, and in May she asked the influence of Johnson's friend, Dr. Taylor, to secure tickets for a fête at Devonshire House. While glad to help her climb, by passing on her request to his friend, Johnson laughingly commented, 'You will become such a gadder, that you will not care a penny for me.'[3] Her letters constantly reveal her delight in numbering the famous people of the day among her intimates, and on June 3 she jubilantly wrote:

Mr. & Mrs. Garrick have been here, so I have heard the Eagle & the Blackbird, & a very pretty Thing it is I think: he is to get us Places for Sherridan's new Play which is *a Thing* it seems, & he is *so* civil & *so* desirous to be intimate &c.[4]

Her thoughts also turned to clothes, and in the same letter she proudly described a new gown of 'plain White Silk which I bought in Paris of a Colour peculiarly elegant—trimmed with

---

[1] Written on a small card (Ry. 629, 29a). When in 1809 Mrs. Piozzi read the published version of Mrs. Montagu's early letters, she commented enthusiastically in the New Common Place Book:

I was unjust enough (who knew her only of late years) to conclude that Lords & Dutchesses were new to her, she seemed so fond of Ton Folks, but 'Twas her rational Taste, she had been bred among them from the Beginning it seems; & was never more at home, or less constrained than in their company. They were I fancy *better* Company in those days than in these.

[2] Ry. 539, 12. To Johnson (undated). Johnson's reply of Mar. 27 (unpublished) indicates the month, but the year is still undetermined. From internal evidence, a reference to hearing an Italian Improvisatore at Mr. Paradise's, &c., I would place the presentation in 1777, in spite of a natural presumption that it must have occurred earlier.

[3] May 19, 1777. See also Ry. 540, 63, 64.

[4] To Johnson. Sheridan's play was *The School for Scandal*. The friendly attitude of the Garricks is evinced by four known letters to the Thrales: Jan. 29, 1777, Feb. 12, 17, Aug. 1. (The years of the last three are not certain.) See forthcoming edition by D. M. Little.

pale Purple & Silver by the fine Madame Beauvais & in the newest & highest Fashion'.

During the summer of 1777 the visits and dinners continued, so that there was a constant round of gaiety. On August 6 Mrs. Montagu came to Streatham for dinner, where she was delighted by her host and hostess and astonished at the splendour of the fruit and flower gardens.[1] On the 13th Mrs. Thrale wrote to Johnson, who was in Lichfield, of another party which she had attended.

Since I wrote last I have dined at Sir Joshua's on Richmond Hill, where we were invited to meet the Pepyses the Patersons, the Garricks &c. there was Mr. Langton, Lady Rothes and their two pretty Babies; I think Miss Langton for an Infant of four Years old the most elegant Creature I have seen, and little George is a fine Fellow too: but very troublesome they were with their Prattle, every word of which their Papa repeated in order to explain; however Miss Reynolds with great composure put them under the Care of a Maid & sent them a walking while we dined; very little to the Satisfaction of the Parents, who expressed some uneasiness lest they should overheat themselves as it was a hot day. In the mean Time Mr. Garrick was taken Ill, and after suffering a good deal from Sickness in his Stomach desired a Table to himself near the open Window: by the Time he was seated the Children returned; and Lady Rothes, who did not much like they should lose their dinner so, had got some Scraps of the second Course—Cheesecakes & such like ready for them at their Return—she then directed them to go to Mr. Garrick's Table, and *eat fair*. He was sick before, and I actually saw him change Colour at their approach, however he was civiller to them than anybody there except myself. Pepys—who had heard you give a Specimen of the *Langtonian* Mode of Life at our house whispered me that he wished them all at the Rope-Walk —& added can one ever come to this oneself? I really never had such difficulty to forbear laughing.[2]

Little George Langton was a proverbially spoiled child. His father once amused the Thrales by claiming that the five-year-old boy had a taste for fortification, and later, when the Langton family retired to live in Kent, Queeney made Johnson laugh by observing that with such help *'Rochester would be impregnable'.*[3]

Later in the month Dr. Burney came to Streatham for a week's visit, and William Weller Pepys and his wife for a brief stay.[4]

[1] Blunt, *Mrs. Montagu*, ii. 269.
[2] Compare Thraliana, Aug. 13, 1777.
[3] Mrs. Piozzi to Queeney, Feb. 30, 1812.
[4] Ry. 540, 69.

Visitors at the Thrales were left very much to their own devices; they might read, talk, or wander about the spacious grounds, whichever suited the inclination of the moment. Dr. Burney often brought his writing, and Pepys, on one visit, wrote to a friend, 'I have bestow'd a great deal of my time here in working through a very large Latin Quarto'.[1] Serious study, interspersed with literary conversation, was the order of the day for Mrs. Thrale and her guests.

Brighton, during the autumn of 1777, offered further opportunity for Mrs. Thrale to widen her acquaintance. With Dr. Burney they moved to the sea-side the last of September, but since their own house was not ready, they were forced to take uncomfortable lodgings for a few days. On October 2 Mrs. Thrale dispatched a hurried note to Johnson in Ashbourne:

> Here we are, not very elegantly accommodated, but wishing sincerely for you to share either our pleasure or our distresses. 'Tis fine bathing, with rough breakers, and my Master longs to see you exhibit your strength in opposing them, and bids me press you to come, for he is tired of living so long without you; and Burney says if you don't come soon he shall be gone, and he does love you, or he is a vile ——. But one woman in the water today,
>
> 'Una et haec audax'
Was your most faithful and obliged
H. L. Thrale[2]

Despite this invitation she was not anxious for Johnson's company until they were comfortably settled. Nor was he very eager to rush to Brighton, a place which only her presence rendered bearable. 'The sea is so cold, and the rooms are so dull; yet I do love to hear the sea roar and my mistress talk— For when she talks, ye gods! how she will talk.' In this same letter of the 6th Johnson referred to his latest literary project, a series of short biographical prefaces which the booksellers had prevailed upon him to write for a new edition of the English poets. 'When I come to town', he added, 'I am to be very busy about my Lives.—Could not you do some of them for me?' Even if meant only in jest, the suggestion must have been very flattering to his correspondent.

Throughout October Johnson remained in the north Midlands, while Mrs. Thrale kept him informed of Brighton gossip.

---

[1] *A Later Pepys*, i. 223.

[2] This letter, which was in the possession of Cecilia Mostyn, was sold at auction after her death. It was published in the *Brighton Herald*, Oct. 17, 1857. The signature, as printed in the newspaper, was H. S. Thrale.

Forced to agree with him about the dullness of the rooms, she commented on the 16th:

We go on here as usual, invite Company to Dinner & daudle in the Rooms at Night, yet my Master & Miss Owen call that Pleasure, & I like it better now I play at Cards, it is a *little* more interesting than before.

Arthur Murphy had joined the company, and it was through him that she met the notorious John Wilkes. 'I like him not,' she remarked to Johnson in the same letter, 'he professed himself a Lyar and an Infidel, and I see no Merit in being either.' Wilkes was unwittingly the cause of a flare-up between Mrs. Thrale and her husband. On the 18th she confided to Johnson:

Wilkes has invited Mr. Thrale to a Dinner of Rakes—Beauclerck, Lord Kelly & the Men of *Worth* & *honour* that are here, & here are plenty too: says Murphy looking at me—he *dares not go*—I would not have him go said I gravely; I am not fond of trying my Power over my husband, nor wish to exert it at all for a new Topknot— but if I could keep him out of such Company—I should think I did him an Act of real Friendship—so who says I have no spirit Mr. Johnson? I got severely rallied for my Prudery & at last lost my Labour for he does go, but I know I did right.

But if she lost her argument about the dinner of rakes, she did prove her husband wrong on another occasion. On November 8 she wrote:

Did I tell you that my Master grew ashamed of his Wife's Peruke since we came here & made me pull it off & dress my own hair, which looks so well now it is dressed that he begins innocently to wonder why he ever let me wear a Wig. I remember well however the why, the when, & the where. My Mother thought it a good scheme to keep young married Women at home.

By this time the season was nearly ended at Brighton, and she commented to Dr. Burney:

The Balls are over and Rooms expire tonight, but Mr. Thrale does not mean to stir till Monday or Tuesday sevennight. We have a *lame* Lord left, a *deaf* Gentleman, and Mr. Palmer who *squints*. My Master therefore *compels* them to come in and we play our cards in the best Parlour.[1]

In the middle of November Johnson joined them for three days, after which they all returned to Streatham together on the 18th.[2]

[1] C. Hill, *The House in St. Martin's Street* (1907), 189. The letter is dated Nov. 6.
[2] Ry. 540, 79. See also *Adam Libr.* i. 64.

Towards the end of the year Mrs. Thrale brought Susan and Sophy from school for the holidays and wrote long accounts of their improvement in the Children's Book. For once, the entries were all in a happy vein; for though expecting another child, her health was better than usual; her children were vigorous, and her husband generous and agreeable. Later commenting on her daughters' return to school and on her plan to take Queeney into London for some gaiety, she added: 'My Master has given me a fine Gown too, & I am going to Court on Monday next with Mrs. Montagu, in little & great things now all goes well.'[1]

Mrs. Thrale had planned only a fortnight's round of pleasure in London, but instead stayed seven weeks. Many things contributed to make this one of the happiest winters of her life: both she and Queeney kept well; there was nothing but good news from the other children; she dined with Mrs. Montagu; a Duchess desired 'leave to visit' her; the King said she spent too little time in London because she lived so near it; and she was delighted and amused by a succession of dinners and entertainments.[2] One morning she accompanied Johnson to the studio of the sculptor Nollekens, whom she had never met. Nollekens called out to Johnson:

'I like your picture by Sir Joshua very much. He tells me it's for Thrale, a brewer, over the water: his wife's a sharp woman, one of the blue-stocking people.'—'Nolly, Nolly,' observed the Doctor, 'I wish your maid would stop your foolish mouth with a blue-bag.' At which Mrs. Thrale smiled, and whispered to the Doctor, 'My dear Sir, you'll get nothing by blunting your arrows upon a block.'[3]

Reynolds's portrait of Johnson was one of a series ordered by Thrale to decorate the library at Streatham. When the collection was finally completed, thirteen pictures by the famous painter lined the walls of the room. Over the fire-place was a full length of Mrs. Thrale and Queeney; Mr. Thrale himself was over the door leading to his study; and spaced around the sides were three-quarter-length portraits of Lord Sandys, Lord Westcote (William Lyttelton), Dr. Johnson, Burke, Goldsmith, Murphy, Garrick, Baretti, Sir Robert Chambers, Dr. Burney, and Sir Joshua himself.[4] Pride in the distinction of their friends was one common bond which united the Master and Mistress of Streatham.

---

[1] Jan. 17, 1778.   [2] See Children's Book, and Ry. 540, 107.
[3] John T. Smith, *Nollekens and His Times*, i (1828), 114. The incident may be dated from Johnson's letter No. 572.   [4] Hayward, ii. 170.

This winter [1778] Mrs. Thrale and Johnson, because of their fondness for the amiable Dr. Burney, actively furthered his efforts to get his son Dick accepted by Winchester College. Although Johnson always had to be stirred up to write letters for anybody, once he started nothing was too much trouble, and, according to Boswell, he actually accompanied the boy and his father to the school.[1] Charlotte Burney, in her journal, is lavish, too, in praise of Mrs. Thrale for her generosity on the occasion. With a kindly thought for the lad's comfort, she had not only presented him with a lot of fine cloth 'to set him up in shirts with but has likewise furnished him with an intire set of school books'.[2] And a few weeks later Dr. Burney himself wrote to the Mistress of Streatham to thank her for one recent gift to the family:

Why, what a Lady Bountiful you are! most People content themselves & others by giving *Boxes* & Tuckies at Xmas; but you are an endless Giver.—never waiting for Times, Seasons, or occasions, but making them at your pleasure.[3]

The two benefactors were, of course, occasionally in the Burney home in St. Martin's Street, and it was probably in February, 1778, that the never-to-be forgotten evening party occurred which has been so delightfully described by Virginia Woolf.[4] The Thrales and Johnson had been invited this time to meet the musician's old patron, Fulke Greville, and his daughter Mrs. Crewe, a notable beauty and Blue-Stocking. But the evening did not prove a complete success. Johnson, better dressed than usual and in a new wig, sat gloomily wrapt in his own thoughts, making no effort to start the conversation, while the others, who had come to hear him talk, were afraid to begin. Greville took a commanding position before the fire, looked supercilious, and said nothing. For entertainment, Dr. Burney had asked one of his friends, an Italian singer named Piozzi, who did his best but had a difficult audience to please. Johnson and the Thrales were wholly unmusical, and many of the other guests were as little interested. After the first number the ominous silence continued, and some of the younger Burneys were called on for a duet, in the midst of which Piozzi casually fell asleep. When the half-hearted applause at the end of the duet woke him up, he unwillingly began another florid aria.

[1] *Life*, iii. 367.
[2] *Early Diary of F. Burney*, ii. 286.
[3] Ry. 545, 4; Mar. 8, 1778.
[4] *The Second Common Reader* (1932), pp. 108–25. See also *Early Diary of F. Burney*, ii. 284–7, and *Memoirs of Doctor Burney*, ii. 101–14.

The situation was too much for Mrs. Thrale, and she decided to liven up the company. Mischievously she slipped behind the panting tenor and mimicked his every gesture, with squared elbows, ecstatic shrugs of the shoulders, and languishing eyes. The near-sighted Johnson failed to notice the scene, but Dr. Burney, completely horrified, tiptoed to the lady and administered a stinging reproof. Mrs. Thrale, who was nothing if not good natured, quietly accepted the rebuke, and returned to her chair like a chastened schoolgirl. The remainder of the evening passed gloomily, unrelieved except for a devastating growl from Johnson, which routed even the conceited Greville.

This was the first meeting of Mrs. Thrale and Gabriel Piozzi, but he seems to have made so little impression that he was immediately forgotten. His day was not yet.

VIII

TROUBLES WITH MASTER

MARCH 1778–JUNE 1779

WHAT sort of woman was this wife of a Southwark brewer who was now being taken up by London society? Less than 5 feet in height, plump and deep-chested, with large, muscular hands, she was certainly not an imposing figure. Her eyes were fine and expressive, light grey in colour; her hair was chestnut brown. A prominent nose and firm chin kept her face from being handsome, but animation undoubtedly made her attractive. Charlotte Ann Burney, indeed, found her so 'blooming and pretty' that she underestimated her age by five years.[1] Perhaps one reason for the mistake was that Mrs. Thrale, according to the accepted mode of the day, kept her cheeks well rouged to offset the pallor of frequent accouchements. Her voice was harsh and unmusical, if we may believe Mme D'Arblay's later recollections, and her manner flaunting rather than reserved.[2] But she carried herself well, and entered a room with the assurance and poise of an acknowledged wit and raconteuse. While never affecting any pretence to beauty, she nevertheless considered herself an unusual woman.[3]

Almost everywhere she went Mrs. Thrale was accompanied by her thirteen-year-old eldest daughter, a constant source of mingled pride and annoyance. The many compliments on the child's obvious good looks filled her with delight, so much so that once she noted in the Children's Book that Queeney 'looked so elegant among the Dowdies I have seen, that I

---

[1] *Early Diary of F. Burney*, ii. 286.

[2] R. Brimley Johnson, *Fanny Burney and the Burneys* (1926), p. 104. Writing to Mrs. Waddington, grandniece of Mrs. Delany, Fanny described Mrs. Thrale [uncertain date]:

She was warm-hearted, generous, sweet-tempered and full of active zeal for her friends, and of fervent devotion in religion. She was replete with wit and pleasantry, and her powers of entertainment exceeded those of almost any woman I ever knew. But her manners were flaunting, her voice was loud, and she had no peace, and allowed none to others, but in the display of her talents.

[3] This composite picture is derived from a variety of sources: Boswell's *Life*, Fanny Burney's journals, and Mrs. Thrale's own entries in Thraliana (May 1778).

restrain my Vanity with the utmost Difficulty'.[1] On the other hand, the child's stubborn refusal to show off in public was always disturbing. Queeney had a haughty, distant air which did not ingratiate her with strangers. Mrs. Montagu, to be sure, found her 'what few young Persons are, an attentive listener',[2] but others ascribed her reserve to less pleasing motives. Fanny Burney's first reaction must have been unfavourable, since she later expunged her original comments and wrote instead that Miss Thrale was 'stiff and proud, I believe, or else shy and reserved'.[3] Fanny's sister, Charlotte Ann, was more frank, and a few years later caustically remarked on one occasion: 'Miss Thrale was, to my no small astonishment, civil to me, and sat by me the whole evening. She has taken it into her head to be civil to people this winter, I hear.'[4]

Queeney had a faculty for putting other people in the wrong. The autumn before at Brighton Mrs. Thrale complained to Johnson:

> Queeney will not dance, and the People twit me that I will not let her, because I dance myself—even Miss Owen who lives with us believes that to be the Case from Queeney's manner & management.[5]

The girl, who 'had from Infancy a Spirit of keeping Secrets', was also suspicious of her mother's scrutiny of everything she wrote, and resorted to the use of code when writing to her most intimate friend, Peggy Pitches (later Lady Deerhurst). One at least of these clandestine letters has survived, possibly the one intercepted by Mrs. Thrale on March 13, 1778, shortly after their return to Streatham.[6] When deciphered, it shows clearly what Queeney thought of parental authority. 'My Mother has scolded me so today and been in such a passion you can't think', she began, and then after some advice to her corre-

---

[1] Oct. 30, 1776.

[2] To Mrs. Thrale, May 16 (no year) (Ry. 551, 7).

[3] *Early Diary of F. Burney*, ii. 152.   [4] Ibid. 306.

[5] Oct. 16, 1777. Probably the reason Queeney would not dance was that it was one thing which she did poorly. In the Children's Book in Oct. 1776 Mrs. Thrale commented how 'incomparably ill' her daughter had danced at every ball.

[6] Mrs. Thrale, after noting in the Children's Book on this date that she had seized the letter, wrote:

> She had from Infancy a Spirit of keeping Secrets, & Baretti long ago told her she was old enough to write her own Letters & have her own Friendships without the Interference of her Mother, in whom she has no Confidence, nor ever had. She is now thirteen years old & a half—rather early I shd. think, but these are forward Times God Knows.

The actual letter which was saved is described in *N. & Q.*, 11th Ser., xi. 298 (Apr. 17, 1915).

spondent about practising their code, added, 'I have just been having such a lecture from Lady Lade as would make you stare. Just such stuff as my Mother talks, about dignity . . . she is getting as bad as my Mother, I think.'

Mrs. Thrale often wondered what was the cause of her daughter's peculiarities, which Johnson attributed to the strange nature of her training.

Queeney he says is made singular by my Education of her; it is not true however, for she is not singular at all. I was myself a very particular Girl; but my Daughter whatever faults she has, has not my faults, of Confidence, Loquacity & foolish Sensibility.[1]

Wondering morbidly what would happen if she should die in childbirth, Mrs. Thrale added that at least her younger daughters would then be brought up like other children, 'which Mr. Johnson says is so *good* a Thing'.

We have no record of what the Master of the house thought of these disagreements between his wife and his children. At home his chief interest was in the kitchen. Besides, he was naturally of a cold, non-committal disposition, never becoming excited over anything, no matter how serious. Indeed he was so tranquil of mind that, as his wife said,

when the house of his favourite Sister was on Fire, & we were alarmed with the Account of it in the Night, I well remember that he never rose, but bidding the Servant who called us, go to her Assistance; quietly turned about & slept to his usual hour. . . . he had built great Casks holding 1000 Hogsheads each, & was much pleased with their Profit & Appearance—one Day however he came down to Streatham as usual to dinner & after hearing & talking of a hundred trifles—but I forgot says he to tell you how one of my great Casks is burst & all the Beer run out.[2]

Thrale was always meticulously correct: he wore the clothes of a person of consequence; he never swore or talked obscenely; he regularly went to church on Sunday and was in theory deeply religious. Even in his vices he conformed to the usual pattern. In appearance he was dignified, with an agreeable countenance and manners so 'free from every kind of Trick or Particularity' that his wife thought him 'out of the Power of Mimickry'. Openly she counted him the handsomest husband in England. The one thing he lacked was a warm-hearted personality; he aroused respect in those about him, but not

[1] Children's Book, Apr. 1, 1778.
[2] Thraliana, June 1777. The description of Thrale which follows is largely derived from this source.

CARICATURE 1772

Undoubtedly intended to represent Henry Thrale

Now in the British Museum

affection. His distaste for terms of endearment was a cause of frequent complaints from his wife, but it is probable that such incompatibility between them is easily exaggerated. In the light of a mass of evidence, all from her side, and in the light also of later events, it is easy to generalize and forget that for the most part they were a reasonably contented couple. During their entire married life they were rarely separated for any long intervals, and in consequence had little occasion for correspondence; but the one letter which has survived clearly shows a cordial relationship. Moreover, this letter, written by Thrale on a visit to Brighton, where he had been accompanied only by Queeney, certainly reveals him in a more amiable character than is usually ascribed to him.

This letter should have been sent by the post last night; but behold there was no post out, and therefore it will come by the *Dili John*. Your verses have been much admired, and particularly by Mrs. Trevor, who I take to be the best judge of ye language: she has taken a copy of them. I make no doubt of seeing some great strokes struck by the time I get home, which will certainly be on Monday to dinner, though, upon second thoughts, you had better not wait after five o'clock, as Major and Mrs. Holroyd have insisted upon my going the Chailey road, and breakfasting with them at Sheffield, which is a longer and heavier road than ours; but as they go, I think, on Saturday in a great measure to show me their place on Monday, I could not decently avoid it. I shall do it upon a promise they have made of calling at Streatham the first time they come to town. Lady Poole is very happy at the honourable mention you make of her, and the Augecock wonders what you think he must be made of to forget all your civilities. He reminds me much of Musgrave, so quick for applause. Puss admires herself much in the glass, and we have breakfasted and dined together every day this week very comfortably. Good night,—it's past one o'clock, and I am to be on horseback at nine in the morning.

Yrs. affectionately
H. Thrale

P.S. If you were always to write such good letters as your last, I should stay where I am and make you play Lady Cotton.[1]

This is an affectionate, appreciative Thrale, not the callous

---

[1] I have not seen the original of this letter, but it is herewith reproduced from a version printed (how accurately I cannot tell) in the *Brighton Herald*, Oct. 17, 1857. It was sold at that time among Cecilia Mostyn's effects. The letter is dated 'Friday morning, 5th. March' [1779]. The postscript refers to a remark of Johnson's about Lady Cotton, who spoke badly but wrote admirably: 'If I were married to that Woman I would always live 200 Miles away from her, and make her write to me twice o' Week' (Broadley, p. 53; also Hayward, ii. 323).

Thrale of tradition. This is the man to whom William Weller Pepys addressed a set of verses, on a wedding anniversary, complimenting him on his temerity in marrying an intellectual woman. Against all precedent, Pepys claimed, Thrale's experience proved that knowledge did not make a wife less loving or faithful.

> Could Ignorance more faithful prove?
> Could Folly's Self more warmly love?
> Then long may this Auspicious Morn
> At each still happier Year's return,
> Tell what Your sweet Experience knows
> That Head and Heart are Friends—not Foes.[1]

To casual observers theirs was a happy marriage. In an undated note, written when Thrale was just recovering from a dangerous illness, Mrs. Montagu insisted 'There is not a moment of my waking hours in which I am not sending you my best wishes. By *you* I mean Mr. & Mrs. Thrale, for you are truly one.'[2]

Yet Thrale, despite his apparent appreciation of his wife's literary efforts, was not an easy man to live with, and from the Children's Book it is possible to discover the marital problems which confronted Mrs. Thrale. For instance, during the autumn of 1776 Thrale had been troubled with an ailment which he refused to take seriously, but which the doctors diagnosed as either cancerous or venereal. To his wife, expecting another child, the prospect was gloomy indeed, but her principal worry was what would become of them all if the Master should follow her children to the grave. She was willing to heave a sigh of relief when the complaint turned out not to be fatal but merely the 'consequence of Folly & Vice'.[3] Could life be spared, everything else might be forgiven. But helping her husband with remedies for such a disease could hardly have served to increase her fondness for him.

Furthermore, his gambling instinct continually kept her apprehensive. When the business was making money, he had

---

[1] Mainwaring Piozziana, i. 85–6. Presented to Thrale Oct. 11, 1776, at Brighton.
[2] In the collection of Mr. A. C. Thomas.
[3] Children's Book. Mr. Thrale's trouble was a swollen testicle, which he asserted was due to a strain occasioned from an accident in France when he had been forced to jump from the Chaise. His wife naturally suspected a venereal infection, and, though not conclusive for us, she felt sure of her diagnosis. The last of Dec. 1776 she wrote: 'Mr. Thrale's Complaint *was* venereal at last—what need of so many Lyes about it! I'm sure I care not, so he recovers to hold us all together.' The trouble, as Dr. Ernest Sadler has informed me, was probably a simple hydrocele which might have been due either to the injury or to some venereal infection.

no thought of saving for a future emergency, but extravagantly spent every penny on which he could lay his hands. To increase the number and size of his brewing vats had become a driving obsession. He was determined to out-do his rivals, Whitbread and Calvert. One spring the idea struck him that a large sum of money with which to increase production might be raised by cutting a part of the beautiful woods at Bach-y-Graig. Shocked at the suggestion, his wife was immediately up in arms to defend her beloved grove. But Thrale coldly warned her:

Ladies have a Charter for teizing—but be pleased to have a Care, & not set your old Bull Dog [meaning Dr. Johnson] upon *me*—for I will hear nothing of that Sort—*except* from a Lady.[1]

Nevertheless she jumped at even this meagre encouragement, and showed her husband a little Triolet made in imitation of some French verses. Included were the lines:

> I shall make a Triolet
> On this Second Morn of May
> Since 'twas on that happy Day
> Favour for my Woods I Won:

The next August she was chagrined to find that, despite all her efforts, some of the trees had been cut.[2]

When the income was increasing, Thrale also delighted in lavish building and improvements at Streatham. During the summer of 1777 a small lake with an island at the far end was dredged out west of the house, and a two-mile walk which circled the property was reconstructed.[3] There were constant additions and redecorations, too, inside the house. This summer Thrale was at his perihelion (to use his wife's expression) so far as finances were concerned, and on one occasion Mrs. Thrale admitted to Johnson that she had been in the city buying finery, 'that I may have my share of the *Years of Plenty*'.[4] But even if not averse to sharing good times, she continued to have forebodings for the future. 'I hope you will not be long away,' she ended her letter to Johnson, 'my Master's Bridle must be held by a stronger hand than that of Your most faithful & Obedient H: L: Thrale.' Since the profits of the brewery had been £14,000 the year before, they may well have led Thrale to feel expansive.[5] He even bought back some of the Welsh property

---

[1] Mainwaring Piozziana, i. 77. Dated in Thraliana, May 2, 1777.
[2] Ry. 540, 69.
[3] Mentioned in Johnson's letters Nos. 538, 551, 554, 558.
[4] Sept. 20, 1777,
[5] From an excised passage in Johnson's letter No. 560 (Oct. 29, 1777), now in the Lichfield Johnson house.

attached to Bach-y-Graig which had been lost while John Salusbury was in Nova Scotia.[1]

Mrs. Thrale, blithely thinking money was unlimited, during the spring of 1778 ordered a new harpsichord for Dr. Burney's use, and in addition treated herself to a new bed, new 'bed gowns' and robes.[2] She was now preparing for her twelfth child, and noted in the Children's Book that for the first time since the birth of her eldest daughter she was buying special baby things. Then suddenly she found that her husband had again allowed his craze for speculation to lead him into difficulties. Caught in a general stringency of credit, he had no reserve funds to meet his obligations. It was a repetition of the old story, but Mrs. Thrale drove to Brighton to borrow again from Scrase, and the immediate danger was averted. On April 20 she wrote:

> I used to say nothing should make me cut my Trees down in Wales & now I offered them Yesterday to pacify My Masters Uneasiness: but he or his Daughter would at any Time rather suffer Misery in a slight degree than receive Consolation or Kindness from me.[3]

Sadly she remembered the dreadful year, 1772, but at least then her efforts had been appreciated. And this time there was actually no desperate need to worry. In a letter to Johnson, who was temporarily staying in town near Boswell, she urged him to speak to Thrale. Affairs, she said, were not dangerous; Perkins paid all obligations 'with a high hand'; and the labourers and tradesmen were satisfied.

> Conjure him not to fret so, when he really has every Reason to be thankful. What shall I do tho' when Burney's fine Harpsichord comes home? he grudges my new Bed so that it makes him half mad, & the other will be twice the Money of my poor Bed.—Oh Dear Me! but he is woeful cross; & glad at heart shall I be to have you with us—for we *grind* sadly else.[4]

[1] Ry. Charter 1025–6. Bodvary estate was purchased from Sir Robert Salusbury Cotton, and on Sept. 28, 1777, leased to Samuel Johnson and John Cator, as trustees.   [2] Children's Book and Ry. 540, 80.

[3] Children's Book. For Mrs. Thrale's other hurried trip to Brighton see p. 93, n. 4.

[4] Ry. 540, 80. The letter is undated, but undoubtedly belongs in the spring of 1778. While Boswell was in London this year Johnson divided his time between the city and the country. Yet Boswell quotes a complaint of Strahan that their friend was so much at the Thrales that 'he was in a great measure absorbed from the society of his old friends' (*Life*, iii. 225). Boswell made a number of visits to Streatham this year and recorded some conversations in which Mrs. Thrale plays a part. In his printed versions Boswell directs several pointed accusations at Mrs. Thrale for her alleged inaccuracy (*Life*, iii. 226, 228, 229, 243). The first does not appear in his contemporary notes; others are substantially as printed.

She could not refrain from commenting in the Children's Book 'that every Man when he begins to wish to *save* Money, always wishes to save it out of his *Wife's* Expenses, & when he wishes to *spend* it, wishes to spend it on *his own*'.

Throughout June Thrale's depression continued, and his wife, restlessly expecting her child, wrote again to Johnson:

Do huff my Master & comfort him by Turns according to your own Dear Discretion: he has consulted you now, & given you a Right to talk to Him about his ill Tim'd Melancholy and do keep your Influence over him for all our sakes.[1]

On the 21st, to her great disappointment, Mrs. Thrale gave birth to another daughter. The child was named Henrietta Sophia, and Mrs. Montagu, who offered herself as godmother, comforted Mrs. Thrale by insisting that she never would have stood for a boy.[2]

Early in July Mrs. Thrale was horrified to learn that her husband was considering discharging his chief clerk Perkins, 'who sets his faults before him somewhat too strongly' for policy.[3] She could not but think that if he hated 'Perkins for telling him Truth, he will of Consequence hate Johnson & me most of all I suppose'. Yet this did not deter the two from exerting all their influence on their Master to bring him to reason. On July 18 she added an account of a long conversation of the night before:

Well! last night Mr. Johnson having looked over my Master's Reste-Book, resolved I suppose to talk to him about his Affairs; for as I came in from walking I found them already entered on the Subject. Mr. Johnson observed that there was no need to be low spirited tho' we had been imprudent, that such was our Capital we might still be rich, might pay all our Debts, & lay up five Thousand a Year, while we lived at the Rate of five Thousand more, if Mr. Thrale would but promise never to brew more than *fourscore Thousand Barrels of Beer* in a Winter. He represented to him that setting his Profits at the low Rate of half a Crown a Barrel, 80,000 Barrels wd. bring him ten Thousand Pounds a Year of wch. says he I will allow you to spend *three* thousand rationally, & *two* Thousand foolishly—in building Digging Planting or what you will—only lay up the other five Thousand for your Children, who really have a

---

[1] Ry. 540, 52. This letter also is undated but was probably written either June 20 or 21, 1778. On it is noted in Johnson's hand: 'written during Labour', and from other evidence it must have been scribbled just before the birth of her twelfth child.

[2] Children's Book, July 3, 1778.

[3] Ibid., July 8, 1778.

Claim to it; & for yourself in Case of any Emergence that we may not be found as now totally unprovided with Money.[1]

Johnson continued by pointing out the great danger of not having a reserve fund for emergencies, and urged him to give up his 'mad Rapacity'.

The Man who will perpetually play double or Quits, must lose at last, & that Loss must be Ruin: & if you thus persist in pouring the profits of the Trade back upon the Trade; that Trade will swell indeed like a Bubble, but like a Bubble it will be sure to burst.

Mrs. Thrale herself then entered the argument and implored her husband to think of the harm to himself and to his children.

Mr. Johnson seconded me by earnest and pathetic entreaties & we at length extorted from him a Promise that he would brew no more than 80,000 Barrels a Year—for five Years to come.

For a time the Master agreed to be conservative, but everyone knew the reformation was only temporary.

During the summer of 1778 Mrs. Thrale's time was not completely taken up with problems of her husband and the brewhouse. There were always new acquaintances to invite to Streatham and new subjects for conversation. One of the sponsors for her youngest daughter, Henrietta Sophia, or Harriet as she was soon called, was a Miss Sophia Streatfeild who had been the last favourite pupil of Dr. Collier. Although the two ladies had heard much about each other, they did not meet until after Collier's death in 1777, and then by chance at Brighton.[2] With a bond of remembrance of their adored tutor, they had quickly become intimate friends. Miss Streatfeild was beautiful, cultivated, and an excellent Greek scholar; but her most astonishing accomplishment was an ability to fill her eyes with tears at any desired moment. It soon became a stock performance at Streatham for Mrs. Thrale to plead in a wheedling voice, 'Yes, do cry a little, Sophy, pray do', and then, wonders of wonders, a pearly tear would course down the cheek of the fair scholar, to the great entertainment of the other guests.[3]

Another addition to the Thrale circle came about through the anonymous publication in January 1778 of a novel called

---

[1] See also Thraliana, July 18, 1778, and Hayward, i. 74.

[2] See Hayward, i. 110–11. In Thraliana, on Nov. 20, 1776, Mrs. Thrale referred to having heard that her old tutor had found a home with the Streatfeilds and was educating the eldest daughter. Collier died May 23, 1777. Miss Balderston tells me that Streatfeild is the traditional spelling of the name, and the one used by the present representatives of the family.   [3] *D'Arblay Diary*, i. 238.

Evelina. By degrees people read and liked the book, and the secret of its authorship further stimulated interest. Although it was possibly not until July that Mrs. Thrale became aware of its existence, she was soon recommending the book to all her friends. When she was told that it was written by the shy, retiring daughter of her beloved Dr. Burney she was dumb-founded, and her first impulse was to urge the Doctor to bring the girl out for a visit. As soon as Fanny Burney heard the news of the excitement her book had caused at Streatham, she was almost overcome. For the celebrated Mrs. Thrale, the goddess of her idolatry, to compliment her writing, and Dr. Johnson!—it was too wonderful to believe. Therefore, her first journey to Streatham early in August was, in her words, 'the most consequential day' she had ever spent since her birth.[1]

The house and grounds which so delighted Fanny Burney in 1778 were far different from those to which Mrs. Thrale had come as a bride. The house now had wings extending on either side, and was surrounded by sloping lawns and shrubbery. To the west was a lake with an island at the far end, where we are told Johnson used to water the laurels. About a hundred yards east of the mansion was the summer-house where he was accus-tomed to meditate and write. To the rear were additional walled gardens for fruit and vegetables. Inside on the ground floor were the library, pantry, and service quarters, together with a dressing-room and six bedrooms, including Dr. Johnson's in the left wing. On the first floor were the dining parlour, drawing-room, and six more bedchambers. In the rear were numerous servants' rooms, while the kitchen, dairy, and scullery were detached from the house.[2] It was a home of luxurious ease, with all the conveniences that wealth and careful planning could provide.

Fanny Burney's record of her reception at Streatham Park has delighted generations of readers. With rapture she described the house, the guests, and particularly her hostess, whose cordi-ality and delicacy in not mentioning *Evelina* made an indelible impression. On August 23 she wrote:

But I fear to say all I think at present of Mrs. Thrale, lest some flaws should appear by and by, that may make me think differently.

---

[1] Ibid. 53.
[2] See H. W. Bromhead, *Heritage of St. Leonard's* (1932), pp. 39–44. The list of rooms is obtained from the catalogue of the 1816 sale of the contents. Since it appears that there were few actual additions after Thrale's day, the description is probably fairly accurate. For other descriptions see *D'Arblay Diary*, i. 53, and *Early Diary*, ii. 255, &c.

And yet, why should I not indulge the *now*, as well as the *then*, since it will be with so much more pleasure? In short, I do think her delightful; she has talents to create admiration, good humour to excite love, understanding to give entertainment, and a heart which, like my dear father's, seems already fitted for another world.[1]

Again on the 26th she compared the Mistress of Streatham to her own father. 'She has the same natural liveliness, the same general benevolence, the same rare union of gaiety and of feeling in her disposition.'[2] Her conversation was particularly captivating:

It is so entertaining, so gay, so enlivening, when she is in spirits, and so intelligent and instructive when she is otherwise, that I almost as much wish to record all she says, as all Dr. Johnson says.

Mrs. Thrale's sweetness of disposition in accepting without anger the vigorous condemnations of Dr. Johnson forcibly struck the young visitor, and on September 21 she recorded the following colloquy:

Last night, when we were talking of compliments and of gross speeches, Mrs. Thrale most justly said that nobody could make either like Dr. Johnson. 'Your compliments, sir, are made seldom, but when they are made they have an elegance unequalled; but then when you are angry, who dares make speeches so bitter and so cruel?'

Dr. J.—Madam, I am always sorry when I make bitter speeches, and I never do it but when I am insufferably vexed.

Mrs. T.—Yes, sir; but you suffer things to vex you, that nobody else would vex at. I am sure I have had my share of scolding from you!

Dr. J.—It is true, you have; but you have borne it like an angel, and you have been the better for it.

Mrs. T.—That I believe, sir: for I have received more instruction from you than from any man, or any book: and the vanity that you should think me worth instructing, always overcame the vanity of being found fault with. And so you had the scolding, and I the improvement.

F.B.—And I am sure both make for the honour of both!

Dr. J.—I think so too. But Mrs. Thrale is a sweet creature, and never angry; she has a temper the most delightful of any woman I ever knew.[3]

Mrs. Thrale knew well that Johnson's rude remarks were involuntary, and if he saw that his adversary was hurt, were always followed by remorse. She herself later told of one

---

[1] *D'Arblay Diary*, i. 68.   [2] Ibid. 85.   [3] Ibid. 128–9.

occasion when Johnson was silently musing by the fire, and Thrale's young nephew, Sir John Lade, called to him suddenly and as he thought somewhat disrespectfully: 'Mr. Johnson, Would you advise me to marry?' 'I would advise no man to marry, Sir,' replied Johnson angrily, 'who is not likely to propagate understanding.' Immediately afterwards he rose and left the room. The poor youth was confounded, but a few minutes later Johnson returned, and drawing his chair up to the company, joined in the general conversation and gradually led the discussion to the subject of marriage. With genial kindness he gave such a dissertation 'that no one ever recollected the offence, except to rejoice in its consequences'.[1] To strangers Johnson's brusque manner was apt to be irritating, but, as his friends knew, he held no grudge after the first paroxysm of anger had subsided.

If Fanny Burney was charmed with Streatham society, the Thrales and Johnson were equally pleased with her. She was a perfect foil for the talkative lady of the mansion, and the Doctor loved to have 'little Burney' sitting at his side. Consequently, for the next few years she spent much of her time in the household, and her vivid, intimate record provides the best description we have of the everyday life of the family. She gives the names of such guests as drove out to the country estate, what they said, and the verdicts of the family upon them. Long conversations about consequential and inconsequential affairs are related with the utmost fidelity. The picture is complete, though coloured perhaps by the extravagant rapture of the diarist, who found herself a modest but delighted celebrity, petted by some of the most outstanding people of her day. Streatham was the scene of Fanny's entrance into the social world, and naturally she describes it with a partial pen.

Fanny Burney's diary shows Johnson in his lighter moments, full of fun and nonsense, ready either for a joke or a romp. This is not the author of the *Rambler*, but a great man relaxing in the genial atmosphere of blandishment and adulation. Johnson enjoyed the society of ladies as much as the more vigorous companionship of the coffee-house and club. Once he remarked to Mrs. Thrale on the power of women to change the habit of men. 'Smoking Tobacco—said Doctor Johnson—must have been a delightful Thing: I wonder it ever went out of Fashion—but the Women, who rule us all, drove it away.'[2]

Fanny's journal has little to say of the Master of the house-

---

[1] *John. Misc.* i. 213–14.   [2] New Common Place Book, p. 273.

hold, for he was still dejected over his financial troubles of the previous spring. In an attempt to divert his mind during the autumn of 1778, a trip was planned to various watering-places in the south of England. Tunbridge Wells was the first stop, where with a crowd of venerable seekers after health they also found Mrs. Montagu, Sophy Streatfeild, and a number of other Blue-Stockings. On October 17 Mrs. Thrale wrote to Johnson, bursting with pride because the Duchess of Devonshire 'had desired to be introduced' to her; but she added of her husband, 'he is not yet a good Tête a Tête but behaves tolerably in Company—every body however says he is *strangely broke*'. Two days later she added in another note:

Mrs. Montagu cannot bear Evelina—let not that be published— her Silver-Smiths are Pewterers she says, & her Captains Boat-swains. The Attorney General says you must all have commended it out of a Joke; My Master laughs to see me Down among the dead Men & I am happy to see him laugh.

All goes on well at the Brewhouse I hear: & the Money that was borrowed when the Leaves were coming out will be paid—or may be—before they are fallen: neither must this be published.

From Tunbridge Wells the Thrales drove on to Brighton, where the Master warded off the menacing 'black dog' of depression by hunting with Sir John Shelley and chatting with Beauclerk and Gerard Hamilton. She spent her time 'dipping' in the sea and exchanging gossip with Pepys, Mrs. Montagu, and Mrs. Byron, wife of the admiral ('Foul Weather Jack') and grandmother of the poet. They had hoped to have Johnson with them at the sea-side, but he was busy writing his *Lives of the Poets* and refused to leave London. Instead, Mrs. Thrale kept him regularly informed with '*prattle* upon *paper*' of her activities and of her grand friends. Once when describing the guests who were to come to her house that night, she chuckled, 'Dearee Me! how I am got all among the Quality of late—Make me thankful—like Murphy's Uncle.'[1] Never a persistent social climber, Mrs. Thrale did enjoy for awhile the novelty of entertaining the nobility. She always sought companions with brains rather than pedigrees, but if she could find the two combined, so much the better. Queeney, on the other hand, was more impressed by 'keeping high Company'—a predilection she was never to lose.[2]

The open-air life on the Sussex Downs restored Thrale's

---

[1] Sat. Nov. 21 [1778]. The reference is to a character in Murphy's play *The Way to Keep Him*.   [2] Children's Book.

health and spirits, and late in November when they returned to Streatham, his wife remarked that he seemed resolved 'to enjoy himself & his Friends as usual'. Yet there was always something to worry about, the new annoyance which Mrs. Thrale had to face being the growing fondness which her husband showed for the beautiful Sophia Streatfeild. She never suspected Sophia of returning the passion, but the fair Greek scholar's appealing glances and soft tender manners proved irresistible to the opposite sex.[1] She was one of those natural coquettes who, with no intention of doing so, seem born with the faculty of attracting married men. Mrs. Thrale, in long passages in her journals, vented her irritation at seeing her husband lavish sentiment on another which he had never shown to her. On December 31, 1778, and on the last page of the Children's Book, she commented, 'Mr. Thrale is once more happy in his Mind, & at leisure to be so in Love with S: S: that it is comical.' Then, after giving a final description of her daughters and of the friends spending the holidays at Streatham, and with a prayer to God for preservation of herself and her family, she squeezed in a small postscript at the bottom of the page: 'I will not fret about this Rival this S. S. no I wont.'

With this typical mercurial touch the intimate, revealing Children's Book comes to an end. It had been her only confidant during the tragic years of depression and difficulty; in it she had transcribed all the clever sayings of those adored little ones now buried in Streatham Church. But that part of her life was over, and no new Children's Book was ever begun. Thraliana alone would now serve to record her whims, her agonies, and her triumphs.

Already Mrs. Thrale was in her third volume of Thraliana. She had been no laggard in filling the pages of this journal with anecdotes, reflections, and reminiscences. Nearly a hundred pages of the second volume had been devoted exclusively to Johnson, including quotations of his *bons mots*, a list of his published works, and hints for his biography. On the other hand, she was just as indefatigable in writing about herself, and filled over seventy pages of the same volume with a complete chronicle of her own life. Thraliana was both to serve her literary ambitions while alive and to be the vehicle of her fame when she was dead.

Mrs. Thrale had not completely given up her old practice of sending contributions to the newspapers, and during the

[1] See Hayward, i. 111–24.

autumn of 1778 she dispatched a number to the *Public Advertiser*. One was a set of political verses addressed to her friend Sir Philip Jennings Clerke, entitled a 'Tale for the Times', which was full of pointed allusions to the issues of the day.[1] Another was an amusing letter, signed Jacquet Droz, which compared the present acceptance of corruption in public office to that in Rome under the Emperor Nerva.[2] As in the case of the famous Partridge hoax of Swift's time, the real Jacquet Droz immediately wrote to disclaim the authorship, but Mrs. Thrale continued the persiflage with further remarks. Here was a perfect outlet for her irrepressible desire to satirize public and private affairs.

Throughout the winter of 1779 Mrs. Thrale remained chiefly at Streatham. During January Fanny Burney, deaf to all pleas to 'come home', lingered in town, but the invitations were so flattering that soon, like Johnson, she was a regular resident of the country house. Fanny, however, set down in her diary only a few interesting conversations for this period, since her time was taken up with writing a comedy—'The Witlings', later doomed by general agreement of a family council. The play purported to be a satire on the Blue-Stockings, and Mrs. Thrale laughingly insisted on finding a resemblance to herself in the character of 'Lady Smatter';[3] but if Fanny was slyly poking fun at her hostess in the composition, she was enthusiastically adoring her in everyday life. For the present the entire Burney family loaded Mrs. Thrale with compliments, and professed to think her the most perfect of goddesses.[4]

During the spring Thrale, who was now 'in high good humour',[5] spent much of his time in town with Sir Philip

---

[1] Printed on Nov. 28, 1778.

[2] Nov. 20, 1778. This letter must have been sent to the newspapers from Brighton. It ends 'In allusion to my Hand-writing, I sign myself, Yours &c. Jacquet Droz.' The real Droz, who was a maker of clocks and mechanical devices, replied in the issue of Nov. 27, insisting that the published letter was a fabrication. Mrs. Thrale continued on Dec. 1 with a highly amusing epistle, in which she made pointed remarks about her neighbour's profession, and again signed his name. To this Droz wisely made no answer. The allusion to Droz's hand probably referred to a contrivance he had invented for the use of persons born with stumps only. See *Public Advertiser*, Feb. 5, 1777.

[3] Constance Hill, *House in St. Martin's Street*, pp. 153–4.

[4] Dr. Burney's letters to Mrs. Thrale, full of slang and cant phrases, and replete with family jokes, are affectionate and amusing. They show why he was such a universal favourite. (Ry. 545.) See also W. Roberts, *J. Rylands Bulletin*, xvi (1932), pp. 115–36.

[5] Ry. 540, 87. Mrs. Thrale to Johnson, dated only 'Streatham, Thursday', but probably Mar. 11, 1779. Thrale had just returned from a trip to Brighton. See p. 163.

Jennings Clerke and his political friends. As his wife later remembered, he

left Fanny Burney and Me very much alone at poor deserted Streatham Park—we said we would write a Weekly Paper & send after them, & call it the *Flasher*—We had a *Way* of calling Things *Flash* that we wanted others to call *Wit* . . . and one Day it was a Chronicle—another Day a Gazette.[1]

One of the messages shows clearly that Mrs. Thrale suspected that the principal reason Thrale remained in London was to be near her rival Sophy Streatfeild. Even if he did always leave his coach in another street in order not to cause gossip, his constant visits to the fair Greek scholar were annoying to his wife.

Late in May the Thrales, with their three elder daughters, Queeney, Susanna, and Sophia, and Fanny Burney drove to Brighton, where they were joined by Arthur Murphy.[2] Johnson, instead of accompanying them, took this opportunity to set out for Lichfield and Ashbourne. At this time of year Brighton was dull, but with Murphy and the Bishop of Peterborough as companions they were kept in constant good humour. For ten days the air of the West Street house was thick with theatrical plans, while Murphy read Fanny's comedy and Mrs. Thrale busied herself with a tragedy by Dr. Delap. Then about the last day of the month they returned to Streatham.

Here, presently, the household was thrown into the greatest disorder. On June 8 Thrale went to the house of his sister, Mrs. Nesbitt, ostensibly to hear the will of her husband who had just died. The two brothers-in-law had been involved together in a number of speculative schemes, and Thrale had stood security for Nesbitt for a very large amount. When the will was read, showing the estate in a precarious condition, Thrale suddenly saw the sword of Damocles again hanging over his own head. The shock was so great that while at dinner his head sank on the table, his speech became confused, and he seemed to know nobody. His sister, instead of calling help, rushed him back to Streatham in a coach.

Mrs. Thrale tells dramatically what followed.[3] When sitting after dinner with Queeney, Dr. Burney, and his daughter, she was startled by the servant Sam opening the door and saying in

---

[1] Mainwaring *Piozziana*, i. 108; also *Thraliana*, Mar. 24, 1779.
[2] For chronology see *Thraliana*, May 21, June 5, 1779, and Ry. 540, 89. For an account of the trip see *D'Arblay Diary*, i. 216–29.   [3] Hayward, ii. 37.

a peculiar manner: 'My master is come home, but there is something amiss.' A black female figure then blocked her way, calling out, 'Don't go into the library, don't go in I say'; but Mrs. Thrale was not to be held back and burst into the other room where she found her husband insensible, with Mrs. Nesbitt calmly holding his hand. At once all was disorder: Dr. Burney hurried in to London for Dr. Bromfield, while the family and servants rushed about, not knowing what to do. By the time the physician arrived, however, Thrale's senses had returned, and the apoplectic seizure was over. For several days afterwards, nevertheless, his mind occasionally wandered, a condition not calculated to quiet the fears of his wife and family.

To Mrs. Thrale one of the most distressing aspects of the calamity was that Johnson was in Lichfield at the time. He always seemed to be away when she needed him most. Nor did he appear to her to be in any hurry to return, a lack of consideration for which he was soundly berated. Johnson was quick to defend himself. 'There is nobody left for me to care about but you and my master,' he insisted; it was not lack of affection that kept him away, but a feeling that he could be of no use even if he were there.[1] As soon as her husband began to improve, however, Mrs. Thrale was mollified. On the 24th she admitted: 'You have been exceedingly kind, and I have been exceedingly cross; & now my Master is got well, & my Wrath over, I ask your Pardon sincerely.—Heberden thinks all quite safe.'

Although Thrale rallied quickly from this stroke, he never quite recovered his full strength. His taciturnity increased, and he found his only pleasure in over-eating—one vice he would not curb. In spite of his physician's orders, he gorged himself with food, regardless of the consequences. No pleading by his family or friends to be temperate ever made any lasting impression. In consequence the Master's health and disposition became the most important consideration at Streatham, and warding off the 'black dog' of depression the one constant thought of Mrs. Thrale.

[1] June 24, 1779.

IX

THE LAST OF MASTER

JUNE 1779–JUNE 1781

AFTER the first stroke, only two things served to rouse the Master from his lethargy—gay company and constant travel. Consequently, for the next year and a half the life of the Thrales was a medley of entertainments and visits. During the latter part of June a succession of guests filled Streatham, and glimpses of this engaging society can be caught in Fanny Burney's letters and journal: the lovely S. S. obediently weeping for Sir Philip Jennings Clerke; William Seward seeking a suitable wife; Dr. Johnson prodigal with compliments; Mrs. Vesey paying a flattering visit; and Dr. Delap pestering the great Doctor for aid.[1] The rector of Lewes was something of a bore with his overweening ambition to become a successful playwright, and he failed completely in his attempt to provide his tragedy with a prologue written by Johnson. The latter was busy with the *Lives of the Poets*, and preferred to spend his spare time tutoring Queeney and Fanny in Latin.[2]

All this time Mrs. Thrale herself was far from well, again *enceinte*, but not progressing so well as usual. The consequent worry over her husband and herself, with numerous petty annoyances, produced an irritation which, as in the past, found release in Thraliana. When writing in her journals, Mrs. Thrale often showed surprising traits of jealousy and spite which seldom appeared in her letters. Perhaps it relieved her to set things down at their stark worst, even to defiant exaggeration; for then she could shake her 'Salusbury fist' at the whole thing, and make that compact with her spirit, so perfectly expressed in the last words of the Children's Book: 'I will not fret . . . no I wont.'

Of course, the irritable entries were apt to be made at times when Mrs. Thrale was in bad health, which may account for the spleen vented, about this period, on the unsuspecting Fanny Burney. While admitting that she was just as fond of her visitor

---

[1] *D'Arblay Diary*, i. 229–54.
[2] See letters from Dr. Delap to Mrs. Thrale (Ry. 547); *Queeney Letters*, p. xv.

as ever, Mrs. Thrale maliciously recorded her displeasure at
Fanny's fear of being patronized.   She had nursed Fanny constantly during a recent short illness, and this was her reward.[1]

With Thrale incapacitated, she was also forced to give more
time to the affairs of the brewery.   Late in June she had written
to Johnson:

I have not been inattentive to Compting House Business since
Mr. Thrale's Illness, though I do not live there; I drove however a
Parcel of Workmen off yesterday with a high hand, just as you
would have had me.—My dear Master is easily subdued just now,
& I fear no Subalterns, *as I told them.* Our trade is in admirable
order, but these Wars & Taxes tear us to pieces.

Then early in August she was suddenly called upon to settle
a quarrel which had developed among the clerks at the brewhouse.   The strain proved too great, and she suffered a miscarriage.[2]   A week later she wrote to Johnson, who apparently
had been away from Streatham at the time,

With a trembling hand do I acknowledge your last kind Letter
which I received in my Bed;—and till today have not been able to
sit up long enough to thank you for it—Ah Dear Sir how very,
very Ill I have been!

Well! but though I have lost the little Companion entrusted to
my Care, though I have lost my Strength, my Appetite &c. you
have not lost your Friend.[3]

As always she found something to be thankful for; 'had we gone
to Spa this would have happened, and happen'd on board a
Ship—what a providential Escape!' Her husband, she added,
looked 'like Death again' and needed some new perspective,
even if a European tour was out of the question. 'As soon as
ever I can travel I must make him go some where, Change of
Scene is actually necessary to his Recovery.'

[1] Thraliana, Aug. 1779. Fanny Burney, in a later letter to Queeney, July 12,
1798, explained her attitude towards Mrs. Thrale's excessive generosity.

She loaded me with obligations which even at this time were oppressive to me,
dearly as I loved her,—& which, even then, when I considered her fondness to
be unalterable, I thought the least pleasant part of it, from an inherent dislike
to all sort of presents, & from an innate spirit of contentment with what I
naturally possessed, however small its proportion to what surrounded me. The
things, indeed, from her, were trifles, her affluence considered,—but my pride
was dearer to me than her gifts, which were forced upon me whether I would
or not, & which hurt me inexpressibly, frequently with a raillery that shewed
she discredited the sincerity of my resistance. But I valued her friendship too
much for any serious dispute—& all other she over-powered. (Lansdowne MS.)

[2] Thraliana, Aug. 15, 1779; *Life*, iii. 397; Hayward, ii. 39.

[3] Ry. 540, 58. This letter is dated only 'Tuesday 17', but seems from internal
evidence to have been written in Aug. 1779.

Many of her friends sent comforting letters, and Dr. Burney wrote on August 29, in his usual light, airy style,

I thought, as how, we were to *throw notes* at each other. I have so long been a dealer in notes, & am now so beset wth. them, that if you liked their fashion, I wd. send you some to *un*bother; as I have had partly enough of them. But, unluckily, a million of my notes wd. not be worth one of yours—*such* a one as I carried off with me, unread, on Tuesday, dated 18 Augt.—& I found your sweet, dear, innocent, sportive little *Soul*, wrapt up in it!—Well, 'tis a good little Soul, as *eefer vaas*—& I likes it.—Who, but a Swan cd. sing so sweetly, when dying?—indeed who but the truly innocent & tranquil can sing at all, in such a situation? pray content yourself, as you will delight me, with singing *worse*, & being *better*.[1]

Paradoxically enough, during this time of illness and depression, when she was oppressed with a feeling that her 'Campaign' was 'quite over', Mrs. Thrale composed her cleverest piece of creative writing, which was called 'Three Dialogues on the Death of Hester Lynch Thrale'.[2] Swift's little poem on his own death, as she admits, gave her the idea. She supposes herself dead, and imagines conversations in various gatherings where she had been familiar. The first dialogue occurs at Mrs. Vesey's assembly, and the characters are Johnson, Burke, Pepys, and Mrs. Montagu. The second is laid at Beckenham Place, the home of John Cator, a retired timber merchant and an intimate friend of Thrale. The guests are another merchant, Mr. Norman, and Baretti. In the third, Seward's lodgings and Lady Lade's house are the scenes of action, and together with Seward appear Dr. Jebb, Lady Lade, Miss Dodson, Thrale, Queeney, and Sir Philip Jennings Clerke.

The dialogues are short and make no pretence to be anything more than simple character sketches, since Mrs. Thrale merely portrays the dominant traits of some of her friends in describing their reactions to her recent death. Johnson is stirred from silent meditation by the well-meaning but annoying Pepys, and is only quieted by the intervention of Burke. Mrs. Montagu shrewdly remarks: 'Mrs. Thrale, among her other Qualifications, had prodigious strong Nerves—and that's an admirable Quality for a Friend of Dr. Johnson's.' The hypochondriac Seward, the independent Baretti, the surly, brooding Thrale, and the garrulous Lady Lade appear in turn, each one sketched

---

[1] Ry. 545, 3. Pepys's letter of Aug. 21 is in the Adam collection, and that from Mrs. Byron of the same day is Ry. 546, 25.

[2] Edited with an introduction by M. Zamick, and printed in the *J. Rylands Bulletin*, xvi (1932), 77–114.

with remarkable skill. It is not the wit which first strikes the reader, but the economy and certainty of the delineation. With a few strokes of the brush the portrait is blocked in, and the subject classified as surely as by a detailed photograph.

Mrs. Thrale's ear was sensitive to peculiarities of everyday speech and manner.[1] She must have studied her friends with an observant eye and ear and carefully filed away for future use the occasional colloquial pronunciations of Pepys and the vulgar phraseology of Cator and Norman. As a result, each person is made to converse in his usual manner, so that even if we did not know more of his history we could characterize him with precision from these short dialogues. If these *jeux d'esprit* may be taken as a sample of Mrs. Thrale's ability in writing the comedy of manners, it is to be regretted that she never tried her hand at a full-length play.

Throughout August and September 1779 Mrs. Thrale was oppressed with a feeling that she was about to die;[2] but her flow of good spirits, like a perennial spring, though temporarily shut off, could never be stopped at the source. As much could not be said of her husband, whose gloom steadily increased. He even lost his former absorbing interest in business and for the first time was content to let Perkins and Mrs. Thrale manage the brewery, while he found his solace in ever-changing society, cards, dinners, and gay company.

In search of diversion the Thrales, with Queeney and Fanny Burney, set out from Streatham on October 5.[3] After a short stop at Sevenoaks they drove on to see the Streatfeilds at Tunbridge Wells, from which place two days later they continued to Brighton. Here, with hunting during the day and constant amusement in the evenings, the Master was kept from brooding; consequently they remained in Sussex for the next six weeks.[4] When the weather became dismal, however, and Thrale fell ill with a bad cold, they hurriedly decided to return to Streatham. The journey north was distressing. Shivering all the way, the sick man suffered a severe chill, and at Reigate, where they had planned to have dinner, his speech grew inarticulate. Fanny,

---

[1] See my article, 'New Light on the Origin of Eastern American Pronunciation of Unaccented "A" ', *American Speech*, x (Oct. 1935), 173–5.

[2] Indicated by entries in Thraliana.

[3] *D'Arblay Diary*, i. 270–311. Oct. 5 came on Tuesday.

[4] During this visit Thrale sought the opinion of Scrase about his will, and Johnson's letters to Mrs. Thrale throughout November show that he was being consulted in the matter (*Letters*, Nos. 640, 642, 645, 647, 648). According to J. Foote (*Life of Arthur Murphy* (1811), p. 259), Murphy superintended the actual making of the will.

frightened almost out of her wits, was of no help, but Mrs.
Thrale speedily took charge, 'worked like a servant: she lighted
the fire with her own hands,—took the bellows, and made such
a one as might have roasted an ox in ten minutes'.[1] After dinner
Thrale seemed better, but by the time they reached home late
that night he was in a comatose condition. Under the doctor's
care he quickly improved; but the month of December was not
a pleasant one for his wife, for to make matters worse, Fanny
also fell ill, so that Mrs. Thrale had two invalids to nurse.[2]

Mrs. Thrale had always disliked living in Southwark, and for
the past few years had spent as much of her time as possible
at Streatham. Especially now that her social ambitions were
rising, and her husband needed constant entertainment to keep
his mind off himself, she was anxious to rent a house in a more
fashionable part of London for the winter. But Johnson vigorously disapproved, pointing out that proximity to the brewery
was imperative, especially at this time.[3] His advice prevailed,
and some time early in the new year the Thrales moved to
Southwark.

During the winter of 1780 Mrs. Thrale was as gay as possible, considering her husband's varying state of health. Fortunately, he was often reasonably well, and even another seizure
on February 21 left him no more depressed than before. Fanny
Burney wrote that she was seeing the Thrales often, and had
been to some charming parties at their house.[4] Together with
Johnson, Mrs. Thrale entertained, and talked, and 'flashed' on
every opportunity. It was possibly at this time that she dined
one evening with Mrs. Montagu and about a dozen literary
friends, among whom was Sir Nathaniel Wraxall. Later she
recalled that Wraxall related on this occasion

a strange (& as it appear'd by the manner of his Audience,) a most
impressive Story:—so I listen'd: hearing him say that he was shut
by Accident up in a Church at Barcelona, where a female Figure
rose from one of the Tombs, &c &c—when all was over, I whisper'd
Mrs. Scott who sate next me—Pray is not this story in the Spectator? Yes surely, she replied; and in one of Smollet's Novels too—
naming it;—where Monimia plays the same Part—or nearly. Going
home in the Carriage I asked Doctor Johnson how he & all those Wise

---

[1] *D'Arblay Diary*, i. 447. This passage is placed in 1780 by the editors of the
diary, but obviously refers to a year earlier. In Thraliana is a similar account
definitely dating the incident as Nov. 23, 1779.
[2] *D'Arblay Diary*, i. 449; Thraliana, early Dec., 1779. This gives further proof
that the passage should be dated 1779.
[3] *Letters*, Nos. 647, 648.　　　　　　[4] *D'Arblay Diary*, i. 318.

Men could sit so cooly, and listen to such Lyes. I did not, replied He, know what they were saying; Wraxall spoke in a low Voice, and I sate a great way off—and the *Wise men* as you call them, were *Fools*.[1]

Mrs. Thrale was gradually becoming intimate with some of the Blues. Proof of her conquest came in a letter from William Weller Pepys on March 7 inviting her and Dr. Johnson to a large party the following Saturday, and also insisting that she steal away and come on Thursday evening also, when she would find 'only two or three chosen people', among whom would be Mrs. Chapone.[2] Pepys then added, 'I am afraid of asking Dr. Johnson, as there will not be variety enough for him to chuse out of in case He shou'd dislike the Dish or two already pre-par'd.' Johnson would be invited to the large parties, but Pepys did not have the courage to brave the sting of his tongue when disappointed in a dinner. Already Mrs. Thrale was con-fronted with something of a choice—between intimacy with high society and allegiance to the old ties.

In his letter Pepys referred to another problem which, besides her husband's health, now occupied much of Mrs. Thrale's time.[3] With the prospect of an early general election, she felt it advisable to begin soliciting aid from prominent people. But Pepys instead suggested that

if nobody is stiring, it may be impolitick to stir first, as that will put others in motion, & bring on the necessity of an open Canvass at a time when you may be oblig'd to acknowledge Mr. T. inability to canvass for Himself, which might possibly not be the Case, if you waited till the Dissolution of Parliament, or at least till somebody else begins to move.

For his part, Pepys added, 'no opposition of Political Principles cou'd enable me to withstand the Request of *such* a Wife engag'd in *such* a Cause'.

Mrs. Thrale readily accepted Pepys's advice; but to take her husband away from the possibility of becoming involved in such concerns she decided to go to Bath late in March, with Fanny Burney as their companion. The first night they only reached Maidenhead Bridge, the second Speen Hill, and the third Devizes. Here they were interested in the astonishing

---

[1] New Common Place Book, p. 103. Written in the spring of 1815.

[2] Ry. 536, 24.

[3] See also letter from the Bishop of Peterborough, Apr. 13, 1780 (*Adam Libr.* iii. 128). Mrs. Thrale had, in addition, to worry about the condition of the brewery. In Thraliana, in Jan. 1780, she noted that they were to brew only 60,000 barrels this year, as against 76,000 the year before and 96,000 the year before that. The war was taking its toll of all business.

skill in drawing displayed by Thomas, the ten-year-old son of their landlady, Mrs. Lawrence.[1] Little did they guess that one day this boy would be President of the Royal Academy.

In Bath they took a house on the left corner of the South Parade, where they had a beautiful view of the Avon. Many London companions were at the watering-place: Mrs. Montagu; Mrs. Lambart, sister of Sir Philip Jennings Clerke; the Dean of Ossory and his family; and Mrs. Byron. Furthermore, from Fanny Burney's diary it appears that this year they made the acquaintance of several people who later were to be numbered among Mrs. Thrale's most intimate friends. There was, for instance, a tall, handsome clergyman named Thomas Sedgewick Whalley, who was also a dilettante and a patron of art. Others included the family of that Thomas Bowdler whose doubtful distinction it is to have contributed a new word to the language; Lord Huntingdon; and Miss Weston, the favoured correspondent of Anna Seward. It was this year, also, that Mrs. Thrale first saw Sarah Siddons as Belvidera in *Venice Preserved*. What was even more gratifying to her pride, the Bishop of Peterborough preached a special sermon in the Abbey at her request.[2] Fanny Burney was treated to a glimpse of such celebrated characters as Mr. Anstey of the *New Bath Guide*, the flamboyant Edward Jerningham, the scholarly Miss Elizabeth Carter, and Lady Miller of Bath-Easton. It was a momentous experience for the authoress of *Evelina*. Herself the celebrity of the hour, Fanny found the society enchanting, and her accounts re-create for us many an amusing scene. Mrs. Thrale, no less pleased with the life, commented to Johnson on May 3:

Mrs. Montagu & I meet somewhere every Night; People think they must not ask one of us without the other, & there they sit gaping while we talk: I left it to her for the first fortnight & she harangued the Circles herself; till I heard of private Discussions why Mrs. Thrale who was so willing to talk at other Times, was so silent in Mrs. Montagu's Company—then I began, and now we talk away regularly when there is no Musick, & the folks look so stupid, except one or two who I have a Notion lie by to laugh, & write Letters to their Sisters &c. at home about us.[3]

---

[1] *D'Arblay Diary*, i. 323–6; see also O. G. Knapp, *An Artist's Love Story* (1904). Mrs. Thrale in Thraliana refers to the proposed journey to Bath on Mar. 28.

[2] For an account of this year's Bath visit see *D'Arblay Diary*, i. 326–426; see also Mrs. Piozzi's letter to Queeney, Feb. 12, 1799 (Lansdowne MS.).

[3] Mrs. Montagu, like Johnson, often talked for victory. 'The Bishop [of Chester] waited for Mrs. Thrale to speak, Mrs. Thrale for the Bishop; so neither of them spoke at all! Mrs. Montagu cared not a fig, as long as she spoke herself, and so harangued away' (*D'Arblay Diary*, i. 364).

Once started, Mrs. Thrale kept her tongue rattling so continually that Fanny wrote of one evening, 'Mrs. Montagu, Mrs.
Thrale, and Lord Mulgrave talked all the talk, and talked
it so well, no one else had a wish beyond hearing them.'[1]
The two rival ladies had a deep respect for each other,
and Mrs. Montagu, when writing to Pepys that Mr. Thrale
was mended in health, insisted that 'the great felicity of his
life, at all times and on all occasions is, his having such a
Wife'.[2]

Mrs. Montagu even attempted to aid the family in urging
Mr. Thrale to use moderation in his eating, his one uncon-
trollable passion. She interests 'herself for him quite tenderly',
Mrs. Thrale added to Johnson, 'complains to Moysey [the
physician] when She sees him eat too much', and uses all her
influence to make him obey. They all knew that if he did not
curb his voracious appetite he was doomed; but what could be
done with a man, his wife sadly asked, 'whose mouth cannot
be sewed up'. On one occasion, however, Mrs. Thrale did not
regret her husband's weakness. When one of their political
supporters came to Bath, ostensibly to bring news, but also to
judge the health of their candidate, she asked the man to dinner,
'& bid him observe (with an Air) that my Master had not lost
his Stomach—that is the Criterion of a good Constitution in
Southwark I believe'.[3]

Johnson had planned to join them for a short visit, but when
it was found that they had no extra room for him in the house,
he contented himself with writing news of himself and of affairs
in London. Political excitement had begun to stir again in the
Borough, and Thrale's friends were anxious to have him on the
spot. Instead, since his physical condition forbade, Johnson
advised Mrs. Thrale to come herself, and although irritated at
having to leave the pleasant company at Bath, she obediently
consented. So, shortly after May 9, she drove to London with
Fanny Burney as companion.

Here she was immediately plunged into a round of tedious
conferences, but on the 15th wrote to Queeney that she had
scarcely begun her task, all her time having been taken up in
thanking kind friends for favours: 'I have not in all seen above
fifty People yet.'[4] Further letters to her daughter tell of the
strenuous campaigning, while replies from such prominent men
as Lord North, Lord Westcote, and Bamber Gascoyne show

---

[1] *D'Arblay Diary*, i. 344.   [2] Blunt, *Mrs. Montagu*, ii. 273.
[3] To Johnson. May 3, 1780.   [4] *Queeney Letters*, p. 128.

how assiduously she was soliciting votes.[1] Johnson had come
to join her in the borough, where he divided his time between
political excitement and the hasty composition of his life of
Congreve.[2] He too described to Queeney the activity of her
mother, who had 'run about the Borough like a Tigress, seizing
upon every thing that she found in her way'.[3] Mrs. Thrale's
only relaxation came in a hurried glimpse of the Royal Academy
exhibition of painting at Somerset House and a dash out to
Streatham to oversee some repairs there. After a strenuous
week she and Fanny returned to Bath, with many promises of
support and the feeling that the effort had been well worth
while. If only her husband's apathy could be kept from the
Southwark electors, all might still be well.

A few weeks later, however, their gay existence was again
interrupted by startling news from London. On June 8, after
returning from a visit to Lady Miller at Bath-Easton, they
heard the first reports of the Gordon riots in the capital. The
next day Bath itself became turbulent, and a new Roman
Catholic chapel was burned. Bursting with excitement, Mrs.
Thrale and Fanny watched the rioting crowds until four o'clock
in the morning. Then suddenly they were themselves involved
in the danger, for mysterious rumours were being circulated
of Thrale being a Papist, and such a report was actually printed
in a Bath newspaper. Terrified by the possibility of their being
attacked by the mob, Mrs. Thrale decided to leave Bath
instantly, and by eight o'clock on Saturday night, the 10th,
they were on their way. They were so frightened, indeed, that
they avoided all large cities, stopping for the most part only in
small villages. In this way they drove in a leisurely fashion
along country roads to Brighton, which they did not reach
until the 18th.[4]

As soon as they were comfortably settled in their own house,
Mrs. Thrale and Fanny left Queeney and Mr. Thrale and
drove to London to see with their own eyes what damage had
been done. On the 23rd Mrs. Thrale wrote to Mrs. Lambart
from Southwark, where Johnson as before had speedily joined
her, that her spirits did 'sink a little, at the nearer View of the

---

[1] See letter from Lord Mulgrave, May 4, 1780 (Myers & Co., London); from
Lord Westcote, May 9; Bamber Gascoyne, May 31; and from Lord North (no
date) (Ry. 892).
[2] *Letters*, No. 666, 672.
[3] *Queeney Letters*, p. 20.
[4] See Hayward, i. 128; letter to Perkins from Salisbury, June 11, 1780; and
Ry. 550, 3, 4.

Precipice we have just escaped'.[1] The mob had actually forced their way into the brewhouse, and in a few minutes would probably have burned it to the ground, had not Perkins, with rare presence of mind, plied the crowd with meat and drink, while Sir Philip Jennings Clerke hurried off to summon troops. All the valuable papers were carried to Chelsea College for safety, and in the end nothing was lost. As a reward for his cleverness, Mrs. Thrale presented Perkins with two hundred guineas and his wife with a silver urn.[2]

After another visit to Streatham to survey the improvements there, Mrs. Thrale returned to Brighton for a vacation at the sea-shore, this time taking along her younger daughters, Susan and Sophy. Fanny Burney had refused to accompany her, much to Mrs. Thrale's annoyance, for the season had not yet begun at Brighton, and she sadly lacked entertaining company. She could not refrain from noting in Thraliana her displeasure at Fanny's pining for her own home, 'always preferring the mode of Life in St. Martins Street to all I could do for her'.[3] Mrs. Thrale could not understand the clannish spirit of the Burneys, who were never long contented away from the family circle.

For the next two months the Thrales remained quietly in Sussex, the head of the house, though 'in rosy health' and joking with Miss Owen, still in no condition to be seen by his Southwark constituents.[4] Mrs. Thrale kept busy with a number of things—chiefly her two strenuous younger daughters and a new project of writing. She had seen little of Susan and Sophia (ten and nine respectively) during the past few years, but now enjoyed watching them make verses, act plays, and swim in the sea. On July 8 she described herself to Mrs. Lambart, one of her regular correspondents, as 'just come from the Sea with my two romping Girls skipping up the street on each side me'. With little society to occupy her time, she could devote herself also to composition. Possibly on the last hurried trip to Streatham something had occurred to remind her of the series of portraits by Sir Joshua Reynolds which lined the walls of the library. Whatever the stimulus, she now decided to finish a series of verse characterizations, begun some years before, of the illustrious company there represented; and in, leisure moments throughout the next months the work was gradually completed. In biting octosyllabic couplets she described with

---

[1] Ry. 550, 4. All the following quotations from letters to Mrs. Lambart are taken from Ry. 550.   [2] *Queeney Letters*, pp. 133–6. See also Thraliana, May, 1780.   [3] July 1, 1780.   [4] *D'Arblay Diary*, i. 431.

considerable insight the strength and weaknesses of her famous friends. Shrewd and incisive, these delineations probably represent her most effective poetry.[1]

There was also Thraliana to be filled. The necessity of keeping her husband away from London had separated her from Johnson, except for two short visits, since the previous April. It was much too long a time, she commented in her journal, and then she added a long entry describing her tenderness for him.[2] All her deep affection for the man who was her intimate friend and adviser was expressed in glowing terms; but in one of the next entries, by a strange irony, she recorded a meeting with the man who was to supplant him.

One morning late in July, when out walking with Queeney, Mrs. Thrale noticed at the door of the bookseller's shop the Italian singer, Gabriel Piozzi. Either she remembered having seen him at Dr. Burney's, or he had been pointed out to her recently by someone else; at any rate she accosted him in Italian, and asked if he would be willing to give her daughter lessons in music while at Brighton. He replied coldly that he had come to the sea-side to recover his voice and to complete some musical composition; but later in the day, upon finding out the name of the lady who had spoken to him, he eagerly offered to do anything she wished. In Thraliana, when noting the incident, she remarked, 'He is amazingly like my Father'— some explanation, perhaps, for her immediate attraction to the man.[3] Shortly after, she wrote to Mrs. Lambart:

I reply to the kindness of dear Mrs. Lambart from the coolest Place I can find in Brighthelmstone the Bookseller's shop: Piozzi the famous singer comes here every Morning and plays on a Publick Instrument wch. stands ready: his Taste is so exquisite, his Manner so fine we have never done adoring him; and I have secured his Instructions for my eldest daughter while he stays here to bathe.[4]

Her husband's spirits, she added, 'are so much increased that he is all on Fire for a Journey to Italy', but she herself viewed such an expedition with anxiety. Worry over all these plans, she insisted, made her melancholy,

and I am glad to see Piozzi coming towards us that his Voice may dissipate the Cloud of Care which gathers round me at this Moment.

This time Mrs. Thrale felt no inclination to mimic the musician behind his back.

[1] Hayward, ii. 170–80; Mainwaring Piozziana, i. 115–25; Thraliana, May 28, 1777; July, Aug. 2, 1780; Jan. 10, 1781.   [2] Thraliana, July 14, 1780.
[3] July–Aug. 1780.   [4] Ry. 550, 2 (no date).

Gabriel Mario Piozzi, who so delighted the ladies of Brighton, was born at Quinzano, in the Venetian State, on June 8, 1740.[1] His parents were of the upper middle class, with a limited income and fourteen children. Originally intended for the priesthood, the young Gabriel early showed his predilection for music and in consequence ran away to Milan, where he found a wealthy patron and friend in the Marquis D'Araciel. Although his voice was never strong enough for opera, he gradually acquired some reputation as a singer; about the year 1776 he arrived in London, where, in addition to giving concerts, he set up as a fashionable vocal teacher, apparently with great success.[2] He soon became a friend of Dr. Burney, who later maintained that 'He was the first who let me know what good singing was'.[3] In the journals of Susan Burney there are numerous references to the touchy Piozzi, playing his compositions and singing divinely in the Burney music room, or jealous of the great favourite, Pacchierotti.[4] Chiefly known as a singer and performer, Piozzi also had more than average ability as a composer, publishing several series of lessons for beginners, some charming songs, and admirable string quartets.[5] Even if his later compositions are largely imitative

---

[1] Hayward, ii. 49, 51. In my possession is a certificate secured by Piozzi in the spring of 1784 giving the date of his christening. In later diaries Piozzi always noted his birthday on June 8.

[2] Piozzi must have been considered a fine teacher, for Charlotte Burney records that the Dean of Winchester paid him 'half a guinea a lesson, twice a week', for each of his daughters (*Early Diary of F. Burney,* ii. 298). Mrs. Thrale wrote in Thraliana at a later date that an article in the newspapers had listed the yearly earnings of various musicians and set Piozzi down for £1,200 (Hayward, i. 151–2). Piozzi's concerts were apparently well attended from his first appearances in England. In the Adam collection is a ticket for one of his early concerts of vocal and instrumental music at the New Rooms, Tottenham Street, Bath, on Apr. 18, 1777. The ticket lists the price of admission as half a guinea, and the number 492 on the back would seem to indicate a fair-sized audience. A critical work devoted to a description of famous living musicians in England, *A.B.C. Dario Musico,* published in Bath in 1780, begins the account of Piozzi by stating that he

> came into this country about four years ago to teach singing, for which he is very capable, having a *flexible* falsetto, though not a clear one. He runs divisions with great facility, and sings with taste, though 'tis the *thousandth* edition of what we hear from Italians in general. (p. 36.)

In this somewhat jaundiced work, where Pacchierotti is described as singing out of tune with a cracked voice, the delineation of Piozzi may be considered as definitely flattering.   [3] To Mrs. Piozzi, Jan. 21, 1807 (Ry. 545, 13).

[4] *Early Diary of F. Burney,* i, p. lxxxviii.

[5] A number of his printed compositions may be found in the British Museum. Opus II consists of six sonatas for harpsichord and violin, dedicated to Lady Caroline Waldegrave, printed and sold by John Welcker, Haymarket. Opus III is a second set of six sonatas for harpsichord and violin, dedicated to Lady Champneys. Opus IV comprises six quartets for two violins, alto, and 'cello, dedicated to

of Haydn and Mozart, they have an engaging, tuneful quality of their own.

At Brighton Piozzi soon became a great favourite with Mrs. Thrale, and on August 13 she wrote in Thraliana:

his Hand on the Forte Piano too is so soft, so sweet, so delicate, every Tone goes to one's heart I think; and fills the Mind with Emotions one would not be without, though inconvenient enough sometimes.

She found him intelligent, discerning, with elegant taste; the only fault in the man was his excessive pride.

Possibly one reason for Mrs. Thrale's sudden interest in music was the paucity of other entertainment. Yet she always made the best of circumstances, and commented to Johnson on the 27th:

I am at the Top of the World here, that I am; & saucy enough most likely, Stephen Fuller who was I think my greatest Favourite, asked me how I, who kept you Company at home, could bear the Society I was in here: I could only reply they were the best I could get, and of high Rank if that was all.

Only her husband's health kept her from tolerant enjoyment of all the place had to offer. He was always on the verge of another stroke; but after one serious attack, from which he rallied after excessive bleeding, he seemed so much better that they accepted an invitation to visit the Shelleys at Mitchel Grove. This visit, in turn, was cut short by the dissolution of Parliament on September 1.[1]

Despite the fact that Thrale was obviously in no condition to make a strenuous campaign, he insisted on returning immediately to Southwark. Faced with the possibility of losing his seat, he was willing to take any risk in order to canvass the voters as vigorously as possible. Johnson came to help, wrote advertisements for the papers, and did all in his power to aid his friend's candidature,[2] but nothing could avail against the

---

the Count de Maltzan, 'Printed for the Author, No. 13 Vere St., Oxford Road'. Opus V has six more sonatas for harpsichord and violin, dedicated to Miss Child, 'London Printed for the Author at his House No. 21 Wigmore Street Cavendish Square'. Opus VI includes three duets and three canzonets for high voice. The copy in the British Museum is signed 'G. Piozzi'. (British Museum Old Music g 293, 432/1 a, 432, 432/2 a, 424 b.) I have heard some of these compositions played from rotograph copies. The sonatas are simple and uninteresting, but the songs are melodic and graceful, and the string quartets are wholly delightful.

[1] Ry. 540, 99, 100; Thraliana, Sept. 2, 1780.
[2] See *Life*, iii. 440. Boswell, while he prints only one, that of Sept. 7, states that Johnson wrote a number of addresses for the newspapers. Others had appeared Sept. 4, and 6, and on the 11th a further solicitation for votes appeared. This

open evidence of Thrale's physical disability. His wife on the 19th described the sequence of events to Mrs. Lambart:

tho' I went with him to every house talked for him, solicited &c. strength would not keep pace with Spirit—& He was again *taken very ill* the day before the Poll, at a Church crowded with Voters, . who came to see the rival Candidates; in whose presence likewise this fatal Accident happened, His friends now considered him as dying, his Enemies as dead; I was to call Physicians, to provide a substitute for him upon the Hustings, to consult Council concerning the Polling Business, & to prove my Husband's Existence by shewing myself in the Streets while my Duty called me to his bedside. I wonder how I kept my Wits for my Part, but my Voice *did* leave me; I grew so hoarse I could hardly articulate any Sounds at all, and the Majority increased so much against us on Monday; that tho' Mr. Thrale rouzed on Tuesday, after losing 26 *more* ounces of Blood, besides Blisters & a dreadful Etcetera; tho' he resolved with unequal'd Spirit to show himself that Day at the polling place; tho' he did actually come thither, among the Shouts and Acclamations of his Friends—which I think are still in my Ears—our Antagonists had gained so much Ground, no Efforts then made could retrieve it.

At the close of the poll Thrale was third on the list, far behind his two successful rivals. Yet even then he refused to accept defeat, and swore he would try for another place. He actually wrote to Lord North of his hopes, asking him to recommend 'some borough where I may be chosen . . . at my Own expense', but his condition being well known, nothing came of the request.[1] The Master's parliamentary career was closed.

As soon as the election was over, Mrs. Thrale took her brooding husband out to newly renovated Streatham, where she hoped he would be quiet for a time. But with his wavering temper he could not be happy anywhere long, and she was forced to plan continual trips round the neighbourhood. Since Fanny Burney was staying with her adored 'Daddy Crisp' at Chessington, the Thrales, on September 20, drove over with Queeney and Johnson for a short visit.[2] Something of Thrale's restless mood at the time is clearly shown in a letter written him some months later by Fanny on another visit to Chessington.

Were I to tell you, my Dear Master, but half the satisfaction I

---

last, which was not signed by Thrale, is probably not by Johnson. The *Gazetteer*, Sept. 12, 1780, described the election at Mill-lane. Mr. Perkins apologized for Thrale's absence, but was interrupted by hisses and groans from his opponents.

[1] The original draft of this letter, probably composed by Johnson, is now in the collection of Dr. Rosenbach. See also Johnson's letter No. 706.

[2] W. H. Hutton, *Burford Papers* (1905), p. 46.

feel in the good accounts I receive of your recovered Health &
Spirits, you would Vow it was all flourish, & only written to shew
off,—& serve my poor Letter as You serve a New's paper Murder,
by calling out 'Come, come, come, let's hear no more on't!' And
therefore, as I am pretty well acquainted with your Taste, & believe
you to have no more respect for the Flowers of Rhetorick than Dr.
Johnson has for the *pipy pipy*, I will try to avoid provoking your
indignation by simply saying I am glad, Sir, you are so well.

'And is that all? you cry,—have you nothing more substantial
for me than a few Compliments? what are become of my Cucumbers? a Man who Eats but once in 2 days, is too sharp set to have
much relish for fine Words, &, like George Bodens, would rather
hear a Jack squeak, than Songs or Orations;—come, therefore, to the
point, let me Nail you to the point, have you any thing to fill—— &c.'

Patience, dear Sir!—the Cucumbers are not quite in order for Eating yet, & Mr. Crisp will not send them to disgrace his Culinary skill.

Miss Kitty Cooke is not yet quite recovered from the dismay into
which she was thrown by your prowling about all the Apartments
here; though she protests the disorder in Mr. Crisp's Room was
nothing to *her*, & that all her concern, like that of Mrs. Frances
Harris, is merely *for the Credit of the House.*

The old lady, too, whose retirement you thought proper to invade,
& whom mortal man had not for many years beheld, still relates
your alarming intrusion with minuteness & wonder, & fancies
there was some secret design in so mysterious a conduct which no
one will tell her.

As to Mrs. Hamilton, her consternation at Dr. Johnson's behaviour to me has made so strong an impression upon her mind
that it dwells there yet; & has rooted from her remembrance all
the other transactions of your memorable visit.

Even the Servants have found ample matter for observation &
discussion since that eventfull period. One of them relates your
general enquiries about the accommodations; another, your
particular Questions concerning the Sequestered old lady;—but
the remarks told by the third, & which were made in the kitchen,
are the most important of all,—for, having examined there what
fare was preparing for Dinner, you cast your Eyes most dolefully
upon a small leg of Mutton, & the servants who watched you
perceived, with no little emotion, that you shrugged your Shoulders
at the Sight! After which, to solace yourself for the impending
disappointment you then foresaw of a Dinner, you called for some
Bread & Cheeze; and those who saw you eat it, having first seen
you descend from a Coach & Four, marvelled as much at the Sight
as Mrs. Montagu at Mr. Burrows, when in a Room full of Company,
he called for his Beer![1]

---

[1] Ry. 545, 20. Probably written Dec. 20, 1780, from Chessington. The term
'*pipy pipy*' perhaps refers to Johnson's known distaste for music.

As Fanny indicates in her best *Evelina* manner, Thrale's chief interest was still centred in food, for although he might on occasions starve himself, he could never adhere to temperance long. He preferred to die rather than give up inordinate eating. So the dinners at Streatham were still worthy of comment for any guest invited to partake of them for the first time. When the recluse Mr. Crisp, after much solicitation, did accept the invitation on September 30, he described the fare in a letter to his sister:

I met a vast deal of Company at Streatham, where everything was most splendid and magnificent—two courses of 21 Dishes each, besides Removes; and after that a dessert of a piece with the Dinner —Pines and Fruits of all Sorts, Ices, Creams, &c., &c., &c., without end—everything in plate, of which such a profusion, and such a Side Board: I never saw such at any Nobleman's.[1]

Thrale was not content, however, to enjoy this magnificence, for his wife wrote to Mrs. Lambart of the peculiar ways in which his illness affected him:

sometimes by Torpor, sometimes by Violence, but he is never querulous or peevish. restless & fanciful to an extream Degree, he will go visiting everybody with whom he has any, or even no Acquaintance; We set out for Berks on Monday next, & have a thousand Projects in View—all of which perplex me so I half run wild at the Thoughts of them.[2]

To keep always on the move, they drove to Brighton about the middle of October. Mrs. Thrale had first begged Fanny Burney to be of the party, but Fanny, with the backing of her father, was obdurate. Already at work on *Cecilia*, she knew that creative writing would be impossible in the bustle of the Thrale household, and she preferred quiet and seclusion for a time.[3] Mrs. Thrale, as in the previous year, was annoyed at the ungrateful Burneys, who did not seem to realize how much better off Fanny would be with her than at home. Johnson rather unwillingly agreed to take Fanny's place. He never had liked the watering-place and was still correcting proof for some of his *Lives*; but in order to be of service to his Master he sacrificed his own inclination.[4]

The company remained less than a month at the shore, for when Dr. Pepys returned to London after the season for bathing was over, they did not dare to linger, as it left them without

[1] Hutton, op. cit., p. 49.   [2] Oct. 5, 1780.
[3] Hutton, op. cit. p. 46.   [4] *Life*, iii. 442.

adequate medical advice.[1] Bath was impossible as an alternative, since their favourite physician there had just died; therefore, to be on the safe side, they stayed at Streatham for the
remainder of 1780.

In spite of all the worry and excitement of the autumn, Mrs.
Thrale had not forgotten the charming singer whom she had
grown to like in Brighton the summer before, and he was soon
asked to Streatham, as part of a crowd of guests invited for the
holidays. Late in December Mrs. Thrale wrote to her aunt
Cotton:

My Master keeps upon his Legs very prettily, & we have had a
merry Xmas: Mr. & Mrs. Davenant—kind Creatures—are with me
still, & I kept Mr. Harry Cotton with me as long as he would stay:
two or three young Men & Maidens of an agreeable sort filled our
Society—& that delightful Mortal Piozzi, the famous Italian singer
spent a day or two in entertaining us with *his* astonishing Powers.
What most amazed the People of the *Ton*, was *his* condescending to
play Country Dances (for the 1st Time of his Life) while we pretty
Masters & Misses set to Dancing. I coax him to teach Hester the
Vocal part of Musick, while Doctor Burney works her at the
Harpsichord.[2]

Evidently she also used Piozzi's singing as a bait to draw guests
to her parties, for Charles Jenkinson (later Lord Liverpool),
who had recently been of service in one of her charitable
schemes, wrote on December 29 that 'not even the Temptation
of the best Singer in Italy & of the fairest & most agreeable
Ladies' could make him break a prior engagement for January 6.[3]
Piozzi was soon a constant visitor at Streatham, where he
taught Queeney singing, played the harpsichord for the entertainment of the Master, and set the Mistress to work translating
Italian poetry.[4] Mrs. Thrale found him increasingly attractive,
and though she had never before had the slightest taste for
music, she now became a most enthusiastic concert subscriber.

At last Mrs. Thrale was to have the pleasure of a London
house in a fashionable district; and strange to say, this time it

---

[1] The date of their leaving Brighton is not absolutely certain. Murphy wrote
on Nov. 11, referring to Johnson's presence at the shore with them (Adam collection), and on the 14th Mrs. Thrale wrote to Mrs. Lambart from Streatham
announcing their return (Ry. 550, 9). Shortly after their return, Thrale was
troubled with a dangerous carbuncle on his neck (*Burford Papers*, p. 57).
[2] Now in the possession of Mr. Francis Edwards, Marylebone, London.
[3] B.M. Add. MS. 38308–59, Dec. 29, 1780. In November Jenkinson had been
of service in recommending a young man to Lord Sandwich for promotion in the
marines (B.M. Add. MS. 38308–39). See also letter of Lord Sandwich of Nov. 20,
1780, to Mrs. Thrale (Ry. 892).   [4] Mainwaring Piozziana, i. 128, &c.

was her husband who most actively urged the change. Having lost his interest in business and desiring constant gaiety at any cost, he looked forward to a London season. Another impelling reason for moving was the comfort of being near their physicians. On January 15, 1781, Mrs. Thrale commented to Mrs. Lambart:

Mr. Thrale talks of a house in Town for the Winter, but cannot suit himself; indeed hunting the House is as much Amusement as having it,—to him, and with Regard to myself, People would not perhaps put the Kindest Construction on my desire of going to London, so I say nothing at all, & sit still to see how it will end.

After much indecision Thrale finally rented a furnished house in Grosvenor Square, to which they moved on January 30.[1] Although his wife always maintained that the change was made solely on account of her husband, it was the realization of her fondest dreams. No longer would she be secluded in dirty Southwark far away from her friends; now she could really entertain the *ton*.

With such a prospect, Mrs. Thrale's thoughts naturally turned to dresses and party clothes, and even before they moved to their new house she appeared at court in a remarkable gown copied from specimens of goods brought from the South Seas by Captain Burney. The dress was splendidly trimmed, Mrs. Thrale wrote to Fanny, 'with grebeskins and gold to the tune of £65—the trimming only'.[2] Susan Burney, greatly excited, went to see the creation at the Davenants in Red Lion Square, where Mrs. Thrale dressed for the ceremony. The next day, January 19, the *Morning Herald* described her appearance.

Mrs. Thrale appeared in a striped sattin Otaheite pattern, trimmed with crape, gold lace, and foil, and ornamented with a profusion of stones, of a new composition, very little inferior in point of lustre to the most brilliant jewels;—the *toute ensemble* of this dress was magnificent as well as singular!

In spite of Society's pronounced preference for late evening parties, the regular dining hour in the Thrale household had always been four o'clock in the afternoon. In Sir Joshua Reynolds's list of engagements he always recorded an invitation to Streatham or Southwark as '4 Mr. Thrale'.[3]

---

[1] Hayward, i. 129; Thraliana, Jan. 29, 1781.
[2] *D'Arblay Diary*, i. 460; *Early Diary of F. Burney*, ii. 265.
[3] See p. 66, n. 2.

Suddenly in the winter of 1781 the terse record was changed
to '8 Mrs. Thrale', indicating that the sturdy, conservative
brewer had finally given way to the dictates of fashion. Mrs.
Thrale had taken her place among the spectacular hostesses
of London, and she wrote to Fanny Burney, who was ill at
Chessington:

Yesterday I had a conversazione. Mrs. Montagu was brilliant in
diamonds, solid in judgment, critical in talk. Sophy smiled, Piozzi
sung, Pepys panted with admiration, Johnson was good-humoured,
Lord John Clinton attentive, Dr. Bowdler lame, and my master not
asleep. Mrs. Ord looked elegant, Lady Rothes dainty, Mrs.
Davenant dapper, and Sir Philip's curls were all blown about by
the wind.[1]

In her usual manner, however, she was so harassed by
vexing personal problems, as well as by her many activities,
that she was unable to enjoy the new-found emancipation.
As she commented to Mrs. Lambart,

here is one Friend writing a Tragedy, & I must read it forsooth, &
do this & t'other to it; here's a second setting up a Concert, & I
must gather Subscriptions—play Patroness &c. here's a Clerk run
away from the Brewhouse, & I must write Dispatches in different
Languages to different Courts, that he may be apprehended, and
obliged to refund his stolen Cash. Here's sweet Fanny Burney very
ill 20 Miles off, and desires to see me directly. Unless there were
52 Hours in the Day, & 100 Weeks in the Year, this *could* not do,
& Mr. Thrale's Health always varying, always precarious,—&
always bad. I really am so lean I shall cut thro' my own skin by
& by.[2]

The first occupation which claimed much of her time concerned her Brighton friend, Dr. Delap, who finally achieved
his lifetime ambition in having his tragedy, *The Royal Suppliants*,
produced at Drury Lane Theatre. The autumn before, Mrs.
Thrale had acted as intermediary between the author and the
manager, Sheridan,[3] and finally she gave further help. Delap
had until the last been hoping for a prologue by Johnson, but
when all his pleas proved fruitless, he turned in desperation
to Mrs. Thrale. Just at this moment the brewery clerk ab-
sconded, and while she was driving about London in the
coach trying to find him, she composed the required prologue.[4]
After numerous last-minute changes the play appeared on
February 17, much to the delight of the author's friends,

---

[1] *D'Arblay Diary*, i. 460–1.   [2] Ry. 550, 15 (undated).
[3] Ry. 547, 2.   [4] Ry. 550, 15; *Thraliana*, Feb. 1, 1781.

particularly Mrs. Thrale, who heard one of her compositions recited on the stage for the first time. Her prologue was printed in the *Gentleman's Magazine* for March with the explanation, 'supposed to be written by Mrs. Thr—le'.[1] It was pleasant to be prominently connected with the production of a play at Drury Lane, even if it was so poor a one as *The Royal Suppliants.*

The other friend who claimed her assistance was Piozzi. She solicited all her acquaintances for subscriptions to his concerts, and actually gathered thirty-four subscribers at 5 guineas each.[2] Never reticent about her likes or dislikes, she now openly showed her admiration for the sentimental musician. He and the Bishop of Peterborough were her acknowledged favourites of all those who came to the house. She adored the Bishop with so much ardour that other old friends pretended to be jealous, and she laughingly admitted to Mrs. Lambart that 'Dr. Johnson & Sir Philip wish to keep *him out* they always say'.[3]

It must not be thought that the removal to fashionable Grosvenor Square had affected Johnson's status in the household; the great man always had a room there ready for his use. Although the incongruity of the situation did not escape Boswell and Hannah More, Johnson himself saw nothing humorous in the matter, only complaining that it was not half so convenient as Bolt Court.[4] His entry into smart London came at an inopportune time, however, for the publication of the last volumes of his *Lives of the Poets* had precipitated him into a bitter quarrel with the Blue-Stockings. These brief biographical prefaces, on which he had been working in a desultory manner for several years, had been largely written while the Thrales were away from London. A few had been composed at Streatham and Southwark, and at these times Mrs. Thrale had helped by acting as amanuensis. Boswell noticed her 'fair hand . . . as one of his copyists of select passages'.[5] And the whole of the existing manuscript of the *Life of Pope* is

---

[1] *Gent. Mag.* li (1781), 134. Three editions of the play appeared, in which the prologue is listed as 'Written by a Friend'. Genest (vi. 180–2) says that the tragedy was acted ten times.

[2] *Thraliana*, Feb. 26, 1781. C. Jenkinson wrote on Jan. 29, 1781, accepting with pleasure 'the honour of having His name in the Book she holds for Piozzi: He will make one of the Party in Harley Street, as often as the House of Commons will allow Him' (B.M. Add. MS. 38308–72). The concerts were held each Friday.

[3] Ry. 550, 14.

[4] H. More, *Memoirs*, i. 207; *Life*, iv. 72.

[5] *Life*, iv. 37.

in her writing.[1] While the work was in progress, as Fanny Burney remembered, Dr. Johnson

would frequently produce one of its proof sheets to embellish the breakfast table, which was always in the library; and was, certainly, the most sprightly and agreeable meeting of the day . . . These proof sheets Mrs. Thrale was permitted to read aloud; and the discussions to which they led were in the highest degree entertaining.[2]

What aroused the controversy with the fashionable literary coterie were his criticisms of Gray and his patronizing attitude towards Lord Lyttelton. As punishment Mrs. Montagu no longer invited the Doctor to her assemblies,[3] a gesture particularly annoying to Mrs. Thrale. She had been assiduously cultivating Mrs. Montagu and her satellites for the past few years, and it was not pleasant to find this friendship threatened by a petty literary feud. Openly she tried to keep from taking sides in the argument, but with Johnson a member of her household this proved a difficult proceeding. There was always the possibility of an unfortunate flare-up, like the well-known quarrel with William Weller Pepys, which occurred at Streatham the following June.[4]

No petty annoyances, however, could restrain the exuberance of her disposition, and, according to Boswell, during the last of March 1781 she was her old, extravagant self. For instance, on April 1 Johnson took her to task for her tendency to exaggeration, maintaining that both her praise and her malice defeated themselves because they were overdrawn.

And yet, (with a pleasing pause and leering smile,) She is the first woman in the World. Could she but restrain that wicked tongue of her's, she would be the only Woman in the World. Could she but command that little whirligig—[5]

Mrs. Thrale's rattling tongue constantly dragged her into difficulties, and when Johnson was her companion, no mistake was ever allowed to pass unnoticed. Only a short time later Boswell recorded after one of her remarks, 'this was illbred, and She was deservedly flogged'. But despite all the nagging, Mrs. Thrale never could control 'that little whirligig', and it must be admitted that this lack of restraint was one of the chief sources of her charm. Everyone liked to hear her

---

[1] MS. now in the Morgan Library, New York City.
[2] D'Arblay, *Memoirs of Dr. Burney* (1832), ii. 177–8; Hayward, i. 27.
[3] *Life*, iv. 73.   [4] *D'Arblay Diary*, i. 498–502.
[5] *Private Papers*, xiv. 186.

chatter, even if occasionally questioning the propriety of her revelations.

Her husband's condition, meanwhile, was steadily growing worse. He slept much of the time and when awake was lethargic and moody. Nevertheless, in spite of the opposing counsel of his friends and physicians, he continued to toy with the idea of a tour to a German spa, or perhaps even to Italy. Johnson had consented to join the party, and Mrs. Thrale was willing to beg Baretti, whom she abhorred, to accompany them because of his facility with foreign languages. Fanny Burney, to her great mortification, was excluded from the plans.[1]

On Monday, April 2, 1781, Johnson, Baretti, and Sir Philip Jennings Clerke were guests at dinner, when their host ate so voraciously that it seemed to all an act of defiance, and to Johnson, almost deliberate suicide. The next morning Mrs. Thrale was so dispirited over the prospect that she confided her fears to Mrs. Hinchcliffe, the wife of her favourite Bishop. Household affairs, however, left her little time to brood, for the Thrales were planning an elaborate party on Wednesday night, for which she had engaged a number of Italian singers and invited a large company, including some Brahmins of India. When Piozzi came to give Queeney her singing lesson, Mrs. Thrale conferred with him about the next day's entertainment and evidently showed her nervous condition so plainly that the tender-hearted Italian was moved to compassion. Taking the only way he knew to comfort her, he seated himself at the harpsichord and sang in his most feeling manner. Mrs. Byron, who heard and watched him, turned to Mrs. Thrale and said, 'You know, I suppose, that that Man is in Love with you.' But the Mistress's mind was far away, and she curtly replied, 'I am too irritated to care who is in Love with me.'[2] For the moment there were far too many other pressing matters for her to admit such sentimental fancies.

That day Thrale seemed in a better mood, full of plans for the musical party, and again he ate an enormous dinner. Late in the afternoon Queeney found her father lying on the floor. 'What's the meaning of this?' she cried out excitedly. 'I chuse it,' replied Thrale firmly, 'I lie so o'purpose.'[3] A messenger was immediately sent for Dr. Pepys, but before he arrived the brewer had suffered a violent attack of apoplexy, from which

[1] Hayward, i. 131–2; *D'Arblay Diary,* i. 463–4.
[2] Mainwaring Piozziana, i. 133. The passage has been scored out, but with patience the words can be deciphered. See also Hayward, i. 132–5, and Thraliana, early Apr. 1781.   [3] Thraliana, early Apr. 1781.

he recovered only to lapse into another. Throughout the night, while Johnson sat faithfully by his bedside hoping always for recovery, Thrale's strength grew weaker.[1] Mrs. Thrale ventured once into the room, but preparations for bleeding proved too much for her sensitive nerves, so that instead of remaining she frantically awaited news in her own room. Early on Wednesday morning, April 4, 1781, Thrale finally succumbed.[2]

Mrs. Thrale's usual reaction to death was to run away. This time, not waiting for the funeral, she hurried with Queeney immediately to Streatham and from there to Brighton, where she remained for two weeks, seeking advice and consolation from her trusted friend, Mr. Scrase. To arouse her own and Queeney's drooping spirits, she wrote jocular French verses on her daughter's ills,[3] and struggled to forget the problems of the moment.

Johnson in London wrote nearly every day with sympathy and news; no death since that of his wife, he maintained, had oppressed him like this.[4] Through the years his early respect had deepened into a sincere affection, and Thrale had been his patron, his banker, his intimate companion. The Master's death, Johnson could not but feel, closed a long, happy chapter in his own life.

While the death of Thrale was naturally a terrible shock to his immediate family, in London it served only to start immediate gossip about the future of his wealthy widow. For years people had wondered about the relationship of Johnson and his Mistress; now many speculated as to their possible marriage. The day after Thrale's funeral, Boswell, with strange lack of taste, composed a set of amusing stanzas, entitled 'Ode by Samuel Johnson to Mrs. Thrale upon their supposed approaching nuptials'.[5] He thought so highly of his verses that he showed them during the next few days to a number of his friends. Even Fanny Burney may have seen this burlesque, for some weeks later she wrote to Mrs. Thrale, 'I have heard some verses, though, about you & Dr. Johnson! such as you so well foretold.'[6] That others too were thinking of

---

[1] *John. Misc.*, ii. 8; i. 96.
[2] Hayward, i. 135. By coincidence it was the seventh anniversary of Goldsmith's death.   [3] *D'Arblay Diary*, i. 472; *Queeney Letters*, pp. 58–9.
[4] Apr. 5, 1781. See also Letters of Apr. 7, 9, 11, 12, 14, 16, 17.
[5] *Private Papers*, xiv. 196. Thrale had been buried at Streatham on Apr. 11. The bill for funeral expenses may be found in Ry. 598, 35.
[6] Ry. 545, 23 (undated).

the same possibility is shown in Boswell's entry on the 18th: 'Scott and I agreed that it was possible Mrs. Thrale might marry Dr. Johnson, and we both wished it much. He saw clearly the Doctor's propensity to love THE VAIN WORLD in various ways.'[1] We may be certain, however, that for her part Mrs. Thrale never even remotely considered such a marriage. Johnson was over thirty years her senior, an old and ailing man. She was only forty, in the prime of life and full of youthful vigour. She reverenced Johnson as a father and confidant, but as a lover—the idea was absurd!

Johnson, too, had other matters to think about. Named as one of four executors of the estate, he threw himself whole-heartedly into the necessary business arrangements following the funeral. Thrale's will, which generously provided for his wife and five daughters,[2] had been read on the 5th in the widow's absence, and in it Johnson had been left only a small bequest of £200. In some quarters it was felt that he should have been remembered by a more substantial legacy, but the Doctor himself made no complaint. Whatever was best for his dear Mistress and her children suited him.

Shortly after April 20, at the insistence of the trustees, who wished to prove the will and transact other necessary business, Mrs. Thrale returned to Streatham, where she was immediately plunged into a round of tedious conferences. The executors, in addition to Johnson, were the retired timber merchant, Cator, the enigmatic Mr. Crutchley, and Thrale's relative, Henry Smith. They, with Perkins, had not only to manage the brewery but also to arrange the financial details of the distribution of the estate. The widow, of course, had to be consulted in every-thing, and in her nervous condition she welcomed the presence of Miss Owen and Fanny Burney in the house. Fanny found her 'dearest Tyo' looking wretched, though showing flashes of her old spirit. Nevertheless, Mrs. Thrale frightened them all

---

[1] *Private Papers*, xiv. 198.

[2] The will was dated Mar. 17, 1781. Streatham was left to Mrs. Thrale for life only, but the contents, as well as those of the Southwark house, were to be hers without qualification. The Crowmarsh estate was to belong to Queeney, and the other daughters received substantial bequests. After a number of smaller sums to Perkins, the executors, &c., it was stipulated that so long as the brewery was in operation, Mrs. Thrale was to receive £2,000 yearly from the profits, and £150 for the maintenance of each daughter under fifteen and £200 for each one under twenty-one. If the brewery was sold, Mrs. Thrale was to receive £30,000, and the remainder to be held in trust for the daughters. It was expressly stated, however, that the will did not revoke the earlier marriage settlement. Mrs. Thrale was made guardian of all the children with the four executors, but it was provided that the daughters should be made wards in Chancery.

several times by fainting dead away, and she confessed her unbalanced condition in a letter to Mrs. Lambart:

one Night I took a panick about Hester & sate up crying till five in the Morning, when nothing of Consequence was befallen her—and I do not know how it is, but I have a Notion of *every body* dying I think.[1]

She appointed three days a week to attend at the counting house, and commented in Thraliana on May 1:

If an Angel from Heaven had told me 20 Years ago, that the Man I knew by the Name of *Dictionary Johnson* should one Day become Partner with me in a great Trade, & that we should jointly or separately sign Notes, Drafts, &c., for 3 or 4 Thousand Pounds of a Morning, how unlikely it would have seemed ever to happen!

The novelty of the experience delighted Johnson, who had counted in pounds rather than thousands, inasmuch as it gave him an added feeling of importance; but for the widow it was merely another vexation. Although determined to follow Scrase's advice and dispose of the business at the earliest opportunity,[2] she did not neglect her present duties, and at first the social world applauded her devotion to business. Public opinion was ever shifting, however, and Fanny Burney on a trip to the city wrote back that when she had last come out to Streatham

I left every body persuaded you would do most wrong to give up the Business, & ought to work at it Day & Night:—well, now I come back, I tell them you purpose the same,—all fly out, & protest *you* will be killed by fatigue, & your Children ruined by fraud and knaveries!—That, now, I am assured, is the *voice of the Town!*[3]

Needing no further urging, Mrs. Thrale was delighted when Perkins found a prospective purchaser in David Barclay, the banker in Lombard Street. And Johnson, although somewhat loath to give up his new-found vocation, was not unaware that the present arrangement of running the brewery by a committee could not continue indefinitely. After some negotiation therefore, an agreement was finally reached with Barclay and Perkins to sell the property to them for £135,000, to be paid in four years. On Thursday, May 31, the documents were signed, and Mrs. Thrale exchanged what Johnson called 'the potentiality of growing rich, beyond the dreams of avarice'

---

[1] Ry. 550, 16.
[2] See letter from Charles Scrase of May 3, 1781, now in the Adam collection.
[3] Ry. 545, 23 (undated).

for the certainty that she and her children would at least be reasonably sure of a regular income.[1] On June 3 she wrote to Mrs. Lambart: 'I have lost my Golden Millstone from my Neck, & float once more on the Current of Life like my Neighbours—I long to salute You in my restored Character of a Gentlewoman.' She was a brewer no longer—but a rich, admired lady of fashion.

[1] Hayward, i. 144–6; *D'Arblay Diary*, i. 487–8; *Life*, iv. 86–7.

X

WIDOW

JUNE 1781–SEPTEMBER 1784

RELEASED from bondage to a sick, morose husband and to an unfashionable business, Mrs. Thrale probably thought her troubles were over. Instead, the next three years were probably the most unhappy of her entire life. Unable alone to cope with practical everyday problems, torn between the lure of new experiences and respect for old conventions, she was tossed like a broken reed by every adverse wind. The story of Thrale's widow is a tragicomedy of frustration and exasperation.

At first there were business worries, for even after the 'Golden Millstone' of the brewery had been thrown off, it was some time before she could dissociate herself completely from the affairs of trade. Throughout the summer of 1781 there were numerous meetings of the executors, and a variety of financial matters to be settled. Perkins, who was one of the new partners, did not have sufficient savings to make up his fourth part of the original payment;[1] and when the trustees refused to allow him to borrow from the estate, Mrs. Thrale permitted him to sell some of her own personal investments instead.[2] On July 1 she wrote to him about the arrangement, adding that she did not wish Dr. Johnson to be told. Since stocks were low, and disposing of them at this time would result in a distinct loss of capital, she was sure the Doctor would oppose any such move. In addition she presented Perkins with all the furniture of the Southwark house, where he and his family were now to reside, for she was determined to reward her former clerk for securing a purchaser for the property. And though temporarily pinched for money, she later lent Thrale's old valet a hundred pounds.[3]

[1] See *Wine and Spirit Trade Record*, Oct. 16, 1935, p. 1250. David Barclay, Robert Barclay, his nephew, Sylvanus Bevan, and John Perkins each had a quarter interest. From July 3, 1781, until the present there has always been a Barclay, a Perkins, and a Bevan in the business.

[2] Discussed in Mrs. Thrale's letters to Perkins of July 1, 1781, and Jan. 17, 1783. Stock of par value £2,000 was sold which realized £1,625 (Perkins MSS.). For the other presents to Perkins see Hayward, ii. 46–8.

[3] Yet she admitted herself that it was at the insistence of Crutchley that Henderson was given the money (to Perkins, Sept. 25, 1781).

She was soon to find, however, that she could not give lavishly as in the past, since a widow's income was neither so elastic nor so extensive as that of a successful business man. But she was hardly prepared for the shock, a few months later, of being told by Cator and Crutchley that her income would be temporarily £1,200 a year instead of £1,600 as originally estimated.[1] This was a sad blow, and characteristically she began to economize at once by dispensing with two horses. Unfortunately Thrale's affairs had been left in some disorder, and none of the trustees took the time or trouble to investigate the precise amount due to his widow. Cator and Crutchley seemed more interested in seeing how little she would take rather than what was the actual obligation. Probably they felt that, being a woman, she would only waste whatever she received, and it was better to keep her ignorant of her full claims. Or perhaps they were themselves unacquainted with the actual provisions of Thrale's marriage settlement. Whatever the reason, this failure to determine the exact provisions of the will ultimately led to bad feeling and interminable lawsuits.

Besides this restriction of her income, Mrs. Thrale found other causes for agitation, particularly since the continuous strain of the last few years had seriously affected her health. While she found some relaxation in the soft voice of Piozzi singing Venetian love songs, even his constant presence in the house throughout May and June was disturbing. This gentle musician stirred up emotions never felt before. Repeatedly in her journals she had insisted that she had never been in love: she had been fond of Thrale, had respected his merits, and borne his children, but there had never been the slightest pretence of romance in their relationship.[2] Now for the first time she began to feel a new and strange agitation, which further ruffled her already perturbed spirits.

Piozzi was preparing for a journey to Italy to see his parents, and on June 10 she presented him with a copy of Johnson's *Rasselas*, possibly for reading on the way.[3] Furthermore, she insisted that he should spend his last day with her, before setting out for France. So, early in July, with the composer, Sacchini, who hoped to rebuild his broken health and fortune at the French Court, Piozzi stopped at Streatham to say fare-

---

[1] To Johnson, Oct. 17, 18, 1781.

[2] Thraliana, Dec. 1777: 'As My Peace has never been disturbed by the *soft Passion*, so it seldom comes in my head to talk of it.'

[3] Now in the possession of Mr. A. Edward Newton.

well. The two musicians sang their final arias with such
exquisite expression that Fanny Burney admitted she had not
had so much pleasure from music since Pacchierotti left
England.[1] As the travellers stepped into their coach to drive
to Margate, Piozzi handed Mrs. Thrale an Italian *partenza*
full of tender expressions of devotion.[2]

As soon as her admirer was gone, Mrs. Thrale's chief concern
was for his safety. By July 21 she had already dispatched two
letters across the Channel, and throughout the rest of the
summer and early autumn she ·was constantly bothering
Perkins about her 'foreign Correspondence'.[3] When the replies
were few and far between, another vexation was added to her
steadily mounting woes.

Fanny Burney's diary gives a detailed and intimate account
of the life at Streatham during the summer of 1781, but little
of the inner struggles of her hostess. Only from the pages of
Thraliana and from Mrs. Thrale's letters do we gain any
insight into the trials which kept her upset and dejected. For
one thing, Crutchley's attentions to Queeney, instead of to
Fanny, caused consternation. As the former's reputed half
brother, he could never be an acceptable suitor.[4] Then early
in September Mrs. Thrale was troubled with a rash which
proved to be St. Anthony's Fire, and the inflammation continued for a whole month.[5] Fanny, too, fell ill, so that Sir
Richard Jebb was forced to make many trips to Streatham to
treat the two invalids.[6]

In October, when Johnson set out for Oxford and Lichfield
and Fanny Burney retired to Chessington for further work on
Cecilia, Mrs. Thrale was even more melancholy. On the 21st
she complained to Johnson:

I was many Years before I felt Sickness, but it is now in no haste
to leave me, I must be still Leaner before I venture to grow fat;
I have now pass'd seven Weeks completely without one comfortable
Meal, & I think seven more must be so spent before I recover.

Her 'sullen' spirits seemed in no hurry to depart, and with
Perkins sick in Southwark and Johnson moping in Lichfield
there was a '*general Gravedo*'. Another old companion, too, was
in desperate straits, as appeared a few weeks later when Cator

---

[1] *D'Arblay Diary*, ii. 20-1. Sacchini (1734-86) was a Neapolitan composer well
known in his day. He later became popular in Paris and received a pension from
Marie Antoinette.   [2] *Mainwaring Piozziana*, i. 133.
[3] See Perkins MSS.   [4] Thraliana, Oct. 15, 1781.
[5] Letters to Perkins, Sept. 1781.   [6] *Burford Papers*, p. 70.

called with a deplorable story of Baretti's poverty. The timber merchant was attempting to collect a small fund to relieve the Italian's wants, and Mrs. Thrale gave five guineas as her share. The next day she wrote to Johnson:

he would I think have fain perswaded me to make my five ten; but if one is to do *all one can do* for a professed Enemy—how does one deserve to have a Friend? I thought five enough.[1]

On October 12 she had noted in Thraliana, 'Yesterday was my Wedding Day; it was a melancholy Thing to me to pass it without the Husband of my Youth'; yet, at the very same time, she was fretting about lack of news from Piozzi. Confidently expecting him back in England the next month, she continued to worry because no word came from Lyons to say that the Alps were safely crossed.[2] It was not until the last of November that the singer reappeared at Streatham. Mrs. Thrale confided in Thraliana on November 25: 'I have got my Piozzi home at last, he looks thin & battered, but always kindly upon me I think.' Piozzi brought with him some Italian poetry, and in particular a sonnet written in his praise by Capello. This Mrs. Thrale immediately translated, but so afraid was he of London gossip that he prudently made her destroy the original.[3] Not unaware of the delicacy of his position, Piozzi tried his best to avoid any overt act which might lead to scandal.

When Johnson, in Ashbourne, heard of the musician's expected return, he wrote: 'Piozzi, I find, is coming . . . when *he* comes and *I* come, you will have two about you that love you.'[4] Again on December 3 he referred to Piozzi's arrival, and added:

Pray contrive a multitude of good things for us to do when we meet. Something that may *hold all together*; though if any thing makes *me* love you more, it is going from you.

On his way home five days later, Johnson pleaded, 'Do not neglect me, nor relinquish me. Nobody will ever love you better or honour you more than . . . Sam: Johnson.'

Many people have believed that Johnson was in love with Mrs. Thrale, and it must be admitted that there is much

---

[1] Sunday, Nov. 18, 1781.

[2] Her letters to Perkins are full of worry because letters had not come from Piozzi. On Nov. 22, 1781, she wrote to Fanny Burney that her heart had been 'pacified by a Paris letter' (*D'Arblay Diary*, ii. 53). None of Piozzi's letters to his future wife has survived.   [3] Ibid., Mainwaring Piozziana, ii. 4.

[4] *Letters*, No. 750; also 752 and 753.

evidence to support such a belief. Yet if he was, Johnson himself would have refused to admit it, in fact would probably not even have allowed himself to consider such a notion. Certainly theirs was a strong bond (her journals and his letters prove that); it was no light acquaintance, no casual friendship based on his fondness for good food and her relish for his talk. Nevertheless, the more than thirty years' difference in their ages, and his constant ill health, forbade a more tender relationship. 'Friend, Father, Guardian, Confident!' she wrote of him a few months later,[1] and Johnson would at once have agreed to this description. But if he refused to think of himself as her lover, he was unwilling to have anyone else usurp this position. He wanted the easy intimacy of the past years to continue; he wanted her to listen to his complaints, to ease his pain, and look after him through the dismal closing years of his existence. He resented any possibility of change, and jealously chafed at every new intrusion. The tragedy of the next few years for Johnson was that life would not stand still.[2]

He, too, had been ill during the autumn, and upon his return to London in December Mrs. Thrale found him much broken. Indeed, the old man's increasing infirmity made him more and more a care, and she confided in Thraliana: 'Queeney works hard with him at the Classicks, I hope she will be *out* of Leading-Strings at least before he gets *into* them, as poor Women say of their Children.'[3] Johnson's chief trouble was 'repelled gout', caused, she thought, by his trick of putting his feet in cold water, which drove the infection to his head and breast.[4] During the remainder of the winter much of her time was spent visiting him in Bolt Court or nursing him in her own house. Late in February Johnson wrote to Malone: 'I have for many weeks been so much out of order, that I have gone out only in a coach to Mrs. Thrale's, where I can use all the freedom that sickness requires.'[5] For her part, Mrs. Thrale commented to her friend Mrs. Lambart, who the year before had gone to Brussels: 'Dr. Johnson has been very ill, & is sadly broken; was he either to die or recover a firm state of Health, I think I should try Continental Air for myself.'[6] Any move depended

---

[1] Thraliana, Feb. 1, 1782.
[2] See a detailed discussion of the relations between Johnson and Mrs. Thrale by Sir Samuel Scott, in *Nineteenth Century* (Sept. 1934), pp. 308–18.
[3] Dec. 17, 1781.   [4] *Queeney Letters*, p. 254; Hayward, i. 167.
[5] *Life*, iv. 141 (Adam collection). Johnson was at Mrs. Thrale's when Levett died.
[6] Ry. 550, 18. In January she had written in much the same mood in Thraliana (*Life*, iv. 502).

on Johnson: she felt she could not leave him behind, nor could she risk taking him with her. More and more she began to chafe, for the present arrangement, while ideal for the sickly Johnson, was hardly so for the lively widow.

On the first day of 1782 Mrs. Thrale had taken a house in Harley Street for the winter season. Craving some company, and yet desirous of avoiding any censure because her year of mourning was not yet over, she was at first cautious in accepting invitations and refused a request from Pepys on January 14 to meet an army of Blues in Wimpole Street.[1] Since she felt that nearly everyone was watching her, trying to guess what she would do, she could ill afford to make a false move. She herself was actually drifting on a sea of indecision. Her own bad health, Johnson's illness, her interest in Piozzi, a wish to see Italy, dread of scandal, everything combined to keep her uncertain and vacillating. Nevertheless, by the 1st of March she finally decided to risk public disapproval by giving a large assembly at her own house.[2] The Blues came in great numbers, there was a whirl of conversation, and she was launched once more on the round of gaiety which she so enjoyed. Not long afterward the *Morning Herald* announced the 'Present state of literary parties—Mrs. Thrale for *Variety*; Dr. Johnson for *Charity*; Mrs. Ord for *Brilliancy*; Mrs. Montagu for *Universality*'.[3]

Mrs. Thrale was included in a set of verses extolling the literary ladies, which was anonymously inserted in the *Morning Herald* of March 12 by Dr. Burney. The Doctor's characterization is interesting as showing how whole-hearted was his admiration at this time.

> *Thrale*, in whose expressive eyes,
> Sits a soul above disguise,
> Skill'd with wit and sense t'impart,
> Feelings of a generous heart.[4]

If the newspapers contained complimentary references, they were just as ready to insert gossip about her eagerness to wed again. Because of such printed reports she was finally forced to send a request to the *Morning Herald* asking it to say no more about her, 'good or bad'.[5] On April 17, once more back at

---

[1] Hayward, i. 165.

[2] *D'Arblay Diary*, ii. 66, 74. Fanny, on Mar. 15, speaks of Mrs. Thrale's first large party as 'about a week ago'.　　　　　　　[3] Mar. 19, 1782.

[4] *D'Arblay Diary*, ii. 78. In the Rylands collection (Ry. 647, 22) there is a copy in Mrs. Thrale's hand.

[5] *Thraliana*, Apr. 1782 (uncertain date).

Streatham, in fair health and '*very* sound of Heart', she wrote in Thraliana of her annoyance at the interest everyone was taking in her possible remarriage. Even Johnson, she insisted, had been joking about it, but she could see no compliment to her in all this bustle. What had she to gain by rushing headlong into matrimony? She was still young, of 'passable Person', 'uncommon Talents', possessor of a large fortune, easily the equal of any man, with

nothing to seek but return of Affection from whatever Partner She pitches on. to marry for *Love* would therefore be rational in me, who want no Advancement of Birth or Fortune, and till I am in Love, I will not marry, nor perhaps then.

This was the one passion in life which she had never experienced; why should she not find it now?

According to Thraliana she was deluged with proposals; even Sir Philip Jennings Clerke, who was already married, made open advances. Tormented day and night with these new embarrassments, she found her only comfort in 'my Dear, my delicate, my disinterested Pıozzı'. It is easy to see why Mrs. Thrale should have been attracted to Piozzi. A woman is apt, we know, to find a similarity between the man she loves and her own father; and from the first Mrs. Thrale had been struck by the physical resemblance of the Italian singer to John Salusbury. Then, too, his soft voice and manner were the exact antithesis of the brusque Thrale and the dogmatic Johnson. With such a man, she felt, it might be possible to capture the delights of romance, to experience that emotion which she had read about in literature, but which had so far escaped her in real life. She wisely kept these dreams to herself; but she could not keep others from wondering.

Johnson may have accompanied Mrs. Thrale to Streatham in the middle of April, 1782, but if so they quarrelled soon afterwards, for he wrote later in the month from the city:

I have been very much out of order since you sent me away; but why should I tell you, who do not care, nor desire to know? . . . Do not let Mr. Piozzi nor any body else put me quite out of your head, and do not think that any body will love you like . . .[1]

He felt his dear Mistress was slipping away from him, but scarcely knew what to do to recapture the old comradeship. Even when Mrs. Thrale brought him back to Streatham on

---

[1] *Letters*, No. 778, Apr. 24 or 25, 1782. See next note.

May 9, he remained gloomy and miserable, for the tension between the two had not relaxed.[1] In consequence, about the middle of June he made a short trip to Oxford, hoping that a change of scene would improve his health.

The rift at Streatham had undoubtedly not escaped the curious eyes of other friends. It was probably at this time that William Seward wrote to Mrs. Thrale:

The whole world here say, you & Johnson have quarrell'd about a sugar dish, pray put an affidavit in the Morning Herald to certify to all whom it may concern that you have not, I get no credit to my assertions that you are as well together, as you have ever been, or when he returns, get you both into an open chaise, & drive thro' Broad Street Cheapside, & Oxford Road, smiling & looking kind at each other . . .[2]

Fortunately the visit to Oxford proved a tonic for Johnson, while Seward's letter was perhaps a warning to Mrs. Thrale. Certainly for the rest of the summer they were on the old footing of intimacy at Streatham. As a friendly gesture, Mrs. Thrale sent the news of Johnson's better spirits to the distant Boswell, who she knew would be delighted with the news. He replied immediately on July 9 with fulsome expressions of joy. 'I kissed the subscription H. L. Thrale with fervency', he insisted, then slyly added his usual wish that she would send him anecdotes of their literary friends, 'particularly of our illustrious Imlac'.[3] Ostensibly on the best of terms with the Mistress of Streatham, Boswell meant to miss no opportunity of preparing the way for a future glimpse of Thraliana.

During the summer of 1782 Mrs. Thrale had time seriously to consider her situation, faced as she was with the major decision of her life. At forty-one, if she were to find romance for the first time, she could not delay; she must act quickly before it was too late. Yet nursing Johnson, who might conceivably live ten years more, would mean giving up all hope of active life for herself. How different would be her chances at fifty-one! Furthermore, Johnson's ill health had sharpened the acerbity of his temper, and his ·idiosyncrasies had a far different effect on the sprightly widow contemplating a second marriage than on the matron absorbed with the varied cares of a family. Conditions had changed. She reverenced the

---

[1] On May 9, 1782, Mrs. Thrale wrote in Thraliana, 'Today I bring home to Streatham my poor Dr. Johnson; he went to Town a Week ago by the way of amusing himself, & got so very ill that I thought I should never get him home alive.' Johnson returned to London on May 18 (*Diaries, Prayers, and Annals*, ed. E. L. McAdam).

[2] Ry. 891, 26 (no date).   [3] Broadley, p. 143; *Boswell's Letters*, ii. 312–13.

Sage as much as ever, but the irritable old man reminded her only too strongly of the passing years.

In many ways the death of Thrale had made a great difference at Streatham. His firm command had kept order in the household, while his large income in the days of plenty had been sufficient for all their needs. Mrs. Thrale had neither the income nor the ability to enforce discipline. A great part of the fortune was now in trust for the girls, leaving only a small portion available for present expenses. To maintain an expensive country estate, as well as a fashionable house in town, required more money than was available. Furthermore, she was threatened with a large loss of capital, because of a suit in Chancery instituted by Lady Salusbury to collect the money paid out by Sir Thomas almost thirty years before to save the estate of Bach-y-Graig.[1] The suit had actually been hanging fire for several years, delayed by Thrale's lawyers, but it was always an ominous menace to his widow's peace of mind, and provided a further reason for immediate and rigid economy.

After some hesitation she finally decided to give up the idea of a London house, to let Streatham, and later to take her three older daughters to the Continent, where they might live inexpensively and at the same time learn foreign languages. With fear and trembling she told Johnson of her scheme. What was her surprise to find him openly approving, apparently not at all upset over the prospect. For once, contrary to his usual habit, Johnson did not show his distress. Her reaction was typically feminine, for she was now very much annoyed that he appeared so willing to allow her to go, and she vented her irritation in a long entry in Thraliana on August 22.[2] Others, including Cator, seemed favourable; only Crutchley, who she felt was in love with Queeney, violently opposed the move.

Once the decision had been made, arrangements were speedily completed. Streatham was let to Lord Shelburne for three years, and final packing and other preparations were hastened. On Sunday, October 6, Johnson, with a kiss, pathetically bade farewell to the Streatham Church, and dined for the last time in the home where his happiest days had been spent.[3] As he looked up at the portraits on the wall of the library, he must have realized that life was closing in.

---

[1] See p. 19, n. 1. For references to the suit see *Queeney Letters*, pp. 60, 133.

[2] She wrote: 'I fancied Mr. Johnson could not have existed without me . . . Not a bit on't! he feels nothing in parting with me, nothing in the least; but thinks it a prudent Scheme, & goes to his Book as usual. This is Philosophy & Truth; he always said he hated a *Feeler*.'   [3] *John. Misc.* i. 108–10; Hayward, i. 177–9.

Goldsmith, Garrick, Thrale were gone—soon he too would be with them. In this spirit he composed a prayer commemorating this farewell to all he held so dear, to the place where he had hoped to pass his declining years. Early the next morning he drove away with Mrs. Thrale and her three daughters to Brighton.

It has often been suspected that Mrs. Thrale's principal reason for leaving Streatham was to get rid of Johnson, but this explanation is too simple. There was also, as has been pointed out, a serious financial reason. Yet it must be admitted that possibly in the back of her mind she had decided to pursue youth rather than cling to age. If the two could not be made to harmonize, then age must be the one to be sacrificed. While she intended no drastic, no sudden or spectacular severance of former ties, her future happiness must now be considered. Giving up Streatham was the first move.

Johnson had been ailing and discouraged before going to Brighton, and the Sussex resort, which he heartily disliked, did not improve his ill humour. When Fanny Burney joined the party on October 26, she found him pretending to be gay, but with little success. Furthermore his bitter tongue had driven away most of the usual visitors, and Fanny commented to her father:

He has raised such a general alarm that he is now omitted in all cards of invitation sent to the rest of us. . . .

Poor Mr. Pepys was so torn to pieces by him the other night, in a party at home, that he suddenly seized his hat, and abruptly walked out of the room in the middle of the discourse. . . . Dr. Delap confesses himself afraid of coming as usual to the house . . .[1]

The next month Fanny added:

Mr. Metcalf is now the only person out of this house that voluntarily communicates with the Doctor. He has been in a terrible severe humour of late, and has really frightened all the people, till they almost ran from him. To me only I think he is now kind, for Mrs. Thrale fares worse than anybody.[2]

If relations between Johnson and his hostess were becoming strained, the general public had no inkling of the situation. The *Morning Post* on October 15 announced that a treaty of

---

[1] C. Hill, *House in St. Martin's Street* (1907), pp. 343–4.
[2] *D'Arblay Diary*, ii. 122. On Nov. 14 Fanny wrote to her father, 'Dr. Johnson was invited to Lord De Ferrars, which is the *only* visit he has made with us since my arrival!—yet not one *refused*.' (Letter in possession of Mr. A. C. Thomas, New York.)

marriage was said to be 'on tap' between Dr. Johnson and Mrs. Thrale, and on the 18th, with unpardonable familiarity, described the coming event. It was stipulated by the Lady, the paper added, that the Doctor should immediately discard his bush-wig, wear a clean shirt and shave every day, give up snuff, learn to eat vermicelli, and leave off red flannel night caps.[1] In succeeding months the papers continued with similar remarks.[2] In the circumstances these quips were particularly inept and did not help to calm the cross-currents in West Street, Brighton.

Mrs. Thrale was considering matrimony, but the newspapers, unaware of her romantic disposition, had suggested the wrong man. All through the summer her fondness for her daughters' music master, Piozzi, had so increased that every thought, every action was centred in him. Even the proposed continental tour was rendered more attractive by the thought of him as guide. On the other hand, we have no unprejudiced evidence of his attitude, for all we know of the affair comes from Mrs. Thrale's own fragmentary and subjective journals. Was Piozzi really in love with the wealthy English widow, with whom he had practically no interest in common? Did he ever declare his affection? Or did she make all the advances? All we may do is to speculate. Yet by August 28 there must have been some sort of understanding, for she noted in Thraliana that Piozzi despondently thought in the end she would give him up. To this she added, '& if Queeney made herself more amiable to me, & took the proper Methods—I suppose I should'.

It was obvious that she could not long keep others in the household ignorant of what was going on, and late in September Fanny Burney openly accused her of being in love with Piozzi. Not too certain of herself, and to clarify her own feelings, Mrs. Thrale made a long entry in her journal,

---

[1] Repeated in the *Morning Herald*, Oct. 16, 1782. See also E. Wead, *Colophon*, New Ser. i., No. 3 (1936), 449–52.

[2] See *Morning Herald*, Dec. 2, 1782, and *Morning Post*, Dec. 11. Under the title 'Amatic Titular Sketches' appeared: 'Dr. Johnson—Timon of Athens, Mrs. Th—e—Love's Last Shift.' One amusing squib, which she believed to have been written by Soame Jenyns, was:

Cervisial coctor's viduate dame,
Opinst thou this gigantick frame,
Procumbing at thy shrine,
Shall catenated by thy charms,
A captive in thy ambient arms
Perennially be thine?

(Hayward, i. 251.) The Hawkins family thought Johnson likely to marry Mrs. Thrale (L. M. Hawkins, *Memoirs* (1926 ed.), p. 56).

considering the affair from every angle. Piozzi was amiable and honourable, but a Roman Catholic, and of neither high birth nor social position. If she became his wife, it would injure the prospects of her five daughters. Yet she had married the first time to please her mother, why not the second time to satisfy herself? Over and over she repeated every argument for and against the step, in the end being as far from a conclusion as at the beginning. Torn between two irreconcilable positions, she could find no answer to her problem. She was certain of one thing alone—that she had found the only man whom she might love.

At Brighton in November she finally made up her mind to throw caution to the winds and declare her intention to wed Piozzi. Laying aside all pride, she begged Queeney to give her consent. Then, after relieving her pent-up emotions by writing a long confession in Thraliana, she showed the passage both to Queeney and to Fanny in a transport of passion. Fanny Burney 'cried herself half blind over it; said there was no resisting such pathetic Eloquence'; but Queeney remained non-committal, though promising to go abroad the next spring.[1]

Following this, on November 20 they drove back to London, where Mrs. Thrale had rented a house in Argyle Street for the winter. Here on the 27th she wrote: 'I have given my Piozzi some hopes,—dear, generous, prudent, noble-minded Creature: he will hardly permit himself to believe it ever can be.' For the moment she was in an optimistic mood, feeling that all obstacles might somehow be overcome.

Though temporarily buoyed by hope, she was still beset with problems, the chief of which was the debt to Lady Salusbury. Cator felt that another appeal in the courts might be advantageous, but Mrs. Thrale was tired of the protracted suit which she seemed sure to lose. Since Lady Salusbury had the documents proving the obligation, there was little prospect of avoiding the payment. Rather, Mrs. Thrale favoured making a compromise offer of £7,500.[2] After repeated conferences a settlement was finally agreed upon, but still there remained the puzzle of how the necessary cash could be secured. She had hoped to raise enough for the purpose by selling much of her

---

[1] Thraliana, Nov. 19, 1782.
[2] Ry. 533, 5. This is a draft of a letter to Dr. Pinfold, pleading with him to aid in effecting a compromise. See also *Queeney Letters*, pp. 29, 60; and Johnson's letters of Nov. 30 (Ry. 543, 8) and of Dec. 11 (now in the Morgan Library).

plate, recovering the sum lent to Perkins, and cutting the woods at Bach-y-Graig; but Crutchley, who had travelled to Wales to see what could be secured speedily there, found it would take too long to realize on the trees.[1] As a substitute, the trustees suggested that the amount might be borrowed from the inheritance of her daughters, giving as collateral security a mortgage on the Welsh property. When this was done, Crutchley, forgetting perhaps that the girls, as heirs, had some interest in saving the estate, brutally told Mrs. Thrale to thank her girls for keeping her *'out of a Gaol'*.[2] Ironically, after this burst of spleen by one of the trustees, none of the Thrale money had to be used, for Cator found the interest and security so favourable that he supplied the necessary sum out of his own pocket.[3] He failed to tell Mrs. Thrale what he had done, however, perhaps thinking it would be salutary for her to consider herself under obligation to her children. Her worry meant nothing to Cator and Crutchley, who felt they could maintain better control over her actions by keeping her ignorant of her own financial condition.

Throughout December 1782 Mrs. Thrale was very gay, and Fanny Burney's diary gives an entertaining record of their many social engagements. Johnson spent part of his time in Argyle Street, where a semblance of the old friendliness still persisted; but for the most part he was fretful and glum. When at his own home, he kept Mrs. Thrale acquainted with his condition by almost daily letters. Thus he wrote plaintively to Argyle Street on December 16, 17, 18, 20, and 21, each note full of his own illness and pain, but with occasional flashes of his earlier sprightliness. The day after Christmas he mentioned his visitors, and pathetically added: 'But I have not seen those of whom I once hoped never to have lost sight.'[4] Evidently the veiled reproach touched Mrs. Thrale's heart, for the next day Fanny found him at Argyle Street, 'comic and good-humoured'.[5] Later in the day, when Mrs. Thrale gave up a

---

[1] Mentioned in a letter from E. Edwards, Sept. 22, 1782 (Ry. 600, 4).

[2] Thraliana, Apr. 1783, *Queeney Letters*, p. 60; Mainwaring Piozziana, i. 132.

[3] Through a change in business conditions, however, Cator actually did not find the proposition to his ultimate advantage. In a letter to Mrs. Piozzi, May 27, 1799 (Ry. 577, 20), John Gillon wrote of a recent conversation with Cator, who complained that he had by 'lending the Money to pay off Lady Salusbury's Claim lost £500 by the Rise of the Funds . . .' In a letter to Salusbury, Dec. 15, 1810, Mrs. Piozzi recalled how Cator had dragged her out of a sick bed to sign the mortgage (Ry. 586, 85), so that the intervening years had evidently made the event seem even more horrible. See also Ry. 586, 158.

[4] J. D. Wright, *J. Rylands Bulletin*, xvi. (1932), 39.

[5] *D'Arblay Diary*, ii. 159–60.

visit to Mrs. Ord's in order to stay at home with him, his happiness was even further increased. With quick reversal of mood, Johnson could still be roused from depression by the slightest consideration from his dear Mistress.

Mrs. Thrale, too, alternated between moments of optimism and fits of black despair. Still hoping to reconcile her family and friends to Piozzi, she found the opposition too strong to be overcome. Her daughters, the trustees, everyone vigorously expressed disapproval. In order to forestall the proposed Italian journey, Crutchley suggested that the Thrale heiresses be made wards in Chancery, a provision stipulated in their father's will but never completely carried out. Fanny Burney, her most intimate confidant, continued to be shocked at the prospect. Years later Fanny, reminded of this troubled time when her friend had been agonizingly trying to come to some decision, wrote:

Sometimes I prevailed entirely:—then she repented her compliance—then she repented her engagement, then her senses seemed to fail her;—then she raved—then she was seized with a sort of stupor—then she used to fall suddenly asleep, and talk aloud . . . frightful period![1]

Vacillating, swayed first by one argument and then by another, Mrs. Thrale could make up her mind neither to accept Piozzi nor to give him up. She needed to remember Johnson's advice to Miss Reynolds on one occasion: 'Ponder no more, Renny,—whatever you do, do it, but ponder no more!'[2]

Her daughters' antagonism is easily understood. As handsome heiresses they had every expectation of marrying into the nobility, or at least into one of the prominent families, and any *mésalliance* made by their mother would certainly prejudice their chances. They had, moreover, no real affection for her which would have moved them to excuse or understand such waywardness. Once she had written in Thraliana: 'They are five lovely Creatures to be sure! but they love not me. Is it my fault or theirs!'[3] It was Queeney, of course, who took the lead, but the younger sisters were easily dominated by her forceful determination. Kept away at school for the most part during their childhood, they never had been thrown so intimately with their mother as had Harry, Lucy, and the other children

[1] R. B. Johnson, *Fanny Burney and the Burneys* (1926), p. 105. Undated letter t Mrs. Waddington, grand-niece of Mrs. Delany. See also Thraliana.
[2] Quoted in a letter from Mme D'Arblay to Queeney, Mar. 23, 1799 (Lansdowne MS.). [3] Sept. 1, 1781.

long since buried in the Streatham churchyard. Seeing their
mother apparently swayed by every whim and passing fancy,
they naturally turned to their firm eldest sister for guidance.
And she now stepped in ruthlessly to oppose what she considered her mother's inexcusable, degrading passion for an
unworthy foreign singer.

Conditions in Argyle Street through January 1783 were fast
approaching a climax. The succeeding scenes, as disclosed in
Mrs. Thrale's journals, resemble a distorted, overacted melo-
drama.[1] On the 25th Crutchley made a last appeal to give up
all thought of taking her daughters to the Continent, and
intimated that strange rumours were afloat in London. The
next day Fanny Burney insisted that she must either marry
Piozzi immediately or renounce him, else her reputation would
be irretrievably lost. When London gossips once started talking,
no woman's reputation could long withstand the assault. As
usual in times of stress, Mrs. Thrale became hysterical and
threw herself on the bed, groaning with anguish, while Queeney
stood by regarding this childish weakness with complete disapproval. 'Susan & Sophy said nothing at all; but they taught
the two little ones to cry where are you going Mama? will you
leave us, and die as our poor papa did?'[2] Moved by such
lamentations, Mrs. Thrale finally consented to abandon the
idea of going abroad. A note was dispatched to Piozzi asking
him to come the next day, her birthday; and after a long night
of restless indecision and prayer she prepared to sacrifice all her
hopes for the best interests of her children.

On the morning of the 27th, after a preliminary emetic, she
saw Piozzi and tearfully announced her decision.

I pleaded Attachment to Miss Thrale, and Entanglement in my
Money-Matters—& beg'd him stay *Two* Years till She should come
of Age. No, No; he was *in Earnest* & he would himself speak to Miss
Thrale. . . . I called her—said I had but one heart for both him &
Her—but that I would break it between them, & give *Ciascheduno
la Metà*. After some Conversation I left them in my Dressing Room
together; whence both of them came out with altered Looks. She
had as I discovered afterwards, touch'd on the Magic String, by
telling him *My Honour* was concerned in our immediate Separation:
That strange Stories were got about, & were finding their Way into
Newspapers (where our Enemies & their Emissaries were daily

---

[1] The following account is based on Thraliana, Jan. 29, 1783; *Queeney Letters*,
p. 61; Mainwaring Piozziana, ii. 11–13. Several pages have been torn out of both
Thraliana and Piozziana at this point, which renders the story incomplete.

[2] Thraliana, Jan. 29, 1783.

putting them), that our Connection would be the ruin of their *Family* forsooth.[1]

Piozzi found such reasoning unanswerable, and yielded,

went home to Wigmore Street at her Command; brought all my Letters Promises of Marriage &c put them into *her* Hand—& flinging mine from him; cried 'Take your Mama—and make it of her a Countess—It shall kill *me* never mind—but it shall *kill her too*!'

Two days later she hysterically wrote: 'Adieu to all that's dear, to all that's lovely. I am parted from my Life, my Soul! my Piozzi.'[2]

The arguments used by Queeney to inspire Piozzi's chivalrous self-sacrifice were undoubtedly cogent. Even though Mrs. Thrale was perfectly honest and open in everything she did, her unconcealed passion for her daughters' music teacher had set London tongues wagging, and scandalmongers were quick to distort and misinterpret. Many rumours were afloat. If Baretti may be believed, there was even a preposterous story that Piozzi was her half-brother, the illegitimate son of John Salusbury and an Italian mother.[3] According to Baretti, the first hint he had of the tale came from Dr. Johnson himself. In addition, the newspapers delighted in coupling her name with sly, obscene remarks about Italian male sopranos.[4] No wonder that Mrs. Thrale's family and friends had been disturbed and urged her to take definite action.

In an attempt to divert her mind from the thought of her submission, Mrs. Thrale made some pretence, during February and March 1783, of enjoying social 'Flash'. Hannah More wrote to her sister on March 7 that the Friday before she had been at a fine party at Lady Rothes', where she had found many friends:

Mrs. Montagu, Boscawen, Carter, Thrale, Burney, and Lady Dartry; in short, it was remarked that there was not a woman in London, who has been distinguished for taste and literature, that was absent.[5]

But Mrs. Thrale could find little pleasure in entertainment, for she was exhausted by the intense emotional crisis through which she had passed.

[1] Mainwaring Piozziana, ii. 11. Compare with Hayward, ii. 52.
[2] Thraliana, Jan. 29.
[3] The claim is made in Baretti's third 'stricture' in the *European Magazine* for Aug. 1788. See p. 324, n. 1.
[4] *Morning Herald*, Feb. 13, 1783; *Morning Post*, Feb. 19, 1783.
[5] H. More, Memoirs (1834), i. 274.

Furthermore, even her parting from Piozzi had not prevented the newspapers from keeping up a stream of inaccurate comment about her future. On March 8 the *Morning Herald*, while announcing that 'the match between Piozzi and Mrs —' had turned out to be merely gossip, added that Mrs. Thrale would soon leave for the Continent accompanied part of the way by Dr. Johnson. On the 26th the same paper stated that she had already left England without her daughters, who had retired to Bath.

It had become apparent to everyone that she and her reputed lover could not be completely separated while both resided in London. Piozzi, accordingly, agreed to leave England permanently and, to prove his good faith, removed the savings of a lifetime from the stocks. Then he gallantly lent Mrs. Thrale at least £1,000 for her present needs—quite in contrast to the rumour that he was being bribed to leave the country.[1] Once this was accomplished, and with the prospect of her lover banished to the Continent, Mrs. Thrale despairingly planned to leave London for Bath, where she might live economically and try to regain her shattered health.

Just how much Johnson knew of all this turmoil is not certain, since she would scarcely have confided to him her feeling for Piozzi. But spending much of his time with the family, he cannot have been oblivious to what was going on. On March 21 Boswell arrived in London and found Johnson with Mrs. Thrale in Argyle Street.

She said she was very glad I was come, for she was going to Bath and should have been uneasy to leave Dr. Johnson till I came. He had told me of her going to Bath, and said they had driven her out of London by attacks upon her which She had provoked by attacking every body.[2]

We know also from Boswell's journal that Johnson was even more depressed than usual. Though on occasion he could rouse himself to talk with his accustomed vivacity, he would often fall asleep after dinner and he seemed morose and peevish. Even Boswell was sometimes hurt by his churlish behaviour.[3] Johnson found his world tumbling in upon him and showed his irritation in his bad temper.

Late in March 1783 Mrs. Thrale was suddenly forced to

---

[1] Hayward, ii. 53; *Queeney Letters*, p. 61. The canard that she paid Piozzi £800 a year while he was on the Continent was repeated in A. K. Elwood, *Memoirs of the Literary Ladies of England* (1843), ii. 16.

[2] *Private Papers*, xv. 174.   [3] Ibid., pp. 176–95.

change her plans because of the illness of her younger daughters. Cecilia went down with whooping-cough, and Harriett had a succession of ills—swollen glands, measles, and a cough. Mrs. Thrale herself had never had whooping-cough, and she had a mortal fear of the disease.[1] For this reason she arranged to have the girls stay with 'old Nurse' and Mrs. Ray at Streatham. From her correspondence with Johnson, however, it appears probable that by April 1 both the girls were considered well enough for her to make the journey. On the 5th she took leave of Johnson, little realizing it was for the last time, and on the 6th parted again from Piozzi. As soon as he was gone, she rushed to pour her suppressed emotions into Fanny Burney's sympathetic ear. Shortly afterwards, with Queeney, Susanna, and Sophia, she drove away to Bath.

Mrs. Thrale expected to find a quiet refuge at the watering-place, where she could forget London and all its complications, but fate was against her. Only a few days after her arrival word came that her daughters at Streatham were worse, and succeeding bulletins were more and more alarming. By Good Friday, April 18, Harriett was dead and Cecilia reported dying. That night, driven frantic by the repeated blows, Mrs. Thrale dashed off a note to Johnson: 'My Children, my Income (of course) and my health are coming to an end Dear Sir—not my vexations . . .'[2] The next morning she added a postscript: 'I have just taken a Vomit, & just received your Letter; I will set out the first Moment I am able.' Leaving Bath at three o'clock, she reached Reading by eleven, and Streatham by nine on Easter Sunday.[3] To her relief she found Cecilia out of danger, but Harriett she laid beside the others in St. Leonard's Church.

As soon as her sad errand was accomplished, Mrs. Thrale returned to Bath. While near London she had attempted to see Fanny Burney, who was out of town, and Piozzi, who refused to see her, prudently thinking there was no need to repeat painful scenes. Wishing only to forget, he was hastening to leave a land where he had received such unkind treatment. But Mrs. Thrale had no intention of allowing him to efface her memory, and as a parting message she sent him a set of verses

[1] Nearly thirty years later she wrote to Queeney (Mar. 28, 1812), 'My Horror of Hooping Cough is such that I actually left Church one Day from hearing the fatal Sound too near me' (Lansdowne MS).

[2] Ry. 540, 108. This appears to be the original of the rewritten version (Ry. 538, 27). See p. 301, n. 2. See also *Queeney Letters*, p. 62.

[3] Thraliana, Apr. 1783.

probably as bad as any she had ever written. Included were the lines:

> Fondly to bless my wandering Lover
> And make him dote on dirty Dover.[1]

Mrs. Thrale's friends had doubtless felt that as soon as the musician had left the country she would return to sanity, but the separation brought no happiness to the despairing woman. Later she described her life at this time.

I sate reading at home, or went wearying heav'n with Prayers to all the Churches & Chapels in town—watching the Post too, & carrying my own long Letters to the Office.[2]

On one occasion she neglected to place the proper postage for foreign correspondence, an omission which resulted in an embarrassed apology from a government official who had opened the epistle and thus become a confidant of her passion. From then on she took more precautions with her letters.

Meanwhile in London, on the morning of June 17, Johnson suffered a stroke which temporarily deprived him of speech. The next day Tom Davies wrote to Mrs. Thrale to acquaint her with the news, adding pathetically, 'He is really much to be pitied, He has no female friend in his House that can do him any service on this occasion . . .'[3] Certainly this was an obvious hint that her presence on the scene was desired! By the 19th, however, Johnson himself was so far recovered that he could write her a long account of his seizure. Though he was bewildered at her coldness, his habit of relying upon her for comfort and advice was too strong to be broken quickly.

I have loved you with virtuous affection; I have honoured you with sincere esteem. Let not all our endearments be forgotten, but let me have in this great distress your pity and your prayers. You see I yet turn to you with my complaints as a settled and unalienable friend; do not, do not drive me from you, for I have not deserved either neglect or hatred.

Under ordinary circumstances Mrs. Thrale would have flown to help him, but she was now in the grip of a severe hypochondria. As she later wrote, 'could I have suffer'd for two People at once—I shou'd have sincerely grieved for *him*—but I was too unhappy to fear much for any thing except myself.'[4]

---

[1] Hayward, i. 206; Thraliana, May 8, 1783.
[2] Mainwaring Piozziana, ii. 16; Hayward, ii. 54.
[3] Ry. 536, 9. Printed in *Life*, ed. Powell, iv. 521–2.
[4] Mainwaring Piozziana, ii. 19.

Her need was for a psychiatrist, not a physician. The active, generous woman of the seventies had been warped by the last years into a listless, psychopathic bundle of nerves. Frustrated, as she thought, in her craving for love, and afflicted by a host of imaginary physical ills, she had developed an exaggerated case of self-pity. Coupled with this was a persecution complex, which kept her convinced that her daughters and friends were cruelly uniting on all sides to thwart her.[1] Consequently, Johnson's touching appeals made little impression. After one half-hearted offer to come to London, she remained morbidly brooding at Bath. Johnson had to content himself with writing frequent accounts of his condition to his distant, callous Mistress.

Throughout the summer of 1783 the situation remained unchanged. Having lost interest in everything except her own misery, she refused to take any part in Bath society, much to the annoyance of her daughters, who were completely bored by their dull existence. She described her unhappy condition in Thraliana:

to teach without Authority, to be heard without Esteem; to be considered by them as their Inferior in Fortune, while I live by the Money borrowed from them; and in good Sense when they have seen me submit my Judgment to theirs, tho' at the hazard of my Life & Wits. Oh, 'tis a pleasant Situation! & whoever would wish as the Greek Lady phrased it *to teize himself & repent of his Sins*:— let him borrow his Children's money, be in Love against their Interest & Prejudice, forbear to marry by their Advice;—and then shut himself up and live with them.[2]

In August they made a short visit to Weymouth for sea bathing. While they were there, Johnson came to Heale, only a short distance away, to visit William Bowles; but sensing his Mistress's mood, as his host recognized, he 'had no great mind to see' her.[3] Nor did she make any move to go to him.

From Fanny Burney's letters to Queeney during the next few months it seems evident that both correspondents suspected that Mrs. Thrale was still determined some day to marry Piozzi. Fanny was completely horrified at such ungovernable passion. 'Poor self-deluded Mrs. T', 'Dear, lost, infatuated Soul'; on and on flow the expressions of affectionate dismay.[4]

---

[1] This is obvious from repeated references in Thraliana to her hard-hearted companions. See also her letter to Chappelow, Mar. 2, 1803 (Ry. 561, 119).

[2] Aug. 14, 1783.

[3] *Life*, ed. Powell, iv. 523; see also *Queeney Letters*, p. 38.

[4] *Queeney Letters*, pp. 72, 76; see also pp. 101, 102. These letters to Queeney show Fanny Burney at her dullest. On June 13, 1784, she wrote that Dr. Burney 'never speaks to me of the matter but with a sigh for the frailty of human nature!' (p. 99).

'How *can* she suffer herself, noble-minded as she is, to be thus duped by ungovernable passions!' It would be better for Queeney, Fanny advised, to 'live single for-ever' rather than follow the terrible example of her mother.[1]

In our day this outcry over the proposed remarriage of a widow of forty-two purely for love appears absurd; yet even to-day an alliance out of one's class is frowned upon. It is but recently that the prejudice against musicians as social equals has been overcome. In the eighteenth century Lord Chesterfield actually forbade his son to learn a musical instrument, since a fiddler could never be considered quite a gentleman.[2] Piozzi was also at a disadvantage in Protestant Britain, as a member of the Roman Catholic Church. Actually, however, the revulsion in the minds of her relatives and friends was due in even greater degree to the fact that throughout she had seemed to be the pursuer. Had she been swept off her feet by persuasive wooing, there might have been only pity for her weak will; but for a rich matron to take the initiative was a sign of degradation.

Conditions at Bath were fast leading up to an explosion. Queeney and her mother had both consulted William Seward in October; when he brutally expressed disapproval of her continued interest in Piozzi, Mrs. Thrale was highly incensed.[3] More and more she felt herself the pitiable object of cruel persecution. Only Mrs. Lewis proved a constant friend and comforter. Then in November Sophia fell desperately ill. Despite her own nervous debility, Mrs Thrale nursed her child through a long, dangerous siege and then collapsed. This last ordeal had broken what little resistance there was left.

For the first time Queeney became genuinely alarmed. All along she must have felt that her mother's melodramatic seizures were assumed for effect, but now there could be no doubt that her health was really undermined. As a result, Queeney capitulated, and at the advice of the physicians gave her consent to Piozzi's recall. If this was the only way to save her mother's life, she was willing to sacrifice her own best interests, though she would never conquer her repugnance to the alliance. A letter suggesting Piozzi's return was dispatched

[1] Ibid., p. 70.
[2] *Chesterfield's Letters*, ed. Dobrée (1932), iv. 1331. Though Piozzi was friendly with men of fashion, he was never accepted without condescension. Thus George Selwyn wrote to Lady Carlisle on Dec. 11, 1781, of meeting 'an Italian fiddler, Piozzi, or some such name', *Hist. MS. Comm.* (1897), xv, App., part vi, p. 549.
[3] *Queeney Letters*, p. 70.

to Milan, late in November, and Mrs. Thrale began to improve.[1]

But now another complication arose. Piozzi was reluctant to return to England without more certainty that his journey would not be in vain. Sophia sent a second urgent message early in January 1784, at Dr. Dobson's suggestion, but still Piozzi delayed.[2] He gave various excuses—the wintry roads, the danger of crossing the Alps, anything to gain time. Knowing too well the situation in England, he had no wish to rush headlong into a series of painful scenes similar to those of the year before. He was not a fearless man, and it required some determination to face the tide of slander and abuse which would be sure to greet his reappearance. Before he would leave agreeable Italy he must be absolutely sure all was well. So throughout the entire winter he lingered, while Mrs. Thrale fumed and fretted at Bath. And the seeming reluctance of her suitor only served to accentuate the distaste of Fanny Burney and her other friends for the match.[3]

Mrs. Thrale still refused to have anything to do with the fashionable society of the watering-place. In her present plight she had no strength for 'Flash', but she did spend some amusing hours with the family of the painter, George James, where she probably met a young man named Samuel Lysons, who had a taste for drawing and literary conversation.[4] Books, however, were her constant resource. Since coming to Bath, she commented to Fanny Burney, she had read to her daughters

the Bible from beginning to end, the Roman and English histories, Milton, Shakspere, Pope and Young's works from head to heel; Warton and Johnson's criticisms on the Poets; . . . and a hundred more.[5]

In spite of the strained relations with her children, she felt in duty bound to continue with their education.

In the spring Piozzi at last prepared to answer the summons to come for his bride. In March he went to Quinzano to secure a certificate of his birth and christening,[6] but it was not until

---

[1] Mainwaring Piozziana, ii. 19–20; Hayward, i. 219; ii. 58; *Queeney Letters*, p. 63. [2] *Queeney Letters*, pp. 64, 86; Hayward, i. 220–1.
[3] *Queeney Letters*, p. 86.
[4] I have seen at Mr. Alfred Goldsmith's, New York, a copy of Père Bouhours, *Pensées Ingénieuses* (Paris, 1692), presented by S. Lysons to Mrs. Thrale at Bath in 1784. In later letters to Lysons Mrs. Piozzi refers constantly to the James family.
[5] *D'Arblay Diary*, ii. 250 (Mar. 23, 1784). See also Thraliana, Mar. 15, 1784.
[6] The certificate which he secured at this time is now in my collection. The document is dated Mar. 24, 1784, at Quinzano, and has the formal approval of the episcopal chancellery of Brescia, dated Apr. 6, 1784. See also Chapter IX, p. 188.

late May or early June that he finally set out. Timorously he waited until repeated letters let him know that everything was prepared for his reception. Still fuming at the delay, Mrs. Thrale spent a few days in London about the middle of May making arrangements.[1] She stayed quietly in Mortimer Street, seeing only the Burneys, and possibly having one last interview with Johnson. Fanny still was a partial confidant, but their relationship was nearing a break.

Mrs. Thrale was beginning to suspect that Fanny might not be the loyal adherent she had formerly supposed. Gradually she became convinced that the sly Miss Burney, with her known dislike for the Piozzi marriage, had from the beginning been encouraging Queeney in her opposition—a suspicion which the existing correspondence goes far to justify.[2] Trying to remain on good terms with both mother and daughter, Fanny had acted as adviser for both. Probably she honestly

[1] *Queeney Letters*, p. 97; *D'Arblay Diary*, ii. 257–8. The exact dates of the visit are not clear. Mrs. Thrale, on her arrival in London, dispatched a note to Fanny dated 'Tuesday Night, May 1784'. On May 17 Fanny wrote to her sister 'the rest of that week I devoted almost wholly to sweet Mrs. Thrale'. The previous published entry in the *D'Arblay Diary* had been on Friday, May 7, so that it would be reasonable to suppose that Mrs. Thrale arrived in London on the following Tuesday, or May 11, and stayed for the remainder of that week. She had definitely returned to Bath by the 23rd, when she wrote in Thraliana about the trip. For the possible meeting with Johnson see *Thraliana*, i. 593.

[2] *Queeney Letters*, pp. 67–100, and unpublished letters in the Lansdowne collection. The disillusionment came slowly and was not complete until after the marriage. By the following August, however, Fanny was definitely considered one of the 'Mischief-makers' who had opposed the union. From Mrs. Piozzi's letter to Queeney of Aug. 17, 1784, it would appear that perhaps Queeney had let slip something of Fanny's efforts on the other side. Piozzi, too, had further widened the breach by complaining that Dr. Burney had never written to him all the time he was in Italy (see letter from Dr. Burney on July 30, 1784, explaining his remissness: Ry. 545, 19). For her part, Fanny Burney described again these last turbulent months in a letter to Queeney, July 12, 1798. Mrs. Thrale, she maintained,

bore all my opposition—which was regularly the strongest the utmost efforts of my stretched faculties could give—with a gentleness, nay, a *deference* the most touching to me—till the marriage was over—And then—to my never ending astonishment, in return to the constrained & painful letter I forced myself to write of my good wishes—she sent me a cold, frigid, reproachful answer, in entirely a new style to any I had ever received from her, to upbraid me that my *congratulations were not hearty!* As if I could write *congratulations* at all! *or meant to* write! How gross must have been such hypocrisy! . . . I wrote then, indeed, an answer somewhat high, for I felt injured, & far from averse to letting her see my resentment. She sent me a reply all kindness & returning affection—to that, you may believe, I wrote with warmth & friendship,—but I never have heard from her since, in any way, good or bad! (Lansdowne MS.)

Fanny suspected that either her last letter had never reached Mrs. Piozzi or that it was Piozzi who had stopped the correspondence. So she wrote, 'I am convinced from the moment of the nuptials she shewed him all my Letters, & probably attributed to me every obstacle that he had found in his way.'

played the double role because she thought it best for all those concerned, but Mrs. Thrale could hardly be expected to approve such a course. Fanny was marked down as a traitress, a false companion who had deserted her in the time of need.

One of Mrs. Thrale's objects in coming to London in May had been to find a governess and chaperon for her daughters. Though Queeney had given her consent to the marriage to save her mother's life, she had no intention of accepting a musician as a stepfather. Mrs. Thrale was clearly given to understand that by her marriage she was cutting herself off from all family associations. Originally she had planned to take her daughters abroad with her, but the trustees had quickly vetoed the suggestion. She was marrying a member of a Church which would tolerate no other religion. Young, impressionable girls might easily be won to the old religion, and the prospect of one of Thrale's heiresses in a convent did not appeal to the blunt, insular Protestantism of Cator and Crutchley. If she persisted in her wish to see her new husband's country, she must leave her children behind. There can be little doubt that at one time or another the alternative was placed squarely before her: she must choose either Piozzi and Italy, or her children. For a woman over forty, in love for the first time, the selection was speedily made. She knew the girls would be well cared for by the trustees, and their attitude towards her proposed second husband left her little option but to accept the temporary separation. Like her grandmother and Katherine of Beraine, she chose love rather than maternal duty.

When word finally came on June 24 that Piozzi was on the way, 'the Misses' made ready to depart for Brighton, where they had decided to spend the summer with their new companion, Miss Nicolson.[1] On the 26th Mrs. Thrale drove with them through Wilton and Fonthill to Salisbury, where mother and daughters parted with some show of affection. Late that night she was back at Bath, tremulously awaiting her lover. Long, excited letters to Queeney during the next few days showed the frayed state of her nerves, as well as those of Piozzi, who at length reached Bath on July 1. On the next day after his arrival she could write in Thraliana: 'The happiest Day of my whole Life, I think—Yes, *quite* the happiest; my Piozzi came home yesterday & dined with me.'

---

[1] *Queeney Letters*, pp. 98, 99. For information about Jane Nicolson see Sir H. J. C. Grierson's *Sir Walter Scott, Bart.*, New York, 1938, p. 46.

If, for over a year, Mrs. Thrale had seen Johnson only once, their correspondence had not lagged. Filled as his letters were with complaints of his own misery and his sleepless nights, there were occasional flashes of intense longing. 'Your letters give me a great part of the pleasure which a life of solitude admits,' he confessed. 'You will never bestow any share of your good will on one who deserves better. Those that have loved longest love best.'[1] Suffering from dropsy, asthma, and a multitude of minor ills, a prey to brooding and regret, he was confined to the house for long periods of time. He cannot have been completely ignorant of the plans of his Mistress, but to the last he probably hoped for a change of heart. Surely all this talk of Piozzi was mere gossip? As late as June 26 he wrote asking for 'some words of comfort', apparently unaware of the situation at Bath. Then suddenly came the cruel shock.

On June 30 Mrs. Thrale sent a formal notification to all the executors of her intentions to remarry, and at the same time enclosed a special apology to Johnson for so long concealing her plans from him.[2] Her only excuse, she maintained, was that she 'could not have borne to reject that Counsel it would have killed me to take'. Receipt of this letter roused the sick, irritable man to a pitch of frenzy. In his first outburst of wrath on July 2 he sent the often-quoted note beginning, 'Madam, If I interpret your letter right, you are ignominiously married'. Yet if she had not already abandoned her children and her religion and forfeited her fame, Johnson continued, he hoped she would grant him one last interview. 'I will come down, if you will permit it.'

To this rough expostulation, Mrs. Thrale replied on the 4th in a dignified but determined tone. 'The birth of my second husband is not meaner than that of my first; his sentiments are not meaner; his profession is not meaner, and his superiority in what he professes acknowledged by all mankind.'[3] Her own fame, she insisted, was 'as unsullied as snow'; and the letter ended, 'till you have changed your opinion of Mr. Piozzi let us converse no more. God bless you.' In order to forestall any attempt of Johnson to come to Bath, the message was hurriedly dispatched by coach instead of by the regular post.

As always, Johnson was sure to suffer remorse for his first

---

[1] Nov. 13, 1783.   [2] *Queeney Letters*, pp. 148–9.
[3] Hayward, i. 240. The original letter is in the R. B. Adam collection. The phrase 'his sentiments are not meaner' may have been added later; it is in different ink and somewhat different hand, though obviously hers. The letter is unsigned, evidently to keep Johnson from knowing she was not yet married.

angry words, and wrote again on July 8 to his once dear Mistress with tender affection.

What you have done, however I may lament it, I have no pretence to resent, as it has not been injurious to me: I therefore breathe out one sigh more of tenderness, perhaps useless, but at least sincere.

I wish that God may grant you every blessing, that you may be happy in this world for its short continuance, and eternally happy in a better state; and whatever I can contribute to your happiness I am very ready to repay, for that kindness which soothed twenty years of a life radically wretched.

After advising her to prevail upon her husband to settle in England, and pointing out a dangerous parallel with Mary Queen of Scots, he closed: 'The tears stand in my eyes. I am going into Derbyshire, and hope to be followed by your good wishes, for I am, with great affection . . .' This was the last letter she ever received from the man whom she had so admired and revered; yet he remained with her in spirit for the rest of her life. His influence on her mind could never be erased.

Johnson's final benediction possibly reached her just before she was leaving Bath. It was necessary to wait twenty-six days before the wedding ceremony could be performed, and in the meantime there was nothing to do but fret and attend to necessary business details. Accordingly, on July 8 Piozzi signed a bond before the Bishop of Bath asserting that there was no lawful bar to the marriage,[1] and soon after drove with Mrs. Thrale to London, where his friend Borghi had prudently hired lodgings for them in different streets. It seems almost certain that they remained in London for at least ten days, consulting lawyers and making final arrangements for the wedding,[2] a fact which renders her last note to Johnson something of a mystery. Dated July 15, 1784, and post-marked Bath, and July 16, it cannot have been transmitted in the ordinary way.[3] How a woman in London could send a letter

[1] A copy of this bond is in my possession. Perhaps it may be taken as further evidence of the insidious rumours which Baretti maintained were being circulated about Piozzi's paternity. See p. 218.

[2] This we know, since she wrote to Queeney from there on July 12, 14, 15. There is no evidence that she went back to Bath between this time and the 23rd, when she was married in London. On July 19 they signed their marriage settlement in London; so the assumption would be that they never left (Ry. Charter 1239). One pleasant feature of this tedious delay in London was that Greenland, her new attorney, in examining her business affairs, found out that a large sum of money was due from the executors, part of which, either by ignorance or design, Cator had thought fit to keep from her (Hayward, ii. 59).

[3] The original letter is addressed to Johnson at Bolt Court, and carries two postmarks, 'Bath' and 'July 16', the former applied in the country and the latter in

from Bath is difficult to explain, perhaps indeed only by the assumption that it had either been left behind with instructions not to send it until later, or had been enclosed in another letter to friends at Bath, who in turn did the actual posting. One thing is certain—that she did not wish Johnson to know she was in London, still unmarried. The strain of a scene with him was more than she could endure. Instead, she wrote affectionately, with many wishes and prayers for his good health and reiterations of her faith in her new husband:

He is a religious Man, a sober Man, and a Thinking Man—he will not injure me, I am sure he will not, let nobody injure him in your good Opinion.

Johnson never answered this defence. He wished only to drive her from his thoughts.

On July 23 she was married to Piozzi in London by a Roman Catholic chaplain;[1] they immediately afterward drove to Bath, where they repeated their vows on the 25th in St. James's English church. After the tension of the past month Piozzi shook so violently during the ceremony that even his bride felt sorry for him. But nothing could mar her thrill of the moment, for at last she was married to the man of her choice. As she wrote at once to Queeney, 'Oh what a disinterested! what a noble Heart has the Man to whom I was this day united.'[2]

Even before the marriage took place, rumour was rife among her friends in the Blue-Stocking circle. On July 15 Mrs. Montagu wrote to Mrs. Vesey.

Mrs. Thrales marriage has taken such horrible possession of my mind I cannot advert to any other subject. I am sorry and feel the worst kind of sorrow, that which is blended with shame . . . I am myself convinced that the poor Woman is mad, and indeed have long suspected her mind was disorderd. She was the best Mother, the best Wife, the best friend, the most amiable member of Society. She gave the most prudent attentions to her Husbands business during his long state of imbecility and after his death, till she had an opportunity of disposing well of the great Brewery. I bring in my verdict lunacy in this affair.[3]

London on arrival. Thus it must necessarily have been posted at Bath only a day or so before the 16th. (Ry. 540, 110.)
[1] Ry. Charter 1242. The certificate of marriage was signed by Richard Smith, July 23, 1784, with an attestation by Jean Balthazar, comte D'Adhemar, July 27, 1784. See, however, *N. & Q.* (Dec. 31, 1932), clxiii. 476.
[2] *Queeney Letters*, pp. 170–1.
[3] R. Blunt, *Mrs. Montagu*, ii. 274. On July 19 Miss Carter wrote to Mrs. Montagu for confirmation of the rumour which seems to have spread even to Deal (*Letters from Mrs. Elizabeth Carter to Mrs. Montagu*, ed. M. Pennington (1817), iii. 215).

Mrs. Vesey in her reply added the information:

Her daughter has told her she can never acknowledge such a Father and she and her three sisters have taken refuge with their guardian at Brighthelmstone. She has cut down the trees on her estate in Wales and would have carried her daughters abroad if the trustees would have allowed . . .[1]

In another letter Mrs. Vesey told of Crutchley's bringing the fatal announcement to Dr. Johnson, who burst into tears and begged Crutchley to stay with him. Piozzi she described as 'black ugly and loves nothing but money'.[2]

The belief seemed general that Mrs. Piozzi had been forcibly separated from her children. Mrs. Scott, writing to her sister, made the assertion:

As soon as the friends of the family learnt her fix'd purpose they informed her the Children must not remain with her, and fetched them from Brighthelmstone, where they were under the care of a Person little older than Miss Thrale.[3]

Even the *Morning Herald* for August 18 reiterated the charge:

Mrs. Thrale, in consequence of her marriage with Piozzi, has the children taken away from her. This the guardians insisted on. The new married couple mean to pass the next winter abroad.

No one knew exactly what had happened, but all realized that by her misalliance Mrs. Thrale had cut herself off from all her old associations.

The love affair of the wealthy widow and her daughters' music master was seized on with avidity by the newspapers of the day. Jokes were cracked about the profession of the bridegroom, and every few days some new absurdity was inserted in the columns of the *Morning Herald*. On August 10 appeared the jingle:

Lines on a Late Piozzified Marriage

Most writers agree, and I know it a truth,
We all love a frolic in days of our youth,
But what shall we say, when such grave ones engage
And frolic in love, in the days of old age.[4]

That a woman of forty-three should consider romance important was astounding.

The Blue-Stockings, too, were outraged by the sight of an

---

[1] Blunt, ii. 275.
[2] The original, now in the Johnson House in Gough Square, London, is merely dated 'Monday 19'.   [3] Blunt, ii. 175.
[4] See also issues of Aug. 6, 12, 14, 17, 18, 27; Sept. 7 and 14.

educated woman succumbing to passion. Mrs. Chapone on August 24 wrote to William Weller Pepys:

there must be really some degree of *Insanity* in that case. for such mighty overbearing Passions are not natural in a 'Matron's bones'. The 4 daughters render it a most frightful instance of human wretchedness indeed! it has given great occasion to the Enemy to blaspheme and to triumph over the Bas Bleu Ladies.[1]

The Queen of the Blues became so obsessed by the degradation of Mrs. Thrale's surrender that she wrote to her sister, Mrs. Scott: 'Mrs. Thrale is fallen below pity. I think the Women and Girls are run mad, Heaven be praised I have no Daughters.'[2] She confided to the same correspondent: 'Dr. Johnson says he did not think there had been so abandoned a Woman in the World.' It was freely suggested that Piozzi would spend his wife's money in riotous living, while she would weep her eyes out in distant Italy, a prey to bitter recollections, once 'her passions subside and give place to reason'.[3]

Meanwhile, the newly married couple were quietly making preparations for their tour of Europe. After remaining in Bath for a few weeks, being entertained by the Jameses and receiving calls from several of their other friends, they came to London on August 11 for final conferences with Cator and the bankers. Further problems had to do with a special travelling carriage built by Hatchet, which Piozzi had ordered fitted with a small portable harpsichord which could be placed under one of the seats. In this way he could carry wherever he went the means of playing the music he loved.[4]

Throughout August Mrs. Piozzi's letters to Queeney kept up a forced gaiety. Although her health was still variable and there were a multitude of annoying arrangements to be made, she would not admit any dampened ardour. At the last, Sophy and Susan were allowed to come to see her, and, according to Thraliana, Queeney also called to bid her a not unkind farewell.[5] Late Friday night, September 3, the packing and financial details having been finally completed, found the Piozzis sitting on trunks, making ready to leave England the next day. The fateful step had been taken, and a new life stretched out before her.

[1] *A Later Pepys*, I. 408.
[2] Blunt, ii. 177, 182. See also E. and F. Anson, *Mary Hamilton* (1925), p. 223. Miss Carter felt that in spite of the great differences in their ages it would have been more suitable for Mrs. Thrale to have married Johnson (*Letters from Eliz. Carter*, op. cit. iii. 221). [3] Blunt, ii. 275.
[4] Hayward, ii. 63; The *Morning Herald*, Aug. 6, 1784.
[5] *Queeney Letters*, p. 185.

HESTER LYNCH PIOZZI

XI

THE FLORENCE MISCELLANY

SEPTEMBER 1784—AUGUST 1785

UPON setting out on a honeymoon tour of Europe, Mrs. Piozzi characteristically selected a fresh note-book into which to set down her observations and reflections.[1] To such an inveterate diarist and commentator it was as important to confide in the written page as to see and enjoy what went on about her. The first entry was made at Dover on Sunday, September 5, 1784.

Last night I arrived at this Place in Company with my dear Husband & faithful Maid,—having left my Daughters reconciled to my Choice, (all at least except the eldest who parted with me cooly, not unkindly:) and my Friends well pleased with my leaving London I fancy, where my Stay perplexed 'em, and entangled their Duty with their Interest.

The next day they sailed for France, and after a windless passage of twenty hours, reached Calais, where Mrs. Piozzi purchased some toys to be sent to her younger daughters in England. After renewing former impressions of Calais, the couple drove in a leisurely fashion to Paris by way of Boulogne, Montreuil, Amiens, and Chantilly, reaching their destination late on Saturday night, the 11th, almost shaken to pieces from jolting over stony roads.

She was rapturously happy. Now that she had escaped from the nerve-racking worries of London, it was possible to relax and enjoy life again. But the contrast of present delights with past afflictions almost overpowered her. As she wrote on the 13th, her new husband's indulgence, the complete absence of anxiety, 'together with that recovered flow of Spirits that new-found health inspires, will go near to make me a Sensualist'. Even remembrance of the birthdays of Queeney and Johnson only served to accentuate the happiness of the moment.

---

[1] Ry. 618. The French portion has been printed in *French Journals*, pp. 191–213. This journal was later used as the basis for her *Observations and Reflections* (1789), but is very different from the printed version. In describing the Piozzis' travels in Europe various authorities have been used: her travel journals, Thraliana, Mainwaring Piozziana; letters to Queeney, S. Lysons, &c.

This is Dr. Johnson's Birthday: may God give him many & happy returns of it; we used to spend these two Days in Mirth & Gayety at Streatham: but Pride & Prejudice hindered my longer Residence in a Place wch indeed had lost its Charms for me. I am Happier at this Moment than I have been these Two & Twenty Years.[1]

All the hectic months of desperation, the agonies of uncertainty, the trials of persecution were a small price to pay for such exhilarating delight.

Paris, none the less, continually brought memories of the visit of 1775. She called on the nuns at Fossée, spent hours with the paintings in the Palais Royal, and watched a balloon ascent of the famous Robert brothers. Beaumarchais's comedy, *The Marriage of Figaro*, at that moment the rage of Paris, she found indecent, though admitting its wit and clever satire. Of new acquaintances made, the celebrated Italian dramatist, Goldoni, proved the most exciting.

Paris was fascinating, but since Italy was their immediate goal, they tore themselves away late in September and drove to Lyons, where letters from her younger daughters contributed further to her good humour. Too late in the year to pass through Switzerland, they proceeded slowly through Savoy to Mt. Cenis. She took passionate delight in the scenery along the route. With an eye for colour, she noticed the carpet of royal-purple wild flowers, the bluish willows, the dull beeches and golden walnuts by the side of the river Yonne, the tender green of winter wheat in the valleys, contrasting with the autumn tints on the vineyard-covered hill-sides. With an appreciation for the unusual, she noted the torrents gushing from the rocks, the little churches perched high on ledges, whose tinkling bells called the natives to prayer. Passage over the Alps naturally thrilled the English traveller, and as soon as they reached Turin she described her feelings to the artistic young Samuel Lysons:

those four Days Journey from Pont Bon Voisin to Novalesa, would be enough I should think to make a Coxcomb of Dr. Johnson, or a Pedant of Mr. James. We often wished for your Company, & said how you would sit upon this Rock & that Rock, taking Views of the Country: I jumped out of the Coach myself at one Place to drink at a beautiful Cascade that came foaming down the Side of the Hill all tufted with various coloured Greens, where I followed *Hyale* among the Bushes (the yellow Butterfly with brown-edged Wings) but could not catch her.[2]

[1] *French Journals*, p. 203.
[2] Oct. 19, 1784. The majority of Mrs. Piozzi's letters to Lysons are now in the

From Turin they proceeded in a roundabout way through Casale, Monferrato, Novi, Genoa, and Pavia to Milan. Piozzi considered Milan his home: here he had spent many of the happiest years of his life; here he wished to remain indefinitely with his new wife. Accordingly, they were soon settled in spacious quarters in one part of the large Casa Fidele, and Mrs. Piozzi described her domestic arrangements in a long letter to Queeney on November 19.

We have a stately Stone Hall & Staircase with Glass Lamps &c. Eating Room, Dressing Room, Bed Chamber & Drawing Room; which in a House at the upper end of Piccadilly would be made to hold ten Card Tables commodiously . . .

All this with coach-houses, servants' quarters, &c., sumptuously decorated, for only £80 a year! The economical soul of her husband must indeed have been delighted.

Mrs. Piozzi had a sentimental reason for wishing to like Italy, for it was her husband's country and should now be her own; nevertheless, the comments in her journal are often shrewd and penetrating. To be sure, the petty inconveniences and annoyances which so enraged other British travellers she largely ignored. She saw no reason to grumble much at the lack of heating facilities, the diet, or the Italian food; these were part of the price one paid for travelling abroad. But however much she tried to keep any insular prejudices from marring her enjoyment and appreciation, there was one custom which, possibly from a lack of perfect understanding, she could not accept. The strange convention of the 'Cavaliere Servente' irritated and frightened her. Deeply in love with her own husband, she resented the necessity of appearing constantly in public with another man. Yet, according to the dictates of fashion, he for whom she had sacrificed so much could not now be her only regular public escort. Amusingly she showed her attitude, when pressed to choose a cavalier from among her husband's friends, by naming an old priest of eighty years. For the most part, however, she threw herself whole-heartedly into the gay life of the city, and occupied her spare time in writing and translating Italian verses.

One of the inherent weaknesses of Mrs. Piozzi's character was an inordinate love of praise. She might be the first to laugh at any pretensions to wit or charm, but in her heart she always

possession of Mr. Lindsay Fleming, Bognor-Regis. Many were published in *Bentley's Miscellany*, xxviii (1850). In the following pages some quotations are made from the original manuscripts and some from the printed versions.

longed for adulation. Thus she welcomed the lavish homage of a group of minor Italian writers and church dignitaries who soon gathered round her. The extravagant toasts offered to the wealthy English signora by these obviously delightful people could not but strike a sympathetic chord. She later remembered the gay, amusing circle:

The Marquis of Araciel, Piozzi's Patron, brought me Presents: The Abbé Bossi made Verses in my Praise, so did Abate Ravasi. I had all the Wits about me; The Abbé Brianconi was excessively civil—The Venetian Envoy Soderini sent to Venice for *Fish* for me: Baron Cronthal of Brera gave me free Access to the public Library—[1]

It was a startling but agreeable contrast to her last days in England.

She could not, however, cut herself off completely from the old life. In Genoa she had received a bitter, vituperative letter from Baretti, accusing her of every crime, but though stung for a moment, she refused to let such taunts destroy her peace of mind.[2] Letters from her daughters were neither so frequent nor so affectionate as she would have wished, but that was to be expected. In compensation, there were a few friends in England, Mrs. Lewis, Mr. James, Sir Lucas Pepys, Dr. Lort, and her new-found disciple Samuel Lysons, who kept her supplied with news and kindly good wishes. To these she replied with gay bravado, emphasizing the civilities showered upon her by her husband's friends, and dwelling with pride on every attention of the talented Milanese. She hoped the news would be retold to those lukewarm Blues who had so betrayed her.

She still thought often of Johnson. Unwilling to forgive the traitorous Fanny Burney and the others, she harboured no resentment towards the sick old man, whose anger she understood and was willing to forget. In a few years, when she returned to London, there might even be a reconciliation and a return to the old relationship. On December 7

---

[1] Mainwaring Piozziana, ii. 27. The Marquis D'Araciel, a nobleman of Spanish extraction who lived in Milan, had aided Piozzi ever since as a young boy the musician had run away from home to escape being made a priest. Piozzi had been a guest in the Palazzo Aracieli in 1784, when recalled to England to marry Mrs. Thrale. See Countess Evelyn Martinengo Cesaresco, *Glimpses of Italian Society* (New York, 1892), p. 11. The Countess Cesaresco also clearly explains Mrs. Piozzi's misunderstanding of the purpose of the custom of the *Cavaliere Servente* (pp. 12–15).

[2] Mainwaring Piozziana, ii. 27. The worst Baretti could say of Piozzi was that he had disputed with an innkeeper about a bill. See also Ry. 552, 4.

she wrote to Lysons: 'Do not neglect Dr. Johnson, you will never see any other Mortal either so wise or so good— I keep his Picture in my Chamber, and his Works on my Chimney.'[1]

Meanwhile, in London the object of her thoughts was dejected and wholly miserable. Deserted by the woman he had adored, racked by pain and disease, Johnson sat and brooded over the faithlessness of the sex. He had written to Hawkins: 'She is now become a subject for her enemies to exult over, and for her friends, if she has any left, to forget or pity';[2] and when Fanny Burney called to see him late in November, Johnson wretchedly confided to her:

> I drive her quite from my mind. If I meet with one of her letters, I burn it instantly. I have burnt all I can find. I never speak of her, and I desire never to hear of her more. I drive her, as I said, wholly from my mind.[3]

It is easy to understand and sympathize with Johnson. His Mistress, so he thought, had deserted her children, her country, and her religion. He had done all he could to save her, but had been cast aside for a foreign musician. And this was the one whom he had often boasted to be the first of womankind.[4] Vainly he tried to throw off the oppressive gloom, to think of other things; but the time left him was too short. In spite of all the doctors and devoted friends could do, he was unable to rally. With a premonition of the end, he settled his remaining worldly affairs early in December, and on the 13th quietly passed away.

The death of Dr. Johnson stirred up further gossip about the absent Mrs. Piozzi. Mrs. Montagu wrote: 'I am afraid Mrs. Thrales imprudent marriage shortend his life', and this view was accepted by many others.[5] Johnson's old friends held her responsible for much of the misery of his last years, and they never forgave what they considered her selfish abandonment of

---

[1] Lysons had met Johnson only once, on June 26, 1784. See L. Fleming, *Memoir and Select Letters of Samuel Lysons* (1934), p. 7.

[2] J. Hawkins, *Life of Johnson* (1787), p. 570.

[3] *D'Arblay Diary*, ii. 271. He did not burn all Mrs. Thrale's letters. See p. 297.

[4] See *John. Misc.* ii. 272; *Letters*, ii. 406. W. Shaw, in his *Memoirs of Dr. Johnson* (1785), p. 178, made the comment:
No event since the decease of Mrs. Johnson so deeply affected him as the very unaccountable marriage of Mrs. Thrale. This woman he had frequently mentioned as the ornament and pattern of her sex. There was no virtue which she did not practice, no feminine accomplishment of which she was not a mistress, hardly any language or science, or art which she did not know.

[5] R. Blunt, *Mrs. Montagu*, ii. 165; also Shaw (op. cit.).

the dying man.[1] All the years of care and devotion which she had lavished on the irritable old man were forgotten; instead, all that was remembered was her failure in his last days.

Occasional references and sly allusions appeared in the newspapers, and many absurd rumours were bandied about by fashionable London society.[2] Mrs. Montagu actually wrote:

Her letters to her Friends from abroad were full of her felicity, it is said accounts are now come that she is confined in a convent at Milan. Her Husband says she is insane, he is the only Person in the World who can say it with an ill grace.[3]

One well-meaning friend carried the news to the youngest Thrale daughters that Piozzi, having rid himself of their mother, was riotously spending her fortune.[4]

The news of Dr. Johnson's death reached Mrs. Piozzi in Milan as a shock and a sad reminder of the past. She had definitely broken with the associations which bound her to the old Streatham coterie; now in a moment she was hurled back into the world she was trying to forget, and forced to make decisions she had hoped to evade for a few years at least. Lysons, writing

---

[1] There were others who defended Mrs. Piozzi. Many years later, on Apr. 24, 1792, Richard Musgrave wrote to Mrs. Piozzi from Ireland:
   I find that one ground of censure of your enemies has been your not having continued to keep Doctor Johnson under your roof. For my part I have expressed great astonishment at your having borne his singular moroseness & peevishness so long. That attention & I may say reverence which you shewed him on all occasions, was often treated with contemptuous petulance & sometimes with abuse. Nothing could compensate the misery which you suffered. In my opinion the British nation are much indebted to you for having kept him alive so long; for I am convinced from the infirmities which he had joyned to his singularities & the neglect of himself which were so well known that he would have died many years before he did but for your unremitting care of his health. (Ry. 892, 27.)
Herbert Lawrence also referred to this criticism on Mar. 3, 1788, and added, 'I have often wonder'd how you bore with him so long: the coarseness and severity of his Behavior to your Friends must have given you exquisite uneasiness' (Ry. 535, 9).
[2] The *European Mag.* for October (pp. 320–1) had printed a selection from the *Vanity of Human Wishes*, as a pointed 'Advice to the Fair Sex'. The *Gent. Mag.* (1784), p. 893, printed a spurious copy of Johnson's letter to Mrs. Thrale, beginning 'If you are already ignominiously married'. The original of this letter, of course, was in the possession of Mrs. Piozzi, but somehow rumours were afloat about it. On Nov. 14, 1784, Wm. Hayley wrote to Anna Seward, 'Can you prevail on the Old Lion to give you a copy or a sight of his Letter to the Widow Thrale? It must be a delightful piece of unsuccessful eloquence.' (*Adam Libr.* iii. 123.)
[3] R. Blunt (op. cit.), ii. 165. This same story kept cropping up for the next few months. The *Morning Post*, Mar. 4, 1785, printed: '*Signora Piozzi*, late Mrs. Thrale, is at present immured in Italy by her husband, who having possessed himself of about 30,000£ of her cash, is striving, with use of it, to dissipate the remains of her affection!'   [4] *Thraliana*, May 1, 1787.

on December 29 of the plans of the various Johnson biographers, warned her that she would be besieged for anecdotes. His prediction was correct, and she was soon approached by the booksellers for anecdotes to be used in the official biography undertaken by Sir John Hawkins.[1] She had, indeed, always planned to write the memoirs of Johnson herself, but his death at this time made it exceedingly difficult. Although she had been collecting material for twenty years with such a work in view, most of these miscellaneous papers and letters were safe in a bank vault in London,[2] and she had only Thraliana with her on which to draw for anecdotes. Of one thing she was certain—she was enjoying her Italian tour too much to consider any speedy return to England. As a result she was in a complete quandary, unable either to give up the idea or to throw herself wholeheartedly into active competition with the other biographers. Replying to Lysons on January 20, she insisted that she had not settled in her own mind what she would do, but asked him to get her all the anecdotes he could find of the early and late parts of Johnson's life, 'the *middle* of which no one knows as well as myself, nor *half* as well'. She warned him, however, that she did not want her intentions known. On the 25th, still in doubt, she confided in Thraliana:

I have recovered myself sufficiently to think what will be the Consequence to me of Johnson's Death, but must wait the Event as all Thoughts on the future in this World are vain. Six People have already undertaken to write his Life I hear of which Sir John Hawkins, Mr. Boswell, Tom Davies and Dr. Kippis are four. Piozzi says he would have me add to the Number, and so I would; but that I think my Anecdotes too few, & am afraid of saucy Answers if I send to England for others—the saucy Answers *I* should disregard but my heart is made vulnerable by my late Marriage, and I am certain that to spite me, they would insult my Husband.

Poor Johnson! I see they will leave *nothing untold* that I laboured so long to keep secret; & I was so very delicate in trying to conceal his fancied Insanity, that I retained no Proofs of it—or hardly any —nor ever mentioned it in these Books, lest by my dying first *they* might be printed and the Secret (for such I thought it) discovered. I used to tell him in Jest that his Biographers would be at a Loss

---

[1] To Mrs. Piozzi from James Robson, Jan. 28, 1785, now in the possession of Ellis & Co., 29 New Bond St., London.

[2] These papers included over 400 letters from Johnson, and at least 25 written to him by a variety of correspondents, including Lucy Porter, Fanny Burney, Charlotte Lennox, Boswell, Langton, &c. There were also the Children's Book and numerous small repositories, as well as miscellaneous loose papers on which she had written down poems and anecdotes.

concerning some Orange-Peel he used to keep in his pocket, and many a Joke we had about the Lives that would be published: rescue me out of all their hands My dear, & do it *yourself* said he: 'Taylor, Adams, & Hector will furnish you with juvenile Anecdotes, & Baretti will give you all the rest that you have not already—for I think Baretti is a Lyar only when he speaks of himself. . . .'

By the latter part of January newspapers and magazines from England had arrived in Milan full of allusions to the recent death of the great lexicographer. These further stirred Mrs. Piozzi's ambition. One of the first in the field, Tom Tyers, published in the December number of the *Gentleman's Magazine* what he called a biographical sketch of Dr. Johnson. This sketch, which was highly complimentary to the Thrales,[1] was reviewed by an anonymous correspondent in the *St. James's Chronicle* of January 8, 1785,[2] who added sarcastic remarks about the cause of Thrale's death, together with insulting gibes at his widow's second marriage. The same unknown writer published a second review on the 11th, in which the Thrales were not mentioned, but in which Boswell's intended biography was highly praised. In far-off Italy Mrs. Piozzi had no means of identifying the author of these articles, whom we now know to have been George Steevens, the editor of Shakespeare; but she immediately suspected Boswell, and recorded her conjecture in Thraliana. The innocent Boswell, who had seen in Edinburgh the article in the *St. James's Chronicle* praising his forthcoming work, was as eager as she to find out the name of the author. Consequently, he wrote a highly characteristic letter to the printers of the paper, in which he thanked the anonymous writer for his compliments and asked him to come forward and avow his name. When Mrs. Piozzi saw this letter of Boswell's, she was convinced that the whole affair had been merely a stratagem of his to rouse public interest in himself. It was more than ever important that she rush into print to retaliate.

Having decided to begin work immediately instead of waiting until her return to England, Mrs. Piozzi wrote to all her old acquaintances whom she could trust, asking for assistance. Lysons replied on February 25:

I fear Anecdotes of the early part of Johnson's life will not be

---

[1] *Gent. Mag.* (1784), p. 904. Tyers quoted Johnson as saying of Mrs. Thrale, 'if she was not the wisest woman in the world, she was undoubtedly one of the wittiest'. He quoted Goldsmith as remarking that after one severe illness Johnson 'owed his recovery to her attention'.

[2] For a more complete discussion of this episode see my article 'The Printing of Mrs. Piozzi's Anecdotes of Dr. Johnson', *J. Rylands Bulletin*, xx (1936), 157–72.

very easily procured, tho' Sir Jno. Hawkins who is writing the life which is to be prefixed to the Édition of his Works, says that he has material sufficient to fill an octavo volume, what he has will of course be kept close 'till the publication. Several others of the Doctor's friends, they say, intend publishing their scraps separate.[1]

Lysons, later in the letter, copied out for her an epitaph 'just arrived from Lichfield', which Johnson was supposed to have written at the age of five, after treading on a duck. This somewhat dubious story she promptly incorporated in her manuscript.[2] On March 22nd she reported progress to the same correspondent:

My Book is getting forward, & will run well enough among the rest; the Letters I have of Dr. Johnson's are two hundred at least I dare say, and some of those from Skie are delightful: they will carry my little Volume upon their Back quite easily.

Do you know who Dr. Taylor gives his Anecdotes to? Mr. Johnson bid me once ask *him* for Memoirs if I was the survivor, & so I would, but I am afraid of a Refusal, as I guess Sir Jno. Hawkins is already in possession of all that Dr. Taylor has to bestow. There lives however at Birmingham a Surgeon Mr. Edward Hector, whom likewise Mr. Johnson referred me to: he once saw Mr. Thrale & me, &, perhaps would be more kind, & more likely to relate such Things as I wish to hear.—Could you go between us? & coax him out of some Intelligence, The story of the Duck is incomparable. Sir Lucas Pepys advised me not to declare to private Friends alone, but to publicly advertise my Intentions of writing Anecdotes concerning Dr. Johnson, you will therefore see it proclaimed in all the papers I hope.

From the beginning Mrs. Piozzi had been undecided exactly what form her compilation should take, but she seems to have contemplated some combination of anecdotes and letters, possibly of the nature of Mason's *Life of Gray*. She constantly referred to her letters from Johnson as the most valuable part of her material. The last of April Mrs. Piozzi wrote to Lysons:

My Book is in very pretty forwardness, but the Letters I have in England are my best Possessions. A propos the Papers said that Sir John Hawkins has had his House burned down, is it true?— Pray enquire for a letter which *I know* Dr. Johnson wrote to Mr. Barnard the King's librarian when he was in Italy looking for

---

[1] Unless otherwise noted all letters from Lysons are in Ry. 552.

[2] *John. Misc.* i. 153. Also, *Life*, i. 40. Lucy Porter always insisted this apocryphal story was true. The verses appeared in the *Daily Universal Register*, Mar. 5, 1785. The story may not have been new to Mrs. Piozzi, for she insisted in a later annotation to Boswell's *Life*, 'I do protest he told them to me himself as I printed them: & I believe he made them' (Isham copy).

curious Books; the Subject was wholly Literary and Controversial, and would be most interesting to the Public; I would give any thing almost to obtain a Copy *now*, and there was a Time when I might have taken twenty Copies.

Realizing her ignorance of Johnson's early life, Mrs. Piozzi constantly wrote to Lysons, to Dr. Lort, and Sir Lucas Pepys asking their aid in collecting information. Unfortunately these men were too busy with their own affairs to be of much service. Dr. Lort, who had been commissioned to apply to Dr. Adams for anecdotes about his relations with Johnson, replied that Adams had little or nothing of any consequence to offer.[1] Lysons was able to report only that Hector had already given his stories to Boswell, and that Seward's collection of Johnsoniana had been 'perused by Kippis & squeezed again by Hawkins'.[2] It was obvious that she could never hope to compete by proxy with such active gleaners of information as Boswell and his rivals. Lysons, however, added as compensation:

I saw the Bishop of Peterborough a few days since, he was much pleased when I told him of your intentions, he thinks it will not be worth while for you to give yourself much trouble in collecting early or late anecdotes of Johnson, for which you must depend on the memory of others, as they will not be expected in your account of him & as those you have, will be infinitely more interesting than any other Period of his life could be supposed to furnish.

Accordingly, as she travelled about, Mrs. Piozzi went ahead transcribing her old jottings from Thraliana, and racking her brain for further memories of the great man. Then, as soon as the work was definitely begun, she wanted her intentions well advertised. Late in March she had given Lysons authority to see that her plans were announced in the papers, but in his replies during April there is no reference to this request. The advertisement did appear, however, in the *St. James's Chronicle* for April 16. Lysons wrote on May 20:

Boswell intends publishing his Hebridian Tour with anecdotes very soon, his Life in Quarto does not appear for some Time. I believe some of Johnson's Biographers are by no means pleased that you should be added to their number—Many ill natured things have been said and a paragraph inserted in the papers to tell the world that it could not be your advertizement, as you was not at present sufficiently at liberty to be the author of it . . .

[1] Ry. 544, 3; May 28, 1785.   [2] Apr. 15, 1785.

Dr. Lort also wrote of the venomous paragraph in the paper,[1] and joined with Lysons in urging her to return to England as quickly as possible, since the only way to put a stop to this canard of her incarceration would be to appear on the spot with her old-time health and vigour. But this Mrs. Piozzi was not yet willing to do.

Although determined to do something with her Johnsoniana, she had no intention of allowing the work to interfere with her enjoyment of the land of romance she had entered. Shortly after hearing of the death of Johnson, she celebrated her birthday on January 27, surrounded by fulsome Italian friends, with a sumptuous dinner and concert. Of her new-found joy she wrote in Thraliana:

> but that of Course which most delights my Heart is the unfeigned Pleasure which I see my Piozzi takes in my Company—God has heard my Prayers, and enabled me to make happy the most amiable of his Sex.—Was I to *wish* for more, I might provoke Providence to lessen the Enjoyments I possess; let me suppress all inordinate Desire of a Child by the Man I so love—*that* only could add to my happiness.

So passes the happiest Birthday ever yet experienced by Hester Lynch Piozzi.

Throughout February and March 1785 the Piozzis continued their carefree existence in Milan. As she wrote to her eldest daughter on February 25, every Monday there was a concert at the 'Casa Piozzi' which was thronged by Italians of all ranks. Life was very pleasant, for 'the Women kiss me, & the Men write Verses about me, & I translated a Sonnet upon an Air Balloon, & they all admired at it'. Among her guests was at least one Englishman, William Parsons, whom she mentioned as having left complimentary verses hidden behind Dr. Johnson's picture which hung, with Queeney's, in their breakfast room.

One flaw, and only one, marred the perfection of this ideal existence. On the surface everything might seem serene, but Mrs. Piozzi sensed uneasily that in a certain respect she was in a difficult position. Difference of religion in Italy was a much more vital consideration than in England. She herself, though brought up a Protestant, had, as she put it, always 'been partial to *Peter* as elder Brother';[2] now she found that in the country of her husband they recognized no other branch of the Church. She had thus become an object for the proselytizing zeal of the

---

[1] Ry. 544, 3   [2] Thraliana, Mar. 1785.

ecclesiastics who frequented their company. At first she took this zealous solicitation good-humouredly enough, and argued with them as she would have done with an English Bishop; but when she found all her ideas casually disdained, she commented in Thraliana, 'these People by treating my notions as Heretical, have made me a *Protestant* in despite of myself'. Gradually, too, she began to feel that the question was more serious than she had at first supposed: if she persisted in open heresy, her husband would be made to suffer; if she was permanently adamant, an attempt might even be made to wean him away from her.[1] To a wife passionately in love such a prospect was a serious challenge. Yet how could she escape from the zeal of the churchmen and still not alienate her husband? Clever woman that she was, she soon found a way to avoid this entanglement; by moving from place to place she would lessen the opportunities of the clerics and keep Piozzi to herself. Constant travel was her only hope.

While announcing their intention of returning to Milan within a year, the Piozzis, after a stay of five months, prepared to depart on a tour of Italy. Leaving all their furniture, fine linen, china, &c., under the care of the kind Abbé Bossi, they set out on April 6 for Venice. Long afterwards, remembering this departure, she wrote:

Well! Now I *did* prepare to be happy; I had my husband to *myself* in the *Coach* which I began to consider as my favourite *home*; no Women to be jealous of, no Priests to be afraid of. We made as short or as long Journeys as suited my health or my Caprice, and I think Lodi was our first Stage, & we went to the Opera *together* at Night: no Party to make—no Lady to lament about, whether she went or no . . . but I had Piozzi with me, & he had his little Piano e forte—& what could we want? The *Places* he took me to, entertained *me* quite enough; my Remarks on them entertained *him*; though I believe he now & then wanted more Auditors than the Gentlemen who showed us the Curiosities.[2]

In a leisurely manner they drove through Cremona, Mantua, Verona, to Padua; and her journals, as usual, were filled with interesting comments on the way. In Padua the Piozzis visited 'Santa Grestina's fine Church', where she delighted to explain to her husband the Biblical carvings around the high altar. All her life a student of the Bible, she found this an excellent chance to display her knowledge. The old ecclesiastic

[1] Mainwaring Piozziana, ii. 37, 38. She confided to Thraliana much about her religious problem.   [2] Ibid. ii. 40–1.

who guided them about the church was astounded, crossed himself, and at last exclaimed: 'Questo è pur un *Portento!*' Such knowledge of the Bible could only be the result of a miracle. But when Piozzi whispered to him that his wife was an Englishwoman and a heretic, an easy explanation of such erudition, the old priest cried out: 'God convert her! She has too great Talents for thy *Enemies*, Oh Lord!' Mrs. Piozzi was much flattered and moved by this tribute, but her husband, seeing the ludicrous side of the incident, rushed out of the church unable to stifle his laughter.[1]

At Padua the Piozzis left their coach and floated on a barge down the Brenta to Venice, accompanied by the music of Piozzi's little piano, which 'never sounded so sweet I think as on that Water, which is used to the Freightage of Musick'.[2] Mrs. Piozzi was completely charmed with Venice. So amiable were the inhabitants and so affectionate their treatment of her; so enchanting the architecture of Saint Mark's, with the moon rising out of the sea on one side and the setting sun gilding the bronze horses on the other; so magnificent the elegant family barges with eight gondoliers, offered by noble Venetians for her evening's entertainment; so amazing the conversations of literary people, who quoted *Clarissa* and repeated Pope's *Essays*; that she filled her letters with rhapsodies about the lovely city and state of Venice. Her journal, too, was crammed with the same encomiums. While in Venice she wrote more comments in five weeks than in five months in Milan. The famous pictures were a never-ending source of delight. She commented to Queeney, 'the Pictures here are all known in England I believe, but nothing can give one a just Idea of them except the Sight'. Such beauty she had long dreamed of, but never before experienced, and she added humourously:

but as I never now speak my own Language except to My Maid, I am more in the way of resembling Mr. Johnson's Madman, who in order to attain perfection said if you remember that it was sufficient to pronounce the Word *bel, bel, bel, bel, bel*: and *this* Word occurs so often in *this* Country that I shall soon arrive at the State he wished for.

In Venice Mrs. Piozzi first met members of her husband's family. A younger brother, Giambattista, greeted them affectionately, but when he tried ineffectually to interest Gabriel in investing some of his wife's money in a speculative scheme,

[1] Ibid. ii. 42.   [2] *Queeney Letters*, 197. To Queeney, Apr. 22, 1785.

the affection cooled.[1] Never a gambler, Gabriel Piozzi had no interest in any wild plans; he was canny, careful and saving, more apt to err on the side of caution than daring.

With regret, '& almost with Tears', the Piozzis left Venice on May 21 and returned up the Brenta again to Padua, where they planned to reclaim their coach. Upon meeting the Professor of Natural History there, she was interested to find that he had been an old acquaintance of Dr. Johnson.[2] On the evening of May 26 they set out under a full moon for Ferrara and Bologna. The latter place offered an opportunity to study the Carracci school of painting, which made an immediate appeal. Guercino, particularly, became her passion, and she filled the pages of her journal with descriptions of his pictures.[3]

Early in June the Piozzis passed over the Apennines to Florence. Upon arrival they arranged to stay at a hotel kept by an Englishman and his wife named Meghitt, and Mrs. Piozzi many years afterward remembered how frantic with joy her maid had been 'to see soft low Beds once again, a Dish of Beans & Bacon, & Currant Tart'.[4] The next morning they learned that 'the House was full of *English* Gentlemen & an *English* Lady—Warwickshire People, Mr. & Mrs. Greatheed: with the Same Friend Mr. Parsons who had left the Verses behind Dr. Johnson's Portrait at Milan'. Then at breakfast time,

we received the civillest of all Notes from our Fellow Lodgers— requesting the honour of our Company—hoping for our Acquain- tance &c. Piozzi was now flattered in the way he wished—said *English* People alone knew how to behave to *him* & to *me*. The Intimacy was then formed, and an Agreement to dine every Day together while we staid—the Greatheeds, Mr. Merry, Mr. Bid- dulph, and Mr. Parsons; to whom Lord Pembroke added his request for admission, and the Dinner was always in my Apartment or Mrs. Greatheeds.

After almost a year Mrs. Piozzi found herself again in a culti- vated circle of her own countrymen. The men flattered her husband, complimented him on his playing and singing, and

---

[1] Mainwaring Piozziana, ii. 44.   [2] Ry. 618.
[3] Mrs. Piozzi was only following tradition when she went into transports over 'not half but wholey divine Guercino'. Lady Miller in her *Letters from Italy* (1776) expressed the typical attitude of the English connoisseur of the period. Further evidence may be derived from a book of prints made by Arthur Pond (*circa* 1735) from the Italian School, where pictures by Carracci and Guercino predominate. (B.M.) In her taste in art, Mrs. Piozzi was not a pioneer, for she came near the end of the English admiration for the Carracci school of painting.
[4] Mainwaring Piozziana, ii. 50-1.

'laughed him out of one Prejudice after another'; for her part, she now had an Englishwoman to stay with when the men went out riding, and a sympathetic group always near by with whom to talk art and literature. It was a welcome change from the constant strain of accommodating herself to new customs and new modes of life.

The three principal members of the group require some introduction.[1] William Parsons, 'of the Sussex Militia', the Piozzis had met both at Milan and Venice. Weak, unstable, inordinately conceited, he thought himself a talented poet, and his head was full of grandiose literary schemes. His friend Robert Merry had more ability if not stability. Of good family, Merry had been educated at Harrow and Cambridge, which he left without a degree; for a time he held a commission in the army, and gambled away a large fortune inherited from his father. He was now settled in the British colony in Florence, carrying on an affair with the notorious Lady Cowper. Merry was undoubtedly endowed with some vein of genius, though he never fulfilled the promise of his youth. The third of the triumvirate was Bertie Greatheed, nephew of the Duke of Ancaster. His verses were no better than those of his companions, but he was a much more balanced character. Many years later the poet Thomas Campbell wrote of him: 'He was a courageous Liberal, at a time when Liberalism was not so safe as at present; a practical philanthropist, and in every respect an estimable man . . . But he was not a man of genius.'[2]

These three, with Mrs. Greatheed and the Piozzis, were the mainstays of the Florence coterie, but also included were a number of others. Shortly after arriving in Florence Mrs. Piozzi met her old friend Manucci, whom the Thrales had first seen on their trip to Paris in 1775. Though he had heard nothing of the Piozzi marriage, Manucci, as an old friend of the singer, came naturally to pay his respects, upon hearing of the latter's coming to Florence with an English wife. When he arrived Mrs. Piozzi was in her apartment; so the two men talked awhile, renewing old acquaintance. Asking particularly for Mrs. Thrale, the Count wondered whether she had married again. Piozzi evaded the question as best he could, until Mrs. Piozzi herself burst into the room to the surprise and delight of

---

[1] For information about Parsons, Merry, and Greatheed, see R. Marshall, *Italy in English Literature 1755–1815* (New York, 1934), and J. M. Longaker, *The Della Cruscans and William Gifford* (Philadelphia, 1924).

[2] T. Campbell, *Life of Mrs. Siddons* (1834), ii. 124.

the astounded Manucci. Over and over he exclaimed: 'Ah, Madame! quel Coup de Theatre!!' Manucci soon joined the agreeable company, the one representative of the old Streatham years.[1]

A number of Italian writers and artists, of far greater merit and more lasting fame than their English friends, were constant guests. Ippolito Pindemonte (by courtesy, The Marquis) was possibly at the time the best poet in Italy, while Count D'Elci and Lorenzo Pignotti were decidedly writers of the first rank. They fraternized with the English amateurs, translating each other's verses, and lauding in turn each new effusion. In 1784 some of this group had united in the publication of a slim volume which they called *The Arno Miscellany*;[2] now they were again toying with the idea of a similar venture.

They were all 'verse mad', Mrs. Piozzi wrote to Queeney, and she confided to Lysons on July 27: 'I have been playing the baby, and writing nonsense to divert our English friends here, who do the same thing themselves, and swear they will print the collection.' Although busily copying out her anecdotes of Dr. Johnson, she was delighted to be included in such a project. For it she completed a long translation of Pindemonte's Ode in praise of England, 'Hymn to Calliope', in return for which he rendered into Italian her 'Three Warnings',[3] and in addition she hurriedly wrote a number of shorter poems. As the summer progressed, the collection began to take form, and possibly was in the hands of the printers some time in August. The title finally decided upon was *The Florence Miscellany*.

The *Florence Miscellany* contains thirty-one contributions by Parsons, who was the moving spirit of the group and acted not only as editor but proof-reader as well, nineteen by Merry, ten by Mrs. Piozzi, six by Greatheed, and fourteen by their Italian colleagues. The book was privately printed, and the expense probably shared by various members of the group. The volume is not of great merit but, it must be admitted, has been much more harshly condemned than it deserves. Perhaps one reason has been its reputed connexion with the so-called 'Della-Cruscan' school of poetry so violently attacked by Gifford in the *Baviad* and *Maeviad*. Strictly speaking, the little group in Florence should not be called 'Della-Cruscans', for it was not

---

[1] Mainwaring Piozziana, ii. 56; also *Queeney Letters*, p. 206.

[2] *Arno Miscellany Being a Collection of fugitive pieces written by members of a society called the Oziosi at Florence*, printed at the Stamperia Bonducciana, 1784.

[3] *Queeney Letters*, p. 202. For Pindemonte's later remembrance of his friendship with Mrs. Piozzi see *Byron's Works*, ed. Moore (1832), iv. 32.

until two years later that Merry, who had actually never been a member of the celebrated Academy, appropriated the signature 'Della Crusca' and thus gave a name to the whole foolish school of poetry which appeared in the columns of the *World* newspaper. Gifford later admitted that he had not examined the *Florence Miscellany* thoroughly when he made his first violent attack.[1]

Mrs. Piozzi has undoubtedly been responsible for much of the misunderstanding of the purpose of the volume. Her preface, while so amusingly written as to arouse the admiration of Horace Walpole,[2] shows that she herself had only a vague appreciation of the aims of some of the members of the group. She apologetically explained their reason for printing the poems:

we wrote them to divert ourselves, and to say kind things of each other; we collected them that our reciprocal expressions of kindness might not be lost, and we printed them because we had no reason to be ashamed of our mutual partiality.[3]

What interested her most were those florid effusions of mutual admiration which appeared throughout the volume, and which she took to be characteristic of the entire work. She was completely oblivious of various undercurrents which influenced much of the writing of her fellow contributors.

As Dr. Roderick Marshall has pointed out, in order to understand the genesis of the *Florence Miscellany* one must take into consideration the political and social conditions in Florence at the time.[4] Many of the poems of the English writers and their Italian confrères have a serious political purpose. The Accademia della Crusca had been the champion of the Italian language, the active defender of the great heritage of Italian literature, and when, in 1783, it was suppressed by the Grand Duke Leopold of Tuscany, lovers of liberty and art everywhere were aroused. Parsons, Merry, and Greatheed, with the liberal enthusiasm of embryo poets, were enraged at this manifestation of despotic rule. Encouraged probably by D'Elci, Pignotti, and Pindemonte, they determined to carry on the ideals of the suppressed Academy. The *Florence Miscellany* was in part the result of that determination. For while a portion of the work is typical *vers de société*, there can be little doubt that some of the authors, certainly the Italians, intended

---

[1] R. Marshall, op. cit., p. 179.   [2] Walpole, *Letters*, xiii. 371.
[3] *Florence Misc.*, p. 5. See R. Marshall, op. cit., p. 178. Reprinted, *Gent. Mag.*, lvii (1787), 3.   [4] R. Marshall, op. cit., pp. 173–99.

their poems to be the expression of liberal, patriotic feeling. In opposition to the tyrannical, corrupted present, they would sing of Italy's greatness in the past, of the days when art and literature reigned supreme along the shores of the Mediterranean.

It is possible, or so it seems to me, to see from the printing of the volume itself further evidence of this serious purpose. Realizing the danger they were encountering in publishing under the rigid censorship from which Florence suffered at the time, the authors arranged to have a number of poems printed with blank spaces at the more critical passages. For the intimate members of the group, slips were printed containing the excised passages, which when pasted in the proper places rendered the verses complete. Yet outsiders, who might chance on a copy, would consider the gaps merely a typesetter's arrangement. Despite the fact that the cancelled lines do not seem to us very incendiary, those referring to the suppression of the Accademia della Crusca, on page 9, and the allusion to the baleful influence of the fierce Austrian Eagle, on page 27, might well have been considered dangerous to publish in a despotic state.[1]

Much of the verse is certainly ingenuous and jejune, but mixed somehow with a strange seriousness. Though occasionally a genuine interest in nature appears, the unifying spirit throughout is a passionate admiration for Italy and its historic past. Even the verse forms, in part, were derived from old Italian rhymes and metres. Italian influence, to be sure, scarcely made itself felt in England until the next century, when Byron, Keats, and Shelley found a similar enchantment in these old rhythms; yet to Parsons and Merry must be given some credit for pointing the way to their more distinguished countrymen. Too long disregarded by the critics because of

[1] My copy of the *Florence Misc.*, with the book-plate of Sir John Salusbury and probably once belonging to Mrs. Piozzi herself, has pasted slips on pages 9, 20, 27, and 215. A copy in the Columbia Univ. Library has similar additions. One without the slips was sold as item 182 in the Isham Sale, Anderson Galleries, May 4, 1933. In my copy Mrs. Piozzi's contributions are initialed throughout, and two additional lines in her hand have been added on p. 209. These occur after line 12 and read: 'Let these last Lines some Truths contain, More clear than bright, less sweet than plain.' Probably this volume is the one referred to by Mrs. Piozzi when writing to her adopted heir, Salusbury, on Apr. 14, 1813.
Is not Mr. Broster a famous Mortal to charge Mrs. Mostyn Ten Pounds for our Florence Miscellany? Pray take Care of that in the Drawer upstairs at Brynbella; it will be worth 50£ in Twenty Years more.
(Ry. 586, 159.) Her prediction as to its ultimate worth has unfortunately for me not been fulfilled.

Merry's later connexion with what is termed the 'Della Cruscan Movement', the *Florence Miscellany* has recently been called by Dr. Marshall 'probably the most important book of [English] poetry on Italian themes to appear in the eighteenth century'.[1]

Just when the *Florence Miscellany* appeared, or how many copies were printed, is uncertain.[2] Since the book was privately printed and thus never published, there were no announcements in contemporary newspapers or magazines. From Mrs. Piozzi's correspondence, however, an approximate date may be determined. She wrote to Queeney on September 17, 1785, 'I shall may be send . . .'; to Lysons on November 4: 'I have sent a few copies to England'; at which time nineteen copies were dispatched by the ship *Roman Emperor* to Cator to be distributed among the few friends who might be interested.

The small stock of copies which the authors had immediately sent as gifts to friends and relatives was speedily exhausted, and in January 1786 Merry proposed reprinting the volume.[3] His English colleagues, on the other hand, were averse to further advertisement of their occasional verses, and nothing came of the suggestion. Nevertheless, the poems were not allowed to sink into oblivion so quickly. One of the copies of the *Florence Miscellany* which had been sent to England fell into the hands of an enterprising journalist, and excerpts were printed in the *European Magazine* for February, March, April, May, and June, 1786, while some portions were repeated in the *London Chronicle* in February, May, and June.[4] When Parsons heard the news, he wrote in haste to Mrs. Piozzi from Berne, quoting from a letter he had just received:

The Editors of the European Magazine have somehow got hold of the Florence Miscellany, and are entertaining their readers every month with selections from it, this month they have inserted the Pleasures of Poetry & La Partenza, & I suppose will go through the volume.[5]

[1] R. Marshall, op. cit., p. 173.

[2] Printed privately by G. Cam, Florence, 1785. The size of the edition, which cannot have been very large, has not been ascertained.

[3] To Mrs. Piozzi, Jan 10, 1786 (Adam collection). After a long passage of effusive compliment, Merry amusingly added, 'don't suspect me of flattery; for I never use it'.

[4] *European Mag.* (1786), 121–2, 203–4, 286, 362–3; *London Chronicle*, Feb. 14–16, May 30–June 1, &c., 1786; *Gent. Mag.* lvii (1787), 257–8. Because of her celebrity due to the publication of the *Anecdotes* nearly all of Mrs. Piozzi's contributions were reprinted in the magazines, but only a portion of those of the other authors of the *Florence Misc.* were included.

[5] Original letter sold at Sotheby's, Jan. 22, 1907, lot 735. It is quoted by

Parsons added that he felt 'most sensibly the hardship of such hasty compositions being submitted to the perusal of the whole world without being at least allowed the liberty of correcting them'. He had written immediately to his friend in England to put a stop to this infringement of their literary rights.

Parsons's anger was soon mollified, if indeed he had ever been even irritated, for upon his return to England the following autumn, he wrote to Mrs. Piozzi:

I have not had an opportunity of hearing much about our Florence Miscellany, most of my Friends to whom I had sent copies being in the Country, but we make a brilliant appearance in the European Magazine, which the Editors have also enrich'd with an Engraving & Memoirs of yourself,—a distinction which they seem not to judge the rest of us worthy of.[1]

This time he seemed more disturbed that one of his collaborators had received the most attention, than that his 'hasty compositions' had been blazoned to the public eye.

The *Florence Miscellany*, in its original form, was never well known in England. Instead, it was chiefly through the excerpts reprinted by the magazines that English readers became acquainted with the verse of Merry, Parsons, Greatheed, and Mrs. Piozzi. These selections, unfortunately not always the best, were considered representative and have largely been used by later critics in an estimate of the publication itself. The contributions by Pindemonte and the other Italians have consequently been almost completely ignored.

Mrs. Piozzi herself always wrote in an apologetic tone about the *Florence Miscellany*, for she had never taken the affair very seriously. While it had been delightful to return to the old occupation of writing and criticizing poetry, she was far more interested in an ambitious publication all her own. Johnson, not Italian politics, would be her stepping-stone to fame.

Edmund T. Silk, 'A Critical Bibliography of Hester Lynch (Thrale) Piozzi', unpublished Master's Essay, Yale Univ., 1927. I am indebted to Mr. Silk for a number of identifications.   [1] Ry. 558, 17; Oct. 1, 1786.

XII

ANECDOTES OF DR. JOHNSON

SEPTEMBER 1785–MAY 1786

IN the spring of 1785 Lysons had advised Mrs. Piozzi to select a publisher in London to take charge of the necessary advance notices of her Johnsonian volumes. Accordingly, on June 7 she wrote to Thomas Cadell in the Strand, offering him her anecdotes, and adding:

As I have a large collection of his letters in England, besides some verses, known only to myself, I wish to delay printing till we can make two or three little volumes, not unacceptable, perhaps, to the public; but I desire my intention to be notified, for divers reasons, and, if you approve of the scheme, should wish it to be immediately advertized.[1]

Cadell gladly accepted her commission, and in his letter of June 28 enclosed a copy of the advertisement placed in the newspapers.

Preparing for the press and will be published with all possible Expedition
Anecdotes of the late Samuel Johnson LLD during the last twenty Years of his Life
By Mrs. Hester L. Piozzi
To which will be added, A Collection of Letters and Verses never before published.
Printed for T. Cadell in the Strand.[2]

At the same time Cadell vigorously urged haste, that the publication might appear while the interest in Johnson was still at its height. He further made the suggestion, to facilitate completion of the work by the following winter, that her letters and manuscripts in England should be sent to Italy. To this proposal, however, Mrs. Piozzi refused to assent. Since Johnson's verses and letters were locked up in a bank with her

---

[1] Hayward, i. 272. Mrs. Piozzi's letters to Cadell were first published in the *Gent. Mag.* (1852) (new series), pp. 136–7, 232–3. Lysons had suggested Cadell as a possible publisher in his letter of Apr. 15, 1785. 'Cadell told me one day he shod. not wish for a better publication than that of Dr. J's letters' (Ry. 552, 4).

[2] Ry. 554, 17. Among other papers, this appeared in the *Morning Post*, June 29, 30, 1785, and the *Public Advertiser*, June 30.

own private papers, she was not willing to entrust the key to
any stranger, to have any busy-body prying into her personal
affairs.¹ As a compromise she proposed that the anecdotes
should be published separately. Instead of the original plan
for a combination of letters and anecdotes, she agreed to print
at once the miscellaneous recollections and stories of Johnson
which she had been compiling during her travels about Italy.
Torn between two impulses, the desire for further travel and
the wish to appear immediately before the public in her guise
of a Johnsonian biographer, she accepted the publisher's lure,
unfortunately for her future reputation, and impetuously set to
work to complete the manuscript at once.

Letters to Lysons constantly referred to the undertaking.
In one she alluded to George Colman's fear that Johnson's
biographers would not show his weaknesses:

> Mr. Colman is right enough in his Conjectures I dare say, but
> those who had a true Knowledge of our great Man's Mind will
> remember that he prefer'd Veracity to Interest, Affection, or Resent-
> ment; nor suffer'd Partiality or prejudice to warp him from the
> *Truth.*—let Mr. Boswell *be sure* to keep that Example in View; his
> old Friend often recommended it to him.²

To find Mrs. Piozzi reporting that Dr. Johnson constantly held
up before Boswell the necessity for veracity is amusing indeed.
Boswell gives the impression that the advice was intended for
her alone.

Young Lysons tried his best to execute her commissions.
Although unable to secure a copy of Johnson's letter to Barnard,
the King's librarian, one plum that all the rival biographers
failed to secure, he did pass on a story told him by Boswell of
Johnson's early laziness.³ Whether the anecdote was new to
Mrs. Piozzi does not appear, but in any case she could not fail
to be pleased at the opportunity to publish in advance one of
her rival's discoveries. And Boswell's surprise and annoyance
when he later read the passage can easily be imagined.

Late in the summer of 1785 Mrs. Piozzi was stricken with
fever in Florence, and after ten days in bed decided to try a
change of scene to restore her appetite. After making plans to
rejoin the Greatheeds later in the south, and exchanging

---

¹ Hayward, i. 273; *Gent. Mag.*, op. cit., p. 136.
² June 14, 1785. Boswell throughout the *Life* impugns Mrs. Piozzi's accuracy,
and indicates that Johnson constantly spoke to her about it.
³ See my article, 'Further Letters of the Johnson Circle', *J. Rylands Bulletin*,
xx (1936), 277.

tearful farewells with Merry, who was sure they would never meet again, the Piozzis left Florence on September 12. Lucca, the first stop, was rendered unendurable by swarms of gnats, scorpions, and spiders; Pisa proved more endurable, but on the 20th they proceeded to Leghorn, where sea air revived her health and spirits.

At Leghorn she finally completed the arrangement of her Johnsonian anecdotes, and a copyist was immediately found to transcribe a clear manuscript to be sent to England.[1] Once the hard labour was over, Mrs. Piozzi could scarcely wait to see the little volume in print. She wrote to Lysons on September 21:

Cadell will have his little Book to print in the Spring, or even earlier if he chooses; the two Volumes of Letters & Verses may very well wait till my return:—People will see by this, that I am *alive and at Liberty.*

She later confided to the same correspondent the hope that her anecdotes would be found 'less trivial than Boswell's', but pleaded as an excuse for even having written them down the fact that she had always felt any trifles connected with Johnson would be welcomed by the public.[2] To Cadell she wrote that since she was 'wholly unused to the business of sending manuscripts to the press', she would rely on him to see that everything was done properly.[3]

As soon as the copy had been dispatched to London, the Piozzis returned to Pisa, where about four miles from the city they found a little house at the foot of the Apennines near a fine cold bath. Here, at the Bagni di Pisa, Mrs. Piozzi wrote verses in admiration of the place and daily bathed in the cool refreshing water. Her pleasure, however, was shortlived, for Piozzi fell ill, and the insects and vermin were so annoying that the travellers packed their belongings and on October 17 set out for Rome.

The Piozzis reached Rome about a week later, and though far from well, immediately plunged into a round of sightseeing. Page after page of her journal was given over to descriptions of the ancient ruins, the fashions of the women, stories told her by the men, and the paintings and sculpture in the palaces. Yet Rome in many ways proved disappointing, possibly because her enthusiasm for ancient history had led her to expect too

---

[1] This episode is described in my article, 'The Printing of Mrs. Piozzi's Anecdotes of Dr. Johnson', *J. Rylands Bulletin*, xx (1936), 163.
[2] From Rome, Nov. 4, 1785.   [3] Hayward, i. 273.

much. The 'disgusting sight of that wretchedness and dirt, which is here everywhere mingled with the monuments of ancient magnificence' spoiled her enjoyment of the beautiful fountains and splendid buildings. The city was like Rembrandt's pictures, 'composed of the strongest lights and darkest shadows possible'.[1]

After spending the month of November in the capital, the Piozzis drove south to Naples, which they entered during a violent electrical storm, while Vesuvius vomited fire and poured a torrent of hot lava down its sides. They secured rooms with a full view of the volcano, to them a constant source of wonder and amazement. Later, like all tourists, they climbed to the top for a view of the smouldering crater, visited buried Herculaneum, wandered through the King's menagerie, and inspected the churches and museums.

Again Mrs. Piozzi found herself in a large company of English visitors. The Greatheeds, the Duke and Duchess of Cumberland, George Coxe, brother of the historian, the Tighes, and the Jervises were her constant companions. The pleasant days in Florence had shown how delightful it was to live with voluntary exiles like herself, and Piozzi found the matter of social distinctions less of a problem among the English than among his own compatriots. Though a gentleman of good birth, Piozzi did not belong to the nobility; consequently at many functions in Italy where his wife, as a foreigner, was welcome, he was excluded. In Florence old Sir Horace Mann, the English Minister, had refused to break with tradition and invite the musician at the same time as his titled guests. But with most of the British travellers the distinction was ignored, so that, ironically enough, the man who had been so disdained by London society the year before, when he dared to marry the widow of a wealthy brewer, now found himself better treated by representatives of this same clique than by the lesser dignitaries of his own country. His wife commented on the fact in a letter to Lysons the last day of 1785: 'Mr. Piozzi always finds friends among my countrymen, and prefers their acquaintance to that of the Italians in the town we reside at.'

Anxiously Mrs. Piozzi awaited word that her Johnsonian manuscript had been delivered into the hands of the printers in England, but unforeseen delays kept it from reaching Cadell until early in 1786. Meanwhile, the reading public had not been allowed to forget Johnson and the Thrales. The great

---

[1] To Lysons, Nov. 4, 1785.

man's private prayers and meditations, many of them composed at Streatham, were printed by Strahan for all to read, and late in September, 1785, Boswell published in London his *Journal of a Tour to the Hebrides with Samuel Johnson, LL.D.* Immediately there was a storm of protest in the newspapers and magazines.[1] Boswell's disclosures of Johnson's actual conversation and his physical idiosyncrasies were considered by many, if not sacrilegious, at least indecorous. What we to-day judge a masterpiece of biographical writing, Horace Walpole called a 'most absurd enormous book . . . It is the story of a mountebank and his zany',[2] and Wilkes is reported to have told the author 'that he had wounded Johnson with his pocket pistol & was about to despatch him with his blunderbuss when it should be let off'.[3] Burke and others of the Doctor's friends were displeased with Boswell's delineation of Johnson's actual behaviour and conversation.[4] James Beattie, writing to Sir William Forbes early in the next year, while agreeing that Boswell probably had meant no harm by his injudicious exposures, added: 'Johnson's faults were balanced by many and great virtues; and when that is the case, the virtues only should be remembered, and the faults entirely forgotten.'[5] The aim of biography, according to Beattie, was to embalm, not to re-create. The general public expected a biographical portrait to be formalized, and to be either panegyrical or openly antagonistic. This very human combination of merit and eccentricity was new and not wholly to their liking.

Since Mrs. Piozzi had had no open quarrel with Boswell, she was treated with civility, but one reference caused immediate excitement and consternation in her old circle. The Blue-Stocking world was profoundly shocked to read that Johnson had admitted that neither he nor Mrs. Thrale had been able to read through Mrs. Montagu's *Essay on Shakespeare*.[6]

---

[1] For examples, see the *Morning Post* for Oct. 1, 5, 8, 10, 11, 19, 1785, &c. On the 1st came the comment, 'Had Dr. Johnson been blessed with the gift of *second-sight*, how it would have tortured him to have known the base advantages which have been taken of his celebrity to make money.' Later references are in a similar vein.   [2] Walpole, *Letters*, xiii. 337.

[3] M. Lort to Mrs. Piozzi, Dec. 31, 1785 (Ry. 544, 5).

[4] Ibid. Lort commented: 'Mr. E. Burke fell hard upon him for the absurdities in that performance.'   [5] Sir W. Forbes, *Life of Beattie* (1806), ii. 184.

[6] Sir Lucas Pepys wrote to Mrs. Piozzi, Dec. 15, 1785, that the opinion 'must have given some Sleepless Hours to Mrs. Montagu' (Ry. 536, 27); and Dr. Lort on the 31st added: 'Poor Mrs. Montagu is almost as much mortified by your opinion of her book as by Mr. Cumberland's Character of her & her bluestocking Club drawn at length in a volume of Essays he has published called the *Observer*' (Ry. 544, 5).

Needless to say, Mrs. Piozzi was at once informed of the resentment this quotation had aroused, and Lysons and Sir Lucas Pepys wrote urgent letters advising complete denial. Yet this she could not conscientiously do. She had seen Boswell's Journal in manuscript, and at the time had made no objection to the offensive passage. She was in a difficult position. After some hesitation she wrote to Lysons:

Mr. Boswell did me very great Injustice in saying I could not get through Mrs. Montagu's Performance, for the Elegance and Erudition of which I hope I am not wholly without Taste or Cognizance; and as for Dr. Johnson, he had, to my certain Knowledge a true Respect for her Abilities, and a very great Regard & Esteem of her general Character.[1]

While attacking Boswell's statement, she did not refute what she probably knew to have been Johnson's decided opinion of the unlucky essay. Instead she tried to evade the issue by insisting on her own personal devotion to Mrs. Montagu. Later she wrote a similar denial to the Queen of the Blues herself, and quasi-refutations to Sir Lucas Pepys and others, being always careful not to attack the veracity of Boswell's statement of Johnson's actual remark. But these guarded replies did not end the matter, for many of her well-meaning friends, chiefly the fashionable physician, Sir Lucas Pepys, felt that some public denial should be included in her forthcoming volume. Taking advantage of her expressed desire for disavowal, Pepys did not wait for further authorization. He wrote to Mrs. Piozzi:

We agreed that a Postscript should be added to your Anecdotes— & by making use entirely of your Own Words in your letter to me, a Postscript is drawn up, which I think you will approve of, & which is sufficiently justified by their being your own Words though in a letter to me.—I have taken Care likewise to have all this Business well explained to Mrs. Montagu.[2]

The printed postscript, which appeared at the end of her *Anecdotes*, repeated the same guarded denial that she had written to Lysons. Sir Lucas Pepys, as he had hoped, stopped further dissension in the Blue-Stocking ranks, but unfortunately, in so doing, he precipitated Mrs. Piozzi into her first open quarrel with Boswell. Sir Lucas thus unintentionally fired the first gun in the public 'wars of Bozzy and Piozzi'.

---

[1] From Naples, Dec. 31, 1785.
[2] Mar. 3, 1786 (Ry. 536, 28); see also 'The Printing of Mrs. Piozzi's Anecdotes of Dr. Johnson' ,op. cit., p. 159.

Because of the slowness and irregularity of the sailing-vessels of the day, Mrs. Piozzi's manuscript was a long time in reaching the publisher. On the last day of 1785 Dr. Lort wrote that her memoirs were still 'performing quarantine' in the river Thames, and that 'all the world is impatient to see them in print'.[1] If Lort might be held guilty of gross exaggeration in saying that all the world was anxious to read Mrs. Piozzi's anecdotes of Dr. Johnson, it must be admitted that public interest in anything connected with the Doctor was still intense. For a number of reasons the general curiosity aroused by the announcement of her forthcoming publication was widespread. Because of her sensational marriage to Piozzi and the accompanying newspaper publicity, many people were anxious to read what she would say about Johnson's disapproval of her choice. And, in addition, it must have been generally felt that she had at her disposal a large mass of Johnsonian anecdotes and letters which would throw a new and intimate light on the personal character of the great man. Even though Boswell and Sir John Hawkins were both preparing comprehensive biographies, the public was aware that the Thrales also had been diligent in collecting material. Only a short time after Johnson's death the *Morning Chronicle* had announced that there were in existence several voluminous records of Johnson's *bons mots*, formed in Thrale's house.[2] According to this account Murphy, Goldsmith, and Hawkesworth had aided the brewer's family in filling the pages of their large blank book with anecdotes of the Doctor. As has been previously pointed out, the story is improbable, but to many readers of the newspapers in 1785 it might not have appeared so; and there can be little doubt that any publication from the Thrale sources was eagerly awaited.

The newspapers, realizing this general interest, kept it alive by occasional bulletins and sarcastic comments over the delay.[3] As Lysons later wrote to Mrs. Piozzi, the copy had been so long on the way, 'that I began to fear it would never arrive, and the Papers began to be witty about it'.[4] The *Morning Herald*, when announcing on January 28 that the manuscript had finally been received from Florence, insisted that it contained 'many

---

[1] Ry. 544, 5.   [2] Jan. 7, 1785. See also pp. 123–4.
[3] References to Mrs. Piozzi had appeared in the *Morning Post* intermittently throughout the autumn. The paper claimed on Oct. 1 that her desire to be remembered as 'the great Johnson's friend' was the sole motive behind her publication, and on the 19th added that 'The *Piozzi* is certainly coming with her brood, without father bred'. On Dec. 17 the paper asked the question: 'What have become of *Signora* Thrale's *Memorabilia* of Dr. Johnson, of which so much has been said and so little known?'   [4] Feb. 7, 1786.

curious particulars of the life of Doctor Johnson for the last twenty-five years'. A few days later the same paper predicted that '*Madame Piozzi's* anecdotes', made up 'from the dressing-room records of that lady', would appear in less than a month, and characteristically added a comment in dubious taste.

Report frequently whispered that a connubial knot would be tied between Mrs. Thrale and Dr. Johnson;—that event never took place, and yet Mrs. Piozzi and the Doctor, it seems, are shortly to be *pressed* in the same *sheets*.[1]

The absent signora was fair game for all the slanderous remarks which might flow from the scurrilous pen of the journalist.

Lysons chanced to be sitting with Cadell when the package was at last delivered, but he had only a peep at the contents, for the publisher was anxious to rush the pages immediately to his compositors. Throughout the month of February the printers were hurrying publication of the *Anecdotes*, and it seems probable that by the 1st of March the sheets were all printed.[2] Then for the first time Lysons was able to read the account from beginning to end. His attention was caught by one passage in particular. Following her transcription of the Latin epitaph which Johnson had written for Thrale, Mrs. Piozzi had added the caustic comment:

Such was the Character of Henry Thrale, when given by Samuel Johnson: but what must be the Character of him, who in a Letter written to the Printer of the St. James's Chronicle—dated 8:th of January 1785 in order to distress the unoffending Survivor, dares even to deride the sacred Dead, and represent the greatest Writer of our Age and Nation, as a wretched Retailer of Latin Scraps, gather'd up to ridicule an Infirmity caused by his best Friend's Illness and ending in his Death! For this Letter too Mr. Boswell is not ashamed I see to return his publick Thanks; accepting with apparent Pleasure the Praises of a Scribbler who delights in the Uneasiness that he can cause to a Family, where Mr. Boswell never received anything but Civilities. Surely such Men make Aaron the Moor a Model for their Imitation! I hoped it was reserved for *him* alone to say,—

> Oft have I digg'd up dead Men from their Graves,
> And set them upright at their dear Friends' Doors,
> Even when their sorrow was almost forgot;

---

[1] Feb. 1, 1786. On Feb. 3 another reference in bad taste appeared: 'Signora *Piozzi*, finding the air of Italy by no means so prolific as she expected, proposes with her *cara sposa* to *people* a *Roman colony*, somewhere in Britain;—Bath, or near it, is the elected spot.'

[2] See p. 257, n. 1.

And on their Skins as on the Bark of Trees,
Have with my Knife carved in Roman Letters,
Let not your Sorrows die tho' I be dead.[1]

This was her reply to the venomous attack of the year before.

Lysons was galvanized into action. Imagining that Boswell might have been perfectly innocent of any malice in his letter to the printer, Mr. Baldwin, he felt that such a bitter rejoinder on her part could only have ill effects on all concerned. After much difficulty he found copies of the *St. James's Chronicle* at the stamp office, and there verified his suspicions. Under the circumstances he was convinced that the passage ought not to be printed, and immediately consulted Sir Lucas Pepys, the Bishop of Peterborough, and Dr. Lort, who all agreed with him that the necessity of the case was such that they should run the risk of her displeasure by leaving out the entire passage. Since the sheets were printed, the vacancy had to be filled, but this was done by inserting an English translation of the epitaph on Thrale hurriedly made by Dr. Lort.

This last-minute change necessitated a cancellation. It seems probable that the entire sheet K, which included the banished passage, was destroyed, and a new sheet *K substituted in its place. Inasmuch as the cancellation of an entire sheet and arranging for the substitute took some weeks, the date of publication was thus further delayed.[2]

The newspapers continually referred to the long-expected publication. On February 8 the *Morning Herald* commented: 'Madame *Piozzi* will not disgrace the Doctor by her Johnsonian Anecdotes, as Mr. Cadell's edition will soon evince. If here and there the wit is softened, it is not *Italianized* in any one instance!' On March 15 the *Morning Chronicle* announced that Mrs. Piozzi's productions would soon see the light of day, 'The Johnsoniana by themselves in one volume. The Bouts Rhymees with the musick of Mr. Piozzi, in another.' No one knew exactly what was in prospect, but anticipation and curiosity were widespread.

Finally on Lady Day, Saturday, March 25, 1786, the *Anecdotes of the late Samuel Johnson LL.D.* appeared.[3] There was an

---

[1] Excised passage in holograph copy of the *Anecdotes* in the Morgan Library, New York City, p. 81. The quotation is from *Titus Andronicus*, v. 1. 135-40. Mrs. Piozzi evidently quoted from memory from a contemporary edition. One original sheet K, retaining this cancelled passage, has survived. See *N. & Q.*, 6th Ser. ii. 442 (Dec. 4, 1880).   [2] See p. 257, n. 1.
[3] Ibid. See also S. Lysons to Mrs. Piozzi, Mar. 28, 1786. In the Adam collection is a small scrap upon which is written: 'March 24, 1786—Mrs. Piozzi's

immediate demand for the little volume, and before nightfall the first edition of a thousand copies was completely exhausted. Even before most of the papers could print an announcement of the publication, the book was out of print, and when the King sent for a copy Cadell was forced to borrow one from a friend to send immediately to His Majesty.[1] The sale was so rapid that Lysons jubilantly compared it to the first rush to buy Fielding's *Amelia*, but since the original impression of *Amelia* was much larger than that of the *Anecdotes*, the comparison is hardly fair.[2]

Since the demand for the book continued strong, Cadell had a second edition of a thousand copies ready on April 5, and from the same type five hundred more as a so-called third edition on April 11. These too were immediately sold, and he was forced to set up another edition, called the fourth, which appeared on May 5.[3]

The daily newspapers at once seized on the new publication and reprinted large portions of the text. While somewhat unfriendly, the *Morning Herald* ran for six numbers a series of excerpts called, 'LEAVES collected from the PIOZZIAN WREATH, lately woven to adorn the Shrine of the departed Dr. Johnson'. The *Public Advertiser*, the *Universal Daily Register*, the *London Chronicle*, and other papers followed suit in selecting special quotations from the new work.[4] On the whole the reception accorded the *Anecdotes* by the newspaper critics was favourable: the *Public Advertiser* for March 28, in making selections from

Anecdotes of Dr. Johnson are proposed at 3/0—kept at 3/3—sells for 4/0—in Boards.' Following this is a list of the booksellers and the quantity each agreed to take. Cadell and Mrs. Piozzi seem to have had no stipulated agreement as to the exact price to be paid for the publishing rights. On Feb. 17, 1786, she wrote to him from Naples that she was perfectly willing to divide the profits equitably after print and paper were paid. Again, on May 20 she instructed him to pay whatever money came from her share to her banker in London (*Gent. Mag.* (1852), pp. 136-7). Nor is it certain how much Cadell finally paid. In one place Mrs. Piozzi claims it to have been £130 (Mainwaring Piozziana, ii. 72), but in others she lists the amount as £150. Possibly the first figure is the one originally decided upon, later raised after the rapid sale of the first four editions.

[1] Hayward, i. 291. C. Selwin wrote that 'the first Edition of your Anecdotes was sold in the space of three or four Hours' (Ry. 556, 171). Selwin added that he had heard Mrs. Montagu 'mentioned it with great Encomiums'.

[2] Ry. 552, 9. See also Hayward, i. 290.

[3] From T. Cadell, May 8, 1786 (Ry. 554, 18). In a well-meant but somewhat abortive attempt to oblige the purchasers, an errata slip was printed, listing eleven mistakes in the first edition. This errata slip, however, is extremely rare. The mistakes were not rectified in the text until the 4th edition.

[4] *Morning Herald* for Mar. 27, 28, 29, 30, and Apr. 4 and 7; *Public Advertiser* for Mar. 28, 31, Apr. 6, 7, 8; *Universal Daily Register* for Mar. 29; *London Chronicle* for Mar. 30, Apr. 4, 15, and 18. Other papers which printed excerpts from the publication are the *St. James's Chronicle*, the *Morning Post*, &c.

'this delightful little book', was highly complimentary; the *London Chronicle* for March 30 called it 'a very lively entertaining miscellany', and insisted that Mrs. Piozzi had given a true picture of the real Johnson. It was only when the persons of fashion began to voice their complaints that the attitude veered to one of general disapprobation.

Throughout April Mrs. Piozzi's treatment of Dr. Johnson was a popular topic of conversation. The Blue-Stockings, for one reason or another, were all antagonistic; Hannah More because of the uncomplimentary remarks about Garrick; Mrs. Chapone because of the mode of writing and the writer; Sir William Weller Pepys (though he himself cut a better figure than he had expected) because of the injurious remarks about his friends.[1] Horace Walpole, commenting to the unfriendly Sir Horace Mann, called it 'wretched; a high-varnished preface to a heap of rubbish, in a very vulgar style, and too void of method even for such a farrago'.[2] Then he added: 'Her panegyric is loud in praise of her hero; and almost every fact she relates disgraces him.'

Walpole, in a few words, expressed the chief objection which many people felt to the publication. While protesting openly and constantly her veneration and admiration for Dr. Johnson, Mrs. Piozzi yet repeated anecdote after anecdote which did not redound to his credit. The puzzled readers could find no consistency whatsoever about the work; nearly every assertion as to his character which she made was contradicted by some episode in the later pages. Mrs. Chapone undoubtedly voiced the general feeling that

it was not handsome to repeat things of him which she must know would mightily detract from the hyperbolical praise she affects to give him. I do not love such inconsistences, & such as blow hot & cold! defend me, when dead from such friends![3]

Yet these same qualities which irritated Johnson's contemporaries give for modern readers a delightfully human touch to the writing. Mrs. Piozzi had attempted, though not so successfully, the same type of biographical method as Boswell, and was greeted with similar criticism. 'This new-fashioned biography',

---

[1] H. More, *Memoirs*, ii. 15; Gaussen, *A Later Pepys*, i. 409; ii. 272.

[2] Walpole, *Letters*, xiii. 372–3 (Mar. 28, 1786). Yet Mrs. Piozzi did not print all she remembered of Johnson's rough behaviour, for sometimes her own pride restrained her. Thus she wrote to Queeney, Sept. 17, 1794, referring to irate remarks at seeing a church turned into a stable in Denbigh in 1774: 'I would not record them in my Anecdotes of him for Shame.' (Lansdowne MS., *Queeney Letters*, p. 253.)

[3] Gaussen, *A Later Pepys*, i. 409.

Hannah More wrote to her sister, forgetting the long passages of enthusiastic praise, 'seems to value itself upon perpetuating every thing that is injurious and detracting.'[1]

The magazines were divided in opinion. The *Gentleman's Magazine*, while admitting that the publication would have been more agreeable 'if a few luxuriant shoots had judiciously been pruned', was on the whole complimentary:

> The foregoing Anecdotes are evidently the production of a vigorous and cultivated understanding; and though the style, in some parts of the volume, bears the marks of haste, the general execution is worthy of the writer, and will not disappoint the expectation of the publick: and when our readers recollect what that expectation has been, and more particularly the high estimation in which the writer's literary powers have been holden, they will regard this as no common praise.[2]

The *English Review* was even more laudatory. 'Of the *nine lives* of this giant in learning, as he is called, which have been promised to the public, Mrs. Piozzi's is the fifth that has been published, and in our judgment the best.'[3] This reviewer pointed out the good sense which she had shown in developing the character of Johnson. The *European Magazine*, though scolding Mrs. Piozzi for relating Johnson's absurdities and follies, made no open attack.[4]

Others were savagely abusive. Ironically, the abuse came from her former friends. Dr. Burney, in the *Monthly Review* for May, indignantly attacked her for 'exposing his [Johnson's] failings and his weaknesses, to the curious, yet fastidious eye of the Public'.[5] The *Annual Register*, with which Edmund Burke was connected, continued the arraignment.[6]

The outcry occasioned by her portrayal of the rougher side of Johnson's nature is difficult for us to understand; the twentieth-century psychological biography demands that the bitter be mingled with the sweet. Other objections appear to us more valid. Dr. Burney, in the *Monthly Review*, indicated what might to-day be considered the greatest defect in the *Anecdotes*,

---

[1] H. More, *Memoirs*, ii. 16. There were some, however, who took the position that recording Johnson's idiosyncrasies was in accord with his own often-expressed opinions about biography. See *Olla Podrida*, No. 13 (Oxford), June 9, 1787.

[2] *Gent. Mag.* lvi (1786), 328, 332.

[3] *English Review*, vii (1786), 255.

[4] *European Mag.* ix (1786), 142–4, 247–52, 317–18. But see x. 128–30.

[5] *Monthly Review*, lxxiv (1786), 374. For identification of Dr. Burney as the author, see B. Nangle, *The Monthly Review* (1934).

[6] *Annual Register* (1786), Domestic Lit., p. 263.

when he asserted that the volume had been planned with only one thought in mind, to excuse the author's behaviour by showing how difficult it had been to live with Johnson.[1] For we might agree with Mrs. Chapone that 'it was not handsome to tell the World how insufferable the friend she had cherish'd & Courted so long was become to her, & that she went to Bath only to shake him off'.[2] It was unfortunate in every way that Johnson's death occurred while Mrs. Piozzi was still smarting under the rebuffs occasioned by her second marriage. In far-off Italy she had been kept well informed of the sneers and lies bandied about London by her former friends and acquaintances; she knew too well that many people held her responsible for deserting the old man in his last illness. There is a possibility, too, that she did not feel herself entirely guiltless. Thus it was perhaps in some measure to stifle her own qualms of conscience that she attempted to vindicate her conduct as soon as possible. The scramble of rival Johnsonian biographers offered what seemed a perfect opportunity.

The *Anecdotes* was consequently begun by Mrs. Piozzi with a divided purpose: to justify her treatment of Johnson, and to achieve fame as one of his biographers. Necessarily, the two plans at cross-purposes injured the quality of her work. As we have seen, she had an abundance of genuine, accurate anecdotes of Dr. Johnson;[3] she had known him intimately for nearly eighteen years; she had been his confidant and inspiration. Had she been unmoved by prejudice, she could have compiled a valuable record of his declining years; and had she returned to England and accepted the advice of her scholarly friends, she might easily have written such a work. Boswell, we must remember, had always at his side Edmond Malone, one of the finest scholars of the age, who willingly revised both the *Tour to the Hebrides* and the *Life*. Mrs. Piozzi had only the advice of her husband, who must have approved of her intention to justify their marriage.

Nearly all she wrote of Johnson is probably true; it is the emphasis that is objectionable. From reports of Fanny Burney, Boswell, and others we know that the Doctor in his last years was often an irascible and difficult companion;[4] yet for years Mrs. Thrale had endured his foibles without complaint for the

---

[1] Op. cit. lxxiv. 373.
[2] Gaussen, op. cit. i. 409.
[3] These were recorded in the Children's Book, in the early journals (now lost), and in the first volumes of Thraliana.
[4] See p. 212, n. 2; p. 219, n. 3; p. 240, n. 1.

sake of his sage advice and stimulating conversation. There can be little doubt that under normal conditions the irritable last years would have been forgotten in the recollection of the earlier happy days at Streatham. Her over-emphasis on this querulousness, because it was serviceable in explaining their final quarrel and separation, is the most serious blot on the *Anecdotes*.

The loyal friends of Dr. Johnson were quick to rush to his defence. They had disliked Mrs. Piozzi for deserting their idol; they now detested her for trying to excuse herself by mis-representing him. They vociferously asserted that she was 'inaccurate', a claim which Boswell reiterated so often in the *Life* that to this day it is the adjective most often applied to her as a writer.[1] Nevertheless, if we are to accept this characterization of her writing, we must be careful to define the word 'inaccurate'. If by this word we imply a constitutional inability to tell the truth, the epithet was inapplicable. To be sure, Mrs. Piozzi was careless in the matter of dates and figures, but a large portion of her recollections of Johnson are based on first-hand information just as authentic and contemporary as that of Boswell. She kept records of his conversations from the earliest years of their acquaintance, so that much of her volume need not be questioned. If, on the other hand, by 'inaccurate' we mean an occasional willingness in this one book to twist evidence in order to further her own ends, there may be some justification for the term.[2] She was also willing, in some instances, to trust to memory rather than to search for further details. One example may be found in a certain rough rebuke supposed to have been administered by Johnson to Thrale when in Rouen in 1775.[3] In remembering the former trip, away from

---

[1] Boswell's aspersions appear throughout the *Life*. Miss Laetitia Matilda Hawkins in her *Memoirs* (i. 65) has reiterated the charge of inaccuracy. She quoted second hand the claim of the Reverend Mr. Evans, the rector of St. Olave's in Tooley St.

> In reading her [Mrs. Piozzi's] representation of facts, as they occurred under his own knowledge, and his report of things said in his hearing, he declared against the fidelity of both; and when reduced to fact, it was often observable, certainly to the credit of her invention but at the expense of her correctness, that the worth of a tale, or the wit of a repartee was furnished by herself.

Miss Hawkins wrote many years after Boswell had made his charge of inaccuracy, and doubtless her attitude was influenced by the generally accepted view.

[2] Miss K. C. Balderston has discovered several examples of real distortion, even amounting to actual shifting of speakers. See the Preface to her edition of Thraliana.

[3] See *John. Misc.* i. 216, and *French Journals*, pp. 46–7, 83–5. Always to be remembered is the fact that Johnson's remark was in English, a language which the Abbé Roffette obviously did not understand.

her contemporary records, Mrs. Piozzi was unable to describe the affair with accuracy. Actually the impolite remark was not even mentioned in her original journal of 1775, a fact which may be explained by the supposition that the entries may occasionally have been read by Johnson and other members of the party. Probably the rebuke did occur at some time during the French tour and had been treasured up in her memory as an example of Johnson's rudeness.[1] One thing is certain: rather than omit the incident altogether, Mrs. Piozzi, in this instance, was willing to print a somewhat garbled account, in order to stress the more disagreeable side of Johnson's character.

Certain of Mrs. Piozzi's idiosyncrasies must also be kept in mind when reading the *Anecdotes*. In matters of age she was apt to be vague, but in some cases what appears on the surface to be a mistake actually confirms the accepted figures, when rightly interpreted. In later life she held the opinion that a person's age should be counted in the same manner as the centuries. Consequently, when a child was one year old, she would speak of his celebrating his second birthday, and from then on he would be in his second year. In the *Anecdotes* Mrs. Piozzi stated that Johnson went to school when 'eight years old', yet other evidence seems to prove conclusively that it was after what we should call his seventh birthday.[2] Again she gives the age of Johnson's father when he died as seventy-six. Actually he was seventy-five. As an old lady Mrs. Piozzi consistently considered herself a year older than we to-day should calculate.

Many statements in the *Anecdotes* are more vague and questionable than they would have been had she been able to

---

[1] The Welsh journal of the year before has no mention whatsoever of any meeting with Windham and Cholmondeley, yet the evidence of Windham himself seems to give support to her other story in the *Anecdotes* of Johnson's rudeness to the two travellers in Derbyshire (*John. Misc.* i. 319; also see p. 271). Compare with R. W. Ketton-Cremer, *The Early Life and Diaries of William Windham* (1930), pp. 145, 255. Mr. Ketton-Cremer indicates that Windham's diary reveals some ire occasioned by the meeting with Johnson, so that in this instance Mrs. Piozzi was probably right, and Boswell's suspicion unjustified. See also *Life of Johnson*, ed. E. G. Fletcher, iii. 400. Remarks of this sort might easily be treasured as amusing anecdotes in the Thrale family and still not find permanent record in her diaries or journals. Boswell in his original notes did not always record Johnson's roughest remarks, yet they were sometimes remembered and printed in the *Life*. See *Private Papers*, vi. 132 (May 7, 1773); *Life*, ii. 247. Johnson's term 'whore', as applied to Lady Di Beauclerk, does not appear in the original version written down by Boswell. See also *Essays and Studies of Eng. Ass'n.* xxiii. 58–69.

[2] *John. Misc.* i. 157; also A. L. Reade, *Gleanings*, iii. 84; see also *John. Misc.* i. 151.

consult all the evidence in her possession in England. For example, in printing the Latin inscription made by Johnson to
put on the collar of Sir Joseph Banks's goat, she vaguely remarked
that it 'was given me by Johnson in the year 1777 I think'.
This may have been true, but on a separate sheet of paper in
her collection she had written down a date for its composition
in 1772.[1]

   In her meagre account of Johnson's early years there are
obviously many mistakes. She was forced to rely largely upon
other people for her record of these years, and it is not surprising
that errors should have crept in. A typical example is the
confusion she made between Johnson's nurse who helped him
to learn to read and the later Catherine Chambers who lived
with his family.[2] A number of other early anecdotes are also
questionable, but so are some of Boswell's for the same period.[3]
In a number of cases what appeared to be an impossible story
has by further evidence been shown to have definite basis
in fact.[4]

   In preparing her anecdotes for publication Mrs. Piozzi did
not merely copy her original journal. Like her rival, she
revised the material to accord with her later ideas. Boswell,
with the hand of genius, in the final reshaping of his early notes
was able to 'Johnsonize' the whole, so that the later wording
was even more typical than the first note.[5] His quotations may
not represent the actual words used, but they are always in
character. Mrs. Piozzi, on the other hand, as she rewrote
her early paragraphs was more concerned with her own style
than with the reproduction of Johnson's remarks with perfect
fidelity. Changes in phrase and wording, she felt, were
immaterial so long as the essential point of the story was
retained. For example, in one of her early note-books she

---

[1] *John Misc.*, p. 195, and Ry. 543, 27. A further example is the death of her
mother, Mrs. Salusbury. In the *Children's Book* she had a full account of all that
happened at that time, and Johnson's behaviour, but not having this journal with
her in Italy her reference in the *Anecdotes* is extremely vague. See also her mistake
about the Preface to Harris's *Hermes* (p. 27, n. 2).

[2] See A. L. Reade, *Gleanings*, iii. 77.

[3] For possible examples see A. L. Reade, *Gleanings*, iii. 78 and 102; vi. 25,
65, 79.

[4] One instance is the story of Johnson's father locking the front door of his
workshop when the back was all open. This referred not to his book-shop, but to
his parchment factory (A. L. Reade, *Gleanings*, iii. 95). Another example may be
found in *Gleanings*, iii. 124. A third is the misunderstanding about the career of
Joseph Simpson (*Gleanings*, iv. 156; viii. 66–9). For explanation see 'Further
Letters of the Johnson Circle' (op. cit., p. 282).

[5] See editorial comments by Geoffrey Scott and Frederick Pottle in Boswell's
Private Papers, particularly in vol. vi.

had recorded Johnson's remarks on the vacuity of life, which began:

one was vicious—follow'd Women or drank Drams in a Corner— he was Idle says Johnson & Life must be fill'd up, a man must do something & he could think of nothing good that was good to do.[1]

After several rewritings the version appeared in the *Anecdotes*:

One man, for example, was profligate and wild, as we call it, followed the girls, or sat still at the gaming-table. 'Why, life must be filled up (says Johnson), and the man who is not capable of intellectual pleasures must content himself with such as his senses can afford.'[2]

Many of the anecdotes in the volume have the true Johnsonian ring. Surely we should not wish to be without the amusing anecdote of his reply to the young man who asked about the advisability of marrying.[3] Others have a definite place in the genuine canon of Johnsonian remarks. Characteristic was his account to Mrs. Thrale of a gentleman with whom she was unacquainted. 'He talked to me at club one day (replies our Doctor) concerning Catiline's conspiracy—so I withdrew my attention, and thought about Tom Thumb.'[4] On another occasion, during the tour to Wales in 1774, he and the Thrales were met by two gentlemen of their acquaintance on the road. Johnson, who was absorbed in reading a book when the travellers approached, seemed oblivious of their presence. When one of them tapped him gently on the shoulder and Thrale told him who it was, Johnson sternly replied. 'Well, Sir! and what if it is Mr. Ch-lm-ley!' hardly lifting his eyes from his book.[5] In spite of Boswell's insinuations, this retort is no more rude than many recorded in his *Life*, and there seems no valid reason for suspecting its genuineness.

Space does not permit a more detailed discussion of the validity of each individual anecdote.[6] Suffice it to say that Mrs. Piozzi was not essentially untruthful or inaccurate. Her contemporary records can almost invariably be trusted. The *Anecdotes*, on the contrary, was produced under extremely unfavourable circumstances, and cannot be accepted without

[1] Ry. 629, 7.
[2] *John. Misc.* i. 251. For a sample of Mrs. Piozzi's accuracy in the *Anecdotes* see *Philological Quarterly*, xviii (July, 1939), 318–20.
[3] See pp. 170–1, Chap. VIII; *John. Misc.* i. 213.
[4] Ibid. i. 202–3.   [5] Ibid., i. 319; *Life*, iv. 345.
[6] For a more complete discussion of the accuracy of Mrs. Piozzi's anecdotes see *Thraliana*, edited by Miss Katharine C. Balderston.

reservation. But in spite of its deficiencies the little volume has value for Johnsonian scholars. It has been our chief authority for many of Johnson's minor poems; it provides evidence of many facets in the great man's character altogether ignored by Boswell. It is filled with information which may in general be relied upon, if only allowance be made for Mrs. Piozzi's motives at the time and for the conditions under which the writing was done.

The postscript which Sir Lucas Pepys had inserted at the end of the *Anecdotes*, referring to Boswell's statement about Mrs. Montagu's *Essay on Shakespeare*, appeared to Boswell an attack on his own veracity. Yet he did not rush immediately into the fray, for he wished his answer to be conclusive. Away from London when the book appeared, Boswell did not return until April 10. On Saturday the 15th he breakfasted with Malone and Courtenay, and with their aid fashioned a reply which appeared in the *St. James's Chronicle* and other papers of the 18th.[1] In this he insisted that Mrs. Piozzi in her postscript had not actually denied the truth of his allegation, in fact had merely dodged the issue; furthermore, he pointed out that years before she had read through his journal in manuscript and had made no criticism of the passage at that time. To many readers Boswell's arguments seemed irrefutable, though others probably felt that Mrs. Thrale's failure to object to the passage might have been due to a disinclination to offend Johnson. In any case, as the *Public Advertiser* of April 21 noted, the retort only served to spread further consternation in the Blue-Stocking ranks.

Mr. Boswell's retort courteous to the stiletto postscript, has played the very devil in the assembly of *stockings*, whose *colour* shall be nameless. It has run amongst the learned legs, flaming and *hissing* like a well charged *cracker*.

Mrs. Montagu, about this time, replied to Mrs. Piozzi in a lengthy, dignified letter in which she accepted her explanation of the affair and completely disavowed all belief in the troublesome Boswell.[2] This doubtless pleased Mrs. Piozzi, but had

---

[1] *Private Papers*, xvi. 184–5. See *A Trifle*, privately printed by Mr. R. B. Adam, Buffalo, N.Y., Aug. 1927, being a facsimile of a manuscript version of the letter written on the last pages of a copy of the *Anecdotes*. *St. James's Chronicle*, Apr. 15–18; *London Chronicle*, Apr. 18–20; *Public Advertiser*, Apr. 18, 1786, &c.

[2] Ry. 551, 2. An extract is printed in *French Journals*, p. 43. A very similar letter, or draft of a letter, from Mrs. Montagu to Mrs. Piozzi (with no date) has been presented to me by Dr. Amos A. Ettinger. Mrs. Montagu wrote:

I must confess I should have been mortified not only that a Person of your taste should have found my work dull but that one in whose conversation I had enjoy'd so many agreable hours should have . . . pass'd some unpleasant ones

little effect in quashing the excited gossip in the London salons. For the next few weeks the chief topic of conversation was the merits and quarrels of the rival biographers. Hannah More wrote that the controversy had spoiled all conversation and ruined a very good evening at Sir William Pepys's,[1] and Walpole and others testify to the widespread preoccupation with this somewhat petty topic.

The general public, too, found much to interest and amuse them in the quarrel. Combined with the argument as to the good taste involved in printing accounts of Johnson's idiosyncrasies, it provided endless opportunity for humorous squibs and epigrams; and the newspapers and journals of the day were filled with attacks and occasional compliments.[2] Walpole wrote to Sir Horace Mann that the rival biographers and their hero were 'the joke of the public';[3] George Colman pointed out that Johnson while alive had written the life of a Savage, but now many a savage wrote his;[4] Soame Jenyns ended an unfavourable epitaph with the lines:

Boswell and Thrale, retailers of his wit,
Will tell you how he wrote, and talked, and coughed, and spit.[5]

Many and various were the overt attacks contained in the newspapers. Philip Thicknesse published a letter in the *St. James's Chronicle* of April 15, signed 'All my Eye', in which he made the absurd claim that Mrs. Thrale before her marriage had been a mantua-maker of mean extraction.[6] Boswell himself arranged in doggerel a number of the Piozzian anecdotes

over some pages of my Essay. however I will confess my mortification was mitigated by the very moderate degree of credit I gave to all Mr. Boswell had ascribed to Dr. Johnson. In the first place poor Mr. Boswell is very often in that condition in which men are said to see double, perhaps in such circumstance their hearing is so much disordered, & then what is still stronger objection to his testimony, he could hardly have had any motive for his publication but that of making it the vehicle of censure & scandal.

[1] H. More, *Memoirs*, ii. 16. The controversy stimulated interest in Mrs. Montagu's *Essay*, and the booksellers brought out a 5th edition on Apr. 26.
[2] One complimentary effusion appeared in the *Gent. Mag.* lvi (1786), 340. The verses, signed A. B., end with the lines: 'For, in the pleasing composition, meet Like punch, the strong, the weak, the sour, the sweet.' Mrs. Piozzi always suspected Sir Herbert Croft was the author. The newspapers were filled with attacks. See letter signed Zed in *St. James's Chronicle* of Apr. 8. The *Morning Post* and the *Herald*, as usual, led the attack. Repercussions appeared in various printed works. See J. Moir, *Gleanings or Fugitive Pieces* (no date), i. 60; J. Towers, *Essay on Life, etc. of Dr. Samuel Johnson* (1786), p. 19. [3] Walpole, *Letters*, xiii. 379.
[4] *Town and Country Mag.* xviii (1786), 384. In S. Lysons's scrap-book (see p. 124, n. 1) the verses are ascribed to Colman.
[5] *Autobiography of Mrs. Delany*, ed. Lady Llanover (1862), vi. 348.
[6] *St. James's Chronicle*, Apr. 15, 1786. Ascription to Philip Thicknesse is derived from Lysons's scrap-book. See above.

of Johnson and inserted them anonymously in the *London Chronicle*.[1] As soon as they were in print, he rushed to Malone's to see if he or Courtenay could guess the authorship. In his journal for the day, after recording his triumph, Boswell complacently added, 'Both liked Them.'

Mrs. Piozzi had been an easy mark for gossip and innuendo in the years of her widowhood and just following her second marriage; now she was again the subject of caricature and open attack. Of the many anonymous attempts at ridicule, one typical example may be selected: *A Poetical Epistle from the Ghost of Dr. Johnson to his Four Friends The Rev. Mr. Strahan, James Boswell Esq., Mrs. Piozzi, J. Courtenay Esq. M.P. from the Original Copy in the Possession of the Editor with Notes Critical, Biographical, Historical, and Explanatory*.[2] In this amusing skit the anonymous editor described a visit to the Elysian fields to find the ghost of Dr. Johnson. Written in doggerel, and illustrated by quotations from the works of the four writers, the epistle attacked Mrs. Piozzi in the usual way. Further proof of continued interest is given by a calendar for the year 1787, printed by Thomas Carnan in St. Paul's Yard. A single sheet, this almanac, as it is styled, had at the top four portraits, ostensibly of the best-known characters of the day: The Prince of Wales, Mrs. Fitzherbert, Dr. Johnson, and Mrs. Piozzi.[3]

The most pretentious, and in many ways the most amusing, of the parodies of the Boswell-Piozzi feud appeared on April 24. This came from the prolific pen of Peter Pindar (Dr. Wolcot), and was called 'Bozzy and Piozzi, a Town Eclogue'. With his usual predilection for a salty story, Wolcot turned from deriding the simple follies of the royal family to the popular quarrels of the Johnsonian biographers. Wolcot imagined Sir John Hawkins, who as yet had not appeared in the lists but was known to be at work on a complete biography, sitting in judgement while Boswell and Mrs. Piozzi engaged in a personal argument, illustrated with all the silliest anecdotes each had recorded of Johnson. An example, to indicate the easy flow and pungency of this popular lampoon, follows:

Bozzy
How could your folly tell, so void of truth
That miserable story of the youth,

---

[1] *Private Papers*, xvi. 185; *London Chronicle*, Apr. 20, 1786. The verses signed 'Old Salusbury Briar' were also reprinted in the *Morning Herald*, Apr. 21, 1786.
[2] Printed for Harrison & Co., London, 1786.
[3] A copy is among Mrs. Piozzi's papers in the John Rylands Library.

Who, in your book, of Dr. Johnson begs
Most seriously to know if cats laid eggs!

Madame Piozzi

Who told of Mistress Montagu the lie
So palpable a falsehood?—Bozzy fie!

Bozzy

Who madd'ning with an anecdotic itch,
Declar'd that Johnson call'd his mother 'b-tch?'

Madame Piozzi

Who, from M'Donald's rage to save his snout,
Cut twenty lines of defamation out?

Bozzy

Who would have said a word about Sam's wig,
Or told the story of the peas and pig?
Who would have told a tale so very flat,
Of Frank the Black, and Hodge the mangy cat?

Madame Piozzi

Good me! you're grown at once confounded tender
Of Doctor Johnson's fame a fierce defender:
I'm sure you've mentioned many a pretty story
Not much redounding to the Doctor's glory.
Now for a saint upon us you would palm him—
First murder the poor man, and then embalm him!

Bozzy

Well, Ma'am! Since all that Johnson said or wrote,
You hold so sacred, how have you forgot
To grant the wonder-hunting world a reading
Of Sam's Epistle, just before your wedding;
Beginning thus (in strains not formed to flatter)
'Madame,
        If that most ignominious matter
        Be not concluded'
                Further shall I say?
No—we shall have it from yourself some day,
To justify your passion for the Youth,
With all the charms of eloquence and truth.

Madame Piozzi

What was my marriage, Sir, to you or him?
He tell me what to do!—a pretty whim.
He, to propriety (the beast) resort!
As well might elephants preside at court.

Lord! let the world to damn my match agree;
Good God! James Boswell, what's that world to me?
The folks who paid respects to Mistress Thrale,
Fed on her pork, poor souls, and swilled her ale,
May sicken at Piozzi, nine in ten—
Turn up the nose of scorn—Good God! what then?
For me, the Devil may fetch their souls so great;
They keep their homes, and I, thank God, my meat.
When they, poor owls, shall beat their cage, a jail,
I, unconfined, shall spread my peacock tail;
Free as the birds of air, enjoy my ease,
Choose my own food, and see what climes I please.
I suffer only—if I'm in the wrong:
So, now, you prating puppy, hold your tongue.[1]

Wolcot undoubtedly caught Mrs. Piozzi's defiant attitude towards the detractors of her second husband. If she ever regretted breaking the rules of English caste, she never admitted it publicly or privately. In her happiness she was callous to what others might think or say. Travelling about sunny Italy with her *caro sposo* was the realization of her fondest dreams, and she could well afford to ignore the carping criticism at home.

[1] *Works of Peter Pindar* (1797), i. 248–51.

XIII

TRAVEL ON THE CONTINENT

MARCH 1786–MARCH 1787

IN Italy Mrs. Piozzi was oblivious of the controversy aroused by her little volume. After spending the early part of the winter in Naples, enjoying the mild climate and interesting surroundings, she and her husband, on February 22, 1786, turned their faces northward. They found Rome in the last throes of carnival week, and Mrs. Piozzi's English sense of decorum was offended by what she considered the vulgar spirit applied to a semi-religious festival. In the Imperial City she saw little of the better class of society, for Piozzi seems to have had few friends there, and social distinctions were even more stringently observed than in northern Italy. Wasting no time in useless lamentation, however, she threw herself, as usual, into the one occupation always open to her.

I have now returned to my old Employment of seeing Palaces & Churches; examining Statues, Pictures &c. and find the Doria & Colonna Palaces exceed all possibility of expectation.[1]

Rome offered a splendid opportunity to indulge her passion for painting, and she wrote to Queeney:

I passed two Mornings in looking at the pictures of Sasso Ferrato and Andrea Mantegna, Names which I used to know only in Books: the Works of Guido *Reni* as the Italians always call him however, give one the real, & true, & unaffected Delight which that Art can afford—and as Goldsmith used to say the way to set up for a Conoscente was to talk a great deal about *Pietro Perugino*, I assure you that in that Merit I have already made many advances.[2]

She was astounded, too, by the profusion and excellence of the sculpture everywhere in the city.

[1] Ry. 618, spread 75. The following description of the Piozzis' travels about the Continent is derived from a variety of sources: Mrs. Piozzi's original travel journals (Ry. 618); the published *Observations and Reflections* (1789); Mainwaring Piozziana; letters to Queeney and S. Lysons, &c. The best discussion of Mrs. Piozzi as a traveller may be found in the Introduction by the Countess Evelyn Martinengo Cesaresco to *Glimpses of Italian Society, etc.* (New York, 1892), pp. 1 41.
[2] *Queeney Letters*, pp. 219–21.

It was said by Vopiscus you remember that there were more statues than Men at Rome in his Time; and as the People are daily popping their heads under Ground, & the Statues peeping theirs above Ground,—I fancy they now nearly double the Number of the Inhabitants.

Seven weeks of sightseeing in the capital proved very pleasant, but on April 19 the Piozzis set out again for Venice. Near Spoleto, high in the Apennines, their coach broke down. Providentially, so it seemed, just at this moment two English gentlemen, a Mr. Shard and the Rev. Leonard Chappelow, drove up and offered their assistance. This offer was gladly accepted, the coach was finally tied together with ropes, and slowly and laboriously they crawled on through Foligno, Ancona, Rimini, and Ravenna to Bologna.

Mrs. Piozzi was immediately attracted to Chappelow, one of their rescuers, and he was equally drawn to the clever, well-informed Englishwoman. A former librarian of Trinity College, Cambridge, a fine classical scholar, naturalist, and would-be poet, he proved a congenial companion and later a delightful correspondent.[1] For the rest of his life he was one of Mrs. Piozzi's most intimate friends.

To the Piozzis' great annoyance, their broken coach could not be satisfactorily repaired in Bologna, but Chappelow and his companion insisted that Mrs. Piozzi and her maid set out for Ferrara in their post-chaise, while they followed behind in the patched up coach with her husband. Ironically enough, the post-chaise lost its hind wheel in the first quarter of an hour, and the women were forced to return to the coach and creep slowly into Ferrara. This latter place she found deserted, and could not but remember how the improvisatore Talassi, in an account of a visit to the Thrales, had written of the village of Streatham as a populous place. Now she found the description less laughable, having seen the empty streets of his native city.

In Bologna Mrs. Piozzi had fallen again under the spell of her favourite painter, Guercino, and was determined to see his birthplace at Cento. Accordingly, she and her husband parted from their new-found friends, arranging to meet them in Padua, and made a detour to see how the painter had decorated his

---

[1] Both sides of the long correspondence are now in the Rylands collection (Ry. 559–63). Chappelow had just published, in 1784, a little volume, *The Looking Glass*, containing imitations of selected fables of Fontaine, 'with Additional Thoughts', &c. A copy presented by the author to H. L. P. in 1792 is now in the Rylands library.

native town. Her expectations were not disappointed, though she could not restrain her indignation at the way he had represented his real name of Barbier over the altar where he was baptized, by drawing God the Father with a long beard. From Cento it was a short journey to Padua, where they rejoined the Greatheeds, who had come north through Perugia, and together once more sailed by barge down the Brenta to Venice. As they floated along, some one in the party read Merry's poem 'Paulina', until the Queen of the Adriatic herself drove all other thoughts from their minds.

In Venice Mrs. Piozzi decided to gratify her love for painting in a more substantial way than merely by gallery attendance. In Rome she had purchased a view of St. Mark's by Canaletto; now she bought an original sketch of Guido's Aurora and a number of pictures by such artists as Canaletto, Salviati, Domenichino, Amigoni, and Bassano.[1] She must have yearned for one by her favourite Guercino, but failing this she was glad to acquire a number of large canvasses of the north-Italian school of painting with which to decorate her house at Streatham.

In Venice she first heard of the success of her *Anecdotes*; yet her letters to Queeney and others had an apologetic tone, and she insisted on emphasizing the difficulties under which the volume was produced. 'These poor Anecdotes', she wrote to Lysons, 'have been published as Philidor is said to make his Moves at Chess, whilst he himself is playing on the Fiddle in another Room.'[2] Gradually, however, the complimentary letters from her friends and the undoubtedly spectacular sale of the little volume raised her spirits, and she soon ceased all apology for the quality of the writing or the numerous errors. Although she herself had not as yet seen a copy, she could now pose as a successful authoress. Heedless of all London disputes, she could enjoy her imaginary fame, unruffled by the 'poisoned arrows of private malignity' which had driven her from her own shores.

Throughout the later part of May and the early weeks in June 1786 the Piozzis remained in Venice. Despite the fact that her zeal for seeing everything was beginning to wane, Mrs. Piozzi still spent most of her time examining fine pictures and libraries with her English friends, Dr. and Mrs. Whalley (whom

---

[1] These pictures were later sold at public auction at Brynbella, Apr. 13–15, 1836. In the catalogue of the sale it was stated that Mrs. Piozzi had purchased the lot in Venice about the year 1786.
[2] May 26, 1786. See p. 236, n. 2.

she had known at Bath), Chappelow, and the Greatheeds. The heat, however, was growing unbearable, and when this, combined with the stench from the small canals, made her ill, they decided to return to Milan. On June 12, the day after the Doge's dinner, they returned to Padua, where they found their coach fully repaired and ready, so the man insisted, to carry them safely round the world should they so please.

They found the road to Verona exceedingly rough, like all those in the Venetian state. As Mrs. Piozzi shrewdly guessed, the senators of Venice, preoccupied with maritime affairs, gave little thought to the comfort of those who chose to travel by land. 'Petruchio & Catherine might well tumble out of their saddles into the Dirt between Padua & Verona.' She was constantly reminded of Shakespearian scenes and characters in northern Italy, and her feeling on passing later through Mantua was to agree with Romeo in lamenting banishment from Verona to this 'disagreeable' town. Verona she found completely enchanting, with an agreeable society of educated ladies, who applauded her husband's playing on the pianoforte and wrote impromptu verses in each other's praise. Mrs. Piozzi preserved a number which she wrote herself, as well as a fine fable presented by the Abbate Bertola to be translated for her daughters.

While they were in Verona, a group of Piozzi's friends and relatives came from Quinzano to see him. Although only a journey of twenty miles, Mrs. Piozzi laughingly recorded, it was considered in the Venetian territory a fearsome trip indeed. Probably the condition of the roads is some explanation of the fact that Piozzi did not take his wife to see his own birthplace; nor did he introduce her to his old father at Brescia. Perhaps he was not anxious to parade his numerous poor relatives before the wealthy Englishwoman, and the difficulty of travelling may have been rather a plausible excuse than an insurmountable obstacle.

The Piozzis moved westward by easy stages and reached Milan on June 21, after an absence of fourteen months. To return again to their own belongings was pleasant, but shortly afterwards the quiet of Casa Fidele was rudely disturbed, when they were nearly robbed by a young Florentine, who had followed them about and attempted to obtain service in their household. In the excitement of the moment Mrs. Piozzi locked herself in a closet for protection against the cut-throats, and remained there until rescued by the police. It all ended like a scene from a comic opera: with the master in mortal terror because he was unarmed, the mistress in hysterics, and the villains calmly dismissed by the lenient authorities. Looking back many years later Mrs. Piozzi could see the humorous side of the incident, but at the time it was a distinct shock to her nerves,[1] and a visit to the northern lakes was needed to restore her equanimity.

Through the heat of July they were near Varese, surrounded by a crowd of gay, care-free friends, experiencing a true Italian *villeggiatura*. They never, she wrote, sat down fewer than fourteen or fifteen at the table, and the gentlemen with good-humoured gaiety composed impromptu rhymes, made comical faces, and engaged in a round of simple and unaffected amusements. She was charmed with the lack of restraint in such a gathering and could not but compare it with the more sedate pleasures of her own country.

Later Count Borromeo extended to the travellers an invitation for a week's stay at his palace on Isola Bella in Lake Maggiore.

> Guess you [Mrs. Piozzi wrote to Queeney] if we made Lago Maggiore resound? having one Barge-full of Friends, another with a band of nine performers the best in Italy, to divert us and them upon the Water. And of an Evening when by Moonlight we returned home to our Calypso-like Dominion, & the Fragrance of the Orange Grove met us by the Time we were half way thither, I really fancied myself in a sort of Mahomet's Paradise.[2]

Here, in celebration of the Piozzis' second wedding anniversary, the Marquis D'Araciel composed a glowing Epithalamium which was sung by the band of musicians. In addition the Marquis had the verses printed in Milan, and presented copies to the happy couple and their friends.[3]

Even in such surroundings, in a spot so perfect that her maid thought it hardly real and confidently expected the palace to disappear by magic, Mrs. Piozzi was not allowed to forget her affairs in England. Friends there wrote constantly about the public reception of her *Anecdotes*, and she replied with fervent thanks for their aid with the cancelled paragraph and the postscript.[4] Although the little volume had been published at

---

[1] Mainwaring Piozziana, ii. 85.   [2] *Queeney Letters*, pp. 228–9.

[3] A copy is in the Rylands collection. On the outside is 'PEL FAUSTO GIORNO DELLE NOZZE AVVENUTE IN LONDRA DEGLI ORNATISSIMI SPOSI PIOZZI. CANTATA EPITALAMICA'. The verses are dated 'Varese 25 Luglio 1786' and signed 'In attestato di vera stima ed amicizia IL MARCHESE DE ARACIEL Ciamberlano di S.M.I.R.A.' The poem was printed in Milan, 'Per Cesare Orena nella Stamperia Malatesta'.

[4] To Lysons, Mar. 25, 1786. See also *J. Rylands Bulletin*, xx (1936), 171

the end of March, she herself had not even seen a copy by July. As she wrote to Lysons, July 6, 'tis a great Plague really not to see how the Book looks'. More of a worry, however, was her proposed edition of Johnson's letters. She had promised the publishing rights to Cadell, who had aroused public expectation by advertisements in the newspapers; consequently she added to Lysons that if her friends thought it advisable she and her husband could hurry to England during the autumn. What was her delight to receive Lysons's reply of July 31, advising the withholding of Johnson's correspondence until after the appearance of the official edition of his works. Almost as pleasing was the approbation of Sir Joshua Reynolds, related in the same letter.

I talked with Dr. Lort about the publication of the Letters, and told him what Cadell said on that subject, he thinks you should not publish them 'till after Sir John Hawkins's Edition of Dr. Johnson's Works, unless you wish them to be serviceable to the Knight, in his compilations—By the way, no great Matters are expected from this promised piece of Biography—I met Sir Joshua Reynolds yesterday at Sir Joseph Banks; and he told me that Dr. Johnson's works were quite printed and that he supposed they would be published on the meeting of Parliament in the Autumn, I was much pleased with Sir Joshua whom I had never before known, he overtook me this morning near Fulham and brought me to Town in his carriage, he speaks very handsomely of your anecdotes, and says he is sure the Letters will be a very valuable publication.

However pleased she may have been that her presence was not immediately required in England, Mrs. Piozzi was determined not to remain permanently in Italy. The constant strain of the ardent proselytizing, which was becoming every day more harassing, and the irritating social distinctions combined to render her position even more insecure than in her native land. But she was too clever to attempt to force any decision on an unwilling husband. She had, indeed, in her last letter to Dr. Johnson expressed the conviction that Piozzi would require little persuasion to settle in England. What was her surprise and delight to learn that he was quite as eager as she to make London their permanent home:

he [Piozzi] had always thought even when a Boy that England should be his home. Milan & even Paris had spread their Charms in vain,—London was the Place he had always wished to shine in:—and to London he would go.[1]

[1] Mainwaring Piozziana, ii. 88.

Once the decision was made, however, she was in no hurry to hasten home. Before leaving she wanted to see the Tyrolean Alps, Vienna, Prague, Germany, Belgium. If only she could get rid of her present difficulties by travelling, she did not care how long their return was delayed.

Wandering about on the Continent, Mrs. Piozzi had been unable to keep closely in touch with her daughters. The youngest, Cecilia, had been left in school at Streatham, while Susanna and Sophia were under the care of a Mrs. Murray in Kensington. Queeney, the eldest, went her own way, and lived in Brighton with an elderly widow, a Mrs. Cochrane, as chaperon. On coming of age (in September 1785) she rented a house in Wimpole Street, thereafter dividing her time between Sussex and London. The younger sisters spent their vacations with the Cators at Beckenham Place and with Queeney in Brighton.[1]

The girls were never very faithful in writing to their distant mother, much to the latter's disappointment. Once she com plained to Queeney:

what can be become of dear Susan & Sophy? who never write themselves, & of whom you say not a Syllable, tho' Mr. Cator's last Letters tell me they are under your Care. Why do you my sweetest Girl, write so coldly and so queerly? & why do you hinder your Sisters from writing at all? is it because I am married to Mr. Piozzi? that Reason (as Shakespear says) *is somewhat musty* . . .[2]

Some weeks later, when the requested letters had arrived, 'in Consequence of my Lamentations', Mrs. Piozzi wrote again to Queeney:

they protest it was nobody's fault but their own that I remained 12 Weeks without hearing of 'em, and when you say it was not yours, I hold myself bound to believe it. That My Name should never be named among you, is too probable for me to doubt; but I must assure you in Confidence that the Ladies *did* do me the favour to write very fondly & familiarly after our parting, & indeed till I left Milan I had perpetual Letters from them, begging me to return, & perswading Mr Piozzi to bring me back. *This* is my Excuse for having written fondly & familiarly to them . . .[3]

Some of her disaffected friends had evidently poisoned the minds of the younger girls against her; nevertheless she continued to send presents to them whenever she found an opportunity, and besought any friend going back to England to see

---

[1] See letters from Cator (Ry. 622, 1, 2, 6).
[2] From Florence, July 26, 1785.   [3] From Pisa, Sept. 17, 1785.

her daughters immediately and report their condition. Shard, one of these, wrote on July 11, 1786:

Mr Chappelow & I took the first Opportunity of making use of your kind introduction to Kensington & were very happy to find both the Miss Thrales well. They inquired very kindly & particularly about you. Mr. C. has hardly recovered the Impression the Eyes of the youngest Lady made upon him & I was equally struck with the mild & pleasing behaviour (for all Dr Johnson says that word has no meaning) of your favorite Sophy . . .[1]

If the connexion with her daughters was only a slender thread, Mrs. Piozzi was determined not to be the one to break it. So in answer to a request from Susanna, and possibly also as a release for pent-up emotions resulting from the recent solicitations of the Roman Catholics, she began on August 13, 1786, a series of short disquisitions on the fundamental tenets of the English Church. This strange work, which consisted of ten chapters discussing the creeds, sacraments, ceremonies, mysteries, and so forth, opened with a preface in the form of a letter to her daughter.

My dear Susanna—

Your Request must be my Excuse for meddling with Subjects which it is the peculiar Province of the Clergy to discuss and to explain; God forbid that I should have an Idea of intruding upon a Profession wch. it is our indispensable Duty to revere; but you used to say my Preachments were the clearest, & that from being accustomed to my Manner of talking on serious Subjects you came away better informed than after listening to Discourses more elaborate, from Lips more learned than mine. The Distance we have now been so long Time from each other, must serve as another Excuse, since we cannot converse as formerly, when ev'ry Sunday Evening glided away in a sort of grave but useful Talk, for which to say the Truth, I have found few People of your Age express so much Taste as yourself. . . .[2]

Having increased her fund of religious information on her recent travels, she added, she was much better fitted to accomplish the task she had in mind. The exposition, when completed, filled over forty folio pages, but whether it was ever presented to Susanna cannot be determined with certainty. The fact that she took so much time to write out the account, however, provides further light on her many-sided character.

[1] Ry. 892, 7. See also from Chappelow, July 4, 1786 (Ry. 562, 1); from Parsons, Oct. 1, 1786 (Ry. 558, 17); and to Queeney, Sept. 27, 1786, concerning a visit from Mrs. Greatheed.   [2] Ry. 634.

Late in August 1786 the Marquis D'Araciel invited the Piozzis to his palace at Bergamo for a week's visit. It was there that she had another glimpse of Piozzi's brother Giambattista who had come to bid them farewell.

He came into the Assembly,—I was dancing; & kiss'd my hand to *him*, tho' the other was held by a Man of Quality—This occasioned a Stir, but never mind; It is *my Brother* said I—& I *will* kiss my hand to Him.[1]

It was particularly hard for an Englishwoman to understand the great gulf which separated men of quality in Italy from the ordinary professional and merchant class. As a foreigner, though, she was able to break social conventions with some impunity, and she naïvely added, 'They admir'd, condemn'd, & *ador'd* me all at once.'

The Piozzis had brought a large quantity of furniture, plate, and table service from England, and had made other purchases on their travels. Confidently expecting to return to Italy for long visits in the future, they decided to leave the greater part of these belongings in care of Piozzi's brother.[2] Packing and farewells occupied the early part of September, so that it was not until the 22nd that the Piozzis left Milan, and she found herself, as she expressed it, again with a coach for her home.

Before starting across the Tyrolean Alps, the travellers spent a few days in Verona. Life here she found as delectable as ever: the Abbé Bertola made impromptu verses, Pindemonte conversed, Piozzi played and sang, while the charming hostesses engaged in a kind of group improvization. This was Mrs. Piozzi's final taste of Italian society, her last opportunity to enjoy the unaffected camaraderie which she felt was this country's most engaging trait. She would always remember Verona as the epitome of all she liked best in Italy.

Although sorry to leave such agreeable company, the Piozzis finally drove north through the mountains to Trent, which they reached on October 3. The next important stop was at Innsbrück, where, in commenting on the increase in cleanliness and comfort as they proceeded northward, she wrote in her journal: 'Here we have all that English People wish for except Language, wch. neither Mr. Piozzi nor I unluckily possess.' Twenty-four hours of hard driving from here brought the travellers to Munich. Upon their arrival they found that the

---

[1] Mainwaring Piozziana, ii. 89.
[2] Included were some portraits of the Piozzis themselves. These are reproduced in *Glimpses of Italian Society* (op. cit.), p. 4.

Marquis Trotti, whom she had met in Paris in 1775, was staying in the same inn, and with him she immediately rushed out to view the picture galleries, recalling her first initiation into the delights of great painting eleven years before. After the expansive paintings of Carracci and Guercino, however, she found German art dull and laboured, 'Italian Sublimity sinking off into German Minuteness'.[1] Breughel, she maintained, 'seems to pique himself on putting upon a 15 Inch Board more than Claude or Poussin would have found sufficient for six large Pictures of four Feet each'. Still more was she discontented with the buildings: 'no more beautiful Architecture, no more half-breathing Statues—but many Figures of Juno & Diana, all of Gilt Lead as the Man who shews 'em off told me with apparent Satisfaction: I thought them a good Emblem of the whole Nation for my part.' Mrs. Piozzi had felt an obligation to understand and admire Italy, her husband's country; she had no similar incentive for Germany and Austria, and allowed her pen considerable liberty in caustic criticism. On the whole, however, her comments and observations in her journals and in her letters were shrewd and understanding. If she was at first bored and disgusted with the matter-of-fact stolidity of the art and the people, she also found much to admire.

From Munich the Piozzis went somewhat out of their way to Salzburg, where Mrs. Piozzi made interesting investigations into her own descent, and firmly believed that she had traced her ancestry back to the original Adam de Salzburg. Then, about the middle of October, they drove on to Vienna. On the very day which brought the travellers to Vienna, Prince Lichtenstein's favourite Spitzberger lapdog presented him with a fine litter of puppies. One of these he gave to the visiting Englishwoman, and for the remainder of the tour Mrs. Piozzi carried with her everywhere she went this new successor to a long line of favourite pets. Flo, as the dog was called, continued for many years a pampered member of the Piozzi household.

In Vienna she was startled by the living conditions: 'five, or six, or seven families all in one house; every one shutting his apartment, or set of apartments, out from the others, by a great iron door, or grate.'[2] She was delighted to find that the public library had sent for copies of her Johnsonian *Anecdotes*, and still more flattered to be told that the book was to be translated into

---

[1] *Queeney Letters*, p. 235.
[2] To Lysons, Nov. 29, 1786.

German.[1] As an established collector of anecdotes, she thought it her duty to transcribe into her journals numerous stories of the Emperor and of the celebrated poet Metastasio.

The music of Vienna made little appeal to her, though her husband must have revelled in the opportunities it afforded. She never acquired any enthusiasm for serious music. Pictorial art was her passion; melody and harmony made little impression upon her feelings. Thus it is strange for us to find that the one acquaintance which she made in Vienna of whom we would like to know more, she does not even mention in her journals. In the spring of this year Mozart had produced his *Marriage of Figaro* in Vienna, and was still living in that city. We have evidence that he and the Piozzis were occasionally at the same parties, but the musician whom we think the greatest of his time made little impression upon the unmusical Englishwoman. If her husband had kept a diary the tale would have been different. We know of the meetings of Mozart and the Piozzis, not from their own records but from the reminiscences of the singer Michael Kelly. Kelly, writing many years later of the celebrated Mme Martines, whose literary and artistic parties were popular in Vienna at the time, added:

Mozart was an almost constant attendant at her parties, and I have heard him play duets on the piano-forte with her, of his own composition. She was a great favourite of his.

At one of her parties I had the pleasure to be introduced to Mrs. Piozzi, who, with her husband, was travelling on the Continent; there appeared to me a great similarity in the manners of these two gifted women, who conversed with all around them without pedantry or affectation. It was certainly an epoch, not to be forgotten, to have had the good fortune, on the same evening, to be in the company with the favourites of Metastasio and Dr. Johnson; and last, not least, with Mozart himself.[2]

Piozzi's one great desire was to see and hear Haydn. Being so near, he planned a little excursion late in October into Hungary, where he meant to visit the great composer at Esterhazy. Unfortunately, in a little country town called Edenbourg Mrs. Piozzi was taken suddenly ill, and they were forced to return to Vienna, disappointed of this ambition. With her passion for history, Mrs. Piozzi was more interested in her proximity to the Turkish Empire than to that of the great musician.

---

[1] *Queeney Letters*, p. 239. I have been unable so far to find any German translation of the *Aneedotes*.

[2] *Reminiscences of Michael Kelly* (1826), 2nd ed. i. 249-50.

After the maddening experience of having all her furs confiscated by the customs officials,[1] Mrs. Piozzi left Vienna on November 23 for Prague, where she wrote to Lysons on the 29th commenting on the miserable housing. But even her insatiable curiosity was now beginning to wear out, and, following a discussion of their proposed route home, she added:

Our coach will hardly hold out more frisks, and one grows tired of seeing the library, and the museum, and the same stuff over again at every place. Mr. Murphy used to say, when we asked him to go with us to look at some gentleman's seat, I remember. 'No, do let me alone,' says he, 'I'll describe it to you when you come home just as exact.' Accordingly, when we returned, he was ready to receive us. 'And well,' says he, 'you ran up a flight of stone-stairs, did not you; turned into an Egyptian hall; then through a magnificent corridor to the picture gallery; the library is in the other wing &c.'

I begin now to be of his mind, and think it would [be] a comfortable thing to sit quiet and stir the fire; a pleasure we never enjoy, for the stoves here warm, but do not divert me; and the double windows tease me to death, I can never get a good look out in the street . . .

From Prague the travellers turned north to Dresden, but finding the roads almost impassible, they put their coach on board a boat and floated down the Elbe for the rest of the journey. She liked Dresden better than any other German city. The famous Gallery with the fine Correggios, the clean streets and squares, the gaiety and good humour of the Courts, all made an instant appeal. As a result, the Piozzis remained nearly a month, not leaving until January 1, 1787.

On Christmas day Mrs. Piozzi was delighted when a French Protestant pastor had a long talk with her husband and gave him a book of devotional exercises. In spite of the fact that she had been much exercised over the efforts of the Romanists to convert her to Piozzi's religion, she was inwardly pleased to think of him as a proselyte to her own. She was happy to note that her husband never 'communicated with the Romanists from the Hour of this Sweet Conversation in Saxony',[2] although it was some time before he actually became a member of the English Church. Years later, looking back at her stay in Dresden, she could write that this Christmas 'was the happiest of my Life'.[3]

---

[1] *Queeney Letters*, p. 237. Mrs. Piozzi's letters to Robert Murray Keith, British Ambassador at Vienna, who finally rescued the furs, may be found in the British Museum (Add. MS. 35538–70, 227). One of his replies is in Ry. 892.
[2] Mainwaring Piozziana, ii. 92.   [3] Ibid.

It was probably in Dresden that Mrs. Piozzi received a letter from Sir Lucas Pepys, written on November 30, containing several suggestions which must have made her indignant. On her return to England, Pepys warned her, she must remember that many of her old acquaintances would not be pleased. But public opinion might be placated to some degree if she could get her younger daughters to share a house in London; or 'perhaps you will find it much more Comfortable to go First to Bath, & not settle in London for the first 6 Weeks or Two Months'.[1] She should crawl back with humility and patiently wait the forgiveness of outraged society. This was unwelcome advice to the woman who not only felt no shame but rather gloried in her second marriage, but Pepys went even further and committed the fatal error of attacking Piozzi's name.

It has been said that an Italian Name makes an awkward Jumble with the Smiths, Thomsons, Jacksons & all the Usual Names of John Bull's Children, & that You being aware of This have Thoughts of getting your Name changed to your Mothers Name of Salisbury; An Excellent Idea & Mr. Cater could get it done for you before you arrive.

Pepys's advice might be safe and discreet, but it did not agree with her belligerent disposition. Never ashamed of her husband's foreign name, she rather insisted on using it at every turn; Thrale was forgotten; for the rest of her life she was H. L. Piozzi, or simply H. L. P. Consequently Pepys's advice fell on stony ground, and though he had proffered the counsel with many protestations of reluctance and hesitancy, it is very probable that the lady never forgave him for his impertinence. Perhaps it is only a coincidence, but in the correspondence from Sir Lucas Pepys now in the John Rylands Library, this letter of advice is the last for many years.

From Dresden the Piozzis crawled along over jolting roads, 'ten Miles o' Day or 15 at the very most', to Berlin, and from there through Brandenburg, Brunswick, Hanover, Münster, Düsseldorf, into the Low Countries. Berlin itself proved a disappointment, being the only place of any consequence from which she felt in a hurry to run away, but Potsdam and the palace of Frederick the Great she found a perfect combination

---

[1] Ry. 536, 29. In the biographical account of Mrs. Piozzi published by the *European Mag.* x (1786), pp. 5–6, the statement had been made that 'Public report hints, that Mrs. Piozzi will return to England in the course of next winter, and that her husband will then be naturalized, and assume the name of Salisbury'.

of 'magnificence, taste, and splendour'. Everything now was seen with jaded eyes, for nothing much mattered except the prospect of letters and news from England. They hurried along as fast as possible through Liège and Louvain, arriving in Brussels at the beginning of February 1787.

In Brussels the travellers found a stack of letters from London, and were cordially greeted by a large number of English visitors, among whom were Dr. and Mrs. Whalley, Lord and Lady Torrington, and Robert Merry, who in Florence had been so sure they would never meet again. Weary of bouncing all winter on German roads, the Piozzis were anxious to return home, but the agreeable company proved so diverting that they stayed nearly a month. There was only one drawback, as she wrote to Queeney on February 5, telling of their recent travels and of the present delights of Brussels society.

We talk nothing but French here, & 'tis quite odd to me who have so long lived in Italy—very mortifying, an't it, to have my Husband speak *two* Languages better than myself—but I shall catch him in my own Country one of these Days.

Mrs. Piozzi's accounts of their reception in Brussels, as well as elsewhere on the Continent, must certainly be taken with a grain of salt; and we may be allowed to doubt whether the Archduchess forced her own children to practise reading English out of the *Anecdotes of Dr. Johnson*, or whether the nobility were so completely overcome by Piozzi's singing, as the diarist later insisted.

There [Brussels] we were fondled & petted till we were proud and ashamed and delighted all at once. The Arch Duchess herself— Gouvernante of the Low Countries—personally invited our Stay . . . no Music pleased her but that of Mr. Piozzi, who told her how good The Queen of France (her Highness's Sister) had been to *him*; Prince Albert stood behind him while He sang at the Duc D'Arenberg's, and *turned over the Book for him*. Princess Pauline . . . learn'd his Sonatas; and Lord and Lady Torington could with Difficulty keep up with the Foreigners in paying us every Attention.[1]

In letters to Queeney and others across the Channel, Mrs. Piozzi was naturally trying to contrast her rapturous acceptance by the people of rank in Europe with the cold sneers of her English acquaintances; yet in her own diaries and journals she can hardly have had the same purpose, and it was not her practice to shirk recording the unpleasant. Undoubtedly they were

---

[1] Mainwaring Piozziana, ii. 95.

well treated by continental society, and it was flattering to her egotism to record these pleasant associations as overwhelming triumphs. That they were not entirely a figment of her own imagination is shown by contemporary foreign dispatches in the English papers. Piozzi played and sang at a grand concert in February; several months later the *World* newspaper in London printed a communication from Brussels mentioning the singer, and ending with the phrase, 'His performance at the Duke d'Aremberg's, is still the topic'.[1]

The Piozzis themselves gave a supper and concert in Brussels attended by sixty-four English visitors, as well as a large number of the local *haut-monde*. With concerts and balls, interspersed with literary conversations with the poet Merry and Dr. Whalley, the days passed quickly. In Brussels she read for the first time the poems of a new English poet who appealed to her immediately. As she commented to Chappelow on February 13:

At *this* place I have read some of your Friend Mr. Cowper's Poems, with sincere Delight to think that there is in the World so good a man, who writes so well, now Johnson has left it.[2]

England urgently beckoned across the Channel. Consequently, on the 1st of March the Piozzis drove on to Antwerp to see Rubens's 'Descent from the Cross', planning to go from there to Ghent, where they would cross the Scheldt by boat. From Antwerp Mrs. Piozzi dispatched a jingling epistle to Mrs. Whalley, beginning:

When I rose to leave Brussels, this morning, I found
That my lips could not utter one audible sound,
For the cold, which had seized on my voice and my hearing,
Had made me a figure not fit for appearing.[3]

To describe all the various sights already seen, she explained:

As my list was so long, then, so straitened my time,
I thought 'twould be easiest to write it in rhyme;
For though Mr. Hayley may think himself clever
To canter in couplets for ever and ever,
I think there is nobody else but what knows
Bad verses are much sooner writ than good prose.

Even when rendered almost speechless with a cold, Mrs. Piozzi could still delight in scribbling English verses on any and every occasion.

---

[1] *World*, May 25, 1787; see also issue of Mar. 8, 1787.
[2] Ry. 559, 5.
[3] *Whalley Corr.* ii. 5–6. The letter is dated Antwerp, Thursday, Mar. 1, 1787.

Because of a high wind they were not able to cross the Scheldt as they planned, and were forced instead to return to Brussels, whence by way of Lille they drove to Calais. The crossing was hurriedly accomplished, and it was with fast-beating heart that Mrs. Piozzi drove along the road from Dover to London. She and her husband had been absent from England for two and a half years; she had seen most of the proudest capitals of Europe; but the fog-wrapped spires of London were in the end the most satisfying sight of them all.

XIV

ENGLAND AGAIN

MARCH 1787–MARCH 1788

THE Piozzis returned to London on Saturday, March 10, 1787. Having established themselves at the Royal Hotel in Pall Mall, they found it was still early, and Mrs. Piozzi suggested going to the play.

There was a small front box, in those days, which held only two; it made the division, or connexion, with the side boxes, and, being unoccupied, we sat in it, and saw Mrs. Siddons act Imogen, I well remember, and Mrs. Jordan, Priscilla Tomboy. Mr. Piozzi was amused, and the next day was spent in looking at houses, counting the cards left by old acquaintances, &c.[1]

This was her answer to Sir Lucas Pepys and his prudent suggestions.

The next morning she sent a note to Queeney, announcing their arrival and explaining that, owing to the confusion and bustle of getting settled, she would be unable to come to see her at once.[2] The truth is, Mrs. Piozzi was somewhat dubious of the way her daughters would view her return; but Queeney and the older girls—always proper and punctilious—soon called and were apparently friendly. Inwardly, however, Queeney had not forgiven her mother for marrying Piozzi, and thoroughly disapproved of her spectacular defiance of London opinion.

The first week was spent in receiving old friends and recent acquaintances, and in making plans for the future. A few of the Streatham coterie were still loyal—Dr. Lort, the Bishop of Peterborough, the banker Selwin—in contrast to Burke, Sir Joshua Reynolds, and others who refused to be cordial to the woman who had treated their friend so shabbily. As she feared, the Blue-Stockings made no move towards reconciliation, and the salons of Mrs. Montagu and her hangers-on were closed to the former Mrs. Thrale. One, and only one, of her former feminine friends seems to have rushed to greet her. Mrs.

[1] Hayward, i. 305.　　[2] *Queeney Letters*, p. 248; Sunday, Mar. 11, 1787.

Lewis, widow of the Dean of Ossory, came in from Reading with her daughter, then suddenly fell ill, and Mrs. Piozzi was forced to nurse an invalid instead of repaying calls.[1]

While some were cold and indifferent, others publicly showed their partiality. On the 17th Dr. Lort gave an entertainment in her honour, to which he asked a number of common friends.[2] Chappelow, the Greatheeds, and Parsons of her gay companions on the Continent eagerly welcomed her return and were just as friendly in England as they had been in Italy. These, combined with the staunch little remnant of her former coterie, made up the nucleus of a very agreeable group. Mrs. Piozzi had no reason to complain of lack of engagements.

Of chief importance was the selection of a suitable home. If she was to brave society, as she planned, her principal need was a large house in a fashionable district where she could entertain in a lavish manner. Streatham was still let, and besides a London house was much more to her purpose. After some search, a satisfactory one was found, and the *World* of March 27 announced: 'Mrs. *Piozzi* has taken a house in Hanover-square. Mrs. *Piozzi*, if not again admitted to the *Blue-Stockings*, will probably establish a similar meeting of her own. The intervals of Conversation to be relieved Music.' Although the house was secured in the first weeks after their return, Mrs. Piozzi was in no hurry to engage in any extensive entertainments, for she wished to decorate and furnish it first as sumptuously as possible, and this involved unpacking and arranging the paintings and works of art sent home from the Continent. Besides, it was desirable to find out the extent of the sentiment against her before risking any avoidable slights.

As might have been expected, the London newspapers hailed her arrival with their usual quips.[3] The *Morning Herald*

---

[1] See letters to Perkins, Apr. 24, 1787, and one undated a few days later. Mrs. Piozzi was forced to decline dining with Perkins in Southwark because she could not leave her sick friend.

[2] Hayward, i. 298.

[3] Even before her arrival the papers had been full of their usual incorrect prognostications. The *World*, Mar. 9, 1787, contained the paragraph:

Mrs. *Piozzi* brings with her the collection of *Sam Johnson's Letters* &c. in much readiness—the Little *Florence* Miscellany by herself, Mr. Greatheed, Sir Horace, and Mr. Piozzi, will probably be reprinted in London.—This will be no small curiosity;—yet, what will be much more curious, would be a publication of her travelling anecdotes and observations!

Nearly every point in this account is wrong, but it is possible that the last phrase may have suggested the later title for her travel book. Other references to Mrs. Piozzi appeared in the *World* for Mar. 8, 17, 22, 27. See also the *General Evening Post*, Mar. 20 and Apr. 7; *Public Advertiser*, Feb. 24, 1787, &c.

of March 17 commented: 'The lady's visit is highly seasonable at this time, as she may survey her learned friend *Dr. Johnson laid in state* by that grave *undertaker* Sir John Hawkins.' Hawkins's official biography was one book she probably found time to read in these first weeks in London, and she cannot have been well pleased. Aside from the naturally jealous reactions of a rival author, there were personal reasons which swayed her judgement, for Hawkins openly discussed the anguish stirred up in the heart of the dying Johnson by what he considered her ignominious marriage. Not very agreeable reading for the lady herself; not very pleasant to have memories of the past so spitefully resurrected.

Mrs. Piozzi was not alone in her distaste for Hawkins's work. The knight's heavy style and his fondness for long digressions were hardly likely to make his book popular. The general attitude may be inferred from a sentence in one of the papers: 'A gentleman, lately arrived in town, has been for several days past afflicted with a lethargy owing to the perusal of three chapters in Hawkins' *Life of Johnson*.'[1] Yet in spite of the almost complete disapprobation, the work is a very valuable one, since it represents the one contemporary biography written after a study of Dr. Johnson's private papers.

With the final appearance of the official edition of Johnson's works, there was nothing now to retard Mrs. Piozzi's own printing of his correspondence. Dr. Lort, writing to Thomas Percy of his entertainment for the Piozzis, added that she 'told me she had been that morning at the bank to get "Johnson's Correspondence" amongst other papers, which she means forthwith to commit to the press'.[2] No time was to be lost in beginning the work which had been her ostensible reason for returning to England. Actually Cadell had been one of the first visitors she had received at the Royal Hotel, and the newspapers printed an amusing fiction that upon his arrival she had failed to rise to greet him, being seated with one foot on Boswell's *Tour to the Hebrides* and the other on Hawkins's *Life*.[3] Cadell immediately offered her five hundred pounds for the right to publish Johnson's correspondence, which was at once accepted.[4] Furthermore, he urged immediate action

[1] From S. Lysons's scrap-book. See p. 124, n. 1. See also *World*, Mar. 22, 1788.
[2] Hayward, i. 298.
[3] *Morning Post*, Mar. 16, 1787.
[4] Mainwaring Piozziana, ii. 96. In Thraliana Oct. 26, 1787, she claimed that her bargain was for 500 guineas, with £50 additional should there be a second edition.

—to launch while the wave of Johnsonian interest was still at its crest. He emphasized that if the publication was to appear at all that year it was advisable it should be before the summer holidays. Mrs. Piozzi agreed, with the result that even before she was comfortably settled in her own house she was plunged into a frenzied attempt to get the material ready for the press.

Having been greatly pleased with the capable assistance of young Samuel Lysons at the time of the publication of her *Anecdotes*, she decided to ask his aid in the arrangement of the correspondence. Lysons, delighted to have his finger in such a controversial pie, eagerly accepted the proffered commission. Which of Johnson's letters to publish was the first important problem; some were too deficient in literary interest, some too short, some too much involved in business matters. Since the success of the venture depended upon the general interest of the public, it was necessary that these should be eliminated, and she welcomed a man's advice in making the choice. It seems evident that she practically constituted Lysons as final arbiter, with full power to select and throw out letters, after conferences with herself. She wrote to him at the beginning:

I enclose you some trifling Letters from Johnson—& some too melancholy for me to endure the reading of—they are on my dear Son's Death: if your Heart is as hard as that *Alexander's* we talk so much of in our Letters, *you* perhaps may like them. Write me word what you do with *my* Stuff, & pray take care to scratch Names out. Yours is a very serious Trust, & tho' you live to be Ld. Tetbury, you will never again have the heart of any one so completely in your hand to rummage every Sorrow out, as you now have that of your . . .[1]

In addition to selecting the letters to be used, it is evident that Lysons also helped to erase names from the manuscripts preparatory to publication. Present-day scholarly consciences are horrified at such a casual treatment of original sources, but this was the usual method of the time, and it would have been surprising had the letters been printed intact. The chief problem of an eighteenth-century editor was to know how much to delete rather than to produce an accurate text.[2]

Among the bundles of Johnson's letters examined by Cadell and Lysons was a packet of her replies. Their presence with

[1] See p. 236, n. 2.
[2] A discussion of the actual treatment of the text will be found in the next chapter.

her papers requires an explanation. During the long years of friendship with Mrs. Thrale Johnson had carefully saved many of her lively notes; and though he burned a number in the dark months following her second marriage, over a hundred escaped the flames and were found by his executors. According to custom, Sir Joshua Reynolds in 1785 had delivered the sealed parcel to Cator, who placed it with Mrs. Piozzi's other effects.[1] As soon as Cadell saw the package, he immediately insisted that some of her own letters should be included with those of her correspondent, having visions of a more varied and sensational production. Mrs. Piozzi, however, though naturally much pleased at the compliment, was doubtful how her notes would be received by the public. Yet another reason for including some of her own letters was the fact that those from Johnson were not sufficient to fill two octavo volumes. On second thought Mrs. Piozzi was convinced that somewhere she had more of the correspondence than had so far been discovered.

It comes in my head seeing these Letters from me dated Bath, that I must have a Heap from him some where which we have not yet looked over: When I have a quiet Moment I'll Search again— and then if we find enough of *his* mine may be excused.

Mrs. Piozzi had in her possession, she knew, all the letters written by Johnson to the Thrale household, with the exception of those directed to her eldest daughter. These last, amounting to over thirty, might provide just the additional number to fill out the volumes; however Queeney coldly refused to surrender them. Her mother visited her on March 24, but to no avail. Queeney deprecated the notoriety attending any literary enterprise, and remained wholly unsympathetic.[2]

Nevertheless, Mrs. Piozzi continued her search. On April 5, Holy Thursday, she wrote jubilantly to Lysons:

I have found about forty Letters of Johnson's in the old Trunk, which may *very well* be printed; some of them exceedingly long ones, and of the *best sort*. I read two or three to Mr. Cadell, & he liked them vastly, but will not abate of *mine*, and for the sake of his

---

[1] See letters from the banker C. Selwin to Mrs. Piozzi, Apr. 19, Aug. 30, 1785 (Ry. 556, 167, 168).

[2] *Queeney Letters*, p. 249. A draft of a letter to Queeney evidently never delivered. Mrs. Piozzi asked whether she should scratch out the name of Queeney or put in 'Miss T', in Johnson's letters. The *Morning Post*, Mar. 25, 1788, announced that Miss Thrale was in possession of letters 'from the Rambler, infinitely superior to those of her Mother . . . but *Miss Thrale* with a resolution that does honour to her delicacy, however unfortunate it may be for the Public, has declared that these *Testimonies of Confidence* shall never see the light'.

partiality I am now resolved to be patiently ty'd to the Stake, and if we can find six or seven tolerable ones for each Volume, he shall have them, but let me look them over *once again*. No need to *expunge* with Salt of Lemons all the Names I have cross'd—let the Initials stand; 'tis enough that I do not name them out; Civility is all I owe them, and my Attention not to offend is shewn by the Dash. The Preface is written, & when I get the Verses from Dr. Lort I will not be dilatory, for I have got a nice little Writing Room, and a very Gentlemanlike Man to deal with in Mr. Cadell.

In spite of her discovery, Cadell and Lysons were still discouraged over the lack of good material to fill two volumes of normal size. To print many of Johnson's shorter notes, largely concerned with intimate details of his own health and medical treatment, having doubtful literary or topical value, would tend to lessen public interest in the edition. And in the four hundred or more letters in Mrs. Piozzi's possession there were many of this type. For all that, she refused to be disheartened, and wrote again on the 12th:

Do not dispirit us, all will do very well; and we will have lines enough; I have a deal to tell you which I should not quite like to write. Come on Tuesday morning, do, at nine o'clock, and bring all the letters, and let us have a good sitting to them; wherever the names can carry displeasure, we will dash them. Miss Thrale refuses her assistance, but we will do without, and very well too.[1]

Just what Mrs. Piozzi had to tell Lysons which she dared not write, we may never know, but in the light of our present knowledge of the publication it is tempting to suppose that it was her proposal to revise and amplify those of her own letters to Johnson which she intended to print. While Lysons was busy with the editing, and Dr. Lort with the poetry, she was weighing carefully Cadell's wish to include some of her own answers. The originals of over a hundred were there in her hands. Why not reword some of them, correcting the grammar, and make them more interesting for the reading public? As far as she could see this procedure would injure no one, and might enhance her own reputation. Furthermore, it would provide an easy way to fill the forthcoming volumes. There can be little doubt that she succumbed to this temptation, and some time during the following months completely rewrote a number of her earlier letters. In some cases they were merely expanded, by rendering the style more literary and formal, while in others whole anecdotes and contemporary stories culled from Thraliana

---

[1] *Bentley's Misc.* xxviii (1850), 541. I have not seen the original of this letter.

were inserted to fill more space. It seems probable, in one instance, that several shorter notes were combined into one long one. Possibly when she began the elaboration nothing quite so drastic was intended, but as she proceeded, the desire to make a good impression became too strong to resist. It was common practice in that day to rewrite one's own letters before publication. It seems probable that Anna Seward completely revised all of hers, and Boswell himself could not withstand the temptation to edit certain passages in his letters to Johnson before printing them in the *Life*.[1]

Even in her own day some readers suspected what Mrs. Piozzi had done. Boswell intimated his distrust in the *Life*; and nineteenth-century editors were willing, for the most part, to follow suit.[2] Yet until recently there has been no definite evidence upon which to base this vague scepticism. Now, however, with the discovery of Mrs. Piozzi's private papers, the problem has been examined by Dr. R. W. Chapman and Dr. Moses Tyson, who have followed clues as devious and intricate as those of a detective thriller, but in the end have gathered a body of proof which is decisive. What follows is a short summary of their findings.[3]

In the John Rylands Collection there are approximately 134 letters, or autograph copies of letters, from Mrs. Thrale to Johnson.[4] Of these, twenty-eight represent the manuscript versions used by Cadell's printers. A careful comparison with the 106 unprinted letters leads to some interesting conclusions. In general, the two classes of manuscripts, the printed and the unprinted, differ both in style and in their actual physical appearance. The majority of those not published are fairly short and deal with personal, family, and business matters; about half show some address, about a quarter bear postmarks, and several have endorsements in Johnson's hand. On the other hand, the published versions are usually longer, in a more literary style; they abound in quotations, allusions, and disquisitions; only one of the twenty-eight bears a 'direction'; none have postmarks or notations in Johnson's hand. Nearly all begin high on the page, as compared with Mrs. Thrale's

---

[1] *Boswell's Letters*, i. 185–7; *Life*, ii. 144–5. Amusingly enough, some of the excised phrases referred to the Thrales.

[2] *Life*, iii. 421–3. Boswell inferred that the published versions had been re-written from a comparison with the style of the one original he had secured.

[3] The following discussion is based almost entirely on unpublished notes by Drs. Chapman and Tyson which they have very kindly placed at my disposal.

[4] Ry. 538–40.

usual practice of leaving some space at the top of her notes. Yet all this is not necessarily conclusive, for eighteenth-century letters, when franked, were often enclosed in a wrapper, so that the original might not preserve any address or postmark.[1] And with longer dispatches Mrs. Thrale would obviously begin higher on the sheet of paper.

Preparation of the manuscripts for the printers offers mixed evidence. Many names are reduced by erasure in a similar manner to that employed with Johnson's original letters, but in a number of cases, 'Mr ——' is so written, where the full name might have been expected.[2] Two of the letters make definite claims to be original. One begins, 'I can find no paper readily, but what is ruled for Children's use'; it is actually written on ruled paper. Another has a postscript (unpublished), 'Here is some confusion with the paper . . . but I stick it together with Thread'; the manuscript still retains some traces of having been sewed.[3]

Internal evidence is more revealing. In the letter written on ruled paper, of February 16, 1782, appears a story first recorded in Thraliana in March 1785 as one of a series picked up in Milan.[4] Another contains a passage resembling an entry in her diary made seven years later. In other cases the wording of a passage, or the implication of meaning, leads to the conviction that it was written by Mrs. Piozzi rather than Mrs. Thrale. Furthermore, an analysis of Johnson's correspondence from Scotland in 1773 would seem to indicate that her printed replies for this period are actually anthologies, made up possibly by combining a number of shorter notes into a longer, more finished production.

All this evidence is presumptive and might possibly be explained away. But a more decisive proof, which cannot by any stretch of the imagination be dismissed, comes from an examination of the paper. A classification and comparison of the watermarks of all the manuscript letters leaves little doubt that a large percentage of those published are late copies. The

---

[1] Most of Mrs. Thrale's letters from Southwark or Streatham to Fleet Street were probably sent by hand, and so would have no postmark. Those sent to a distant address were usually franked, and if heavy would probably be enclosed in a cover.

[2] Mrs. Piozzi may have made her revisions thinking only of improving the literary style, and afterwards excised the names from the copies before publication.

[3] Ry. 538, 25, 13. A possible suggestion might be that the use of the ruled paper and thread was merely a subterfuge to stop suspicion, but since only printer's compositors would see the evidence, this is difficult to believe.

[4] Ry. 538, 25; Thraliana, Mar. 1, 1785. Compare also Ry. 538, 15 and Thraliana, June 8, 1783.

paper does not agree with that used during the Thrale years, but is definitely that in use in 1787. Eight of the versions are written on the same paper as the first draft of the Preface for the edition of Johnson's letters; others compare exactly with miscellaneous scraps in her hand for notes to the volumes. To be sure, not all the twenty-eight published letters are re-visions. Four seem to be genuine originals, and a number of others may be.[1] The remainder, however, cannot be the actual versions read by Johnson. Mrs. Piozzi had not been able to withstand the temptation to augment her literary reputation at the expense of accuracy. Yet with all her careful planning to escape detection, all her devious shifts to fool Cadell's com-positors, she forgot one thing—the paper she was using.

Just what happened to the originals when the copies were made cannot be determined, but it seems probable that they were destroyed. In one instance, however, it appears that, whether by accident or by some mischievous trick of fortune, both the first letter and the later revision have survived.[2] Two versions written Good Friday night, April 18, 1783, contain the same information but differently worded; 'a Vomit' becomes 'an Emetic', and 'Vexations' is turned into 'Sorrows'. The second version is amplified to more than twice the length of the first, by describing her illnesses and cares in a more dis-cursive manner. Mrs. Piozzi undoubtedly had the general public in mind rather than Johnson when she prepared the copy to be printed.

Once the decision to rewrite her own side of the correspon-dence had been made, probably in April 1787, Mrs. Piozzi realized that she needed more time to complete the task.

[1] After examining and tabulating the various watermarks, I feel reasonably sure that the evidence is conclusive for at least half of the published versions. Two watermarks, 'PRO PATRIA', and 'C PATCH', appearing on fourteen letters, do not appear in any letter before 1787. One other, 'J W', appearing on four letters, possibly represents a completely new paper, since in that exact form it does not appear in any of the genuine Thrale letters. I would tentatively list the letters of July 17, 1770 (538, 3), May 1773 (538, 4), Friday (June 1773) (538, 6), and that of no date [July 13, 1775] (538, 13) as genuine originals. Those of Nov. 2, 1781 (538, 24), and Aug. 30, 1783 (538, 29) are merely suspicious. Those of Aug. 9, 1775 (538, 14), June 14, 1782 (538, 26), and June 30, 1784 (538, 32) may possibly be original.

[2] Ry. 538, 27; 540, 108. The unpublished version is postmarked, 'Ap. 21' and 'Bath', definitely directed to Johnson at Bolt Court, and is undoubtedly the letter actually sent. It contains about 130 words, while the published version has over 350. In one other instance the genuine letter may have been found. Mrs. Thrale's letter of Oct. 2, 1777 (see p. 155, Chap. VII) seems to be the first letter written after their arrival at Brighton, and would cast grave doubt on the printed letter of Oct. 1, 1777 (538, 17).

Moreover, Lysons, her conscientious co-editor, was still not satisfied with the amount of good material so far unearthed, and urged her to secure additional letters from Johnson to other people.[1] Both of them, therefore, willingly agreed to put off the publication until the next winter. About the 1st of May the work was temporarily laid aside, and Mrs. Piozzi was free to give thought to other matters.

In the first place, her business affairs needed attention. During the Piozzis' sojourn on the Continent Cator had acted as agent, collecting their income and forwarding enough for necessary expenses. Because of Piozzi's thrift the disbursements for their travel had been less than the receipts, so that in the two and a half years a considerable sum had accumulated with which to relieve the estate from debt. Consequently, early in May she was able to pay the mortgage assumed in 1782 to settle Lady Salusbury's claim, and she was amazed to learn that the money had not been borrowed from her daughters' inheritance as she had always understood.[2] This concealment, which necessarily engendered some suspicion of Cator's integrity, probably also suggested the advisability of a thorough investigation of her financial condition. The report later showed that the Piozzis, in addition to receiving income from landed property at Streatham, in Wales, and Oxfordshire, were possessed of a liquid capital of over £65,000 in the Funds.[3]

There was therefore no lack of money to finance her intended

---

[1] The editors sometimes could not make up their minds which letters to use, changes being made in two instances even after the sheets were printed. This involved later cancellation of sheet F in volume i, and sheet C in volume ii. Letters 300, 301, 302 were substituted for 285. 1, 286. 1, 289. 2 in volume i; and 576, 583 for 561. 1, 660. 1 in volume ii. Pages from the original cancelled sheets are bound up in Samuel Lysons's copy, now in the possession of Lord Harmsworth. The excised letters have been published in Broadley, pp. 111–15. Unfortunately it is impossible to tell just when these changes were made, but it was probably in the autumn of 1787.

[2] Mainwaring Piozziana, ii. 97. For the date of the meeting see Thraliana. The passage in Mainwaring Piozziana telling of what occurred, together with all paragraphs of a controversial nature referring to her daughters, has been crossed out, presumably at some later date. With care, however, the original entry can be deciphered under the erasures. See also p. 215, n. 3.

[3] Shortly after, Piozzi began to investigate the exact state of his finances. On January 26, 1788, J. Madison wrote from Charing Cross:

According to your Request I have examined the Books of the Transfer officers at the Bank respecting the £30,000, money which was to be invested in the Funds, and I find that that sum, has produced a Capital in the 3 P. cent. Consolidated Annuities of £51,865 ″ 1 ″ 8 ″ the half-yearly Dividend of which amounts to £777 ″ 19 ″ 6. (Ry. 601, 31.)

In addition there was £13,400 in the reduced funds, so that the Piozzis' liquid capital was well over £65,000.

assault on the stronghold of British society. While she realized that it would not be an easy conquest and would perhaps take a long time, by May 1 she began to feel reasonably sure of the result. She wrote in Thraliana:

> It was not wrong to come home after all, but very right. The Italians would have said we were afraid to face England, & the English would have said we were confined abroad in Prisons or Convents or Seraglios or some Stuff.[1]

Throughout April and May she had been gathering a group of friends, old and new, upon whom she might depend for support, and by the middle of May was confident enough to plan a spectacular entertainment as a test of strength. Dr. Lort, writing to Thomas Percy of the coming rout, commented: 'then will be seen who of her old acquaintance continue such.'[2] On the 18th the day arrived, and Mrs. Piozzi's first large public assembly proved a distinct success. In Thraliana the next day she made the entry:

> We had a very fine Assembly last Night indeed, in my best Days I never had finer; there were near a Hundred people in the Rooms which were besides much admired.

Several days later the *World* carried the statement that 'Mrs. Piozzi's assembly, the other night, was one of the fullest private meetings, this year has seen at any private house'.[3] Probably curiosity brought many of the guests, curiosity to see the notorious lady and her house, but many who came were connexions and acquaintances made during the recent years in Europe. Always adept at making friends, why should she despair if the old Streatham companions refused to reinstate her? She felt perfectly capable of gathering another circle about her, just as interesting and even more distinguished socially.

One disappointment rankled deeply—the absence of her daughters—who instead of accepting their mother's invitation insultingly drove by the door on their way to another affair.[4] The girls had decided to hold themselves aloof from her ostentatious hospitalities. They had done their duty in calling, but hesitated to risk their own social positions by any further

---

[1] At the same time Mrs. Piozzi noted what Cecilia confided to her that Mr. Smith, one of the guardians, had actually insisted the year before that her mother was locked up in Milan and fed on bread and water.

[2] Hayward, i. 299. The date should be May 13, 1787.

[3] May 25, 1787.

[4] Mainwaring Piozziana, ii. 97.

connexion. Mrs. Piozzi had ironically commented in Thraliana some weeks before:

As for seeing our Daughters why we never do see them here, any more than when the Sea parted us—or hardly. The eldest has called twice, and we have called twice on Susan & Sophy, who refused dining here at our Invitation; perhaps from an Idea that *they* are superior to the petty Sovereigns of Germany.[1]

Though the elder daughters resisted her authority, Cecilia, the youngest, was only ten years old, and legally still under her mother's control. Mrs. Piozzi was determined to assert this right, even if it meant a quarrel with Queeney, who during her mother's absence had constituted herself guardian of all the sisters. Cecilia was accordingly brought from school to become a member of the household in Hanover Square.[2]

Mrs. Piozzi's one pretentious assembly in the waning London season having proved reasonably successful, she set out in the middle of June 1787 with her husband and Count Martenengo, one of their continental friends, for Bath, where she found Mrs. Byron not completely estranged and many others openly glad to see her. Cecilia had been left in school at Streatham, but Queeney, seizing the opportunity to outwit her mother, removed her sister to London, where the child fell ill. When Mrs. Piozzi heard the news she was furious. Resentfully she wrote to Queeney on July 7:

If London however disagrees with her—why is She there? I left her in the Country at Mrs. Ray & Fry's School Streatham, where She enjoyed the Air of her *native Place*, and if you removed her thence, on pretence of Improvements which you now say are Trifling Matters at so early an Age—it will be found necessary perhaps some Day for you to produce your Authority for so doing. That I am her Mother & Guardian appears by her Father's Will, which expresses that no Marriage made by her while under Age shall be held legal if it has not my Consent: and it is no longer ago than last Month, that I was called with Mr. Piozzi to the Chambers of an Attorney to sign Settlements & Papers relative to her Fortune.

Mrs. Piozzi was not to be tricked out of her right to Cecilia. Feeling that having one daughter under her roof might be a partial sop to convention, she would allow nothing, not even her desire to be friendly with Queeney, to stand in the way. As it happened, the dispute resulted in so wide a rupture that

---

[1] Thraliana, Apr. 29, 1787.
[2] On Apr. 24 Mrs. Piozzi gave a children's party in their Hanover Square house especially for Cecilia. See letter to Lysons, Apr. 23, 1787.

there was no communication between the mother and her elder daughters for many years.

Queeney's attitude may be guessed from her correspondence with Fanny Burney. She angrily asserted that the little Cecilia would be corrupted by the insidious influence of her mother, an idea which shocked even the pliant Miss Burney, who wrote early the next year protesting that she could hardly see how Cecilia was irretrievably lost; the old scandal was now safely buried in the past, and there was no new stain to render Mrs. Piozzi a dangerous guardian.[1] But Queeney stubbornly refused to change her opinion, and Fanny was forced to write again:

> I have done, my dear Miss Thrale, compleatly done,—upon this unhappy subject you have now finished my interference. The word *corrupt* must silence me for-ever, unless I had the means with the wishes of washing it away, & obliterating the dreadful image it brings to view.—*Corrupt*, indeed, I did not think her![2]

All Fanny's objections only seemed to irritate the determined Queeney, who now accused her of wavering in her allegiance, and intimated that any further defence of the former Mrs. Thrale must necessarily end their intimacy. Fanny pathetically ended her letter: 'Favour me with an answer to this, my Dear Miss Thrale & let me not have the grief to find that in trying to unite Both, I have been able to retain neither?'

Irony of ironies! The author of *Evelina*, who had wished to act as mediator between Mrs. Piozzi and her daughter, was now considered a traitress by both. It is perhaps significant that in the correspondence of the former confidants there is a gap of five years after this letter. The uncompromising Miss Thrale would brook no disaffection. The tragic part of the affair was that Mrs. Piozzi never knew of this attempt of Fanny's to act as her advocate, and continued to consider all the Burneys as her bitter enemies.

Because of the news of Cecilia, the Piozzis were forced to return to London in July.[3] At Hanover Square on the 25th they celebrated their third wedding anniversary with the few friends who still remained in town. Shortly afterwards they set out again for the west of England, this time accompanied

---

[1] Lansdowne MS. Jan. 5, 1788.

[2] Ibid., Mar. 22, 1788. Fanny suggested that they come to a tacit compromise, and 'preserve for each other the good will so long held, that we mutually make allowances for the difference of our sentiments, & that we agree to maintain our friendship & regard, however we may dissent upon Her who first brought us together'.

[3] See letter to S. Lysons, July 17, 1787.

by Cecilia, whom Mrs. Piozzi would not risk leaving behind again.

For several weeks in August they visited the Greatheeds at Guy's Cliffe in Warwickshire. During their stay Greatheed read to his guests a poetic tragedy he had written, which made such an impression on Mrs. Piozzi that she urged him to take it to London to show to the managers. From Guy's Cliffe Mrs. Piozzi led her husband on to see Hagley, The Leasowes, and the other show places which had so pleased her in the past. By August 22 they had come to the Swan Inn in Lichfield, where she had stopped with Dr. Johnson in 1774.

Mrs. Piozzi's chief purpose in coming to Lichfield was to secure more of Dr. Johnson's letters to fill up the second volume of her proposed edition. Lysons had written on the 16th that the first volume was almost printed, but that without resorting to typographical devices of 'driving out' there was not enough left to fill a similar second volume.[1] He urged her 'to procure some of these Lichfield Letters'. Her first move, therefore, was to get in touch with all the old friends and acquaintances of the Doctor.

The belle of Lichfield's social and literary society was the sparkling but sarcastic Anna Seward. For various reasons Mrs. Piozzi and the so-called 'Swan of Lichfield' had never met, though each was anxious to sample the other's conversation. Their common friend Dr. Whalley had promised to write a formal introduction, but unfortunately he was dilatory, and the Piozzis arrived in Lichfield before the letter. Miss Seward was in a quandary: uncertain whether to break the laws of etiquette, or to lose the pleasure of the travellers' company. Fortunately her qualms were soon overcome, and at the insistence of several local friends she made the first move of welcome. As a result, the Piozzis spent the evening of August 22 at the Seward home, where a number of the local literati were invited to meet them.

In a later letter to Dr. Whalley, Anna Seward described some of the guests who that night had applauded Piozzi's singing and his wife's ready wit.[2] One was her cousin Henry White, who, she wrote, 'when perfectly awake from an intellectual torpor, which is apt to overcloud him, is very ingenious';

---

[1] Ry. 552, 13. Malone kept Boswell, who had himself been scouring the country for Johnsoniana, informed of his rival's search. See *Fettercairn Cat.*, No. 560.

[2] *Letters of Anna Seward* (1811), i. 335. This letter to Whalley is dated Oct. 6, 1787, but obviously must have been written late in August or early in September. For the question of the dates of Anna Seward's letters, see also p. xiv, n. 2.

another was Colonel Barry of Worcester, a successor of the unfortunate Major André both in his passion for Honora Sneyd and in his appointments in America. Ending her description, Miss Seward used the characteristic phrase, 'The evening was Attic'. The next day, Henry White, who had evidently dispersed the torpor which was 'apt to overcloud him', invited the Piozzis to his house, but they were forced to decline since they were engaged to drink tea in the forenoon with Mr. Peter Garrick. Instead they invited White to call upon them later at their inn.[1] Anna Seward, too, wishing to see more of the charming visitors, brought other friends to call, and the second evening was spent like the first with music and stimulating talk.

Piozzi, as a musician, made a great impression on Miss Seward. She confessed to Dr. Whalley that she had been 'charmed with his perfect expression on his instrument, and with the touching and ever-varying grace with which he sings'. 'Surely,' she continued, 'the finest sensibilities must vibrate through his frame, since they breathe so sweetly through his song, though his imperfect knowledge of our language prevents their appearing in conversation.' Writing to the poet Hayley, she repeated her eulogium:

Dr. Johnson told me truth when he said she had more colloquial wit than most of our literary women. It is indeed a fountain of perpetual flow;—but he did not tell me truth when he asserted that Piozzi was an ugly dog, without particular skill in his profession. Mr. Piozzi is an handsome man, in middle life, with gentle, pleasing, and unaffected manners, and with very eminent skill in his profession.[2]

It must be admitted that Anna Seward is not an unbiased witness, wholly to be believed, when writing about Dr. Johnson or his friends. Her rapturous descriptions of Piozzi may have been written more to prove Johnson wrong than to express her true feelings. One thing, however, is certain; the two literary ladies were much pleased with each other, and their letters during the next year are full of reciprocal compliments.

Mrs. Piozzi's reason for visiting Lichfield had not been

---

[1] Mrs. Piozzi to Henry White, Thursday, Aug. 23. Original at Dr. Johnson's Birthplace, Lichfield. See *Life*, iv. 372, for references to White.

[2] Op. cit. i. 339–40. This letter, like that to Dr. Whalley, is obviously misdated and probably rewritten. The wording, therefore, may not be exact. See also i. 391, where Miss Seward, in writing to Helen Maria Williams, insisted, 'There has been no exaggeration, there could be none, in the description given you of Mrs. Piozzi's talents for conversation.'

merely to make the acquaintance of the local literati. As we have seen, she was searching for relics of Johnson, and despite the fact that Boswell had long before secured copies of many letters here, she found there were still more to be culled. Anna Seward, too, proved an able ally, for she was indifferent to Boswell and was willing to help one of his rivals. The principal quarry described by Miss Seward was a series of letters written by Johnson to Miss Hill Boothby in the years 1755 to 1756, which Boswell had been promised, but which, as far as was known, he had not yet secured. Here was a splendid opportunity to get ahead of her adversary, and Mrs. Piozzi gladly welcomed Miss Seward's offer to apply to Sir Brooke Boothby for permission to transcribe the letters written to his sister. Solicitation of other old friends of Dr. Johnson did not prove very successful; Mrs. Cobb and Miss Adey were away on a visit, and all that could be done was to leave messages asking their aid in the coming edition.

From Lichfield the Piozzis drove through Ashbourne on their way to Buxton and Wales. She called on Dr. Taylor at the Mansion, where she was surprised to find that the Boothby letters had been deposited with him. Here, too, she saw other papers written by Johnson, but Dr. Taylor was in no mood to part with any of his treasures.[1] As she reported to Lysons, shortly afterwards, 'promises and anecdotes picked up at Lichfield and Ashbourne' were all that she had to show for her effort 'to swell Cadell's second volume for him, with matters less trifling than familiar nonsense scribbled by myself a dozen years ago'. But there was still hope in the promises.

After a few days in Buxton, viewing the new buildings with their friend Parsons, they passed on to Manchester, where Mrs. Piozzi wrote to Lysons a summary of their plans for the next few weeks: 'we are going on to Liverpool, Chester, Flint, Denbigh, and dear Bachygraig; then back through Wrexham, Shrewsbury, &c., to Warwickshire again—and then to town, where all shall be settled for our spring publication.'[2]

One of the great disappointments of her life had been the lack of appreciation of Welsh scenery displayed by her first husband and Dr. Johnson in 1774. To an ardent Welshwoman any slight to her country was regarded as directed against herself. What, then, was her joy to find Piozzi delighted with Wales, especially with the Vale of Clwyd, which he maintained resembled his beloved Lombardy more than any other portion

[1] Ry. 559, 7. To Chappelow, Oct. 18, 1787.   [2] Sept. 9, 1787.

GABRIEL PIOZZI
Artist unknown
Now in the Hyde Collection

of the island he had seen. As a result, she eagerly showed him the haunts of her childhood, the ruins and fine country houses near by, and introduced him to the agents in charge of her Flintshire properties. He had shared his country with her; now she would do the same with hers.

On the way back to Warwickshire Piozzi was taken very ill at Shrewsbury, which forced them to drive the remainder of the distance to Guy's Cliffe in a day. Because of his fever they had to remain at the Greatheeds' longer than they had planned, and while there Mrs. Piozzi wrote an epilogue for her host's tragedy. This poetic drama, later produced as *The Regent*, was the topic of the hour at Guy's Cliffe, and almost as much so in London, where they also saw much of each other the second week in October. As Mrs. Piozzi commented to Chappelow on October 9, the day after their arrival:

> I have much to say about literary stuff, & no body in Town to talk to except dear Mr. Greatheed, whose Head is full of his own new Tragedy, which will fill every body's Mouth too when it once appears.

In order to advance the interests of the play Mrs. Piozzi shortly afterwards gave a dinner for the Greatheeds and Mrs. Siddons, but warned Chappelow that not a word must be breathed of her schemes until something definite had been decided.

If she found London in October barren of acquaintances with whom to discuss her literary problems, she had been regaining some of her old friends. In July, seeing Arthur Murphy one day in a shop, she stopped her carriage to upbraid him for not coming to call.[1] Murphy gladly accepted an invitation to dine, and for the rest of his life he was a constant member of her intimate circle, one representative of the early days at Streatham. Step by step Mrs. Piozzi was rebuilding her lost friendships.

Throughout October the Piozzis remained in Hanover Square, but not from choice. It was her Johnsonian editing for Cadell which kept her in the deserted city. Even if the summer tour apparently had not gleaned much new material for the second volume, it was not wholly unproductive. Anna Seward wrote long effusive letters and busily made good her promise to secure the Johnson–Boothby correspondence.[2] In

---

[1] *Nichols' Illustrations*, vii. 771. To Bishop Percy from T. Campbell, Clones, Oct. 25, 1787. Campbell apologized for not knowing Mrs. Piozzi was in London until just before he left. See also *Dr. Campbell's Diary* (1947), p. 99.

[2] Ry. 565. For a more detailed account see my article, *J. Rylands Bulletin*, xx. (1936), 278–80.

this instance, indeed, she was indefatigable. At first Sir Brooke Boothby had qualms about allowing the letters to be published, and insisted, possibly as he thought to end the matter, that his son, who was in Paris, must give permission before anything was done. In reply Miss Seward urged that 'Mr. Boothby's offer to permit my copying those in question for Mr. Boswell' made it unnecessary to wait for his consent to give them to Mrs. Piozzi. But Sir Brooke remaining adamant, a letter was immediately dispatched to the son in Paris. Yet even when, after a long delay, a favourable reply was received from France, the problem was not solved, for the Boothbys and Dr. Taylor, who had the letters in his possession, had quarrelled over a local matter and were not on speaking terms. 'The Swan', however, was equal to any task, and on October 13 the choleric Dr. Taylor wrote to Mrs. Piozzi that he had sent the letters 'at Miss Sewards Request, by Mr. Boothby's Direction'.[1]

Although he had grudgingly complied, Dr. Taylor was not pleased to be of service in bringing to public notice his old friend's letters, and urged that Mrs. Piozzi change her resolution to print the correspondence.

Dr. Johnson's Mental Powers and extreme good Heart, all men very well know, and his Enemies acknowledge; but I shall be greatly grieved to see the ridiculous Vanities and fulsome Weakness's which he always betray'd in his conversation and Address with his amiable female friends, exposed . . .

It was not exactly an appeal which could have carried much weight with one of Johnson's 'amiable female friends' herself. Mrs. Piozzi, instead, eagerly snatched at the short series of letters to swell her volumes, and in addition welcomed an epitaph on his aunt which the young Boothby sent from Paris.[2]

The Lichfield visit brought one other addition when Miss Mary Adey wrote enclosing a copy of Johnson's letter to her cousin Joseph Simpson. With ingenuous candour she admitted that since Boswell had been given a transcript some time before, she could see no reason for withholding a copy from his rival.[3] This acquisition, too, was welcomed by Mrs. Piozzi, despite the opinion of Dr. Lort that it would be better for Dr. Johnson's reputation if it were consigned to the flames.[4] All she could

---

[1] Ry. 892, 13.
[2] Ry. 892.
[3] Ry. 892; and *J. Rylands Bulletin*, op. cit., 280–2.
[4] Ry. 892. In his letter of Nov. 16 Dr. Lort called Johnson's reasoning in the Simpson letter 'idle and sophistical'. See also *Letters*, No. 134; *Life*, i. 346–7.

think of now was the problem of filling the extra pages of the second volume.

One obvious recourse was to write down a number of new anecdotes about Johnson which she had picked up on her travels.[1] Another was the old idea of enlarging her own letters. Writing to Chappelow on October 18 of Greatheed's tragedy, she added: 'I had more need be thinking of *my own* Stuff, & beg Mercy for those Letters of Mrs. *Thrale's* which are mingled among Dr. Johnson's. Oh do come & help them along a little for the Regard you kindly bear to Mrs. Piozzi.' Just how Chappelow could help her, if she was merely to send the originals to the printer, does not appear; but the request gives added evidence of her revision.[2]

It was not until early in November that, leaving the finished copy in Cadell's hands, the Piozzis were able to drive to Bath. Here Mrs. Piozzi tried to escape from the problems of her literary venture, and except for occasional disturbing messages, referring to vain solicitations of Barnard the King's librarian, she was content for the time to forget her work. As she commented to Lysons from Alfred Street on November 17:

> With regard to my own Book if no one thinks more about it than I have done since I saw you, Woe betide Cadell! if anybody has *stolen* a Letter of mine, they will add little to their Guilt, tho' much to their Shame by publishing it.

Lysons had possibly stumbled on the trail of the one note from Mrs. Thrale to Johnson which Boswell later printed in the *Life*. But how Boswell secured it—Mrs. Piozzi later made the charge that he had bought it from Francis Barber for half a crown—we may never know.[3]

In Bath many of Mrs. Piozzi's old friends were gradually won over to accept her new husband. So on January 1, 1788, she wrote in Thraliana of the capitulation of several of the quasi-Blues: Mrs. Byron was gradually converted by Piozzi's assiduity, and Mrs. Lambart told everybody she was in love

---

[1] See *Letters* (1788), ii. 378–90.

[2] See also pp. 298–301. A comparison of watermarks of the paper leads to the assumption that Mrs. Piozzi at this time rewrote a number of her letters. The paper used in other correspondence, and in the miscellaneous anecdotes of Johnson written down as a result of her trip to Lichfield and Ashbourne, is the same as that of more than ten of the revised letters to Johnson. It is almost possible to tell exactly which letters were rewritten in the spring and which in the autumn.

[3] *Life*, iii. 421–3. Dr. L. F. Powell, pp. 536–7, prints Mrs. Piozzi's marginal note:

> This is the famous letter with which Boswell threatened us all so; He bought it of Francis the Black for half a crown to have a little Teizing in his Power.

with him. In addition there were always new acquaintances to fill the gaps, this time chiefly Harriet Lee and her sister, Sophia, later authors of the *Canterbury Tales*.

On January 2 the Piozzis left for London. On the way, while visiting Mrs. Lewis at Reading, Mrs. Piozzi was seriously ill and suffered a miscarriage.[1] Such an end to her last attempt at child-bearing was a bitter disappointment, for if there was anything in the world which she wanted passionately, it was a child by Piozzi to inherit her Welsh estate. Her husband, however, seems to have accepted her misfortune philosophically. Perhaps he had never really expected a son of his own from a wife almost forty-seven years old. At any rate he refused to be dejected over his loss, and comforted his wife as best he could. She was not so easily consoled, but business in London left her little time for vain regrets.

She was plunged immediately into last-minute conferences with Lysons and Cadell, combined with steady correction of proof. On the last day of January she hurriedly wrote to Lysons:

> I recollect a gross Mistake in the printed Sheet you show'd me this Morning—it was in a Letter of my own from Bath, in which *Torquato Tasso* is mention'd, and the Reply he made to one who asked him what use he made of his Philosophy.
>
> Do me the favour to let me have that sheet again . . .[2]

Since this was one of her recent revisions, it was necessary to be particularly careful.

Search for additional letters from Johnson finally resulted in securing one written to Miss Cotterell in 1755, and five to Francesco Sastres during the closing months of 1784. Possibly for this reason it was decided to omit all her own translations from Boethius, except those in which she had collaborated with Johnson by producing alternate verses.[3] This sacrifice must have cost her many a pang, but she was forced to bow to the superior judgement of her scholarly friends, who probably felt that the public was only interested in the compositions of the Doctor, and not in those of the former Mrs. Thrale. Even the announcement that the publication would contain both sides of the correspondence brought forth some unfavourable criticism. It was probably to answer this that the *World* of February 22 carried the notice that 'Mrs. Piozzi's Work is to

---

[1] Mainwaring Piozziana, ii. 99; Thraliana, Jan. 7, 1788.
[2] For reference to Tasso see *Letters* (1788), ii. 254.
[3] Sheet Ee of volume ii was cancelled and the poetical excerpts rearranged. See p. 302, n. 1.

contain but very few Letters, which are not Dr. Johnson's, and those only 'needed to illustrate each reply'.

Occasional references in the London newspapers throughout January and February 1788 kept the public in an expectant mood.[1] Naturally the most curious of all was Boswell. He could not refrain from indulging in a little detective work of his own, and wrote to Thomas Percy from London on February 9:

> Mrs. (Thrale) Piozzi's collection of his letters will be out soon, and will be a rich addition to the Johnsonian memorabilia. I saw a sheet at the printing-house yesterday, and observed Letter cccxxx, so that we may expect much entertainment. It is wonderful what avidity there still is for every thing relative to Johnson.[2]

Although the sheets were probably all ready early in February, it was decided to withhold publication for a few weeks. Just at the moment the sensational trial of Warren Hastings was overshadowing any literary production; nothing else could hope to compete with it as a topic of conversation. The *World* of March 3 explained that 'amongst other effects of the Trial, it has delayed the publication of Mrs. Piozzi's Letters—nobody had then time to read'.

Finally, early in March 1788, the two volumes of letters appeared, and Mrs. Piozzi was again the centre of acrimonious controversy.

---

[1] For example: *Morning Post*, Jan. 21, Feb. 29, 1788. The *World* published several poems by Mrs. Piozzi: 'Enigma' on Feb. 5 and 'On an Air Baloon', on Feb. 11.
[2] *Boswell's Letters*, ii. 340.

XV

JOHNSON'S LETTERS

1788

LETTERS to and from the Late Samuel Johnson, LL.D. appeared on Saturday, March 8, 1788.[1] At first the sale was fairly rapid, but since Cadell had printed 2,000 copies of the first edition, there was no immediate shortage, as had been the case with the *Anecdotes*.

As usual, the newspapers were filled with quotations and comments, being divided as to the propriety of publishing anecdotes and letters of the great man. The *Morning Post* for March 10 and 12, while including excerpts from Mrs. Piozzi's Preface and from some of Johnson's letters, was unfavourably critical both of the subject-matter of much of the correspondence and of the value of the poetry.[2] On the 14th the same paper returned to the attack. 'Mrs. Piozzi', it pointed out, 'has converted her private epistles into hard *cash*; so that every letter sent her by Dr. Johnson had a *double value*—the *value* of *informing*, and the value of a *bank note*.' The same censure was aimed at the editor; that she had '*heaped up* every thing that could tend to *expose the weaknesses* of her *old friend*', for the sole purpose of attaining notoriety by her connexion with such a famous figure.

Although the *Morning Post* was hostile, the *World* was decidedly complimentary. For once in her life a newspaper defended Mrs. Piozzi in the literary and social quarrels of the day. Charles Este, editor of the *World*, was himself a member of the London group in which she moved, and his newspaper was filled with gossip about his friends and acquaintances. Mrs. Piozzi's plans had therefore been heralded from the first by the *World*, and the edition received a laudatory review.[3]

---

[1] *Morning Post*, Mar. 8, 1788, and other newspapers of the same date. It was sold at 12s. in boards. See also Thraliana. There was no second edition, possibly because of the appearance immediately of a Dublin edition, and the inclusion of many of the letters in the 1792 issue of Johnson's works.

[2] On the 12th the *Post* maintained that the letters of Johnson formed 'a salmagundy composed of *bulls, cows, calves, cats* and *Mr. Piozzi*'.

[3] *World*, Mar. 11, 1788.

In addition to heaping high praise on the Preface, Este declared that Mrs. Piozzi's own letters and poems compared favourably with those of Johnson. He even claimed that in the Boethius excerpts which they translated together some of her lines were superior. Of Johnson's letters Este later wrote 'that they are such as the frivolous will think frivolous—and the wise know to be wise—while the good universally, will feel that they are good'.[1]

Reviewers in the monthly magazines were also divided in their opinion. Many people felt that printing an account of Johnson's everyday affairs was of no literary value, and the *European Magazine* actually went so far as to question whether the 'epistolary correspondence of any man be a fit subject for publication'.[2] The *Gentleman's Magazine*, however, refused to agree:

We cannot say that we think there is any thing unjustifiable, as some seem to imagine, in such a publication as this. Johnson himself would have answered those who think it unjustifiable, in some such way as this, perhaps:

'No, sir; I cannot see any harm in the business. Do the Letters deduct from the man's good fame? Do they prove him to be in any respect less a man of virtue, or more a fool? No sir. Then where is the harm? He has written to women as wise men write when they write to women; and he has written to children as wise men write when they write to children.

'Sir, a laurel has its small branches as well as its large ones. Sir, when you come to be a great man, you will know that such trifles as these go to make up a great man's fame . . .'[3]

The *Gentleman's Magazine* added, in referring to Mrs. Piozzi's Preface, that it was 'elegantly characteristic and female'.

The *English Review* for May praised the volumes in no uncertain terms.

In this publication the republic of letters has received a valuable present, conveyed to them by the hands of a lady to whose genius, discrimination, and fertility of composition they have already been considerably indebted. Such, however, is the ingratitude, and such the caprice, of the readers of literary publications, that Mrs Piozzi has incurred from many a considerable degree of sarcasm and censure for a conduct that has merited nothing but applause.[4]

---

[1] Ibid., Mar. 18, 1788. This article points out how few errata could be found in the two volumes, in contrast to Lord Lyttelton's nineteen pages of errors prefixed to his history. (Actually 7 changes are listed on the errata slip, 4 in vol. i. and 3 in vol. ii.) [2] *European Mag.* xiii (1788), 165.
[3] *Gent. Mag.* lviii (1788), 233. [4] *English Review*, xi (1788), 352.

The writer compared the letters with those of Swift to Stella, though admitting that they were not so interesting because of the nature of the subject-matter. Insisting that Mrs. Piozzi was not to be blamed for her break with Johnson, he only lamented that 'mutual talents' and understanding had not been sufficient to ensure the happiness of the two intimate friends.

Arthur Murphy, writing in the *Monthly Review*, pointed out that in his private letters to Mrs. Thrale the public could see the human Johnson, the Johnson of everyday life, and that such a picture did not detract from his greatness. 'We see him in his undress,' Murphy asserted, 'that is, the undress of his mind, which, unlike that of the body, was never slovenly.'[1]

In the literary society of London Johnson's letters became the subject for continued discussion. Hannah More wrote: 'They are such Letters as ought to have been *written*, but ought never to have been *printed*', and quoted Burke as saying to her, in allusion to the many books and anecdotes written about Dr. Johnson, 'How many maggots have crawled out of that great body!'[2] Yet Walpole thought better of Johnson after reading his letters, and Cowper was pleased with the epistolary style.[3]

Despite the fact that many readers blamed Mrs. Piozzi for publishing the private letters of her old friend, some were forced to admit that the work decidedly increased her reputation. Fanny Burney wrote to Queeney: 'I see Her, however, rising from their Contents,—she is more admired, & meets with greater allowances, from these undoubted proofs how well she stood with so great & good a man.'[4] After the storm of abuse of the past few years, strangers were startled to find a Mrs. Thrale quite different from what they had imagined.

Fanny Burney at Windsor had seen a copy of the first volume in January, and thus was able to record her reactions and those of the Royal Family before the edition actually appeared. As might have been expected, Fanny's sensibilities were offended,

---

[1] *Monthly Review*, lxxviii (1788), 326. For identification see B. Nangle, *Monthly Review* (1934).

[2] H. More, *Memoirs*, ii. 100–1.

[3] *Life*, iv. 314; *Corr. of William Cowper*, ed. T. Wright (1904), iii. 295. Thomas Green made the entry in his diary, Jan. 17, 1805, 'Finished *Johnson's* Letters to Mr. [*sic*] Thrale. They raise him, if possible, still higher than ever in my esteem and veneration.' (*Gent. Mag.* i. (new ser.) (1834), 472.)

[4] Jan. 5, 1788 (Lansdowne MS.). Fanny wrote while the first volume was being perused by the royal family at Windsor. Characteristically she insisted that she 'must grieve at the whole of such a publication, sacred as I hold all letters, *written* or *received*, by those still living'. On the whole, however, she found the publication 'less generally injudicious than I had feared'.

but her chief objection was that she felt sure the letters had been published complete, not judiciously pruned in accordance with the accepted procedure of the time.[1] This attitude comes as a distinct shock to us to-day, since one of the most valid criticisms recently levelled at Mrs. Piozzi has been her mutilation of a few of Johnson's letters. While the twentieth century deplores her excision of the slightest word or phrase, the eighteenth generally felt she had allowed too much to be exposed to public scrutiny. It is thus important for us to consider carefully Mrs. Piozzi's actual treatment of the text. How did she prepare Johnson's correspondence for publication?

It was the practice in the eighteenth century, when publishing private correspondence, to send the original letters directly to the printer. Mrs. Piozzi followed this procedure, and as Dr. R. W. Chapman has pointed out, it was fortunate that she did so, for the printers probably made fewer mistakes in reading Johnson's difficult hand than any copyist she might have employed.[2] But in sending the actual letters to the printer it was necessary to mark and deface the originals to indicate the editor's wish for minor excisions or changes in the text. An examination of a large number of letters which have survived shows them marked in various ways. Printers' numbers appear, as do brackets and other marks inserted by the compositors. The formal conclusions of the letters are struck off with red ink, and reduced to a simple '&c'. Personal names are often crossed out with a simple stroke of the pen, or reduced to a single initial, and even in many cases completely eradicated by the use of a knife or lemon and salt. In some cases, in addition to inking out the name, Mrs. Piozzi or Lysons pasted over the erasure an additional scrap of paper. The varied methods used in dealing with the proper names probably depended upon how anxious Mrs. Piozzi was to keep secret

---

[1] *D'Arblay Diary,* iii. 366. Fanny wrote on Jan. 9: 'She has given all—every word—and thinks that, perhaps, a justice to Dr. Johnson, which, in fact, is the greatest injury to his memory.' Mrs. Piozzi evidently herself thought that she had been particularly circumspect in her treatment of Johnson's letters. Many years later, in Piozziana, iv. 73, she wrote of Anna Seward's correspondence:

> Her keeping Copies too of her own Letters! how astonishing! Copies of one's own Letters! She might well complain for want of *Time* when she wrote every Trifle so—Twice over.—Mr. Samuel Lysons could have informed her how little I weeded Doctor Johnson's correspondence—and how certain it was, that had not *he* preserved my Letters, they would not ever have been seen by Lysons or Cadell.

[2] *Johnson, Boswell and Mrs. Piozzi—A Suppressed Passage Restored* (Oxford, 1929); see also R. W. Chapman, *R.E.S.* xiii, No. 50 (1937), 139–76. I am indebted to Dr. Chapman for personal help in the following discussion of Johnson's letters.

the identity of the person mentioned, not only from the general public, but from the compositors and printers themselves. She may have suspected that Cadell's workmen were not above regaling their acquaintances with choice quotations from these letters. At any rate her suspicions led her to deface many references so thoroughly that it is impossible even with the most modern scientific aids to decipher what Johnson originally wrote.

In addition to removing proper names from the text, whole sentences and paragraphs are occasionally omitted. Usually, when this was done, the paragraph in question was merely crossed through with a red line, but on at least one occasion the entire passage was blocked out, covered with a blank white sheet, and another paragraph cut from a different letter superimposed on this.[1] For the most part, the passages marked to be omitted from the printed text had to do with either health or business.[2] They contained remarks which Mrs. Piozzi felt it would be inadvisable to print at the time, either because the reference was of a private nature or because it contained business information which involved the brewery. Examples may be found in the paragraphs referring to the fatal illness of Mrs. Salusbury in Johnson's letters of June 25, 1771, and April 2, 1773; and the comments on the price of malt and the probable profits of the brewery in that of October 29, 1777.[3]

If many of the passages which Mrs. Piozzi excised from the printed text of Johnson's letters are of little interest even to-day, at least one is of great importance. This is the paragraph discovered by Dr. R. W. Chapman in Johnson's letter of June 19, 1775, praising Boswell's *Hebridean Journal*, and calling Boswell himself 'a very fine fellow'.[4] When Mrs. Piozzi came to this passage in 1787 she must have been in a quandary, since the remarks of Johnson in 1775 not only indicated that she had had the journal in her possession at the time, but also clearly put Johnson's absolute stamp of approval on the contents. Although she might not have wished to print this high commendation of her rival under any circumstances, it was out of the question after the quarrel of the year before over Mrs. Montagu's *Essay on Shakespeare*. Boswell had defended his

[1] R. W. Chapman, op. cit.
[2] It has been obviously impossible for me to examine all of the original letters, and this generalization is made from the large number actually seen. See also p. 94, n. 2.
[3] Originals at Dr. Johnson's Birthplace, Lichfield.
[4] See p. 317, n. 2.

revelation of Johnson's and Mrs. Thrale's adverse opinion of Mrs. Montagu's *Essay* by pointing out that both of them had read through his journal and had not objected to any part of it. To publish a passage so completely proving her rival's contention would have been humiliating. So, possibly with Lysons's approval, the paragraph was obliterated, and a quotation neatly clipped from another letter was pasted over the blank space. In this way she felt sure no one would ever be able to read the sentences which would have stirred up another whirlwind in the Blue-Stocking ranks.

The combination of *naïveté* and guile shown by Mrs. Piozzi in her treatment of Johnson's letters was very characteristic. Torn between the desire to publish the correspondence exactly as it had been written, and the determination not to allow certain of her friend's opinions to become known, she adopted a compromise. Except for the excisions of whole sentences and paragraphs, she did not tamper materially with what Johnson had written. She may, on rare occasions, have added a missing article or a small word the absence of which obviously rendered the sense incomplete;[1] but in general the letters were printed in the proper order and with only the few omissions which she felt to be imperative. In contrast with the ruthless editorial methods employed by Mason, who cut and reassembled Gray's correspondence with little regard for chronology or facts, or those of Lockhart in his *Life of Scott*, her changes seem venial and unimportant. Even if she did not have Boswell's ardour for an accurate text, Mrs. Piozzi's long association with Johnson had imbued her with some feeling for order and exactness.

The reception of Mrs. Piozzi's own revised letters, which were printed with those of Dr. Johnson, was on the whole favourable. A few bitter enemies suspected they were fabrications, and others, like Hannah More, found it 'odd to print one's own letters while one is alive and merry'; but Miss More herself thought them 'good sprightly letters', and most readers accepted them as typical examples of Blue-Stocking art.[2] Mrs. Montagu, though objecting to an occasional vulgarity of style, admitted that she had been amused by Mrs. Thrale's letters. 'She writes like a Woman of parts', continued Mrs. Montagu; 'her accounts of things are lively and clever, and her observations often very ingenious and sensible.'[3]

---

[1] In several of the originals in the Adam collection I have noted one or two words seemingly introduced into the text to supply deficiencies.
[2] H. More, *Memoirs*, ii. 101.   [3] R. Blunt, *Mrs. Montagu*, ii. 278.

Two letters in particular were usually singled out for praise: the one addressed to Jack Rice in 1773 after his marriage to Fanny Plumbe, and the one of June 24, 1775, describing the regatta on the Thames. The former, usually called 'Advice to a new Married Man', was often reprinted. It first appeared in the *European Magazine* for April 1788, then in the *Annual Register* for the same year, and later in a number of collections of sample letters published in England and America.[1] The regatta letter was highly complimented in the *World*,[2] and generally held in esteem by Mrs. Piozzi's own personal friends. Watermark evidence would seem to indicate that the letter to Rice had not been tampered with, but that the description of the regatta had either been rewritten from memory or was a late revision of an earlier note.[3]

Although Boswell had caught a glimpse of some sheets at the printer's in February, he did not have an opportunity to read the entire edition until the day before publication. Then on March 7, when his good friend Dilly sent him the volumes, he hurriedly scanned the whole series of letters. His immediate reaction was one of personal disillusionment.

I was disappointed a good deal, both in finding less able and brilliant writing than I expected, and in having a proof of his fawning on a woman whom he did not esteem, because he had luxurious living in her husband's house; and in order that this fawning might not be counteracted, treating me and other friends much more lightly than we had reason to expect. This publication *cooled* my warmth of enthusiasm for 'my illustrious friend' a good deal. I felt myself degraded from the consequence of an ancient Baron to the state of an humble attendant on an Authour; and what vexed me, thought that my collecting so much of his conversation had made the World shun me as a dangerous companion.[4]

Obviously what irritated Boswell most was the fact that his name rarely appeared in the long series of letters. The warmth of expression used by his hero in writing to his dear 'Mistress' at Streatham appeared in too great and obvious contrast to the few casual references to his friend Boswell. Yet two days later, after a talk with Courtenay and Malone, who both thought highly of the letters, he was willing to admit that upon looking at some of them again 'they improved upon me'. The next

---

[1] *European Mag.* xiii (1788), 282–4; *Annual Register* (1788), Essays, pp. 149–51; *A Series of Letters on Courtship, etc.* (Elizabeth-Town, printed by S. Kollock, 1796).

[2] *World*, Apr. 18, 1788.

[3] See pp. 298–301. The Regatta letter is written on 'Pro Patria' paper.

[4] *Private Papers*, xvii. 74–5. For following references see also pp. 76, 80, 83–4, 93.

Saturday he wrote that he and Langton joined in thinking that
Johnson 'appeared to disadvantage, as shewing a studied
shunning to speak of the friends whom he valued most, in
terms such as to make her at all jealous of them. This was a
stooping in the high mind of Johnson'.

Boswell was genuinely upset, and his friend Wilkes only
made matters worse by seeming 'to take a mischievous pleasure
in pointing out how often Johnson had written slightingly of me
to Mrs. Thrale'. As a result, his zeal for the *magnum opus* considerably flagged during the last weeks of March. Why should
he give his life to perpetuate the fame of a man who had been so
two-faced? Then suddenly the dejection disappeared as if by
magic. Boswell had a long talk with Lysons, with whose aid
he 'filled up a great many of the blanks in Dr. Johnson's *Letters
to Mrs. Piozzi*'. After this conversation there were no further
complaints, for Lysons had evidently let slip some remarks
about the censorship employed in certain letters. Not knowing
exactly what had been excised from the correspondence,
Boswell naturally assumed it had been complimentary references to himself. Here was the explanation of the Doctor's
seeming neglect. Consequently Johnson was again in the ascen-
dancy, but his quondam friend Mrs. Thrale was now marked
out for complete destruction.

Boswell, nevertheless, was not ready for immediate revenge;
the full force of his anger was only to find release in his great
Life of Johnson. In the meantime he would merely annoy the
lady with various anonymous attacks. Possibly brooding over
various methods of retaliation, he finally decided to publish a
humorous *jeu d'esprit* written seven years before. This was
Johnson's supposed nuptial ode to Mrs. Thrale, which had
been dashed off only a few days after Thrale's death, and which
Wilkes had once threatened to show to Johnson himself.
Originally only intended to be passed around among Boswell's
personal friends, it should now, he determined, have a wider
and more varied audience. On May 9 he was hobbling about
on a sprained ankle, arranging for the anonymous publication
of the verses.[1] Highly amusing, though indelicate and in
execrable taste, the ode probably did not have an extensive circulation. It served merely as a temporary release

---

[1] Ibid. 109. *Ode by Dr. Samuel Johnson to Mrs. Thrale, upon their supposed approaching Nuptials* (London, Printed for R. Faulder, 1784). (The pamphlet obviously
was predated.) See also F. A. Pottle, *Literary Career of James Boswell* (1929), pp. 131,
295, 311; the *Monthly Review*, lxxviii (1788), 528; and *Critical Review*, lxvi (1788),
252-3.

of his wrath; it was too outrageous to damage Mrs. Piozzi materially.

The most bitter attack which followed the publication of the letters—in fact the most violent castigation of her entire life—came from the vituperative pen of her old enemy Baretti. It will be remembered that Baretti and Mrs. Thrale had always been antagonistic, ever ready to quarrel over children's punishments or household arrangements. She had tolerated his presence in the house only because of admiration for his great talents, and he remained because the Thrale home offered a pleasant refuge from misery and want. Her marriage to his fellow countryman, Piozzi, a careful, parsimonious musician—just the opposite of Baretti's own impulsive, lavish disposition —increased his animosity. Mrs. Piozzi, in her preoccupation with other things, had probably largely forgotten her quarrel with Baretti, but he had been brooding for years in poverty over the many fancied or real slights from the Thrale family. Reading his name in Johnson's letters in no flattering terms roused him to a pitch of fury. And when provoked, as every one familiar with his life will know, Baretti usually allowed his anger to carry him far beyond the bounds of common decency. In this case the vials of his wrath were poured out in a series of long, bitter 'Strictures', which appeared in the *European Magazine* during the spring and summer of 1788.

On March 20 he wrote to the editor of the magazine, warning readers not to place too much confidence in Mrs. Piozzi's publication because the letters had been mutilated and falsified throughout.[1] (Baretti egotistically and erroneously assumed that the unflattering references to himself in Johnson's letters had been inserted by the editor merely for revenge.) If the true letters were published, he insisted, a completely different story would be told, and Johnson's reputation, as well as that of many of his real friends, enhanced rather than degraded. He promised to regale the readers of the magazine with a series of revelations in which he would tell the truth about the false signora. The promised 'Strictures' were printed in the *European Magazine* in the issues of May, June, and August, 1788.[2] To us it is somewhat surprising that any editor could have been found ready to print the fierce invective with which

---

[1] *European Mag.* xiii (1788), 147. As has been demonstrated, there is no evidence of any widespread falsification of Johnson's correspondence.

[2] Ibid. xiii. 313–17, 393–9; xiv. 89–99. The 'Strictures' have been reprinted in G. Baretti, *Prefazioni e Polemiche*, ed. L. Piccioni (2nd ed., Bari, 1933), pp. 333–82.

Baretti denounced that 'frontless female, who goes now by the mean appellation of Piozzi'. Mrs. Piozzi herself believed the editor to have been the younger Charles Burney, which in her eyes made the insult even more unforgivable.[1]

In the first 'Stricture', with many gibes at her degrading marriage to a musician, Baretti worked himself into a fury of rage over her assertion that after Harry's death he alone had proved unsympathetic. Instead, for the edification of his readers he gave his own detailed account of the episode.[2] Unfortunately Baretti's memory, after twelve years, was faulty, and his chronology so mixed that it is almost impossible to separate fact from fancy. His most severe remarks are often based on wrong assumptions which destroy their historical value.

In the second outburst, published in June, Baretti continued his discussion of Mrs. Thrale's cruelty to her daughters. What particularly produced this diatribe was a phrase in Johnson's letter of July 15, 1775, in which he referred to Baretti's tyranny over the Thrale children. If there had been any oppression, the Italian insisted, it was the mother who exerted it, enforced by fear of her 'Salusbury fist'. A heartless, silly, erratic mistress of the household, she had been distrusted by every one in it.

The third and final 'Stricture' appeared in August, and exceeded all the others in frenzied hate and absurd misrepresentations. After first pointing out a number of glaring mistakes

---

[1] See letter to Queeney, Mar. 25, 1811 (Lansdowne MS.), and to Mrs. Byron, June 8, 1788 (Ry. 546, 4). Many years later she gave Lord Fife as her authority for connecting the Burneys with the *European Mag.* (Hayward, ii. 70; i. 301). I have not been able to find any conclusive evidence bearing on this claim.

[2] Baretti objected to a passage in her letter to Johnson, dated May 3, 1776, from Bath (See Chap. VII.) He assumed that the passage had either been fabricated in order to annoy him, or had been written Apr. 3 on the first trip to Bath directly after Harry's death. We now know that this letter was one of her revisions, but there is no reason to doubt that the allusion to the Italian represented a genuine contemporary feeling. It may possibly have been part of an original version actually dispatched to Johnson some time in May after the latter's return to London. Numerous references throughout show that the letter definitely must be assigned to the second journey to Bath, and her irritation was largely due to Baretti's wrath at the decision to give up the Italian tour. Yet even if Baretti's assumption had been correct, that the passage referred to the earlier trip, his own account of the period would justify her comment. His bitter invective against her amateur attempts at doctoring might well have been considered by the distressed mother as particularly unsympathetic. Baretti does not mention the quarrel over the decision to postpone the continental journey at all. It is perhaps useless to point out all of Baretti's errors in chronology, &c. He insists that Thrale presented him with £100 for bringing Mrs. Thrale and Queeney safely back from Bath, not mentioning the fact that it was to recompense him for expenses involved in the proposed Italian tour. For other examples of his overstatement, see *French Journals*, pp. 234–57.

in the *Anecdotes of Dr. Johnson*, Baretti warmed to his subject
and related the sensational story that Mrs. Thrale had imposed
Piozzi on Thrale as her own half-brother.[1]

The excessive malignity of Baretti's attack defeated its own
end, since complete strangers were instinctively prejudiced
against the author of so vicious an attack. Thus a friend of
William Weller Pepys wrote to him: 'I know neither of the
Parties, but will venture to pronounce Mr. Baretti in the wrong,
at all events.'[2] The violence may have amused many of the
readers of the day, but they undoubtedly did not take such
unusual charges seriously. Anna Seward, on the contrary, was
greatly exercised. Writing to Dr. Whalley on June 19, she
insisted that 'the whole literary world ought to unite in repro-
bating publicly such venom-mouthed railing', and in a later
letter to the same correspondent she protested that something
ought to be done about 'Baretti's scoundrel libels'.[3]

Probably while he was at work on his 'Strictures', Baretti
filled the margins of his copy of the *Letters* with spiteful annotations.[4] Like his published fulminations, these represent rather a
release of hatred than any desire to establish the truth. For
instance, Johnson on November 24, 1781, referred to Piozzi's
return from France in the words: 'when *he* comes and *I* come,
you will have two about you that love you.' Opposite this
Baretti exploded:

Impudent Bitch! How could she venture upon forging this
paragraph! Johnson to put himself abreast with such an ignorant
and stupid Dog as Piozzi! You lie, you Bich, and Johnson never
wrote this damn'd paragraph.

On page after page appear similar recriminations. Strangely
enough, many years later Mrs. Piozzi was given the opportunity
to purchase for ten guineas this annotated copy of the *Letters*.
She was approached through Lysons, who advised that since
the marginal references were so gross and brutal, and contained no valuable original anecdotes, she had better not waste

---

[1] See p. 218. Though obviously an incredible fabrication, the libel may have been
circulated by London gossips, and may have been partly responsible for the
general distaste for the Piozzi marriage.   [2] *A Later Pepys*, ii. 95.

[3] *Whalley Corr.* 11, 27, 29. Miss Seward suggested that a reprobation should
be placed in all the papers, signed by 'all our literati—Hayley, Mason, and Gibbon
to lead the male division, Mrs. Montagu, Mrs. Carter, and Miss More the female'.
Nothing was ever done, since obviously most people thought it best to ignore such
preposterous accusations.

[4] Now in the British Museum. George Steevens evidently had the volumes in his
possession at some time, for he had the annotations recopied into his own copy.
(Once in the possession of Mr. A. Edward Newton.)

the money. He added that he had told the owner that he felt sure she would not wish to purchase the volumes, for two reasons:

first because the MSS notes were so libellous that no one would think it safe to publish them, if they were so disposed, and secondly because, Baretti had in his life time published much of the same sort of trash, which no body ever paid any attention to.[1]

Mrs. Piozzi evidently agreed with Lysons and saved her ten guineas; but had she known the extensive use which a later celebrated Johnsonian scholar, Dr. Birkbeck Hill, would make of these same slanders, she might have purchased the copy and destroyed it.

Even the long 'Strictures' in the *European Magazine* and the copious jottings in his copy of the *Letters* had not exhausted Baretti's malevolence. A strange man, Baretti—brilliant linguist, lexicographer, scholar, he yet could stoop to the meanest devices for revenge. His life was one long series of quarrels, of friendships made and broken, of chances acquired and thrown away. One patron after another, attracted by his genius, tried to help him, only to find that his fierce independent spirit and sensitive pride repaid their benefactions with insult.[2] A few friends, Cator, Gawler, and Malone, never deserted him, but were unable to brighten his last fretful, brooding years. He died in May 1789, as he had lived, in poverty, rancour, and despair, alienated from most of his companions and mourned by few; though the caustic remark of the *Morning Post* was exaggerated—'The death of Baretti has, perhaps, excited regret in no human being.'[3] What an epitaph for one of the most gifted Italians ever to migrate to English shores!

[1] Nov. 23, 1798 (Ry. 552, 21). The volumes were held by a 'printseller at Lambeth', who had approached Cadell & Davies as a possible purchaser.

[2] Baretti's own attitude towards the many patrons who had tried to help him is shown in a long letter to Fanny Chambers, Apr. 3, 1786. After listing his grievances and disappointments in the past, he wrote:

Then I knew the great Brewer Mr. Thrale, and had the honour to teach him Spanish every Sunday, and to teach occasionally his sweet wife Italian and Spanish, and, above all, his pretty Daughter, during no less, than six years and a half, most incessantly; and, occasionally too, two more of his Daughters, and a Son. Very well! The Rascal died almost in my arms, and as a token of his love, esteem, and gratitude, what has he left me? A shilling, less than a shilling; which was as little as he could possibly leave me.

(Formerly in the possession of Mr. A. C. Thomas—now owned by Prof. C. B. Tinker.)

[3] May 11, 1789. The writer insisted that Baretti was 'a snarling old brute with some literature, but wholly destitute of genius and liberality'. Only Johnson's patronage, the journalist added, had brought him into prominence. About as true as many similar references to Mrs. Piozzi, the comment serves to show the slanderous nature of the *Morning Post* during this era.

Baretti's executors, according to Mrs. Piozzi, remembering his bitter writings of the past few years, thought best to burn all his papers;[1] but one of the most virulent escaped, possibly because it was already in the hands of a printer. This was his last brutal stab at the false signora, his final Gargantuan guffaw at the absurd household of the Thrales. At the end of his second 'Stricture' Baretti had predicted that the public might some day be entertained 'with a laughable comedy in five long acts, entitled with singular propriety: *The scientific mother*'.[2] And the *Morning Post* of May 9, 1789, shortly after his death, remarked:

If Barretti had not unfortunately *slipped his wind*, the world would soon have been favoured with some anecdotes respecting the musical *Signora* of Hanover-Square and her *pseudo-brother*, of a very interesting kind.

There can be little doubt that what was referred to was a comedy printed by James Ridgway in St. James's Square and published anonymously in the latter part of June, entitled *The Sentimental Mother   A Comedy in Five Acts; The Legacy of an Old Friend and his Last Moral Lesson to Mrs. Hester Lynch Thrale, Now Mrs. Hester Lynch Piozzi*.[3]

The scandalous plot and personal malignity of *The Sentimental Mother* have blinded many critics to much brilliant writing in the play. Indisputably, if the central situation be disregarded, it does no discredit to Baretti's genius. Yet it was probably not even very widely read in its own day, although several years later, when the notorious Frederick Hervey, Earl of Bristol, chanced on a copy, he admitted to being 'convuls'd with fits of laughter . . . c'est de la main d'un maître'.[4] Hervey was anxious to find out who the master was, but his suspicion of Greatheed was undoubtedly far from the mark, for internal evidence points unmistakably to the author having been one of the old Streatham circle.

---

[1] Hayward, i. 316.   [2] *European Mag.* xiii (1788), 398.

[3] The *World* for June 26, 1789, announced the publication of *The Sentimental Mother*. In the Bodleian Library, Oxford, is a copy of the play with identifications of the characters on the fly-leaf, seemingly in Mrs. Piozzi's hand. The play was reviewed in the *English Review*, xiv (1789), 385. The reviewer, after asking if there is any possible resemblance between the portrait and the original, added, 'if there is not, as the author has so plainly pointed out the original, we must say that he has been guilty of the worst species of assassination, and ought to be avoided as the pest of society'. (See also Thraliana, Jan. 1790.) Nevertheless, as a well-written diatribe against the cult of sentimentality the play deserves more critical attention than it has yet received.

[4] W. Childe-Pemberton, *The Earl Bishop* (1925), ii. 440.

The characters of the play are fashioned to represent members of the Thrale family, though in many cases obvious theatrical types are inserted rather than lifelike portraits. Lady Fantasma Tunskull is a malicious caricature of the lively Mrs. Thrale, while Signor Squalici, the music master of the young ladies and favourite of their mother, is a loathsome creature with no possible merit of any kind. The story is a queer mixture of farcical situations and obscene insinuations, repeating in more graphic detail most of the accusations made by Baretti in his 'Strictures'. Obviously not intended to offer any credible evidence as to actual occurrences in the Thrale household, it does provide some sidelights on the character of Mrs. Piozzi.

Baretti's particular abhorrence was the affected sensibility of the late eighteenth century. He felt that Mrs. Thrale's chief weakness was a tendency to adopt this cult of superficial sentiment. Thus in order to reveal her character, even Lady Tunskull's reading is described with the jaundiced eye of the irate classicist. According to Bellamy, a suitor for one of the daughters, her favourite books are 'the Persian Letters, Nouvelle Heloise and Tristram Shandy', and it is Sterne and Rousseau whom she openly admires. Throughout the play Lady Fantasma is the very epitome of insincere 'gushing', which the English disciples of Rousseau seemed to consider the proper way to let the heart speak. Bellamy constantly moralizes on this contemporary curse. 'O how I hate sentiments!' he says, 'They are in manners, what fanaticism is in religion, the cover of insidious hypocrisy; the bane of every good disposition.' Again and again he comes back to the attack. 'Every turgid brute affects to be tremblingly alive all over; and every brawney vixen whom nature designed for the coarsest duties of the kitchen; and whose nerves are like packthread; is ever affecting delicacy or weakness.'

The lack of sympathy between the chief character and her husband mirrors the old situation at Streatham. Lady Tunskull is made to say, '*There was never anything sentimental even in my hasband's love:* our children are common children.' Later she continues with the same complaint: 'There is not a person about me, who has the least share of sensibility; and I am like one dropt out of the clouds among Indians.' Overdrawn as it is, the characterization has some modicum of truth; Mrs. Thrale had never been understood by the other members of her family, the usual fate of any enthusiast in a commonplace household.

Even if Baretti's railings were too exaggerated to gain
credence, Mrs. Piozzi must have heaved a sigh of relief on
hearing of his death in 1789. Yet when the immediate danger
of further persecution was over, she tried to harbour no resentment. On May 8, 1789, she wrote in Thraliana:

Baretti is dead—Poor Baretti! I am sincerely sorry for him, &
as Zanga says—If *I* lament thee, sure thy Worth was great. He was
a *manly* Character at worst; & died as he lived, less like a Christian
than a Philosopher.

And when her favourite newspaper, the *World*, possibly out of
partisan loyalty, failed to notice his death, Mrs. Piozzi wrote a
letter of mingled praise and condemnation which appeared in
a somewhat garbled form in the issue of May 11.[1] As Collison-
Morley, the English biographer of Baretti, remarks, 'Mrs.
Thrale was as good-natured and forgiving a woman as ever
lived, but the malice in her description shows how deeply
rooted her hatred of Baretti was. She never really pardoned
him, and it would have been strange if she had.'[2] Over thirty
years later she still thought him 'a bad man'.[3]

In addition to the vicious attacks of Boswell, Baretti, and
other old friends, the publication of Johnson's letters brought
out a multitude of lampoons and amusing squibs.[4] One
anonymous satirist arranged twenty-five verses of doggerel
quotations from Johnson's letters, attempting to show the
ridiculous character of the subjects treated by the writer.[5]

---

[1] Este revised Mrs. Piozzi's letter before printing, and she found it 'more altered
than improved'. Compare the *World*, May 11, 1789, and Hayward, i. 317.

[2] Collison-Morley, p. 356.   [3] E. Mangin, *Piozziana*, p. 3.

[4] The *Morning Post* every few days printed some sneering remark. See the
issues of Mar. 10, 12, 14, 15, 17, 20, 21, 24, 25, 27, 28, 29; Apr. 1, 3, 26; and
June 2, 12. Some of the comments are indecent; others merely insulting; none may
be implicitly believed. For example, on April 26 the paper stated

The squabble between Baretti and Mrs. Piozzi has brought out a curious
piece of information, which the Lady thought proper to suppress in her Anecdotes, namely, that Dr. Johnson, in a reasonable time after Mr. Thrale's death,
put the question of matrimony to her. The negative that followed, was the real
cause of their separation, and of the coolness that subsisted between them during
the remainder of the Doctor's life.

The *World* contained numerous complimentary references, and occasional remarks were printed in other papers. Miscellaneous squibs appeared in books and
magazines. Thus in *Miscellanies in Prose & Verse* (Edinburgh, 1791; published
anonymously but by Francis Garden, Lord Gardenstone), p. 224, appear the lines:

He told the Brewer's crazy wife
How well he lov'd a stomach load
And stay'd but once in all his life
At home, when ask'd to dine abroad.

See also B.M. Add. MS. 30349.

[5] Called 'The Quintessence of Johnson's Letters to Mrs. Piozzi'. Broadley,
p. 116.

Sayer, the noted caricaturist, made Mrs. Piozzi the subject of a print in which a pretty woman seated at her writing-table is confronted by the ghost of Dr. Johnson. Beneath this caricature appeared four stanzas:

> Madam (my debt to Nature paid),
> I thought the Grave with hallow'd shade
>   Wou'd now protect my name:
> Yet there in vain I seek repose,
> My friends each little fault disclose,
>   And murder Johnson's fame.
>
> First, Boswell, with officious care,
> Shew'd me as men would shew a bear,
>   And call'd himself my friend;
> Sir John with nonsense strew'd my hearse,
> And Courtney pester'd me with verse;
>   You torture without end.
>
> When Streatham spread its plenteous board,
> I open'd Learning's valued hoard,
>   And as I feasted prosed.
> Good things I said, good things I eat,
> I gave you knowledge for your meat,
>   And thought th' account was clos'd.
>
> If obligations still I owed,
> You sold each item to the croud,
>   I suffer'd by the tale:
> For God's sake, Madame, let me rest,
> Nor longer vex your quondam guest—
>   I'll pay you for your ale.[1]

Mrs. Piozzi expected another open attack by Dr. Wolcot, the ex-physician and West Indian slave-driver who wrote under the pseudonym of 'Peter Pindar'. This time she was determined to be ready to meet his mud-slinging with a rejoinder in the same style:

> Now Peter Popgun, Pill-Box Pindar! Hail!
> Feast for one Week on Johnson and on Thrale;
> Or to that Rhyme if Readers should grow dozy,
> Change it at once to Johnson and Piozzi.
> With hungry haste dispense your dirty Drug
> And clasp these Letters with a Cornish Hug.

---

[1] Sayer's caricature appeared Apr. 7, 1788, and was entitled *Frontispiece to the 2nd Edition of Johnson's Letters*. It was printed in the *European Mag.* xiii (1788), 248. See also Broadley, pp. 101–2.

Haply some choice Expression they contain
May guide the skilful Hand to give fresh Pain:
The unoffending Editor to torture,
And bruise both Husbands in your Brazen Mortar.
All will assist: even now Methinks I see,
A Motley Heterogeneous Coterie;
Press round their Bard, his Incantations aid,
And cast her Character in hateful Shade.
Each full-filled Enemy, each Traytor Friend,
Recounts his Powr's to hurt and to Offend;
And skill'd of Wit and Sense to stop the Growth,
One churns the Venom, and one spits the Froth.
Now Pigmy Colman speeds his feeble Dart,
Now merry Boswell—hopes it in her heart,
Baretti begs the *Murderous Style* to guide,
And pliant Burney bows from Side to Side.
Mosquitoes thus, beneath that Sultry Sky
Where the keen Whip the harden'd Drivers ply,
And Hawkins' Self might learn Malignity.
Mosquitoes thus round the fresh Banquet crowd
Clap their Thin Wings for Joy & buz aloud.[1]

To her surprise Wolcot did not immediately seize on the new publication as a subject for his ridicule, and her verses were not printed. They serve to show Mrs. Piozzi's skill in satire, however, as well as to indicate the names of those whom she considered her chief enemies.

Letters to and from the Late Samuel Johnson, LL.D. brought many things to Mrs. Piozzi: £500 in currency; the most savage abuse of her entire career; higher estimation in the minds of many readers; definite, if temporary, celebrity in literary London of the time.[2]

[1] Mainwaring Piozziana, ii. 123–4.
[2] Proof of Mrs. Piozzi's temporary notoriety may be found in *The Wreck of Westminster Abbey* (London, Stalker, 2001) (published anonymously in Apr. 1788, but probably by Sir Herbert Croft). In this series of imaginary epitaphs, including royalty and the most famous people of the day, that of Mrs. Piozzi stands first and in the most prominent position.

XVI

LONDON SOCIETY AND TRAVEL

DURING the winter and spring of 1788, though occupied with the publication of Johnson's letters, Mrs. Piozzi also had time for a variety of other interests. Chief of these was the production at the Theatre Royal in Drury Lane of Greatheed's tragedy, *The Regent*. Before her marriage Mrs. Siddons had lived with the Greatheeds at Guy's Cliffe, as a genteel helper, and she felt a personal responsibility for the success of the play. She and her brother agreed to take the principal parts, were active in advertising the coming production, and used all their influence to secure a favourable reception. As a close friend of the playwright, Mrs. Piozzi was greatly excited over the preparations, especially since her epilogue was to be spoken by Mrs. Siddons on the opening night. The tragedy finally appeared on Saturday, March 29;[1] Kemble and Mrs. Siddons were at their best, and the society partisans of the author were vociferous in their applause. Mrs. Piozzi's epilogue was well received—at least so Este said in the *World* the following Monday. He showed his partiality by printing it in full a few days later with further encomiums.[2]

After this auspicious start *The Regent* had to be withdrawn temporarily because of the illness of Mrs. Siddons. Greatheed, however, went ahead with the publication of the text, which included Mrs. Piozzi's epilogue.[3] Preparatory to the re-opening she also wrote a prologue, but for some reason it was never used.[4] Finally, the *World* for April 28 announced a packed house for *The Regent*, again with the same prologue and epilogue. A week later this paper stated that on the fourth

---

[1] The exact date of the first performance is given in Mrs. Piozzi's engagement-book, and in an announcement in the *World* of Mar. 29, 1788.

[2] Apr. 5, 1788. Reviews and complimentary references to the play appeared in the issues of Mar. 31, Apr. 1, 2, 5, &c.

[3] *The Regent a Tragedy as it is acted at The Theatre Royal in Drury Lane* (1788). At least two editions were printed this year. The work contains a dedication to Mrs. Siddons, a prologue by the Rev. Mr. Williams, and the epilogue by Mrs. Piozzi. [4] Mainwaring Piozziana, ii. 121; see also the *World*, Apr. 18, 1788.

night the receipts had been £300. Although the actual merit of the play was slight, the energetic sponsorship of Mrs. Siddons ensured a temporary triumph, and it continued to be popular, even being produced in various provincial theatres during the summer.

The success of Greatheed's tragedy naturally drew many of his personal friends into close connexion with the playhouse. As Mrs. Piozzi later remembered, 'We were now thinking of Plays and Prologues & Theatres, *Day & Night*.'[1] Indeed, throughout the spring of 1788 Mrs. Piozzi's circle was theatre mad. And they were not alone in this preoccupation, for amateur theatricals were the rage among a certain group of the nobility in London, with the Duke of Richmond as the prime mover. At Richmond House a number of performers, including the Earl of Derby and the Honourable Mrs. Damer, were continually presenting plays for the amusement of themselves and their intimate friends. In rehearsing for Lee's *Theodosius*, the favourite singer, Miss Hamilton, decided she needed a special song as part of the stage action. When none could be discovered exactly suited to the situation, Miss Hamilton, at her wits' end, came to Mrs. Piozzi for aid. After much searching they found an Italian air by Sacchini which pleased the singer, but no English words to set to it. Nothing daunted, Mrs. Piozzi had her husband play the tune over and over until she learned the rhythm, and then dashed off a set of verses embodying the desired sentiment. It was a happy chance for Mrs. Piozzi, since the improvisation gained her admission not merely to the present performance but to society more exclusive than she had ever entered before.[2]

An invitation to the entertainments given by the Duke of Richmond was a distinct feather in Mrs. Piozzi's cap. But what pleased her most of all was that her husband, contrary to their experience in Italy, was always included in the invitation. Piozzi more than ever was satisfied to remain an exile from his native land.

For once in her life Mrs. Piozzi's ability for easy rhyming proved a social asset. She scribbled off prologues, epilogues,

---

[1] Mainwaring Piozziana, ii. 101.

[2] Ibid. ii. 102. In Thraliana the account is dated Mar. 27, 1788. See also *Atlantic Monthly*, vii (1861), 620. In her 1788 engagement-book Mrs. Piozzi listed Richmond House for the first time on Mar. 15, with later invitations to the same place on Apr. 28, May 1 and 19. On May 1 the *World*, in a list of guests the night before at Richmond House, included Mrs. Piozzi, Mrs. Damer, Mr. Walpole, &c.

lyrics for anyone who asked. For Mrs. Greatheed's friend,
Mrs. Hobart, she wrote a scene to end a little one-act comedy
by Le Texier.[1] For Mr. Fector of Dover, who had allowed all
their belongings to come through the Customs unexamined
the year before, she wrote an epilogue to be spoken by his son,
who was appearing in a production of Young's tragedy *The
Brothers*. About this she later remarked with characteristic
naïveté, that it had 'saved the Play I heard—and the Performer'.[2]

Mrs. Piozzi could never be satisfied with such ephemeral
pieces. Many years later she remembered that about this time,

having been so often solicited for Prologues Epilogues &c. my Heart
began to pant for Dramatic Celebrity; & bring something—I knew
not what—upon the *Stage*.

Johnson's Fountains would do well for A Masque—in the Manner
of Milton's Comus I thought; where Sentiment and Show might
supply the Place of Terror Pity or Merriment.

Kemble & his Sister saw the Two first Acts in 1789 as I remember,
profess'd to like & bring it forward—so I *finished*—& They *shelf'd it*.[3]

She explained in detail just what her intentions were in
adapting Johnson's prose tale to the stage.

Certain that I could neither make People laugh nor Cry my hope
was to please by Interesting Obscurity as to the Plot, and Interesting
tho' in nowise uncommon Characters upon the Stage. A good Style
—without Tumid or too Flat Language was all I aimed at: but It
would *not do* The Managers wanted more Pepper & Salt to It.

Examination of the surviving manuscripts of 'The Two
Fountains', as she named the piece, confirms the adverse
judgement of Kemble and Sheridan, even if it is possible to
discover some admirable passages.[4] It was unfortunate that
Mrs. Piozzi tried to produce a poetic masque, for her talent did
not lie in pure imagination. Had she attempted a comedy of
manners, filled with wit and sprightly conversation, she might
well have produced a successful play. The dialogues written
in 1779 are enough to show her special aptitude for such composition. Instead she tried this faery spectacle, which collected
dust on the shelves of a succession of managers.

We have two contemporary sources of information about
Mrs. Piozzi's social activity during the next few years: her own

---

[1] Ibid. ii. 109–12.   [2] Ibid. ii. 104.
[3] Ibid. iii. 1; also ii. 125. According to Thraliana, Jan. 1790, she was then
working on the play.
[4] Ry. 649; Mainwaring Piozziana, iii. 1–49; another copy was sold at Sotheby's,
June 4, 1908. See also New Common Place Book, p. 163, where she refers to
Sheridan's pretending to like the masque. Also E. Mangin, *Piozziana*, p. 44.

engagement books and the *World* newspaper.[1] In the former, side by side with the names of many titled personages, appear those of a number of friends of long standing. General Paoli seems to have been a constant guest, and the Bishop of Peterborough, Dr. Lort, Mrs. Byron, Mrs. Lewis, Lady Hesketh, the cousin and correspondent of the poet Cowper, and the Hornecks were frequently included. Nevertheless, it was her recent acquaintances, the Greatheeds, Mrs. Siddons, the Kembles, Merry and Parsons, Samuel Lysons and Chappelow who are mentioned most often. It was a heterogeneous group: visiting foreigners, popular writers of the day, a sprinkling of the nobility, scholars and prelates, a few actors and musicians.[2] For one concert in February 1789 the invited list included fifty-one men and fifty-four women. One notable change, besides the character of the guests, might be seen in the nature of Mrs. Piozzi's entertainments. Music now assumed the first place; the best amateur and professional singers vied with the talkers for pre-eminence. Needless to say, the Johnsonians were conspicuous by their absence. The *Morning Post* had not been far wrong when it jokingly remarked, in announcing one of the Piozzis' large concerts, that 'it is supposed that a vast crowd will assemble on this occasion, though but a very few *friends* of Dr. Johnson are expected'.[3]

As the years moved on, however, Mrs. Piozzi renewed her intimacy with a few of the Blue-Stockings. In January 1789 she wrote in Thraliana:

Mrs. Siddons dined in a Coterie of my unprovoked Enemies yesterday at Porteus's—She mentioned our Concerts & the Erskines

---

[1] Engagement books for 1788 and 1790 are in the Rylands collection (Ry. 616), and that of 1789 in my own. They are far from complete, but give some record of her invitations and the names of her guests.

[2] Names of guests appearing in 1788 are: Major Barry, Mrs. Bunbury, Mr. Byng, Mrs. Byron, Miss Carter, L. Chappelow, Lady Clive, C. Este, Mr. and Mrs. Greatheed, Mrs. Hamilton, Lady Hesketh, Mrs. Horneck, Dr. and Mrs. Lort, S. Lysons, R. Merry, Arthur Murphy, Baron Nolcken, General Paoli, W. Parsons, The Bishop of Peterborough, Miss Pitt, Mr. Sastres, Miss Shelley, C. Selwin, Mr. and Mrs. Siddons, Miss Weston, William Windham.

Others in 1789 are: Count Andriani, Sir Wm. and Lady Ashhurst, Mr. Bartolozzi, Mr. Borghi, the three Miss Beavers, Mr. Cosway, Dr. Delap, Lord and Lady Dudley, Miss Farren, Lord Fife, Count Frieri, Mrs. Garrick, Mr. Greville, Mrs. Hobart, Lord Huntingdon, Sir Charles and Lady Hotham, Mr. Jerningham, Mr. and Mrs. Kemble, the Bishop of Killaloe, Mrs. Lambart, Mr. Le Texier, Dr. Moore, Hannah More, Miss Nicolson, Miss Owen, Dr. and Mrs. Parker, Mr. Perkins, Mr. Swale, Helen Maria Williams, Count Zenobio, to mention only those most familiar.

New names in 1790 are: the Pennants, Pindemonte, Miss Palmer.

[3] Mar. 15, 1788.

lamented their Absence from One we gave two days ago, at which Mrs. Garrick was present, & gave a good Report to the *Blues*. Charming Blues! blue with Venom I think; I suppose they begin to be ashamed of their paltry behaviour . . . Mrs. Garrick more prudent than any of them, left a Loophole for returning Friendship to fasten through, and it *shall* fasten.[1]

The widow of the great actor and Hannah More appeared regularly at her fêtes, and Mrs. Piozzi often used Mrs. Garrick's box at the theatre. According to Mrs. Piozzi, others were anxious to resume friendly intercourse. 'Mr. Pepys, Mrs. Ord, &c.', she wrote, 'now sneak about, & look ashamed of themselves.' Even the Queen of the Blues may have contemplated a reconciliation.

Mrs. Montagu wants to make up with me again; I dare say she does; but I will not be taken & left, even at the Pleasure of those who are much dearer and nearer to me than Mrs. Montagu. We want no flash, no flattery; I never had more of either in my Life, nor ever lived half so happily.[2]

It was inevitable that she and Fanny Burney should one day meet. After several narrow escapes—one on the terrace at Windsor in the summer of 1787[3]—the encounter finally occurred on March 17, 1790. The next day Mrs. Piozzi wrote in Thraliana of seeing her former confidant at Mrs. Lock's assembly, when the hostess had insisted on acting as peacemaker. Fanny appeared 'most *fondly* rejoyced', but both were on their guard and chatted with studied ease about everything except what was most in their thoughts. 'And all ended', Mrs. Piozzi added, 'as it should do with perfect Indifference.' The moment which Fanny had so long dreaded yet desired failed to bring a reconciliation.[4] Ignorant of her efforts to soften Queeney's cold heart, Mrs. Piozzi no doubt judged too harshly. Yet how could she ever forget the desertion of Fanny when

---

[1] Jan. 17, 1789. The *World* of Jan. 13, 1789, referred to Mrs. Piozzi's concert of the night before last.   [2] Thraliana, May 1, 1789.

[3] Late in the summer of 1787 (dated Aug. [?]; postmarked Sept. 10) Fanny Burney wrote to Queeney Thrale:

> your poor Mother has been at Windsor!—she was here, it seems, 3 days,—yet I knew not of it till long after, when I heard it from Mr. Fisher, one of the Cannons, . . . To have had her so near me—yet not to have seen her,—I can scarcely express the strange emotion the intelligence raised in me.—a *very* few years ago—how should we have flown to each other!— . . . She walked, it seems, upon the Terrace;—& Mr. Fisher tells me I was there myself, accidentally, but the very Day before:—suppose we had met there!—good God, what a meeting it must have been! (Lansdowne MS.)

[4] *D'Arblay Diary*, iv. 361.

she most needed her support; how forgive her lack of courage
to defy the smug snobbery of the day in her defence? The two
might continue to meet with pleasure, but they could never
return to the old intimacy.

Mrs. Piozzi saw nothing at all of her elder daughters. Once
she wrote to Mrs. Byron: 'My Misses are cold & cruel, & so
their Sweethearts say as well as their Mother: I wish some of
them were once well married. Cecilia is not like them, either
in their good or ill Qualities.'[1] But Mrs. Piozzi was always
avid for information about them. Having no illusions as to their
feelings towards her, she always hoped that perhaps time would
render them more kindly in their treatment of her. So she
commented to Mrs. Byron on September 4, 1788:

My fair Daughters have been seen at Bath I hear; is it not silly
to feel delighted that they are well & happy? who wish me no good
I am sure either of Health or any other Enjoyment—as they have
done their utmost to deprive me of all: Yet glad I am at my Heart—
for after every thing is said they *are* my Children—

Of all her new friends the one most admired was Mrs.
Siddons. The actress was then at the peak of her popularity,
both professionally and socially, and Thomas Campbell in his
biography of her wrote of these years:

At this period our great actress was the courted favourite of an
intellectual circle, whose acquaintance made her prouder than even
the notice of Royalty. Often have I heard her boast of the times
when every other day she had a note or a visit from Sir Joshua
Reynolds, from Mrs. Piozzi, or from Erskine, Burke, Sheridan, or
Malone.[2]

In this list it is interesting to note that Mrs. Piozzi was the only
woman whom Mrs. Siddons mentioned on a par with Reynolds,
Burke, and Malone. On her side Mrs. Piozzi elevated the
actress to the pedestal left vacant by Collier and Johnson. Her
temperament always needed some one to adore, some one to
look up to and serve proudly, some one to nurse when sick and
entertain when well. Mrs. Siddons now became this most
intimate companion, and the correspondence between the two
gives proof of the lasting quality of the relationship.[3]

About this time an incident occurred which made her
question the loyalty of Sam Lysons.

---

[1] Oct. 11, 1787. All letters to Mrs. Byron are in Ry. 546.
[2] T. Campbell, *Life of Mrs. Siddons* (1834), ii. 129–30.
[3] Ibid., and Ry. 574. References throughout Thraliana also indicate the
devotion of Mrs. Piozzi.

Sammy Lysons invited us all to his Chambers, & gave us a Breakfast: when he shewed me a little Collection of Books, Tracts, Pamphlets, Ballads &c on a Corner of his Shelves—& *Look there* said he, 'There are, I flatter myself, all the Things that ever were written *against You* either Serious or in Ridicule—All, All; not one left out that could be found by the most diligent Research.' Thank you was all my Reply. Why observed John Kemble as we came home, 'tis Lysons's *Way*: He made it his Business & bounden duty to call on me every Morning after I had been on the Stage—*one whole Season*; to tell me every Illnatur'd Remark, every bitter Sarcasm; every Criticism he had heard.—& when I said Don't my Dear Fellow come Spoiling my Breakfast so every Morn: Why replied he, You shall have your Compensation next Week & I'll ask the Greatheeds & Piozzis to meet you on Saturday & so he did.[1]

Mrs. Piozzi need not have been worried over Lysons's collection, for it contained merely newspaper clippings embodying the old charges which had been levelled against her so often in the past. But not being allowed to examine the scrap-book, she always felt uncomfortable about its contents and distrustful of its compiler.

Nearly everything Mrs. Piozzi did was described in the *World*: her spectacular concerts, her presence at the Duke of Richmond's entertainments, her travels about England. As a public character she had no privacy. The *World* and Charles Este, its editor, are remembered to-day largely because it was in this paper that the long series of 'Della Cruscan' verses first appeared. As has been previously pointed out, the little group who published the *Florence Miscellany* in 1785 were not properly 'Della Cruscans'. It was not until two years later, in June 1787, that Robert Merry, while still on the Continent, sent his first poem with this signature to the English newspapers, to be followed by a long succession of florid verses under the same pseudonym. Della Crusca had been answered in the columns of the *World* by an unknown writer who signed herself Anna Matilda, and throughout the autumn of 1787 there had been a series of complimentary poems between the two. To-day the poetry appears artificial and vapid in the extreme, but it exactly suited the society verse-makers of the time. And Este, being a clever editor, and gauging the popular approval aroused by his anonymous poets, did all in his power to stimulate the interchange with comments and suggestions. Other writers who signed themselves Ruben, Arley, Laura Maria,

---

[1] New Common Place Book, p. 263. Written July 1, 1819, upon hearing of his death. See also Hayward, ii. 442. For Lysons's scrap-book see p. 124, n. 1.

Eliza, Benedict, Melissa, and The Bard joined in the game, and the *World* became the repository for a mass of occasional verse which we to-day classify under the contemptuous term 'Della Cruscan'.[1]

Mrs. Piozzi herself never belonged to this movement, except as a friend and confidant of some of the principal participants. Even if a few of her poems did appear in the *World*, they were almost all reprinted from her published works and under her own signature. Nevertheless, her friendship with Este and Merry, together with the many flattering remarks about her in the former's newspaper, resulted in a general tendency to consider her as an active 'Della Cruscan'. In a *Catalogue of Five Hundred Celebrated Authors of Great Britain Now Living*, which appeared in 1788, and which gave Mrs. Piozzi more space than her rival Boswell and many other more gifted writers, the author went so far as to make the conjecture that Anna Matilda was none other than Mrs. Piozzi herself.

As a matter of fact, the identity of the unknown correspondent was as much a mystery to Mrs. Piozzi and Merry as to everyone else, and trying to guess the name of the lady was an endless source of conversation in the Piozzi circle. To many, Anna Seward seemed the most likely candidate, but Merry eliminated her as a possibility:

I rather doubt Miss Seward being Anna Matilda, as she says in her last Ode
'Love on my couch has pour'd each sweet' now tho' the circumstance is very possible, yet the confession is hardly probable for a *Miss*.[2]

For many months Anna Matilda successfully maintained her incognito, and Merry allowed his romantic imagination to run wild. Finally, however, when an actual interview revealed the lady as the authoress Mrs. Cowley, neither young nor physically attractive, his ardour suddenly cooled, and with a long carefully worded poem, 'The Interview', the verses to Anna Matilda came to an end.

The complete story of the 'Della Cruscan' episode is too long to tell here; nor is there space to describe the petty quarrels and jealousies of Este's group, so amusingly revealed in Merry's excitable letters to Mrs. Piozzi.[3] Envy and spite had turned the

---

[1] For a description of the Della Cruscan episode see J. M. Longaker, *The Della Cruscans and William Gifford* (Philadelphia, 1924); and R. Marshall, *Italy in English Literature 1755–1815* (New York, 1934).
[2] To Mrs. Piozzi, Feb. 27, 1788 (Ry. 558, 2).   [3] Ry. 558.

chief authors of the *Florence Miscellany* into bitter enemies. Merry and Greatheed refused to speak to each other; Parsons was always at odds with either one or the other; so that Mrs. Piozzi, as a friend of all three, was often placed in an embarrassing situation. Yet she managed somehow to keep the peace, for their names constantly appear in the lists of her invited guests.

Her new-found group had not the depth or stability of the old Streatham coterie, but for the time it would suffice until she could draw more people of genius about her. The prominence of the Greatheeds and their friends at least allowed her to take an enviable place in London society, and so to ignore the slights and sneers of her elder daughters and the vengeful Blues. Though she always preferred intellect to position,[1] for a time the latter might be used as a means to regain the former.

It must not be supposed that in the gay round of fashion Mrs. Piozzi forgot her literary ambitions. Probably even before the actual appearance of Johnson's letters she had begun to plan her next large publication, which was to be a detailed account of her experiences in southern Europe during the years immediately following her second marriage. On April 3, 1788, the *World* announced that Mrs. Piozzi was again at work, this time on her travels, and several weeks later Este remarked that the hand which had written the regatta letter would surely produce something unusual.[2]

Allowed little time for serious labour in the hectic London season, she planned a quiet summer at the sea-side, where she could revise her travel journals for publication. The notes and observations jotted down as she moved about the Continent were to be the basis of her volumes; but to make a more pretentious and readable work, these would need to be expanded and rewritten, just as her old letters to Johnson had been. Accordingly, the Piozzis left London on June 4, stopping first at Reading, where Mrs. Piozzi dispatched a note to Mrs. Byron, adding a message of apology to Mrs. Lambart for not writing: 'let her remember that I have with me for the constant Occupation of my Thoughts, a Husband, a Child, & a Book.'[3] Leaving Reading, they spent a few idle weeks in Bath, and then went on through Exeter to Exmouth.

---

[1] Cecilia, many years later, wrote to her mother after referring to some news of 'these Dukes & Marquisses', 'You scorn a *Lady* so much that I did not think of telling you all my Tales of *Ladies* of which my Letters are filled' (Ry. 572, 28).
[2] Apr. 18, 1788. See also issue of June 5.
[3] June 8, 1788. See also Thraliana, July 1, 1788, and the *World* of June 5.

Mrs. Piozzi, who had been seeking a secluded spot far from all disturbance, wrote to Mrs. Byron on June 29 from Exmouth, very much pleased with her surroundings, although her husband and Cecilia found the place exceedingly dull.[1] She admitted that she was not working very hard at the task, doing only ten pages of long folio paper a day, with a complete rest on Sunday. 'Mr. Este', she added, 'and two or three other Friends spirited me up to this Folly—if it does not succeed I shall fall hard up on *them*.'

She quickly adjusted herself to the simple life.

Mr. Piozzi laughs at my facility of accommodating my self to every Place: *here* I bathe & write, (by the by the 1:st vol: is done) and go to Bed at 10 o'Clock, & comb my Hair clean out of the Powder, washing it every Morning in the Sea, and on Sundays tell my Friends at a Distance how I love them.[2]

Exmouth was not without some agreeable company. Lord Huntingdon obligingly read her manuscript, gave her advice, and in general proved so congenial that she commented to Lysons that when she fell in love next it would be with him.[3] Piozzi, on the other hand, finding little to amuse him, after a few weeks was glad to trump up an excuse for a business trip to London. While he was away, his wife continued with her transcribing, and by August 11 she could comment to her steady correspondent, Mrs. Byron, 'the Book I have really not *read* yet, only *written*, wch. sounds odd, but *so it is*. I shall now read, correct & copy it over—beginning next Thursday at soonest, for just now I hate the Sight of it.'[4] Composition did not take all her time, since she had also the discouraging task of educating her youngest daughter. Resignedly she commented: 'I cannot make a Scholar of Cecilia, I never shall; tis impossible, but there are Scholars enough in the World without her: She has many good Qualities.'

Like many present-day sea-side towns, Exmouth had a summer theatre, and though preoccupied with other affairs, Mrs. Piozzi could not refrain from taking an interest in the makeshift dramatic company trying its fortune in the vicinity. So the London newspapers in September were able to print an 'Occasional Prologue' written by Mrs. Piozzi for the Exmouth theatre on August 27.[5] In typical eighteenth-century fashion she compared their local group with that of the fabled company

---

[1] See Hayward, ii. 453.   [2] To Mrs. Byron, July 13, 1788.
[3] Aug. 23, 1788 (*Bentley's Misc.* xxviii (1850), 624).
[4] See also Thraliana, Aug. 1, 1788.   [5] *London Chronicle*, Sept. 27, 1788.

of Thespis, with the contrast that 'They had a cart—and we have a barn'.

The Piozzis remained at Exmouth until late in September 1788. Then through Exeter and Plymouth they drove in a leisurely manner back to Bath, where they stayed throughout October. On their way, from an inn at Exeter, she wrote:

I wish my dear Mrs. Byron saw me with all my Papers for the *Book stuff* and the People coming in every Moment, and the Dog flying at 'em, and Cecilia's Task to look over; and My sullen Maid with *Ma'am this Guinea won't pass*, and my husband crying Come, shut away this Work *do*, and write to dear Mrs. Byron.

Her work was far from completed, for on October 9 she admitted that what would make four hundred printed pages still remained to be recopied. But her husband, who never could understand why she should spend so much time over a stack of foolish papers, remarked that 'never had Man so diligent a Wife'. She soon found, however, that in Bath there would be less leisure to devote to her task than at Exmouth. 'If People drop in every Moment so, how can I finish it?' was her complaint; yet undismayed she struggled on with the long job of transcription.[1]

Meanwhile Este kept his readers in London constantly informed of her progress,[2] and inserted a dispatch from Bath of November 9: 'Some few People, about 500, at the Rooms, talked about Mrs. Piozzi's coming Tour—Miss Hartley's Drawings, and some New Work, we know not what, of Miss Lee.' In order further to stimulate interest in the lady and her writing, Este published in the *World* her verses written at Calais the year before and the corresponding rhymes completed after the trip across the Channel.[3]

With the tedious copying finally completed, Mrs. Piozzi wrote to her publisher, Cadell, on November 14, offering him the right to publish the volumes for the substantial sum of 500 guineas.[4] Calculating that the work would run to nearly a thousand printed pages, she suggested printing in three small volumes of the same size as the *Anecdotes*. Mrs. Piozzi never

---

[1] To Mrs. Byron, Oct. 21, 1788. Mrs. Piozzi wrote her first version in seven folio note-books, using her special travel journals and Thraliana as groundwork. She then corrected and revised, and recopied into 3 other volumes to send to the printers (Ry. 619–22).
[2] *World*, June 21; Oct. 6, 11; Nov. 17, 24, 28; Dec. 4, 6, 29, 1788, &c.
[3] *World*, Oct. 6; Nov. 17, 1788.
[4] Hayward, i. 322. According to Thraliana her copying was completed by Nov. 10.

hesitated to ask her price, but it is doubtful if she received it this time. Although Cadell agreed to publish the travels, the complete details of their financial arrangement are not known.

Late in November the Piozzis left Bath, and after a short visit to Mrs. Lewis in Reading, returned to London, where they were again installed in their house in Hanover Square.[1] The gaiety of English society during the autumn and winter of 1788–9 was much damped by the critical illness of the King. The opposition immediately demanded a regency, with the Prince of Wales acting for his father, and the political rancour and general nervousness so increased that in London this possibility became almost the only topic of general conversation. Uncertainty over this situation was undoubtedly responsible for some delay in printing Mrs. Piozzi's new work.[2] To bring out a frivolous travel book while all the reading public was thinking of more serious concerns would have been poor business. Another effect of the mania of the King was the shelving of Greatheed's tragedy. Preparations had been made to continue the run of *The Regent* at Drury Lane, after its undoubted success of the year before, but in the circumstances the Lord Chamberlain refused permission for its revival.

If the King's illness had acted as a pall over society throughout the early months of 1789, his sudden return to sanity resulted in a whirl of rejoicing. Houses were illuminated; the streets were filled with shouting men; London hailed the event with gay abandon. As Mrs. Piozzi later described it: 'every Day produced a Fête and every Night produced a Gala—Public; private—We were Mad with Joy. The Women wore Restoration Caps at one fine Show, Loyal Bandeaus at another —Mr. Piozzi was enchanted with the Bustle.'[3] She herself wrote verses on the recovery and joined whole-heartedly in the celebration. The *World* of March 11, listing some of the loyal houses conspicuous for their decorations, named that of Mrs. Piozzi in Hanover Square, 'alight—from the roof to the area. With a Transparency in the Heart of the building—God Save the King. . . .'

Throughout the spring of 1789 Mrs. Piozzi's travel book was still in the printer's hands. Early in May the *World* and the

---

[1] *The World* on Nov. 24, 1788, announced that 'Mrs. Piozzi leaves Bath this day', and on the 28th added that she was on a visit to Berkshire.

[2] According to Thraliana the book was sent to press by January [Feb. ?] 5, 1789, but did not appear until late spring. See also the *World*, Jan. 9, 1789.

[3] Mainwaring Piozziana, ii. 109.

Morning Post both predicted that it could be expected soon;[1] and on June 2 the *World* advertised it as 'this month will be published'. The official publication day appears to have been June 4, though it is not clear exactly when copies were available to the general public. The *World* of June 5, in an account of the King's birthday, lists Mrs. Piozzi's new work as among the other reasons for rejoicing. On the other hand, Horace Walpole did not begin writing his unflattering comments to his correspondents—the first to the learned Miss Elizabeth Carter—until June 13.[2]

The work consisted of two octavo volumes of about 400 pages each, and was entitled: *Observations and Reflections made in the Course of a Journey through France, Italy, and Germany*. The newspapers, as usual with all Mrs. Piozzi's publications, immediately printed numerous excerpts, and the *London Chronicle* of June 20, after giving up the entire first page to selections, added: 'From this entertaining work we shall occasionally select such passages as may be most easily detached, for the perusal of our Readers.'[3] Other papers followed suit. The reactions of the newspaper critics, as might have been expected, were varied. The *Morning Post*, her particular enemy, remarked on June 15 that 'the literary crudities of this lady afford a lamentable proof of what *vanity* will do when it is associated with wealth', while the *World* and other papers were as openly enthusiastic.

The principal censure this time was directed at Mrs. Piozzi's mode of expression. In her first printed prose work, the *Anecdotes of Dr. Johnson*, many readers and reviewers had commented on what they considered her slipshod writing; Walpole being upset by her 'vulgar style'; the *Monthly Review* by the occasional 'ungraceful' terms; and the *Town and Country Magazine* by the use of 'colloquial barbarisms, and professional allusions, not happily applied'.[4] Again with *Observations and Reflections* there was the same outburst of annoyance.

The chief complaint in both cases was that the author had filled her pages with language not suited to the printed page. Walpole once more contemptuously referred to the 'excessive vulgarisms so plentiful in these volumes', and added, 'her

---

[1] *World*, May 7, 1789; *Morning Post*, May 12, 1789.

[2] *World*, June 2, 4, 5, 1789; *London Chronicle*, June 4; Walpole, *Letters*, xiv. 128–9, also 137, 140, &c.

[3] More excerpts appeared June 23, 27, 30. Also in the *Public Advertiser*, June 23, 29, &c.

[4] Walpole, *Letters*, xiii. 372; *Monthly Review*, lxxiv (1786), 382; *Town and Country Mag.* xviii (1786), 288.

friends plead that she piques herself on writing as she talks: methinks, then, she should talk as she would write'.[1] Anna Seward was shocked at the corruption of Mrs. Piozzi's style which she found so loaded with colloquialisms. In an age when 'language has acquired its utmost degree of refinement, its last polish', Miss Seward could not understand how the accomplished conversationalist who had delighted her in Lichfield could condescend to use to such a jargon of barbarous phrases.[2] Priding herself upon her frankness, she could not resist expressing her criticism directly to the person involved. The following December she wrote to Mrs. Piozzi, filled with wonder that the friend of Johnson should publish a work,

in wh. while she frequently displays a *power* of commanding the most beautiful style imaginable, she sullies almost every page with inelegant & unscholarlike *dids*, & *dos*, & *thoughs*, & *toos*, producing those *hard angles* in sound, that stop-short, & jerking abruptness in the close of sentences, wh. are fatal to *grace*, & *flow* of style.[3]

The reviewers in the magazines continued the onslaught. The *European Magazine*, while admitting

that many of the defective parts of this work appear to be rather the result of negligence, and the affectation of an easy, playful, and familiar stile, than an ignorance of the art of composition,[4]

was disgusted that this attempt

should have betrayed her into the frequent use of such mean and vacant terms as '*to be sure*', '*sweet creature*', '*lovely theatre*', '*though*', '*vastly*', '*exactly*', '*so*', '*charming*', '*dear, dear*', and many others of the like nature with which the work abounds.

Mrs. Piozzi, like Addison, Sterne, and possibly a few others of the century, was convinced that non-scholarly books might be written in the same idiomatic language employed by ordinary people in conversation. In spite of a classical education at the hands of Collier and Johnson, she was disgusted by the ornate, florid prose adopted by the majority of the authors of her day. Why, she wondered, should there be one set of words for writing

---

[1] Op. cit. xiv. 129. Hannah More wrote to Walpole on July 27, 1789, after repeating one of Mrs. Piozzi's favourite phrases, 'You see I stand a good chance of adopting all her pretty colloquial familiarities, but as I am aware that I shall never be half so knowing and so witty, I do not see what right I have to pretend to be as barbarous, and as vulgar' (*Memoirs*, ii. 164). See also W. M. Tartt, *Essays*, i (1876), 218.   [2] *Letters of Anna Seward*, ii. 287, 294, 299, 336, &c.

[3] Ry. 565, 9. This is the original of the letter published (ii. 336) as of Dec. 21, 1789. The actual date on the letter is Dec. 31. This letter serves to show how Anna Seward rewrote and redated her letters before publication. See p. xiv, n. 2.

[4] *European Mag.* xvi (1789), 332.

and another for speaking? Could not the same vocabulary be used in both? If novelists could use a colloquial style, why not other writers? She, at least, would try the experiment of using all the everyday expressions to render her account less artificial. Chappelow exactly described her purpose when he said of the *Observations and Reflections*, 'to read 20 pages and hear Mrs. P. talk for 20 minutes is the same thing',[1] The 'lovely's', the 'dear, dear's', the 'charming's' were purposely included to give a feminine, garrulous quality to the whole.

To the twentieth century such a desire arouses neither surprise nor horror. We are used to the intrusion of the slang of the street into our books. A 'context crowded with familiar phrases and vulgar idioms'[2] would certainly not prejudice most modern readers. Even if we might still dislike many of her affected phrases, others probably would scarcely be noticed.

In her own day many people, though puzzled by the colloquialisms, were pleased in spite of themselves. George Selwyn, the wit and friend of Walpole, admitted to Lady Carlisle that the book 'with all its absurdities, has amused me more than many others have done which have a much better reputation';[3] and William Cowper, reading the volumes to the ladies after supper, wrote to his friend William Rose: 'It is the fashion, I understand, to condemn them. But we who make books ourselves are more merciful to bookmakers.'[4] James Edward Smith, in his three-volume *Sketch of a Tour on the Continent in the Years 1786 and 1787*, besides prefixing a quotation from Mrs. Piozzi on his title-page, added of her work (in an appendix devoted to lists of guide-books and other aids for future travellers):

This publication is too well known, and its authoress too celebrated, to need a criticism here. It is stamped with the character of genius, and few books are more full of ideas. . . .

I know not whether we have a right to censure the style of this publication, or to regret that passages of the most dazzling beauty are introduced amid inaccuracies of composition, which might be taken for carelessness, were they not evidently laboured to represent ease. The whole is so peculiar, and so masterly in its own way, we

---

[1] To Mrs. Piozzi, June 18, 1789 (Ry. 562, 4). Chappelow insisted: 'should anyone say to me, that twas a desultory Publication, I shall immediately reply—Twas intended to be so.' [2] *European Mag.*, op. cit.
[3] *Hist. Manusc. Comm.*, 15th Report—App. Part VI (1897), p. 679. See also Climenson, *Diaries of Mrs. Philip Lybbe Powys* (1899), p. 243.
[4] *Cowper's Corr.* iii. 396.

have no standard to judge it by, and had better, perhaps, submit to be pleased, though we do not know exactly why.[1]

Smith's perplexity, and his admission that there was no real criterion by which to judge Mrs. Piozzi's effort, probably represented the attitude of many of the readers of the day. Since the pseudo-Johnsonese style of most of the lesser writers was beginning to become unbearable, some were instinctively reaching out for an easier, freer mode of expression. Mrs. Piozzi's endeavour to write as she talked was welcomed, if at the same time it was misunderstood.

It must be admitted that she was not wholly successful in her stylistic experiment, even according to twentieth-century standards. Her character was too mercurial to produce any consistent, serious work. Consequently the composition was uneven throughout—light, conversational passages alternating with occasional involved and stilted descriptions in the more usual manner. While this lack of uniformity detracts from its absolute merit, *Observations and Reflections* remains a fascinating and delightful attempt to popularize travel literature.

The volumes may well be recommended to-day as an accompaniment to an up-to-date Baedeker, if certain shortcomings are always kept in mind. Many of the paintings described are now in the Louvre, brought there as the spoils of war by Napoleon.[2] Some of her information was erroneous, because of the credulity and the ignorance of the local guides; in other cases her smattering of Roman history led to fanciful reconstructions not acceptable to-day. Her comments, however, always have a personal touch, and are often illuminating as well as amusing; her anecdotes, while sometimes absurd, are never dull; and her observant eye and insatiable curiosity, together with a strong desire to understand the social conditions of her husband's country and to interpret them sympathetically for her uncomprehending countrymen, render the account a valuable exposition of life in Europe in the seventeen-eighties.

Observations and Reflections seems to have been widely circulated at the time, despite the fact that Cadell, as in the case of

---

[1] Smith's *Sketch* was published in London in 1793. The Appendix follows vol. iii. Prefixed to the first volume is a quotation from Mrs. Piozzi (i. 288). 'Italy is only a fine well-known academy figure, from which we all sit down to make drawings, according as the light falls, and our own seat affords opportunity.'

[2] In regard to art she was familiar with the two Richardsons' *An Account of Pictures and Statues in Italy,* and had undoubtedly read Lady Miller's *Letters from Italy,* first published in 1776. Her taste was influenced by these and other authorities, but her comments are nearly always personal.

Johnson's *Letters*, did not find it necessary to issue a second edition. A Dublin edition was issued in 1789, and in the following year it was translated into German and appeared as *Bemerkungen auf der Reise durch Frankreich, Italien und Deutschland von Esther Lynch Piozzi, aus dem Englischen mit einer Vorrede und Anmerkungen von Georg Forster.*[1] That Forster, who was a well-known writer, should have been connected with this translation shows the interest displayed on the Continent in Mrs. Piozzi's travel reminiscences.

In succeeding years the *Observations and Reflections* continued to be read, and Mrs. Radcliffe used some of Mrs. Piozzi's descriptions to give local colour to her novels of terror.[2] But the sustained attacks of her enemies, Boswell, Gifford, and others, gradually resulted in a tendency to ignore the book, as the production of a foolish woman. To-day many competent scholars know nothing of it except perhaps Gifford's couplet in his attack upon the Della Cruscans:

> See Thrale's grey widow with a satchel roam,
> And bring in pomp laborious nothings home.[3]

Mrs. Piozzi's comments and anecdotes, whatever they may be, are certainly not 'laborious nothings'. Possibly Gifford had never actually opened the work he was condemning. But standards change with the years, and time has been kind to Mrs. Piozzi; for some modern critics are even more enthusiastic over the *Observations and Reflections* than were the admirers of her own time. In 1892 the Countess Evelyn Martinengo Cesaresco, reprinting selected passages as *Glimpses of Italian Society in the Eighteenth Century from the 'Journey' of Mrs. Piozzi*, gives the impression that of all the English visitors to the Continent during this period, including Addison, Young, Smollett, and Sharpe, Mrs. Piozzi came the nearest to an appreciation and understanding of the life and manners of the countries through which she passed.[4] And another reader insisted that 'it still remains for our nineteenth century to produce a book which will read

---

[1] Published in Frankfurt and Mainz, 'bei Barrentrapp, und Wenner', 1790 (2 vols.). See appendix for other editions.
[2] Thomas Green in his diary for Nov. 25, 1800, wrote:
> Read the first volume of Mrs. *Piozzi's* Travels in Italy. Tolerably amusing, but for a pert flippancy, and ostentation of learning. Mrs. *Radcliffe* has taken from this work her vivid description of Venice, and of the Brenta, but oh! how improved in the transcript.

(*Gent. Mag.* civ. (1834), 10.) Dr. Marshall, on the other hand, feels that Mrs. Radcliffe owed more to Beckford than to Mrs. Piozzi (*Italy in English Lit.*, p. 167).
[3] W. Gifford, *Baviad and Maeviad* (8th ed. 1811), p. 10.
[4] Published by Scribner, New York, 1892.

as well a hundred years hence'.[1] That the narrative can still rouse admiration can be seen from the printed recommendations of such diverse critics as Mr. Osbert Sitwell and Dr. Roderick Marshall.[2] Indeed, although Johnsonians may always prefer the *Anecdotes*, for the majority of modern readers *Observations and Reflections* will remain Mrs. Piozzi's most valuable and entertaining publication.

The years of wandering had accustomed Piozzi to a life of constant change, and he was not content to stay long in one place. He was vaguely considering another journey to Italy, but Mrs. Piozzi was loath to quit England and give up control of Cecilia, whom she was determined to keep under her wing. Instead, to satisfy her husband and temporarily evade the issue, she planned various tours about England. Ever since Johnson's visit to Scotland in 1773, she had wanted to see the northern part of the island, and this seemed a perfect opportunity. Consequently the Piozzis, with Cecilia and their favourite dog Flo, left London on June 3, 1789, not even waiting for the actual publication of her volumes.

In Edinburgh, which they reached on July 7, after passing through Scarborough, Durham, and Newcastle, Mrs. Piozzi heard from Lysons and Dr. Lort of the success of her book.[3] Here also she met some of the local literati, but her correspondence contains little of interest about any of them except Dr. John Moore, the author of *Zeluco*.[4] At the same hotel, however, was a wealthy young Englishman who later became one of her intimate friends in London. His name was Samuel Rogers, and many years afterward he recorded his version of the meeting:

My Acquaintance with Mr. and Mrs. Piozzi began at Edinburgh,

[1] *Maggs Bros. Cat.*, No. 653, 1937. The writer is listed as M. S. Stillman. He added:

Mrs. Piozzi wrote wittily, describing scenes vividly, relating anecdotes with humour and point, never allowing her English prejudices to interfere with her judgment or to spoil her enjoyment of the scenes so new to her. Her knowledge of Italian must have been very thorough, she detected so readily the slightest differences in the dialect of each of the cities she visited. Her book remains a most valuable record of Italian society in the eighteenth century. It is delightfully written, and leaves an impression of extreme accuracy.

[2] O. Sitwell and M. Barton, *Brighton* (1935), p. 69; R. Marshall, op. cit., p. 201.
[3] Lysons's letter has apparently not survived, but is referred to in her reply of July 8, 1789. Dr. Lort wrote on July 11 that her book met with as favourable a reception as she could wish or expect, and insisted that he expected to read it himself three or four times (Ry. 544, 10).
[4] See her letters to Mrs. Byron (Ry. 546) and to Sam. Lysons (see p. 236, n. 2). During July the *World* contained comments on the Piozzis' tour. See issues of July 9, 17, 29, 30. Mrs. Piozzi is listed as having met Campbell, Erskine, Cullen, Murray, Robertson, and Blair in Edinburgh.

being brought about by the landlord of the hotel where they and I were staying. He thought that I should be gratified by 'hearing Mr. Piozzi's piano-forte:' and they called upon me, on learning from the landlord who I was, and that Adam Smith, Robertson, and Mackenzie had left cards for me.

I was afterwards very intimate with the Piozzis, and visited them often at Streatham. The world was most unjust in blaming Mrs. Thrale for marrying Piozzi: he was a very handsome, gentlemanly, and amiable person, and made her a very good husband. In the evening he used to play to us most beautifully on the piano. Her daughters never would see her after that marriage; and (poor woman) when she was at a very great age, I have heard her say that 'she would go down upon her knees to them, if they would only be reconciled to her'.[1]

Though wrong in stating that Mrs. Piozzi's daughters would never see her after her second marriage, Rogers was right in stressing her vain longing for reconciliation.

As usual, Mrs. Piozzi kept a separate journal devoted to an account of her itinerary and experiences along the way. Having just completed her observations on continental life, perhaps she contemplated a feminine Scotch 'Tour' as a continuation. Naturally her predecessor's account was always in her hand (the Doctor's, not Boswell's), and she commented to Mrs. Byron on July 11:

Were you ever much a Reader of Johnson's Tour to the Hebrides? Tis one of his first Rate Performances—I look it over now every day with double Delight—Oh how the Scotch do detest him!

Perhaps it was the influence of this work which rendered her own day-by-day account, filled as it is with descriptions of scenery and local monuments, deficient in the usual personal interest.[2] Intimate gossip about people on this journey is to be found in her correspondence rather than her journal.

Mrs. Byron inadvertently showed one of Mrs. Piozzi's long descriptive letters to Mr. Este, who immediately printed part of it in the *World*.[3] Feeling that this was a bit high-handed, Mrs. Piozzi was indignant. Probably she did not mind appearing in public print, but it was annoying to have her frank comments on Scotland published while she was still in the

---

[1] S. Rogers, *Table Talk* (1856), pp. 45–6.
[2] Ry. 623. This journal may some day be edited by Mr. J. D. Wright of the University of Manchester, and for this reason only a cursory description of the tour is here included.
[3] *World*, July 31, 1789. The editor quoted from 'what she says of *Edinburgh* to an accomplished friend of hers'.

country. An editor friend was not always an unadulterated blessing.

After a stay of about three weeks the Piozzis drove from Edinburgh to Glasgow, where they left their coach and 'scrambled' about Loch Lomond, Glencoe, and Inveraray in the carriages of the country. The original plan to follow Johnson through the Highlands had been given up because of bad weather and Mrs. Piozzi's ill health. Glasgow itself she did not find very entertaining, the city having 'much merit but no attraction', but the rambles through the Scottish lakes were more enjoyable. From Glasgow their route led south through Kendal, where she visited her old friend Mrs. Strickland, whom she had last seen in Paris in 1775,[1] and Cumberland, which provoked an immediate comparison with the northern Italian lakes. By August 19 they had reached Liverpool and their friends the Kembles; but with their immediate goal now the Vale of Clwyd, they did not linger long even in such congenial company, and by the end of August they were ensconced in Denbigh, seeing old acquaintances and relatives and settling business affairs with their agents. This, however, proved no easy task.

Piozzi, an Italian who could hardly understand English, could not readily understand Welsh methods of procedure; nor was Mrs. Piozzi much wiser. As she confessed to Mrs. Byron, they were at the mercy of unprincipled agents:

these nasty Steward's Accts. crack my Brains. I know no more of Business *now* than Cecilia does: and have best just Sense enough to see that I am cheated, without knowing how to extricate myself. Had not God given me always a large Fortune, I must have been in Prison Years ago.[2]

Too clever to be fooled by the schemers, she was not sufficiently mathematical to cope with them. As a result she became a shuttle-cock, driven back and forth between the various groups of agents caring for her affairs.

In spite of business worries she found time to show her husband her beloved Vale, and to her immense delight he declared it more beautiful than anything they had seen on their long tour. They both particularly admired the view from the road as it neared the top of Dymerchion Hill, just above her old family property of Bach-y-Graig. Here, she may have thought,

---

[1] See *French Journals*, pp. 59–64. Mrs. Strickland had been Cecilia Townley whom Mrs. Piozzi had first known when they were children together in London.
[2] Denbigh, Sept. 19, 1789 (Ry. 546, 24).

would be a perfect spot for a house. But this was a dream for the future; for the present there were problems enough in London.

The *World*, which had been keeping its readers informed during the summer of Mrs. Piozzi's movements about the island, on October 1 carried the notice: 'From the Vale of Clwyd to Mr. Greatheed's from Guy's Cliffe to Bath and from Bath to London form the remainder of the Piozzis' tour which will be welcome news.' Este was looking forward to early entertainments in Hanover Square, but Bath was alluring. 'Who would not love pretty Bath!' Mrs. Piozzi wrote to Lysons late in November, 'I am sure we prove our affection for it, by coming every autumn so.'[1] Since Mrs. Siddons, Mrs. Byron, Mrs. Lewis, General Burgoyne, and other of her intimate friends were also there, she was loath to leave. Nevertheless, she added to Lysons, 'But 'tis time to get home after so long a ramble.' It was not until December 27, 1789, however, that they finally arrived at Hanover Square, after a journey which she computed as over 1,300 miles.

[1] Nov. 28, 1789. About this time, for some reason, she sent a communication to the *Public Advertiser*, for this paper on Dec. 16, 1789, printed Johnson's verses 'In Theatro' together with her translation and an explanatory letter signed H. L. P.

XVII

STREATHAM RENEWED

1790–1794

IN the autumn of 1789 Mrs. Piozzi had referred to her mansion in Hanover Square as 'home'; yet in less than a year she was to move back to a house filled with memories of other days. Streatham Park, it will be remembered, had been let to Lord Shelburne in 1782, when Johnson had breathed a sad farewell to the home he had loved so deeply. Other tenants followed, but the lease of the last of these, Thomas Steele of the Treasury, came to an end on April 10, 1790.[1] After some deliberation, the Piozzis decided not to let the house again; instead they would live in it themselves.

By Thrale's will, a life interest in the house and grounds of Streatham was left to his wife, but the property would revert to the daughters at her death. While Mrs. Thrale was required to keep the place in reasonable repair, any extensive improvements to the buildings might thus be considered almost as a gift to her heirs. The tenants who had been living in the house had, nevertheless, taken such poor care of the place that much had to be done to render it habitable. As a result, his wife recorded, Piozzi spent through the spring of 1790 over £2,000 in a renovation of the entire property.[2] The house at Streatham was redecorated with a continental splendour unknown in the days of Thrale. Filled with costly vases and pictures brought back from Italy,[3] with rich fabrics and rarities, the

---

[1] Lord Shelburne had been followed as a tenant by General Dalrymple. In Oct. 1786 Cator, acting for Mrs. Piozzi, let the place to Thos. Steele for a year and six months. (See letter from Cator of Aug. 8, 1786, and the agreement signed Oct. 10, 1786, by Cator and Steele—Ry. 602, 3, 4.) This agreement had been extended for two additional years. In a letter of Apr. 1, 1790, Cator refers to the termination of the lease (Ry. 602, 7). In her daily note-book for 1790, on Apr. 10, Mrs. Piozzi made the notation, 'took possession of Streatham', but they did not actually move into the house until the middle of May (Ry. 616, and Thraliana, May 17, 1790).

[2] Mainwaring Piozziana, ii. 112; Hayward, ii. 71; *Whalley Corr.* ii. 343.

[3] Among the pictures was one supposed to be by Titian, one by Murillo, and others by Cipriani, Domenichino, Ruysdael, Canaletto, &c. Ancient Etruscan vases from Cicero's villa in Tusculum and numerous Italian art objects filled the rooms (*1816 sale cat.*). See also *Whalley Corr.* ii. 343.

comfortable, sedate English country house was changed into an Italian villa.

On July 25 the Piozzis gave a gay and splendid party to open the house for inspection, and with characteristic bravado Mrs. Piozzi selected the sixth anniversary of her second marriage to celebrate her reoccupation of the house of her first husband. Dinner guests filled the library and the adjoining rooms, while musicians played outside under the trees, which were illuminated with coloured lanterns. According to Horace Walpole, who unfortunately was not there himself, 'in the evening was a concert, and a little hopping, and a supper'.[1] Villagers and neighbours came from miles around to admire the decorations, and Mrs. Piozzi recounted that 'many Friends swear that not less than a Thousand Men Women & Children might have been counted in the House & Grounds, where tho' all were admitted, nothing was stolen, lost, broken, or even damaged'.[2]

Looking back years later her only wonder was where the money had come from for such extravagance, but Piozzi knew how to spend as well as save. In little matters he was parsimonious and careful; he kept detailed accounts of every sixpence spent in the kitchen; he listed every bottle of wine removed from the cellar; yet in large affairs he knew how to be lavish in the grand manner, and he was eager to show his Italian friends how he could shine far from his native land. Now master in the house where he had once been a lowly singing-instructor, he delighted to act the part of the generous host.

Piozzi was equally active in trying to increase the family income in every way possible. Over forty years before, John Salusbury, on the ill-fated attempt at colonization of Nova Scotia, had received grants of land near Halifax, of little value at the time, but by 1790 not to be ignored. What was more reasonable than to claim this long-forgotten heritage in the New World? John's daughter might finally be repaid for all those unhappy years of the past. Unfortunately, all efforts proved unavailing, for letters from officials in Halifax revealed that the property had years before been redistributed to other more active settlers. Unwilling to attempt expensive legal redress, the Piozzis wisely decided to drop the matter.[3] But it was a disappointment.

---

[1] Walpole, *Letters*, xiv. 278.   [2] *Thraliana*, July 28, 1790.
[3] Ry. 601, 34, 41; see also *Bentley's Misc.* xxviii (1850), 312, and *Thraliana*, May 3, 1790.

Another attempt to find ready money nearer home proved equally fruitless. Piozzi had always been suspicious of Cator, particularly since the revelation of the latter's duplicity about the payment of Lady Salusbury's claim; now he tried to secure some definite accounting of past income and expenses of the Thrale estate. The timber merchant, however, was not to be moved, and Mrs. Piozzi wrote to Perkins on Nov. 10, 1790, 'Mr. Piozzi cannot force from him any Book or Paper relative to my Affairs by any decent Methods, and so what he received or paid at that Time—Heaven knows—not I.'[1] Cator thought best not to humour a woman and her foreign husband with actual figures, which he probably suspected they would not understand.

In 1790 Cator's definite refusal to show any accounts proved effective, but it hardly served to allay the suspicions in the minds of the occupants of Streatham. Two years later a new set of legal advisers urged the Piozzis to substitute action for surmise. In a letter of September 5, 1792, J. F. Vandercom wrote that he did not wonder that Mrs. Piozzi had not sooner investigated her rights under Thrale's will and settlement, because her mind had been more nobly employed; 'but', Vandercom complained, 'what have your Trustees—what your Attorney, been about, not to know all this before? & so permit your income for several Years to suffer so material a diminution.'[2] In spite of the fact that no action had been taken over treatment by the old trustees, the new adviser continued, she still had a right to collect past obligations. One thing was evident; the matter should be investigated immediately. After some hesitation Vandercom's advice was taken, and for the next few years Mrs. Piozzi's affairs were kept in a constant turmoil of lawsuits, investigations, and conferences.

Although Mrs. Piozzi was increasingly plunged into business and legal complications, her chief interest continued to be people and conversation. At Streatham she entertained a succession of visitors from the Continent;[3] she occupied herself with occasional acts of kindness, such as persuading the famous Dr. Parr to accept two sons of Perkins for his school (vastly pleased she was at old Parr's flattering answers to her solicitations!);[4] and she busied herself with the various literary affairs

---

[1] Letters to Perkins. See p. 106, n. 3.   [2] Ry. 606, 5.

[3] Their names may be found in her engagement books and in Thraliana. The Marquis de Pindemonte, who had aided in the *Florence Miscellany*, was in England at this time and was a frequent guest.

[4] Hayward, i. 305; letters to Perkins, Nov. 10, Dec. 10, 1790.

of her guests. That new acquaintances made their appearance —the radical Helen Maria Williams, Sophia Weston, the friend of Anna Seward, the Misses Lee from Bath—was to be expected; nevertheless the old favourites—Dr. Whalley, Chappelow, Samuel Lysons—were not supplanted. With two exceptions, Mrs. Byron and Dr. Lort, whom death was to remove from the circle, the coterie of Hanover Square now moved out to Surrey.

Mrs. Siddons was still high on the pedestal of adoration. In the new Streatham she stood in the place of Johnson, and even while the workmen were still busy with the improvements to the house, the ailing actress, who because of her nervous condition was not appearing in London during the season of 1790, spent much of her time with Mrs. Piozzi. In a post-script to one of the latter's notes to Miss Weston, Mrs. Siddons wrote of her hostess: 'There are many disposed to comfort one, but no one knows so rationally or effectually how to do it as that unwearied spirit of kindness.'[1] The old companion of Dr. Johnson was a past mistress at relieving mental dejection.

For the next five years, except for two winters spent at Bath, and several trips to Wales, Mrs. Piozzi remained for the most part at Streatham.[2] It was here that she read with consuming interest Boswell's great biography, which appeared on May 16, 1791.[3] 'I have been now laughing & crying by turns for two Days over Boswell's Book', she wrote in Thraliana.[4] The sudden re-creation before her very eyes of whole episodes in the past brought much anguish of heart; the reading of the story of her son's death made her 'very ill indeed'; while the numer-ous humiliating, and even unjust, references to herself in the book stirred immediate indignation.

In spite of the fulsome language employed in their corre-spondence, Boswell and Mrs. Thrale had never become intimate friends. Each was jealous of the other's influence over their common idol; yet as long as she remained Mrs. Thrale, Boswell had always hoped to secure her aid in his proposed biography. As soon as he found, however, that she was to be a literary rival, his dislike became an open one. The quarrels ensuing from his quotation about Mrs. Montagu's *Essay on Shakespeare* deepened the rift, and her publication of Johnson's letters had

---

[1] *Letters to Pennington*, pp. 27–8.
[2] The Piozzis were in Bath from early Feb. to early Apr. 1791; and from late Jan. to the end of Mar. 1792. They were in Denbigh from Sept. 15 to the second week in Oct. 1792; and from July 25, 1794 to Apr. 9, 1795.
[3] F. A. Pottle, *Literary Career of James Boswell* (1929), p. 166.
[4] May 25, 1791.

stirred up a bitter antagonism. The woman who he must have felt had excised all the complimentary references to himself from the great man's published letters deserved no polite consideration on his part. As a result, in writing his biography Boswell included, near the end, a violent attack on the former Mrs. Thrale and her *Anecdotes*. But on a later revision, with the help of his friend Courtenay, he lightened his animadversions on the lady—for his own credit.[1] He must have seen that open attack would defeat his purpose—that there was a surer, more insidious way of demolishing his feminine rival. Consequently, in the *Life of Dr. Johnson* Boswell does not allow his animosity to show on the surface. Hardly any reference can be pointed out as offensive, though the sum total of the allusions is overwhelming. What Boswell has done is to undermine her character, little by little, by a long series of insinuations and qualifications. As an artistic achievement in depreciation it remains a masterpiece.

We know from various sources that Johnson often spoke warmly in praise of his 'Mistress of Streatham'. Miss Frances Reynolds, who should have been an unprejudiced observer, wrote: 'On the praises of Mrs. Thrale he used to dwell with a peculiar delight, a paternal fondness, expressive of conscious exultation in being so intimately acquainted with her.'[2] Miss Reynolds continued:

One day, in speaking of her to Mr. Harris, Author of *Hermes*, and expatiating on her various perfections,—the solidity of her virtues, the brilliancy of her wit, and the strength of her understanding, &c. —he quoted some lines . . .

'Virtues—of such a generous kind,
Good in the last recesses of the mind'.

Other observers also testify to the Doctor's overwhelming partiality for her. Whether Johnson was completely wrong in his estimate of the lady or not is beside the point. In his own day it was a matter of common knowledge that, before Piozzi came upon the scene, the Doctor was loud in the praise of his Mistress. Boswell's failure to record similar encomiums, to be sure, may be explained by the fact that in Boswell's presence Johnson may have been less complimentary.[3] What would appear on the surface to be wilful manipulation of the evidence

---

[1] *Private Papers*, xviii. 109 (Feb. 22, 1791).
[2] *John. Misc.* ii. 272. The quotation is from Dryden's translation of Persius. See also *Letters of Anna Seward*, iii. 72.
[3] His occasional praise is lost in qualifications. See *Life*, iv. 82.

may be merely a one-sided view. In any event the final effect in depreciation of the lady is much the same.

As has been pointed out, any study of Boswell's evidence must take into consideration the fact that his contemporary accounts of Johnson's conversation were often revised before publication in the *Life*. Boswell was not the parrot-reporter that some nineteenth-century critics supposed him; he was a conscious artist with high creative and dramatic gifts.[1] And today we are coming more and more to appreciate this artistry, as well as his basic integrity as a reporter. In many ways he produced a more consistent and amusing Johnson than verbatim accounts of the great man's conversation would have shown. Boswell's superiority over his rival biographers, therefore, lies not only in the completeness of his picture of Johnson, but also in the significant definition, the delicate shading, and the general coherence of his portrait. He justifies himself as a creative artist.

Of chief importance here is the fact that, while usually he did not greatly change Johnson's actual statements,[2] Boswell did sometimes show his bias in the manner of presenting them. Consequently, the general effect of numerous passages referring to one of his enemies, Mrs. Piozzi for example, is decidedly adverse, and the portrait that emerges is not a fair one. For this reason in the preceding pages, as far as possible, only remarks found in Boswell's original notes have been quoted. A reading of these contemporary jottings gives us a very different picture of Johnson's Mistress of Streatham from that developed in the *Life*. As first written, without Boswell's later allusions and covert attacks, the accounts certainly bring us closer to the real scenes described. Thus Boswell's belittling of his rival, Mrs. Thrale, in the *Life*, can now be better understood, and a more just estimate secured.

Boswell must have known that many people of his own day would question the authenticity of his accounts. To meet this

---

[1] See the introductory remarks of Geoffrey Scott and Frederick Pottle throughout the various volumes of the *Private Papers*. See also H. Pearson, 'Boswell as an Artist', *Cornhill Magazine* (Dec. 1932), p. 704. For an example of how Boswell revised his original quotation to make a better story, compare *Life*, iv. 275, and *Private Papers*, vi. 172.

[2] Compare the accounts for Apr. 1, 1781, *Life*, iv. 82, with *Private Papers*, xiv. 185-6. Though a printer's change of punctuation, it was allowed to stand. Compare also *Life*, ii. 328, with *Private Papers*, x. 160. In this account, for Mar. 28, 1775, Boswell in his printed version points the episode at Mrs. Thrale, and then introduces another sentence into the mouth of Dr. Johnson generalizing on what had preceded.

contingency he went to superhuman lengths to consult every possible source of information, and to check every statement he made. Yet in a considerable portion of his work, despite his rigorous approach and the mass of his facts, Boswell had to rely on second-hand evidence. In this part of the fabric it was easy to find flaws. For example, Mrs. Lewis, the former Miss Cotterell, found much to criticize in Boswell's account of the first meeting of Johnson and Sir Joshua Reynolds. On August 23, 1791, she wrote to Mrs. Piozzi, after reading the first volume of the new biography, 'if the other anecdotes are as inaccurate as those relating to the Miss Cotterells the trouble he took in fixing dates was very Ill bestow'd'. Mrs. Lewis then proceeded to point out the errors in time and circumstance in Boswell's account, insisting, '& as to the *agreable conversation*, he puts into the mouth of Mr. Reynolds it is wholly imaginary . . .'[1]

In this case the biographer had probably accepted Sir Joshua's own account of the affair, which so many years later was sure to be vague in minor details. In other places, too, Boswell's dramatic instincts led him to take some liberties in painting the scenes round his major figure. Fanny Burney's niece, Marianne Francis, is responsible for the story that Lady Rothes was very angry with Boswell for printing details which he knew to be untrue about one of her dinner parties. He replied that 'in telling a Story, one is *forced* to embroider it a little—like putting trees in a Landscape, that's all'.[2]

This realization that people would look for mistakes in his evidence probably led Boswell to hit upon the obvious scheme of diverting the attack instead against his rivals. Neither Sir John Hawkins nor Mrs. Piozzi was popular with the general public; the former with his unsociable manner, and the lady made vulnerable by her sensational second marriage, were

---

[1] *French Journals*, p. 44. On the other hand see Francis Hardy, *Memoirs of Charlemont* (2nd ed., 1812), i. 401, and an autograph memorandum of Sir George Beaumont, Sept. 12, 1826 (*Adam Libr.* iii. 23). Boswell's method of reporting Johnson's conversation was satirized by a number of contemporary writers. As a sample see A. Chalmers, *A Lesson in Biography, or How to Write the Life of One's Friend, etc.* (1798), and 'Dialogues of the Dead. Boz and Poz in the Shades', included in Wm. Mudford, *Critical Enquiry* (1803). Yet others recognized that Boswell was trying to reproduce an actual three-dimensional picture of Johnson. Arthur Murphy, in 1792 (Ry. 548, 7), while apologizing to Mrs. Piozzi for not having attacked Boswell with all the severity in his power, not desiring a paper war on his hands, added: 'I contented myself with calling him indirectly the *Careful Theobald of a Whale.*' Murphy quoted Wilkes as saying,
    Who tells whate'er you think, whate'er you say,
    And if He Lies not, must at Least betray.
[2] *J. Rylands Bulletin*, xvi (1932), 12.

easy marks, and necessarily without many active defenders. Throughout his book, accordingly, Boswell constantly kept pointing out the mistakes and errors made in Hawkins's official biography and Mrs. Piozzi's *Anecdotes*.[1] His continued expression of open disbelief in many of the lady's accounts has resulted in neglect for over a century of much interesting detail about Dr. Johnson.

It would be impossible in the present volume to analyse carefully each allegation of inaccuracy made by Boswell in his *Life of Dr. Johnson*. Some can easily be substantiated, while others may as obviously be disproved. In a large number of cases we have no external evidence on which to base decision, and the problem becomes merely a question of whose word to accept. Though Mrs. Piozzi, in annotating her own copy of the *Life*, reiterated her claim to the veracity of her anecdotes,[2] Johnsonians have always preferred to accept the word of her more successful rival. This is reasonable, and probably right. Boswell had in general a much clearer zeal for the truth. Nevertheless, it must be admitted that a number of his carping criticisms are unsupported by corroborating evidence and cannot be definitely proved.

Boswell, throughout his volumes, carefully insinuated that Doctor Johnson had had less unqualified admiration for the former Mrs. Thrale than was generally supposed. This was to be his revenge for the treatment allotted him in her publication of Johnson's letters. The lady herself was quick to feel the implication. 'If Johnson was to me the back Friend he has represented,' Mrs. Piozzi wrote in Thraliana, 'let it cure me of ever making *Friendship* more with any human Being.'[3] Others realized that the biographer had hardly been fair to several individuals. Horace Walpole, no friend of either Mrs. Piozzi or Boswell, wrote to Miss Mary Berry that Boswell had treated Mrs. Piozzi, Mrs. Montagu, and Bishop Percy shamefully.[4] Boswell's occasional willingness to yield to prejudice is a minor blemish on his otherwise remarkable accomplishment.

Before Boswell's masterpiece appeared, upon her return to Streatham from Bath in April 1791, Mrs. Piozzi had begun

---

[1] *Life*, iii. 226, 243, 404; iv. 83, &c.
[2] Hayward, ii. 123–31. See also Minna Steele Smith, 'Manuscript Notes by Madame Piozzi in a Copy of Boswell's Life of Johnson', *London Mercury*, v (1922), 286–93. In one instance she wrote opposite Boswell's expression of doubt: 'He told me this *himself*; I did not dream it, & could not have invented it, or heard it from others. I will *Swear* he told me as I tell the Public.'
[3] May 25, 1791. [4] Walpole, *Letters*, xiv. 438.

writing a new book. Always experimenting, always trying new forms, she decided this time to write a series of dialogues to be called 'Una & Duessa', in which she would discuss the literary, philosophical, and artistic problems of the day. All through the late spring and early summer she worked hard at these dialogues. By July a hundred and forty-nine pages of her blank book were filled, and six dialogues completed; then the composition was put aside.[1]

Although Mrs. Piozzi maintained in Thraliana that the decision to shelve 'Una & Duessa' was due to the advice of her husband, she undoubtedly recognized that publication of the dialogues would not enhance her reputation.[2] This particular form hampered her easy style, with the result that the language was laboured and turgid, far from her usual idiomatic prose. She was not fitted to write a serious philosophical work, and it is to her credit that she quickly recognized that the dialogues were a failure. Nor did she ever seem to regret the sacrifice, for scarcely any references can be found to the manuscript in her voluminous correspondence and diaries. This was simply an experiment to be forgotten.

Possibly we too should accept this verdict and allow 'Una & Duessa' to sleep on undisturbed; yet the dialogues may to-day be read with interest, if with little pleasure. From the verbose, stilted repartee of the two Spenserian characters, with their long-drawn-out harangues, some insight may be gained into the late eighteenth century's attitude towards the revolutionary tenets of the day. Mrs. Piozzi was a staunch monarchist, an unbending conservative in political matters, as befitted a friend of Dr. Johnson. Filled with horror by the radical books of her friend Helen Maria Williams, she felt that the unrest emanating from across the Channel was a disease to be dreaded. Thus Una inveighs against the French philosophers, 'that pernicious School of Falsehood', whose notions if permitted to spread would endanger all humanity.

See you not that they are seeking to infect England with their Folly? & set that happiest of all Nations against itself & its best Friends—as the great Plague which desolated Mankind a Century ago was said to proceed from a pestilential Vapour bursting out of a fissure in some Part of the Kingdom of Cathay—so this Intellectual, but equally morbid and Epidemic Disease, that appears in larger or smaller Tokens of Putridity, over the civilized Nations of

---

[1] Ry. 635. With note in Mrs. Piozzi's hand, 'begun in April and ended in July 1791'.   [2] Thraliana, July 1791.

Europe, owes its Original Birth to the *Boue de Paris*—can you say that it does not Duessa?

The dialogues are filled with many such expressions of fear of the French democrats.[1] Reading 'Una & Duessa', one might easily imagine it to have been written by a twentieth-century conservative viewing with alarm the current Red menace. There is the same horror, the same sense of impending doom, the same feeling that civilization is coming to an end. Yet Mrs. Piozzi lived calmly through the Napoleonic wars almost to the reign of Victoria.

'Una & Duessa' is not all political propaganda. Interspersed are occasional references to Garrick, Mrs. Siddons, Dr. Johnson, and other well-known people of the day, but for the most part these are embedded in long, dreary excursions into aesthetics and philosophy. As a sample, which also shows Mrs. Piozzi's attitude towards style, a short quotation may suffice. Una, who had been discussing the philosopher Bernard Mandeville, makes the remark:

had he but defin'd Vice and Virtue! had he once drawn the Boundary—his Antagonists could scarcely have obtained such Advantages over him; but something will always be wanting—among *my* Votaries; while yours err from Redundance in almost every Science—Colours too much varied—Words too much accumulated—notes too much confused, & cluttered all together.

DUESSA. Shall we then recommend Simplicity as the only Charm? old Ballads as the best Poetry?—Addison went near to do so; and Percy in these latter Days would fain have revived the Fancy; but course Prose like Mandeville's would scarcely be read now, when Writers are forced to cull every Flower of Rhetoric to induce lazy Mortals to open their Books at all. Burke & Della Crusca shew the true Taste of this Age in England is ornament & plenitude, for I will not call it Redundance.

UNA. Simplicity will charm every Age when accompanied with Majesty or Pathos; Great Thoughts have little need to be adorned or amplified . . .

.   .   .   .

For Historical, Political or Moral Truth, the plainest Diction is the best—Information is clouded by Multiplicity of ideas however elegantly expressed, while the Reader looks in vain for his lost Position, & receives only Delight in lieu of the Instruction he sought for.

'Una & Duessa' had been all-engrossing throughout the

[1] See also J. M. Thompson, *English Witnesses of the French Revolution* (1938), pp. 1-2.

spring of 1791, but as summer advanced, and the conviction grew that the work could never be published, inspiration flagged. Early in August, instead of continuing her writing, Mrs. Piozzi accepted an invitation to visit Mrs. Siddons at her country retreat at Nuneham, on the banks of the Thames below Oxford, while Piozzi took two continental friends, the rich young Marquis Trotti and his tutor the Abbé de Buchetti, on a tour through Wales and western England.

The Piozzis had met the young Trotti and his cultivated companion in Paris in 1784, and since that time had kept up a friendly intimacy with them. On the present trip to England the Marquis had fallen in love with one of Mrs. Piozzi's younger friends, Harriet Lee, later a popular authoress of the day. The sentimental Mrs. Piozzi, who was delighted to further a romance between two members of her set, filled her letters through 1791 and 1792 with references to the affair. Considerations of social position and religion, however, stood squarely in his way. Such barriers might have appeared insuperable to many English-women of the day, but not to Mrs. Piozzi. Writing to Miss Weston, she related a recent conversation with the lovesick Trotti, and ended with the remark:

Who would have pressed him further to tell that which I know already, and which no power on earth can cure; the difference of Birth, Religion, and Country? If however he has but *love enough*, all those three things which would drown him if he tried to swim across, may be *leaped* over; and I, who have taken the jump before him, never cease to show him how well I feel myself after it. . . .[1]

Mrs. Piozzi had been willing to brave the upheaval, but Trotti could not bring himself in the end to risk all, as she had gladly done.

While the three travellers wandered through Wales, Mrs. Piozzi remained quietly at Nuneham, writing verses and help-ing to nurse the ailing Mrs. Siddons; but after a few weeks the latter's health was so much improved that Mrs. Piozzi was able to accept an invitation to visit Miss Owen at Shrewsbury, at which place late in August she was rejoined by her husband on his way home.

Miss Owen was one constant link with the past, but not many others remained. Arthur Murphy, to be sure, during the next few years renewed his old intimacy with Streatham, and in Bath in the winter of 1792 she met the Irish clergyman, Dr. Thomas Campbell, who had been a constant visitor in South-

---

[1] *Letters to Pennington*, p. 41.

wark seventeen years before. Campbell, engaged in gathering information for a life of Goldsmith, asked her for anecdotes. She mentioned the fact in a letter to Murphy, who, in reply, related a long amusing story of Goldsmith's behaviour on the night of the first production of *The Good-Natured Man*. This, he suggested, Mrs. Piozzi might 'dress up for Doctr. Campbell' in her own manner, which was 'allways Extremely happy'.[1] From our knowledge of Campbell's memoir, however, we cannot tell how much she actually did pass on to him and Dr. Percy of her recollections of 'Doctor Minor'.

Upon her return to Streatham from Bath in the spring of 1792, Mrs. Piozzi found it necessary to occupy herself with another incipient romance, this time more annoying than pleasing. Her youngest daughter Cecilia, though only fifteen years old, had acquired a determined admirer, a certain James Drummond. From the existing correspondence Drummond appears to have been a fortune hunter, probably more interested in the Thrale dowry than in the beauty of his beloved; but he was properly sentimental and acted the part of the distressed lover in true stage fashion. At first undoubtedly a trifle dazzled, Cecilia soon agreed to the banishment of her lover. Drummond, however, refused for some time to accept his dismissal, and annoyed the family with his melodramatic importunities. In the end he finally disappeared from sight, but not until he had caused Mrs. Piozzi much vexation.[2]

Cecilia, for one reason or another, was a constant trial. The following autumn, when on a visit to Denbigh in Wales, the girl was taken so ill with a cold that the doctors feared her lungs were affected. To the horror of all the household Cecilia actually began to spit some blood. Her mother wrote despairingly in October, 'Indeed, indeed, Cecilia has, between her lovers and her illness, worked my poor heart very hard this year.'[3] Then to make matters worse their coachman, Jacob, fell ill and Sally Siddons, who had accompanied the party as a companion for Cecilia, was suddenly stricken with an alarming attack of asthma. On the return journey home on October 14, Mrs. Piozzi wrote from Guy's Cliffe to Miss Weston, 'if no new affliction arises we shall be at Streatham Park on Thursday night, 18, and you shall see what yet remains of your poor H. L. Piozzi.'[4] It was all reminiscent of the days of the Children's

---

[1] Ry. 548, 6; Mar. 14, 1792. See also K. C. Balderston, *Percy's Memoir of Goldsmith* (1926). [2] Ry. 572, 3–9.
[3] *Letters to Pennington*, p. 66; Thraliana, Sept. 10, 1792. [4] Ibid., p. 70.

Book. Whenever there were children in the household, she was never free from worry.

During the winter of 1793 Cecilia, soon her lively self again, led her mother a merry chase. With the handsome good looks of her father's family, Cecilia combined her mother's gay, volatile disposition. As a result she never lacked a train of ardent admirers, a fact which, though it flattered Mrs. Piozzi's pride, was also a source of continual concern. One of the girl's suitors was the banker-poet, Samuel Rogers, whom the Piozzis had met in Scotland in 1789. Rogers had found more to admire at Streatham than his hostess's conversation, and in January 1794 actually made formal proposals for Cecilia's hand, only to be refused. As Mrs. Piozzi amusingly noted in Thraliana, 'he is too ugly to hope Acceptance: who but himself could fancy She would think of *him*? . . . She wants neither Money nor Verses I suppose, & like the Girl in the Comedy would rather have a Husband with white Teeth.'[1] Cecilia was like her mother in many ways; romance rather than social position was what she sought in a husband. Meanwhile she flirted with every man who entered the house, and kept Mrs. Piozzi in a continual state of nervous anxiety.

The early winter of 1793 was spent at Streatham, and Mrs. Piozzi wrote to Miss Weston, now married to a Mr. William Pennington, master of ceremonies at the Clifton Hot Wells:

I'm told London has a violent Influenza in it, and will keep my Miss out while I can, but one's arms do so ache with pulling at an unbroken Filly that longs to hurt herself by skipping into some mischief or other, that, like the old Vicar in Goldsmith's Novel, I get weary of being wise, and resolve to see people once happy in almost any way.[2]

By March she was able to take Cecilia into London for a series of parties. 'I have covered Cecy with finery, and sate up till morning at every place without repining, while she was diverted, I hope,' she wrote to the same correspondent on March 12. Late hours and London 'Flash', however, were beginning to lose their charm, and she longed to get back to 'counting my Poultry, and kissing my *Canes*'.

On this visit to London a very exciting event occurred. Not since the summer of 1787 had she held any communication with her elder daughters except about business matters; then suddenly on March 16 Piozzi received a short note from Queeney

---

[1] Thraliana, Jan. 23, 1794; see also *Letters to Pennington*, p. 107.
[2] *Letters to Pennington*, p. 76; Jan. 17, 1793.

asking to see him the next morning. Attending her summons, he was startled to learn of the intention of the three sisters to call upon their mother the next day. After six long years, this was the first move for reconciliation.[1]

As she sat in her lodgings nervously awaiting the visit, Mrs. Piozzi's mind must have been in a turmoil. There was so much to plan: the breakfast things set for four daughters instead of one, safe topics for conversation, ways to ensure a return of the old intimacy. To have Queeney, Susanna, and Sophia with her again in the same room—it was breath-taking even to consider.

There was, of course, the chance that at the last minute the girls would refuse to come—but surely this time all would be well.

The morning arrived; the three 'Miss Thrales' appeared; they had breakfast; they seemed in high good humour. Queeney and her mother, not to be daunted by any difficult situation, chattered away about 'popular subjects'; for in spite of the tenseness in the air, neither was willing to let the other see that there was anything unusual about the occasion. Later Mrs. Piozzi told Mr. Richard Greatheed, who had dropped in by chance, to tell Mrs. Siddons how well (like Rosalind) she had '*counterfeited*'. Everything ended with great propriety; the next day the visit was returned, and the daughters invited to Streatham for Easter Monday. But though apparently Mrs. Piozzi managed to remain cool and collected, the nervous strain of the excitement did not wear off for several days. On the 20th, after her return to the country, she admitted to Mrs. Pennington that 'her spirits were so oddly kept afloat', that she had 'never been *sleepy* since Saturday that Piozzi received the letter, and this is Wednesday morning'.

In the midst of the tension she could not but see the humorous side of the affair. Referring to the prospect of having the girls for dinner on Easter Monday, she added:

All the Town would buy *tickets* I'm sure, with pleasure, could they procure 'em, and pass through danger itself willingly, *to see the sight*. I told my Master it would have been best to take the little Theatre, and give them the whole show at once.

[1] Ibid., p. 83. The following description of the reconciliation with her daughters is based on letters to Mrs. Pennington, a series of unprinted notes from Queeney (Ry. 533, 13, 18), and Mrs. Piozzi's replies (Lansdowne MSS.). Miss Balderston suggests that it is possible the girls now sought a renewal of friendship because of certain business problems having to do with the affairs of their uncle Nesbitt. See letter from Mrs. Piozzi to Queeney, May 15, 1793, &c., also p. 175.

None the less, nearly two weeks later, when the three daughters arrived for the day as promised, Mrs. Piozzi's joy was complete. She was 'content to be happy', and not too inquisitive of the reason. 'All is vastly well,' she maintained to Mrs. Pennington, her regular correspondent, 'they are contented to take me up, as they set me down, without alledging a reason; and I am contented to be taken and left by *them* without reasoning on the matter at all.' Merely to sit and admire her eldest daughter was enough; long ago she had given up any thought of securing real affection. Yet it was impossible for her not to notice the restraint and reserve shown by the other two. 'The Girls seemed less shy of Mr. Piozzi than of me, comical enough! But he is *so* good, and *so* attentive to them! How you would love him!' The daughters had decided to go through the outward form, but had no intention of returning to real intimacy.

Through April the public reconciliation continued. On April 21 she wrote:

Nothing serves them but fagging me out, that we may show ourselves *in public*, Susanna says; so out I march, and do not laugh nor cry, though under perpetual temptations to both, for why did we not always do so? or what has happened to make us do so *now* . . . Cecilia thinks 'tis a merry life, and when she is in a calm, as mine Hostess Quickly says by Doll Tearsheet, she is *sick*.

To outsiders the *rapprochement* probably seemed complete, and during the spring of 1793 Streatham Park again resounded to the laughter of all the Thrales. In June Mrs. Piozzi wrote:

Mr. Murphy too is now almost perpetually in our society, and my own Lasses beat up our quarters whenever London affords little of that tumultuous amusement which delights the first 30 years of life.

At least for a time the tongues of the gossip-mongers would be stilled.

Although the last few years had largely been given up to society and entertaining, Mrs. Piozzi could never remain long without some literary iron in the fire. As soon as the cumbersome dialogues between 'Una & Duessa' had been put aside, her active mind began to consider other possibilities. Living constantly with a foreign husband and his friends, Mrs. Piozzi could not but notice the great difficulty which they had in selecting the right English words in normal conversation. The large number of synonymous terms constantly in use in the language proved an insurmountable obstacle to persons not accustomed from birth to sense the minute shades of meaning involved. She found, moreover, that many cultivated Englishmen used words in wrong connotations, with little regard for the true meaning of the terms. Long association with a dictionary-maker made this a constant vexation. Would it not be possible, she thought, to devise a simple list of the most common groups of similar words, with an analysis of the differences in implication and suggestions for their use? Girard's French compilation was familiar to her, but she knew no similar volumes of English synonyms. Even as early as December 1791 she had considered such a publication, and by the next March was definitely engaged in preliminary work.[1] Throughout 1792, whenever she had a moment's spare time, Mrs. Piozzi worked away at her task.

By the summer of 1793 the composition was well advanced. On August 1 Mrs. Piozzi wrote to Queeney, 'You said I should copy out my *own* Book,—my *own* self: so I this Morning set about it.'[2] Evidently a first draft of one portion at least was completed. While her husband hurried away for a short business trip to Wales, she seriously began the final revision, and largely because several friends had insisted that she did not have enough copy, she decided to enlarge in her usual manner at the same time the final copy was made for the printer. On August 10 she wrote again to Queeney, who was now a constant correspondent:

You see I steal Time to laugh with you tho' I do make believe busy; and if you send me a Set of Synonymes for the second Volume or the latter end of this, I'll insert them for the sake of doing something in Johnson's Phrase 'to hold all together.' Your Theme must be after H—— however, unless your Answer comes quicker than this last, because like Hardham's hapless Brat who was getting the Dictionary by heart 'I am past Letter C already.' and added the Old Man, 'he never reach'd D, for he died on't.'

Mrs. Piozzi's request must have brought a querulous response

[1] *Thraliana.* The Abbé Girard's *Synonymes François* passed through many editions, and it is impossible to guess which one Mrs. Piozzi used. She seems to have assumed that there had been no English imitation, possibly being unfamiliar with *The Difference between Words esteemed Synonymous, in the English Language; and the Proper Choice of them determined,* 2 vols., published by Dodsley in 1766. This work contained a translation of part of Girard's preface and employed much the same method as the French work.

[2] Lansdowne MS. The following letters to Queeney and the elder Thrale daughters are all from this collection. My quotations are from typescript copies generously provided by the late Lord Lansdowne.

from her eldest daughter, for on the 22nd another letter was
dispatched to Queeney in Southampton.

Oh Serpentella! and who thought of asking Help for the Synonymes?—I would not accept help from Doctor Johnson as you well
know, or I should not have waited for his Death before I commenced
Authour—in good Time! *such* an Author! but the Fact is, I meant
a String of Parallel Words; *Spring, Fountain, Source, Well*—or *Bush,
Briar, Thorn* &c. the Theme in that manner given by *you*, and *I* to
write the Stuff. *now* you understand me. I really do work very hard
tho' seriously—ten pages o' Day copying, besides a little Composition now & then to stretch and swell: but this is my best Time for
Diligence, as Mr. Piozzi is in Wales, and there is nobody near to
drop in and disturb one at this Time o' Year. I should like to make
it two thin Octavos like Brown's Estimate and sell it like Merlin as
dear as I can, *to buy pretty Gown, and pay little Expence* &c.

By keeping conscientiously at work, copying and enlarging
her volumes, she was able to write to her eldest daughter at the
end of October that the last was nearly copied out. She was
now interested in finding a publisher who would buy the copyright, for which she confidently expected a large sum. It was
Queeney, strangely enough, who encouraged her mother in
this desire. The usually sensible Miss Thrale wrote, 'I think
you ought to have a very good Price for your Synonymes, & I
do not doubt would have anything you asked almost but that
Money is so scarce now. . . .'[1]

The manuscript was submitted to Robinson of Paternoster
Row, who asked his good friend Arthur Murphy to give him
his advice as to what it was worth. Recognizing the handwriting, Murphy immediately offered his services as intermediary in making arrangements for the publication.[2] On the
12th of November he wrote to Mrs. Piozzi that he had come
to an agreement with the publisher, who would give her £300
for the copy, payable £100 on the day of publication, £100 in
three months from that day, and £100 six months later.[3]
Robinson stipulated that the volumes should contain at least
400 pages each. Later, on the 29th, Murphy added that he was
preparing a contract embodying much the same provisions as
he had outlined in the previous letter, which seems to have been

---

[1] Ry. 553, 3. From Bath, Nov. 22, 1793.
[2] See Mrs. Piozzi's letter to Chappelow, Feb. 24, 1800 (Ry. 560, 90).
[3] Ry. 548, 8, 9. In Thraliana, Jan. 23, 1794, Mrs. Piozzi maintained that she
was to receive £500 for the copyright, but she explicitly stated in a letter to
Queeney in February that Robinson was giving her £300 for 500 pages of her
large handwriting.

accepted, though actually she received the entire £300 on the day of publication rather than by instalments.[1]

Late in November Mrs. Piozzi was temporarily forced, by the illness of her husband, to give up work on her new book. Earlier in the year Piozzi had suffered a very severe attack of gout, at which time he had lain on a 'rack of torment' for fifty hours, able to doze for only a few minutes at a time. Now came another violent seizure. 'For Twenty Hours', his wife wrote to Queeney, 'he screamed like a Woman in Labour: I did not know (like Doctor Johnson & the Tart) that Gout could have been *so bad*.' Nor did the affliction pass away as rapidly as it had appeared, for on December 21 Mrs. Piozzi added, 'these Dismals have kept back my Synonymes, & I am as nerve-shaken as possible'. As the invalid himself once put it, he seemed to advance towards recovery like the lobsters—backwards.[2]

Although Piozzi had always been susceptible to gout, it had not proved much of an annoyance during the early years of their marriage. But from this time on the seizures came more frequently, and his wife's plans had always to be dependent on his health. In this instance three successive attacks throughout December and January plunged the whole household into gloom. Nevertheless, early in February 1794 he was so much improved that, to amuse Cecy and to expedite Mrs. Piozzi's publication, they arranged to spend part of each week in London, staying in their former house in Hanover Square. It was their custom to go in every Tuesday, returning again to Streatham on Saturday. Now that her book was in the press, Mrs. Piozzi was kept busy correcting proof. On February 23 she wrote to Queeney that she had just finished the last sheet of the first volume and that she found producing a book a very tedious operation indeed. Moreover, she was beginning to get nervous about its reception by the public, although her chief worry seems to have been that Robinson was not sufficiently active in advertising the coming work.

The newspapers certainly were tardy in announcing *British Synonymy*, and as a consequence it is difficult to tell exactly when the two volumes appeared. Since, however, Mrs. Piozzi noted in Thraliana on April 3 that the 'Synonymes' were published, and on April 10, 1794, received her payment for the copyright, it may be assumed that the exact date was some time

---

[1] The receipt for £300, signed by Hester Lynch Piozzi, Apr. 10, 1794, is in the Adam collection (*Adam Libr.* iii. 196).

[2] *Letters to Pennington*, p. 78.

early in the month.[1] On the 16th Horace Walpole wrote that he had run through both volumes, further evidence that by this time some readers at least had received their copies.[2]

In considering *British Synonymy* one must always remember the non-English public for whom it was first written. In the second volume Mrs. Piozzi relates that Prince Gonzaga di Castiglione, when once in England, dined in company with Dr. Johnson at the house of a friend. Thinking it would be both polite and gay to drink the Doctor's health with some proof that he had also read his works, the Prince called out to Johnson across the table, 'At your good health, Mr. Vagabond.' He meant, of course, to say 'Mr. Rambler', but a confusion of partly synonymous words led him into an error which was probably as amusing to the other guests as it was annoying to the Prince.[3] It was to prevent mistakes of this sort that Mrs. Piozzi wrote her volumes. The subtitle itself was self-ex-explanatory: 'An Attempt at Regulating the Choice of Words in Familar Conversation. Inscribed, with Sentiments of Gratitude and Respect, to such of her Foreign Friends as have made English Literature their peculiar Study.'

The method employed was simple. Groups of words having similar meanings but used in different connotations were defined as clearly as possible, and then used in sentences to show their correct usage. As an example, the words 'Eagerness, Earnestness, Vehemence, Avidity, Ardour in Pursuit' were used in a single sentence showing typical uses in conversation. 'A man is said to follow pleasures with EAGERNESS, to seek knowledge with EARNESTNESS, to press an argument with VEHEMENCE, to thirst for power with ambitious AVIDITY, and drive a flying enemy before him with ARDOUR of pursuit.'[4] Finally, in order to give added interest to her definitions, she included in many cases personal anecdotes of well-known characters exemplifying the usage in question. To-day these last provide much the most interesting reading in the book.

If Mrs. Piozzi had been willing to limit herself to simple explanations of the different shades of meaning in English words, amplified with anecdotes of famous men, there would be little to censure in her work. She could not, however, refrain from numerous excursions into the realm of etymology, where

---

[1] See p. 369, n. 1. The published price of the two volumes, octavo, was 12*s*. in boards (*London Chronicle*, May 1, 1794).   [2] Walpole, *Letters*, xv. 284.
[3] *Brit. Syn.* ii. 358. Also *Life*, iii. 411. This incident probably occurred in 1777. See *Letters*, No. 513.   [4] Ibid. i. 187.

she was distinctly out of her depth. Her derivations, in the light
of present-day knowledge, are often ludicrously wrong, and
even in her own day competent linguists found much to contradict.[1] On the other hand, although Mrs. Piozzi does not
merit remembrance as a philologist, it must be admitted that
a lifelong interest in words gave her an ear sensitive to shifting
values in the everyday speech of her time.

Modern historians of the English language can find something of value in *British Synonymy*. For example, Mrs. Piozzi
records temporary popular reaction in the seventeen-nineties
to particular words and phrases. The word 'dubious', she
insists, had for the time being been thrown into disrepute for
the simple reason that it had been constantly mispronounced
by a clown in a popular comedy some years before. In good
society the word had thus taken on a comic connotation, and
people grew afraid of using it in serious conversation.[2] She
lists the gradual entrance of words into the language, fleet-
ing changes in meaning, alterations in utility, variations in
acceptability. Though often hidden among a mass of mistaken
notions and long classical allusions, these records of contemporary speech give *British Synonymy* some usefulness even
to-day.

Most modern readers, if any should by chance pick up the
volumes, will find their chief interest in the anecdotes of Dr.
Johnson and others which are scattered throughout. Concentration on her earlier *Anecdotes* has blinded many students
to the fact that in later works Mrs. Piozzi continued to draw
on her great store of recollections of her famous friend. Actually
Johnson is mentioned fifty times in the two volumes of *British
Synonymy*, and eighteen of the references occur in original
anecdotes.[3] To illustrate the word 'prodigality', his verses on
Sir John Lade's coming of age, written years before in 1780,
were here printed for the first time.[4] To serve as a sample of
the power of fascination she related:

'When Foote told a story at dinner time,' said Dr. Johnson, 'I
resolved to disregard what I expected would be frivolous; yet as the
plot thickened, my desire of hearing the catastrophe quickened at
every word, and grew keener as we seemed approaching towards
its conclusion. The fellow *fascinated* me, Sir; I listened and laughed,

---

[1] Horne Tooke's copy (now at Bowood) is copiously annotated with derogatory
remarks. See Lansdowne, *Johnson and Queeney* (1932), p. xxvi. See also p. 373, n. 2.
[2] *Brit. Syn.* i. 173.
[3] See particularly i. 24, 82, 218, 323; ii. 120, 123, 183, 256, 354, 358.
[4] Ibid. i. 359-60.

and laid down my knife and fork, and thought of nothing but Foote's conversation.'[1]

Despite the fact that some of the stories which she included did not add much point to her differentiation between words, all those about Johnson are amusing in themselves. A case in point is her recollection:

And I well remember one day at Sir Joshua Reynolds' house, some gentlemen coming in with a foreigner, to shew him the pictures, and pointing out Johnson's, when he asked whose was *that?*—Johnson the philosopher, says one in company—Johnson the great WRITER, cries another interrupting him—Our famous AUTHOR, sir, said the master of the house. *N'est-ce pas là le* POETE? enquired our visitant. When the Doctor came in half an hour after, I asked him which he loved best of his panegyrists.—I love none of the rogues, replied he—merrily—and am only sorry it was not Reynolds who called me the POET. That dog of a Frenchman took it for *Ben's* portrait, I'm afraid.[2]

Not all the anecdotes relate to Dr. Johnson; there are stories of Goldsmith, Chesterfield, and a host of other personages, some dead, some still alive when the book appeared. They are hard to find, but will repay a patient student of the times.

The public reaction to *British Synonymy* was very similar to that accorded to her other books. The *Morning Post* was scornful,[3] but the reviewer for the *European Magazine*, while admitting that he had come to the work with 'equal hope and fear', insisted that he had been agreeably surprised at the ingenious turns and substantial merit which the work possessed.[4] Some of the reviewers actually hinted that Mrs. Piozzi had had some fragments left by Dr. Johnson as the basis for her work. Notwithstanding the flattering implication, she was quick to deny the charge, and wrote to Queeney after the reviews appeared,

The Reviewers tho' lavish in their Praises, do me much wrong in supposing I had any Fragments of his upon Synonymy to consult— the Public has been denied nothing written by him which I possess'd, & I never had a Moment's Talk with him on the Subject. You may perhaps recollect *Your Father's* partiality for Abbé Girard's Work, when it was in one Volume only; and his tormenting me to read, & commend, & recommend it to *you*, I have thought a Thousand Times how *he* would have been pleased with the Performance,

---

[1] *Brit. Syn.* i. 24. Boswell tells the story, but instead of 'fascinated' he uses the word 'irresistible' (*Life*, iii. 69–70).   [2] *Brit. Syn.* ii. 122–3.

[3] *Morning Post*, Apr. 22, May 2, 1794.

[4] *European Mag.* xxv (1794), 361. The *Annual Register* (1794) in Essays, pp. 400–6, printed excerpts from the work.

but Johnson had never one Thought upon't I'm very sure. Some of my Friends, particularly Mr. Chappelow, work themselves up to fancy a new Edition with added Words will be call'd for; but Politics must take a different Turn, if anything *but* Politics are read this Year I think; & by this Year I mean 1795.[1]

William Gifford was the most severe critic of the work. In a note to one of the later editions of the *Baviad* he insisted that as a qualification for such a work Mrs. Piozzi had only

a jargon long since become proverbial for its vulgarity . . . an utter incapacity of defining a single term in the language, and just as much Latin from a child's Syntax, as sufficed to expose the ignorance she so anxiously labours to conceal.[2]

The irate classicist was incapable of generous appreciation of any writer whom he suspected of being secretly in sympathy with the detested sentimental romanticism of the Della Cruscans.

Horace Walpole was delighted to have the volumes as a subject on which to exert his cutting wit, and willingly annotated his friends' copies with copious remarks. In writing to Mary Berry, just after the work appeared, he made the criticism:

Here and there she does not want parts, has some good translations, and stories that are new; particularly an admirable *bon mot* of Lord Chesterfield, which I never heard before, but dashed with her cruel vulgarisms.[3]

Again it was the same complaint. Mrs. Piozzi's use of vulgar words, her flippant experiments with style, her obvious attempts to write in the light manner of everyday speech; all these irritated people brought up to believe that good style must obey certain immutable laws. After pointing out many flaws in the volumes, Walpole added to Miss Berry, 'I have picked out a motto for her work in her own words, and written it on the title-page: "Simplicity cannot please without elegance!" '[4] Mrs. Piozzi's attempted mixture of simplicity with

---

[1] Lansdowne MS., Dec. 19, 1794. See *Monthly Review*, xv (1794), 241–51 371–80; *Critical Review*, xii (1794), 121–8.
[2] W. Gifford, the *Baviad and Maeviad* (8th ed., 1811), p. ix. See also Seeley, p. 303.
[3] Walpole, *Letters*, xv. 284; Apr. 16, 1794. Another dig at Mrs. Piozzi's vulgarisms appeared in his letter to Mary Berry of May 1. See also *Berry Papers*, ed. L. Melville (1914), p. 123. Mrs. Piozzi's own friends, on the other hand, were openly complimentary. See letters from Chappelow, Dec. 14, 1794 (Ry. 562, 20); from Dr. Gray, Apr. 17, 1794 (Ry. 571, 3); and from Mrs. Siddons, Apr. 11, 1794 (Ry. 574, 10). Mrs. Siddons complained that her husband was so taken with the work that he read in it an hour after he went to bed, with the result that she had not had a glance at the volumes until he was done.   [4] Op. cit. xv. 284.

Blue-Stocking erudition did not wholly please, but she had sensed a pompous quality in the prose of her own age, and instinctively groped for something more easy and natural.

No matter how scorned by the English literati, *British Synonymy* seems to have been appreciated by the public for which it was especially written. Ten years after its first appearance, in 1804, large portions were reprinted in Paris by Parsons and Galignani as volumes 14, 16, 18, 20, and 22 in their so-called *British Library*. In the preface to the first instalment, the editor, while pointing out Mrs. Piozzi's indebtedness to the famous Abbé Girard, wrote of her English imitation: 'We shall not enter into any discussion of its merits, the successive editions it has passed through being the best proof of the estimation in which it is held.'[1] He further added: 'To foreigners, who study and wish to improve in the English language, it ought to be an inseparable companion.' In the last instalment an announcement was made that the sale had so far surpassed all expectation, and the Press had been so commendatory, that other projected issues had been postponed in order to complete the *British Synonymy* as quickly as possible. The editor further informed his readers that several of the numbers would be reprinted on common paper without engravings for the use of schools, and to make the work more accessible. After the jeers of the English, the reception of her volumes abroad must have proved extremely gratifying.

With the publication of *British Synonymy* another epoch in the life of Mrs. Piozzi came to an end. The gay parties in London, even the more sedate entertainments at Streatham, were beginning to pall. At fifty-three she found the idea of a quiet country estate in far off Wales more and more alluring, and to end her days where they had begun seemed eminently fitting. From Wales she had come; back to Wales she would go.

---

[1] Published by Parsons and Galignani, Paris, 1804. The first instalment has a portrait of Mrs. Piozzi as a frontispiece. For surviving editions of *British Synonymy* see Appendix. Years later a long series of extracts from *British Synonymy* were reprinted in the *Gent. Mag.* xxxi (new ser. 1849), 43–5, 158–60, 494–5; xxxii. 21–4, 135–6, 269–72, 602–5; xxxiii (1850), 34–5.

XVIII

BRYNBELLA

1794–1801

VARIOUS considerations were responsible for the determination of the Piozzis to build a country house in Wales.
Nor was the decision sudden or whimsical. Mrs. Piozzi's
ardent Welsh patriotism had always been a vital part of her
nature; she was prouder of old Bach-y-Graig than of all the
spacious grounds of Streatham Park; she had been deeply hurt
in 1774 by the bland distaste shown by Johnson and Thrale
for her Flintshire patrimony; now she was overjoyed to find
her second husband openly enthusiastic.

But it was more than mere national pride which led Mrs.
Piozzi to consider leaving the environs of the capital. The
constant struggle for social recognition, while it had proved
partly successful, was becoming wearisome. Although she had
built up a new circle of friends, they were not the equals of
those whose portraits still lined the walls of the Streatham
library. With vivid memories of Johnson, Burke, and Reynolds,
she rarely found the present race of wits and writers stimulating.
Writing to Mrs. Pennington in June 1793, she complained,
'Well! I tried a little raking myself this year, but it does not
suit me somehow, I can make too little sport out on't, and the
people tell me nothing which I did not know before, and
that is what *I* want from company always.'[1] Her eager, in-
quiring mind was always seeking information; the shallow
repartee of polite society was never enough. What she sought
was the sound judgement of a Johnson, and this she could
not find in her London circle of the early nineties.

Her position, too, in the social world was uncertain. However much her guests might seem to flatter and adore her, she
could not be sure that they were not laughing at her pretensions behind her back. Without any inherited rank of birth or
family, with a disdained foreign musician for a husband, she
was able to retain her position only by constant vigilance and

---

[1] *Letters to Pennington*, p. 91.

persistent endeavour. Although she had forced Piozzi on society, he was only tolerated with a kind of half-hearted patronage. The gentle musician might be admired for his art, but he was never quite accepted as an equal. For instance, on July 20, 1793, Farington, accompanied by the artist Dance and Samuel Lysons, went out to breakfast at Streatham. The diarist made the entry: 'Mr. Piozzi obligingly played on the pianoforte and sung in a charming taste. He is a very obliging, unaffected man, and as much English as a foreigner can be in manner and way of thinking.'[1] On this occasion Farington described his host, in a condescending way, as being almost English in manners; but in later references he recorded amusing examples of the musician's inability to understand the essentials of British culture.[2] According to these accounts Mrs. Piozzi was constantly annoyed by her husband's lack of knowledge of English literature and the drama. Whether this is true or not, one thing is certain; she never allowed any pique to show in her own intimate journals and letters. She herself respected Piozzi's complete devotion to the art of music; at the same time she knew from sad experience that in the polite circles of London such a preoccupation was accepted as a sign of social inferiority.

Piozzi was also anxious to get away from city life. Since conditions on the Continent were precarious, there could be no immediate return to Italy; and with constantly recurring fits of gout, he must have thought with delight of retiring to the rolling hills of Flintshire, which was so like his own beloved Lombardy.

At first the Piozzis considered repairing or rebuilding Bach-y-Graig, but the old house, built by Sir Richard Clough in the sixteenth century, was damp and inconvenient, as well as badly situated. It nestled at the bottom of 'Dymerchion' Hill (now spelt Tremeirchion), just in the edge of the thick wood, and afforded a poor view of the surrounding country. They sensibly decided to build a completely new house, not close to Bach-y-Graig, but near the top of the hill, where for generations travellers passing along the old road had paused to gaze across the fertile valley of the Clwyd. Mrs Piozzi herself had often stopped her coach at this spot, and thought what a perfect situation it would be for a house. On the left one could

---

[1] *Farington Diary*, ed. J. Greig, 4th ed. (1923), i. 3. The drawings of Mr. and Mrs. Piozzi made by Dance on this occasion are now in the National Portrait Gallery, London. [2] Ibid. iii. 102, &c.

see the ruined battlements of Denbigh Castle, and far to the right the sea, occasionally dotted with glinting white sails, with the great Orme, a constant landmark, stretching out into the blue. And on very clear days the distant Snowdonia range appeared grey and austere far across the other side of the Vale. It was an inspiring prospect, satisfying every mood.[1]

Just when the Welsh building project was first discussed is not certain, but according to Mrs. Piozzi it was in the summer of 1791 that her husband began to make plans for the new house on the hill.[2] Actual surveys were started in the autumn of 1792, when the Piozzis, with Cecilia and Sally Siddons, spent almost a month near by at the Crown Inn in Denbigh. Despite the fact that they had at first only intended building a small 'cottage', they found themselves in the end constructing an imposing Italian villa. Piozzi drew the original plans, and with the aid of a local contractor and architect he attempted to supervise the construction.[3] Since they wished to build just where the road crossed the side of the hill, permission to change the road to encircle this proposed site was required.[4] Once this was accomplished, during the winter of 1793 preliminary work was begun on the foundations.

Of great importance to Mrs. Piozzi was the proper choice of a name for her new home. No ordinary one would do, and soon the first suggestion of 'Belvedere' gave way to a more sentimental, hybrid form 'Brynbella'. Since 'bryn' is Welsh for a hill or eminence, the resulting Cambro-Italian form might be translated as 'Beautiful hill'. What, she felt, could be more appropriate? What more suitable for a happy couple than such a combination of their native languages?

Delayed by workmen's strikes, difficulty in securing the proper materials, and most of all by the fact that the owners were not near by, work continued on the house in a desultory manner throughout 1793 and early 1794. Finally, in July 1794, the Piozzis with Cecilia drove to Wales in order to hurry things up, arriving just in time to celebrate their wedding anniversary

---

[1] Through the hospitality of the former occupants of Brynbella, Mr. and Mrs. Herbert Evans, I have been able to enjoy this marvellous view on a number of occasions.

I regret to record that Mr. and Mrs. Evans died during the war and their collection of Piozzian MSS. is in the National Library of Wales, Aberystwyth.

[2] *Letters to Pennington*, p. 61; Hayward, ii. 71.

[3] Several long series of letters from the contractors and agents in Wales—C. Mead, J. Oldfield, T. Lloyd, W. Shackfield, &c.—give the complete story of the building of the house. See Ry. 601, 603, 604, 607, 608, &c.

[4] Documents formerly at Brynbella describe this transfer.

on the 25th. Brynbella they found still full of scaffolding and without floors.

The Piozzis remained in lodgings in Denbigh until Brynbella could be completed, and Mrs. Piozzi could see the new house from her windows, a white patch in the green, far across on the other side of the vale. When not busy with contractors and workmen she had much to divert her: gossiping with old cronies of her father, discussing literature with the local scholars, climbing about the ruins of old Denbigh Castle. This last she found a source of inexhaustible entertainment, as she admitted to Queeney, though Cecilia wondered how she could amuse herself day after day with the same scenery. It was not the same, the older woman insisted, since it varied constantly with the different lights and the gradual change of the seasons.

It was natural that here in the country of her youth her thoughts should turn to other days. On September 17, Queeney's birthday, she wrote to her daughter:

I wish you & myself Joy of this Day my dearest Child with all Sincerity and Affection. After half a Century Spent in this empty yet bustling World—here am I like a Hare ending at the Place I set out from. This Day ten Years I pass'd in France, how changed since that Hour! this Day Twenty Years we were in Wales together, and dined at Gwaynnyog: the Master and Mistress of which both are dead—but Rector Myddelton, the poor Colonel's Brother & his Lady remember you with Admiration—*they* are the present possessors, and often observe how unlike You Cecilia is.—a Fact none remain however so well convinced of as myself: they say at the same time that She resembles Mr. Thrale, which in part has some Foundation. Well! this Day Thirty Years I spent at the Borough of Southwark—in cruel Agony & Labour of my darling Queeney: This Day Forty Years I presented my Uncle at Offley Park with a Petition in Verse from an old Hunter that he called Forester, and had condemn'd to the Guillotine of those Times for being old & worthless; and this Day Fifty Years I past at Bodvel in North Wales —most probably in my Mother's Lap or my Nurse's Arms—A curious Recapitulation! & now I write Political Ballads and feel much pleased that you like my 'King-killers'.

During the summer Piozzi had been unusually well, but late in the autumn his old enemy, the gout, caught him unawares. On December 2 his wife wrote to her eldest daughter, 'this is the 15th: Day that my poor Husband has lain on his Back screaming out like a Man upon a Racking Wheel . . .' Fortunately they had found in Denbigh a young Doctor Thackeray (great-uncle of the novelist) who seemed to understand Piozzi's case, who prescribed the same remedies as Sir Lucas Pepys, and who was a scholar and interesting conversationalist as well as a skilled physician. Such a paragon appealed both to the patient and his nurse; as a result, for the next twenty years he was to play a large part in the life of the Piozzis. Because of this present attack of gout, all thought of a trip to Bath was given up, and during the winter Mrs. Piozzi and Cecilia were forced to make the best of the restricted life in Denbigh.

Mrs. Piozzi found escape, as usual, in books and letters, and though confined through a long autumn and winter in a little country town, she never complained of lack of things to do. Reconciliation with her three older daughters had provided additional correspondents to whom she could send letters or verses almost every fortnight. Ending her note of December 2, she confessed:

> The reading Ladies of Denbigh find our Mysteries of Udolpho a Treasure, I sent for it from London to divert them. Cecilia says that like Emily the moment my Mind or my Teeth are at Ease for an Instant, I set about *arranging* a few Stanzas. but there are none ready *now*; nothing but honest Prose in which to send my Dear Girls all our Love . . .

She even began to toy with the idea of another major literary project. Writing to Queeney in January 1795 of the dazzling changes exhibited by the world in these last days, she tossed off the suggestion:

> Yet I could make a pretty Book too to bring out on the last Days of 1799 or the first of 1800 could I get Materials cleverly round me, and Time for Study: as *Anecdotes* of the late Century—not a History.

Her idea was to leave out all the weighty matter which usually filled historical books; instead to try to compile two or three volumes of entertaining anecdotes of famous characters. Nevertheless, she did not wish her idea to be known just yet. 'Say nothing of my Project tho'. I could not make the Pamphlet Scheme answer, so have given it quite up.'[1]

Cecilia, as a gay, fashionable girl of seventeen, found more difficulty than her mother in accustoming herself to rural Denbigh. Having been seriously ill on her last trip to the little town, she hated the place with an unreasonable dislike. Moreover, she had her father's distaste for Wales and told her

---

[1] It is not clear what Mrs. Piozzi meant by 'the Pamphlet Scheme'. Possibly this refers to some project which had been mentioned to Queeney, but never actually begun.

mother that Mr. Piozzi bored her to death with his openly
expressed admiration of the scenery. Far from balls, beaux,
and fashionable society, she found life very dull. At first,
to pass the time, she took violent exercise, and then began to
devise various pranks to enliven the neighbourhood. On one
occasion, unknown to any one but the stewards, she invited a
large company of the local squires to a ball at the Crown Inn,
where she danced and laughed to her heart's content, while
her stepfather paid the bill and worried over the indignation
of the older people whom she had failed to invite. Another time
she and a friend roamed about Denbigh disguised as gipsies,
repeating impromptu verses which Mrs. Piozzi had accom-
modatingly scribbled, not realizing Cecy's purpose. The
frolicsome girl made quite a stir in quiet Denbigh, and kept
her mother constantly apprehensive.[1]

Gradually, as she drew other gay companions about her,
Cecilia found her attitude towards Wales beginning to change.
In a letter to Queeney on March 14, 1795, Mrs. Piozzi wrote:
'Cecilia gets Balls and Admirers as you say I get News and
Knowledge, tho' we do live in a Corner of the World:—but
every one will get what they look for.' Cecy was no longer
bored. It was particularly the attentions of a handsome young
Welsh squire that had altered her point of view, for she was
fast falling in love. At the end of March Mrs. Piozzi confided to
Chappelow that 'Cecy has a Mind to be married', and added
that the young man had her entire approval.[2] To the mother
the fact that he was John Meredith Mostyn of Segroid, a
member of a fine old Denbighshire family and grandson of an
intimate friend of her father, John Salusbury, was recommendation enough. On the other hand, she was quick to
recognize serious objections, chief of which was the age of the
young couple—Cecilia only eighteen and Mostyn not much
older. Since Cecilia was a ward in Chancery, some better reason
than mere sentiment would have to be presented to the Lord
Chancellor, Lord Loughborough, before his consent could be
gained. Mrs. Piozzi's precarious relations with her other
daughters further complicated the affair. Now outwardly on
good terms with the elder 'Miss Thrales', she was very anxious
to avoid another quarrel.

Should Cecilia die before coming of age, her sisters were
legally her heirs. Under normal circumstances Cecilia's

---

[1] Cecilia's pranks are described in letters to Queeney of Sept. 1, 17; Nov. 19,
1794.   [2] Ry. 559, 29.

husband, on receipt of her dowry, would have been required to make a settlement in return, which would stand in lieu of her estate in case of accident. But Mostyn, being under age, could make no legal settlement; and if Cecilia married him, her fortune would be irrevocably lost to herself and to the other Thrale sisters.[1] In view of this Mrs. Piozzi felt that she could not give her consent to such an injury to their legal rights, especially since she and Queeney were already on the verge of another quarrel over the Crowmarsh estate, which the latter's legal advisers, not understanding the provisions of Thrale's marriage settlement, were urging her to claim.[2] Mrs. Piozzi, therefore, refused to give her consent to the marriage of Cecilia and Mostyn until he should come of age.

Having made this difficult decision, and thinking it best to take Cecilia away from temptation, the Piozzis returned to Streatham Park the middle of April 1795. But young Mostyn was not to be balked in his suit, and followed his love to London, where the Piozzis, making the best of an embarrassing situation, welcomed him to Streatham on the 18th. He remained in the house as a guest for the next two months.[3] Torn between sentimental liking for the youth and a realization of the awkwardness of her position, Mrs. Piozzi was in a quandary. Her dilemma, however, did not last long, for the young, hot-headed lovers, unwilling to wait until Mostyn was twenty-one, soon took matters into their own hands. In a letter dated Saturday, June 6, Mostyn wrote to Mr. Ray, one of the Piozzis' trusted advisers:

> I feel allmost ashamed after your repeated advice to the contrary, to tell you that I hope Cecilia Thrale and myself shall determine no longer to wait for Mrs. Piozzi's consent but go to Scotland this night—Now Sir You may be assured that on my coming of age the most honourable & proper settlement shall be made for her & Children, to that I pledge my word.[4]

Immediately throwing sensible advice to the winds, they slipped away to Gretna Green, where they were married late on Monday night. On Tuesday morning, June 9, Cecilia dashed

---

[1] Mrs. Piozzi explained her predicament in a letter of June 12, 1795, to Dr. Thackeray.

[2] Ry. 606, 39. In the 1763 marriage settlement Mrs. Thrale had been granted £200 a year from Crowmarsh while her husband lived and £400 afterwards. In his will Thrale left the estate to Queeney but did not revoke the former provisions, so that the annual payment to Mrs. Piozzi was still chargeable against the estate.

[3] From a notation in the front of Piozzi's 1797 diary (Ry 616).

[4] Ry. 572, 16.

off a long letter to her mother, telling of the rapid journey
north and of their marriage.[1] 'It seems so odd to be here
without you', she wrote, and then added a multitude of questions about the reaction of the family to her elopement.
Especially she wanted to know what 'Papa' thought: 'what
does he say to the Affair? *may godda bless—never I* see such a
people.—give my love to him—how will he be able to live
without *Miss Cecil* to scold . . .'

Cecilia, who was delicate and, like her mother, easily upset
by excitement, soon fell ill amid the bustle of her elopement;
but fortunately she was as soon better, and the young couple
drove to Wales by easy stages, stopping on the way to see Mrs.
Strickland at Kendal. Further agitated letters asked anxiously
how her sisters felt about the runaway match, invited them all
and the Siddons girls to visit her and her husband immediately
in Wales, and always ended with affectionate messages to
'Papa'.[2]

However much they may have deprecated their sister's
elopement, Queeney and the other sisters made no open
objection and seemed quite willing to welcome Mostyn into the
family. What else could have been expected of the child, with
the example constantly before her of a mother who had married
for love? It would have been useless to expect Cecilia to regu-
late her life from motives of prudence. Such a denouement
had been obvious to them from the beginning, and they were
willing to accept with equanimity an event which proved them
in the right.

Throughout the summer of 1795 the Piozzis were busy
preparing to move to Brynbella. Boxes of books, linens, and
other necessities were shipped by sea to the Welsh coast;
lighter belongings were packed for conveyance by coach.
Although several years before some furniture had been sent to
Wales from their house in Hanover Square, many new pieces
were now especially constructed for the house by the firm of
Gillow at Lancaster.[3] Streatham was left untouched, for
Piozzi could make up his mind neither to let nor to dismantle
his wife's old home, preferring to have it kept ready for use

---

[1] Ry. 572, 18 (postmarked June 12, 1795, and Gretna Green). In the Nat.
Portrait Gallery (Leverton Harris collection, D-IV-2, 372) is a photograph of the
marriage certificate dated June 7, 1795, signed by Cecilia and Mostyn. The exact
date of their arrival in Gretna Green is not quite clear.

[2] Letters of June 15, 17, 1795; Ry. 572, 19, 21.

[3] One such piece is now in the possession of the Misses Pennant, Egerton
Crescent, London. Altogether, £2,000 was spent on new furniture for Brynbella.

whenever they returned to London. Nevertheless, several years later, when the lavish expense of keeping up two large establishments while they used but one, and the annoyance of having friends and acquaintances continually asking to use the house for visitors became too irksome, the Piozzis finally decided to let Streatham Park again.[1]

The loss of Cecilia made a great difference in the household, for she had been constantly with her mother and stepfather since the summer of 1787. With her other daughters, Arthur Murphy, the Siddons girls, and others as frequent guests, however, Streatham was not lonely. It was not until the middle of August that Mrs. Piozzi wrote to Queeney, 'Mr. Piozzi & I dined *Tête a Tête* for the *first* Time since our Return from abroad.' It was almost as if embarking on another honeymoon journey that they made ready to set out for a home of their own building.

Finally, on September 11, 1795, they drove away. Cecilia and her husband met them at Chester, and they reached their destination on the 17th, Queeney's birthday, in time to drink her health in the new house. She, with Susanna and Sophia, had promised to visit the Vale of Clwyd the next autumn, to see their new brother-in-law and Brynbella, and Mrs. Piozzi scribbled off a note to them on the day after her arrival.

The House is half finished & full of Workmen & noise, & nothing in order; but you shall have Beds, & Dinners, and kisses; and a hearty Welcome: and help us scold about *one* thing, and praise another, & so on. Mrs. Mostyn will entertain you much in the same manner at Segroid, & you will see how we live in Wales.

While their own house, Segroid, was being made ready, Cecilia and her husband stayed for a month at Brynbella. Mrs. Piozzi was overjoyed at their presence, since her husband was suffering from gout, and she needed help and advice. In spite of workmen's hammers and Piozzi's groans resounding through the house, she refused to be unhappy, revelling in the glorious weather and the hills of her beloved vale.

Happily, Piozzi was better by October, when all the four Thrale daughters were reunited under his roof. They were constantly together for the next month, even when the Mostyns

---

[1] Several times Cecilia and her husband stayed at Streatham and entertained their friends there without asking the Piozzis' permission. At another time Mr. MacNamara, the Duke of Bedford's agent and close friend of the Prince of Wales, asked to use the house for quarters when his own house was filled with guests. (See letters to Mrs. Pennington and from Arthur Murphy.)

removed to their own home. On October 21 Mrs. Piozzi wrote
to Mrs. Pennington that her husband 'gallants his wife's four
daughters to Holywell Assembly tomorrow'.[1] Throughout most
of November Mrs. Piozzi was kept busy with her daughters,
showing them the sights of the vale, getting their advice in
decorating her new house, and entrusting them with long lists
of commissions to execute for her in London when they left
on November 25. Books, pens, ribbons, dress goods, pamphlets
of Hannah More—the list of her needs was unending! Mrs.
Piozzi may have felt that one way to ensure a continuance of
the present friendly relationship was to enlist her daughters'
interest and assistance on all occasions. Fortunately, Queeney
was amenable, and her packets kept the new mistress of Brynbella steadily supplied with household necessities as well as
gossip and news. Mrs. Piozzi was always avid for the latter,
and thanked her daughter on January 27, 1796, for 'the little
Bundle of Chat with which I may now if I please divert the
Friends who dine here'.

However much she delighted in close contact with the world
of fashion, Mrs. Piozzi did not find Welsh society dull, for she
soon discovered a number of congenial friends in the neighbourhood. There she met again her distant relative, Thomas
Pennant, the famous naturalist and traveller, who lived near
by at Downing. Their casual acquaintance, first begun by an
exchange of property when Brynbella was building, soon
ripened into intimacy, and she was proud to be called cousin
by such a celebrity, whom she later came to think of and to
use as her 'Dictionary'.[2] There were also other excellent
scholars in the vicinity, such as Mr. Lloyd of Wickwar, who was
ever ready to drive over to discuss science or the forged Shakespearian manuscripts, Dr. Myddelton and the vicar of Tremeirchion, who were available for classical arguments. The Williams
family at Bodylwyddan across the vale proved congenial
friends, giving frequent concerts and parties.[3] Even though
missing the stimulating round of London society, she found
many pleasures and few disadvantages in her peaceful existence
in Wales.

There were further compensations in the country itself. The
inspiring scenery on every side, the ever-changing colours of the

---

[1] *Letters to Pennington*, p. 130.
[2] See Ry. 575 and Mrs. Piozzi's letter to Queeney, Mar. 19, 1799.
[3] Over 600 letters still exist from Mrs. Piozzi to the Williams family (now in
the possession of a descendant, Sir Randle Mainwaring). Letters to John Roberts,
the vicar of Tremeirchion, and Mr. Lloyd also have survived (see Appendix).

beautiful Vale of Clwyd, its vistas of distant hills, the blue wisp of ocean to the north, are described again and again in letters of this period. In order to see more of the country-side the Piozzis set up a fine telescope in front of the house. Mrs. Piozzi wrote to Queeney on January 8, 1796, that they had just been watching a fleet of forty-one sails pass by in the distance. Their neighbour, Mr. Lloyd, who was something of an astronomer, initiated her into the absorbing study of sun-spots and planets.[1] The telescope proved diverting in more ways than one, for there is an amusing story, still current in the vale, that one day Sir John Williams at Bodylwyddan lost his watch, and spent almost an hour searching for it around his house. Just as he had about given up, a messenger arrived from Mrs. Piozzi asking if he had found what he had lost. Scanning the horizon from Bryn-bella, five miles away, she had seen her friend crawling about on his hands and knees, and her curiosity gave her no rest until she had found out what had occurred.

Although throwing herself whole-heartedly into the business of gathering a new circle of friends in Wales, she was not allowed to forget those left behind in London. Mrs. Siddons, ill and annoyed by various public rumours, wrote mournfully, 'I now wish myself with you at dear Streatham, where I could, as usual, forget all the pains and torments of illness and the world.'[2] Arthur Murphy, who continued to spend long periods of time in the deserted house, found it, with the mistress absent, strangely altered.[3] The Lysons brothers, the Hamiltons, Mrs. Pennington, and others, in the same letters which kept her constantly supplied with news, wistfully looked forward to the day when she should return.

Instead she invited her old intimates to Brynbella to see for themselves what a paradise she had discovered. In February 1796 Chappelow came to visit for three weeks. For the local gentlefolk he was a well of gossip about the great world of Society; for Mrs. Piozzi, as she wrote Queeney, he was 'a good Classical Scholar & a sensible Friend and an agreeable Companion when all these *desirable* Topics are gone away with the Visitors—and we are left alone'. Yet even to Chappelow she made no mention of her new literary project, for she was guarding her secret jealously from everyone but her daughter. 'I tell nobody' that but *You*, and I am dying to see whether

---

[1] Letters to Queeney of Jan. 8, 1796, and July 9, 1798.
[2] T. Campbell, *Life of Mrs. Siddons*, ii. 197.
[3] Ry. 548, 17–19.

you will like it.' While her historical plan was gradually taking shape, she wanted no critical comments from the public.

During the next few years many friends came to visit Brynbella: the Lysons brothers, Miss Owen, and other occasional travellers, such as Philip Francis (the reputed author of *Junius*), were eagerly welcomed.[1] There was no lack of social events. One autumn Mrs. Piozzi was selected to act as Queen of the local County Assembly with Lord Kirkwall as King Consort; at other times episcopal entertainments with the Bishop and the Dean of St. Asaph provided adequate if somewhat solid mental fare.[2] Piozzi found neighbours with musical tastes, anxious to listen to his Italian songs or to play duets on the harpsichord, while his wife was busy with her scholarly arguments. For both of them the Vale of Clwyd proved a hospitable and satisfying home.

Nevertheless, the Piozzis did not intend to spend all their time in Wales; the travelling instinct was too strong. Brynbella was to be their principal retreat, but occasional summer excursions and winter visits were to vary the monotony of the simple country life. Thus large portions of the winters of 1797 and 1798 were spent in London and Streatham, and in succeeding years the inclement months were almost always passed at Bath.[3] Piozzi's recurrent attacks of gout were the determining factor, either speeding or retarding the journey to gayer surroundings.

One of the joys of the early months at Brynbella had been the close proximity of Cecilia and her new husband; constant visits back and forth kept alive the old intimacy of mother and daughter. But this happy state of affairs did not last. Mrs. Piozzi had been very much attracted to the good-looking John Meredith Mostyn before his marriage to her youngest daughter, but further acquaintance tended to make her doubt her good judgement. Mostyn was inconsiderate, dilatory, and enamoured of high society. He preferred to lounge about with the London rakes rather than to transact even necessary business. Notwithstanding his definite promise to make a settlement on his bride, he found procrastination more to his liking. Both

---

[1] Names of visitors may be found in Piozzi's diaries, and in Mrs. Piozzi's letters to Queeney, Mrs. Pennington, Chappelow, &c.

[2] *Letters to Pennington*, pp. 168, &c.

[3] The Piozzis were at Streatham and in London from Dec. 31, 1796, to Aug. 12, 1797; from Feb. 24 to late in May, 1798; and from Oct. 28, 1800, to Jan. 19, 1801. They were in Bath from early Dec., 1798, to early March, 1799; from Dec. 12, 1799, to March 3, 1800; and from Jan. 26 to March 28, 1801. From May 10 to the middle of July, 1796, they were at Beaumaris, Anglesey.

Queeney and her mother consulted Arthur Murphy on the matter, who tried his best to bring Mostyn to task. Beginning in July 1796, and throughout the next year, there is a long series of letters from Murphy to Mrs. Piozzi which tell the story of his attempts to settle the Mostyn matter in or out of court.[1]

At first it was thought Mostyn would make good his word and agree to a normal settlement, but when confronted with the document devised by a neutral lawyer, he called it 'extortion'. It was next suggested that Cecilia's fortune should be placed in Chancery, for in spite of the fact that Cecilia was already a ward of the court, her financial affairs had remained in the hands of the old trustees. If the whole were now placed in Chancery, Mostyn would be forced by the Lord Chancellor to make a fitting settlement on his wife, before he could himself receive her fortune. But Mostyn's plan was to avoid any action until his wife came of age, at which time he would be free to do exactly as he pleased; and so the matter was purposely delayed.

Then suddenly, in October 1796, Mrs. Piozzi was precipitated into a quarrel with Cecilia herself. A rumour was current in the neighbourhood that Mostyn was having an affair with his wife's maid, and with her usual ineptitude in dealing with her children, Mrs. Piozzi immediately insisted that her daughter should do something about it. Wisely taking her husband's side, Cecilia preferred to ignore the whole business. But when Mrs. Piozzi was aroused she could not be restrained, and she wrote long letters to Queeney, Murphy, and her other friends about this flouting of local opinion. The result was that relations between Segroid and Brynbella became very strained, and another factor was introduced into the legal complications over Cecilia's fortune. Mrs. Piozzi's struggle to secure a settlement out of Mostyn now became a crusade. She wrote to Queeney:

What a Blessing her Fortune has not been paid into the Hands of such a Man!!!
The little Power *I* have shall be exerted he may assure himself, to keep it long out of his Reach.

Mrs. Piozzi was a person of violent moods; she could turn quickly from intense admiration to vigorous hate. Though she had thought young Mostyn the pattern of all the virtues before his marriage to Cecilia, she was now convinced that he was the lowest of the low. Desire to save her daughter from the clutches of such a man drove her to impulsive plans for retaliation.

[1] Ry. 548.

Since Mostyn and his wife proved so stubborn, Piozzi was determined to make them pay for Cecilia's expenses incurred before the marriage. Technically all Cecilia's bills while under the roof of her mother were supposed to be paid out of her own fortune; but the Piozzis had been careless in submitting accounts to Cator, and possibly had not intended to keep any definite reckoning of minor expenses. Nevertheless, bills kept coming in for goods bought by Cecilia without her mother's knowledge until the whole amount reached a large sum. As a counter attack, in order to force Mostyn into some action, Piozzi demanded an accounting from Cator to settle all of Cecilia's old bills. Cator, who had to represent the best interests of all the children, was placed in a very trying position. He wrote to Mrs. Piozzi on November 12, 1796, expostulating with her for acting under the motives of violence, passion, and revenge, carefully explaining that he was doing all he could to force Mostyn to make a proper settlement, but that he could not act in settling the Piozzis' claims without an order from the court.[1] But Mrs. Piozzi and her advisers were not to be mollified, though unfortunately all they could accomplish was to drive Mostyn and Cator into friendly co-operation.

Murphy's efforts throughout the last months of 1796 having proved unavailing, he urged Mrs. Piozzi to come to London to expedite matters by her presence. Accordingly, she left Brynbella late in December, and soon was plunged into a maze of legal complications, which ruined the entire winter for her. Murphy and her other advisers actively pushed her forward, while Cator and her daughters openly took the other side.

Vacillating continually from one side to the other, Mrs. Piozzi showed she did not possess the temperament of a successful legal disputant. She was extremely anxious not to alienate her elder daughters, and when she found them gradually beginning to side with Mostyn, did not know what to do. Murphy was completely disgusted. By June 1797 his Irish temper gave way, and with characteristic vigour he denounced her lack of decision, and called her recent letters 'veering and shifting from one point to another, Capricious, *flickering* Inconsistent, and Contradictory'. Possibly with half-jocose irony he ended his castigation with the wish that she might enjoy 'that Peace, that cold Indifference, and Lazy Apathy, which you so much admire,' signing himself 'Your Emancipated Slave Arthur Murphy'.[2] The Irishman, feeling himself in the right,

---

[1] Ry. 602, 17. [2] Ry. 548, 37.

could not understand the motives which kept Mrs. Piozzi from pressing her claims through every legal recourse.

The story of these interminable legal proceedings is a complicated one which need not here be unravelled.[1] The one net result, which Mrs. Piozzi had feared and later tried to avoid, was that her relations with all four daughters were again strained to the limit. She seemed to have a fatal facility for doing exactly what would distress her children, and her advisers now widened the breach.

The Piozzis remained in London and at Streatham, involved in the interminable conferences and legal discussions, all through the winter, spring, and early summer of 1797.[2] Then, in spite of Murphy's protests, they returned to Wales. Cecilia Mostyn was expecting her first child, and at such a time Mrs. Piozzi felt all differences might well be forgotten. Torn between a desire to punish the despicable Mostyn and a determination to keep what affection she could of her own children, Mrs. Piozzi tried to seize the opportunity to be of service to her youngest daughter. But she had underestimated the animosity on the other side. Though the mother of twelve children herself, she was allowed no part in the birth of her first grandchild. Queeney it was who came to take charge; Queeney it was who supervised all the arrangements. Thus the long battle to rule at least one of her daughters ended in failure; the matter-of-fact Queeney was finally triumphant, and all the Thrale daughters were united in opposition to their mother.

In his diary for 1797 Piozzi noted that several visits had been paid to Segroid in August; but when Cecilia became seriously ill, and her mother sent word that she was 'ready to fly at her Command', no call came.[3] On August 30 Piozzi made the entry: 'Miss Thrale refused to Mrs. Piozzi to go to Segroid to see her daughter Cecilia Mostyn which she brought a dead child.'[4] On September 3 he added: 'Mrs. Piozzi went to Segroid with Miss Thrale permission.' After that she did not see her daughters again until they called on October 14 and

---

[1] Ry. 611 is a 'Memorial of H. L. Piozzi against John Cator, Esq.', in which her side of the argument is outlined. A long brief prepared by Cator in defence, together with numerous financial schedules showing the distribution of the Thrale estate, is now in the possession of Mr. Herbert Warren, London.

[2] Piozzi's diary for 1797 (now at Brynbella) lists their many engagements this winter. Constant meetings with the Thrale sisters, with Murphy, Mrs. Siddons, &c., are recorded.

[3] Lansdowne MS.; Piozzi's diary for 1797; *Letters to Pennington*, p. 146.

[4] See also letters to Queeney; to Chappelow, Sept. 18, Oct. 3, Oct. 20, 1797 (Ry. 560, 59–61).

November 17. Denied admittance to her own daughter, Mrs. Piozzi felt crushed by this last cruel stroke of fate. And when Arthur Murphy heard the news, he too was greatly roused, but reminded her that it was exactly what he had predicted.[1]

This painful incident further stirred the troubled waters, and litigation with Mostyn and Cator continued for the next few years. As might have been expected, nothing was ever really settled. In 1800 Cator did finally agree to a compromise in which he paid a small sum to the Piozzis' banker in settlement of past claims;[2] but this was only a temporary concession, since Queeney's lawyers immediately afterwards revived the old argument about Crowmarsh, the Oxfordshire estate. The claim was again put forward that the estate had been left to Queeney by Thrale in his will, and that her mother had been illegally receiving income from this source for many years. They even threatened to make Mrs. Piozzi repay all the money received from Crowmarsh since 1781. After another long series of conferences this too was finally allowed to drop, since Queeney could not substantiate her claim.[3] But the daughters continued to suspect their mother of grasping selfishness, just as she was confident that Cator and the trustees had cheated her out of part of her income.

In spite of all this bickering and legal argument, Mrs. Piozzi was determined to keep up the appearance, at least, of being on good terms with her daughters. She wrote to Mrs. Pennington, after one particularly annoying attack by her daughter's lawyers, that she meant to harbour no resentment. 'I wrote to the girls by yesterday's post', she added, 'exactly as if no such transactions had passed among us.'[4] In her heart she knew that they would never have any affection for her, but she did not desire another open breach if she could possibly avoid it. And so the letters to Queeney and the others continued, with slight intervals, through the rest of her life.

The never-ending quarrels with her daughters undoubtedly

---

[1] Ry. 548, 48.　　　　　　　　　　[2] Ry. 577, 47.
[3] The trouble resulted from the same old inability to harmcnize the 1763 marriage settlement with Thrale's later will. Queeney's advisers had discovered a flaw in the wording of the settlement, but were unable to prove that this definitely invalidated Thrale's intention to leave his wife a yearly income from the Crowmarsh estate. Actually Mrs. Piozzi had not been paid all that she legally might have claimed in the past from this source, and nearly £1,000 was due to her. See Ry. 577 and *Letters to Pennington*, pp. 189-93. As Mrs. Piozzi wrote to Mrs. Pennington, the trouble was that in Thrale's settlement and will 'nothing has been *worded* so as to preclude discussion among eager disputants, diligent to catch and cavil' (pp. 189-90).　　　　　　[4] *Letters to Pennington*, p. 195.

served to augment Mrs. Piozzi's overpowering desire for a male heir to inherit the Welsh estate and perpetuate the name of Salusbury. Since it was too late now to have a son of her own, she gradually came to the determination to adopt a boy who would take the place of her beloved Harry. In 1793 Giambattista, her husband's younger brother, whom they had seen twice in Italy, had named one of his sons John Salusbury Piozzi, out of compliment to his rich aunt and doubtless with an eye to the future. It may be—but it is the merest conjecture —that the boy was so named at the express desire of Mrs. Piozzi herself. Be that as it may, in 1794, when the boy was a year old, Giambattista suggested sending him to England; but the Piozzis decided that they would rather wait until he was older before undertaking the responsibility for his care.[1] The adoption, though decided upon, had thus been put off until an indefinite future date.

The ravages of war in northern Italy in the late seventeen-nineties left Giambattista's family homeless; in the wake of Napoleon much of the family property had been destroyed and the old grandfather frightened out of what remained of his life. For a long time no word was heard of the survivors, but when, in 1798, communication was again possible, Mrs. Piozzi and her husband decided not to wait any longer but to send for the little boy, who was now five years old.[2] It is not hard to understand the motive which urged the Piozzis to bring little John Salusbury Piozzi to England. Mrs. Piozzi avowed her reason in Thraliana. He would be naturalized and educated, and then 'we will see if He will be more grateful, & rational, & comfortable than Miss Thrales have been to the Mother they have at length *driven to Desperation*'.[3]

The child arrived in England late in November 1798, and was cared for by Mrs. Piozzi's friends in Streatham during December.[4] Mr. Ray brought him to Bath for Christmas with his aunt and uncle, while they debated what to do with him. He was sturdy and fearless, but shocked Mrs. Piozzi with his stories of war-torn Italy. As she walked with him across the

[1] Mainwaring Piozziana, iii. 60.
[2] The child had been born, Sept. 9, 1793. See copy of baptismal certificate made Oct. 4, 1798, upon his departure from Italy (J.R.L. Charter 1247). Also Hayward, i. 347.   [3] Jan. 17, 1798.
[4] Mrs. Piozzi wrote to her Streatham coachman, Jacob Weston, on Dec. 18, 1798, 'I am glad you like our dear little Boy. . . . We are very impatient to see him: he is in the right to say that his name is John Salusbury, for so he was christened just five years ago, & he is my child now.' (Now at Brynbella.) See also letter to Mrs. Piozzi from Davies, Dec. 6, 1798 (Ry. 573, 6).

Bath market, he said to her, '*These are* Sheep's Heads are they not Aunt? I saw a Basket of *Men's heads* at Brescia.'[1] As the little boy spoke no English, it was finally decided to place him in school under the Reverend Reynold Davies at Streatham. Neither Piozzi nor his wife felt well enough to struggle with the difficulty of language, and they logically felt he would be better taken care of by a professional teacher.

Above all things, Mrs. Piozzi felt, his education was most important. On January 14, 1799, writing to Lady Williams of Bodylwyddan of the arrival of the boy, she added that, as he 'has nothing but his Talents & Education to depend upon, *he must be a Scholar* & we will try hard to make him a very good one'. A year later, after hearing good reports of the boy's progress, she wrote to Davies:

> Dear little Boy! he has worked hard, you say. I am very glad: my Heart tells me he will be a valuable Creature with God's Blessing and your kind Care. Let him dance by all means; and let me see him all that a fond Mother can fancy—and a true Friend wish.[2]

Yet in spite of her ambition to make the child a scholar, she warned the tutor not to push him ahead too quickly. Sadly she had to confess that her efforts with her own children had been largely unsuccessful because she had been too ambitious to make them all prodigies. 'Little phials', she continued to Davies,

> must be filled with a Tunning-dish however; else much Learning is spilt by the way, and the fragile Bottle is in danger of bursting. I did not know that as well when I was 25 years old as I know it now . . . but I began teaching before I had learned, and writing before I had read enough—always—and that made me do both so ill.

Bringing her husband's little nephew to England was an exciting event, but for a number of years it made little difference in Mrs. Piozzi's mode of life. Except for occasional vacation trips to Wales, the boy was kept constantly at school in Streatham. Until he was older and had become more used to English manners and customs, she was content to let others struggle with his education. If only she might continue to hear good reports of his progress, she would be satisfied.

[1] Letter to Lady Williams, Feb. 10, 1799. See p. 384, n. 3. All quotations from letters to the Williams family are from this source.

[2] Broadley, p. 49. Davies's school was called 'Streatham University' and was built on ground leased from Mrs. Piozzi. See H. W. Bromhead, *First Elementary Education in Streatham* (Streatham, 1936), p. 4.

Besides, she was preoccupied with other matters. In spite of interminable legal proceedings, quarrels with her daughters, illnesses of her husband, Mrs. Piozzi always found time for various literary projects. Less than a year after the publication of *British Synonymy*, she had been toying with the idea of writing a popular historical work; but it was not until February 1796 that the work was begun. She wrote on the 10th to Queeney:

Well! tis a Sign my Spirits are not low, for last Monday I begun upon a Literary Work of no inconsiderable Magnitude. Its Title would be anticipated if I let any body know it, but when we meet I shall tell it *you* under promise of Secrecy, & shew you as far as it will be gone by that Time:—but I do not work hard.

On March 10 she asked Queeney to help her find various old historical books to aid in her writing.

Oh! do look over some Bookseller's Catalogues for Knollys's *History of the Turks*: second hand *Rums* of that Sort are very cheap, and 'tis necessary *for my Work*: which if I can complete by the Year 1800 will do very well: but 'tis amazing how slowly it goes on. These Visits & sleeping at Neighbours' houses so—cut off the Mornings cruelly.

A great many of her standard reference works were at Streatham, and she hesitated to have them all moved to Wales. Consequently she was forced to borrow a fine copy of Gibbon's *Decline and Fall* from a neighbour, but was in constant fear of getting it soiled. Like Doctor Johnson she was interested in what was inside books, not in the expensive bindings. So on the 23rd she made the comment to Queeney:

I hate a fine Book and a famous Edition a little more ev'ry Year than other: You would laugh to see my Anguish about Mrs. Heaton's *beautiful Infidel Gibbon*—lest a Spot of Ink should penetrate the Papers I have wrapped him in, and make him black on the *Outside*.

In the same letter she referred in a cryptic vein to her project:

'Tis much my Wonder what *you* would think of my new Undertaking? *I* think that Wit's Work done by a Scholar, never pleases the Public; but that Scholar's Work done by a Wit, always pleases.

In her letter, on April 7, she ceased insinuations and promised to tell her daughter exactly what she was doing, but not at once.

Meantime I am the foolishest among them all: undertaking a Work wch. should be written in All Souls College Oxford, that I might have Books at hand, just where I have *no* Books to consult;

& one hates to buy what one has already So I will keep Secrets
No longer but tell *you* in my next Letter what I'm about, & you
shall help judge what most will be wanted.

Amusingly enough, on the 11th she still could not bring herself to divulge her secret.

Here 's no Room left for the Literary Secret, but tho' a Mannerist
in Style, you will not find me one in Subject—Mercy on me! What
Buffets I shall get if I live to publish this *last*—but *Tentanda via est.*

It was not until April 16 that she wrote a long explanation
of her proposed scheme:

My Book will be a Summary of Events for the whole 1800 Years
interspersed with Reflections &c. and a Table of immense Length
in the last of four 8vo. Volumes with the Names of all Cities mentioned in Course of the Work, as called by Ancients & moderns;
French Italian English and Latin—Some Rivers *to run thro'* besides—
& the whole to have for its Title *Retrospection.*

The title, she thought, would make her fortune; but it was an
arduous undertaking, and it would be necessary to collect all
the old histories she could find for consultation in her work.

What Mrs. Piozzi planned was obviously a popularized
history of the world since the birth of Christ, illustrated with
amusing anecdotes and comments. Though not an *Outline of
History*, her design was amazingly in the spirit of the twentieth
century. She felt that there was a need for a review of the outstanding events which had occurred in the world, written in a
colloquial style for the everyday reader. With a project so
suited to her tastes, she threw herself enthusiastically into sifting
and arranging the historical material. She commented to
Queeney a few days later:

Mean while the eternal Difficulty is to judge where to contract
most, & where to amplify—lest one at last should resemble Johnson's Macbean, whom he set a long Time ago to compile a Geographical Dictionary, and looking it over said that he had dwelt
too little on the Article *Athens*. 'Ah Doctor!' says the Man, 'but if
I make so much writing about *Athens*, what Room will be left for
me to talk of Abingdon?' After this Conversation—cries Johnson,
You may be sure we talked no more of Work.[1]

During the spring of 1796 Mrs. Piozzi kept hard at her
writing, while Queeney in London supplied her with books and
information, as well as with dress goods and ribbons. But the
expenses of building Brynbella had reduced their income, and
she was forced to expostulate with her daughter for her zeal

[1] See also *Life*, i. 187.

in supplying her wants: 'send me no more *expensive* Books
sweet Love, for they will undo me . . . we are really as poor as
Rats, with so many Bills to pay.'[1] Even while spending a
vacation at Beaumaris in Anglesey during the summer of 1796,
Mrs. Piozzi kept plying her daughter with historical questions
and requests to look up quotations from books not available
in Wales. The social diversions of the place, her husband's
gout, and the fact that Lord Bulkeley, who had offered the
use of his fine library, forgot to leave her the key, interfered with
the writing, but her mind was never free of the project. Later
in the summer, when back at Brynbella, she commented to
Queeney:

I had been thinking pretty seriously one Day here about such
Sort of Stuff, and dreamed the Night after that my Head ached
cruelly, & that complaining to you about the pain—Your answer
was 'Why it all comes from Studying Etymologies, you had much
better read Homer's Iliad.'

Instead, she added, she was reading Mme D'Arblay's new
novel, *Camilla*, which she liked immensely, though troubled
about the style.

Through the spring of 1797, for once free from legal conferences in London, she struggled on with her compilation,
and remarked to Queeney on May 5:

I work hard at the *Stuff*; & resolve to take your Method of a more
equal Distribution than I at first intended. How will you like my
Death of Thomas o'Becket I wonder! & how will the Whigs &
Democrates like it?

Mr. Godwin's new Book is quite a Literary Curiosity, Davies
brought it, & I read it Night & Day—Any thing but Sleep you Know.

Reading Godwin and worrying about the French 'Democrates' diverted Mrs. Piozzi's mind from her researches into the
Middle Ages. Like her old friend Burke she was horrified at
the 'reds' across the Channel and the radical economists of her
own nation, who were, she felt, undermining the English
Constitution. In the unpublished dialogues between Una and
Duessa she had attacked those who sympathized with the
French assassins; in *British Synonymy*, while ostensibly explaining
the meaning of words, she had taken occasion to point political
morals; in her voluminous correspondence throughout the
nineties she continually expressed her detestation of the new

---

[1] Brynbella cost over £20,000 (Mainwaring Piozziana), but since Piozzi was
a careful manager, he conserved the rest of her fortune so that they always had
sufficient for their needs.

principles; finally came the urge to disseminate her strong convictions even more widely.

The desire to enter the lists herself became so strong that Mrs. Piozzi put aside *Retrospection* for a time and hurriedly composed a political pamphlet which she called *Three Warnings to John Bull before he dies.* Signing herself only 'an Old Acquaintance of the Public', and using as a framework the old tale written over thirty years before, she warned the British public of the danger which threatened. England must reform or be lost; either the people must resolve unanimously to support the government, defend the Established Church, and amend their manners, or dire consequences would surely follow.

Let the Constitution alone, preserve it as it is—revere, support, obey it, touch it not—When the French Fools tried to reform and quack their own;—what did they? instead of letting Blood in the *safe* Vein, they stabbed it in the temporal Artery, & fierce Convulsions followed—Listen not to the Excitement of those Men who instigate John Bull to his undoing: false Friends, who mean to mount upon the People's Shoulders, whence better to strike at the King's head. have a Care of them. Their song about Liberty and Equality is the Syren's Song, to follow it is Death. Twas thus the pied Piper that we read of seduced the Men of Halberstadt or Hammelen: Standing in the Square he piped first all the Rats away, & that was so fine a Thing—the Magistrates beg'd of him to pipe again, & so he did, and then he piped the Children all away: and with the last Set of the fools that he infatuated, the Piper himself went away into a hollow Cave,—its Mouth closed, & they came out no more. Such will be the fate of our Street Orators, or like it. But let us rather remember the Wise Man's Warnings, and not suffer these half-hatch'd Notions to be presented so before the Public, who ought not to be fed with addle Eggs; as if in its Dotage, and unable to discern good Food.[1]

The pamphlet appeared in April 1798, shortly after the Piozzis' arrival in London. Since it was published anonymously, only a few of Mrs. Piozzi's intimate friends guessed her connexion with it, but they were highly complimentary.[2]

---

[1] Ry. 642, 8–9. This holograph version has written on the wrapper 'MS. of a political Pamphlet, 1798, Mrs. Piozzi, Warrens Hotel'. See *French Journals*, p. 52. A copy of the printed version is in the British Museum.

[2] J. F. Vandercom wrote, May 4, 1798:

Your inestimable Sermon the Three warnings to John Bull (which I have just receiv'd & read with delight, & thank you for) will I'm sure have a good effect; & will notwithstanding the concealment of your name, be discovered to be yours, & add another sprig of laurel to your literary fame.

(Ry. 606, 53.) See also *Letters to Pennington*, p. 155, and a letter from the Ladies of Llangollen, July 16, 1798 (Nat. Lib. of Wales).

Nevertheless, it is doubtful if the sale, outside the circle of the authoress, was very great; certainly not many copies of the printed versions have survived. Practically unnoticed in her own day, the brochure will never be more than a rare curiosity for the Johnsonian collector.

While in London in the spring of 1798 Mrs. Piozzi was active with a number of literary projects: she translated for a news-paper (the *True Briton*) a recent letter from Piozzi's brother in Venice telling of the ravages of the French;[1] and she gave a quantity of intimate biographical information about herself to a journalist who published a fairly accurate account of her life in *The Monthly Mirror* for June and September.[2] This is perhaps the most authentic short biography of Mrs. Piozzi to appear in print during her life, but unfortunately it was never very well known.

During the past few years Mrs. Piozzi had been less in the public eye than in the late seventeen-eighties, for the 'scandal-sheets' had found other targets for their barbed arrows. Nevertheless, attacks and compliments appeared occasionally in print. In two biographies of Johnson, following that of Boswell, she received diverse treatment: Murphy (1792) mentioned the Thrales with friendly courtesy, though making no attempts to defend them from the slurs of their enemies;[3] Dr. Robert Anderson (1795) repeated the old allegations in regard to her cruel treatment of Johnson.[4] Of other general writers, William Gifford attacked her violently in his two outbursts against the Della Cruscans, the *Baviad* and the *Maeviad*;[5] but Pigott was strangely complimentary in his ribald *Female Jockey Club*, which appeared in the spring of 1794.[6] Pigott defended her second marriage, and shrewdly pointed out that socially a musician should have been the equal of a brewer. In addition he ad-mitted some admiration for Mrs. Piozzi's ability as a writer.

Her life of Johnson is full of requisite information, certainly far superior to any similar production from her *learned* male competitors. Her poetry is by no means contemptible. The account of her travels

---

[1] *The True Briton*, Mar. 8, 1798. Mrs. Piozzi wrote to Mrs. Williams that she had translated the letter and printed it in this paper (Mainwaring MS.).
[2] *The Monthly Mirror*, v (1798), 323–6; vi. 137. I am indebted to Professor D. Nichol Smith for the information that Mrs. Piozzi's letter to the editors of this magazine, supplying the facts used in the biography, is now in the Huntington Library. See also *European Mag.* xxxiv (1798), 101–2. Comment on the sketch may be found in letter of J. Gillon, July 13, 1798 (Ry. 577, 8); and in Ry. 552, 21.
[3] *John. Misc.* i. 422–3.   [4] *Life of Johnson* (Edinburgh, 1795).
[5] See pp. 347, 373. See also J. Toulmin, *The Injustice of Classing Unitarians with Deists and Infidels* (1797), p. 5, where a statement in *British Synonymy* drew a stinging rebuke.   [6] pp. 122–3.

with her present beloved lord and master is enriched by accurate observations, as well as by a faithful delineation of national character, and may be reckoned her best *literary* production.

The spring of 1798, with various journalistic enterprises, with a round of entertainments, with pleasant hours spent in the company of Mrs. Siddons and other old friends, was almost a revival of old times. In spite of these attractions, however, the Piozzis were determined to make Bath their winter residence and to give less and less time to London. Accordingly, after vainly offering Streatham rent free to Queeney and her sisters, they let the house to a Mr. Giles for three years.[1] This happily accomplished, they returned to Wales, where Mrs. Piozzi again threw herself whole-heartedly into her historical researches.

Retrospection was gradually taking shape; it provided a constant source of interest and amusement wherever she might be. The following winter in Bath offered an opportunity to consult other scholars and to browse about in bookstores and libraries. She remarked to Queeney, January 24, 1799, that 'Mr. Piozzi is on his Feet again thank God, & I am scarce ever off mine; running about to see and hear and pick up living Intelligence to animate the heavy Stuff one collects in solitary Study.' But information was hard to get, she complained, for even the celebrated authorities knew little about many of the problems which puzzled her. After consulting the younger Dr. Charles Burney, the celebrated Greek scholar, about a mysterious 'Abraxas' stone, she confided to Queeney that

those *steady Scholars* will be often found neglectful of what would not disgrace them to know: They keep polishing and brightening the *Key* of Knowledge, but think not of opening the *Door* with it; & so you & I run up our Rope Ladder & climb in at Window sometimes, & bring away a bit of Plunder—and if our Rope does not break & we fall down & disgrace ourselves—*we* look wise for a Moment, & *they* look foolish.

In the same letter, referring to Queeney's expressed opinion that she must be a valuable subscriber to Bull's lending library, she added that Bull

hates the very Sight of me the while. because I come to his Shop at 8 or 9 o'Clock in the Morng always—the only Leisure hour the Man has from Readers who sit round his Table all Noon, & Footmen who ferret after him for Novels all Night—: and I make him clamber for me & reach Books which do not answer, & then he has to mount the Steps again, & so we go on . . .

[1] *Letters to Pennington*, pp. 142, 156; Thraliana, June 3, 1798.

During the summers at Brynbella, despite the lack of library facilities or scholars to consult, she kept busily at her task. In August 1800 Lord Henry Petty, afterwards Lord Lansdowne, stopped over night. Many years later, remembering his host and hostess, he gave an interesting account to Hayward.

When in my youth I made a tour in Wales—times when all inns were bad, and all houses hospitable—I put up for a day at her house, I think in Denbighshire . . . I remember her taking me into her bed-room to show me the floor covered with folios, quartos, and octavos, for consultation, and indicating the labour she had gone through in compiling an immense volume she was then publishing, called 'Retrospection'. She was certainly what was called, and is still called, blue, and that of a deep tint, but good humoured and lively, though affected; her husband, a quiet civil man, with his head full of nothing but music.[1]

By the summer of 1800 *Retrospection* was finally nearing completion, and the problem of finding a publisher was uppermost in Mrs. Piozzi's mind.[2] Since Robinson had published *British Synonymy*, she turned first to him. As early as 1798 she had shown him rough drafts of several chapters, but no definite contract had been arranged. Now Robinson determined to have nothing to do with the proposal, alleging that he was old and in ill health. Possibly another reason for his disinclination was that, with naïve egotism and with the mistaken idea that the labour involved should be the measure of the worth of a manuscript, Mrs. Piozzi had determined to ask £1,000 for the copyright. To Chappelow, her agent in the matter, she wrote on June 30, 1800, defending her expectation of so large a sum, and adding that the publisher must surely get his money back by printing an octavo four-volume edition 'for use of Schools' after the original quarto edition was exhausted.[3] She explained to Chappelow that her sole purpose was to abridge history for the everyday reader, to make popular what had always proved so fascinating to herself.

Negotiations for the sale of the manuscript throughout the summer having proved unsuccessful, the Piozzis left Brynbella for London the second week in October 1800, stopping at several places on the way, particularly in Oxford, where she consulted some authorities in the Bodleian Library. By the end

[1] Hayward, i. 345–6. The date of his visit, about Aug. 15, 1800, is derived from Thraliana.

[2] In Thraliana the date of completion is given as shortly after July 15, 1800.

[3] Ry. 560, 98. See also letters to Chappelow of June 9, 10, 1800 (Ry. 560, 95, 96). Davies also spoke to Robinson about the book (Ry. 573, 21).

of the month they were at Streatham visiting her tenant Mr.
Giles. She had brought back to Streatham all the broken sets
of books which had been taken to Brynbella for use in writing
Retrospection, a proceeding which must have amused and to some
extent annoyed her husband, for she commented to Queeney,
'Mr. Piozzi says if I was to undertake any thing ever again
(which I shall not) the best way would be to take a House at
Oxford & study in some College Library'. All this worry and
absorption in old musty books was a constant puzzle to the
simple-hearted musician; yet he was sympathetic with her
vagaries and never openly interfered.[1]

Because of her determination to have the book ready for the
public by January 1, 1801, Mrs. Piozzi's one idea now was to
come to terms with some publisher immediately. Robinson's
reluctance to consider the matter forced her to go to Stockdale,
the well-known publisher in Piccadilly. Her price was still
£1,000, but she soon found that no one would guarantee such
a return. Instead Stockdale offered her half interest in the profits of the publication, he to pay all expenses of printing and
publication. Under such an arrangement she would run no risk
whatever and would retain her right to half of all that the copyright of the work would produce. While hesitating at this combination of author and publisher, she considered it was the best
offer she could secure, and on November 3 signed an agreement
with Stockdale covering these provisions.[2] The publisher rushed
the manuscript to the printers, and by November 14 she wrote
to Chappelow that Stockdale plied her hard with proofs.[3] That
same day the Piozzis left Streatham and moved into an hotel
at 25 Leicester Square to be near the printer's shop.

Throughout December she kept hard at her work of correcting proof, which was only interrupted by week-end visits
to Streatham, evenings in the playhouse to see Mrs. Siddons,
a meeting with her daughters on their way to Brighton, and
journeys with Sam Lysons to the British Museum to examine
manuscripts necessary for last-minute changes in her text.[4] Her
desire to have the work completed by 1801, the beginning of
another century, actually forced printing at too fast a rate, and
hundreds of errors of fact and typography went uncorrected.

---

[1] In Mainwaring Piozziana, iii. 113, Mrs. Piozzi once described her husband
'whose kindness for his Wife's Vanity never forsook him'.
[2] Ry. 557, 201.   [3] Ry. 559, 105.
[4] Every Saturday, Sunday, and Monday were spent with Giles at Streatham
and the middle of the week in London (Thraliana, Apr. 7, 1801). See also *Letters
to Pennington*, p. 206.

Personal friends did all in their power to further the success of the undertaking, and John Gillon, her business adviser, secured ninety orders from his own acquaintance.[1] On New Year's Day, at a dinner given for her and her publisher, toasts were drunk to the coming volumes and the air was electric with gay expectation. But not all was plain sailing, for labour troubles delayed the publication. On January 4 she wrote to Queeney: 'Stockdale advertising the Book for New Years Day has brought in a Crowd of Orders & we have no Copies to send out in any Degree answerable to the Demand.' She added that

the Country Booksellers too are quite clamourous, & if it had not been for the Secession of Compositors Devils &c. who retired to Mons Sacer, & refused to Work; we should have been out of Print during the first Fortnight: such Mortification would have made an Aristocrate of any one.

Being interested both as book-seller and book-writer, Mrs. Piozzi urged all her friends to recommend the work to every one they saw. She asked Queeney not to lend anyone her copy, because that would injure the sale: 'cry Charming! & keep it at home, if you mean good to the bustling Author.'

The title of the work, when finally printed, was *Retrospection: or A Review of the most striking and important Events, Characters, Situations and their consequences, which the last Eighteen Hundred Years have presented to the View of Mankind.* It appeared in two volumes, quarto, and altogether comprised over 1,000 pages. Prefixed to the first volume was an unflattering portrait of the author, which caused much annoyance to her more intimate friends.[2]

Mrs. Piozzi was greatly distressed by the multitude of typographical errors caused by the haste in printing. Her letters to various friends are full of comments on the numerous mistakes; 'the Words are perpetually transposed,' she wrote to Queeney, '*Yet as*, for *as Yet*,' and she insisted that she was 'desirous of a new Edition chiefly on Acct of these vexatious *Lapses*—but not of *my Pen*'. For this reason, in spite of the delay in completing all of the first edition, a second was proposed almost immediately. From Reading on January 21, while on her way to Bath, she wrote to Mrs. Pennington, 'Stockdale was hurrying to drive out a new edition before we left London, and I was

---

[1] *Letters to Pennington*, p. 207.
[2] Murphy insisted the print looked more like the 'Witch of Endor' than Mrs. Piozzi (Ry. 548, 50). The manuscript is now in the Hyde collection.

forced to *hold him in*. We shall hear all *our* faults, and the printers too, when the Reviews make their appearance.' When corrections were made, she felt, it would be better to make them all in one unhurried printing.

With the probable sale of *Retrospection* a constant source of worry, she wrote to Chappelow on February 2, particularly lamenting the printers' strike and the resulting numerous errors, especially in the quotations, for she found that people were delaying their purchases, hoping to get a corrected second edition.[1] She urged Stockdale to print an errata slip immediately to still at least some of the criticism. (None seems ever to have been printed.) The problem of the new edition was uppermost in all their minds, but they could come to no definite agreement. According to Chappelow, who wrote from London on February 4, Stockdale did not wish to make the new printing octavo, but was insisting on quartos again; Mrs. Piozzi herself vacillated between desire for a correct text and the wish to wait to see what the reaction of the reviewers would be.[2] As a result, the reprinting was put off from month to month. In the meantime Mrs. Piozzi corrected the copies of her intimate friends, and filled her letters with comments on printing errors and discussions of favourite chapters.

Retrospection cannot be recommended to modern readers. Although some portions are undoubtedly written with insight and cleverness, on the whole it is Mrs. Piozzi's most uninteresting book. She seemed unable, in the dreary and tedious summaries of Roman and medieval history, to combine her talent for telling a good story with the miscellaneous information she had culled from her wide reading. Many people in her own day, as Chappelow said, preferred the second volume to the first;[3] yet even in her later accounts the same inability to combine various sources intelligently is apparent. The twentieth century is much more adept at popularized world history, but it must be remembered that Mrs. Piozzi did not have many models to consult.

Most of the work was based on supposedly standard historical sources, but in many cases the author failed to note her authority. Consequently, errors and false deductions which she had lifted wholesale from out-of-print volumes were often imputed to her own fertile imagination. In other places where her meaning was not quite clear, critical readers made the wrong inference. Add to all this an uneven style, partly chit-chat and

---

[1] Ry. 560, 108.   [2] Ry. 563, 70.   [3] Ibid.

partly Johnsonese, and it is easy to see why the unprejudiced readers of the time did not take the volumes seriously.[1]

While anxiously awaiting the verdict of the critics, the Piozzis remained at Bath; then late in March they started back to Brynbella. On April 13 Chappelow wrote of severe attacks appearing in the *Anti-Jacobin* and in the *European Magazine*, but insisted that nobody minded these short-lived publications.[2] It was the *Critical* and *Monthly* reviews which were of the most importance. Everything depended on the attitude which these two publications would take.

Finally in May the *Critical Review* published its discussion of *Retrospection*, and Mrs. Piozzi was staggered. Condemning the publication in no uncertain terms, the arrangement, the accuracy, and particularly the style, 'rendered abrupt and quaint, by the pursuit of what the French call "esprit",' the reviewer maintained that the work was unsuitable for any class of reader.[3]

> To the learned, it must appear as a series of dreams by an old lady; and many of the mistakes are so gross, as not to escape the general reader. Far less is it fit for the perusal of youth, of either sex; since the numerous errors, and the air of sufficiency with which they are written, might leave impressions difficult to be eradicated by the genuine page of history.

What was even worse, after emphasizing the minor errors in the volumes, the reviewer imputed to the authoress responsibility for the many silly mistakes resulting from faulty typography. Although hardened to newspaper abuse, Mrs. Piozzi could not bear this last, for she seems to have ignored the fact that an author was at least partially responsible for improper reading of proof. With impulsive haste she attempted to vindicate herself, and wrote a long letter to the bookseller Robson, which was published in the *Gentleman's Magazine* for July 1801.[4] In this letter Mrs. Piozzi replied to her critics with decided

---

[1] One writer has called *Retrospection* an

Ancient History in dishabille, in a dimity morning gown, her slippers down in the heel, and her *front* awry; and *Modern* History in a cotton gown, and pattens, just returned from shopping, with a new cambric pocket-handkerchief, three yards of pink ribbon, a cake of Windsor soap, and an ounce of all-spice in her reticule.

(*Love Letters of Mrs. Piozzi* (1843), p. 9.)

[2] Ry. 563, 71. In the *Anti-Jacobin*, viii (1801), 241–6, the reviewer called the work, 'History cooked up in a novel form reduced to light reading for boarding school misses, and loungers at a watering place'. The writer in the *European Mag.* xxxix (1801), 188–93, sneered at the portrait prefixed to the work and the lack of dates. See also pp. 271–6.

[3] *Critical Review*, xxxii (1801), 28.   [4] *Gent. Mag.* lxxi (1801), 602–3.

spirit. Before it was actually printed she wrote to Queeney of her refutation of the reviewer's criticisms, asking her daughter's approbation of the step, explaining at length her opponent's mistakes, and ending with the plaint: '*do* say something about my Battle with these odious Reviewers—'Tis a Manuscript Battle merely on my Side, but I could not bear to be called such a Blockhead.' Queeney, who had admitted enough interest in *Retrospection* to read it through twice (a task we may not much envy her), refused to commend her mother's undignified public retort to her detractors. As late as August Mrs. Piozzi was still vainly trying to draw some expression of opinion on the matter from her daughter, for Queeney probably remembered Dr. Johnson's quotation of Bentley's dictum that 'no man was ever written down, but by himself'.[1] In the end it was only through the interposition of her husband that Mrs. Piozzi stopped railing at the reviewers, an interposition which seems the one instance where Piozzi took an interest in her literary affairs.[2]

Though the *Critical Review* contained the most devastating attack on *Retrospection,* other periodicals poked sly fun at its many weaknesses. A writer in the *Gentleman's Magazine* in June suggested that most of the work was actually written in rhythm, and selected passages which he asserted naturally took the form of blank verse though printed as prose.[3] The next year the *British Critic* reiterated this amusing charge, printing further excerpts arranged as poetry.[4] Mrs. Piozzi's style continued a perennial source of amusement and argument to her readers.

The sale of the book, which at first had been rapid, slackened as quickly. As soon as her friends had been supplied and the first adverse reviews made public, few additional purchasers appeared; yet by Easter Stockdale himself had sent all his stock to the booksellers, and Lady Williams was having difficulty in finding a copy.[5] At that time an octavo second edition was still planned, but as soon as the *Critical Review* appeared with its slashing attack, Stockdale gave up any intention of reprinting a corrected version. For her part Mrs. Piozzi was not so easily disheartened, and for some time continued to cherish a vague hope that her copyright might still prove valuable. But her hopes were vain. The long years of patient study brought no

---

[1] *Life*, v. 312.　　　　　　　　[2] *Letters to Pennington*, p. 224.
[3] *Gent. Mag.* lxxi (1801), 493–4. The letter is dated June 7, and is signed L. S.
[4] The *British Critic*, xix (Apr. 1802), 355–8.
[5] Letter of Easter Eve (Mainwaring MS.).

financial reward. The final accounting with Stockdale showed
her net profit on the venture to be £124. 3s. 9d., and this was
further reduced to less than a hundred pounds by charges for
complimentary copies sent to friends.[1] Only 516 sets were
actually sold in 1801 of the first and only edition of 750 copies.

Both as a commercial venture and as a vehicle to enhance
her literary reputation, *Retrospection* had proved a failure; but
for the rest of her life Mrs. Piozzi remained loyal to it, and
freely annotated and corrected every copy which came into her
hands. While she realized that the decision not to quote
authorities had been her undoing, she still believed footnotes
or citations would have spoiled a popular work of the type she
had planned. Here, too, Mrs. Piozzi proved herself a fore-
runner of popular twentieth-century writers, but an effective
innovator herself she was not.

[1] Ry. 557, 202, 203.

XIX

GOUT

1801-1809

DESPITE her troubles with *Retrospection*, Mrs. Piozzi's exuberant spirit was unaffected. In February 1801 Hannah More wrote from Bath to Dr. Whalley:

Your lively friend, Mrs. Piozzi, is our next neighbour, and the expense of strength and spirits which two such quartos would suppose, have not one whit diminished her gaiety, animation, and cheerfulness.[1]

It was probably about this time that a neighbour in Wales met her on the way to Wynnstay,

skipping about like a kid, quite a figure of fun, in a tiger skin shawl, lined with scarlet, and *only* five colours upon her head-dress—on the top of a flaxen wig a bandeau of blue velvet, a bit of tiger ribbon, a white beaver hat and plume of black feathers—as gay as a lark.[2]

She still retained her eager interest in public and private affairs. In one thing only was she disillusioned—the joys of authorship. Though long inured to the sneers of the critics, she had been hurt and dismayed by the cool public reception of *Retrospection*. Furthermore, she was forced during the next few years to spend most of her time nursing a sick husband, and had little strength for anything else. Nostrums for gout became, for the time being, of more importance than the exploits of Prester John.

Gabriel Piozzi was slowly changing into a typical English squire, in his illnesses as well as his tastes. As a well-to-do country gentleman, he found aching toes and disgruntled farmers of almost as much importance as a string-quartet by Haydn or an aria of Mozart. He had become a naturalized British subject in 1793,[3] and while it was not until some years later that he received the sacrament from an Anglican vicar, to all

---

[1] *Whalley Corr.* ii. 188.
[2] Hayward, i. 346–7. The date given is Jan. 1803, but since the Piozzis were at Bath from Dec. 1802 until Apr. 1803, this year cannot be correct.
[3] His denization papers are dated Aug. 8, 1793 (Ry. Charter 1245, 1246).

HESTER LYNCH PIOZZI

Drawing by JACKSON, 1810
Now at the Johnson House, Gough Square, London

intents and purposes he had become a member of the English Church.

To be sure, Piozzi was never able to master the intricacies of the English language. In his yearly diaries, which record every little expenditure in addition to the names of guests who came to dine, the entries are made in a sort of 'pidgin English'.[1] For example, in 1803, when his wife fell ill at Bath, he recorded: 'Mrs. Piozzi she got the influenza, and find herself very ill with fever.' Four days later he added, 'Mrs. Piozzi, she is a little Better this Morning'. And like Mrs. Garrick, Piozzi never learned to speak without a decided accent; nor could he distinguish between the colloquial shades of meaning which a native knew by instinct. An amusing story is told that Piozzi, calling once upon some old lady of quality, was told by the servant 'she was indifferent'. 'Is she indeed?' answered Piozzi huffishly, 'then pray tell her I can be as indifferent as she,' and walked away.[2]

When at Brynbella he hobbled about, supervising the labourers, planning the crops, visiting the tenants. He became interested in the neighbouring farm hands, and in April 1800 was appointed overseer of the poor of his parish. Letters from the Dean of St. Asaph at this time show how seriously he took the responsibilities of his office.[3] Personally investigating the poverty-stricken families in the vicinity, he tried his best to improve their condition; and on July 25, 1800, to celebrate his wedding anniversary, Piozzi arranged a dinner for thirty-five haymakers. As Mrs. Piozzi wrote to Mrs. Pennington, this year 'instead of feeding the rich, we fed the poor'.

Notwithstanding his careful counting of every penny, Piozzi found the means for extensive building. There were always improvements at Brynbella, changes in the house, or additions to the stables. Bach-y-Graig, too, needed attention. The old house had badly needed repair in 1774, when Dr. Johnson viewed its high tower and lack of floors; now it was almost in ruins. Neighbours advised pulling it down completely and building a snug farm-house from the materials, but Mrs. Piozzi's sentimental regard for the home of her ancestors turned the scale against such a proceeding. Instead, the old house was renovated and made habitable for a new tenant. In typical fashion she

---

[1] Piozzi's daily diaries and account books for 1801, 1802, 1803, 1806, and 1808 have survived, some in the possession of Mrs. Herbert Evans of Brynbella and others in my possession. These are important in establishing the chronology for the period and in giving further insight into his character.

[2] T. Moore, *Memoirs* (1853), iv. 329. [3] Ry. 557, 193–5.

had a stone placed in the front of the building which stated that the Mansion had been 'repaired and beautified by Gabriel Piozzi Esq. in the year 1800'.[1] Defiantly and proudly she honoured at the same time her Welsh forefathers and her Italian husband.

Further repairs were made at Bach-y-Graig in 1803, and at the same time extensive additions were begun to the little church at Tremeirchion. Mrs. Piozzi explained to Queeney that they were

paving, Glazing, slating painting it &c and we give them a new Pulpit, Desk, & Cloths besides—with a brass Chandelier.—It *was* a Place like a Stable you know; and we have made a Vault for ourselves & my poor Ancestors. . . .[2]

One ever-threatening interruption to all this activity was Piozzi's susceptibility to gout. Some years he escaped almost entirely, but in others the attacks followed each other in quick succession. In 1797 he was housed in his upstairs room from October to Christmas Day, and even then could only be wheeled about in a chair. In 1798, 1799, 1800, 1801 there was always at least one relapse. In the spring of 1803, after an attack of influenza at Bath, he was again crippled. Mrs. Piozzi wrote to Queeney from Brynbella on July 10:

Mr. Piozzi is forced to make me the Operative Farmer now— The frequent returns of Gout leave his Feet so sore he cannot move but in a Bath rolling Chair—yet is his general Health & Strength unimpaired, and he has even consented to lend me out for a Day or Two at a Time to dear old Lleweney Hall, where they expect an Heir every Day, & Lady Kirkwall almost *insists on* my Attendance as a Twelve-Times-experienced Matron.

Though the years had brought anxiety and sickness, Mrs. Piozzi still adored her disabled husband, and tossed these impromptu verses across the table to him on July 25, the anniversary of their marriage:

> Accept, my Love, this honest Lay,
> Upon your twentieth Wedding Day.
> I little hoped that life would stay
> To hail the *twentieth* Wedding Day.
> If you're grown gouty, I grown gray,
> Upon our twentieth Wedding Day,
> 'Tis no great wonder; Friends must say
> Why 'twas their twentieth Wedding Day.

[1] *Letters to Pennington*, p. 198. This tribute unfortunately no longer remains at Bach-y-Graig. See also letters to Queeney, Aug. 7, Sept. 20, 1803.
[2] Sept. 20, 1803. The church was also enlarged in the gallery.

Perhaps there's few feel less decay
Upon a twentieth Wedding Day:
And many of those who used to pay
Their court upon our Wedding Day,
Have melted off, and died away
Before the twentieth Wedding Day.
Those places too, which, once so gay,
Bore witness to our Wedding Day,
Florence and Milan, blythe as May,
Marauding French have made their prey.
If then of gratitude one ray
Illuminates our Wedding Day,
Think, midst the wars and wild affray
That rage around this Wedding Day,
What mercy 'tis we are spared to say
'We have seen our twentieth Wedding Day.'[1]

She further showed her contentment by lending encouragement to others who gave up social advantages for love[2] or whose marriage was similar to hers, and the next year she wrote to Dr. Thackeray:

Mr. Piozzi *should* feel a *particular* Interest in the Choice you have made of a Widow with children. . . . *We* have lived together now 20 years, wanting only a Month; and may you my Dear Sir find yourselves as well pleased with the Anniversary of the Day that united you as are your true Servants & Friends at Brynbella.[3]

During the summer of 1803 Piozzi was so lame that he could hardly walk a hundred yards; however he was able in October and November to pay several long visits to old Lleweney, where four generations of Lord Kirkwall's family gaily kept open house. Every move is described in Piozzi's diary. Suddenly on November 28 he made the entry: 'I went to Bed with the Gout'; and for the rest of the year there were only a few scattered entries.[4] His wife wrote to Dr. Thackeray on December 7,

I never saw a human Creature so Irritable as Mr. Piozzi *now*, so

[1] *Letters to Pennington*, p. 259; Mainwaring Piozziana, iii. 75, &c. The Piozzis had been married nineteen years, but, of course, it was their twentieth wedding day, counting the first as one.

[2] In 1803 Mrs. Holman (*née* Jane Hamilton) came to Brynbella for a visit of seven weeks (Piozzi Diary, 1803). She was closely related to the Duke of Hamilton, but on marrying Joseph George Holman, who acted at Covent Garden from 1784 to 1800, had been ostracized by her family and friends.

[3] Mrs. Piozzi's letters to Dr. W. M. Thackeray are owned by Mr. Albert Ashforth, Jr., of New York City. Unless specifically noted, the following quotations are taken from Mr. Ashforth's collection.

[4] Piozzi's 1803 diary, which is in my possession, shows the intimacy of the Piozzis and the owners of Lleweney.

that between Passion & Strangling with his horrid Cough, I verily thought he would have burst in my Hands last Night: My Fingers are not yet steady from the Terror.

By Monday, December 19, the invalid was able to come to the dining-room, but immediately afterwards Mrs. Piozzi was forced to dispatch a hurried appeal to Dr. Thackeray in Chester imploring him to come at once. Galloping over as quickly as he could, the doctor found Piozzi in the throes of the worst attack he had yet experienced. The pain from the inflammation in his chest and throat was so intense that he became delirious. Late Christmas night Mrs. Piozzi reported to the doctor·

His poor Head has been far from home all Day,—& all last Night.—The Back I am told looks better but tho' he rambles in his Talk about Mrs. Mostyn's being poysoned, & Doctor Myddelton's inviting him to Dinner,—he knows us all; & takes your Draughts willingly. . . . What a Life we do lead.

Three days later she described her plight to the sympathetic Chappelow: 'half destroyed with anxiety Watching & Fatigue. Eleven Days & Nights without taking my Clothes off.'[1] Gradually the disease wore itself out and she could relax, but from this time on Piozzi's attacks became every year more virulent, and the intervals between them less restorative. To recount them is like compiling a list of horrors.

The next summer (1804) Mrs. Piozzi wrote to little John Salusbury Piozzi, still at school in Streatham:

My dearest little Boy

It was very good natured in Mr. Davies to carry you half a Crown, and *exceedingly* good natured in him to make you write that bit of a Letter, which was worth Two Half Crowns to *me*; because I wanted Comfort very much, your Uncle is so bad of the Gout, and cries out terribly.[2]

Then in the following December came a recurrence of the same painful scenes. On the 17th Mrs. Piozzi sent word to Dr. Thackeray that her husband was 'stretched on a Bed of Agony himself; one Foot worse than ever I knew it—getting him out of Bed is sad screaming Work, & sets all *my* Nerves in a hurry' To Queeney, on the last day of the month, she added:

Mr. Piozzi has but just done Shrieking, & tis hoarseness, not

---

[1] Ry. 561, 128. She here describes the trouble as internal gout which had settled in the lungs. For the terrible cough and low pulse, Dr. Thackeray prescribed draughts of strong madeira.

[2] July 1, 1804 (seen at the Brick Row Bookshop, New York City).

happiness makes him leave off *now*. A Succession of 3 frightful
Abcesses in 3 different Parts of his Feet, have set Opiates & Pacifiers
all at Defiance; & kept him nine Days without our daring to move
him, or change his Linen or his Bed. Two Men Two Women &
myself did however accomplish it on the 10th Morng: when he was
kept with the utmost Difficulty by dint of Wine & Cordials, from
bursting in our Arms with Rage & Pain united.

The following day: 'but all's Over now:—*till the next Time.*'

As usual, once the acute attack was over, improvement was
gradual but sure; however, it was like living over an active
volcano, this dread of a certain 'next Time'. By 1805 Piozzi
was almost a complete invalid, wheeled about constantly in his
Bath chair, seldom attempting any gaiety without a relapse.
On July 25 the Piozzis celebrated their wedding anniversary at
nearby Prestatyn by feeding forty-eight poor children with
plum-pudding; but the next day Piozzi was seized with pain,
and carried in torments back to Brynbella.[1] Perhaps he, too,
had sampled the pudding. Then in October, after ten days'
sea-bathing at Abergele, an abscessed foot drove him back to
his own room at Brynbella.

Writing to Queeney on November 2 of her husband's sufferings, Mrs. Piozzi recounted a strange occurrence of a few days
before. One stormy night, sitting reading in the little upstairs
music-room with the west wind howling outside, she had suddenly been startled by a deep-drawn sigh seemingly near by.
Her husband lay quiet under an opiate and there was no dog
in the house. Another hollow respiration added further to the
mystification, until she found on examination it came from
the organ pipes. Then, 'it was my Turn to sigh *with* the Organ
pipes: which never-*never* more will feel the Hand of their Master
—& certainly never such a hand'.

If life seemed one violent shock after another, there were
peaceful interludes. Even after the discouraging summer and
autumn of 1805, upon arriving at Bath early in December,
Mrs. Piozzi could write the joyful news to Queeney that
'Mr. Piozzi has *walked upStairs* today—*with help*, but in short
not carried in Arms, as he has been ever since we were at

---

[1] Mrs. Piozzi to Queeney, Aug. 10, 1805. On another trip to Prestatyn Mrs.
Piozzi composed a set of verses for Queeney. It much amused Lady Kirkwall to
think that anyone should write serious poetry on such a bleak spot (Mainwaring
Piozziana, iii. 76). During these years Mrs. Piozzi constantly scribbled verses on
every and no occasion, and Thraliana and her other Common Place books are
filled with the effusions. In the present volume only occasional attempts can be
mentioned.

Abergeley'. Actually, by waiting patiently until each attack had run its course, they were able to spend a part of nearly every winter at Bath, and a few weeks occasionally in London.[1]

The difficult journeys to Bath were usually broken by visits on the way to the famous Ladies of Llangollen, Miss Ponsonby and Lady Eleanor Butler, two feminists who braved the displeasure of the world at their views and lived in retirement in the Vale of Llangollen; to Miss Owen in Shrewsbury; or to Mrs. Pennington at Bristol. Jolting over the rough roads in the coach was often painful, but with short leisurely runs travel was not impossible.

When at Bath Piozzi was forced to divide his time between a couch and his wheeled chair; yet when convalescent, he recorded in his diary a succession of parties and concerts especially arranged for him. Rauzzini was usually the principal performer, but there were also charming young ladies willing to play for the disabled musician. Piozzi's own fingers had become so gnarled and twisted by the ravages of gout that, as his wife wrote, 'the poor Pianoeforte no longer a Resource of Comfort to him, presents only a painful Retrospect of Times long past'.[2] Once a little girl of five, noticing his bandaged hands, said:

'Pray, Sir, why are your fingers wrapped up in black silk so?' 'My dear,' replied he, 'they are in mourning for my voice.' 'Oh, me!"' cries the child, *is she dead?*' He sung an easy song, and the baby exclaimed, 'Ah, Sir! you are very naughty—you tell fibs!'[3]

Pathetically the skilled performer, who had charmed the musical connoisseurs of Europe, was forced to be a passive listener.

In spite of her husband's continual illness Mrs Piozzi found much to amuse her at Bath. On March 7, 1805, she wrote to Queeney:

You know my Character exactly; I never want for Amusement when thrown upon Society, & tho' we go out very *very* seldom at Night, I pick up some entertaining Chat in my Morning Rambles.

Even when, two years later, Piozzi was so much worse that she was able to leave him only an hour each morning, for exercise

---

[1] The Piozzis were in Bath from early in Jan. to May 13, 1802; from Dec. 6, 1802, to Apr. 25, 1803; from early Feb. to May 6, 1805; from Dec. 2, 1805, to May 6, 1806; and from Dec. 9, 1806, to Mar. 31, 1807. They were in London from the middle of May to July 20, 1802; from early Feb. to Apr. 30, 1804; from early Apr. to June 1, 1807. Except for a trip to Cheltenham and Tenby in the summer of 1802, the remainder of the time was spent in north Wales.
[2] To Queeney, May 26, 1806.   [3] Hayward, i. 355.

and to gather news, she did not have far to go for gossip, since, as she wrote to her daughter, she visited 'at no fewer than 15 Houses in my own Street'.[1] Other diversions, too, varied the monotony of this valetudinarian existence: lectures on chemistry by Dr. Archer, talks by famous explorers, or exhibitions of natural wonders. But it was the wide circle of friends at the watering-place which made life pleasant, for nearly everyone came to Bath at one time or another.

On the street one day, in the winter of 1799, she met Richard Graves of Claverton, the friend of Shenstone and author of the *Spiritual Quixote*. The old man, who at the time failed to recognize her, in an apologetic letter of February 1 promised to pay her a visit as soon as the hill was passable. At eighty-three Graves admitted that, like the hero of her poem, he had had more than his three warnings, but was still vigorous enough to answer Gifford's 'illiberal' attacks in a set of complimentary verses.[2] There were other links with the past. In 1802 Mrs. Piozzi rented a house next door to Hannah More, whose knocker and patience, she laughingly admitted, she was daily wearing out.[3] In 1805 she accidentally met Perkins in the pump room, into whose deaf ears she shouted questions about the death of Cator and affairs of the brewery. In 1807 she impulsively dropped in one day to see the ageing and broken Dr. Burney, who also was spending the winter at Bath. The old quarrel might well be forgotten, she felt, with illness and death staring both of them in the face. Later, Dr. Burney wrote an account to his daughter Fanny:

We shook hands very cordially, and avoided any allusion to our long separation and its cause; the *Caro Sposo* still lives, but is such an object from the gout that the account of his sufferings made me pity him sincerely; he wished, she told me, 'to see his old and worthy friend,' and, *un beau matin*, I could not refuse compliance with his wish. She nurses him with great affection and tenderness, never goes out or has company when he is in pain.[4]

---

[1] Feb. 10, 1807. See also letter to Miss Williams, Nov. 29, 1806. Mrs. Piozzi's letters to Miss Williams, the sister of Sir John Williams of Bodylwyddan, have been inherited by Sir Randle Mainwaring.

[2] Graves's letter and a copy of the verses in his hand are in my possession. See also Ry. 560, 75.   [3] To Queeney, Jan. 6, 1802.

[4] *D'Arblay Diary*, vi. 46. Another version is given in the *Memoirs of Dr. Burney* (1832), iii. 378–81. In each case the date of the letter is given as 1808, though in different months (June and Nov.). Nevertheless, Mrs. Piozzi must have met the doctor in Jan. 1807, for a number of reasons: she refers to him in a letter to Queeney of Feb. 10, 1807, while he wrote to her, commenting on their recent meeting, on Jan. 6, 1807 (Ry. 545, 13), and again on the 21st (*Adam Libr.* iii. 44). This is another instance of the untrustworthy chronology of the *D'Arblay Diary*.

For her part Mrs. Piozzi wrote to Queeney that the doctor was 'still amiable, still sprightly; still a *particularly* pleasing Companion'.[1]

The passing of old acquaintances touched her deeply. Once she wrote to Queeney, "tis a melancholy Thing—as Floretta found it in Dr. Johnson's Tale—to outlive Lovers & Haters, & Friends & Foes; & find ones' self surrounded by those with whom one has no Ideas in common'.[2] But, as in her youth, Mrs. Piozzi lost no time in vain regrets. She found making new friends more worth while, and followed Johnson's advice by keeping her friendships in constant repair.

One such new link came from a chance meeting in 1805 with a lively girl named Marianne Francis. At first merely attracted by the beauty and vivacity of the new acquaintance, Mrs. Piozzi was startled later to find that the young lady was the granddaughter of Dr. Burney and niece of Mme D'Arblay.[3] The gay, witty girl assiduously flattered her grandfather's former friend, and for the next decade carried on with her a frequent and intimate correspondence. Marianne, like her aunt, was fascinated by the mercurial, sharp-tongued Blue-Stocking: a woman equally at home in a salon, a sick room, or a library; as ready to give a medical prescription as to argue over the latest philosophical theory; to repeat the juiciest tit-bit of scandal, or prove the importance of the Book of Revelation. Mrs. Piozzi had always been a bundle of contradictions; now, as she grew older, the idiosyncrasies became more apparent. As Sophia Lee once cried out, 'Oh here comes Mrs. Piozzi like Nebuchadnezzar's Statue, with a Head of *Gold* & *Feet* of Clay.'[4] To the brilliant young Marianne, nevertheless, the older woman proved a constant source of delight, while Mrs. Piozzi herself must have been amused to find another Burney enrolled among her satellites.

---

[1] Mrs. Piozzi showed, however, that she had not forgiven her old friend, when writing in her New Common Place Book (p. 39) after his death in 1814,

Burney—dead at last I am told at 89 Years old; and in the full possession of his Faculties:—They were extremely fine ones. He *thought* himself my Friend once I believe, whilst he *thought* the World was so:—when the Stream turned against the *poor* Straw, he helped retard its Progress with his *Stick*: & made his Daughter do it with her *Fingers*——The Stream however grew too strong, and forced the little Straw forward in *Spite of them*—Oh then they cowr'd, & sneaked again, and would again have plaid the *Parasite*.

[2] Mar. 19, 1799. Graves had just informed her that Seward was dying. In her letters Mrs. Piozzi constantly referred to the passing of friends and acquaintances. In 1806 she wrote verses on the death of her former friend, the Dean of Derry, which she sent to the *St. James's Chronicle*. (Mainwaring Piozziana, iii. 91; and letter to Queeney, Apr. 17, 1806.)

[3] To Queeney, Jan. 30, 1806.   [4] Ibid., Jan. 6, 1802.

Occasionally Piozzi was well enough to undertake short visits to London. While these were made ostensibly for business reasons, they also served to keep Mrs. Piozzi in touch with her daughters and old friends living there; and they were no doubt a welcome change from the quiet life at Bath and Brynbella. In 1802, after a particularly gay two months, the economical Piozzi gleefully told his wife that they had 'dined from home no fewer than 30 times'.[1] In 1804 her daughters were more than usually cordial, and the family group was augmented by the presence of Cecilia's three sturdy boys. In 1807 only Sophia of her daughters was in the city, but was most attentive; indeed, Mrs. Piozzi wrote to Queeney that Sophia with her charitable disposition left them 'very little alone'.[2] During these short stays in London Mrs. Piozzi renewed her intimacy with many old favourites: 'Dear Mrs. Siddons', the Kembles, Parsons, Dr. Gray, the Misses Lee; she also met after many years Sophia Streatfeild and Richard Cumberland; to whom were added a young poet named Thomas Campbell, and Thomas Moore, 'a sort of English Improvisatore'.[3] One constant joy on every visit was the opportunity to see beautiful pictures. In 1807, after viewing Lord Stafford's exhibition of art with Sophia, Mrs. Piozzi commented to Queeney: 'Painting is a Luxury I can never enjoy but in a Metropolis & my Avidity for it makes her laugh now & then.'[4]

As we have seen before, even when at Brynbella she was not completely cut off from the outside world. A succession of visitors—Chappelow, the Lysons brothers, Dr. Whalley, William Clarges, to name only a few—found their way to Flintshire and were hospitably welcomed to the Vale of Clwyd. In 1805 came William Siddons, husband of the actress; an invalid himself, he and his host had become fast friends, with two bonds in common—illness and celebrated wives.[5] Sometimes travellers arrived at inconvenient times, as did the Countess of Cork and Orrery, who drove up for a fortnight's stay just when Piozzi was writhing in agony. With her husband's groans echoing in her ears, Mrs. Piozzi found it difficult to amuse

---

[1] *Letters to Pennington*, p. 245.

[2] See also letters to Miss Williams, Mar. 31, Apr. 3, 1807.

[3] Mrs. Piozzi met Sophia Streatfeild, Campbell, and Moore in 1802, and Cumberland in 1804 (*Letters to Pennington*, pp. 241, 243, 265; Ry. 554, 38).

[4] May 12, 1807. On June 18, 1806, Mrs. Piozzi had commented to Queeney, 'Pictures are to *me* much as Romantic Scenery to Abbe Nicholls, & my heart often feels a void Place which they were once accustom'd to fill up.'

[5] The letters from Wm. Siddons to the Piozzis (Ry. 574) show how intimate had been the relationship between the two families.

her guest. Referring also to Queeney, who was exploring the Hebrides at the same time, Mrs. Piozzi somewhat acidly commented to Mrs. Pennington: 'Ladies appear now to travel all Autumn upon a foraging plan of gleaning talk for their Spring parties.'[1] Usually, however, the chance wayfarers were greeted with open arms, as welcome purveyors of news themselves.

During the early eighteen-hundreds Mrs. Piozzi found little time or inclination to begin any new literary venture; yet she could never long resist the perennial urge to authorship. In 1803 conditions on the Continent set her at work again, and she wrote to Queeney on September 9 that she was

Translating & compressing Dumouriez's Sketch of Europe written seven Years ago—into a Miniature Picture. There will be no Name to it; & I will make it *so* small, People *shall* read it: Nothing ever was written so true or so Wise; but Wisdom & Truth like Gold & Silver must be alloy'd, & I have put a little Copper to Dumouriez that he may *run Current* among us. . . .

This time her enthusiasm was suddenly quenched, for she wrote again to her daughter on the 20th.

Mr. Chappelow called here & says Dumouriez's Tableau de L'Europe has been translated already; I live out of the World,— & resemble the Recluse who asked if *Jealousy* would not be a *new* & admirable Subject for Dramatic Composition? *you* should have stopt me from touching it.[2]

In 1804, when she was in London attending the grand ceremony performed in celebration of the memory of the Duc D'Enghien, Lumley St. George Skeffington besought her to write a prologue for his play, to be called 'Friends and Enemies'.[3] This she obligingly did, much gratified at the thought of appearing again in the public eye. Four years later, in May 1808, Skeffington wrote to her at Brynbella requesting an epilogue for his play, *The Mysterious Bride*. Still more flattered at his remembrance, Mrs. Piozzi again complied with alacrity, and sent a set of verses which were used on the first appearance of the drama on June 1. According to Skeffington's

---

[1] *Letters to Pennington*, p. 253 [1802].

[2] See also letter from Chappelow, Sept. 29, 1803 (Ry. 563, 79). Two drafts of Mrs. Piozzi's translation exist, the second being a revision (Ry. 640, 641).

[3] Discussed in notes to Queeney of Apr. 30, May 13, June 21, 1804. It appears that her daughter had been giving Mrs. Piozzi advice and acting as an intermediary in the matter of the prologue. The play was not produced this year, and whether Mrs. Piozzi's prologue was ever used is not certain.

partial report, the epilogue was loudly acclaimed and his play was received 'with unbounded applause'.[1]

These occasional minor effusions were not enough to keep her mind from stagnating; the authoress of *Retrospection* needed more substantial fare. Confined to the house at Brynbella for long autumn months, Mrs. Piozzi was consequently driven again to study. In the late summer of 1805 she confided to Queeney,

> No, No, my Dear Girl I am not going to say any thing clever, I am o' going to *do* something very Clever tho'—if I can accomplish it; I am at least *wishing* to read my Bible in Hebrew before I dye— 'Tis the only Study that would not be more ridiculous than estimable perhaps, at my Time of Life. Can you give me any Assistance?

With the vicar of Tremeirchion, John Roberts, as her tutor, Mrs. Piozzi struggled valiantly for several years with the intricacies of the Hebrew tongue. At the beginning she found the grammar exceedingly perplexing, and on September 12 amusingly commented:

> My Tutour—a profound Scholar, *does* lead me a Thorny Road *I know*; & terribly scratched & torn am I with the Brambles: making me form long Paradigms of irregular Verbs,—& in persing, give Acct: for every Letter radical & servile. . . . Farewell! I am surrounded by no fewer than five Hebrew Grammars . . .[2]

Still zealous to learn at sixty-four, still not afraid to begin the study of a complicated oriental language; she would be a true Blue-Stocking to the end.

This unquenchable thirst for information is Mrs. Piozzi's most characteristic trait. But she needed a common-sense Dr. Johnson ever at her side to override the vagaries of the moment. Without any such restraining influence she was led into a variety of silly speculations. Numerology became a fad, and she filled Thraliana and other Commonplace books with long disquisitions seeking to prove that Napoleon was the Beast in the Apocalypse. Other equally futile pursuits dissipated much

---

[1] Skeffington to Mrs. Piozzi, June 2, 1808 (Ry. 892). On May 10 he had written of the play, and on the 16th outlined the plot, at the same time asking her to write the epilogue (*Maggs Bros. cat.*, 605, 1935). On June 20 he sent her a copy of the epilogue as spoken by the actor, Russell, and asked her consent to print it as corrected. Later letters of Sept. 19 and 26 add further information about the play (Sotheby sale, Dec. 6, 1904). The epilogue may be found in Mainwaring Piozziana, iii. 109, &c.

[2] In the Rylands collection are miscellaneous notes on Hebrew grammar in her hand (Ry. 631). In her later journals she often used Hebrew characters and attempted many etymological conjectures.

of her energy. Her eager inquisitiveness seized on every weird story she heard of natural monstrosities or miracles, and these were copied at length into her journals. Fascinated by anything new or strange, she no longer had the critical judgement necessary to sift and evaluate evidence. In the later years Thraliana thus became a repository for fantastic stories and improbable suppositions, all of far less interest than her records of the *bons mots* of London wits or the latest dictum of Dr. Johnson.

From time to time during vacations Brynbella was enlivened by the presence of a noisy, growing boy. Little John Salusbury Piozzi, however, was still too strenuous for his uncle and aunt. In 1801 the latter found him 'blithe as a bird, almost as wild', and later she constantly referred to him as a 'pug'.[1] Unused to the obstreperous energy of an active boy, the elderly couple could endure his company for only short periods. Accordingly, Salusbury, as his aunt called him, remained until 1806 with Davies at Streatham, and then, when twelve years old, and ready for more scholarly tutoring, was placed under the Rev. Thomas Shephard at Enborne near Newbury.[2] Yet even if she found the boy's companionship too exhausting, Mrs. Piozzi did not lose interest in his future. 'Virtue Literature and Manners' were the three essentials she prescribed as imperative for a gentleman,[3] and she was determined he should have every advantage. When the boy grew old enough to understand, she wrote him long, delightful letters, full of Welsh gossip, puns, and literary jokes.[4]

With her own daughters Mrs. Piozzi kept up a casual intercourse. The bitter quarrel with Cecilia had been laid aside, if not forgotten, and Piozzi's diaries show Cecilia constantly in and out of the house. For one thing, Mostyn had become too sick to be an active enemy. His lazy apathy, which at first had appeared to be moral frailty, later turned out to be the result of physical weakness. In 1807 he died of tuberculosis, leaving Cecilia, at thirty, a widow with three strapping sons.[5]

---

[1] *Letters to Pennington*, p. 228.

[2] Apr. 18, 1806 (note at the back of Piozzi's 1806 diary).

[3] To Rev. T. Shephard, Jan. 23, 1807 (Johnson House, Gough Square, London).

[4] Nearly 500 letters from Mrs. Piozzi to John Salusbury Piozzi have survived (Ry. 585–90). She filled these letters too full of moral precepts to be very effective with a high-spirited boy; yet some are highly amusing.

[5] Mostyn's unkind treatment of Cecilia had been a common subject of conversation in the neighbourhood. See E. Œ. Somerville and M. Ross, *An Incorruptible Irishman* (1932), p. 170. Charles K. Bushe, writing to his wife on Sept. 28, 1805, of a visit to the recluse Ladies of Llangollen, added of Mostyn,

he uses his Wife abominably and it is well known that he is anxious (to use Lady E's phrase) to get her into a *scrape*, and lays traps and gives opportunities

In the same year in which Cecilia lost her husband came word of the engagements of two other Thrale daughters. On hearing that Sophia had accepted Henry Merrick Hoare, Mrs. Piozzi immediately wrote congratulations, and then to Queeney added her fervent hope: 'May her Husband never cease being her Lover! May that Passion which has not yielded to refusal ... Be Proof against Possession too—it is a harder Tryal.' Since Sophia loved 'the modern Artists', in October Mrs. Piozzi sent her as a wedding present a beautiful landscape painted by Gainsborough.[1]

Queeney, a few months later, finally achieved the ambition of her life and married a lord. She was now forty-four, and Admiral Lord Keith, the man of her choice, was sixty, a widower with a grown daughter. With characteristic common sense she selected an elderly man of wealth and position, of congenial habits and tastes. News of Queeney's engagement, although not unexpected, came as a shock to Mrs. Piozzi, and she wrote to Susan on November 9:

Your eldest Sister & I having passed *Twenty* Years closely united, & never three Days out of each other's Sight—Some Castles in the Air would now & then rise up in a Musing Hour,—as if we might *once more* meet in a like familiar Manner—Those Misty Fabricks now are quite dissolved—& She has fixed *her* Castle—*in the Rock*.[2]

Of all her children Queeney had been the most admired. From the days of the Children's Book Queeney was the one to whom she always turned for advice, the one whose good opinion was most desired, the one whose affection she had vainly tried so hard to secure. The prospect of her marriage was definitely exciting. Piozzi rummaged about through stacks of old manuscript music to make up a packet of songs as a nuptial gift, and in addition set about composing a Nautical March to celebrate the event.[3] Years before he had taught Queeney singing; now he wished her to possess some of his music, the one interest which they had in common. When Queeney finally became Lady Keith, it seemed to her mother that another door had been closed on the past.

and furnishes temptations in addition to the provocation of neglect and ill treatment, for the very purpose.
On Oct. 12 Bushe wrote from Cheltenham of having seen Cecilia whose 'beauty is fast going, almost gone—The change is great and I am sure the result of Care'.
    [1] To Queeney, Aug. 4 and Oct. 17, 1807. After sending Sophia the Gainsborough painting (now at Bowood), Mrs. Piozzi wrote a long poem, 'A Winter in Wales', to send to her daughters (Mainwaring Piozziana, iii. 104).
    [2] Lansdowne MS. The last remark is a pun on Lord Keith's name, Elphinstone. See also Hayward, i. 357.   [3] To Queeney, Nov. 22, Dec. 4, 1807.

During the summer of 1806, taking advantage of one of the rare intervals between attacks of gout, the Piozzis made a ten-day trip to the Welsh 'Highlands'. Mrs. Piozzi had long wished to show her birthplace to her second husband. Thirty-two years before, she and Johnson, with Thrale and Queeney, had travelled over the same roads. What pictures every town and mountain must have brought before her eyes! What memories every inn and country house revived! Yet even if Piozzi was more enthralled by the glorious prospects than the near-sighted Johnson, there is no mention that he bought any memento in Pwllheli 'in memory of his little Mistresses' Market Town'.[1]

This vacation trip provided a pleasant breathing spell, and they hoped to get to Bath before any relapse, but October brought a return of the old symptoms. Mrs. Piozzi wrote sadly to Queeney of their altered plans:

No Food will pass his Lips I dare say for at least Three days longer, & he shut them close last Wednesday, leaving me 18 Turkeys to devour before we set out.

When the invalid steadily grew worse, she was forced to send a hurried appeal to Dr. Thackeray from 'melancholy Brynbella',

Come to me Directly my dear Dr. Thackeray I am in great Distress; indeed I am. Cough, Spasms; everything come again to torment that poor hapless Husband of mine, who endured so much at Bath.

Watching the man she loved suffer torture on the rack tore away the affected veneer of the witty Blue-Stocking and revealed the real woman beneath. The glittering, unfeeling front which she showed to the world at large was only a protective coating; there was always hidden underneath the distraught wife and mother. If, then, the following pages seem to the reader a probing of harrowing details much better forgotten, it must be remembered that this is a side of Mrs. Piozzi's life which has been completely ignored by her biographers. The selfish, egotistical caricature so often accepted as a true representation of her character is no complete portrait. No one can read the long series of pathetic notes to Dr. Thackeray, enumerating the sufferings of the crippled Piozzi, and not be convinced of the essentially kindly nature of the writer herself. Nowhere does Mrs. Piozzi show more clearly than in the early years of the

---

[1] Compare Broadley, p. 203. Piozzi's diary for 1806 gives an accurate itinerary for this journey. See also Mainwaring Piozziana, iii. 96.

nineteenth century the contrasting shallowness and depths of her character.

At the end of November 1806 Mrs. Piozzi wrote to Miss Williams that 'poor Brynbella smells now like the Bath Pump room', and Bath itself proved no more hospitable, for there in January Piozzi actually thought himself dying; indeed he was so ill that, after his wife suggested calling a priest, he willingly received the sacrament from the rector of the neighbouring English church.[1] The recurring attacks finally rendered Piozzi a permanent invalid. On occasions he might still crawl about with the aid of his valet, but for the most part he was confined to his room. Never again would he be able to leave it for long. The summer and autumn of 1807 were consequently spent quietly in Wales, and then, fearing to attempt any journey on stormy roads, they reluctantly gave up all plans for a visit to Bath in the winter of 1808. To the sick man there seemed to be nothing to look forward to but pain. 'He can now', Mrs. Piozzi confided to Queeney on February 1, 1808, 'scarcely bear to hang his Legs down whilst the Men wheel him from Room to Room.' On the 25th, when writing that her husband had not risen from bed for nineteen days, she added,

I write from poor Mr. Piozzi's Dressing Room, with the Door open to his Bed;—near which no one but myself & his tender Attendant Dunscombe dare venture . . . A small TeaCup might be turned in the grand Abscess, & more will break—nay indeed more are breaking.

Nevertheless she continued: 'He is so kind & so patient & so much more concerned for us than for Himself, that it is Melancholy to see.'

Piozzi was not always so considerate; but his wife in all her letters and journals never complained of the care and nursing which kept her an exile from the society and the literary world that she loved. She never blamed him or murmured, no matter how disagreeable conditions might be. Yet hers was a dreary existence. As she wrote to Salusbury, 'if I did not love Reading what would become of me?'[2] Books and study alone could while away the tedious hours spent watching near the bedside of the dozing patient; they furnished the one sure retreat from anxiety and sorrow.

The entire year of 1808 was spent in Wales. In June, following a visit from Dr. Whalley, the Piozzis drove to Chester

[1] To Miss Williams, Jan. 27, 1807; Hayward, i, 355; Mainwaring Piozziana, iii. 102.   [2] Ry. 585, 4; Jan. 28, 1808.

for medical consultation, but when Piozzi was brought home screaming, they were forced to abandon plans for other journeys. For a man in his condition travelling was out of the question. During the summer Salusbury came for his vacation, and Sophia with her new husband stopped for a few days on a tour of Wales; but nothing served to rouse Mrs. Piozzi's jaded spirits. She had no time or inclination for entertaining visitors; nor could the usual round of local gossip do more than temporarily drag her thoughts from the suffering of her adored husband. Reading *Marmion*, or worrying over foreign affairs, alone seemed to rouse her old enthusiasm. She admitted to Dr. Thackeray in December, 'See how I can preach Courage in *public* Affairs! when to Your Knowledge & my own I have not a Grain to keep my Pulse in Motion, when anything ails Mr. Piozzi.'

The new year, 1809, brought little hope, with dreary weather outside and foreboding within. Even Salusbury's presence in the house for the Christmas holidays could not dispel the gloom. All she could do was continue with the never-ending regimen of draughts and medicines, and when conditions grew too bad, dispatch a pathetic note to Dr. Thackeray: 'We can go on no further without You; Come and comfort us.' On February 17 she confided to the doctor:

we are all alone now; for Mrs. Mostyn appeared no more after you were called on that dreadful Night—and Salusbury went back to Berkshire last Wednesday—so our Life is a dull one enough—I watch for Primroses with desiring Eyes, & listen for a Thrush to tell me Spring is at hand & that these Stormy Winds will be hushed *some Time*.

The whole world seemed to Mrs. Piozzi to be approaching rack and ruin, 'Scenes of Wickedness & Folly' meeting her eyes everywhere, prices rising, quality decreasing. Yet her wails always ended with an amusing personal touch; even public affairs became subjective when viewed through her eyes. 'I never thought', she wrote to Queeney on February 19, 'to see the *Necessaries of Life*—such are to *me* Pens printed Books & Paper; become so costly, & so unsupportably bad beside all.'[1]

---

[1] In her New Common Place Book, p. 31, Mrs. Piozzi wrote 'Books are grown terribly dear of late, and more than ever necessary to my well-being . . . When I was half wild with Distress of Mind, Low Spirits, & Perplexity this last Feb. & March 1809—no Books would take off my Attention from present Misery, but an old French Translation of Quintus Curtius—and Josephus's History of the Siege of Jerusalem. Romances & Novels did *nothing* for me: I tried them all in vain.'

Piozzi's condition had steadily grown so much worse that he could be kept free from pain only by the constant use of narcotics, one opiate after another rendering him partially insensible to all about him. Late in February he relapsed into what his doctors, for want of a better name, called a fit of 'red raging Gout', but by March 1 he appeared better, and his wife found time to write to Queeney:

We have often read that no Artificial Torture equals natural Pain, & I am sure it *is* so.—When Mr. Piozzi suffer'd from a Carious Finger two Months ago; & the 5 Cavities flung up excrescent Flesh, which was burned off daily in 5 Places by the Lunar Caustic;—his Jaw was locked by the Anguish:—& when set free, he lamented his Case with Cries—but kept his Wits sound.—The *natural* Gout brought on immediate Delirium and he was insensible to any but imaginary Afflictions. Thank God 'tis all over now; at least for some time.

She was too optimistic, for on March 5 another hurried appeal had to be sent to Dr. Thackeray.

This fine Fit of red hot Gout which Mr. Moore bade me hope so much from—seems to me likely to finish in a never-ending Delirium. My poor Husband lives here in a World of his own Creating, and talks *to* the Company & *of* the Company till he makes me almost wild.—& when I went down Stairs at Two o'clock this Morning Dunscombe protested *he* had felt a Shock of an Earthquake; whilst his poor Master no longer requiring Wine or Water or anything else—kept him constantly employed in brushing away Flies & driving Birds (which never existed) from his Bed. Come & see us before we have *all lost* our Wits.

On the 18th she sent word to Salusbury that the delirium was gone, but the patient's back so covered with deep ulcers that it was a pitiful sight. No wonder the torture made him frantic. Everyone suspected that the end was near; yet on the 21st he was so much better that Mrs. Piozzi tore up a letter to Salusbury summoning him. The next day, however, a message was dispatched, and on the 23rd she wrote in her diary: 'Sleeps perpetually—Life ebbing out.'[1] During the last days he knew nobody, but continued to suffer intolerable anguish when his wounds were dressed. Though the doctors prayed for his release, he lingered on until 'the slow-spreading Gangrene reached his Spinal Marrow'. On the morning of March 26 with a trembling hand his wife dashed off a note to Lady Williams at Bodylwyddan: 'We hope his Sufferings begin to

[1] 1809 Daily Diary (in the possession of Mrs. Herbert Evans, Brynbella).

remit now: Nature is nearly exhausted.' At the bottom is scrawled in another hand, 'Mr. Piozzi expired at 2 o'clock'.[1]

Though long expected, the shock left Mrs. Piozzi in a state of complete collapse, so that not until the 30th could she enter the dread tidings in Thraliana: 'all is over; & my Second Husbands Death is the last Thing recorded in my first husband's Present. Cruel Death!' After the years of outcries and confusion, the sudden silence in the house was appalling.

On Monday, April 3, Piozzi was buried in the vault at Tremeirchion Church.[2] The next day she wrote to Queeney:

My dearest Girl

has written very kindly—so have you *all*; *all* very good and very amiable; and I have less *Right* & *Claim* to my little Hoard of Sorrow than I *wish* for in my present State of Mind—but to part as I did yesterday *for ever* from the Man who has engross'd my heart for so long a Course of Years, must cost a cruel Pang—*You know* it must.

Salusbury and Charles Shephard, son of his tutor and a Counsellor of Lincoln's Inn, remained in the house doing all in their power to divert her morbid thoughts, but the short entries in her daily diary show her despondent mood. 'Every day dismal', 'Blank Sorrow'. On the 8th she confessed to Dr. Thackeray:

My Head seems quite *stunned*, & Sleep like my Pulse runs away from me quite frighted. I must leave this Place awhile & go to London to my Daughters for 3 or 4 Weeks. . . . The girls have asked me to *their* Houses, but I cannot bear either Society or Solitude *just now*: and at a Hotel I can shut them both out by turns; & rest my half crazed head . . .

One of Piozzi's last desires had been that Queeney should have his little travelling pianoforte which he had taken under the carriage seat all over Europe. Arranging for its transporta-

---

[1] Mainwaring MS. Dr. Ernest Sadler has kindly diagnosed Piozzi's symptoms, summarized as follows: First he had typical attacks of acute gout in the feet and hands, in addition to a more chronic deposit of chalk-stones (uric acid) in the smaller joints of the hands, &c. The next stage was the addition of internal gouty troubles—bronchitis, fibroid disease of the heart, and disease of the blood-vessels, giving rise to orthopnoea with a tremendous cough and low pulse. Next came abscesses of the feet due (1) to inflammation of the veins (phlebitis) which broke down into ulcers; and (2) to inflammation and thickening of the abscesses gradually stopping the circulation. The latter condition led to the final stage of gangrene. Piozzi's delirium, Dr. Sadler infers, was more the result of the constant drugging with opiates than of pain. 'A death certificate would probably have given the cause of death as gangrene, secondary to gouty arteriosclerosis.'

[2] The date is ascertained from her letter to Dr. Thackeray of Apr. 8, 1809, describing the funeral and enclosing a paragraph for the newspapers.

tion took up some of her time;[1] but when Salusbury and Shep-hard drove away on the 11th she was left disconsolate, and in her diary she made the entry: 'All alone—arranged my Spars and specimens; & antique Curiosities.' Anything to keep her mind from dwelling on the past or the future!

'All alone' the cry continued; the one human being she had loved with her whole heart was gone. For him she had sacri-ficed family, social position, personal comfort; year after year she had nursed him tenderly without complaint; now in the end all she would remember was their love, 'which made twenty years passed in Piozzi's enchanting society seem like a happy dream of twenty hours'.[2]

[1] To Queeney and Dr. Thackeray, Apr. 10, 13, 1809.
[2] Hayward, ii. 43–4.

XX

BATH-BLUE

1809–1821

THE death of her second husband left Mrs. Piozzi overcome with grief. For years every move, every decision had depended upon his state of health; now she suddenly found herself alone, with nothing to worry about except herself. It was a difficult transition. And yet, as it proved, she still had twelve more years—twelve reasonably happy years—ahead. But in spite of everything which was to come, her devotion to the memory of the gentle musician never wavered, and for her remaining years she always wore black, though varying it in summer by the addition of a white hat.[1]

On April 18, 1809, she left Brynbella, rendered gloomy by sad associations, and journeyed by easy stages from Chester to London. On the 21st she noted in her diary, 'Got safe to Lichfield—ask'd for old Acquaintance—all dead!!'[2] She did see the daughter of Johnson's old servant, Francis Barber, and for a guinea bought back a pocket-book which many years before she had given to Johnson; but inquiries for her silver tea kettle, portrait, and the chair which Mrs. Salusbury had presented to the great man in 1772 proved fruitless. By the 23rd she had arrived at the Crown Inn, Dunstable, in which she had been ill with measles fifty-seven years before, and which she had not seen since;[3] the next day she was settled in a dirty hotel in Duke Street, Manchester Square, London.

Mrs. Piozzi was not long left to herself, for her daughters, Mrs. Siddons, and a host of others immediately called, and as she wrote to Salusbury on the 26th, she received 'Kind Letters

[1] Hayward, ii. 375.
[2] Of Mrs. Piozzi's daily diaries kept after Piozzi's death, those of 1815, 1816, 1820 are in my possession; those of 1809, 1811, 1812 in the possession of Mrs. Herbert Evans, Brynbella; and those of 1810, 1817, 1818, 1819, 1821 in the John Rylands Library (Ry. 616). Other smaller note-books for these years also exist (Ry. 616).
[3] The attack of measles had occurred in Dec. 1752. See letters from Sir Thomas Salusbury of Dec. 21, 24, 26, 1752 (Ry. 530, 23, 24, 25).

from Absent Friends all the Day long, & Visits innumerable'.[1] The same day she scribbled a note to Dr. Thackeray telling how ill she had been on the way, adding, 'I shall present my *Hand & Pulse* to my old Friend Sir Lucas Pepys, who saved my Life 30 years ago.'[2] Her daughters and their husbands were with her almost every day, so that she had no reason to complain of their cold hearts this time. But she was still too exhausted nervously to enjoy much society. As she wrote to Lady Williams at Bodylwyddan on May 1, the first time she went to church 'the loud Organ pealing in my Ears, who have not heard a Musical Note, or seen 25 People together for 25 months; affected me too strongly: and I was very near fainting away'.

Fortunately, the kind ministrations of Dr. Pepys were so successful in calming her nerves that throughout May she was able to attend to business affairs. Piozzi's will was proved, one of her own duly signed and witnessed, and arrangements made for settling the estate. Piozzi had left everything to his wife, with the exception of £4,000 to be divided among his Italian relatives.[3] His own savings, gathered together before his marriage to the English heiress, he rightly thought should go back to his own family. Mrs. Piozzi heartily agreed, and despite the fact that the depressed value of the stocks made it necessary to sell securities costing approximately £6,000 to settle these claims at once, she would consider no delay.[4] Her one obsession now was to arrange for the future of Salusbury, whom she intended to make her heir. He must be naturalized, his name legally changed to John Salusbury Piozzi Salusbury, and then confirmed in the English Church.[5] Some day, she was sure, he would be a son of whom she might well be proud.

[1] Ry. 585, 22. Dr. Whalley's kind letter of condolence, Apr. 6, 1809, is held by Myers & Co., London. Mrs. Pennington, who had quarrelled years before with Mrs. Piozzi, wrote to Whalley on May 31, 1809: 'But I think I was still more sensibly affected by the death of Mr. Piozzi, which has cost me many tears. I can only now remember his matchless talents, his kind hospitality, and the many, many pleasant and happy days I have passed under his roof' (*Whalley Corr.* ii. 332). Many old friends called whom she had not seen for years, among whom were Sir William Weller Pepys, Sir Lucas Pepys, Samuel Rogers (who told her Cumberland would call), Sir John Lade, Lady Rothes, &c. Her more recent friends were equally solicitous; among the principal ones constantly appearing in her diary are her four daughters, with Merrick Hoare and Lord Keith, Charles Shephard, Mrs. Siddons, the Lysons brothers, Dr. Robert Gray, Chappelow, Marianne Francis, Mrs. Barrett and Miss Burney, Miss Gilpin, Mrs. Holman, Lumley Skeffington, Mrs. Broadhead, Lady Bradford, Dr. Myddelton, Jackson, &c. (1809 Diary).

[2] Ashforth collection. Mrs. Piozzi described her trouble as 'Languor, Tremor, Diarrhoea, every Torment bad Nerves could bestow'.

[3] Ry. Ch. 1249–56; Ry. 585, 35.   [4] Ibid.

[5] See letters from Lord Deerhurst (Ry. 554, 56, 57) and to Salusbury (Ry. 585, 24–6). Salusbury was to be made to conform in every way to the genteel English pattern.

After arranging these business details, Mrs. Piozzi returned to Brynbella the middle of June, joined on the way by Salusbury, who planned to remain with her in Wales for the summer. While in London she had begun to read the recently published early letters of her old friend Mrs. Montagu. Petty jealousy had no part in Mrs. Piozzi's nature, and she raved to Queeney about their sparkling superiority. From Brynbella on June 28 she wrote:

> Farewell; and dont *go about* as the Children say to compare my Letters with Mrs. Montagu's, because there is no Comparison—but mind & make me acquainted with Walter Scott and Joanna Baillie when I come next to London.

With her buoyant zest for life Mrs. Piozzi could never long be downcast. In the old days, after the death of a favourite child, she had forced herself as quickly as possible into gay society; now she again began to grope instinctively for new contacts with life. It was not that she was callous, or incapable of real feeling, but merely that she felt useless grieving a weakness. No one could ever say that she had not loved Piozzi devotedly; but now that he was gone she saw no reason to mope in futile misery. There were always new friends to be made, new places to be seen, and new stories to be heard. So, instead of writing about the dead, Mrs. Piozzi asked her daughter for an introduction to Walter Scott and Joanna Baillie.

During the summer and autumn of 1809 she remained quietly at Brynbella, busying herself with a proposal to beautify the estate by enclosing part of 'the Bryn' behind the house. As she admitted to Queeney, 'one *must* have something in Prospect, or the Ties to Life would relax too fast'. Queeney was expecting a child, and at her age it was a source of worry to all the family. Mrs. Piozzi was greatly excited, and wrote to Salusbury on September 9:

> She *may* find her Life endanger'd; & she *may* (possibly) feel her Tenderness rekindled towards a Mother who so long adored her: & she *may* request my Presence at her Delivery.[1]

No such possibility had entered her daughter's head, however, and the baby was born in December without the benefit of her grandmother's presence. Nothing would ever change Queeney's feelings towards her mother.[2]

---

[1] Ry. 585, 32.

[2] *Queeney Letters*, p. xxiii. Queeney wrote to Mme D'Arblay in 1813 after a talk with Cecilia:

We have often agreed that her and I have been the great sufferers from

With no invalid now to consider, Mrs. Piozzi was able to go back to her old plan of spending the summers in Wales, and the winters at Bath and London. Her life at Brynbella was simple: hours of absorbing study and composition in the writing-room, interspersed with visits in the neighbourhood for informal chat and gossip. Books remained the one sure source of pleasure, and in 1814 she wrote to young John Williams, who was then at Cambridge: 'I am glad you are a Reading Man, Dear Sir, it is the best Thing after all. . . . What would have become of me These last years at Brynbella had I not loved Reading?'[1] Hospitable neighbours welcomed her to their houses. Once after a week's visit to Bodylwyddan she described how the days had been spent: 'Readings in the Morning for those who did not go out with Dog and Gun. Music every Evening.'[2] Occasionally one of her old circle from London would come for a stay at Brynbella, as did Chappelow in September 1811, bringing with him a long manuscript poem called 'The Sentimental Naturalist', which Mrs. Piozzi carefully read and criticized. She even added copious notes and a preface, but in the end failed to persuade him to publish the work.[3]

Sometimes, to be sure, she found time hanging heavy on her hands, but there was always one answer to such a situation— a new subject for her active pen. In 1810 she decided to write an account of all her poetical compositions for her adopted heir. On October 15 she began the task with a Preface addressed to Salusbury, in which, after apologizing for copying out all the worthless trifles of her youth, she insisted that at seventy it was surely better than vicious pleasures.[4] For the next few years,

---

having been so much more exposed to injuries from a quarter where it was least to be expected in the common course of nature. *She* is convinced that it was from original and persevering dislike, and real hatred of us all from her hatred of our father.

Queeney's attitude had not even allowed her to give her mother credit for unselfish attention to the ailing Piozzi. On Mar. 23, 1799, Mme D'Arblay wrote to Queeney,

Mr. P. was terribly gouty, & she shewed him unremitting attention in the short time Charles saw her,—but, by what you say, I should imagine this was only to *look pretty* to strangers.

(Lansdowne MS.)

[1] Mainwaring MS., Mar. 13, 1814.   [2] To Miss Williams, Jan. 21, 1814.

[3] The original manuscript of the poem, with Mrs. Piozzi's notes and corrections, is now in the Cambridge University Library. The shy clergyman could never bring himself to brave the reviewers. On Nov. 1, 1811, he had intimated to Mrs. Piozzi that he would publish privately, but nothing came of his plans (Ry. 563, 95).

[4] The work finally filled five 4to volumes, of approximately 570 pages. On the title-page appears: 'Poems on Several Occasions.' Following this is: 'Poems &c Little Characters—Anecdotes &c Introductory to The Poems.' Throughout the present biography I have arbitrarily referred to the work as Mainwaring Piozziana,

whenever at Brynbella, she persistently kept at the work, and from occasional references it seems evident that she hoped the account might be published after her death. Undoubtedly she felt Thraliana contained too many sensational passages which might some day have to be destroyed; instead there should be a less controversial history of her literary life designed not to offend a squeamish reader or to betray secrets best forgotten. Accordingly, she filled five red-bound volumes with her juvenile and mature poetical efforts, interspersed with long autobiographical explanations. It is a garrulous, rambling account, but more chronological than Thraliana. If Salusbury was pleased with this laboured production, at least he never thought fit to have the volumes published; indeed it was not until recently that even their existence was known. Mrs. Piozzi's longing for remembrance as a poet was never to be gratified.[1]

In Wales there were few interruptions to the peaceful current of her life. Once, late in January 1812, following a pleasant Christmas spent at Segroid with Cecilia and her boys, Mrs. Piozzi epitomized her existence in a note to Lady Williams. 'My 71st. Birth Day was like my *Life*,' she wrote, 'Stormy & rainy Morning and Afternoon; but clearing up fine *late in the Evening*;—& the *Night* very tranquil & brilliant.' Despite her optimism there were still squalls ahead.

During the winters and late springs Bath continued to prove satisfying and London a tonic.[2] Here she could see Queeney's baby, whom she found 'very pretty indeed like the Mother exactly', and at the same time enjoy some parties.[3] On May 16,

since the volumes are now in the possession of Sir Randle Mainwaring. See also *Whalley Corr.* ii. 343, and letter to Chappelow, Mar. 16, 1811 (Ry. 561, 144).

[1] In addition to copying all her poems into Thraliana and the Mainwaring Piozziana, she filled at least three other volumes with the same effusions (in the Rylands collection and in the possession of Dr. A. S. W. Rosenbach). Yet in spite of all this recopying, few have been published.

[2] Mrs. Piozzi was in Bath from Dec. 1, 1809, to Apr. 9, 1810; from Feb. 3 to June 1, 1812; from mid-May to June 6, 1813; for two weeks in the late summer of 1814; from early in Nov. 1814, to July 23, 1815; from Aug. 8, 1815, to Mar. 27, 1816; from Apr. 8 to Aug. 4, 1816; from Sept. 13, 1816, to Aug. 17, 1817; from Sept. 2, 1817, to July 10, 1818; from Sept. 15, 1818, to July 7, 1819; and from Oct. 24, 1819, to June 10, 1820. She was in London from Apr. 24 to June 10, 1809; from Apr. 12 to May 28, 1810; from Apr. 5 to May 1, 1811; from Apr. 13 to May 11, 1813; from May 27 to late Aug. 1814 (Streatham); from July 24 to Aug. 7, 1815; from Mar. 28 to Apr. 7, 1816; from Aug. 20–31, 1817; and from Sept. 4–12, 1818. From Feb. 3 to Apr. 1, 1811, she was at Cheltenham. She visited Mendip Lodge, Somersetshire, in June 1813; and Condover Park near Shrewsbury from late Sept. to early Nov. 1814.

[3] 1810 Diary. In the spring of 1810 Mrs. Piozzi saw much in London of the Whalleys, Mrs. Siddons, Lord Erskine, Marianne Francis, and her four daughters. Jackson painted her picture in May. Visits in other years were much the same.

1810, a little over a year after Piozzi's death, she noted in her diary, 'a good Frolic, a fine Day, a bad Dinner, but good Companions'. The Blue-Stocking was herself again.

She was always forced in London to give up a large part of her time to business conferences, for her affairs were still involved. In 1811 Streatham Park was again the problem. Her tenant there had gone bankrupt, and she had to decide what was to be done with the place. Thrale in his will had left his wife a life interest in the house and complete possession of the contents; but Dr. Whalley now suggested that perhaps her daughters would purchase this right, and thus relieve her of the worry and expense of an estate which she never used. The daughters, however, disdained the proposal. Seeing no reason to purchase what would probably be theirs in a few years anyway, as Mrs. Piozzi wrote to Dr. Whalley, they were 'very bitter' about the matter.[1]

The problem was not easily solved. The next spring, on May 30, she wrote to Dr. Thackeray from Bath:

My Nerves have had a new Shock in the Anger of my beautiful Daughters for a Fault committed (if a Fault) most unintentionally on my Part. but having heard that they threw out Menaces of making my Successor amenable for Dilapidations at Streatham Park —I resolved to repair, & partly resolved to inhabit it when repaired, instead of paying House Rent every Spring—while that Place was tumbling down. By all means said my wise Counsellor Mr. Charles Shephard, By all means said my wise Steward Leak; & both agreed there was plenty of Timber on the Premisses, which really wanted cutting. So I sent Mead—my old Surveyor who you know built Brynbella, & bid him set to Work, & I called Charles Shephard— *Ranger* but the Ladies were enraged, said *their Property* was ruining by my Agents; & the Letters were dreadful; and I am at my Wits end; while the Men complain that my Daughters *insult them*; and *they* storm at the Men for injuring their Place.[2]

[1] *Whalley Corr.* ii. 343. In 1807 Streatham had been let to Abram Atkins, who agreed to pay £500 a year, without deduction for taxes (to Miss Williams, May 28, 1807; original in the Victoria and Albert Museum, London). A lawsuit with Giles, her former tenant, was finally settled in 1808, when he paid what was demanded (Ry. 585, 9).

[2] See also ibid. ii. 353. The other side is shown in the correspondence of Lord and Lady Keith. On May 13, 1812, Lord Keith wrote to his wife to stop proceedings if she could. On the 15th he wrote again:

I do not believe your Mother has any Right to cut Trees at that Rate . . . Mr. Shephard is a Vagabound and finds it his interest to Inflame a Mind too apt to be so against her Children and she by a Momentary approbation from a flattering cur is soothed from the Reflection of her improper Conduct, which I daresay Ranckles her now and then, if Vanity would permit her to Confess it—The Act is the Most uncivil I ever heard of . . .

It was her daughters' contention that Mrs. Piozzi should keep up the property out of her other income, while she, who had no use of the house herself, felt that it should be made to pay for itself. The net result was that bickering over Streatham provoked another quarrel with Queeney, and there was a break in their correspondence for over a year. One thing was imperative: the property must be repaired. A long succession of careless tenants had ruined the furniture and allowed the house and grounds to lapse into a distressing condition. Thus Mrs. Piozzi, who was legally responsible for the upkeep, was forced to begin an expensive restoration, little suspecting at the beginning how costly it would be.

In this instance her willingness to give way brought about another temporary truce with Queeney, although the latter's lawyers continued to find errors in Thrale's settlements.[1] During the spring of 1813 Mrs. Piozzi was accompanied to Streatham several times by her daughters, to see the improvements under way.[2] When the work was all completed, in the spring of 1814, at a total cost of £6,500, she had 'new fronted the house, new fenced the whole of the 100 acres completely

Three days later he insisted that the affair was premeditated
> to excite an opposition on your parts . . . and thereby furnish pretexts for her Complaints of unfeeling undutiful and the like. As to right I am satisfied, she has none to sell an inch.

On May 20th came the final reference,
> I am sorry for the times at Streatham and for all you have suffered first and last. you have a heart capable—it were well others had the like, even at the expense of some Learning.

(Lansdowne MSS.)

[1] See letters to Salusbury of Apr. 14, 17, 19, 20, 21, 23, 24, 26, 28, 29, 30, and May 1, 3, 4, 5, 6, 7, 8, 9, 11, 1813 (Ry. 587, 158–80). The trouble seems to have been with the 1775 settlement. The daughter's lawyers maintained that in some way the document had been fraudulently changed. On the 17th Mrs. Piozzi wrote to Salusbury:
> Doctor Johnson I see could not escape lending *his* Name to a Business he never could have investigated; it is written on an *Erasure* in the Parchment, no fewer than four Times: of which he was wholly unconscious, & signed the Deed as directed by Robson & Norris—Tho' himself a Doctor of Laws, and very Learned in Jurisprudence.

However, since it was discovered that no fine had been levied, the deed was a '*Nullity*', and since, in any case, the property legally belonged to Mrs. Piozzi, she had discretionary power over it. The daughter's lawyers, nevertheless, felt that Thrale should have secured the inheritance for his own children. On Apr. 19 Mrs. Piozzi quoted Robinson as saying:
> 'I only say that Robson & Norris deserved a Horse Whipping—& I wish I had the giving it Them. They have Jockied these charming Ladies out of their Estate'—Out of *mine* You mean Sir, I suppose was the pointed Reply of your H. L. P.

[2] *Queeney Letters*, p. 261. This spring she let the Reynolds portraits of Johnson, Burney, Baretti, and Goldsmith be shown in Lord Stafford's exhibition, but refused all requests to have them copied (to Queeney, May 15, 1813, &c.).

round; repaired stables, out-buildings, barns which I had no use for; and hothouses which are a scourge to my purse, a millstone round my neck'.[1] For the inside a splendid set of furniture was purchased from Gillow. Thrale's legacy proved an expensive burden.

All through the years it had been Mrs. Piozzi's custom to lavish affection upon someone, and for a time following her husband's death Salusbury assumed first place in her thought. All her plans, all her hopes for the future were vested in him. On February 27, 1810, she wrote to him,

> I am no *Egotist* you Know—rather a *Dualist*, according to Greek Grammar; thinking always of *You & me*. . . . Ah Salusbury! how Love of Thee does recall me to scenes of Business & of Life! when I have scarce Strength or Skill left to sit at the *helm* & watch the Changes of the Wind.[2]

Uppermost in her mind was the problem of his education. In 1810 she stopped at Oxford on her way back to Brynbella, to use all her influence that Salusbury might be accepted by one of the better colleges. Determined that he should be a gentleman and a scholar, she left no stone unturned to accomplish her purpose. The little, dark, Italian refugee would need every help to gain acceptance in snobbish England; yet if only she could get the right people on her side the battle would be won. So she arranged for him to call on the Ladies of Llangollen on one of his vacation trips to Wales, and solicitously introduced him to all her titled acquaintances. She was continually scheming to get her London friends to stop and see the boy at his school, using as her pretext the plaint that she wanted first-hand reports of his health. Having no illusions about the difficulties in her path, she still refused to be daunted.

After spending the year 1810 in being tutored in Greek and making other preparations for university life, Salusbury was finally accepted the next year by Christ Church as a 'Gentleman Commoner'. Lady Kirkwall presented him with a set of china for his rooms, and Mrs. Piozzi lavishly provided for every whim.[3] Her pride was at its highest when she stopped at Oxford in May 1811, and saw him 'happy in a Square Cap'. Nevertheless, there were constant warnings in her letters that he must step warily, for all her enemies would be quick to pounce on any mistake.

---

[1] To Dr. Gray, Nov. 27, 1814 (Hayward, ii. 269).   [2] Ry. 585, 49.
[3] To Miss Williams, May 25, 1811. Mrs. Piozzi gave Salusbury an allowance of £125 every quarter while in college (Ry. 586, 102).

There seemed to be an ironic fatality which thwarted all of Mrs. Piozzi's ambitious schemes for her children. She had no sense of fitness, no innate ability to judge the capabilities of those around her. She had attempted to make intellectual prodigies out of the daughters of a stolid Southwark business man; she had struggled in vain to force sentiment from the naturally prosaic Queeney; she had alienated Cecilia, the only one of her daughters having a temperament similar to her own, by attempting to meddle in her domestic affairs; now she tried to make an English scholar out of a lazy, indifferent, Italian *émigré*. To anyone else her failure would have been evident from the beginning; even she was finally convinced when a year later Salusbury earnestly begged to be allowed to leave Oxford. All along he had felt himself unsuited for the scholastic life. Only his aunt's insistence had pushed him on. In May 1812 he begged to be allowed to try some other career. At first the Army was suggested, but his heart was fixed on settling down in Wales as a country squire. It was a bitter disappointment to Mrs. Piozzi, but in spite of a determination to make him 'a gentleman, a Christian, and a scholar', she resignedly admitted in a later letter to Dr. Gray, 'when one has succeeded in the first two wishes, there is no need to fret if the third does fail a *little*'.[1]

One of the reasons why Salusbury had been so anxious to leave the University was that he had fallen in love with Harriet Pemberton, the sister of an old school friend from Condover Park near Shrewsbury. Such an appeal to Mrs. Piozzi's romantic heart was irresistible, and she decided to give Brynbella and all her Welsh property to her future heir at once, to make possible an early marriage. She herself would alternate between newly beautified Streatham and Bath. Waiting for Salusbury to come of age, arranging the legal details of the gift, all this delayed the happy event; but finally on November 7, 1814, the couple were married and went immediately to Brynbella, their future home.[2] At last one of the fondest dreams of her life had come true: a Salusbury, though an adopted one, to be sure, again was master of old Bach-y-Graig.

Mrs. Piozzi was again the victim of her impulsive generosity. Rendered poor by the lavish expenditure at Streatham, she

---

[1] Hayward, i. 349. See also Ry. 586, 146, and letter to Miss Williams, Aug. 26, 812.

[2] All the legal difficulties, all the annoying complications, were described in letters to Miss Williams (Mainwaring MS.).

JOHN SALUSBURY PIOZZI SALUSBURY

Painted by JACKSON

Now in the Hyde Collection

could ill afford the loss of all income from the Welsh properties.
A few months spent at Streatham during the summer of 1814,
with Mrs. Siddons and other old friends as guests, had convinced her that living there was far beyond her limited means;
and after repeated efforts to get the Hoares to take the place,
she finally agreed to let it to Count Lieven, the Russian Ambassador.[1] In consequence, after Salusbury's wedding Mrs. Piozzi
retired to Bath, where she hoped to find a peaceful haven for
her last years. Hard pressed for money, she was able to afford
only dingy lodgings at 17 New King Street, instead of the usual
fine house in Pulteney Street.

The choice of Bath for her last permanent home is not difficult to understand. Even as a child Mrs. Piozzi had occasionally visited her aunts there, and she vaguely remembered
having been carried in the arms of Beau Nash. Throughout
the ensuing years she had found the watering-place just to her
taste. The informal visiting and unending gossip suited her
garrulous nature; just as the constant flow of visitors to the
watering-place provided a never-failing source of entertainment. Here people had time to linger in the pump room and
chat to their heart's content; here a lively old lady of seventy-
four was sure to find congenial company. It was an ideal
residence for one with her positive genius for making friends;
and she soon gathered around her a new circle of admirers.

In every period of her life Mrs. Piozzi had one intimate friend
whom she placed on a pedestal, and to whom she confided all
her perplexities. She was not long in finding at Bath a person
to take the place of Collier, Dr. Johnson, and Mrs. Siddons.
On January 1, 1815, she noted in her daily diary, 'I dined at
Lutwyche's, met an agreeable Sir James Fellowes'.[2] Fellowes
had been a naval surgeon, had travelled widely, had published
a number of professional monographs, and was something of a
linguist and a raconteur. Although much younger, he was
immediately attracted to the witty and versatile Mrs. Piozzi,
so much so that for the rest of the winter the two saw each
other nearly every day. Later, when separated, they carried
on a spirited correspondence filled with scholarly arguments
and personal discussions. It was to Sir James that she now
turned on every occasion for consolation or advice.

[1] Ry. 588, 240.
[2] Entries throughout the winter show how often he called to see her. See also
Broadley, pp. 253–77. Mrs. Piozzi's letters to Fellowes are printed in Hayward,
vol. ii.

Fellowes became so charmed by her anecdotes of the past that he began to play Boswell to her Johnson. Delighted at such deference, Mrs. Piozzi answered all his questions, profusely annotated copies of all her works for his shelves, presented him with some letters from Dr. Johnson, and in December 1815 wrote out for his sole use a detailed autobiographical sketch. This last, which Sir James carefully preserved, has until recently been the chief source of information about her early life.[1] Doubtless most of the facts were derived from Thraliana, but since in this instance there was no pretence of chronological arrangement, they must always be used with caution.

She also showed Fellowes a manuscript upon which she had been labouring for some time. Like Dr. Johnson, whom she remembered reproving a lady of quality for having christened her daughter Augusta, since the girl would certainly never be majestic,[2] Mrs. Piozzi had always felt that names were often bestowed upon children without any proper regard for their suitability. Yet the only book she knew devoted entirely to the etymology of names was that of Lyford, published in the seventeenth century.[3] It struck her that there was a need for a new reference work on this subject, and some time after Piozzi's death she had begun to gather the necessary information. A first draft was far enough along in the summer of 1814 to be shown to one publisher at least; but when he considered it a doubtful risk, she began a complete revision, hoping to make it more attractive.[4]

The title which she chose for the work was highly characteristic: 'Lyford Redivivus or A Grandame's Garrulity'. Signing herself merely 'An Old Woman', she insisted in an apologetic preface that at least the volume would 'be read "once" by every one who has a Name,—if it be but to look for his own'. Then followed some 900 familiar and unfamiliar names, with conjectural derivations and stories of their use. If Mrs. Piozzi had contented herself, as she had largely done in *British Syno-*

[1] It was printed by Hayward (ii. 6–30). The manuscript is now in the possession of Mrs. D. F. Hyde. On Nov. 5, 1815, she sent Sir James a copy of *British Synonymy*, her favourite work, and about this time he took down at her dictation the story of Johnson's composition of the *Fountains*. See p. 63, n. 2. Her letters to Fellowes are full of recollections that show how eagerly he was pumping her for information.

[2] New Common Place Book, p. 20.

[3] Lyford, *Etymology of Christian Names*, London, 1655. Mrs. Piozzi's copy was listed in the 1823 sale.

[4] See letter to John Williams, July 13, 1814, and to Miss Williams, Oct 18, 1814 (Mainwaring MS.). Also Ry. 588, 243.

nymy, with simple illustrations of the proper use of words, the work might have had some value; but her recent introduction to Hebrew, combined with an already faulty grounding in etymology, resulted in innumerable absurd conjectures and unsuitable excursions into Jewish history and philosophy. For every name possible she gave the Hebrew equivalent, and then often tried to trace connexions in German, Welsh, or English. Occasionally, this time more rarely than usual, anecdotes of her former famous friends were used as illustrations. Two examples may serve to show the nature of the commentary.

> *Harold* A Lover of Arms says one Expositor—a Lord well beloved says another—I side with the last. The word is of Saxon Etymology, and *Her* is *Lord* in German. There is a strange Affinity in Language: *Herus* was always Master in Latin, & the Asiatic Researches shew us how the Orientals at this Moment cry Hail to thee *Heri* Lord of the Universe! The Low Dutchman recognizes *Myn Heer* as his Superior,—and *Harold* was Lord of our Armies in England, till William the Norman Conqueror killed him in the field of Battle at Hastings—where he resigned his Kingdom only with his Life.
>
> *Clarissa* is another Name deduced from Clara—with whose Story Richardson was of course familiar; his Novel has made it deservedly a favourite—*His* Novel!—developing every fold of the human heart, yet Doctor Johnson said the Name was not well chosen because the Heroine sometimes justified her Parents at the Expense of Truth. It was however in his Opinion a prodigious Work formed on the stalest of all empty Stories. . . .[1]

In January 1815 Edward Mangin, one of her Bath admirers, upon being shown the manuscript had 'seemed to like it', and in March, after the recopying was all completed, he had offered to find a publisher.[2] She herself was not sanguine of success. With Napoleon escaped from Elba, she rightly judged, 'people cannot be thinking on Books or Bargains, during Times of such agitation'. In this instance Mrs. Piozzi's fears proved well founded, for in the troublous period just before Waterloo no one could be found willing to risk issuing such a work. Nor did it ever in succeeding years find a publisher. 'Lyford Redivivus' shows how Mrs. Piozzi's predilection for abstruse philology, of

---

[1] The completed manuscript is now in the possession of Mrs. Donald F. Hyde. Further quotations may be found in Mangin's *Piozziana*, pp. 13–18. For her absorbing interest in etymology see New Common Place Book, pp. 147, 225, &c.

[2] 1815 Diary, and New Common Place Book.

which she had no accurate knowledge, rendered all her serious writing in her later life unfit for publication.

During the years at Bath the terse entries in Mrs. Piozzi's daily diaries give an accurate, and sometimes amusing, picture of her regular life. Monday was the day for settling accounts, and according to the state of her health and finances was variously described as 'Milk White Monday', 'Light Grey Monday', 'Dark Grey Monday', 'almost Black Monday', 'Coal Black Monday'. Every letter sent and received, every invitation, every visitor, was carefully noted. Constant in her attendance at Laura Chapel, there was always a comment on the sermon, sometimes far from flattering. Historic events in Europe, however, rarely found an echo in these jottings, which were supposed to be merely the record of her private life; literary and political observations were kept in other journals. Although Thraliana had been closed for ever after the death of Piozzi, she never ceased to be an indefatigable commentator, and each amusing bit of gossip, each new or startling tale she heard, was immediately jotted down in one of her numerous repositories. One of these, the 'New Common Place Book', begun in 1809, is a strange jumble of *jeux d'esprit*, aphorisms, bits of doggerel written by herself and her friends, and shrewd comments on the state of the nation.[1] Literature, as in the Johnsonian years, was her chief interest; yet in all the discussions of books and authors there is little evidence that she was as much interested in the new writers as in the new science and philosophy. Since her taste in reading had been formed by Collier and Johnson, she could never quite accept the full flowering of the romantic movement. Of Wordsworth and Coleridge she seemed completely oblivious; of Southey she was aware but scornful; in the rapidly maturing Keats and Shelley she had practically no interest. Referring once to her youthful passion for Ossian, she added that she

never till Walter Scott founded as it were a *new* Academy in Literature, *again* felt that Enthusiasm which Novelty alone can inspire. The Byromania succeeded—but I am not sure *any* of these Worthies will like Pope, Addison, Swift & Young last their Century out, and become *Classical*. . . . The old Court Dress will go on, whilst the feather-headed Indian will be forgotten:—as Cards will continue to

[1] Now in the possession of Mrs. Donald F. Hyde. On the front inner cover is written: 'Begun in 1809 at Brynbella; Thrown by—after writing about *fifteen* Pages—and begun again at Streatham Park in the year 1814. carried on in *New King Street Bath* 1815.' The whole comprises about 276 pages, the last entry being made at Penzance, Nov. 16, 1820.

be an Amusement, when Jonas & Breslau & others who shew'd
Tricks on them will be forgotten—Tho' the Tricks were excellent.[1]

It was natural that Byron, the grandson of her old intimate
friend, should fascinate her, and she thought his *Corinth* a marvellous example of the use of horror; nevertheless she insisted
'Lord Byron like his own Greece, suffers from Redundancy;
unchecked, unguided by wise & wholesome Laws'.[2] Though
something of an experimenter herself in the matter of prose
style, in poetry she preferred orderly design to the new lack of
restraint. As one might suppose, it was Crabbe who pleased
her most of all the modern writers.

Crabbes Poems please me better than any of the modern Productions—They leave something behind them. Lord Byron gives
you frightful Images, but they fade away in Phantasmagoria.
Southey sends you to Bed in the Horrors not knowing why: Walter
Scott's Marmion is very fine certainly, and his Lay—very Interesting:—They seized my Imagination forcibly on their first Appearance
but I return to Crabbe. As in Miss Linwood's Gallery we look with
Grief upon the Jepthah's Daughter, with awe upon the Lyons in
their Den: but go back with Pleasure to the Girl picking a Leaf—
& cry out Oh how natural![3]

Literature did not monopolize the New Common Place
Book; wit still claimed its share of her pages. Never prudish
in her tastes, she enjoyed a good story as well as in the Streatham days, and recorded a number which she thought amusing
in spite of their *risqué* character.

Lord Gwydir's Story of the Soldiers never knowing when to
expect a Battle from any Word that should drop out of the General's
Mouth is excellent: his Officers however learned to make Surmises
at last by observing the favourite *Lady* of the Week, Month or Year,
who was used to be near Duke Wellington on other Occasions:
commanded to the *Rear* of the Army—on which some of them very
cleverly called her—*hors* de combat. Tis an incomparable good
Joke, or Pun, or Flim-flam . . .[4]

---

[1] New Common Place Book, p. 46. Written in 1814.
[2] Ibid., p. 139; Feb. 1816.   [3] Ibid., p. 265; 1819.
[4] Ibid., p. 121; Nov. 1815. An example of Mrs. Piozzi's taste in repartee might
be the following:
   I believe we have done talking of Athenian Perfection *now*, except in Lord
Byron's oddly constructed Poems; but when Mr Stuart first came over, The
London Folks were mad for Greek Faces, & Greek Vases; & nobody durst laugh
except Frank Hayman: who when Athenian Stuart said, Painting is my Wife
I think, & Architecture my Mistress—replied What Pity 'tis then Sir, that you
have *no living Issue by either*!
(p. 54, spring, 1814.)

She even transcribed a somewhat indelicate anecdote, told her by General Donkin, of a quarrel said to have occurred once between Mrs. Montagu and Charles Fox,

whose Politics did not agree with *hers*, and that he replied to her arrogant Speech impromptu—Thus.

> Mrs. Montagu tells me, and in *her own House*,
> That She values *my* Thoughts not Three Skips of a Louse;
> No Matter: I must not regard what she said
> Because Women will talk of what *runs in their head*.[1]

Mrs. Piozzi must have shocked some of her more decorous companions with the blunt vigour of her speech; but she had been brought up in an environment where humour had been considered more important than refinement. She continued to find fun where she could, to laugh with gusto at absurdity no matter how coarse.

The round of quiet pleasures at Bath was at times disturbed by business worries. Streatham, in particular, was a perpetual problem; and when on March 14, 1815, Count Lieven informed her that because of the uncertain conditions he would be forced to cancel his lease, she was desperate.[2] Writing to Dr. Whalley on April 8, she explained her difficult position, having now an income of only £600 a year, while many of the Streatham bills were still unpaid.[3] What could she do? How escape from this financial labyrinth into which she had so blithely pushed herself? The entries in her diary for the next few weeks show clearly Mrs. Piozzi's indecision. On April 14 she wrote to Salusbury suggesting that she give the whole of Streatham to her daughters and so be spared all this worry and expense; but in reply he urged her to sell her interest and give him the money. Now sure of Brynbella, Salusbury schemed to get more from his adoring aunt; yet this time his tactics were too apparent for success. On May 17 Mrs. Piozzi wrote in her diary: 'Sate at home in the Evening & pitied poor Mrs. Piozzi—squeezed and despised between two Rapacious Families.'[4] In

---

[1] New Common Place Book, p. 98; Apr. 1815.

[2] The original note from Count Lieven is in the possession of Myers & Co.. London. [3] *Whalley Corr.* ii. 395.

[4] 1815 Diary. Her changing moods are further shown in letters to, Salusbury (Ry. 588). For some time her steward, Alexander Leak, had been stirring up trouble between Mrs. Piozzi and her heir. Leak wrote from Streatham on Mar. 12, 1815,

I hope Your Labours at the Book will not be lost but that it will after all bring You in a good sum of Money, But wile You are working at Your Book to get Money, Mr. Salusbury go an easier way to work to get it, by cuting down a Thousand Pds worth of Timber in Poor Old Bachagreag Woods—which

her dilemma every counsellor offered a different suggestion. And she again attempted to interest Lord Keith in the house, but in vain. Meanwhile, the expenses of Streatham without a tenant were exhausting her funds, so that she was forced to live in dirty lodgings at two guineas a week.

In desperation she drove to London in July 1815 for conferences with her daughters. After a talk with Sophia's husband had bolstered up her hopes, 'a cold dry note' informed her that Lord Keith would have nothing to do with the matter. This was the end, and she wrote to Dr. Whalley, upon returning to Bath:

All my scruples and delicacies are therefore at an end; and if you hear, when in Italy, about May or June 1816, that H. L. P.'s house is advertised for public sale, believe it.[1]

She had tried to be fair to her girls; now she was compelled to think only of herself.

The sale was set for the following spring, but before the house was completely dismantled it had one more temporary occupant. In March 1816, when Sir James Fellowes married an heiress, Mrs. Piozzi offered him Streatham Park for his honeymoon, rejoicing that someone she liked might once again enjoy her treasured belongings. On March 28 she herself arrived in London to make final arrangements for the sale. Her plan was simply this: to sell the contents of the house, which had been left solely to her by her first husband, and thus pay the debts incurred in repairing the house and grounds; then to let the empty house at a reduced rent for the remainder of her life. The first week in April was spent with the auctioneer. On the 3rd she jotted in her diary: 'Squibb & Catalogues took up the Morng. China examined. Reading Writing and Laughing filled the day'; two days later she added: 'Hard Work all day, making the China & Books into Lots.' This was the last of Thrale Place, the final dismantling of the home where Johnson had spent the happiest years of his life.

The sale took place on May 8, 1816, and following days, and brought a total of £3,921. 7s.[2] Nearly half of this amount came from the famous Reynolds portraits, of which Mrs. Piozzi

---

You were so Tender about. the Plate I suppose will go for sale next, for I understand He is about Building a New Farm Yard, which will cost 1000£ I am certain. He will be soon in the situation of the Man who sold all his Land to Build a Barn.
(Ry. 609, 6.)   [1] *Whalley Corr.* ii. 405; Aug. 13, 1815.
[2] In my possession is a marked copy of the sale catalogue. Mrs. Piozzi did not attend the sale, but her daughters bought a few objects which they wanted.

reserved for herself only two, those of Thrale and Arthur Murphy, the only one of the group, she wrote, 'equally attached to both my husbands'.[1] Finally, when all the furniture, bric-a-brac, and books were completely dispersed, the bare house was let to a Mr. Elliott, who agreed to pay all repairs and taxes and a rent of £260 a year for the remainder of her life. At last Mrs. Piozzi felt herself a free woman. With all debts paid and money in the stocks, she could leave the two miserable rooms in New King Street for a more fashionable dwelling. She wrote happily to Dr. Whalley:

Now, dear sir, wish me joy that I have shaken off this load of splendid misery, that I have by these means set my income free, and enabled myself to live in a decent style, such as neither of my husbands would be shocked to witness.[2]

To celebrate her new freedom, Mrs. Piozzi now leased a fine house near the Crescent, at 8 Gay Street.[3] While it was being repainted and redecorated, she drove to Brynbella to see Salusbury and his children. She found Brynbella much changed and, after agreeable Bath, very dull. '*No* Newspapers, & *no* Company; *no* Books, and *no* Conversation.'[4] Since Salusbury and his wife were more interested in social position and money than in literature, Mrs. Piozzi had to go to some trouble to beg 'a Book out of Mr. Salusbury's Study' for her own amusement. It was a strange alteration from the days when even the floors were piled high with weighty tomes. After almost a month she was not sorry to return to Bath.

Inevitably Mrs. Piozzi and Salusbury were drifting apart. She was made to feel that he and the Pembertons only wanted her money, while he was jealous of her generosity to other people. In the next few years, whenever she was able to save any money, he appeared to wheedle it from her. She was not unaware of his scheming, but pride in the name of Salusbury outweighed any wounded feelings; pride was the ever-present

---

[1] Hayward, ii. 339. After long solicitation by Mr. Watson Taylor, she finally sold him the Murphy portrait in 1819. See pp. 427, 431, and Ry. 557, 211. See also Mrs. Piozzi's letters to Leak now in the possession of Mr. Oswald Bourne, Surbiton, Surrey.

[2] *Whalley Corr.* ii. 429–30. Her Steward Leak came to Bath in June 1816 to settle the accounts, and while staying in her house fell seriously ill. The increasing height of her diary entries dramatically showed Mrs. Piozzi's excitement. On June 19 came the entry: 'Leak very ill'; the 20th, 'Leak safe'; the 21st, 'Leak not safe at all'; the 22nd, 'Leak dying'; and 23rd, 'Leak dead'.

[3] For a description of the house which had been designed by the elder Wood, see M. A. Green, *Eighteenth Century Architecture of Bath* (Bath, 1902), pp. 140, 204–12.

[4] 1816 Diary.

touchstone to open her purse-strings. In 1817, probably on the recommendation of friends, Salusbury was made sheriff of Flintshire, and arranged to carry up an address from his county. On March 4 Mrs. Piozzi wrote in her diary, 'Salusbury came'; on the 5th she added, 'Gave Salusbury £200—he went away directly'. Then on April 17 came another hurried visit, and on the 24th she made the entry, 'Sir John Salusbury returned'. The presentation of the address, after the proper negotiations, had resulted in his being knighted.

To think of her heir as Sir John was delightful, but to a proud Welshwoman it was more important that the honour should be passed on to succeeding generations. So, when she received a letter from a Mr. Cathron of the College of Heralds, intimating that a certain nobleman had the nomination for a baronetcy which might be secured for a 'valuable Consideration',[1] Mrs. Piozzi immediately asked the terms. Cathron's reply, unfortunately, named five thousand guineas as the necessary inducement for the noble Duke, which was much more than she could possibly pay, and she sadly gave up the idea. Negotiations, however, had only just begun. On July 19 Cathron made a new offer of three thousand guineas, with the understanding that the nobleman was 'willing to exert his Influence at Carlton House on the Condition of no Success no Pay'. This was more to the purpose, and on August 17 Mrs. Piozzi set out for London to see her correspondent personally. After a talk with Cathron on the 25th, she noted in her diary: 'I think we shall agree.' She was perfectly willing to exchange her present and future savings to ensure a succession of Sir John Salusburys in the Vale of Clwyd. Then, just as the affair seemed nearing completion later in the year, the death of Princess Charlotte necessarily forced a postponement. For the moment out of the question, the scheme was not forgotten.

Mrs. Piozzi had only one more glimpse of her beloved Wales —during the summer of 1818, when she spent six weeks at a sadly changed Brynbella. What hurt her most this time was to find that Salusbury's need for money had made him cut and sell much of the wood from old Bach-y-Graig. After courageously rescuing these trees from the designs of her first husband, after cherishing them as her most prized possession, she felt a stab of pain to find the wood 'stript stark naked'. Nevertheless young trees were growing, and she had no legal right

[1] The letters from J. Cathron, some of which he ineffectually tried to get Mrs. Piozzi to burn, are in Ry. 554, 24–30.

to complain. What had been freely given could not now be
taken back. But the incident cut her to the quick.

On this last visit Mrs. Piozzi was amusingly tormented by
a never-ending stream of mendicants. She had always been
lavish in gifts to the poor in the neighbourhood, much more so
than her successor, so that the news of her return to the vale
brought a crowd of former dependants. On July 22 she noted
in her diary: 'I am devoured by Beggars, and Sir John Displeased at seeing them'; the next day: 'no Rain—nothing but
Beggars'; then on the 24th: 'Beggars increasing, Sir John displeased, but who can help it?' In the detailed list she kept of
her benefactions to nearly two hundred different people, the
total amounted to well over £20.[1]

Sir John was unsympathetic to more than her philanthropies;
he had no interest whatsoever in any literary aspirations, and
even urged her to burn Thraliana.[2] The volumes evidently
had been left at Brynbella, but after this suggestion she took
them with her on her return to Bath. After all her high hopes,
what a disappointment it was to find her adopted son turning
into an ordinary country squire. Books and literary talk were
the staple of her diet; she had no wish to emulate Dr. Johnson
and 'learn to talk of runts'.[3] Congenial Bath seemed more and
more the perfect home.

What Sir John objected to in his aunt's insatiable ambition
as an author was not the wasting of time in useless scribbling,
but the possibility of more scandalous notoriety of the type that
had been unleashed against her in the late seventeen-eighties.
If ever Thraliana, or any of her other diaries, should be made
public, the resulting furore might jeopardize his social position
in Flintshire. It was just the attitude Queeney and her sisters
had taken in the past. To be sure, Mrs. Piozzi recognized that
Thraliana in its present condition was unsuitable for publica-

---

[1] In my possession is a separate sheet of accounts in Mrs. Piozzi's hand, undated,
but presumably of this year.˝ 119 minor expenditures are listed, all but a few
being small gifts to beggars, &c. A few sample entries follow:

'Long-faced Molly of the Bryn—0=2=0', '8 Beggars in a Bunch—0=6=0',
'Screaming Woman—0=2=6', '18 Beggars in a Troop—0=2=6', 'Simple
Neddy's Wife—0=2=6', 'Man 99 Years old—0=2=0', 'Poor Man upon the
Road—0=1=0', 'Woman in a Fit—0=2=0', 'Six Women & a Boy & Girl
& 2 more—0=4=6', 'Tom Cowman—0=1=0', 'Whooping Cough Woman—
0=1=0', 'Poor Fool forgotten—0=1=0', 'Woman with a foolish Husband—
0=1=0', '3 old Labourers—0=6=0', 'Long faced Molly—0=2=6', 'Man
& Woman Waunt—0=2=0', 'Other Beggars—0=3=0', 'Black Nancy—
0=6=0'.

[2] 1818 Diary, July 16. See also New Common Place Book, p. 240, and p. 146,
n. 3.   [3] *Life*, iii. 337.

tion. At Brynbella she had glanced through some of the painful episodes recorded in the past, and in consequence lost her sleep for a week; but late in November of the same year, when she calmly examined the volumes with Sir James Fellowes, she 'left off in a cheerful Humour enough'.[1] With Sir James as one of her executors, she felt perfect confidence that the precious journals would be properly treated.

Throughout her later years Mrs. Piozzi only occasionally found her name in newly printed books or papers. Though a well-known figure at Bath, she was only a legend and a relic of a past age in London and elsewhere. To the end, however, she would be the subject of mingled compliment and abuse. Thus in 1815 it had been pleasing to read Sir Nathaniel Wraxall's estimate:

Mrs. Thrale always appeared to me, to possess at least as much Information, a mind as cultivated, and more wit than Mrs. Montague; but she did not descend among men from such an eminence, and she talked much more, as well as more unguardedly, on every subject.[2]

In 1816 she engaged in a lengthy correspondence with Richard Duppa, who proposed to print Dr. Johnson's journal of the Welsh tour of 1774.[3] She willingly explained many of the entries, which naturally proved puzzling to a complete stranger, but at a distance it was impossible to clear up all his uncertainties. Consequently, Duppa's edition, when it appeared, was full of inaccuracies. The publication caused some reverberations; as she noted in her diary of November 8, 'saw the Review laughing at me & Mr. Duppa'. In 1817 William Beloe attacked her with all the merciless vigour of a Baretti. Mrs. Piozzi's chief characteristic, he insisted,

was vanity; acute, ingenious, and variously informed, she undoubtedly was; but there was a pert levity about her, which induced a perpetual suspicion of her accuracy, and an affectation also, which it seems wonderful that Dr. Johnson could ever have endured.[4]

Beloe then added a long inaccurate account of the adoption

---

[1] New Common Place Book, p. 242.

[2] *Memoirs*, 1904 edition, pp. 92–3. In her New Common Place Book, p. 103, Mrs. Piozzi made various comments about Wraxall's accuracy, and set down a story told her by Mr. Wansey of his early predilection for telling a tall story.

[3] Duppa's letters of Aug. 6, 21, 28; Sept. 11; Oct. 11; Dec. 4, 1816, have survived (largely in the Rylands collection). Mrs. Piozzi did not meet Duppa personally until Nov. 9, 1816, after the publication. See also *Life*, v. pp. xv, 427.

[4] *The Sexagenarian* (1817), i. 386. See also Hayward, ii. 384. For a typical unfavourable journalistic résumé of her career, see *Biographical Dictionary of Living Authors* (London, Colburn, 1816), p. 274.

of Piozzi's nephew in order to disinherit her own children, together with a claim that her second husband had pulled down old Bach-y-Graig. Never free from slander, Mrs. Piozzi had long ago learned not to worry too much over such attacks. Happily settled at Bath, in a comfortable house, with a host of devoted friends, she found life very much to her liking.

For the next few years her daily diaries give a pleasant picture of constant 'Droppers in', literary chat, and entertainments: 8 Gay Street became the centre of a Bath group, another miniature Blue-society. It was chiefly talk which filled the days and nights, for Mrs. Piozzi's powers of conversation remained undimmed and unrestrained. Mrs. Whalley wrote to her husband in the autumn of 1816,

> It is uncommonly entertaining to listen to Dr. Gibbes and Mrs. Piozzi; for though their conversation was above our flight to join in, it was both instructive and amusing.[1]

She was always the centre of the talkers. According to Mangin,

> She told a story incomparably well; omitting every thing frivolous or irrelevant, accumulating all the important circumstances, and after a short pause (her aspect announcing that there was yet more to come), finished with something new, pointed, and brilliant.
>
> To render all this more fascinating, she would throw into her narrative a gentle imitation—not *mimicry*, of the parties concerned, at which they might themselves have been present without feeling offended.[2]

Sir William Pepys, many years later, added the weight of his evidence when he admitted that 'he had never met with any human being who possessed the talent of conversation in such a degree'.[3]

Mrs. Piozzi did not, however, expect to monopolize the talk. Mangin insisted that 'she excelled in the delicate art of exciting and encouraging others to talk', and easily adapted herself to the interests of her companions. She contrived 'to appear at first less learned than she really was', and her eagerness to learn had the effect of making the others think 'that their agreeableness was the cause of hers'. It was no wonder that a continual round of visitors came to Gay Street to enjoy the repartee of this most famous of the 'Bath-Blues'.

Being a local celebrity just suited Mrs. Piozzi's tastes, for age

---

[1] *Whalley Corr.* ii. 438.
[2] E. Mangin, *Piozziana*, pp. 19–20.   [3] *A Later Pepys*, i. 146.

had not dimmed her delight in flattery. She once passed on to Sir James Fellowes a remark made by another Bath friend:

That grave Mr. Lucas brought his son here, that he might see the *first woman in England*—forsooth. So I am now grown one of the curiosities of Bath, it seems, and *one of the Antiquities.*[1]

Even receiving an unexpected visit from one whose genuine friendship she suspected was in the main flattering. On December 16, 1815, she noted in her diary: 'Madame D'Arblaye came!!!', and the next day added, 'Madame D'Arblay's Visit must be returned—Amicitiae Sempiternae, Inimicitiae placabiles . . . said my Lord North'.[2] Five days later she returned the call and later saw her old friend a number of times. Reading their later correspondence, one might be led to suppose that the old friendship had been renewed; but under the surface the resentment smouldered, and the next year, after one long chat, Mrs. Piozzi noted in her New Common Place Book:

Madame D'Arblay—always smooth always alluring;—pass'd two or Three Hours with me to day—— My perfect Forgiveness of l'aimable Traitresse, was not the act of Duty, but the impulsion of Pleasure rationally sought for, where it was at all Time sure of being found—In her Conversation. I will however not assist her Reception in the World a *Second* Time—'else She'll betray more Men' as Shakespear says; and she is no favourite with the present Race of Talkers here at Bath.[3]

Not many of the old Streatham company remained. Early in 1818 Sir William Pepys wrote to Hannah More: 'You and I, Mrs. Garrick and Mrs. Piozzi, are all I can now recollect of those who have surviv'd the wreck of our former society.'[4] At seventy-seven Mrs. Piozzi herself had little time to regret

[1] Hayward, ii. 307; Oct. 30, 1815. In Hayward's first edition this letter was dated Oct. 19.

[2] Marianne Francis had been trying for years to bring about a reconciliation. On Aug. 5, 1812, Mrs. Piozzi noted in her diary: 'Letter from Marianne says Madame D'Arblaye is come to London with her Son Alex. . . . a Letter from Clem says What a Regard She has for *me*!!! Too bad—Too bad *indeed*.' (See also W. W. Roberts, *J. Rylands Bulletin*, xvi (1932), 134.) In 1813 they narrowly escaped meeting. After some hesitation, hearing from Marianne that Mme D'Arblay was ill in London, Mrs. Piozzi called on her old friend only to find her out. The next day, May 12, Mme D'Arblay returned the visit, but found Mrs. Piozzi gone to Bath. See C. Lloyd, *Fanny Burney* (1936), p. 277, and Ry. 583, 113.

[3] p. 177 (summer of 1816). On July 13, 1816, Mrs. Piozzi noted in her diary, 'Madame D'Arblay & her Son came in the Evening, extremely agreeable *both*.' Mme D'Arblay wrote to Queeney on Nov. 7, 1816, describing one visit. 'We talked, both of us, in Dr. Johnson's phrase, "our *best*", but entirely as two strangers, who had no sort of knowledge or care for each other, but were willing, each to fling, & to accept the Gauntlet, *pour faire la belle conversation*' (Lansdowne MS.).

[4] *A Later Pepys*, ii. 334.

lost friends; she was too busy making new ones, and she found
more pleasure in the visit of a rising celebrity than in that of
one long since forgotten. Thus on April 28, 1819, she made
the entry in her diary: 'Lady Charlotte Fitzgerald brought
Anacreon Moore to see *me*.' He recorded of this visit:

> Breakfasted with the Fitzgeralds. Took me to call on Mrs. Piozzi;
> a wonderful old lady; faces of other times seemed to crowd over her
> as she sat,—the Johnson's, Reynoldses, &c. &c: though turned eighty,
> she has all the quickness and intelligence of a gay young woman.[1]

If only there had been an opportunity, she would have enjoyed
meeting others of the coming race of poets. Once in 1818 she
wrote to Queeney: 'I wonder if this Mr. Shelley is a Sussex
Cousin of Ours? The heavy Dumpling Diet of that Country
was unlikely to produce a Modern Prometheus.'[2]

As she grew older, Mrs. Piozzi became an even more indefatigable letter-writer, and thousands of these 'miniatures of
herself', as she called them, to a number of old and new friends,
have survived. Making it her practice to suit the tone of the
epistle to the taste and education of her correspondent, she
wrote gay letters, serious letters, dull letters. Each series shows
a different personality; yet all are tinged with the colloquial
smartness which characterized all her writing. To be sure, Mrs.
Piozzi will not be remembered among the great eighteenth-
century letter-writers, Walpole, Gray, Cowper, but she undoubtedly deserves a place only slightly lower. It is not as
a biographer, as an historian, or as a philologist that she will
be remembered, if indeed she will be remembered at all by
future students of the past; it is as a diarist and correspondent.
In her journals and letters, still for the most part unpublished,
Mrs. Piozzi captured the spirit of her age. At the same time
that they reveal her own many-sided character, they accurately
portray everyday life around her. They are miniatures not only
of herself, but of the century.

As might be expected, her correspondence was filled with
memories of Dr. Johnson and the great company who once
thronged her house. A chance remark, a visit to a place
haunted by ghostly reminders, an allusion in a book; anything
was apt to start the train of recollection. So passing through
Chester brought the comment:

> Dr. Johnson used to say he had lived with his Mistress—meaning

---

[1] T. Moore, *Memoirs* (1853), ii. 299. Mrs. Piozzi was so much struck by the
conversation that she wrote a long account of it to Conway at Birmingham (not
found).   [2] Feb. 13, 1818. There was no close relationship.

me—near 20 Years & never saw her out of Humour except once
upon CHESTER WALL.[1]

Or listening to heated political arguments:

Dr. Johnson was a wise Man, and he said History was a foolish
Study; for it tells said he of *Consternation* filling the Towns and
People, when in Truth no one was *consternated*, but Men minded
their Shops and counted their Money, and Women looked to their
Crockery Ware & minded their Mops, whether under one form of
Government or another.[2]

A business problem might bring forth:

Dr. Johnson advised in a similar Case once; 'If the Fellow is
refractory Sir—send a rough Att[y] to him, & all will be well;[3]

as might current events:

Do you trouble your head about Mr. Carlisle's Tryal? it is over
by now I suppose, I remember seeing a wretched Man pelted once
in the Pillory; & lamenting his Fate at Dinner;—Doctor Johnson
said Let us think no more of him Dear Madam: assure yourself of
his Safety: I nothing doubt but he is drunk by now.[4]

Vignettes such as these from her former life were scribbled
not only into letters and journals but also on the margins of
the books she read. She filled hundreds of volumes which
passed through her hands with notes, comments, and stories,
and often these original anecdotes are nowhere else available.[5]
As she read, she wished to record her own opinion, her own
version of the matter, either for the amusement of her intimate
friends or for posterity. And these marginalia, now unfortunately widely dispersed owing to a series of auction sales
beginning in 1823, are of real importance in any estimate of
her capabilities, for they provide the most unquestionable proof
not only of the variety of her reading but of her knowledge as
well.[6] They are the answer to those who have followed Boswell
in sneering at both her intellect and her character.

---

[1] To Salusbury, Apr. 9, 1813 (Ry. 586, 154).
[2] To Miss Williams, Aug. 25, 1819. Compare with *Piozziana* (Mangin), p. 118.
[3] To R. Davies, Apr. 15, 1803 (now owned by Mr. S. C. Roberts).
[4] To Miss Williams, Oct. 17, 1819. Compare *Letters to Pennington*, p. 339.
[5] The auction sale catalogues of her library (1823 following) list well over a
hundred sets of volumes containing annotations in her hand.
[6] A number of Mrs. Piozzi's marginal annotations have been published. In
addition to Hayward, i. 280–5, ii. 75–162, see: J. P. R. Lyell, *Mrs. Piozzi and
Isaac Watts* (1934); P. Merritt, *Piozzi Marginalia* (1925); Minna Steele Smith,
'Manuscript Notes by Madame Piozzi in a Copy of Boswell's Life of Johnson',
London Mercury, v (1922), 286–93; P. Merritt, 'Piozzi-Johnson Annotations', *Gazette
of the Grolier Club* (New York, May 1922), p. 58; Boswell, *Life* (ed. E. G. Fletcher

As Mrs. Piozzi approached her eightieth birthday, and by this she meant the day on which, according to our reckoning, she would be seventy-nine years old, she became more and more determined to make the celebration one of the most spectacular of her entire life. Six months ahead invitations were dispatched to 'all parts of the world', and throughout the year 1819 the coming party was uppermost in her mind. To conserve strength, and build up new vigour, she spent the summer first at Clifton and then at Weston-super-Mare. At the latter place, since the hotel was expensive, she rented a small cottage near by, but was not pleased with the accommodation. As she wrote to Mangin on July 11,

Doctor Johnson would have said that the negative catalogue of comforts in this place was of an immeasurable length indeed. . . . Not a book in the place, but one Bible and one Paradise Lost; I have got *them*, so am best off again. But Cocker's Arithmetic would be as great a wonder here, as Johnson's present of it was to the wench in the Hebrides.[1]

Nevertheless, sea bathing made up for the lack of other comforts, and it was not until October that an epidemic of typhus fever drove her back to Bath. For the remaining months of 1819 the approaching celebration occupied all her time: Sir John and his wife were coming from Brynbella; there were vague hopes of the presence of her daughters; and letters from many old friends assured her of their determination to be present.[2]

On January 27, 1820, the great day arrived.[3] A company of over six hundred persons gathered at the Assembly Rooms for a concert, ball, and supper. After her health was drunk to a round of cheers, Mrs. Piozzi opened the ball with Sir John Salusbury, and danced 'with astonishing elasticity' until early

for the Limited Editions Club, 1938); Marjorie Nicolson, 'Thomas Paine, Edward Nares, and Mrs. Piozzi's Marginalia', *Huntington Library Bulletin*, No. 10 (Oct. 1936), 103–33. Miss Nicolson maintains that the notes show that Mrs. Piozzi knew Hebrew, Latin, Greek, and had a wide knowledge of the Bible and modern science. [1] E. Mangin, *Piozziana*, pp. 110–11.

[2] See *Letters to Pennington*, p. 292, &c.; Hayward, ii. 440, 449. Cecilia Mostyn, who was in Italy and would not be back in time, promised to come for her ninetieth birthday.

[3] As previously pointed out, Mrs. Piozzi was seventy-nine years old, but it was her eightieth birthday. Dr. Johnson himself counted in the same way. On Sept. 18, 1764, he wrote, 'this is my fifty-sixth birth-day, the day on which I have concluded fifty five years' (*John. Misc.* i. 31). Mrs. Piozzi was, to be sure, always vague about her age, and sometimes insisted she had been born in 1740 (*Letters to Pennington*, p. 277); consequently in this instance it is not clear just which method of counting she was using.

in the morning. Yet the next day her callers found her 'mirthful and witty as usual', and she delightedly wrote in her diary, 'Lysons called, surprised to see me up—and at Breakfast, at 10 o'clock'.[1]

This spectacular birthday party was the crowning achievement of Mrs. Piozzi's life at Bath. Once again at seventy-nine she had shown to the world that irrepressible energy which was her dominant trait. Some might criticize her lavish expenditure, others her brazen ostentation,[2] but all were forced to admire the ageless vigour of her spirit. After almost eighty years of ceaseless activity, life was still as thrilling as it had been when she had watched the fireworks celebrating the Peace of Aix-la-Chapelle. She had witnessed stirring times, as the world had moved in an ever-widening cycle from Quebec to Waterloo, Johnson to Shelley, Hogarth to Turner. Her own family group had been often broken by sickness and death, but through it all she had passed unchanged. To the last she was as ready as ever for a dance, a joke, or a serious argument.

The epitome of youth herself, Mrs. Piozzi never ceased to be interested in the young people about her, and one of these, a tall actor named William Augustus Conway, who appeared regularly at the Bath theatre, roused more than casual interest. Tall, handsome, gentlemanly, he looked the hero, and the mystery of his birth made him a truly romantic character.[3] The son of a Mrs. Rudd who was the proprietress of a lodging-house and several cottages at Clifton, he was firmly convinced that his father was Lord William Conway; but like the ill-fated Richard Savage he had been unsuccessful in proving his paternity. This mysterious background alone would have been enough to enlist the sympathies of Mrs. Piozzi, but in addition Conway was unhappily in love with a young girl at Bath named Charlotte Stratton, whose family bitterly opposed the match. The combination proved irresistible, and in 1819, with a number of other old ladies at Bath, Mrs. Piozzi actively undertook to further his suit. The entries in her diaries reveal the ensuing complications.

---

[1] For a complete description of the fête, see E. Mangin, *Piozziana*, pp. 159–61. On the 28th there was a servants' party, and she noted: 'Sir John Salusbury & I danced with them.'   [2] See comment of H. Wickham in *Whalley Corr.* i. 11.
[3] Manuscript note in copy of *Love Letters, &c.* (1842) (see p. 470), in the Victoria and Albert Museum, London. Also G. and P. Wharton, *Queens of Society* (1860), ii. 164. The claim is made that Conway was the illegitimate son of the daughter of a farmer and Lord William Conway, from whom he inherited his gigantic stature. The actor was born and brought up in the West Indies where his mother had been sent to hush up the scandal.

Early in May 1819, when Conway accepted an engagement
in Birmingham, Mrs. Piozzi commented, 'Charlotte half
drown'd in Tears'; yet less than a month later she added,
'Charlotte seems resolved to jilt poor Conway after all. I feel
quite shocked at her Behaviour.—4 weeks today since he left
us, & now—jilted.' The following autumn Mrs. Piozzi interested her old friend Mrs. Pennington, recently reconciled,
in the actor, and late in December all three met at Clifton.[1]
Conway's love affair was still the principal source of worry. On
December 30 Mrs. Piozzi recorded: 'Mrs. Stratton met Conway—*alone*; & they had their own Talk quite out in my Room
—uninterrupted'; but seemingly to no avail, for the following
February, 1820, she noted that he had 'half destroyed me by
the Tale he told'. In the end, despite all their efforts, Conway
and Charlotte were as far apart as in the beginning.

One trouble was that Conway was not a good actor, his
height making him unsuitable for many parts. Even his future
on the stage was thus unpromising. The romantic old ladies,
nevertheless, refused to be discouraged: Mrs. Piozzi wrote him
long, ardent letters, which were later to be so grotesquely misunderstood,[2] took charge of his money, tried to get him engagements, actively planned for his future. 'Our Chevalier', as she
and Mrs. Pennington called him, took the place of Queeney,
Cecilia, and Salusbury, who had all cast her off; she even wrote
of him as her 'youngest adopted child'. Conway for his part
willingly listened to her tales of former years, and gratefully
accepted profusely annotated copies of her published works.
His name constantly appeared in her diary: 'Conway came &
dined with us; & read & talked all Eveng. *so* sweetly', 'Conway
came (God bless him)', 'wrote to dear Conway'. It was almost
as if she were keeping a Children's Book again.

Sir John Salusbury was not unaware of his aunt's growing
interest in the impecunious actor, and knowing her generous
nature, began to fear for his inheritance. During the past few
years she had accumulated £6,000 in the stocks which she had
promised to leave to her heir. He thought it best to get this
into his own hands now, before she either spent it or gave it
away. Accordingly, the old proposal of the baronetcy was
revived, and Cathron wrote on June 7, 1820, that there was

---

[1] *Letters to Pennington*, pp. 291–2. Mrs. Pennington and Mrs. Piozzi had quarrelled in 1804, and there is a gap in their correspondence until 1819.
[2] See *Love Letters* (1842), described on pp. 470–1. On Feb. 26, 1820, with Miss
Williams as a witness, he deposited a box of valuables with Mrs. Piozzi.

a good opportunity to be included in the coming coronation
lists, the average price being now about five thousand guineas.[1]
Later letters urged her not to delay. Sir John himself arrived
on June 16, and she wrote in her diary, 'we had a long Business
Talk, unpleasant of Course'. A second day of conferences
brought no decision, but on the 18th she noted, 'Quickening
Letter from Cathron. answer'd it'. At the bottom of the page
in deep black letters she added, 'my poor 6000£. gone—Addio!
—I trust they will leave me the Dividend'. The next morning
Sir John hurried away, his task accomplished. In succeeding
months various entries in Mrs. Piozzi's diary refer to continuing
negotiations, but in the end the baronetcy was never secured.
Obviously, what Sir John wanted was the money, not the title.

The expense of the lavish birthday party had temporarily
driven Mrs. Piozzi into debt. With numerous tradesmen's bills
to be paid out of her restricted income, she decided to let her
house at 8 Gay Street and to live more economically for a while
away from Bath. After a month at Clifton, where the first entry
in her diary was, 'Talk with Mrs. Rudd about Conway', she set
out on July 19, 1820, for Cornwall. At Penzance she hoped to
combine warm sea bathing with pleasant inexpensive lodgings,
but after hunting for several days she found it no easy task to
find a suitable place to live in, and finally was forced to take
a small 'nutshell of a cottage', though hoping for a better house
in the autumn. Like Weston-super-Mare, Penzance had only
negative recommendations. '*No* Milliner's Shop,' she wrote to
Susan Thrale, '*no* Rooms, *no* Theatre, *no* Music Meeting—*no*
Pleasure, but *no* Expence. I had too much of *both* the last
Winter at Bath.'[2] Later in the autumn she was joined by an
old Bath friend, Miss Willoughby. 'But for *her*', Mrs. Piozzi
commented to Mrs. Pennington, 'I should have pass'd many
a dreary hour.'[3] Gradually, however, she found a few interesting acquaintances, and there were always books to read and
letters to write.[4] Her diary was largely devoted to long lists of
the latter, together with constant complaints of the dilatory
manners of her correspondents. Conway in particular never
seemed to write.

Mrs. Piozzi's chief purpose in retiring from society had been
to retrench her finances, and throughout the remainder of the

---

[1] Ry. 554, 29, 30.   [2] Lansdowne MS., Sept. 25, 1820.
[3] *Letters to Pennington*, p. 364; see also p. 341.
[4] On Oct. 7 she 'corrected one Vol. of Retrospection for Dr. Forbes & his
Penzance Library' (Diary). Forbes was a frequent visitor and praised her writing
highly. There would always be flattery wherever she went.

year her diary shows numerous payments to Bath tradesmen. As she wrote to Mrs. Pennington on November 2, 'I continue to do what I came hither to perform, eat cheap fish, and pay old debts. . . . Had I dreamed of losing £6000 at a stroke so, I would have been more prudent.' Though often annoyed and dismayed at what she considered Sir John's heartless conduct, she considered him her heir and meant to leave him an unencumbered estate. In spite of continual grumbling she conscientiously kept to her self-appointed task.

The late autumn and early winter of 1821 passed drearily, far away from congenial Bath company; then finally in March she decided to return to civilization. On Saturday, the 10th, she reached Exeter, but instead of retiring immediately sat up until early morning writing letters. Later, as she tried to climb, unaided, into the high bed of the period, the chair used as a stool slipped from under her, and she suffered a severe fall. Nevertheless, even with a badly bruised leg she was able to reach Clifton on the 12th, where she found temporary quarters at 10 Sion Row until Mrs. Rudd could receive her at the Crescent. She had chosen Clifton rather than Bath, she wrote to Queeney, 'as Gulliver made himself a Mash of Oats & Milk, and eat it with the Sorrel Nag, when not Up to the Houhynm Society—and above that of the Y——s'.

Although the fall at Exeter had been both a physical and a nervous shock, it did not affect her vivacity, and she laughingly wrote to Miss Willoughby on March 18, 'Dr. Forbes will be very sorry, for poor H. L. P., always a blue, now a black and blue, lady, bruised, say you, from top to toe?—"My Lord, from head to foot."[1] A few days later when writing to Sir James Fellowes, she indulged in further puns about the 'l.e.g.—my elegy'. Salusbury, she commented, had been worried about the long expensive journey if she had died at Penzance, but now he could come to the river Severn, 'to look after the demise and the legacy (leg I see)'.[2]

Life was gradually, but perceptibly, closing in. Even Mrs. Piozzi herself seemed to have a premonition that this was the end. Yet in spite of her injured leg she was determined to be present at Conway's benefit on March 25. Accordingly, she drove over to Bath 'in high spirits', saw 'dear Conway more inimitable than ever in Mirandola', and dined with the Fellowes family. It was her last 'Flash'. The seemingly inexhaustible energy was beginning to flag, and throughout April

[1] Hayward, ii. 462. [2] Ibid. ii. 463.

she remained quietly at Clifton. But even as her physical
vitality slowly lessened, she showed in her diary the same
amusing attitude towards herself. On the 7th came the entry:
'I rec'd a saucy Letter from Salusbury. care the less about my
Debts.' For the next few weeks the entries continue, indicating
continued gaiety and curiosity over what was going on about
her; then finally on April 27 the insatiable diarist laid down
her pen, and the succeeding pages are blank.

By this time it was apparent that she was dying, and word
was sent to her daughters and to Sir John, whom, according
to Mrs. Pennington, she had never expressed any desire to see.[1]
She left him her property, what little remained of it, but at the
last her heart turned to the children of her own flesh and blood.
When told of the arrival of Queeney and Sophia, late on the
evening of May 1, she characteristically remarked, 'Now I shall
die in state'.[2] The next day Queeney wrote to her husband,
Lord Keith, telling of the hurried journey, and of seeing her
mother that morning.

I am happy to say she *knew us* & appeared pleased at our being
by Her Bed side, & whenever she is awake puts out a Hand to each
of us—but the Medicines they give her, keep her in a dozing state.[3]

Belying her sarcastic tongue, the outstretched hand mutely
expressed one last appeal for affection.

As the dying woman lay quietly watching her daughters by
the bedside, what thoughts of other days must have drifted
through her consciousness: childish memories of Bodvel, perhaps—of Lleweney, or Bach-y-Graig—of summer hours at
Offley—lessons with Dr. Collier. How far away those first years
at Streatham must have seemed. Anxious days and troubled
nights in the nursery—little Queeney carrying a puppy about
the lawn, or drawing a smile from Doctor Johnson—darling
Lucy and manly Harry! Or did she only remember those later
days with Piozzi—his expressive face—his voice singing Venetian love songs—his delight in the splendid entertainments at
Hanover Square—his constant fear of annoying her daughters?
Here were Queeney and Sophia now holding her hands,
Susanna on the way, Cecilia too far away to come. Why had
there been all those futile quarrels? Had it been somehow
her fault? Why had she never been able to pierce Queeney's

---

[1] Ry. 596, 9, Conway to Sir John Salusbury. Also *Letters to Pennington*, p. 369,
and Queeney to Lord Keith (Lansdowne MS.). Queeney was in Scotland when
she heard of the fatal illness of her mother (*Athenaeum*, Apr. 11, 1857).

[2] Seeley, p. 330. [3] Lansdowne MS.

self-contained, cold exterior? That was the one complete failure of her life. But now she was too tired to worry about anything. All she wanted was rest.

So gradually life ebbed away, with no particular pain and no anxiety.[1] It was simply that her physical energy was near the end. Yet, weak as she was, Mrs. Piozzi would have one last whimsical joke; when her old favourite, Dr. Gibbes, came over from Bath, she had just strength enough left to trace with her fingers the outline of a coffin in the air.[2] Then, shortly after the arrival of Susanna, late on the evening of May 2, she passed quietly away.[3] The active, curious mind and the whirligig tongue at last were stilled for ever.

[1] Mrs. Pennington insisted that Mrs. Piozzi's death was not due to the injury to her leg, but merely to 'inanition' and physical exhaustion. See *Letters to Pennington*, pp. 369–74.

[2] E. Mangin, *Piozziana*, p. 8. See also *Gent. Mag.* xci (1821), 470–1. The biographical account is full of inaccuracies.

[3] It has formerly been assumed that Mrs. Piozzi died at 36 Royal Crescent, Clifton, but the evidence seems to indicate that she was still at 10 Sion Row at the time of her death. Conway's letter to Sir John Salusbury of Apr. 30, 1821 (Ry. 596, 9), intimated that Mrs. Piozzi was in furnished rooms at his mother's house in Sion Row, a fact which he used as an explanation for his writing. When Queeney and Sophia arrived, Mrs. Piozzi insisted that they stay in the newly decorated house on the Crescent (Lansdowne MS.), and it was here that the will was later read, which may explain the later assumption that Mrs. Piozzi herself had died in the house.

EPILOGUE

ON May 16, 1821, Mrs. Piozzi was laid to rest beside her second husband under Tremeirchion Church in the Vale of Clwyd. But she was not soon forgotten. Something vital still lived on—call it fame, personality, what you will. Though her voice was stilled, the voices of her friends and enemies were not; and the indomitable spirit of the Mistress of Streatham has, for a hundred years or more, been as provocative of scurrilous attacks, unmeasured praise, and acrimonious controversy as in her own day. She had accurately predicted the result early in July 1820, when she noted in her diary: 'At my Death the Battle about my Merits & no Merits will be renewed over my Memory. Friends wishing to save it—Foes contending for the Pleasure of throwing it to the Dogs like the Body of Petroclus in Homer.'[1] Nor was such a prospect evidently displeasing, for above all things she wished to be remembered.

The reactions of her own intimate circle following her death were what might have been expected. There seems little need to describe the official mourning of Sir John Salusbury, or of Queeney, Susanna, and Sophia, decorously formal yet tinged with an obvious sense of relief, for they need no longer fear disagreeable publicity from their mother's eccentric caprices.[2] Nor is it necessary to comment on the real grief of her true friends— Edward Mangin, Sir James Fellowes, Mrs. Pennington, and Mrs. Siddons.[3] We need not reprint the eulogy written for the Bath newspaper by Mrs. Pennington, who was convinced that she would never 'look upon her like again',[4] or Mme D'Arblay's complimentary comparison of her former friend to Mme de Staël.[5] And we may justifiably pass over, too, the immediate settlement of Mrs. Piozzi's bequests, which led to a bitter quarrel between Sir John and Mrs. Pennington about a silver teapot.[6] All this is of minor interest. What is more important is to trace the underlying forces which have kept Mrs. Piozzi from being fully understood.

[1] Ry. 616. [2] Lansdowne MSS.; Broadley, p. 72, &c.
[3] For example, see T. Campbell, *Life of Mrs. Siddons*, ii. 373; Broadley, pp. 72-4; *A Later Pepys*, i. 149; Ry. 596, 9, &c.
[4] *Letters to Pennington*, pp. 371-3. [5] *D'Arblay Diary*, vi. 399-400.
[6] *Adam Libr.*, iii. 212; *Letters to Pennington*, pp. 375-6. Also see Ry. 596, 10; 597, 5.

It will be remembered that Mrs. Piozzi had asked Sir James Fellowes to act as her literary executor, to cull what poems and anecdotes he might think fit from Thraliana and her miscellaneous papers, and to publish them as her final bid for fame. Like Boswell, she had been certain that her great collection of journals and letters would provide a valuable record for later generations; but, as in the case of Boswell, it was her own heirs who temporarily thwarted this desire. Sir John Salusbury had no inclination for literary notoriety, and when Sir James Fellowes eagerly tried to secure possession of the necessary papers to carry out the behest, Sir John proceeded to store them at Brynbella, while he put off his fellow-executor with vague promises.[1] It seems probable, moreover, that he actively forestalled another immediate attempt to make Mrs. Piozzi better known as a writer. The Williams family at Bodylwyddan had saved at least six hundred notes and letters from Mrs. Piozzi, and they had access also to those written to the Reverend John Roberts of Tremeirchion, who had been her tutor in Hebrew. Feeling that some of these were admirable examples of the art of familiar letter writing, John Williams, shortly after her death, proposed an edition of her correspondence, and actually sent about a hundred originals and copies to the publisher Longman in London.[2] Only the threat of a legal injunction by Sir John forced the abandonment of these plans. He, indeed, was more interested in finding which of his aunt's belongings might be converted into ready cash without undue publicity, than in furthering her reputation as a Blue-Stocking.[3] While he lived, no one was allowed to see the great store of manuscripts packed away at Brynbella.

Sir John's opposition could not keep occasional compositions or memorials of his aunt from appearing in print, but it was responsible for the fact that throughout the remainder of the century public opinion about her was based almost exclusively on the authority of Boswell and Mme D'Arblay. Even if there were occasional attempts to revive interest in Mrs. Piozzi's writings—Mangin printed some of her letters and excerpts from 'Lyford Redivivus'; Hayward was allowed to publish long selections from Thraliana[4]— most Victorian writers were content to

---

[1] *Adam Libr.*, iii. 212; Ry. 597, 3, 5.

[2] These, together with some of the correspondence referring to the projected edition, are now in the Victoria and Albert Museum in South Kensington.

[3] On Sept. 17–25, 1823, in Manchester, Sir John sold a large part of Mrs. Piozzi's library, pictures, prints, plate, and valuable curiosities. Again on Apr. 13–15, 1836, in Liverpool, he sold additional paintings, prints, and household effects.

[4] See Bibliography.

accept a casual, warped portrait of the lady. It was Macaulay who set the fashion; it was his blighting criticism, enforced by the weight of his balanced style, that kept Mrs. Piozzi's star in eclipse. As with Boswell, Macaulay found her wayward natural-ness, her inherent disregard for convention in literature and society, intolerable. His attitude dominated the mid-nineteenth-century mood so thoroughly that the sporadic efforts of others in opposition were largely ignored. Not until our own century has this strange mixture of abuse and praise begun to fade, and Mrs. Piozzi been able to emerge as a real figure.

The present revival of interest is chiefly due to the gradual dispersal of her large mass of manuscripts;[1] for with the avail-ability of this new evidence, private collectors have found the lady a fascinating subject for inquiry. In consequence, there has come a sudden increase in writing about Mrs. Piozzi—editions of her travel journals and letters, sentimental apprecia-tions and character sketches—so that she is beginning to assume a more important position among the talented women of the eighteenth century. This re-estimate, however, is not complete. Still only a small fraction of her literary remains has been critically examined; still the major portion of her correspon-dence is unpublished. But with the printing of excerpts from the Children's Book in the present volume, with a selected edition of her correspondence in prospect; and with the un-censored publication of Thraliana in its entirety, most of the facts of her life will be available.

What, then, will all this new evidence show us about Mrs. Piozzi? Will the new volumes radically change our estimate of Boswell's 'lively' lady? The answer is undoubtedly, No. We shall, it is true, be able to understand more clearly the motives which led to many of her otherwise incomprehensible actions. But we shall probably never be able to discover the main-spring of her character. Still Mrs. Piozzi will defy concise characterization; and it is just this human unaccountability which is her most engaging quality. A bundle of contradictions, she fascinates at the same time that she puzzles the reader. At one moment apparently self-centred and brazen, and the next unselfish and considerate; on occasion grasping and penurious, and then with sentimental generosity capable of giving away almost all she had; at times a fretful wife and mother, but seldom shirking disagreeable tasks; garrulous to the extreme, yet,

[1] Sotheby sales Dec. 14, 1901; Dec. 6, 1904; Jan. 22, 1907; June 4, 1908; Jan. 30, 1918, &c.

according to Mangin, always ready to listen to the other person;
widely read in both classical and modern literature, but never
a thorough scholar; sensitive to words and having a naturally
fluent style, yet uneven in her writing; endowed with a real
genius for making friends, and at the same time having an
uncanny faculty of losing them—Mrs. Piozzi was as unpre-
dictable as the weather. But one thing is certain: she was almost
always interesting. As Charles Eliot Norton aptly remarked,
'Dulness was, in her code, the unpardonable sin. Variety was
the charm of life, and of books. She never dwelt long on one
idea'.[1]

Her two most distinguishing traits were a boundless vitality
and a never satisfied curiosity. She was interested in practically
everything—politics, science, literature, religion—but like Johnson, she found people and social relationships the most fascinating study of all. These traits found expression through her
impulse to record for others the incidents and stories which she
found so entertaining. Thus her diaries and letters provide an
enduring record of people and events, a kaleidoscopic picture
of the age in which she lived. This is her chief claim to remembrance; this her value to the social historian of to-day.

[1] C. E. Norton, 'Original Memorials of Mrs. Piozzi', *Atlantic Monthly*, vii (May,
1861), 617.

APPENDIXES

APPENDIX A

FAMILY RECORD

(S. = Streatham; Swk. = Southwark.)

Name	Birth	Christened	Died	Buried
Henry Thrale	1728–9? (Swk.)	?	Apr. 4, 1781 (Grosv. Sq.)	Apr. 11, 1781 (S.)
Hester Lynch Salusbury	Jan. 27, 1741 (Bodvel) (Jan. 16, Old Style)	Feb. 21, 1741 (Llanner)	May 2, 1821 (Clifton)	May 16, 1821 (Tremeirchion)
Hester Maria Thrale (Queeney)	Sept. 17, 1764 (Swk.)	Sept. 24, 1764 (Swk.)	Mar. 31, 1857 (London)	
Frances Thrale	Sept. 27, 1765 (Swk.?)	Oct. 3, 1765 (Swk.)	Oct. 6, 1765	Oct. 8, 1765 (S.)
Henry Salusbury Thrale	Feb. 15, 1767 (Swk.)	Mar. 3, 1767 (Swk.)	Mar. 23, 1776 (Swk.)	Mar. 28, 1776 (S.)
Anna Maria Thrale	Apr. 1, 1768 (S.)	Apr. 17, 1768 (S.)	Mar. 21, 1770 (Dean Street)	Mar. 23, 1770 (S.)
Lucy Elizabeth Thrale	June 22, 1769 (S.)	July 16, 1769 (S.)	Nov. 22, 1773	Nov. 26, 1773 (S.)
Susanna Arabella Thrale	May 23, 1770 (Swk.)		Nov. 5, 1858 (Knockholt)	
Sophia Thrale	July 23, 1771 (S.)	Aug. 11, 1771 (S.)	Nov. 8, 1824 (Sandgate)	
Penelope Thrale	Sept. 15, 1772 (S.)	Sept. 15, 1772 (S.)	(lived 10 hours) (S.)	Sept. 16, 1772 (S.)
Ralph Thrale	Nov. 8, 1773 (S.)	Dec. 5, 1773 (S.)	July 13, 1775 (Brighton)	
Frances Anna Thrale	May 4, 1775 (S.)	May 21, 1775 (S.)	Dec. 9, 1775	Dec. 11, 1775 (S.)
Cecilia Margaretta Thrale	Feb. 8, 1777 (S.)	Feb. 17, 1777 (S.)	May 1, 1857 (Brighton)	
Henrietta Sophia Thrale	June 21, 1778 (S.)	July 12, 1778 (S.)		Apr. 25, 1783 (S.)
Gabriel Mario Piozzi	June 8, 1740 (Quinzano)	(the same day)	Mar. 26, 1809 (Brynbella)	Apr. 3, 1809 (Tremeirchion)
John Salusbury Piozzi Salusbury	Sept. 9, 1793 (Brescia?)	Sept. 12, 1793	Dec. 18, 1858 (Cheltenham)	(Tremeirchion)

APPENDIX B

CHIEF PUBLISHED WORKS

Florence Miscellany. Florence. Printed for G. Cam, Printer to His Royal Highness. With Permission, 1785. (Mrs. Piozzi provided the Preface, and nine poems.) 8vo.

Anecdotes of the Late Samuel Johnson, LL.D., During the Last Twenty Years of His Life. London: for T. Cadell in the Strand, 1786. 8vo.
—— The Second Edition. London, 1786.
—— The Third Edition. London, 1786. (Actually a reissue of the second.)
—— The Fourth Edition. London, 1786 (so-called).
—— Another Edition. Dublin, 1786. 12mo.
—— A New Edition. London, T. and J. Allman, 1822. 8vo.
—— Another Edition. London, Longmans, 1856. 8vo. (Vol. 16 of the Traveller's Library.)
—— Another Edition, in *Johnsoniana*, collected and edited by Robina Napier. London, Bell, 1884. 8vo.
—— Another Edition. London, 1887. (A volume of Cassell's National Library, with introduction by Henry Morley.) 16mo.
—— Another Edition, in *Johnsonian Miscellanies*, edited by G. Birkbeck Hill. Oxford, 1897.
—— Another Edition, edited by S. C. Roberts. Cambridge, 1925.
—— Another Edition of the same. Cambridge, 1932.
—— Another Edition. Freeport, N.Y., Books for Libraries Press, 1969.
—— Another Edition. Westport, Conn., Greenwood Press, 1971.
—— Another Edition, reprint of Dublin edition of 1786, in series The Life and Times of Seven Major British Writers: Johnsoniana. New York, Garland Publishing, 1974.
—— Another Edition, edited by Arthur Sherbo. London, Oxford University Press, 1974.
——*Dr. Johnson by Mrs. Thrale: The 'Anecdotes' of Mrs. Piozzi in Their Original Form,* edited with an introduction by Richard Ingrams. London, Chatto & Windus, 1984.

Letters to and from the Late Samuel Johnson, LL.D. to which are added some Poems never before Printed. Published from the Original MSS. in Her Possession. London, Printed for A. Strahan and T. Cadell, in the Strand, 1788. 8vo. (2 vols.)
—— Another Edition. Dublin, 1788. 8vo.

Observations and Reflections Made in the Course of a Journey through

France, Italy, and Germany. London, Printed for A. Strahan and T. Cadell in the Strand, 1789. (2 vols.) 8vo.

—— Another Edition. Dublin, 1789. 8vo.

—— A German translation, *Bemerkungen auf der Reise durch Frankreich, Italien und Deutschland von Esther Lynch Piozzi.* Aus dem Englischen mit einer Vorrede und Anmerkungen von Georg Forster. Frankfurt und Mainz, bei Barrentrapp, und Wenner, 1790. (2 vols.)

—— Another Edition, edited by Herbert Barrows. Ann Arbor, Mich., University of Michigan Press, 1967.

The Three Warnings, Kidderminster, printed by John Gower, 1792. (A separate publication of the Tale originally appearing in Miss Williams's *Miscellanies in Prose and Verse,* London, 1766.)

British Synonymy; or an Attempt at Regulating the Choice of Words in Familiar Conversation. Inscribed, With Sentiments of Gratitude and Respect, to such of her Foreign Friends as have made English Literature their peculiar Study. London: Printed for G. G. and J. Robinson, 1794. (2 vols.) 8vo.

—— Another Edition. Dublin, 1794. 8vo.

—— Another Edition. Published in five instalments in Parsons and Galignani's *British Library* (vols. 14, 16, 18, 20, and 22). Paris, 1804. (Contains additional notes by the editors.)

—— Reprint, facsimile of first edition. Menston, Yorks., Scolar Press, 1968. (2 vols.)

Three Warnings to John Bull before He Dies. By an Old Acquaintance of the Public. London, Fauldner, 1798. (Political pamphlet.)

Retrospection: or a Review of the Most Striking and Important Events, Characters, Situations, and Their Consequences, which the Last Eighteen Hundred Years Have Presented to the View of Mankind. London, Printed for John Stockdale, Piccadilly, 1801. (2 vols.) 4to.

Autobiography, Letters and Literary Remains of Mrs. Piozzi (Thrale), edited by Abraham Hayward. London, Longman, 1861. (2 vols.)

Reprint, Women of Letters series. New York, AMS Press, 1975. A revised version edited by J. H. Lobban, *Dr. Johnson's Mrs. Thrale: Autobiography, Letters and Literary Remains of Mrs. Piozzi* Edinburgh, Foulis, 1910.

The Intimate Letters of Hester Piozzi and Penelope Pennington 1788–1821, edited by Oswald G. Knapp. London, John Lane, 1914.

'Minced Meat for Pyes', extracts edited by Percival Merritt in *Piozzi Marginalia* Cambridge, Mass.: Harvard University Press, 1925.

'Three Dialogues on the Death of Hester Lynch Thrale', edited by M. Zamick, *BJRL* 16 (1932), 77–114.

Reprint, as pamphlet. Manchester, Manchester University Press, 1932.

The French Journals of Mrs. Thrale and Dr. Johnson, edited by Moses Tyson and Henry Guppy. Manchester, Manchester University Press, 1932.
Reprint. New York, Haskell House, 1973.
Thraliana, edited by Katherine C. Balderston. Oxford, Clarendon Press, 1942; 2nd edition 1951. (2 vols.)
'The Children's Book or rather Family Book' edited by Mary Hyde in *The Thrales of Streatham Park*, pp. 21–218, Cambridge, Mass.: Harvard University Press, 1977.

APPENDIX C

DIARIES AND JOURNALS KEPT BY
MRS. THRALE (PIOZZI)

1757 and 1761—Fragmentary daily diaries and account books. (Ry. 616.)

THE CHILDREN'S BOOK, OR RATHER FAMILY BOOK, begun Sept. 17, 1766, and continued to the end of 1778. Unpublished MS. 94 folios. 8vo. (Now in the Hyde Collection, Somerville, New Jersey.)

JOURNAL OF JOHNSONIAN ANECDOTES. (Conjectural.) Begun probably before 1770. (Three torn leaves from this Journal still exist—Ry. 629. See pp. 76, 85–8.)

JOURNAL OF MISCELLANEOUS ANECDOTES. (Conjectural.) Begun definitely before 1770. A number of leaves from this Journal still exist—Ry. 629. See pp. 85–6.

1773—Fragmentary note-books. (Ry. 616.)

WELSH JOURNAL, July 5 to Sept. 30, 1774. MS. of 48 folios, 4to. (Published by A. M. Broadley, 1910. Original MS. in the Hyde Collection.)

FRENCH JOURNAL, Sept. 15 to Nov. 11, 1775. MS. of 74 folios, 4to. (Ry. 617. Edited by Dr. Moses Tyson and Dr. Henry Guppy, Manchester University Press, 1932.)

THRALIANA, begun Sept. 15, 1776, and ended Mar. 30, 1809. Six vols., 4to, comprising over 800 folios of MS. (Now in the possession of the Huntington Library, Pasadena, Cal. Edited by K. C. Balderston, 2 vols. (Clarendon Press, 1942; 2nd ed. 1951.)

ITALIAN AND GERMAN JOURNALS, from Sept. 5, 1784, to Mar. 1787. Two 4to MS. note-books. In all 168 folios of MS. (Ry. 618. Early portion printed with *French Journals* in 1932.)

SCOTCH JOURNEY, from June 3, 1789 to Dec. 27, 1789. Unpublished MS. of 20 folios. (Ry. 623.)

1788, 1789, 1790—Fragmentary lists of social engagements. (Ry. 616, &c.)

MINCED MEAT FOR PYES. (A collection of jottings, extracts, quotations, verses, &c.) MS. folio blank book of about 27 folios, to which have been added at various times about 150 additional pages. Begun about 1796. (Portions published by Percival Merritt in *Piozzi Marginalia*, 1925. Now in the Houghton Library, Harvard University.)

NEW COMMON PLACE BOOK. 1809 to 1820. An unpublished MS. of 138 folios. (Now in the Hyde Collection.)

POEMS ON SEVERAL OCCASIONS with Anecdotes, &c., introductory to the Poems, Piozziana and Scrap and Trifle Book. (Designated by me as MAINWARING PIOZZIANA.) Five MS. volumes, 4to, comprising approximately 285 folios. Begun Oct. 15, 1810, and ended May 2, 1814. Unpublished. (Now in the Houghton Library, Harvard University.)

DAILY DIARIES for 1808, 1809, 1810, 1811, 1812, 1815, 1816, 1817, 1818, 1819, 1820, 1821. Kept regularly every day from Aug. 1808 to her death. Unpublished. (Ry. 616, Columbia University Library Rare Book Collection, and the National Library of Wales, Aberystwyth.)

MISCELLANEOUS NOTE BOOKS, 1812–17. (Ry. 616.)

APPENDIX D

LETTERS FROM MRS. THRALE (PIOZZI)
WHICH HAVE SURVIVED

(For the locations and a description of Hester Lynch Piozzi's letters, see the forthcoming edition of her correspondence for the period 1784–1821, edited by Edward A. and Lillian D. Bloom (Newark: University of Delaware Press; London and Toronto: Associated University Presses); 'Portrait of a Georgian Lady: The Letters of Hester Lynch (Thrale) Piozzi, 1784–1821', *Bulletin of the John Rylands University Library of Manchester*, ix, No. 2 (Spring 1978), 303–38.—*Editor*.)

140 to Dr. Samuel Johnson. (1770–84.) Thirty-seven complete letters have been printed, and excerpts from 18 more. (Hayward; Broadley; *Queeney Letters*; 1788 edition of Johnson's letters; *Life*; various publications of the John Rylands Library, &c.) About 20 have been rewritten. Almost all are now in the John Rylands Library—Ry. 538–40.

15 to the Rice family. (1773–6.) Excerpts have been printed in the *Fortnightly Review*, No. 440, New Series, Aug. 1903. The originals are held by Messrs. Myers & Co., London.

47 to John Perkins. (1773–90.) Excerpts from a few letters were printed by Hayward. The originals are now in the possession of Major C. A. Carlos Perkins, London.

2 to James Boswell. (1775–6.) *Fettercairn Catalogue*.

c. 250 to the Burney family. Some have been published in the *D'Arblay Diary*, and in C. Hill, *The House in St. Martin's Street*. Many originals are in the British Museum and the New York Public Library.

4 to Miss Margaret Owen. (1778–1805.) Now in the National Library of Wales, Aberystwyth. Published in *Cornhill Mag.*, Sept. 1939.

367 to the Thrale daughters. (1780–1821.) Forty-eight have been printed in *Queeney Letters*. In the possession of the Marquis of Lansdowne.

21 to Mrs. Lambart. (1780–8.) Ry. 550.

35 to Dr. Thomas Sedgewick Whalley. (1784–1820.) Published in *Journals and Correspondence of Thomas Sedgewick Whalley, D.D.* (1863.) Present ownership unknown.

62 to Samuel Lysons. (1784–1814?) The majority have been published in *Bentley's Miscellany*, xxviii (1850). A large portion of the originals is now held by Mrs. Donald F. Hyde.

154 to Leonard Chappelow. (1786–1818.) Ry. 559–61.

24 to Mrs. Sophia Byron. (1787–9.) Ry. 546.

206 to Mrs. Penelope Pennington (Sophia Weston). (1788–1804, 1819–21.) Excerpts published in *The Intimate Letters of Hester Piozzi to Penelope Pennington* (1914). The originals are now in the Princeton University Library.

9 to Daniel Lysons. (1794–1802.) Published by Hayward.

38 to Jacob Weston. (1793–1801.) All but one in the possession of the late Mr. D. F. Pennant, Nantlys, N. Wales.

97 to Dr. Thackeray. (1795–1816.) In the possession of Mr. Albert Ashforth, Jr., New York.

602 to the Williams family of Bodylwyddan. (1796–1821.) Nineteen originals and copies of 81 are in the Victoria and Albert Museum, London; nearly all the remainder are held by Brig. Hugh Salusbury Mainwaring, St. Asaph, N. Wales.

c. 100 to Dr. Robert Gray. (1797–1821.) Twenty-five printed by Hayward, the remainder examined by him. Present disposition unknown.

16 to the Rev. John Roberts. (1804–20.) Seven originals and 9 copies are now in the Victoria and Albert Museum.

472 to John Salusbury Piozzi Salusbury. (1804–21.) Ry. 585–90. Excerpts from 18 have been printed in the *Athenaeum*, No. 4602 (Feb. 1916).

130 to Harriet Pemberton Salusbury. (1813–21.) Ry. 592–3.

c. 135 to Alexander Leak. (1814–16.) The majority are in the possession of Mrs. Donald F. Hyde, Somerville, N.J.; 35 were sold at Sotheby's, Dec. 1, 1938, and 7 on Mar. 19, 1940.

21 to Mrs. Pemberton. (1814–18.) Ry. 594.

130 to Sir James Fellowes and family. (1815–21.) Published by Hayward. The originals have been largely dispersed.

94? to Edward Mangin. (1816 20.) Excerpts published in *Piozziana* (1833).

c. 80 to a variety of other correspondents (53 different people).

APPENDIX E

LETTERS TO MRS. THRALE (PIOZZI) WHICH HAVE SURVIVED

(Since letters are constantly turning up, this check-list is obviously only tentative. The present ownership of large collections is given; the remainder have been widely scattered through a series of auction sales.)

c. 107 from Dr. Arthur Collier. (1758?–63.) Ry. 534.

13 from Herbert Lawrence. (1758–88.) Nine included in Ry. 535.

c. 377 from Dr. Samuel Johnson. (1765–84.) (Mrs. Thrale also had in her possession a good many written to other members of her family.) Widely dispersed.

60 from Arthur Murphy. (1768–1801.) Almost all in Ry. 548 and 892.

8 from James Boswell. (1769–82.) (Also 3 to Henry Thrale.) Widely dispersed.

1 from Oliver Goldsmith. (1773.)

12 from Joseph Baretti. (1773–6.) Eight in Ry. 541.

16 from Dr. Michael Lort. (1774–89.) Thirteen in Ry. 544.

3 from Edmund Burke. (1774–81.)

9 from William Seward (1775–82?) Six in Ry. 536.

6 from William Weller Pepys. (1777–82.)

c. 17 from Dr. Charles Burney. (1777–1807.) Many in Ry. 545.

4 from David Garrick or Mrs. Garrick. (1777–?)

1 from Sir Joshua Reynolds. (1778.) Adam.

c. 50 from Fanny Burney. (1779–83.) Many in Ry. 545.

6 from Sophia Byron. (1779–82.) Ry. 546.

15 from Dr. John Delap. (1779–97.) Thirteen in Ry. 547.

40 from Elizabeth Montagu. (1780–86.) Thirty-five in Ry. 551.

49 from the Thrale daughters. (1784–1815.) The majority in Ry. 553 and 572.

26 from Samuel Lysons. (1784–1814.) Twenty-five in Ry. 552 and 892.

9 from Sir Lucas Pepys. (1784–1813.) Eight in Ry. 536 and 892.

21 from John Cator. (1785–96.) Ry. 602.

15 from Robert Merry. (1786–9.) Eleven in Ry. 558.

127 from Leonard Chappelow. (1786–1818.) Ry. 562–3 and 892.

39 from Dr. Thomas Sedgewick Whalley. (1787–1816.) Thirty-seven in Ry. 564.

14 from Anna Seward. (1787–90.) Twelve in Ry. 565 and 892.

151 from Mrs. Pennington (Sophia Weston). (1788–1821.) Ry. 566–8.

13 from Helen Maria Williams. (1791–6.) Eleven in Ry. 570.

73 from Dr. Robert Gray. (1791–1820.) All but one in Ry. 571.

41 from the Rev. Reynold Davies. (1792–1814.) Ry. 573.

37 from Sarah and William Siddons. (1793–1812.) Twenty-six in Ry. 574.

21 from Thomas Pennant. (1793–8.) Twenty in Ry. 575 and 892.

13 from Daniel Lysons. (1794–1821?) Ry. 576 and 892.

24 from The Ladies of Llangollen. (1796–?) Twenty-three in Ry. 581 and 892.

154 from John Gillon. (1798–1808.) Ry. 577–9.

163 from Marianne Francis. (1806–20.) Ry. 582–4 and 892.

22 from Clement Francis and family. Ry. 584.

26 from John Salusbury Piozzi Salusbury. (1808–21.) Ry. 591.

22 from Edward Mangin. (1815–19.) Twenty in Ry. 595.

8 from William Augustus Conway. (1819–21.) Ry. 596.

c. 430 from T. Lloyd, J. Ward, J. F. Vandercom, C. Mead, J. Old-field, A. Leak, &c. (business letters). (There are in addition a large number of other letters addressed to Henry Thrale and Gabriel Piozzi.) Ry. 603–9.

At least 300 from a variety of other correspondents. (Over two hundred different people, including James Beattie, Sir Philip Jennings Clerke, George Colman, J. Crutchley, Thomas Davies, R. Duppa, C. Este, Sir James Fellowes, Elizabeth Fry, Richard Graves, Bertie Greatheed, J. Hamilton, Bishop of Peterborough, Lord Huntingdon, George James, P. Kemble, Harriet Lee, Mrs. Lewis, Hannah More, Richard Musgrave, William Parsons, Bishop Percy, R. B. Sheridan, L. Skeffington, Dr. John Taylor, Dr. W. M. Thackeray, Henry S. Thrale, Joseph C. Walker, among others.)

SELECT BIBLIOGRAPHY

(Only books and articles containing new or little known Piozzian source material are listed. Usual standard reference works on other major figures of the period, such as Prior's *Life of Edmond Malone*, or Blunt's *Mrs. Montagu, 'Queen of the Blues'*, have not been included.)

The First Guide to Weston-Super-Mare in 1822. (Reprint, edited by E. E. Baker, Weston-Super-Mare, 1901.)
  (Contains letter from Mrs. Piozzi.)

P.[ENNINGTON], S. S. *Poems Addressed to Various Literary Characters.* Weymouth, 1827.
  (Includes some of Mrs. Piozzi's verses.)

Blackwood's Magazine, xxvi (Nov. 1829), 753–55.
  (Prints a letter from Mrs. Piozzi about her first meeting with Johnson.)

BOSWELL, J. *Life of Johnson*, edited by J. W. Croker. London, 1831.
  (Croker evidently had access to some of Mrs. Piozzi's unpublished letters, chiefly those to R. Duppa.)

MANGIN, E. *Piozziana; or, Recollections of the Late Mrs. Piozzi.* London, 1833.
  (A strange mixture of fragmentary letters, personal reminiscences, and extracts from some of her unprinted works. Reviewed in *Gentleman's Magazine*, ciii (Apr. 1833), 334–6; *Fraser's Magazine*, vii (Apr. 1833), 471–5, &c.)

Gentleman's Magazine, ciii (May, 1833), 418.
  (Prints a letter from Mrs. Piozzi about Miss Owen.)

CAMPBELL, T. *Life of Mrs. Siddons.* 2 vols. London, 1834.
  (Prints a number of Mrs. Piozzi's letters to the actress.)

Diary and Letters of Madame D'Arblay, edited by C. Barrett. London, 1842.
  (Includes many of Mrs. Thrale's letters to the Burneys.)

Love Letters of Mrs. Piozzi, written when she was eighty to William Augustus Conway. London, 1843.
  (For the complete evidence in regard to this diabolical fabrication see P. Merritt, *The True Story of the So-called Love Letters of Mrs. Piozzi*, Cambridge, Mass., 1927. Also see *T.L.S.*, Mar. 22, 1928; L. F. Powell, *Review of English Studies*, v (July, 1929), 362–3; and R. W. Chapman, 'A Literary Fraud', *London Mercury*, xxii (June, 1930), 154–6. Immediately after the calumny first appeared, on Jan. 24, 1843, Mangin wrote to the editor of the *Bath Herald*, denouncing the insinuation. See also

E. Mangin, *Miscellaneous Essays*, London, 1851, p. 68. The first complete exposure appeared in the *Athenaeum*, No. 1811 (July 12, 1862), p. 50; and in No. 1815 (Aug. 9, 1862), pp. 169–72. This was repeated in the *Living Age*, lxxv (Oct. 18, 1862), 102–10. In spite of all these refutations, however, the canard still is believed by many casual students of the eighteenth century. For instance, see *The Bellman*, xii, No. 297 (Mar. 23, 1912), p. 361. Readers have preferred to believe a salacious lie, rather than the less sensational truth.)

Bentley's Miscellany, xxviii (1850), pp. 73–82, 163–71, 307–15, 438–47, 535–43, 620–8.

(Forty-five letters from Mrs. Piozzi to Samuel Lysons are here printed.)

Gentleman's Magazine, xxxvii (new series) (Feb., Mar. 1852), pp. 136–7, 232–3.

(A series of letters from Mrs. Piozzi to T. Cadell.)

HAYWARD, A. *Autobiography Letters and Literary Remains of Mrs. Piozzi (Thrale)*. 2 vols. London, 1861.

(Hayward was the first to make any extended search for manuscript source-material. He was allowed by the Rev. Augustus Salusbury, son of Sir John, to quote some passages from Thraliana; he had access to all the letters and notes saved by Sir James Fellowes, and those written to the Lysons brothers, Dr. Gray, &c. These he hurriedly threw together, with no pretence of chronological arrangement; and the ill-digested mass appeared late in Feb. 1861. The work was extensively reviewed, much space being devoted to Hayward's obvious attempt to rescue the lady from the disrepute into which Boswell's *Life of Johnson* and Macaulay's essays had thrust her. Typical reviews may be found in *Blackwood's Edinburgh Magazine*, xci (Apr. 1862), 412–23; *All the Year Round*, v (Apr. 20, 1861), 82–7; *Athenaeum* No. 1735 (Jan. 26, 1861), 111–13; *Fraser's Mag.* lxiii (Mar. 1861), 368–84; *The National Review*, xii (Apr. 1861), 376–92; *Edinburgh Review*, cxiii (Apr. 1861), 501–23. A copy of the *Edinburgh Review*, which attacked both Hayward and Mrs. Piozzi in no uncertain terms, fell into the hands of the Rev. Augustus Salusbury, who annotated his copy with copious marginal notes pointing out the mistakes of the reviewer (now in my possession). Impressed with the fact that the Thraliana diary explicitly proved certain of the claims of the reviewer to be false, Mr. Salusbury immediately offered Hayward additional long extracts from this unprinted source to be used in refutation. Furthermore, Charles E. Norton had discovered some of the ill-fated Conway's effects in the United States and published a few of the more interesting details as 'Original Memorials of Mrs. Piozzi' in the *Atlantic Monthly*, vii (Boston, May, 1861), 614–23. Accepting all this new material now available, Hayward issued a second edition of his work late in the same year (1861), which should, whenever possible, be consulted rather than the first. Even in this revised and largely augmented second edition, however, Hayward made no real attempt at orderly arrangement, and his volumes are probably as exasperating as any in the entire field of English literature. It requires infinite patience and long acquaintance with his subject-matter to use the work for reference, perhaps one explanation for the fact that the contents have been so often overlooked by succeeding scholars. For a later attempt to prune and rearrange Hayward, see Lobban, J. H., *Dr. Johnson's Mrs. Thrale*, London, 1910.)

WICKHAM, H. *Journals and Correspondence of Thomas Sedgewick Whalley*, D.D. 2 vols. London, 1863.
(Contains Mrs. Piozzi's letters to Whalley.)

MURCH, J. *Mrs. Barbauld and Her Contemporaries.* London, 1877.
(Includes letter from Mrs. Piozzi.)

Sotheby Sale Catalogues, Dec. 14, 1901; Dec. 6, 1904; Jan. 22, 1907; June 4, 1908; Jan. 30, 1918, &c. (Sales of Piozzi papers.)

GREEN, M. A. *The Eighteenth Century Architecture of Bath.* Bath, 1902.
(Includes facsimile of one of Mrs. Piozzi's letters to Sir James · Fellowes.)

ELLIS, M. A. 'Some Unedited Letters of Mrs. Thrale', *Fortnightly Review*, No. 440, new series (London, Aug. 1903), pp. 268–76.

HILL, CONSTANCE. *The House in St. Martin's Street.* London, 1907.
(Prints further letters of Mrs. Thrale to the Burney family.)

BROADLEY, A. M. *Doctor Johnson and Mrs. Thrale.* London, 1910.
(Prints Mrs. Thrale's Welsh journal, as well as many original letters.)

HUGHES, C. *Mrs. Piozzi's Thraliana.* London, 1913.
(Consists of short excerpts from the unpublished diary, evidently to stimulate interest and further a sale of the manuscript.)

The Intimate Letters of Hester Piozzi and Penelope Pennington 1788–1821, edited by O. G. Knapp. London, 1914.

HUGHES, C. 'Mrs. Piozzi and Her Heir: Some Unpublished Letters', *Athenaeum*, No. 4602 (Feb. 1916), pp. 63–5.
(Selections from a few letters to Salusbury.)

'Two Miniatures of Mrs. Thrale by S. T. Roch', *The Connoisseur* (Sept. 1917), pp. 43–4.

NEWTON, A. E. 'A Light Blue Stocking', *Atlantic Monthly*, cxxi (Boston, 1918), 783–94. See also *The Amenities of Book Collecting and Kindred Affections*, Boston, 1918, pp. 186–225.
(Describes some of the author's Piozziana.)

SMITH, M. S. 'Manuscript Notes by Madame Piozzi in a Copy of Boswell's *Life of Johnson*', *London Mercury*, v (Jan. 1922), 286–93.

MERRITT, P. 'Piozzi–Johnson Annotations', *Gazette of the Grolier Club* (New York, May, 1922), No. 3, p. 58.

MERRITT, P. *Piozzi Marginalia.* Cambridge, Mass., 1925.
(Includes excerpts from Mrs. Piozzi's Common Place Book.)
The R. B. Adam Library Relating to Dr. Samuel Johnson and his Era.
Buffalo, N.Y., 1929–30.
LADY CHARNWOOD. *An Autograph Collection and the Making of It.*
London, 1930.
(Prints letter of Mrs. Piozzi.)
Bulletin of the John Rylands Library, xv (July, 1931), 467–88; xvi (Jan.
1932), 9–15, 32–136, &c.; xx (Jan. 1936), 157–72; xx (July–
Aug. 1936), 268–85.
(Excerpts are here printed from the great collection of Piozzi
manuscripts now in the Rylands Library.)
TYSON, M., and GUPPY, H. *The French Journals of Mrs. Thrale and
Doctor Johnson.* Manchester, 1932.
(In addition to the travel journals, many quotations are made
from hitherto unknown letters and documents.)
LANSDOWNE, MARQUIS OF. *Johnson and Queeney.* London, 1932.
(An illustrated edition of Johnson's letters to Hester Maria
Thrale. These were reprinted by Lord Lansdowne in *The
Queeney Letters*, London, 1934; and in this later volume selec-
tions were also given from the letters of Fanny Burney and
Mrs. Piozzi to Queeney. Lord Lansdowne included also
an admirable, but somewhat unsympathetic, study of Mrs.
Thrale during the troubled years of her widowhood and second
marriage.)
BROMHEAD, H. W. *The Heritage of St. Leonard's Parish Church, Streat-
ham.* London, 1932. Pp. 22–45.
(Contains much valuable information about the Thrales'
connexion with Streatham.)
BROWN, A. T. *One or Two Johnsonians.* Privately printed, Liverpool,
1933.
(A description of Susanna Thrale and Sir John Salusbury.)
LYELL, J. P. R. *Mrs. Piozzi and Isaac Watts.* London, 1934.
(Mrs. Piozzi's annotations on a copy of Watts's *Philosophical
Essays.*)
NICOLSON, M. 'Thomas Paine, Edward Nares, and Mrs. Piozzi's
Marginalia', *Huntington Library Bulletin*, No. 10 (Oct. 1936),
103–33.
BOSWELL J. *Life of Johnson*, ed. F. G. Fletcher, Limited Editions
Club, 1938.
(Prints Mrs. Piozzi's marginal annotations.)
CHARLES, B. G. 'Peggy Owen and Her Streatham Friends', *Cornhill
Mag.*, clx (Sept. 1939), 334–51.
(Prints Mrs. Piozzi's letters to Miss Owen.)

ADDITIONS TO SELECT BIBLIOGRAPHY

Thraliana: the Diary of Mrs. Hester Lynch Thrale (later Mrs. Piozzi),
1776–1809, edited by Katharine C. Balderston. 2 vols., Oxford,
1942; revised 2nd edition, 1951.
(The standard edition, admirably edited.)
CHAPMAN, R. W. 'Did Johnson Destroy Mrs. Thrale's Letters?'
Notes and Queries, clxxxv (Aug. 28, 1943), 133–4.
CHAPMAN, R. W. 'Piozzi on Thrale', *Notes and Queries*, clxxxv (Oct.
23, 1943), 242–7.
(Her later attempts to restore suppressions in Johnson's
letters.)
EWING, MAJL. 'Mrs. Piozzi Peruses Dr. Thomas Browne', *Philolo-*
gical Quarterly, xxii (Apr. 1943), 111–18.
(Her marginal annotations on a copy of the *Pseudodoxia*
Epidemica.)
KRUTCH, JOSEPH WOOD. *Samuel Johnson*, New York, 1944.
(Contains excellent analysis of the relationship of Johnson
and Mrs. Thrale.)
CLIFFORD, JAMES L. 'Mrs. Piozzi's Letters.' *Essays on the Eighteenth*
Century Presented to David Nichol Smith in Honour of His Seventieth
Birthday, Oxford. 1945, pp. 155–67.
(A general estimate of their merits.)
CHAPMAN, R. W. 'Mrs. Piozzi's Omissions from Johnson's Letters to
Thrales', *Review of English Studies*, xxii (Jan. 1946), 17–28.
CHAPMAN, R. W. 'Mrs. Thrale's Letters to Johnson Published by
Mrs. Piozzi in 1788', *Review of English Studies*, xxiv (Jan. 1948),
58–61.
BUSBY, J. H. 'The Hertfordshire Descent of Henry Thrale', *Notes*
and Queries, cxciii (Nov. 13, 1948), 495–8.
(Controverts Mrs. Piozzi's assertions as to the obscure origin
of the Thrale family.)
BALDERSTON, K. C. 'Johnson's Vile Melancholy', *The Age of John-*
son: Essays Presented to Chauncey Brewster Tinker. New Haven,
1949, pp. 3–14.
(Presents startling evidence of Mrs. Thrale's knowledge of
Johnson's masochistic tendencies.)
HEMLOW, JOYCE. 'Dr. Johnson and Fanny Burney: Some Additions
to the Record', *Bulletin of the New York Public Library*, lv (Feb.
1951), 55–65. Reprinted in *Johnsonian Studies*, ed. Magdi
Wahba. Cairo, Egypt, 1962, pp. 173–87.
(Passages cut out of the published *D'Arblay Diary*, some about
Mrs. Thrale.)

CLIFFORD, JAMES L. 'Hester Thrale-Piozzi', *Bath Weekly Chronicle and Herald*, June 10, 1950, p. 16; June 17, p. 16.
(Prints new diary references to her connexion with Gay Street, Bath.)

Three Centuries. London: Barclay, Perkins Co. 1951.
(A history of the brewery.)

CHAPMAN, R. W., ed. *The Letters of Samuel Johnson, with Mrs. Thrale's Genuine Letters to Him*. 3 vols. Oxford, 1952.
(Many of her letters printed here for the first time.)

FLETCHER, EDWARD G. 'Mrs. Piozzi on Boswell and Johnson's Tour', *University of Texas Studies in English*, xxxii (1953), 45–58.
(An annotated copy of Boswell's *Tour* at Harvard.)

GILMOUR, J. 'Mrs. Piozzi and the Metres of Boethius', *Notes and Queries*, cc (1955), 488.

ALLISON, JAMES. 'Mrs. Thrale's Marginalia in Joseph Warton's *Essay*', *Huntington Library Quarterly*, xix (February 1956), 155–64.

BOSTETTER, EDWARD E. 'The Original Della Cruscans and the *Florence Miscellany*', *Huntington Library Quarterly*, xix (May 1956), 277–300.

Boswell in Search of a Wife, edited by Frank Brady and Frederick A. Pottle. New York, 1956.
(Boswell's first visit to Streatham Park.)
(Other references to the Thrales in later volumes of the Yale Boswell Edition.)

HEMLOW, JOYCE. *The History of Fanny Burney*. Oxford, 1958.
(Uses manuscript material unavailable in 1941. Of major importance for understanding the relations of Mrs. Thrale and the Burneys.)

HEMLOW, JOYCE. 'Dr. Johnson and the Young Burneys', in *New Light on Dr. Johnson*, edited by F. W. Hilles. New Haven, 1959, pp. 319–39.
(Quotes from new evidence.)

GREENE, DONALD J. *The Politics of Samuel Johnson*. New Haven, 1960.
(Discusses Thrale's political affiliations.)

HAYMAN, JOHN G. 'On Reading an Eighteenth-Century Page', *Essays in Criticism*, xii (October 1962), 388–401.
(Uses *British Synonymy*.)

WALKER, RALPH S. 'Charles Burney's Theft of Books at Cambridge', *Transactions of the Cambridge Bibliographical Society*, iii (1962), 313–26.
(Evidence comes from Mrs. Piozzi.)

HEMLOW, JOYCE. *Morning at Streatham: from the Journal of Susannah Elizabeth Burney*. Privately printed, Princeton, 1963.
(Cf. p. 143, note 3. Further information.)

LONSDALE, ROGER. *Dr. Charles Burney: a Literary Biography*. Oxford, 1965.

(Contains new information. See also *Johnson, Boswell and Their Circle: Essays Presented to Lawrence Fitzroy Powell.* Oxford, 1965, pp. 21–40.)

FLEEMAN, J. D. 'Dr. Johnson and Henry Thrale, M.P.', in *Johnson, Boswell and Their Circle: Essays Presented to Lawrence Fitzroy Powell.* Oxford, 1965, pp. 170–89.
(Prints all known election addresses drafted by Johnson.)

The Catalogue of Burney Correspondence, edited by Joyce Hemlow and assistants. New York Public Library, expected in 1967.
(Lists all correspondence of Mrs. Thrale-Piozzi with the Burney family.)

The Journals and Letters of Fanny Burney (Madame d'Arblay), edited by Joyce Hemlow and others, 12 vols. Oxford: Clarendon Press, 1972–84.

HYDE, MARY MORLEY. *The Impossible Friendship: Boswell and Mrs. Thrale.* Cambridge, Mass.: Harvard University Press, 1972.

WAIN, JOHN. *Samuel Johnson.* New York: Viking Press, 1974.

SPACKS, PATRICIA MEYER. *The Female Imagination.* New York: Knopf, 1975, pp. 197–207.

HYDE, MARY MORLEY, *The Thrales of Streatham Park.* Cambridge, Mass.: Harvard University Press, 1977.

BATE, WALTER JACKSON. *Samuel Johnson.* New York: Harcourt Brace, 1977.

BROWNELL, MORRIS R. 'Hester Lynch Piozzi's Marginalia', *Eighteenth-Century Life,* iii (1977) 97–100.

MOERS, ELLEN, *Literary Women.* New York: Anchor Press/Doubleday, 1977.

BLOOM, EDWARD A. and LILLIAN D. BLOOM. 'Portrait of a Georgian Lady: The Letters of Hester Lynch (Thrale) Piozzi, 1784–1821', *Bulletin of the John Rylands University Library of Manchester,* lx, No. 2, (Spring, 1978), pp. 303–38.

BROWNLEY, MARTINE WATSON. '"Under the Dominion of *Some* Woman": The Friendship of Samuel Johnson and Hester Thrale', in *Mothering the Mind,* ed. Ruth Perry and Martine Watson Brownley. New York and London: Holmes & Meier, 1984, pp. 64–79.

McCARTHY, WILLIAM. 'Hester Piozzi' entry in *A Dictionary of British and American Women Writers 1660–1800,* ed. Janet Todd. London: Methuen & Co., Ltd.; New York: Rowman & Allanheld, 1984, pp. 253–6.

McCARTHY, WILLIAM. *Hester Thrale Piozzi: Portrait of a Literary Woman.* Chapel Hill, N.C.: University of North Carolina Press, 1985.

BLOOM, EDWARD A. and LILLIAN D. BLOOM. *The Letters of Hester Lynch (Thrale) Piozzi.* Newark, Del.: University of Delaware Press; London and Toronto: Associated University Presses. Forthcoming.

INDEX

Abbas and Mirza, 61.
A.B.C. Dario Musico, 188.
Abergele, 411–12.
Abingdon, 36, 394.
Abingdon, Mr., 111.
Abraxas stone, 398.
Adam de Salzburg, 4, 286.
Adams, William, 242, 244.
Addison, Joseph, 12, 56, 344, 347, 361, 438.
Adey, Mary, 308, 310.
Albion Manor, 37.
Alexander, Mr., 97, 296.
Amiens, 235.
Amigoni, Jacopo, 279.
Ancona, 278.
André, John, 307.
Andriani, Count, 334.
Anecdotes of Dr. Johnson, see Piozzi, Hester Lynch.
Anna Matilda (pseudonym of Hannah Cowley), 337–9.
Anstey, Christopher, 141, 183.
Antwerp, 291.
Araciel Marquis, d', 188, 238, 281, 285.
Arblay, Alexander d', 447.
Arblay, Mme d', see Burney, Frances.
Archer, Lady Betty, 22.
Arenberg, Duke d', 290–1.
Arne, Thomas, 37, 89.
Arno Miscellany, The, 250.
Ashbourne, 114, 308, 311.
Ashhurst, Lady, 334.
Ashhurst, Sir William Henry, 334.
Athens, 394.
Atkins, Abram, 431.
Austria, 286–7.

Bach-y-Graig, 7–9, 11, 114, 308, 350, 375–6, 434, 446, 455; description, 5, 19, 166; inheritance, 39, 41, 106, 128; Johnson trustee for, 129; mortgage, 19, 211, 215; repaired, 407 8; threatened loss, 13, 16, 19; woods at, 165, 215, 440.
Bagot, Lewis, Bishop of St. Asaph, 386.
Baillie, Joanna, 428.
Baldwin, Henry, 263.
Balthazar, Jean, 229.
Banff, 107.

Banks, Sir Joseph, 270, 282
Barber, Francis, 275, 311, 426.
Barclay, David, 201, 203.
Barclay, Robert, 203.
Baretti, Joseph, 66, 74, 101, 118, 121, 122, 125, 136, 140, 157, 161, 179, 198, 228, 432; annotations, 67, 96, 324–5; poverty, 206, 325; character, 242, 323, 325, 327 8; death, 325–6, 328; letters from, 107, 114, 140, 238, 468; newspaper attacks on, 325–6, 328; on Mrs. Salusbury's fatal illness, 103; Epistolario, 114, 134; Prefazioni e Polemichi, 137–8, 322; Sentimental Mother, 326–7.
— and the Thrales: early relations, 109, 325; teaches languages, 109, 111, 142, 144, 325; care for the children, 114, 116, 128, 140; describes Harry's death, 136; attacks and strictures on H.L.P., 113, 137, 218, 238, 322–8, 330; trip to Bath with H.L.T., 137–8; French and Italian tours, 129 32, 134, 138–9; rupture with, 143–4.
Barnard, Mme, 36.
Barnard, Sir Frederick Augusta, 243, 256, 311.
Barnard, Thomas, Bishop of Killaloe, 334, 414.
Barrett, Charlotte Frances, 427, 470.
Barry, Col. Henry (?), 307, 334.
Bartolozzi, Francesco, 334.
Bassano, Jacopo (da Ponte), 279.
Bates, friend of Johnson, 89.
Bath, 23, 82, 188, 193, 289, 297; Alfred St., 311; Bishop of, 228; Gay Street, 442, 446, 453; New King Street, 435, 438, 442; H.L.P. at, 137–40, 182–5, 219–31, 304–5, 311–12, 323, 339, 341–2, 351, 355, 386, 398, 401–3, 406–8, 411–14, 421, 430–1, 435–53; houses occupied by Thrales, 139, 183, 311, 435, 442; Johnson at, 139–40; Pulteney Street, 435.
Bathurst, Dr. Richard, 88.
Batton, Capt., 22.
Baviad, The, 250.
Beaconsfield, 116.
Beattie, James, 91, 101, 104, 106, 109, 121, 151, 259, 469.
Beauclerk, Lady Diana, 269.

Beauclerk, Topham, 156, 172.
Beaumarchais, P. A. C., 236.
Beaumaris, Anglesey, 386, 395.
Beaumont, Sir George, 358.
Beckenham Place, 179, 283.
Becket, Thomas à, 395.
Beckford, William, 347.
Bedford, Francis Russell, 5th Duke of, 383.
Bedford, John Russell, 4th Duke of, 34.
Belgium, 283.
Belle, Mrs. Salusbury's dog, 67, 70.
Belvedere, suggested name for Brynbella, 377.
Bentley, Richard, 404.
Bergamo, 285.
Berkeley, Bishop George, 25.
Berlin, 289.
Berne, 253.
Berry, Mary, 359, 373.
Bertola, Abbate, 280, 285.
Bevan, Sylvanus, 203.
Biddulph, Mr., 248.
Billinge, Richard, 3.
Billinge, Thomas, 3.
Birmingham, 96, 448, 452.
Blair, Hugh, 348.
Blake, a boy from Loughborough school, 134.
Blue-Stockings, 122, 150, 172, 174, 229–ß1, 259–60, 265–6, 272–3, 293–4, 319, 334.
Bodens, George, 53, 191.
Bodvary estate, 166.
Bodvel Hall, 8, 9, 10, 14, 103, 378, 455.
Bodylwyddan, 384–5, 423, 427, 429, 458.
Boethius, 57–8, 312, 315.
Boileau's Épistle to his Gardener, 61.
Bologna, 248, 278.
Bolognese school of painting, 132.
Booth, Mr., 142.
Boothby, Sir Brooke, the elder, 67, 308, 310.
Boothby, Sir Brooke, the younger, 310.
Boothby, Hill, 308–10.
Borghi, Luigi, 228, 334.
Borromeo, Count, 281.
Boscawen, Mrs. Frances, 150, 218.
Bossi, Abbé, 238, 246.
Boswell, James, 64, 69, 75, 76, 88, 91, 103, 111, 113, 117, 121, 134, 135, 137, 143, 158, 166, 189, 196, 241, 261, 265, 267, 328–30, 436, 458–9, 466; characterizes Goldsmith, 86; biographical style, 259, 357–8; contemporary suspicions of, 273, 358; accuracy, 319, 358; letters from, 468; *Life of Johnson*, xiv, 267, 270, 299, 311, 321, 355–9;

Tour to the Hebrides, xv, 75, 105, 106, 244, 259–60, 267, 295, 318, 349.
— visits: Hebrides, xv, 105–6, 125, 348–9; Southwark, 92, 122–5; Streatham, 78, 84, 166; Bath (1776), 139–40; Grosvenor Sq., 197; Argyle St., 219.
— and the Thrales: early attitude, 92, 105, 123–5, 210; first meeting with H.L.T., 77; reaction to J.'s letters to H.L.T., 313, 320–1, 356; attacks H.L.P.'s accuracy, 256, 268, 271, 347, 358–9, 471; and her scholarship, 76, 449; rivalry with H.L.P. after J.'s death, 241–2, 244, 256–7, 259–60, 272–6, 295, 306, 308, 310–11, 321–2, 330, 338, 355–9; Ode on J. and Mrs. Thrale, 199–200, 321–2; Piozzian verses, 273–4.
— *Letters*, 77, 92, 210, 299, 313.
Boswell, Mrs. Margaret, 75, 92.
Bouhours, Père, 224.
Boulogne, 235.
Bowdler, Thomas, 183, 195.
Bowles, William, 222.
Bowood, 371, 419.
Bozzy and Piozzi, 274–6.
Bradford, Lucy Elizabeth, Countess of, 427.
Brandenburg, 289.
Brent, Charlotte, 89.
Brenta, the, 247–8, 279.
Brescia, 224, 280, 392, 461.
Breughel, Jan, 286.
Brianconi, Abbé, 238.
Bridge, Miss, 13.
Bridges, Edward, 12–17, 19, 23, 31–2, 38, 53, 106–8, 114.
Bright, Henry, 80, 88.
Brighton, 58, 59, 81, 84, 93, 126–9, 148, 155–6, 161, 163, 166, 172–5, 180, 186–9, 192–3, 199–200, 212–14, 226, 283, 301, 400, 461; home of Thrales in West Street, 81, 155.
Bristol, 109, 412.
Bristol, Frederick Augustus Hervey, 4th Earl of, 326.
British Synonymy, see Piozzi, H. L.
Broadhead, Mary, 427.
Bromfield, Robert, 110, 119, 120, 136, 176.
Brooke, Francis, 75.
Brooke's Menagerie, 135.
Broster, Mr., of Chester, 27, 252.
Brunswick, 289.
Brussels, 207, 290–2.
Brynbella, *see* Piozzi, Hester Lynch.
Buchetti, Abbé de, 362.
Bulkeley, Lord, 395.

Bull, of Bath library, 398.
Bunbury, Mrs. Catherine, 334.
Burgoyne, General John, 351.
Burke family, 116, 151.
Burke, Edmund, 151, 361, 375, 395; portrait by Reynolds, 157; and Boswell, 259; and Johnson, 64, 84, 316; and Mrs. Siddons, 336; and the Thrales, 66, 85, 96, 116, 121, 179, 266, 293, 468.
Burney, Dr. Charles, 147, 154–5, 157, 166, 169, 175–6, 187, 192, 432; criticizes *Anecdotes*, 266–7; pleasant companion, 149, 414; verses in *Morning Herald*, 208; and J., 151–2, 155, 158–9; and the Thrales, 149, 151–2, 155, 158–9, 193; and Piozzi, 188, 222, 225, 330, 413, 414; and H.L.P., 158, 174, 179, 330, 413–14, 468.
Burney, Charles, the younger, 323, 398, 429.
Burney, Charlotte Ann, 158, 160, 161, 188.
Burney, Frances (Mme d' Arblay), 69, 94, 160, 186, 194, 198, 215, 218, 220, 267, 358, 414, 458; at Chessington, 190, 195, 205; letters, 199, 216, 241, 468, 473; *Camilla*, 395; *Cecilia*, 192, 205; *Diary*, ix, xiv, 115, 168 *et passim*; *Evelina*, 169, 183, 192, 305.
— and J., 197, 239, 316–17.
— and the Thrales: at Bath, 182–5; at Brighton, 175, 180–1, 212–14; relations with Queeney, 161, 222–3, 305, 316, 335, 428–9; description of Thrale, 56–7.
— and H.L.P.: first meeting, 151–2; first visit to Streatham, 169–71; later visits, 174–5, 177–8, 200–1, 205; nursed by, 178, 181, 205; deplores her gifts, 178; and Piozzi marriage, 213–14, 216–17, 222–5; break with, 225–6, 447; defence of, 305, 335; later meetings, 335, 447; compares to Mme de Staël, 457.
Burney, James, 194.
Burney, Richard, 158.
Burney, Sarah Harriet (?), 427.
Burney, Susan, 49, 143, 188, 194.
Burroughs, Samuel, 33.
Burrows, 191.
Bushe, Charles K., 418–19.
Bute, John Stuart, 3rd Earl of, 37.
Butler, Lady Eleanor, *see* Llangollen.
Buxton, 308.
Byng, —, 334.
Byron, Lord, 150, 252, 438–9.
Byron, Sophia, wife of Admiral Byron,
172, 183, 304, 311, 334, 355, 439; letters from, 179, 468; letters to, 323, 336, 339–41, 348–51, 466; tells H.L.T. Piozzi is in love with her, 198.

Cadell, Thomas, publisher, 255, 257–8, 262–4, 282, 295–301, 308–9, 311––12, 314, 317–18, 341–2, 346, 471.
Calais, 235, 292.
Calvert, Felix, 165.
Cam, G., 253, 461.
Cambray, 132.
Campbell, —, 348.
Campbell, Thomas, 249, 336, 415.
Campbell, Rev. Thomas, 74, 122, 123, 125, 309, 362–3.
Canaletto, Antonio, 279, 352.
Capello, 206.
Carlisle, Caroline, Countess of, 223, 345.
Carlton House, 443.
Carnan, Thomas, 274.
Carracci, Lodovico, 286.
Carracci school of painting, 248.
Carter, Elizabeth, 150, 151, 183, 218, 229, 231, 324, 334, 343.
Carter, —, 119–21, 126.
Casa Fidele, Milan, 237, 245, 280.
Casale, 237.
Castiglione, Prince Gonzaga di, 370.
Cathron, J., 443, 452–3.
Cator, John, trustee for Welsh property, 128, 166; friendship for Baretti, 143, 205–6, 325; character in H.L.T.'s dialogues, 179–80; executor for Thrale, 200, 204–6, 211, 214–15, 226, 228, 231; agent for H.L.P., 253, 289, 297, 352; takes care of Thrale daughters, 283; later financial quarrels with H.L.P., 302, 354, 388–90; and Mostyn, 388–90; death, 413; letters from, 468.
'Cavalier Servente', 237.
Cento, 278.
Cervantes, Life of, 21.
Chambers, Catherine, 71, 270.
Chambers, Sir Robert, 104, 105, 157; his wife, 325.
Champneys, Lady, 188.
Chantilly, 132, 235.
Chapone, Hester, 150, 151, 182, 231, 265, 267.
Chappelow, Leonard, meets H.L.P., 278, 280; friendship for H.L.P., 294, 334, 355, 410, 416, 427; visits Brynbella, 385, 415–16, 429; on H.L.P.'s style, 345; aids H.L.P. with publications, 373, 399–403; visits Thrale daughters, 284; friendship for

Cowper, 291; letters from, 61, 468; letters to, 222, 308, 309, 311, 380, 386, 389, 466; *The Looking Glass*, 278; *The Sentimental Naturalist*, 429.
Charlemont, James Caulfield, 1st Earl of, 23, 24.
Charles, B. G., 140, 473.
Cheltenham, 412, 419, 430, 461.
Chessington, 190–1, 195, 205.
Chester, 308, 383, 410, 421, 426, 448–9.
Chester, Bishop of, *see* Porteus.
Cholmondeley, George James, 269, 271.
Cibber, Colley, 122.
Cipriani, Giovanni Battista, 352.
Clarges, William, 415.
Clarke, Rev. Edward, 22, 27.
Claude Lorrain, 286
Clerke, Sir Philip Jennings, 174–5, 177, 179, 183, 186, 195–6, 198, 209, 469.
Clifford, Mr., 22, 32.
Clifton, 450–6, 461.
Clinton, Lord John, 195.
Clive, Lady, 334.
Clones, 309.
Clough family, 10.
Clough, Sir Richard, 4, 5, 376.
Clwyd, Vale of, xii, 114, 308, 350–1, 376, 383, 385–6, 415, 443, 457.
Cobb, Mrs. Mary, 308.
Cobham, Richard Temple, Baron, 34, 35.
Cochrane, Mrs., 283.
Coleridge, Samuel, 438.
Collier, Dr. Arthur, 25, 56, 168, 336, 435, 438; and H.L.S., 26, 27, 36, 39–43, 344, 455; letters to H.L.S., 22, 37–43, 114, 468.
Collier, Jane, 25.
Collier, Margaret, 25.
Colman, George, the elder, 76, 256, 273, 330, 469.
Combermere, 11, 114.
Condover Park, 430, 434.
Conway, Lord William, 451.
Conway, William Augustus, 448, 451–6, 469, 471.
Cooke, Miss Kitty, 191.
Cork and Orrery, Mary, Countess of, 415.
Cornwallis, Hon. Edward, 14.
Correggio, Antonio Allegri, 288.
Corsica, 77, 78.
Cosway, Richard, 334.
Cotterell, Charlotte, *see* Lewis, Charlotte.
Cotton, Elizabeth Abigail, wife of Sir Lynch, 22, 115, 142, 163.
Cotton, Harry, 193.
Cotton, Hester, cousin of H.L.S., *see* Davenant, Hester.

Cotton, Hester Maria, *see* Salusbury, Hester Maria.
Cotton, Sir Lynch, 13, 14, 15, 22, 38, 41, 44, 45, 53, 114.
Cotton, Dame Philadelphia Lynch, grandmother of H.L.S., 7, 8, 15, 18, 31.
Cotton, Sir Robert Salusbury, uncle of H.L.S., 5–8, 10–13.
Cotton, Sir Robert Salusbury, son of Sir Lynch Cotton, 133, 135, 166.
Cotton, Sidney Arabella, aunt of H.L.S., 40, 45, 52, 81, 193.
Cotton, Sophia, aunt of H.L.S., 40, 52.
Cotton, Thomas, cousin of H.L.S., 21, 133.
Cotton, Thomas Salusbury-, 15.
Coulson, Rev. John (?), 89. [356.
Courtenay, John, 272, 274, 320, 329, Cowley, Hannah, 337–9.
Cowper, Lady, 249.
Cowper, William, 291, 316, 334, 345, 448.
Coxe, George, 258.
Crabbe, George, 439.
Cradock, Joseph, 56.
Crane, Dr. E., Prebendary of Westminster, 14, 22, 38–9, 107.
Cremona, 246.
Crewe, Mrs. Frances Anne, 158.
Crisp, Samuel, 152, 190–2.
Croft, Sir Herbert, 273, 330.
Cronthal, Baron, of Brera, 238.
Crossby, 121.
Crowmarsh estate, Oxfordshire, 45, 200, 302, 381, 390.
Croxall, Samuel, 120.
Croydon, 51, 83.
Crutchley, Jeremiah, 98, 200, 203–5, 211, 215–17, 226, 230, 469.
Cullen, William, 348.
Cumberland, Anne, Duchess of, 258.
Cumberland, Henry Frederick, Duke of, 258.
Cumberland, Richard, 259, 415, 427.
Cumberland lakes, 350.
Cumyns, Mrs., 111, 114, 117, 135.

D—g, Sir Edward, 98.
D—n, Mrs., 98.
Dalrymple, Maj. Gen. William, 352.
Damer, Hon. Mrs., 332.
Dance, George, 376.
Dann, Count, 28.
Daran, Dr., 98.
Dartry, Lady, 218.
Davenant, Corbet, 193, 194.
Davenant, Hester, 49, 193, 194–5.

Davies, Rev. Reynold, 391–2, 395, 399, 410, 418, 449, 469.
Davies, Thomas, 221, 241, 469.
Dead-Man's Place, Southwark, 52.
Deal, 229.
Deerhurst, George William, Lord, 427.
Delany, Mrs. Mary, 150, 151, 160, 216.
Delap, Rev. John, 64, 175, 177, 195, 212, 334, 468.
Della Cruscan school of poetry, 250–2, 337–9, 347, 361, 373, 397.
Denbigh, 4, 265, 308, 350, 363, 378–81.
Denbigh Castle, 377–8.
Derby, Edward Stanley, 12th Earl of, 332.
Derry, Dean of, *see* Barnard.
Devizes, 182.
Devonshire, Georgiana, Duchess of, 172.
Devonshire House, 153..
Dilly, Charles, 137, 320.
Dobson, Matthew, 224.
Dr. Anecdote, and Mrs. Thralia, a dialogue, 121.
Dodsley, Robert, 367.
Dodson, Miss, 179.
Domenichino (Domenico Zampieri), 279, 352.
Donkin, General Sir Rufane Shaw, 440.
Dornford, Josiah, 81.
Douay, 132.
Dover, 221, 235, 292.
Downing, home of Thomas Pennant, 384.
Dresden, 288–9.
Droz, Jacquet, 174.
Dryden, John, 30, 80, 356.
Dudley, Julia, Viscountess, 334.
Dudley and Ward, William Ward, 3rd Viscount, 334.
Düsseldorf, 289.
Dunquerque, 132.
Dunscombe, Piozzi's attendant, 421, 423.
Dunstable, 426.
Duppa, Richard, 445, 469–70.
Durand, John, 120.
Durant, Mr., 59.
Durham, 348.
Dymerchion, *see* Tremeirchion.

East Hyde, Bedfordshire, 15, 16, 103.
Edenbourg, 287.
Edinburgh, 242, 348–50.
Edwards, Edward, 215.
Edwards, Frances, 193.
Effingham, Catharine, Countess of, 121, Elba, 437.
Elba river, 288.
Elci, Count Angelo d', 250–1, 254.

Elliott, Robert, 442.
Elphinstone, George Keith, *see* Keith.
Elphinstone, Hester Maria, *see* Thrale.
Enborne, 418.
Endovellicus, 21.
Erskine, Thomas, 1st Baron, 334, 336, 348, 430.
Este, Charles, 314–15, 328, 331, 334, 337–41, 349–51, 469.
Evans, Herbert, 377.
Evans, Mrs. Herbert, 60, 70, 130, 377, 407, 423, 426.
Evans, Rev. Mr., 268.
Exeter, 339, 341, 454.
Exmouth, 339–41.

Farington, Joseph, 376.
Ferrars, Lord De, 212.
Farren, Elizabeth (later Countess of Derby), 334.
Fector, Mr., 333.
Fellowes, Sir James, 5, 6, 63, 98, 435–6, 441, 447, 454, 457–8, 467, 469, 471.
Ferrara, 248, 278.
Fielding, Henry, 25, 133, 264.
Fielding, Sarah, 25, 27.
Fife, James Duff, 2nd Earl of, 323, 334.
Fisher, Canon, 335.
Fitzgerald, Lady Charlotte, 448.
Fitzherbert, Maria Anne, 274.
Fitzpatrick, Dr., 53.
Fleming, Lyndsay, 58, 73, 237, 239, 466.
Fletcher, Edward G., 269, 449, 473.
Flint, 308.
Flo, Mrs. Piozzi's dog, 286, 348.
Florence, 248–50, 252, 256–7, 409.
Florence Miscellany, 250–4, 294, 337, 354, 462.
Foligno, 278.
Fonthill, 226.
Foote, Samuel, 180, 371–2.
Forbes, Dr., of Penzance, 453–4.
Forster, Georg, 347, 462.
Fossée, Austin nuns at, 236.
Fox, Charles James, 440.
Francis, Clement, 447, 469.
Francis, Marianne, 358, 414, 427, 430, 447, 469.
Francis, Sir Philip, 386.
Frankfurt, 347.
Friend, Thomas, 81.
Frieri, Count, 334.
Fry, Elizabeth, 469.
Fuller, Stephen, 189.

Gainsborough, Thomas, 419.
Gardenstone, Francis Garden, Lord, 328.

Garrick, David, 12, 35, 78, 80, 84, 96, 153–4, 157, 212, 265, 361, 468.
Garrick, Mrs., 153–4, 334–5, 407, 447.
Garrick, Peter, 307.
Gascoyne, Bamber, 184.
Gawler, Mr., 325.
Genest, 196.
Genoa, 237–8.
George III, 36, 37, 86, 118, 132, 157, 264, 342.
George IV, 274, 342, 383.
Germany, 283, 288–9.
Ghent, 291.
Gibbes, Sir George Smith, 446, 456.
Gibbon, Edward, 324, 393.
Gifford, William, 250–1, 347, 373, 393, 413.
Gilbert, Charles, 81.
Giles, Mr., 398, 400, 431.
Gillon, John, 215, 397, 401, 469.
Gilpin, Katherine (?), 427.
Glasgow, 350.
Glencoe, 350.
Goldoni, Carlo, 236.
Goldsmith, Alfred, 224.
Goldsmith, Oliver, 106, 124, 157, 212, 242, 261, 277, 372, 432, 468; friend of, J., 64, 85; weakness in conversation, 86; death, 121, 199; life by Campbell and Percy, 363.
— and the Thrales, 66, 80, 84, 96, 99, 106, 109.
— *Good Natur'd Man*, first night, 363; *Vicar of Wakefield*, 364; *Works*, 85; *Letters*, 91.
Gordon riots, 185–6.
Graves, Richard, 413–14, 469.
Gray, Robert, 373, 415, 427, 433–4, 467, 469, 471.
Gray, Thomas, 30, 123, 197, 319, 448.
Greatheed, Bertie, described, 248–9; friendship for Piozzis, 258, 279–80, 294, 306, 334, 337, 339, 351; compositions for *Florence Miscellany*, 250–1, 254; *The Regent*, 306, 309, 311, 331–2, 342; suspected of being author of *Sentimental Mother*, 326; letters from, 469.
Greatheed, Mrs., wife of Bertie Greatheed, 248–9, 258, 279–80, 284, 294, 306, 309, 333–4, 337.
Greatheed, Richard, 365.
Green, Thomas, 316, 347.
Greenland, Angus, 228.
Gretna Green, 381–2.
Greville, Mr., 334.
Greville, Fulke, 158.
Guadagni, Italian singer, 89.

Guercino (Giovanni Francesco Barbieri), 248, 278–9, 286.
Guido Reni, 277, 279.
Gunning, Elizabeth and Maria, 35.
Guy's Cliffe, Warwickshire, 306, 308–9, 331, 351, 363.
Gwaynynog, 378.
Gwydyr, Peter Burrell, Baron, 439.

Hagley Park, 35, 116, 306,
Halifax, George Montagu Dunk, 2nd Earl of, 13–14, 17–18, 22, 32, 38–39, 44.
Halifax, Nova Scotia, 18, 353.
Halley, Edmund, 6.
Halsey, Edmund, 34.
Hamilton, Douglas Alexander, Duke of, 409.
Hamilton, Jane, 332, 385, 409, 427, 469.
Hamilton, William Gerard, 82, 172.
Hamilton, Mrs., 334, 385.
Hamilton, Mrs., of Chessington, 191.
Hampstead, 15.
Hanmer, Sir Thomas, 8.
Hankin, Mr., 104.
Hanover, 289.
Hanson, Richard Locke, 21.
Hardham, Mr., 367.
Harley, (Thomas?), 119.
Harris, James, 26, 27, 55, 86, 151, 356; *Hermes*, 27, 270, 356.
Harris, Mrs. James, 55, 56, 122, 151, 191.
Harrow, 50, 249.
Hart, Polly, 51, 98.
Hartley, Miss, 341.
Hastings, Warren, 313.
Hawkesworth, John, 124, 261.
Hawkins, Sir John, 74, 213, 239, 241, 243–4, 261, 274, 282, 295, 329–30, 358, 359.
Haydn, Joseph, 189, 287, 406.
Hayley, William, 240, 291, 307, 324.
Hayne, Mrs., 15.
Hayman, Frank, 439.
Hayward, Abraham, 399, 458.
Heale, 222.
Heaton, Mrs., 393.
Hebden, 12.
Heberden, William, 176.
Hebrides, Johnson's journey to, xv, 103, 105, 106, 125, 348–50, 450; Queeney's visit to, 416.
Hector, Edmund, 123, 242–4.
Henderson, Thrale's valet, 203.
Herne, William, 120.
Hervey, Mr., 135.
Hesketh, Mrs. Harriet, 334.

Hills of Tern, Lord Berwick's family, 12.
Hinchliffe, John, bishop of Peter-borough, 175, 182–3, 196, 198, 244, 263, 293, 334, 469.
Hoare, Henry Merrick, 419, 422, 427, 435, 441.
Hobart, Mrs., 333–4.
Hodge, Dr. Johnson's cat, 275.
Hogarth, William, 23–4.
Hogmore Lane, 117.
Holman, Joseph George, 61, 409.
Holman, Mrs., see Hamilton, Jane.
Holroyd, John Baker, first Earl of Sheffield, 163.
Holywell, 384.
Horneck, Mrs., 151, 334.
Horneck, Miss, 151.
Hotham, Sir Charles and Lady, 334.
Houghton, Richard Monckton Milnes, first Baron, 105.
Hudson, Thomas, 24.
Hume, Alexander, 59.
Hunter, John, 119, 120.
Huntingdon, Lord, 183, 334, 340, 469.

Innsbrück, 285.
Inveraray, 350.
Isola Bella in Lake Maggiore, 281.

Jackson, Humphrey, 93, 97.
Jackson, John, 427, 430.
James, George, 224, 231, 236, 238, 469.
James, Robert, 110.
Jebb, Sir Richard, 136, 137, 150, 179, 205.
Jenkinson, Charles, 193, 196.
Jenning's Free School in Southwark, 133.
Jenyns, Soame, 150, 213, 273.
Jerningham, Edward, 183, 334.
Jervis, Mr., 258.
Jervis, Mrs. Sophy, 258.
Johnson, Samuel, 85, 109, 110, 121, 142, 145, 147, 161, 236, 284, 287, 344, 361, 367, 393, 404, 417, 435–6, 438, 444, 447–8; described by Hogarth, 24; character, 55, 56, 195, 310; physical appearance, 55, 68; melancholia, 64, 75, 102–3; fabricated story of battle between Russians and Turks, 67; roughness in conversation, 68, 170–1, 182, 240, 265, 268–9, 271; possible place in Parliament, 74; fears of insanity, 75, 241–2; riding and swimming ability, 82, 155; distaste for music, 89, 158, 191; scientific experiments, 90–1; illness, 96, 101, 141, 149, 151, 205, 207, 208, 221, 227; eye trouble, 101;

Doctor of Laws, 123; refusal to speak French, 130; late hours, 149; portrait by Reynolds, 157, 372, 432; kindness, 171; newspaper gossip about, 208, 213, 328; bad temper, 212, 219, 240; paralytic stroke, 221; death, 239; anecdotes in *British Synonymy*, 360–2.
— trips to Brighton, 59, 81–2, 84, 148, 156, 192–3, 212–14; journey to the Hebrides, xv, 103, 105, 106, 125, 348–50, 450; preparations for Italian tour, 134–5; life in Grosvenor Sq., 196–8; life in Argyle St., 215, 219.
— opinions: on Addison, 56; Baretti and the Thrales, 143, 322–3; Bath, 140; being mistaken for Ben Jonson, 372; Boswell, 318; Brighton, 155, 192; children's education, 162; *Clarissa*, 437; counting birthdays, 450; dreams, 112; expressing feelings, 211; Foote's conversation, 371–2; Goldsmith's conversation, 86; James Harris, 27; heaven's joys, 112; history, 449; indulging grief, 139; Macbean's geographical dictionary, 394; madman, 247; marriage, 171, 271; Milton, 56; negative comforts, 450; reading, 76, 112; revisal of past life, 148; scenery, 115; smoking, 171; suitability of Christian names, 436; *Tom Thumb*, 271; using an attorney, 449; vacuity of life, 130, 271; veracity in biography, 256; wasting sympathy on a man in the pillory, 449.
— relations with others: Blue-Stockings, 122, 152, 196–7, 259–60; Bowles, 222; Burney, 149, 152, 158–9; Fanny Burney, 170–1, 191; Carter, 120, 126; Prince Castiglione, 370; Cholmondeley, 271; Lady Cotton, 163; Delap, 177, 195; Mrs. Montagu, 152, 197, 259–60, 318–19; Arthur Murphy, 54, 123; Nollekens, 157; W. W. Pepys, 179, 182; Ralph Plumbe, 88; Anna Williams, 61–3.
— — Mrs. Salusbury: early jealousy of, 67; later concern about, 94–5, 97, 103, 318; present from, 95, 426; remarks during her last hours, 103; epitaph for, 126.
— — Thrale family: introduction to, 54–6; love for the children, 69–70, 81, 91, 112, 133–4, 137; at Streatham Park, 64, 65, 67, 69, 74, 78, 84, 85, 96, 104, 106, 166, 169, 211–12, 236, 352; in Wales, 113–16, 308, 375, 420.

—— Henry: epitaph for, 34, 262; misspells his name, 55; his conversation, 57; political aid for, 59, 60, 72–4, 116–17, 184–5, 189–90; respect for, 68, 91, 98, 176, 199; business aid for, 93–4, 97, 104, 165–8, 200–2, 318; called Bulldog by, 165; legal matters for, 180; sorrow at death of, 198–9; executor for, 200, 203; legacy from, 200; and sale of brewery, 201–2.

—— Hester Lynch: opinion of her poetry, 36, 50; compliments her, 58, 68, 74, 101, 115, 118, 155, 197, 239, 242, 307, 356; dependence on, 74, 101, 111, 149, 215–16, 221, 227, 242; on her learning, 76; gives comfort to, 83, 118, 125; affection for, 88, 105, 132, 152, 200, 206–7, 209, 215, 221, 227–8; scandal about, 99, 199, 200, 212, 213, 218, 262, 274, 328; letters in French to, 102; help in her benefactions, 118–21; trustees of her Welsh property, 128–9, 166, 432; on correspondence with, 129; advises her on keeping a journal, 145, 146; on her social ambitions, 153; on her accuracy of narration, 166, 197; on her good nature, 170, 448–9; J. characterized in her dialogues, 179–80; jealousy of other admirers of, 196, 206, 209, 227, 307; harshness to, 197, 212, 227, 231, 240; break with, 209–10, 212, 215, 219, 221–2, 225–8, 239, 328; farewell to, 220; letters on her second marriage, 227–9, 240, 275; later grief over her marriage, 230, 239.

—— Hester Maria (Queeney): interest in, 91, 109, 112, 177, 207; tutors her and Fanny in Latin, 177, 207.

—— Lucy Elizabeth: sponsor for, 81, 84.

— writings: inscription for Sir Joseph Banks's goat, 270; translations of Boethius, 57–8, 312, 315; life of Congreve, 185; The False Alarm, 73, 74; The Fountains, 61, 63, 333, 414, 436; In Theatro, 89, 351; Journey to the Western Islands, 118, 349; Latin ode to H.L.T., 105; Lives of the Poets, 155, 172, 177, 192, 196, 224; Patriot, 117; Prayers and Meditations, 259; Rambler, 171; Rasselas, 66, 100, 204; Salusbury family papers, notes on, 4, 6, 11, 17–18, 37, 51, 60, 114; Shakespeare Preface, 58; Taxation no Tyranny, 118; Vanity of Human

Wishes, 240; Verses, 90, 243, 255; Welsh journal, 114, 445.
— Letters to and from (1788), 101–2, 138; H.L.P.'s bargain with Cadell, 295, 330; Boethius excerpts in, 57; cancellations in, 57–8, 302, 312; collecting material for, 306–13; editions of, 462; errata slip for, 315; preparations for, 243, 255, 257, 282, 294–302, 306–13, 322; printing of, 314, 347; criticisms of, 310, 314–17, 322–3, 328–9.
Jonson, Ben, 372.
Jordan, Dorothea Bland, 293.
Junius, 386.

Katherine of Beraine, 3, 4, 34, 226.
Keats, John, 252, 438.
Keith, George Keith Elphinstone, Visc., 3, 419, 427, 431–2, 441, 455.
Keith, Viscountess, see Thrale, Hester Maria.
Keith, Robert Murray, 288.
Kelly, Michael, 287.
Kelly, Lord, 156.
Kemble, John Philip, 331, 333–4, 337, 350, 415, 469.
Kemble, Mrs., 334, 350, 415.
Kendal, 350, 382.
Kennington Common, 51.
Kensington, 114, 117, 137, 140, 283, 284.
Killaloe, Bishop of, see Barnard.
King, Cotton, 31.
King, Mrs. Sarah, see Salusbury, Sarah.
King, Hon. William, 33.
King, Captain, 15.
King, Mrs., see Cotton, Lady.
Kingston, Lord, 33.
Kippis, Andrew, 241, 244.
Kirkwall, Anna Maria, Lady, 408, 411, 433.
Kirkwall, John, Viscount, 409.
Knockholt, Kent, 461.
Knollys, Mrs. William Edward, 3.
Kollock, S., 320.

Lade, Anne, sister of Henry Thrale, 53, 93, 104, 106, 137, 162, 179.
Lade, Sir John, nephew of Thrale, 88, 171, 371, 427.
Lambart, Mrs. (née Jennings), sister of Sir Philip Jennings Clerke, 183, 185–7, 190, 192–6, 201–2, 207, 311, 334, 339, 466.
Lambeth, 325.
Lancaster, 382.
Lane, Mr., 22.

Langton, Bennet, 64, 94, 95, 154, 241, 321.
Langton, George, 154.
Langton, Miss, 154.
Lansdowne, Henry Petty-Fitzmaurice, 3rd Marquis of, 399.
Laura Chapel, Bath, 438.
Lawrence, Herbert, 19, 37, 38, 73, 240, 468.
Lawrence, Lucy, mother of the artist, 183.
Lawrence, Sir Thomas, 183.
Lawrence, Dr. Thomas, 102, 110, 133, 136, 150.
Leak, Alexander, 431, 440, 442, 467, 469.
Leasowes, 306.
Lee, Harriet, 312, 341, 355, 362, 415, 469.
Lee, Nathaniel, 332.
Lee, Sophia, 312, 355, 414–15.
Leeds, Thomas, 4th Duke of, 12.
Leghorn, 257.
Lennox, Charlotte, 241.
Leopold, Grand Duke of Tuscany, 251.
Lester, brewery clerk, 99.
Le Texier, M., 333–4.
Levett, Robert, 207.
Levicz, Mr., 22, 111.
Lewis, Charlotte, wife of the Dean of Ossory, 183, 223, 238, 294, 312, 334, 342, 351, 358, 469.
Lewis, John, Dean of Ossory, 183.
Lewis, Mrs., of Bloomsbury, 7.
Lichfield, 63, 165, 318; Johnson at, 91, 95, 96, 114, 126, 129, 134, 137, 154, 175 6, 205, 306, H.L.T. at, 114, 306–8, 311, 344, 426.
Lichtenstein, Prince, 286.
Liège, 290.
Lieven, Count, 435, 440.
Lille, 132, 292.
Linwood, Miss, 439.
Little, David M., 153.
Liverpool, 308, 350.
Liverpool, Lord, see Jenkinson.
Llangollen, Ladies of (Lady Eleanor Butler and Miss Sarah Ponsonby), 396, 412, 418, 433, 469.
Llanner church, 8, 461.
Lleweney, 5, 10, 12, 114, 115, 408–9, 455.
Lloyd, Mr., 384–5.
Lloyd, Richard, 9, 44, 114.
Lloyd, Thomas, 377, 469.
Loch Lomond, 350.
Lock (or Locke), Mrs., 335.
Lodi, 246.
Lombardy, 308.

London, Argyle St., 214, 217; Broad St., Cheapside, 210; Charing Cross, 302; Charles St., St. James's Sq., 15; Dean St., Soho, 19, 52, 83; Duke St., Manchester Sq., 426; Fleet St., 61, 300; Great Queen St., 13; Grosvenor Sq., 194, 196–8, 461; Hanover Sq., 294, 304–5, 309, 326, 342, 351–2, 355, 369, 382, 455; Harley St., 196, 208; Johnson's Court, 64, 77, 96; Jermyn St., 19; King St., Soho, 11; Leicester Sq., 400; Lincoln's Inn, 424; Masefield St., St. Anne's, 36; Mortimer St., 225; Oxford Road, 210; Parliament St., 149; Paternoster Row, 360, Piccadilly, 400; Red Lion Sq., 194; St. James's Sq., 326; Wimpole St., 208, 283.
Lort, Michael, 121, 238, 244–5, 348; aids with *Anecdotes*, 244–5, 261, 263; with *Letters*, 282, 295, 298, 310; letters from, 259, 348, 468; loyal to H.L.P., 293–4, 303, 334; death, 355.
Lort, Mrs. Michael, 334.
Loughborough, Alexander Wedderburn, 1st Baron, 380, 387.
Loughborough School, 133.
Louis XVI, King of France, 130–1.
Louvain, 290.
Lucas, Charles (?), 447.
Lucca, 257.
Luttrell, Henry Lawes, 53, 73.
Luttrell, Simon, 53.
Lutwyche, Mary, 435.
Lysons, Samuel, 253, 277, 279, 281, 282, 334, 348, 355, 376, 385 6, 400, 415, 427; aids with *Anecdotes*, 241–5, 255–7, 260–3; with *Letters*, 282, 296–8, 302, 306, 312, 317, 319, 321; his 1788 copy, 57, 302; on Baretti's annotations, 324–5; his scrap book, 63; first meets H.L.T., 224; party for Piozzis, 337; letters to, 235–7, 340, 466, 471, *passim*; letters from, 238, 243, 468.
Lyttelton family of Hagley, 116.
Lyttelton, George, 1st Baron, 197, 315.
Lyttelton, William Henry, Baron, 35, 157, 184.

McAdam, Edward L., 55, 58, 90, 210.
Macaulay, Mrs. Catharine, 140.
Macaulay, Thomas Babington, 64, 459, 471.
Macbean, Alexander, 394.
McDonald, Sir Alexander, 275.
Maclean family, xv.
MacNamara, Mr., 383.
Macpherson, James, 37.

Madison, John, 302.
Maeviad, The, 250.
Maggiore, Lago, 281.
Maidenhead Bridge, 182.
Mainwaring, Sir Watkin Randle Kynaston, 70, 133, 384, 413, 430, 464–5, 467.
Mainz, 347.
Malone, Edmond, 207, 267, 272, 274, 306, 320, 325, 336.
Malvern water, 95.
Malzan, Count de, 189.
Manchester, 308, 458.
Mandeville, Bernard, 361.
Mangin, Rev. Edward, 24, 76, 437, 446, 450, 457–8, 460, 467, 469–70; *Miscellaneous Essays*, 471; *Piozziana*, 23, 76, 98, 328, 333, 437, 446, 449–51, 456, 467, 470.
Mann, Sir Horace, 258, 265, 273, 294.
Mantegna, Andrea, 277.
Mantua, 246, 280.
Manucci, Count, 133, 135, 136, 249–50.
Margate, 205.
Marie Antoinette, Queen of France, 131, 205, 290.
Maria Christina, Archduchess, 290.
Marriott, Sir James, 30, 31, 44.
Martenengo, Count, 304.
Martines, Marianna, 287.
Mary Queen of Scots, 228.
Mason, William, 30, 243, 319, 324.
Mather, Dr., rector of Whitechapel, 27.
Mathias, Mr., 32. 107.
Mayans y Siscar, Don Gregorio, 21.
Mead, Clement, 377, 431, 469.
Measles, 105, 426.
Meghitt, Mr. and Mrs., 248.
Mendip Lodge, Somersetshire, 430.
Meretriciad, 98.
Merlin, John Joseph, 368.
Merrick, James, 54.
Merry, Robert, 248–54, 257, 290–1, 334, 337–9, 361, 468; *Paulina*, 279.
Metcalfe, Philip, 212.
Milan, 188, 224, 237–8, 245–6, 280–5, 300, 303, 409.
Miller, Anna, Lady, of Bath Easton. 183, 185, 248, 346.
Mills, Sir Thomas, 121.
Milton, John, 30, 56, 224, 333, 450.
Molly, maid of H.L.T., 136.
Monferrato, 237.
Montagu, Mrs. Elizabeth, 150, 157, 161, 172, 179, 181, 191, 208, 218, 293, 324, 359; compliments from, 152, 164, 264; courts Johnson, 152; her talk, 183–4, 445; quarrel with Johnson, 197; first meeting with

H.L.T., 122; Queeney's impression of, 140; opinion of H.L.T., 151, 184, 319; characterized by H.L.T., 153, 195; visit to Streatham, 154; interest in Thrale, 164, 184; godmother to Henrietta, 167; on the Piozzi marriage, 229–31, 239–40; wish for reconciliation with H.L.T., 335; at Bath, 183–4; opinion of Boswell, 273; quarrel with Fox, 440; *Essay on Shakespeare*, 259–60, 272–3, 275, 318–19, 355; her letters, 428, 468.
Montreuil, 235.
Moore, John, 334, 348.
Moore, Thomas, 250, 407, 415, 448.
Moore's Carpet Manufactory, 135.
More, Hannah, 384, 447; a Blue-Stocking, 218, 324; criticisms of the *Anecdotes*, 265–6, 273, of the *Letters*, 316, 319, of the *Observations and Reflections*, 344; friendship for H.L.P., 334–5, 406, 413; on Johnson and Grosvenor Square, 196; letters to H.L.P., 469.
More, Miss, companion of Nesbitt, 141.
Mostyn, Cecilia, *see* Thrale, Cecilia Margaretta
Mostyn, Elizabeth, 18, 19.
Mostyn, John Meredith, 380–2, 383, 386–90, 418–19.
Moysey, Abel, 184, 193.
Mozart, Wolfgang Amadeus, 189, 287, 406.
Mudford, William, 55, 56, 358.
Münster, 289.
Mulgrave, Constantine John Phipps, Lord, 184–5.
Munich, 285–6.
Murillo, Bartolomé Esteban, 352.
Murphy, Arthur, 35, 59, 109, 124, 193, 261, 401; attacks Goldsmith, 86; and Johnson's vulgar remarks, 123; introduces Johnson to Thrales, 53–6; at Brighton with Thrales, 156, 175; Harry Thrale's favourite, 133, 155; aids with Thrale's will, 180; friendship with H.L.P. renewed, 309, 334, 362, 366, 383; legal adviser to H.L.P., 387–90; on Mrs. Salusbury's fatal illness, 103; portrait by Reynolds, 157, 442; opinion of sightseeing, 288; criticises Johnson's *Letters*, 316; *Essay on Johnson*, 358, 397; on Boswell's *Life*, 358; aids with *British Synonymy*, 368–9; at Streatham, 383, 385; *The Way to Keep Him*, 172; letters from, 468.
Murray, David (?), 348.
Murray, Mrs., 283.

Musgrave, Richard, 163, 240, 469.
Myddelton, Dr., 378, 384, 410, 427.

Naples, 258, 277.
Napoleon Bonaparte, 346, 391, 417, 437.
Nares, Edward, 450, 473.
Nash, Richard (Beau), 435.
Nesbitt, Arnold, 71, 175, 365.
Nesbitt, Mrs. Arnold, 53, 141, 175-6.
Nesbitt, Arnold, Jr., 141.
Netto, Isaac, 20.
New Bath Guide, The, 141, 183.
Newbury, 418.
Newby, Mrs., 120.
Newcastle, 348.
Nicholls, Rev. Norton, 415.
Nicolson, Jane, 226, 334.
Nicolson, Marjorie, 76, 450, 473.
Nolcken, Baron, 334.
Nollekens, Joseph, 157.
Norman, Mr., 179-80.
Norris, Mr., 432.
North, Frederick, second Earl of Guilford, 73-4, 104, 184, 190.
Novalesa, 236.
Nova Scotia, 13, 14, 16, 17, 18, 166, 353.
Novi, 237.
Nuneham, 362.

Observations and Reflections, see Piozzi, Hester Lynch.
Offley Park, Hertfordshire, 16, 18, 20, 26, 29, 31, 32, 33, 36, 103, 106-8, 378, 455.
Ogilby's translation of Homer, 9.
Oglethorpe, General James Edward, 92
Oldfield, J., 377, 469.
Oliver, William, 27.
Ord, Mrs., 195, 208, 216, 335.
Orkney, Mary, Countess of, 3.
Ossianic poems, 37, 438.
Ossory, Dean of, 183.
Owen, Margaret, of Penrhos, 140, 148-51, 156, 161, 186, 200, 334, 362, 386, 412, 466, 473.
Oxford University, 34, 104, 120, 399-400, 433-4; Johnson at, 72, 74, 77, 96, 126, 134, 205, 210.

Pacchierotti, Gasparo, 188, 205.
Padua, 246-8, 278, 280.
Paine, Thomas, 450, 473.
Palmer, Mary, 334.
Palmer, Mr., 156.
Paoli, Pascal, 92, 334.
Paradise, John, 121, 153.
Paris, 129-32, 235-6, 286.

Parker, Dr., 27, 28, 334.
Parker, Mrs., 142.
Parr, Samuel, 354.
Parsons, William, 245, 248-54, 284, 294, 308, 334, 339, 415, 469.
Paterson, Wm. (?), 114.
Pauline, Princess, 290.
Pavia, 237.
Pearson, H., 357.
Pemberton family of Condover Park, 442, 467.
Pembroke, Henry Herbert, 10th Earl of, 248.
Pennant, D. F., 467.
Pennant, Thomas, 3, 4, 8, 55, 334, 384, 469.
Pennick, Rev. Richard, 72.
Pennington, Mrs. Sophia, 355, 362-5, 385-6, 390, 407, 427, 452-4, 470; and H.L.P., 183, 334, 412, 455-7, 466-9.
Pennington, William, 364.
Penrice, Anna Maria, see Salusbury, Anna Maria.
Penrice, Sir Henry, 16, 18.
Penzance, 438, 453-4.
Pepys, Sir Lucas, 150, 293; aids with Anecdotes, 243-4, 259-60, 263, 272; letters from, 238, 289, 468; physician to Thrales, 127, 192 198, 379, 427; his pronunciation, 112.
Pepys, Sir William Weller, 184, 231, 273, 324; his pronunciation, 112, 180; friend of Blue-Stockings, 150, 172, 195, 447; visits Streatham, 154-5; dines in company with H.L.T., 154, 182; character in H.L.T.'s dialogues, 179-80; her relations with H.L.P., 335, 427; on H.L.P.'s conversation, 446; fears Johnson, 182; quarrels with, 197, 212; opinion of Anecdotes, 265; letters from, 468; verses on Thrale's wedding anniversary, 164.
Percy, Anne, wife of Bishop Percy, 93.
Percy, Thomas, Bishop of Dromore, 94, 295, 303, 309, 313, 359, 361, 363, 469.
Perkins, Major C. A. Carlos, 106, 466.
Perkins, John, clerk at the brewery, 97, 99, 104, 135, 166-7, 180, 200; saves brewery in riots, 186; becomes partner, 201, 203; political aid for Thrale, 190; sons tutored by Dr. Parr, 354; letters from H.L.T., 9, 106, 185, 203, 206, 294, 354, 466; examines Welsh property, 106-8; borrows from H.L.T., 203, 213; directs her foreign correspondence, 205-6; invites H.L.T. to Southwark,

294; last meeting with, 413; at Harry's party, 133.

Perney, 'Old', 134.

Perron, Madame du, 130.

Perugia, 279.

Perugino (Pietro Vannucci), 277.

Peterborough, Bishop of, *see* Hinchliffe.

Philidor (Daniçan, Francois André), 279.

Piccioni, Luigi, 114, 134, 137, 322.

Pignotti, Lorenzo, 250.

Pindar, Peter, *see* Wolcot.

Pindemonte, Ippolito (Marquis of), 61, 250–1, 254, 285, 334, 354.

Pinfold, Dr., 214.

Pinkstan, Dr., 110, 136.

Pinto, Mrs., *see* Brent.

Piozzi, Gabriel: birth, 188, 461; personal appearance, 187, 209, 307, 349, 376; early life, 188, 238; concerts, 188, 196, 291; at Brighton, 187–9; homes in London, 189, 218; musical ability, 187–9, 193, 290, 307, 349, 376, 412, 427; musical compositions, 188–9, 290, 419; teaches Queeney, 193, 198, 419; singing, 195, 290, 306–7, 376; early trips to Italy, 204–6; attitude towards society, 223, 230, 293–4, 376; recall to England, 223, 238; portable piano, 231, 246–7, 424–5; thrifty disposition, 237–8, 248, 302, 323, 353, 395, 407, 415; religion, 246–7, 288, 406, 421; relations with his own family, 247–8, 280, 285; social barriers against in Italy, 258, 277, 285; preference for London, 282; fondness for Wales, 350, 375–6; spending, 352–3, 407–8; attacks of gout, 369, 378–9, 383, 398, 406, 408–13, 415, 420–4; lack of English culture, 376, 399, 407; diaries, 386, 389, 407, 409, 418, 420; interest in the poor, 407, 411; naturalization, 406; death, 424, 461; his will, 427.

— and H.L.T., 198, 205–6, 213, 217, 245; first meeting, 158–9; lends her money, 219; renounces her, 217–21; marriage, 229; loss of their child, 312.

Piozzi, Giambattista, 247–8, 285, 391, 397.

Piozzi, Hester Lynch: genealogical claims, 3; birth, 8, 90, 269, 450, 461; early education, 9, 15; personal appearance, 23, 118, 160; model for Hogarth, 23–4; learns Latin, 26; inheritances, 27, 39, 52, 107, 200, 427; finances, 31, 200, 204, 252–3, 302, 350, 354, 435, 440–2; suitors, 31–3, 44,

209; marriages: Thrale, 46; Piozzi, 229; marriage bond and settlement: Thrale, 45, 128–9, 200, 204, 381, 390, 432; Piozzi, 228; brewery business, 92, 94, 96–7, 104, 107, 166–8, 177, 180, 195, 200–3; sale of brewery, 201–2; attempts at economy, 95, 166–7, 204, 435, 453–4; scandal about her, 99, 217–19, 240, 262, 273, 303, 324–6, 445–6; illnesses, 105, 141, 177–81, 200–2, 205, 222–3, 426–7, 454–6; travel, 113–16, 207–8, 235–8, 245–8, 257–8, 277–92, 348–50, 420; revisal of past life, 148; morbid mental condition, 149, 203, 221–3; clothes and personal appearance, 153, 156–7, 194, 406; portraits, 157, 254, 285, 374, 401, 430, 472; miscarriages, 178, 312; income after Thrale's death, 204; newspaper attacks, 208, 213, 218–19, 230, 240, 242, 244–5, 261–3, 314, 328; fear of whooping cough, 220; newspaper compliments, 303, 314–15; sale of pictures, 279, 352, 458; rumoured change of name, 289; grandchildren, 389, 428, 430; described in *Sentimental Mother*, 326–7; disillusioned by society, 375–6; eightieth birthday celebrations, 450–1; death, 454–6; burial, 457, 461; possible epitaph, 149.

— character, xi–xiv, 49, 122, 125, 127, 156, 162, 177, 217, 414, 417–18, 420–1, 428, 434, 451, 459–60; described by others, 151–2, 157, 160, 169–70, 184, 197, 208, 216, 229, 323, 327, 399, 406, 414, 431–2, 445, 448; accuracy of narration, xiii–xiv, 103, 147, 166, 243, 256, 265–72, pride in Welsh ancestry, 3, 115, 308, 350, 375, 407, 443; youthful precocity, 9–10, 12, 28; scholarly attainments, 76–7, 373, 449–50; taste in wit, 132, 439–40; sentimentality, 147, 327, 362; social ambitions, 153, 172, 181, 194–5, 294, 303, 332, 334, 339, 375–6; conversational ability, 183–4, 307, 446; flattery, delight in, 237, 447; reaction to death, 199; need of hero-worship, 336, 435; love, attitude towards, 204, 209; dependence on reading, 421–2, 429.

— interests, &c.: Bible, 134, 224, 246–7, 417, 450; card playing, 156; etymology, 370–1; foreign languages, difficulties with, 130, 134, 285, 290; French, 11, 12, 15, 20, 27, 61, 130; Greek, 26, 76, 450; Hebrew, 417,

437, 450; Italian, 20–31, 193, 206, 245, 250, 397; Italian society, 237–8, 245, 280–1, 285; music, lack of interest, 89, 158, 287; names, 436–8; painting, 132, 236, 277–9, 286–7, 415; philanthropy, 118–21, 158, 193, 444; religion, 245–7, 282, 284, 288; science, 90, 413, 418; sea bathing, love of, 81, 155, 340, 450, 453; of sightseeing, 277–80, 288; Spanish literature, 20; speech, 112, 179, 366–7, 371; the theatre, 195–6, 331–3.

— relations with others:

— — Baretti, 109, 118, 128, 137; gifts to, 138, 206; early rupture with, 143–4; later attacks of, 238, 322–8; final estimate of, 320.

— — Blue-Stockings, 122, 150–1, 182, 197, 208, 218, 229–31, 238, 259–60, 265–6, 272–3, 293–4, 303, 319, 334–5, 339.

— — Boswell: first meeting, 77; early attitude towards, 92, 123–5; rivalry with, 242, 244, 256–7, 259–60, 262–3, 355–9; his treatment of her in *Life of Johnson*, 355–9.

— — Burney, Fanny, *see* Burney.

— — Cator, 204, 215, 354, 388–90.

— — 'Cavalier Servente', 237–8.

— — Cecilia, *see* Thrale.

— — Chappelow, 429.

— — her children: births, 54, 59, 71–2, 81, 83, 91, 94, 107, 126, 150, 167; deaths, 59, 82, 110, 127, 133, 136, 220; illnesses, 59, 82, 105, 110, 118, 125–8, 132–3, 135–8, 140, 144–5, 220, 223, 304, 363; education, 70, 79, 111–13, 133, 136, 144, 222, 224, 340–1, 392, 432; occasional harshness to, 95, 113, 143, 323; changing attitude towards, 144–5, 216, 222, 226; their opposition to her second marriage, 216–18, 222, 349; reconciliation marriage, 231, 235, 283–4, 293, 303, with, 365–6; relations after second 5, 336, 349, 364–6, 380–4, 387–91, 398, 415, 418–19, 424, 426–7, 434, 444, 455–7.

— — Collier: affection for, 32; letters from, 25–6, 37–43.

— — Cotton, Sir Robert, 10–11.

— — Cowper, 291.

— — Della Cruscans, 248–54, 337–9, 349, 373.

— — Fellowes, 435 6.

— — Hawkins, 295.

— — Johnson: discusses family papers with, 4; J. suspected of literary help, 62–3, 368, 372; at Streatham, 64–5;

attempts to alleviate his melancholia, 64, 75, 102, 355; his effect on her, 66–7; collecting anecdotes of, 75–6, 173, 241, 257, 268, 311; disputes with, 78, 123, 132; affection for, 88, 187, 207, 239–40; feeling for, 200, 207, 211, 336; dependence on, 96–7, 99, 128, 176; amanuensis for *Lives of the Poets*, 196; gossip, 199–200, 213, 219; gradual break, 208–10, 212–13, 215, 219, 221–2, 225–8, 328; leave-taking, 220; her forgiveness, 238–9, 291; blamed for J.'s death, 239–40, 334; letters to, 91, 297, *et passim*; letters from, 227–9, 240, 275, 296, 298, 317–19.

— — Lysons, 239, 336–7.

— — Marriott, James, courted by, 30–1.

— — Mrs. Montagu: friendship with, 151–2, 335; compliments from, 152, 264; compared with, 153, 428, 445.

— — Moore, Tom, visited by, 448.

— — Mostyn, quarrel with, 386–90.

— — her mother, affection for, 32, 45, 103 4.

— — Mozart, meeting with, 287.

— — Piozzi: first meeting, 158–9; letters to, 205, 221; marriage, 229.

— — Salusbury, Sir John, 391, 434.

— — Salusbury, Lady, 19, 53, 106–8, 211, 214–15, 302, 354.

— — Seward, 223.

— — Streatfeild, Sophy, 173, 175.

— — Thrale, 49–50, 97, 104, 126, 142, 163–4, 206, 327; his courtship, 36–8, 43–5; marriage, 46; political attitude to, 73, 117, 182, 184–5, 189–90.

— — Thrale's nephews, 88.

— — Wilkes, meeting with, 156.

— — Wraxall: on his conversation, 181–2.

— places:

— — Bach-y-Graig: entail of, 19; her feeling for the woods of, 165–6, 440–1, 443.

— — Bath: love of, 351, 435, 444, 446 Gay St. House, 442.

— — Brighton: house at, 81, 155, 175.

— — Brynbella: building, 376–8, 382–3, 395, 407, 441; choice of name, 377; move to, 382–3; life at, 383–7, 389, 399, 407–11, 415–18, 420–3, 428–30, 442–4.

— — London: residences in, 11–13, 15, 19, 36, 194, 208, 214, 294; going to court, 153, 157, 194; return to, from the Continent, 289, 292–3.

— — Streatham Park: redecorating

and repairing, 352–3, 431–3; tenants, 211, 294, 352, 431, 435, 440, 442; sale of contents, 440–2.
—— writings:
—— — biographical method, 265, 270; prose style, 265, 319, 343–6, 360, 373–4, 403–4; proof correcting, 312, 369, 400; marginal annotations in books, 243, 359, 449; disposition of her papers, xii, 458–9.
—— — 'Albion Manor', 37.
—— — *Anecdotes of Dr. Johnson*, 55, 59, 86, 106, 253, 279, 281–2, 286, 290, 314, 328, 341, 348, 371; composition, 241–5, 250, 255–7, 265, 267, 270, 279; printing, 260, 262–3; editions, 264, 287, 462, errata slip, 264; cancelled sheet K, 262–3; financial agreement, 264; newspaper references, 244, 255, 261–5, 272–4; criticism, published, 264–7, 273–6, 356, 337; style criticized, 343.
—— — literary autobiography written, xiii, 429–30.
—— — biographical sketch for Sir James Fellowes, 5, 13, 436.
—— — biographical sketch for *Monthly Review*, 397.
—— — Boethius, translations of, 57–8, 312, 315.
—— — Boileau, translation of, 61.
—— — *British Synonymy*, 393, 395, 397, 399, 436, 462; composition of, 366–9; contract for, 368; publication date, 369–70; Paris edition of, 374, 462; published criticisms, 372–4.
—— — Children's Book, xiii, 70, 173, *et passim*.
—— — daily diaries, 22, 426, 438, 464–5, *et passim*; later censorship of, 148, 198, 217, 302.
—— — dialogues on her own death, 179–80.
—— — Dumouriez's Sketch of Europe, translation of, 416.
—— — engagement books, 332, 334, 354, 464.
—— — Exmouth Theatre, prologue for, 340–1.
—— — *Florence Miscellany*, 250–4, 294, 337, 354, 462.
—— — journals, early, 76, 85–8, 124–5, 148, 464.
—— — letters, ix, xiii, 448, 466–7 *et passim*; to the Burneys, 466; to and from Johnson, *see* Johnson: to Johnson, 91, 297, 311, *et passim*; some rewritten, 220, 297–301, 311–12, 319–20, 339, 466; to Piozzi, 205, 221; to

Queeney, 367 *et passim*; to Jack Rice, 101, 320.
—— — Lyford Redivivus, 436–8, 458.
—— — Minced Meat for Pyes, 464, 473.
—— — New Common Place Book, xiii, 23, 98, 112–13, 171, 182, 333, 337, 414, 422, 436–40, 444–5, 447, 464.
—— — Nova Scotian journals, her father's marked by, 17, 114.
—— — *Observations and Reflections*, 235, 277; composition, 339–42; German translation, 347, 462; literary style, 343–6; publication, 343, 462; published criticisms, 343–8, 397–8; worth of, 346, 348.
—— — political satires, 37, 73, 174, 378, 395–6.
—— — prayers, 82, 83.
—— — Racine, translation of, 27–8.
—— — *Regent*, epilogue for, 309, 331.
—— — *Retrospection*, 417, 453, 462; plans for, 379, 385, 393–4; composition, 393–5, 398, 400; typographical errors, 401–2; publication, 401, 405; style of, 402–4; published criticisms, 403–4.
—— — Scottish journal, 349, 464.
—— — Spanish, translations from, 20–2.
—— — travel journals, 115, 130, 235 ff., 286, 339–41, 346, 349, 464.
—— — *Thraliana*, xii, 145–8, 173, 417–18, 430, 444–5, 458, 464, 471.
—— — *Three Warnings to John Bull*, 396–7, 462.
—— — Una and Duessa, 360–2, 366, 395.
—— — Verse: on an Air Balloon, 245, 313; on Ash Tree at Offley, 29; on Blessings of Peace, 37; at Calais, 341; on Collier's dog Pompey, 36, at Dover, 341; on the English Poets, 29–30; Enigma, 313; on Forrester, 29, 378; *In Theatro*, translation of, 89, 351; on Offley Park, 36; on Peter Pindar, 329–30; to Piozzi at Dover, 221; for Richmond House, 332; on Robin Redbreast, 51; on Streatham portraits, 186–7; Three Warnings, 61–2, 250, 462; Two Fountains, 333; Winter in Wales, 419; youthful verses, 28–30; nursery rhymes, 73; epistles, 141–2, 291; later verses, 411.
Pisa, 257.
Pitches, Peggy, later Lady Deerhurst, 161.
Pitt, Miss, 334.
Plumbe, Fanny, 99–101, 121, 320, 466.
Plumbe, Ralph, 88.
Plumbe, Alderman Samuel, 71, 99–101.
Plumbe, Mrs. Samuel, 53, 100.
Plymouth, 14, 18, 341.

Ponsonby, Sarah, *see* Llangollen.
Poole, Lady, 163.
Pope, Alexander, 28, 30, 34, 79, 80, 102, 196, 224, 247, 438.
Porter, Lucy, 67, 96, 241, 243.
Porteus, Beilby, Bishop of Chester, 183, 334.
Portsmouth, 141.
Postmarks, 228–9, 301.
Potsdam, 289.
Pott, Percivall, surgeon, 125.
Poussin, Nicolas, 286.
Prague, 283, 288.
Prestatyn, 411.
Prior, Matthew, 28, 78.
Pwllheli, 8, 10, 114, 115, 420.

Queeney, *see* Thrale, Hester Maria.
Quin, James, 12.
Quinzano, 188, 224, 280, 461.

R.—?, Mrs., 99.
R-d-h, Mrs., 98.
Racine, Louis, 27, 28.
Radcliffe, Ann, 347, 379.
Ranelagh, 37, 128.
Rauzzini, Venanzio, 412.
Ravasi, Abate, 238.
Ravenna, 278.
Ray, Robert, 381, 391.
Ray, Mrs., at Streatham, 220.
Ray and Fry's school, Streatham, 304.
Raymond, Samuel, 122.
Reading, 220, 312, 339, 342, 401.
Regent, The, 309, 331–2, 342.
Reigate, 180.
Reynolds, Frances, 151, 154, 216, 356.
Reynolds, Sir Joshua, 358, 375, 448; Johnson's friend, 64, 84, 293; first meeting with Thrales, 66; note books, 66, 194; entertains Thrales, 96, 122, 151, 154, 372; Oxford degree, 104; at Streatham, 106, 121; Streatham portraits, 157, 186, 432, 441; friend of Mrs. Siddons, 336; approves of *Anecdotes*, 282; Johnson's executor, 297; letter to H.L.T., 468.
Rice, Fanny, *see* Plumbe.
Rice, Jack, 99–101, 121, 320, 466.
Richardson, Mr., 22.
Richardson, Samuel, 150, 247, 437.
Richmond, Charles Lennox, 3rd Duke of, 332, 337.
Richmond and Gordon, Duke of, 24.
Richmond, Surrey, 105.
Richmond House, 332.
Rickmansworth, 141.
Ridgway, James, 326.

Rimini, 278.
Robert brothers, 236.
Roberts, John, 384, 417, 458, 467.
Robertson, William, 348–9.
Robinson, Mr., 432.
Robinson, George, 368–9, 399–400.
Robson, Bateman, 107, 129, 432.
Robson, James, 241, 403.
Roch, S. T., 472.
Rochester, 154.
Roffette, Abbé, 130, 268.
Rogers, Samuel, 348–9, 364, 427.
Rome, 113, 257–8, 277–8.
Rose, William, 345.
Rothes, Mary, Countess of, wife of Bennet Langton, 154, 958.
Rothes, Lady, wife of Sir Lucas Pepys, 195, 218, 427.
Rouen, 130, 268.
Rousseau, Jean Jacques, 28, 327.
Rudd, Mrs., 451, 453–6.
Rush, Mr., 93.
Russell, Samuel Thomas, 417.
Ruysdael, Jacob, 352.

Sacchini, Antonio Maria Gasparo, 204–5, 332.
St. Albans, 34.
St. Asaph, Dean of, 386, 407.
Salisbury, 185, 226.
Salisbury, misspelling for Salusbury, 289.
Sally, Thrale's maid, 106.
Salusbury family history, 3–5.
Salusbury, Anna Maria (*née* Penrice), first wife of Sir Thomas, 16–18, 20, 21, 25, 31, 36, 72.
Salusbury, Rev. Augustus, 471.
Salusbury, Harriet Pemberton, wife of Sir John Salusbury, 434, 436, 467.
Salusbury, Harry, 5, 6.
Salusbury, Hester Lynch, *see* Piozzi, Hester Lynch.
Salusbury, Hester Maria (*née* Cotton), mother of H.L.S.: family history, 3–5, 7; description, 5; marriage, 7; at Bodvel, 8–10; birth of daughter, 8; reconciled to brother, 10, 11; in London, 12–15; educates daughter, 15, 25; forces her marriage to Thrale, 43–5; health, 15, 91, 94, 97; fatal illness, 94–5, 97, 103, 318; divides possessions, 95, 426; death, 103, 270; epitaph by Johnson, 126.
— at Streatham with Thrales, 49, 53; and Dr. Collier, 43; annuity not paid, 53; and Johnson, 67; and grandchildren, 71, 81–3; savings lent to Thrale, 93.

Salusbury, John, father of H.L.S., 4, 41, 145, 166, 187, 209, 218, 380; birth and education, 5; youthful adventures, 6, 7; marriage, 7; life at Bodvel, 8; quarrels with Sir Robert Cotton and Sir Thomas Salusbury, 11, 36; lead mine, 12; letters and journals, 14, 16–19, 22, 114; experiences in Nova Scotia, 16–19, 353; debts paid by brother, 19; friendship with Hogarth, 23; opposes daughter's suitors, 31; death, 38; misrepresented in Thraliana, 147.

Salusbury, Sir John, husband of Katherine of Beraine, 4, 5.

Salusbury, Sir John Salusbury Piozzi, nephew of Piozzi: birth, 461; adoption, 391–2; education, 392, 418, 433–4; naturalization, 427; marriage, 434; negotiations for baronetcy, 443, 452–3; knighted, 443; letters from, 469; letters to, 215, 418, 421, 423, 433, 449, 467; his copy of *Florence Misc.*, 252.

— and H.L.P.: her executor, 457–8; her affection for him, 410, 433; at her birthday celebration, 450–1; his lack of sympathy with her, 440, 442–4, 452, 454–5, 458; with her in Wales, 418, 422, 424–5, 428, 442–4; attitude towards her writing, 429–30, 444.

Salusbury, Lucy, 5, 6, 7, 9.

Salusbury, Sarah (formerly King), second wife of Sir Thomas, 19, 33, 36, 38, 41, 53, 106, 108, 211, 214–15, 302, 354.

Salusbury, Rev. Thelwall, 32, 36.

Salusbury, Sir Thomas, uncle of H.L.S., 14, 22, 25, 30, 32, 46, 72, 106, 426; birth, 5; education, 6; death, 107; Welsh family debts, 7, 9, 13; marriage to Miss Penrice, 16; inherits Offley, 18; pays off Bach-y-Graig mortgage, 19, 108, 211; and the widow King, 33, 36, 38, 41; his marriage to her, 53; financial support to brother's family, 31, 39, 41, 44, 45; introduces Thrale to Salusburys, 33; negotiations with Collier about H.L.S.'s fortune, 41–4; encourages H.L.S. in poetry, 29, 32, 378; relations with H.L.T., 53, 104, 106–8.

Salusbury, Thomas (15th century), 3.

Salusbury, William, 5.

Salusbury-Cotton, Thomas, 15.

Salviati, Franceso Rossi, 279.

Salzburg, 286.

Salzburg, Adam de, 4, 286.

Sam, servant of Thrales, 175.

Sandgate, 461.

Sandwich, John Montagu, 4th Earl of, 193.

Sandys, Lord, 157.

Sasso Ferrato (Giovanni Battista Salvi), 277.

Sastres, Francesco, 312, 334.

Saurin, Jacques, 69.

Savage, Richard, 273, 451.

Savoy, 236.

Scarborough, 348.

Scarlett, Miss, 22.

Scheldt, river, 291–2.

Scott, Sir Samuel, 207.

Scott, Sarah Robinson, sister of Mrs. Montagu, 181–2, 230–1.

Scott, Sir Walter, 422, 428, 438–9.

Scott, Sir William, later Baron Stowell, 200.

Scrase, Charles, 81, 93, 104, 128–29, 166, 180, 199, 201.

Segroid, Mostyn residence, 380, 383, 387, 389, 430.

Selwin, Charles, 264, 293, 297, 334.

Selwyn, George, 223, 345.

Sevenoaks, 180.

Severn river, 454.

Seward, Anna, 183, 240, 355; anger at Baretti's strictures, 324; entertains Piozzis in Lichfield, 306–7; aids with Johnson's *Letters*, 308–10; her own letters rewritten, xiv, 308; letters to H.L.P., 468; on H.L.P.'s style, 344; suspected of being Anna Matilda, 338.

Seward, William, 124, 150, 177, 179, 210, 223, 244, 414, 468.

Shackfield, William, 377.

Shakerley, George, 9.

Shakespeare, William, 30, 52, 58, 224, 280, 283, 447.

Shard, Charles, 278, 284.

Sharpe, Samuel, 347.

Sheffield, home of the Holroyds, 163.

Shelburne, William Petty, Earl, 1st Marquis of Lansdowne, 211, 352.

Shelley, Sir John, 172, 189.

Shelley, Percy Bysshe, 252, 438, 448.

Shelley, Miss, of Sussex, 334.

Shenstone, William, 413.

Shephard, Charles Mitchell Smith, 424–5, 427, 431–2.

Shephard, Thomas, 418.

Sheridan, Richard Brinsley, 153, 195, 333, 336, 469.

Shrewsbury, 308–9, 362, 412, 430, 434.

Siddons, Sally, 363, 377, 383.
Siddons, Sarah, 147, 333–4, 361, 365, 389, 398, 400, 415, 426–7, 430; at Bath. 183, 351; at Nuneham, 362; admired by H.L.P., 336, 435; affection for H.L.P., 355, 385, 547; letters to H.L.P., 469; reading *British Synonymy*, 373; as Imogen, 293; in *Venice Preserved*, 183; in *The Regent*, 309, 331–2.
Siddons, William, 334, 373, 415, 469.
Silk, Edmund T., 254.
Simpson, Joseph, 270, 310.
Skeffington, Lumley St. George, 416–17, 427, 469.
Skye, 105, 243.
Smith, Adam, 349.
Smith, Henry, 200, 303.
Smith, Richard, 229.
Smollett, Tobias George, 347.
Sneyd, Honora, 307.
Snowdonia, 377.
Soderini, M., 238.
Southampton, 141, 368.
Southey, Robert, 438–9.
Southwark, 68 *et passim*.
Speen Hill, 182.
Spoleto, 278.
Squibb, auctioneer, 441.
Staël, Mme de, 457.
Stafford, George Granville, Marquis of, 415, 432.
Stalker, Mr., 330.
Steele, Thomas, 352.
Steevens, George, 73, 242, 324.
Stella (Esther Johnson), 316.
Sterne, Laurence, 327, 344.
Stillman, M. S., 348.
Stockdale, John, 400–5.
Stonehenge, 141.
Snowe, 34, 35.
Strahan, George, 259, 274.
Strahan, William, 166.
Stratton, Charlotte, 451–2.
Stratton, Mrs., 452.
Streatfeild, Sophia, 168, 172–3, 177, 180, 195, 415.
Streatham Park, or Streatham Place, description of, 50, 104, 151, 165, 169, 352–3; reopened by H.L.P., 352–3; 435; later repairs, 352–3, 431–3; 1816 sale of contents, 169, 440–2; secured by Ralph Thrale, 34; tenants, 211, 294, 352, 383, 398, 431, 435, 440, 442.
'Streatham University,' 392, 410, 418.
Strickland, Mrs. Cecilia, 150, 350, 382.
Stuart, James (Athenian), 439.

Surman, Elizabeth, 54.
Swale, Mr., 334.
'Swan of Lichfield', *see* Seward, Ann.
Swift, Jonathan, 25, 174, 179, 316, 438, 454.

Talassi, Angelo, 153, 278.
Tasso, Torquato, 20, 312.
Taylor, George Watson, 442.
Taylor, John, 96, 126, 140, 153, 242–3, 308, 310, 469.
Tenby, 412.
Tetbury, Lord, imaginary title for Lysons, 296.
Thackeray, Dr. W. M., 378–9, 381, 409–10, 420–4, 427, 431, 467, 469.
Thames regatta, 1775, 126, 320.
Theatres: Drury Lane, 195–6, 331, 342; Globe, 52.
Thelwall, Edward, 4.
Theobald, Lewis, 358.
Thicknesse, Philip, 273.
Thomas, Dr., 97, 100, 111, 114.
Thrale, Anna Maria, 72, 74, 80, 81, 82, 83, 84, 127, 145, 461.
Thrale, Cecilia Margaretta, 81, 217, 252, 283, 303, 339–41, 377, 410, 418, 452, 461; birth, 150; illnesses, 220, 304, 363, 382, 389; guardianship by her mother, 304–6, 348; characterized, 336, 378–80; education, 340–1; admirers, 363–4; high spirits, 364, 366, 379–80; elopement, 381–2; quarrels over her fortune, 386–90; husband's unkind treatment, 418–19; her boys, 415, 418, 430; distaste for Denbigh, 379–80; in Wales, 383–4, 387, 389, 418, 422, 430; in Italy, 450, 455; her copy of Yorke's *Royal Tribes of Wales*, 3; sale of her effects, 69, 155, 163.
Thrale, Frances, 59, 64, 461.
Thrale, Frances Ann, 126, 132–33, 461.
Thrale, Henrietta Sophia (Harriet), 167–8, 217, 220, 461.
Thrale, Henry, birth, 34, 461; character, 49, 55–7, 92, 94–5, 97–9, 108, 115, 119, 126, 128, 134, 149, 157, 162–4, 166, 192, 195; venereal complaints, 98, 144, 164; mental depression, 167, 172, 176, 178–9, 190, 198, 216; strokes, 175–6, 180–1, 189–90, 198–9; death, 199; funeral, 199; will, 180, 200, 352, 390, 431.
— introduction to Salusburys, 33; life after college, 35; parliamentary career, 35–6, 59–60, 71–4, 116–17, 132, 182, 184–5, 189–90; election

addresses, 59–60, 72, 116–17, 189–90; robbed on highroad, 51; mistresses, 51, 98–9; interest in eating, 51, 176, 184, 191–2, 198; in hunting, 51, 81, 180; rakish friends, 53, 66, 156; power over Johnson, 68, 91; purchase of Brighton house, 81; business speculation, 92–4, 164–8; brewing experiments, 93, 104; newspaper scandal about, 97–9; degree of D.C.L., 104; social interests, 156, 177, 194–5; fondness for Sophy Streatfeild, 173, 175; learns Spanish, 109, 325; plans for Italian journey, 113, 187, 198; presents address to the king, 132; extravagant spending, 165; portrait by Reynolds, 157, 442; partiality for Girard's *Synonymy*, 372.
— and H.L.S.: courtship, 36–8, 43–4; reasons for choice of, 52; marriage, 46; marriage settlement, 45, 381, 390; affection for, 118.
Thrale, Henry Salusbury, (Harry) 84, 103, 106, 115, 119, 127, 145, 151, 216, 455; birth, 71, 461; amiable disposition, 80, 133; measles, 105; education, 111, 114; birthday party, 133–4; last illness and death, 135–7, 144, 153, 323; and Johnson, 91, 112; hatred of Goldsmith, 109; his mother's favourite, 110, 145, 391; letters from, 133, 469.
Thrale, Hester Lynch, *see* Piozzi, Hester Lynch.
Thrale, Hester Maria (Queeney), birth, 54, 378, 461; Johnson's interest in, 69–70, 112, 297; makes purse for Johnson, 80; in Children's Book, 70–1, 78–80, 109–11, 145, 160–1; character, 79–80, 161–2, 305; clever remarks, 79–80, 109, 139–40, 154; letters from, 91, 297, 473; letters to, 32, 38, 69, 473; her tutors, 109, 134, 142, 177, 207; Baretti, 109, 134, 142; feeling for Baretti, 143; dislike of Goldsmith, 109; illnesses, 135–8, 150; opinion of Bath, 140; musical study, 149, 193, 198, 419; clandestine letters, 161–2; letters from Fanny Burney, 178, 222–3, 305, 316, 447; love of society, 172, 216; opposition to Piozzi, 213–14, 216–18, 222–3, 226, 293; visits Hebrides, 416; marriage, 419; her child, 428, 430.
— and her mother: given ornaments by, 21; opinion of, 161–2, 216, 305, 336, 389, 428–9, 431; parting from, 226, 230–1; later reconciliation, 365; business quarrels with, 381, 390,

431–2; later help for, 384, 393–5, 416; *Retrospection* discussed with, 401–4; with her at death, 455–6; letters from, 367 *et passim*.
— and Cecilia, 304–5, 382–3, 387–90, 428.
Thrale, Lucy Elizabeth, 79, 81, 84, 110, 127, 133, 144, 145, 216, 455, 461.
Thrale, Margaret, 33.
Thrale, Penelope, 94, 461.
Thrale, Ralph, Sr., 34, 35, 93.
Thrale, Ralph, 107, 115, 118, 125–8, 461.
Thrale, Sophia, 139, 145, 157; birth, 91, 461; at Mrs. Cumyns's school, 117; at Brighton, 175, 186; and the Piozzi marriage, 217, 224, 231, 283, 293, 303–4; at Bath, 220, 223–4; under care of Mrs. Murray, 283; Chappelow visits, 284; at Brynbella, 383–4, 422; marriage, 419; quarrels about Streatham, 435, 441.
— and her mother: taught by her, 136, 144; reconciliation with, 365–6; kindness to, 415; letters from, 466; with her at death, 455–6.
Thrale, Susanna Arabella, 84, 145, 157, 419, 453, 473; birth, 83, 461; sponsor for Francis Brooke, 75; at Mrs. Cumyns's school, 111, 117, 135; one of Johnson's favourites, 112; at Brighton, 175, 186; and Piozzi marriage, 217, 231, 283, 303–4; at Bath, 220; interest in religion, 284; at Brynbella, 383–4; and her mother, 365–6, 455–6, 466.
The Three Warnings, 61–2, 250, 462.
Tibson, 'Old Nurse', 106, 114, 220.
Tighe, Mr. and Mrs., 258.
Tollemache, Lady Betty, wife of Sir Robert Cotton, 5.
Tooke, John Horne, 371.
Torrington, Lord and Lady, in Brussels, 290.
Townmalling, Kent, 75.
Townsend, —, 94.
Townshend, Charles, 27.
Tremeirchion, 17, 350, 376.
Tremeirchion church, 384, 408, 417, 424, 457, 461.
Trent, 285.
Trevor, Mrs., 163.
Trotti, Marquis, 286, 362.
Tulip, Thrale's dog, 142.
Tunbridge Wells, 172, 180.
Turin, 236–7.
Tusculum, 352.
Ty-coch, 16.
Tyers, Thomas, 242.

Ty-mawr, 16.
Tyrolean Alps, 283, 285.

Una & Duessa, *see* Piozzi, H.L.

Vandercom, J. F., 354, 396, 469.
Vanessa (Hester Vanhomrigh), 26.
Vansittart, Robert, 142.
Varese, 281.
Venice, 188, 247–8, 278–80, 397.
Vernon, Frederick, 19.
Verona, 246, 280, 285.
Versailles, 131.
Vesey, Elizabeth, 150, 151, 177, 179, 229–30.
Vesuvius, 258.
Vienna, 283, 286–8.
Viry, François-Marie-Joseph, Comte de, 104.

Waddington, Mrs. M. A. Port, 160, 216.
Wager, Sir Charles, 62.
Waldegrave, Lady Caroline, 188.
Walker, Joseph Cooper, 469.
Walpole, Horace, friend of Blue-Stockings, 150; criticisms of *Anecdotes*, 265, 273, 343; of Boswell's *Tour to the Hebrides*, 259; of *Life*, 359; of *British Synonymy*, 370, 373; of *Florence Miscellany*, 251; of *Johnson's Letters*, 316; of *Observations and Reflections*, 343; at Richmond House, 332.
Wansey, Henry, 445.
Warburton, William, 19, 20.
Ward, J., 469.
Warton, Thomas, 224.
Watermarks, 300–2, 311, 320.
Welcker, John, 188.
Wellbury, 39.
Wellington, Duke of, 439.
Westcote (William Henry Lyttelton), Baron, 35, 157, 184.
Weston, 52.
Weston, Jacob, coachman, 363, 391, 467.
Weston, Sophia, *see* Pennington.
Weston-super-Mare, 450, 453, 470.
Weymouth, 19, 20, 222, 470.
Whalley, Thomas Sedgewick, 306, 324, 406, 446; in Brussels, 290–1; at Brynbella, 415, 421; in Venice, 279; letters from, 468; letters from H.L.P. to, 466, about Streatham, 431, 440–2;

first met H.L.P., 183, friendship for, 355, 427, 430.
Whalley, Mrs. (*née* Jones), 279, 290–1.
Whalley, Mrs. (widow of General Horneck), 446.
Whitbread, Samuel, 165.
Whitchurch School, 5.
White, Henry, 306–7.
Whitefield, George, 78.
Wickham, H., 451, 472.
Wilkes, John, 37, 40, 53, 72, 73, 116, 156, 259, 321, 358.
Williams family, 384, 413.
Williams, Lady, of Bodylwyddan, 392, 397, 404, 423, 427, 430, 458, 467.
Williams, Miss, sister of Sir John Williams, 413, 415, 421, 431, 433–4, 436, 449, 452, 458, 467.
Williams, Rev. Mr., 331.
Williams, Anna, 61–3, 63, 93, 119, 462.
Williams, Helen Maria, 307, 334, 355, 360, 469.
Williams, Sir John of Bodylwyddan, 385, 413, 458, 467.
Williams, John, son of prec., 429, 436, 458.
Willoughby, Miss, 82, 453–4.
Wilson, Dr. Bernard, 14, 27.
Wilton, 226.
Winchester, Dean of, 188.
Windham, William, 269, 271, 334.
Windsor, 106, 316, 335.
Woburn Abbey, 34.
Wolcot, John, 274–6, 329–30.
Wood, John, 442.
Woodhouse, James, 55, 56.
Wordsworth, William, 438.
Wraxall, Sir Nathaniel, 181–2, 445.
Wrexham, 308.
Wright, J. D., 88, 102, 215, 349.
Wycombe, 141–2.
Wynn, Morris, 4.
Wynn, Lady, 22.
Wynnstay, 406.

Yorke, Charles, 86.
Young, Arthur, 347.
Young, Edward, 224, 333, 438.
Young, Owen D., 466.

Zamick, M., 179.
Zeluco, 348.
Zenobio, Count, 334.
Zoffany, John, 70.